5

LEARNING FOUNDATIONS OF BEHAVIOR THERAPY

SERIES IN PSYCHOLOGY

LEARNING FOUNDATIONS OF BEHAVIOR THERAPY

Frederick H. Kanfer
University of Cincinnati

Jeanne S. Phillips
University of Massachusetts

JOHN WILEY & SONS, INC.
NEW YORK · LONDON · SYDNEY · TORONTO

To George Saslow, whose enthusiasm and receptiveness to new ideas and their critical appraisal have been happily contagious for us.

To Ruby, Ruth, and Lawrence Kanfer, whose faith and patience made our work possible.

Preface

This book had its beginnings when we were both in the Department of Psychiatry at the University of Oregon Medical School. We were actively engaged in the psychological research, the day-to day clinical practice, the supervision, and the teaching that is usual in such settings. In this combination of activities we were confronted with repeated requests to help our students by bringing the available substantive material from basic psychology to bear more directly on their clinical problems. Specifically, graduate students in clinical psychology, interns, residents, and experienced clinicians wanted instruction in the behaviorally oriented therapeutic practices that were then already attracting increasing and widespread attention.

In our attempts to deal with these requests and questions we became aware of the clinician's great need for a storehouse of behavioral psychological principles. Both the potential and the realized relevance of these principles to clinical problems would make them immediately useful in guiding therapeutic operations and clinical research. Rapid changes in clinical practice, simultaneously occurring in many different areas and directions, seemed to underscore the clinician's need to understand not only the technology of a particular behavioral technique but also the underlying principles. So armed, any professional should be able to judge for himself the appropriateness of a given technique for his own cases or research. He should be able to construct idiosyncratic treatment programs to suit the circumstances of a particular clinical situation. He should be able to adapt to the changes and innovations that are inevitable and necessary in a new and often unproven field. By his grasp of the ties between theory, laboratory investigation, and application, the professional should understand the utility and limitations of various techniques. At the same time, such a compilation should permit the student, who is not a clinician, to recognize how work in his own discipline can lead to a variety of clinical applications, and how, in turn, investigations in the laboratory can be stimulated by problems first raised in applied settings.

This book is the product of our efforts to provide an integrated storehouse. It was initiated by an invitation from the series editor, George Mandler, to the senior author (FHK) to write a short volume on behavior therapy. The junior author (JSP), whose interest in behavioral approaches to clinical practice has been whetted by collaboration with the senior author, was then invited to join in the planning and writing. The volume soon outgrew the size of its initial charge. It has become a text appropriate for courses surveying clinical and psychotherapeutic methods; it is equally intended for practitioners or researchers who wish to have an understanding of the basic principles and problems in behavior therapy.

In writing this book, each of us accepted initial responsibility for drafting individual chapters, but shared so extensively in the redrafting that all chapters represent joint undertakings. Throughout, the senior author carried final responsibility for the material. For many chapters, items from his bibliography supplied the foundation even when the chapter was written by the junior author. Although the work cited in each chapter is necessarily selective, it is the result of a relatively exhaustive literature review through the winter of 1968. Thereafter, only especially significant or novel items were added to the bibliography.

As must be true for a volume that reviews the experiments and theories of a large field, we have been influenced not only by personal contacts but by the many writers and colleagues whose efforts have created the field of behavior therapy. J. R. Kantor deserves particular recognition as a teacher who has deeply influenced the senior author's view of human behavior. George Saslow gave us personal support and encouragement, and also the benefit of years of vigorous discussion with him about clinical practice, teaching, and behavioral approaches to clinical problems. As our department chairman, he provided us with the opportunity and stimulation to pursue our own professional growth and development, and to devote our energies to writing this book. A number of friends and colleagues helpfully reviewed early drafts of many chapters. We thank George Mandler, Warren Garlington, Kenneth Craig, Allen Marlatt, and Isaac Marks for their critiques. Finally, we express appreciation to Kathryn Hall who aided us with care and devotion in the typing and preparation of the manuscript and the collection of references.

Our basic conviction that research and practice can and must coexist for progress to occur in clinical psychology is illustrated by the simultaneous development of our work in both areas. Specific acknowledgment is due to the National Institute of Mental Health, which has generously supported the senior author's research from 1955 to the present. Almost all of the research cited in this text of which he is author or coauthor was funded by NIMH; completion of the text was facilitated by his current grant. Similarly, NIMH provided a Special Research Fellowship to the junior author during a sabbatical year in England and California, which was devoted to the study of behavior therapy techniques and their bases.

FREDERICK H. KANFER
JEANNE S. PHILLIPS

Contents

LEARNING FOUNDATIONS OF BEHAVIOR THERAPY

Introduction

The field of clinical psychology has changed so rapidly in the past two decades that it defies any unitary characterization of its methods, its basic principles, or its goals and professional problems. Today's clinicians are roaming freely across boundaries of scientific disciplines, sometimes adopting techniques demonstrated for the first time only weeks previously, sometimes modifying traditional clinical methods by combining them with new approaches, and at other times using well-established tests or therapy methods. Clinicians are constantly evolving new methods for delivering their services and for adapting available methods to the local requirements of their communities. Prominent among the changes in clinical practice is a shift from a medically oriented to a social-behavioral view of psychopathology. Concomitantly, there is a remarkably rapid development and spread of what are commonly termed "behavior therapies." The goal of this text is to select, from among the welter of new behaviorally oriented treatments, the principles, methods, and issues that appear likely to have some temporal durability. From them the clinician is most likely to be able to develop particular case management techniques suited to the realistic demands of a unique problem and to take advantage of the resources available in the individual case.

This book was not written as a manual for clinicians, however. Its main purpose is to present the research and theory underlying the current application of learning principles and techniques to therapeutic change, as well as to point out the problems involved in practical usage. More specifically, our purpose is to concentrate on laboratory and clinical research relating learning principles to modification of behaviors that are selected as therapeutic targets (behaviors labeled "symptomatic," "sick," "abnormal," or deviant). The student who has some familiarity with learning principles and is interested in their application to practical behavioral problems will gain some understanding of how basic scientific findings

1

from general psychology have been put to work for the betterment of human life through ingenious extrapolation. Clinical practitioners and students already familiar with traditional and behavioral therapeutic procedures hopefully will gain a firmer grasp on the empirical bases of the behavior therapies. They also will gain an awareness of the insufficiencies of behavior therapies, and of the reasons for their increasing importance in clinical practice. Students interested in research with humans will gain greater appreciation of the rich research potentials in the field of clinical psychology since clinically based research can advance the understanding of normal and abnormal behavior and also the methods for appraisal and treatment of human suffering. This book was written, then, as a text for readers who have some familiarity with basic principles of psychology and learning and who wish to know more about the manner in which these principles have been adapted for practical use.

We intended to provide a cohesive framework for a general understanding of behavior therapy methods instead of a series of illustrative case studies. We emphasize and cover basic behavior theory as it applies to the treatment of behavioral problems, rather than dwelling on the causes of human maladjustment or the significance of the person's behavioral disturbance in his own life. While these are recognized as legitimate and, indeed, vital areas of inquiry, they were not of major concern to us in writing this book. We did not intend to cover the many variants of behavior therapy currently under study or in use but, instead, to illustrate major trends with some examples. At the same time, the vast number of investigations in learning and other areas of experimental psychology are drawn upon as they are needed to illustrate their utilization in the applied area and as bases for the clinical procedures that evolved from them. A huge body of literature relevant to the development and change of problem behaviors deals with biological variables and social and cultural processes. These areas are hardly touched upon, despite their obvious significance for the full understanding of disordered behaviors and the processes of therapeutic change with which we are concerned. We emphasize that these omissions are a function of focus (not relevance) and of the limitations of the authors in providing expertise for such an encyclopedic endeavor.

The choice of approaching the field of clinical behavior change from the point of view of learning principles is rooted in our deep conviction that this approach offers two unique advantages over previous clinical presentations: (1) it provides a more flexible and broader frame of reference than any other approach for the clinician or researcher analyzing human behavior or planning for behavior change. Since its methodology and its contents are shared with other fields of psychology, it can profit from continuing enrichment as the other fields advance in knowledge and understanding; (2) the viability of this presentation, its practical utility, and the minimal constraints it places on the conditions under which a patient or a social unit can be examined and treated, promise finally to place clinical psychology in the position of an applied science, and to permit contributions both to human welfare and to the further understanding of human behavior.

The reasons for writing any text are numerous. Clinical applications of behavior therapy models and efforts to bolster (with additional research) those areas with insufficient bases for application are increasing at a rapid pace, suggesting the students' need for an integrated introduction to the subject. A relatively comprehensive presentation may help prevent tendencies toward premature closure of thought or orthodoxy within the behavior therapies. It may emphasize the fact that even the most elegant technological developments in this field require the exercise of mature judgment by the person who applies these developments. We hope that by our presentation of techniques and their related principles within the same framework, the reader will become aware of the research still to be done; careful investigation is still needed to verify hypotheses concerning human psychological processes and to understand the success of many techniques.

We hope that our presentation helps the reader not just to remember techniques, studies, and significant findings, but mainly to broaden his perception of human behavior, both in his professional and personal life. Despite the enlightenment and the vast technological advances in this scientific age, in everyday life beliefs about the nature of human behavior and attitudes toward social institutions and cultural and human values have not yet been reexamined from the perspective of our scientific knowledge. The cultural lag between the data of the social sciences and their use in everyday human pursuits presents a major problem in contemporary human affairs—be they economical, political, social, or psychological. As the methods of behavioral analysis and experimental psychology are jointly applied to a critical examination of human problems, myth after myth about human nature crumbles. We believe that a scientific approach, which emphasizes constant monitoring of the methods of observer or therapist and makes constant demands for verification of apparent truths or assumptions, will help the reader better understand the techniques used for treatment of individual neurotic or psychotic patients. It will also give him a better perspective of himself, his fellow men, and our social institutions as products of human ingenuity and folly—remarkable and awe-inspiring in their diversity yet open to study and understanding by the methods of the social sciences.

ORGANIZATION OF THE BOOK

The organization of this book is based on the view that the locus of psychological problems is in the interaction of people with their social environment, and not in their mental apparatus. We do not expect a diagnostic label to result in the selection of a therapy uniquely suited for that diagnostic category. We do not believe that the model for behavior disorders should be based on the medical disease concept in which diagnosis of a disease manifestation leads to assignment of treatment; nor do we accept the utility of the current psychiatric diagnostic system for treatment decisions. Behavior therapy does not involve itself with "schizophrenia" or the "compulsive character," but with a series of responses that create difficulties for the patient or his environment. From our behavioral viewpoint, problems are described and defined by the therapist in an analysis of the patient's total life setting, and appropriate treatment methods are then selected. Thus, we chose to organize treatment techniques on the basis of the learning principles from which they are derived. In any treatment program, practical considerations may demand simultaneous or successive attacks on separate problems in the same person by different methods. Overlap among therapeutic methods is the rule, not the exception; whereas purity of learning techniques is the exception, even in laboratory studies. The chapters on therapy methods represent clusters of basic techniques which have evolved around a set of learning procedures and a body of experimental findings.

The material in this book has been roughly divided into three sections. Part One introduces a behavioral learning model and its relevance to clinical psychology. Parts Two, Three, and Four describe the structure and application of various learning models. Part Five deals with more general issues of importance in all clinical enterprises, regardless of the particular learning paradigm employed.

Discussion of various learning models has been arbitrarily divided into parts and chapters for expository convenience. As we indicate early in the book, it is rare that a therapeutic program encompasses only one single model to the exclusion of all others. However, it is possible to differentiate methods which rest *primarily* on one of the few basic learning paradigms. Some approaches to behavior change utilize a classical conditioning model (Chapter 3); others are mainly based on the operant conditioning model (Chapter 6). In other chapters we find patterns that involve both models. In some instances there are theoretical and practical reasons for general disagreement about proper assignment of even the basic experimental paradigms to one or the other type of conditioning. When the mechanisms underlying a given operation may involve both classical and operant conditioning, the operation may be discussed in several different places. This is the case, for example, with application of noxious stimuli which may include both classical (aversive conditioning) and operant (punishment) components, and hence it appears in both Chapter 3 and Chapter 7. When one therapeutic procedure operates on both the antecedents of the target behavior and the consequences, the model is a mixed one. Thus Chapter 4, which describes desensitization as a complex therapeutic procedure defying easy classification, is titled "Mixed Models."

In addition to modification of behavior through direct manipulation of the stimulational environment or the behavioral consequences of an act, learning can also occur through indirect or mediated means. The models of vicarious learning (Chapter 5), learning by verbal mediation (Chapter 8), and self-regulation (Chapter 9) are useful as foundations for therapeutic devices. Their theoretical explanation, however, is more difficult, so that each has been accorded a separate chapter.

Effectiveness of therapeutic behavior change procedures depends on utilization of appropriate learning mechanisms, the setting in which learning occurs, and the biological and social characteristics of the individuals involved—learner and behavior modifier. Brief consideration of a sample of these factors and a discussion of behavioral methods of assessment comprise Chapter 10. The final chapter (Chapter 11) reviews broader issues associated with the execution of behavior change procedures in contemporary society. Some implications of the behavioral models for professional practice are discussed in the context of traditional ethical and social requirements of the clinician. Chapter 11 also reviews weaknesses in the foundations of behavior therapy and areas in which further research is needed.

Part I

Overview of a Behavioral Approach to Clinical Psychology

CHAPTER 1

Clinical Psychology and Its Relation to the General Field

Since the end of World War II the practice of clinical psychology has been undergoing continuous change. Innovations in treatment methods have kept pace with increasing demands for the services of psychologists beyond the field of behavior disorders. Although individual diagnosis and therapy still remain the popular image of the psychologist's activities, current practices in community mental health clinics, schools, hospitals, and public institutions have changed. They have moved toward application of the subject matter of psychology to the task of describing, predicting, or altering human behavior under many conditions. The consumption of psychological services is no longer the mark of abnormality. Motives for application of psychological principles are as diverse as the methods.

Reduction of human misery and inefficiency caused by behavior disorders, mainly the neuroses and psychoses, still ranks high among the concerns of practicing psychologists. But increasing attention is also given to prophylactic measures in human development in order to assist men in using their personal and environmental resources to their full extent and to help people achieve the satisfactions which our society values. Some clinical psychologists are engaged in helping individuals in social or industrial groups to work more effectively with their peers. Some are drawn into the planning of social changes associated with the country's attempts to solve its social, economic and political problems. Despite this divergence in interests and purposes, there remain common features which characterize the clinical psychologist's skills. Most important is the knowledge of principles of human behavior and skill in their application to any of the numerous problems that arise in the attempt to understand or alter man's actions or the social environment that controls such actions.

The clinician's changing spheres of action and the wide range of approaches required to handle diverse problems have modified the emphasis of training. Today, a clinician is engaged as much in the analysis of a patient's social environment as in the analysis of thought processes, as much in observation of social behaviors as in description of emotions and feelings. The mark of a good clinician is no longer only sensitivity and intuitive capacity for understanding another person; it includes also knowledge and skill in using learned techniques and principles from general psychology applied to particular problems.

These latter aspects of the clinician's work, his academic skill and knowledge of the field, can be taught formally. Only when he is equipped with such knowledge can the clinician benefit from experiences and improve his judgment and ability to appraise and analyze problems in the execution of programs for behavior change. As in any profession, simple "book learning" is insufficient for practice. Surgeons, lawyers, and other professionals must combine general knowledge of their basic field with good judgment and flexibility to apply their knowledge to the individual case.

But the differences between the psychologist who is a practicing clinician and his colleague who is a researcher have not often been clarified. The image of the clinician as a "scientist-professional" has remained the guiding principle in the training and personal conduct of many clinicians. This role model was formalized in the 1949 Boulder Conference, a two-week-long discussion of doctoral training programs for clinical psychologists, attended by 71 representatives of psychology and related disciplines. The model was intended to reduce the divergence between practitioners and scientists by proposing that the psychologist be prepared to understand and conduct research, although his primary function may be clinical service. The clinical psychologist was envisaged as "one who will be able to contribute through research and scholarship to the development of the techniques and methods of the profession, one who can choose sound procedures and reject worthless ones because he can react critically to the evidence behind new theories and methods, in short an alert and constantly growing, rather than a passive and stagnating, member of his profession" (Cook, 1966, p. 340). Although the desirability of this idealized model has caused many debates and disagreements, the increased utilization of experimentally derived methods for individual psychotherapy and change of social climates has demonstrated the necessity for the practicing clinician to be thoroughly grounded in the research of his science.

In addition to alterations within clinical psychology, there have been greater social changes affecting institutions and living patterns at a rapidly increasing rate. The whole pattern of daily living of the ordinary person in our society is constantly being altered by new ideas, technical innovations, and scientific discoveries. Public attitudes toward science have changed dramatically as the result of the spectacular impact of the Scientific Revolution on everyday life. The imminent conquest of space, automation of large industries and services, miniaturization of electronic equipment and communications systems, control of diseases, and similar contemporary accomplishments have profoundly changed man's view of himself and his environment. Advances in the physical sciences and biology seem to have softened the time-honored opinion that human behavior falls outside the domain of scientific method. Although doubts about the amenability of mental phenomena to a scientific analysis still prevail, there has been wider acceptance of innovation and experimentation in the fields of applied psychology. Most important, there is less resistance to a fresh analysis of the assumptions about human behavior and about the cultural institutions in which man lives.

Technological achievements in the areas of physics, electronics, and other "hard sciences" have also altered the traditional view that progress must evolve slowly from basic laboratory research, through tentative exploration, to eventual application to practical problems. Physicists and engineers have recently called attention to the fact that in the physical sciences the flow of ideas is no longer a one-way street from basic principles to practical application. Engineers no longer wait to start a project until laboratory research provides them with the necessary information. Social demands have provided an impetus to the advance of scientific knowledge by outlining practical goals and defining areas of study in which financial and manpower resources can be concentrated. For example, the social decision to embark on a moon landing before developing new modes of land transportation or prevention of environmental pollution, has resulted in priorities for scientific efforts to solve basic problems associated with space travel and with survival in a gravity-free atmosphere. This decision has not only freed scientific manpower for a particular area of inquiry, it has also firmly established the return flow of information from practical experience to the laboratory. Observations by astronauts on their space travels have raised new scientific questions with suggestions both for "basic research" and for reformulations of earlier theories. In the social sciences, decisions to modify educational systems, prisons, urban communities, or industrial organizations have led to renewed interest in analysis of basic variables associated with relevant social phenomena. These decisions have served as stimuli for investigations of phenomena which had been observed only accidentally.

The practice of clinical psychology has been deeply influenced by technological developments, changes in moral and sexual standards, different vocational opportunities, new educational and medical methods, changing population distribution, and the shifting structure of the community and family. All of these changes have brought with them tolerance of deviations from narrow traditional norms. They are also destroying many assumptions about the universality of pathogenic experiences, the nature of behavior disorders as disease entities, and the limits of adaptability of the human organism. It is therefore difficult to predict to what phenomena the application of psychological principles may be needed most in the future. The most proper strategy for training the psychological practitioner thus lies in acquainting him with the empirical foundations of psychological knowledge instead of with specific procedural methods. Similarly, the viability of any approach to behavior change appears to depend largely on its capacity to accommodate to society's changing criteria for effective social behaviors and changing clinical practices, which reflect the new social demands on the behavioral sciences.

The current field of psychological science, particularly clinical psychology, has been characterized as enduring a transition. In psychotherapy, the decreased prominence of psychoanalysis and the growing diversity of approaches appear to some writers to signal imminent revolutionary changes in the field (see, for example, Colby, 1964). Colby calls attention to Kuhn's (1962) attempt to analyze the historical progress in science. In psychotherapy, the downfall of old models, the current crisis-state, and the invention of alternate theoretical explanation all fit Kuhn's statement of preconditions for the emergence of new paradigms. Kuhn's view of scientific progress suggests that the sequence of (1) discontent, (2) search for alternatives, and (3) revolution by replacement of old paradigms with new ones is the course of scientific progress through discontinuous episodes. All of these conditions are reflected in the recent reexamination of older theories of psychotherapy and personality development, and in the richness (in patches) of theoretical constructs in explaining components of personality and social interactions. As yet, no single comprehensive theory has been offered that covers in depth as many different areas of human life as have been touched upon by psychoanalysis.

BEHAVIORISTIC CLINICAL PSYCHOLOGY

Among several new theoretical models for clinical psychology is one based on neobehavioristic methodology and experimental learning data. The behavioral learning model and the methods of behavior modification derived from it seem to be especially well suited for incorporating changes in cultural content and "miniature" theories from experimental psychology because the model is primarily content-free. It does not describe the behavioral ingredients of "normalcy" or "good adjustment." It does not attempt to pinpoint the content of a given experience (for example, a childhood trauma) as the cause of a mental illness. It is not limited only to learning processes, but includes perceptual, motivational, and biological phenomena. Unlike its predecessors, the main contribution of the behavioral learning model lies in an emphasis on methodology. It seeks to specify general functional relationships between independent variables and response classes and to discover anew in each case the particular parameters which affect these relationships. Thus, it can be applied to wide ranges of behavioral problems, many of which involve not only individuals but social groups. Its application has already extended far beyond the scope of earlier clinical models. The openness of the behavioral model is not limited to clinical psychology alone. In a survey of the status of the profession of psychology in 1962, Webb suggests that contemporary psychology, in all its diversity, is bound by the single common principle—that human behavior is lawful. From this assumption follow two corollaries: "(1) the understanding of human behavior can best be achieved by systematic analysis; (2) systematic methodologies may be derived which will permit effective predictions and modifications of behavior" (Webb, 1962, p. 32). This belief (that human behavior is lawful) represents a strong bond among psychologists whose views may diverge on other issues. It also contrasts with the beliefs of some practitioners that (1) the laws of man's behavior should be generated not from behavior but from understanding of the structure and functions of the mind, and (2) intuition, introspection, and spiritual communion—not systematic analysis—are the proper methods for psychology.

The general principles of psychology form the scientific substrata of behavior modification methods, but particular clinical enterprises require a unique combination of procedures to fit individual cases. For example, two patients may present similar phobic reactions, aggressive behaviors, or sexual difficulties. Yet in each case the particular living pattern of the patient, his responsiveness to clinical intervention, and the degree to which the symptoms interfere with his daily life will be among the factors which determine the treatment method. The resources in the patient's environment that can be enlisted to facilitate the therapeutic process include the patient's level of social and vocational skills, and many other crucial features in endless combinations. Consequently, the presentation of many individual cases in great detail would still leave the student in the field with little *specific* preparation for the next case. Until the parameters of persons, complaints, environments, and therapists which govern therapeutic outcome are better understood, it is impossible to prescribe specifically the multitude of concrete steps that make up the clinician's work with each patient. A presentation of general methods and their underlying principles can, at least, provide the clinician with alternative strategies. At the present time, personal ingenuity and experience still remain the main resources for the selection of the most promising technique.

On the scientific side, a similar problem exists. No theory can hope to encompass all of the events of ordinary human behavior. The vast richness of ongoing behavior presently defies any abstraction into a few simple event classes for attack by simple standardized laboratory procedures. However, this does not mean that detailed guidelines for practical behavior modification are unattainable. On the contrary, the construction of better catalogs of therapeutic procedures is a goal that both behavior theorists and clinical investigators seek. But even if it were presently possible to prescribe a given technique (we are approaching the time when this may be possible) and to indicate the type of personality, social conditions, symptomatic behaviors, and therapeutic resources that would represent modifying parameters in the therapeutic equation, selection among such techniques would still depend very much on the particular goal for an individual patient. Beyond that, the lack of a comprehensive system for describing and understanding behavior, the therapist's personal predilections, skills, and beliefs, and other practical factors still would allow some choice among treatment programs.

It is highly questionable whether complete understanding of human behavior or a high accuracy of prediction for all aspects of a person's functioning may even be necessary for effective therapeutic intervention. An analysis of human behavior may be complete when it has pragmatic usefulness rather than aesthetic appeal, practical utility rather than complete coverage. Skinner (1964) has stated the issue this way:

"No scientific analysis of behavior 'will be as rich as *The Brothers Karamazov*,' nor will the physicist's analysis of the world be as rich as walking around the campus. They are 'not there to be rich.' Whatever view of human nature emerges from the science of behavior will be different from any we now have, but 'I cannot imagine anything which is less likely to be regarded as poverty-stricken than a genuinely effective understanding of human behavior.' (p. 104) '. . . psychology needs to learn one very important lesson, and that is that it cannot answer every question which is asked of it' " (p. 99).

In this book, the choice of a learning model as a basis for organizing recent behavior modification methods has been dictated by two considerations. First, despite its limitations and the certainty that even its basic features will change in proportion to advances in such areas as motivation, perception, thinking, and brain function, the learning model has successfully integrated the largest body of available research about behavior change, although it is an incomplete model. Second, the learning model has served as a base for developing most of the clinical techniques that are described in this book, and its pragmatic utility is now widely accepted. From among the available theoretical orientations in learning we have selected one that generally tends toward the point of view expressed by Skinner. It also includes elements from social learning, cognition, and other areas when they appear particularly pertinent to a therapeutic technique. The viewpoint expressed here and shared with Davison (1967), Ullmann (1969), and others, is that behavior therapy techniques should utilize all the findings of experimental psychology, instead of those that are limited to learning and conditioning alone.

In surveying experiments on learning, a large body of data is encountered in the animal learning area. In fact, these animal studies represent the basis of contemporary learning principles. Extrapolations from animal laboratory data to complex social behavior, however, become precarious when they involve generalizations to symbolic or thinking behaviors, self-attitudes or other processes that cannot be directly tested at the animal level and have been only partially explored at the human level. Indeed, the data cited in this book are offered only as anchor points for clinical application. They represent a cross section of a rapidly moving stream of knowledge, and they illustrate approaches and issues that comprise the field of behavior therapies at the end of the 1960s. Many of the general principles described here will undoubtedly endure relatively unchanged. Other principles may be expanded or superseded; and some of the proposed issues may be resolved shortly after this volume is in the reader's hands. The most important lesson to be learned from this presentation is not the factual content. We consider it important to recognize that the main tools that animal laboratory research and the work of experimental psychologists have made available to clinicians are (1) a scientific methodology, and (2) a few basic principles from which extrapolation to practical situations can be made. On these foundations the clinical researcher will have to build a progressively better approximation to a model of human behavior.

In this chapter we introduce the reader to the viewpoint of behavior therapy. Since it is based on a relatively well-articulated philosophical orientation, it dictates methods of observation and, to some extent, determines what is observed. Therefore, a comparison of clinical and laboratory methods is made in order to highlight the adjustments and changes necessary as one shifts from the investigation of well-controlled laboratory phenomena to exploration of clinical problems. Finally, we briefly discuss current research strategies and deficiencies in the clinical area. This is to illustrate strategies that can maximize rigor of method and generality of conclusions, although experimental subjects may be individuals in natural environments, and execution of ideal research designs may be tempered by practical necessity and social limitations.

BEHAVIOR THERAPY AS A POINT OF VIEW

Some behavioral therapeutic techniques were employed long before learning theories existed, but their rationale was based on common sense or observations instead of experimentation. For example, a pediatrician in 1830 proposed a treatment for enuresis that included most elements of a conditioning therapy (Lovibond, 1964). Franks (1966) reports that Pliny, the Elder, proposed a number of intriguing techniques for establishing a revulsion for alcohol. Kantorovich's application in 1929 of Pavlovian conditioning principles introduced controlled testing of these techniques to establish conditioned aversion to alcohol. The Mowrers' 1938 bell-and-pad conditioning device—explicitly derived from the same Pavlovian model—produced a treatment for enuresis.

It is not surprising that some earlier therapy methods resemble current behavior therapies. Modern learning theories describe processes and parameters presumed to govern all human learning, obviously available for early technological exploitation despite the absence of behavior theories or empirical data from which technology could be derived. As Ullmann (1967a) has noted: "There are elements of behavior therapy in the writings of people as diverse as Albert Ellis, Hobart Mowrer, Alfred Adler, George Kelly, and Dale Carnegie" (p. 1). What is novel in the behavior therapies is their adoption of methods that shift from laboratory to clinic and back to the laboratory in self-conscious testing of the utility and validity of their operation, and with a data-oriented, hypothesis-testing frame of reference within the treatment setting itself. In the past, for example, the wealth of literature on verbal conditioning and microscopic analysis of dyadic verbal therapy operations had almost no influence on the format of psychotherapeutic interviews or on the behavior of the interviewing therapist (Kanfer, 1966a). The voluminous research on abnormal behavior had little effect on the traditional psychiatric classification system. In contrast, behaviorally oriented therapists and their laboratory colleagues have recently urged and attempted extrapolations of experimental findings to clinical methods, proposing testable hypotheses and describing the steps required for making these extrapolations. This tendency to mix experimental and clinical areas is clearly shown by Goldstein, Heller, and Sechrest (1966). They draw upon cognitive dissonance research for hypotheses about maximizing a therapist's interpersonal influence on a patient, and upon social psychological research about operations within small groups to formulate testable propositions regarding methods for enhancing effectiveness of group therapy. Their book has been heralded by some psychologists as an excellent example of expanded clinical use of scientific psychology without sacrificing either humane values, or objectivity and rigor.

Other investigators in the field of behavior modification have similarly urged breadth in technique and theory:

"Why should behavior therapists limit themselves only to 'experimentally established principles of learning against the background of physiology' and ignore other areas of experimental psychology such as studies on perception, emotion, cognition and so forth? And why should behavior therapists avoid using such techniques as self-disclosure, dyadic interactions, and other methods, as long as they can be reconciled with reinforcement principles? Finally, one might inquire to what extent Wolpe's reference to a 'stimulus-response model' is a vague and meaningless abstraction. If the current upsurge of interest in behavior therapy is to expand and mature, we must beware of oversimplified notions, limited procedures, and extravagant claims which could conceivably undermine our efforts. The field of therapy and its many facets needs anything but yet another closed system" (Lazarus, 1968, p. 2).

This open viewpoint places an increased responsibility on the behavior therapist for broad acquaintance with current research and for making careful experimental tests of the relevance of new findings to actual clinical applications. Ultimately, he needs to discover the parameters and relationships which govern extrapolation of findings from laboratory to clinic. The more we recognize that these areas are germane to clinical work, the less clear-cut becomes the distinction between behavior therapies and other behaviorally oriented interview therapies.

BEHAVIOR THERAPY AND OTHER APPROACHES

What distinguishes behavior therapies from more traditional approaches? Behavior therapists tend to select specific symptoms or behaviors as targets for change, to employ concrete, planned interventions to manipulate these behaviors, and to monitor progress continuously and quantitatively. A patient's early life history is largely ignored, except as it may provide clues about such factors as currently active events which maintain symptoms, or hierarchies of reinforcers. Behavior therapists tend to concentrate on an analysis of particular symptoms. They devote far less attention than other clinicians to subjective experiences, attitudes, insights and dreams. Their tools include electronic equipment and devices which permit precise measurement of behavior. Their programs tend to give less consideration to evidence based on empathy than on observations. Their "show me" attitude puts the burden of proof on the outcome of an attempted therapeutic move rather than on the social preconceptions of what should be beneficial for a person. Critics have demonstrated possible pitfalls of the behavior therapy approach. Dangers lie not in the methods themselves, but in their use by an unskilled clinician who may conceal his shortcomings in judgment in a maze of numbers and graphs as effectively as the secrecy of doubled-door psychoanalytic offices can screen an analyst's errors. Use of mechanical devices adds to the clinician's burden of alertness; focus on the *human* problem must constantly be remembered, even while technological problems arise in therapy.

Behavior therapy is most distinguishable from other approaches after a program with a carefully outlined procedure has been established for treatment of a defined problematic response. Treatment in which a patient's nervous tic is conditioned by applying an aversive stimulus whenever the tic occurs is markedly different from the psychodynamic treatment of the same problem by repeated interviews attempting to ascertain conflicts of which the tic is said to be a manifestation. On the other hand, assignments to a subassertive patient to note and record his subassertive behavior or to practice assertive behaviors in planned situations, or the use of relaxation and hypnosis in therapy during recall of embarrassing or anxiety-arousing situations are much more likely to be found among various schools of psychotherapy. The essential distinction of behavior therapy seemingly may be most vivid in its unique methods, but it actually lies in the approach of the clinician, from his very first contact with the patient. The questions asked about the patient's complaints, sources of various schools of psychotherapy. The essential distinction of behavior for therapeutic attack, the rationale underlying all of these, not just the actual techniques used, are the hallmarks of behavior therapy.

The differences in procedures are based on the differences between traditional and behavior therapy with regard to several important assumptions about the nature of the problem, including:

1. With regard to etiology, behavior therapies do not accept the concept of psychological problems as "diseases" due to early faulty personality development.
2. The behavior to be altered is not viewed as a superficial "symptom" or manifestation of an underlying disease process, but as the patient's problem. The target behavior is not a substitute for a conflict or an unconscious expression of a blocked desire, but is a learned response

which has detrimental consequences for the patient or his environment, regardless of how it was acquired.

3. Treatment is aimed at the problem behavior, not at the hypothesized disease, conflict, or unconscious struggle within the patient's personality.

4. Treatment techniques are tailored to the individual patient's problems, not to the diagnostic label attached to his condition or personality.

The behavior therapies differ in their entire conception of abnormal behavior from the traditional view of the nature of neuroses, psychoses, and other personality disorders. Ullmann and Krasner (1969) present a detailed discussion of the behavioral approach to abnormal psychology, and several other recent books (for example, Lundin, 1969; Mischel, 1968a; Aronfreed, 1968; and Bandura and Walters, 1963) describe the kind of behavioral conceptions of personality development on which behavior therapy is based.

CRITICISMS OF BEHAVIOR THERAPIES

Two kinds of criticism have been leveled against behavior therapies. On one hand, the new techniques have been attacked for their failure to retain roots in firm scientific evidence. On the other hand, they have been accused of offering a mechanistic technology that dehumanizes both its administrator and consumer. Each group of opponents raises serious questions about the risks involved in adopting behavior therapy methods, and the implications of their criticisms are worthy of further discussion.

The Science Issue

We have already noted that utilization of a learning model requires extrapolation from animal data, since these data represent the core of learning research. Such extrapolations run the risk of losing contact with their "scientific" base when applied to complex human phenomena. Breger and McGaugh (1965) sharply criticize the learning theory approach to psychotherapy on several grounds. The sufficiency of learning principles for explanation of many of the laboratory experiments, let alone for the complexities of human learning behavior, is questionable. "When we look at the way conditioning principles are applied in the explanation of more complex phenomena, we see that only a rather flimsy analogue bridges the gap between such laboratory defined terms as stimulus, response, and reinforcement and their reference in the case of complex behavior" (Breger and McGaugh, 1965, p. 344). But apart from the problems of finding appropriate transitions from the laboratory to the clinic, criticisms can be made against the comprehensiveness of the psychology of learning itself. The basic processes described by concepts like reinforcement or memory are still not clearly understood. Thus there exists the danger that behavior therapists may lend an air of scientific respectability to their work by use of terminology and constructs from a body of science that is still in a primitive state.

There is indeed occasional evidence in reports of behavior therapy procedures of the use of oversimplification, imprecision, and loose terminology. Some examples will be encountered in our review of early experiments. At the same time, clinicians who pioneered in the area of behavior therapy found themselves defending an approach against well-entrenched alternate approaches to psychotherapy. Incompletely worked out methods and tenuous procedures were often reported with a "pejorative, excoriative tone in some of the earlier writings in this field . . . [some pretentions] to a precision and scientific status not yet achieved, an overreaching quite out of character with the public intellectual posture of working scientists" (Hunt and Dyrud, 1968, p. 140). Uncontrolled clinical trials of new techniques sometimes resulted in claims of high success rates that critics readily viewed as extravagant and misleading. With the behavior therapists' growing maturity and confidence in their methods, the trends described by Breger and McGaugh and by Hunt and Dyrud seem to have been countered by more modest claims of accomplishments and scientific status. In recent writings there is increased emphasis on the need for detailed study of the mechanisms and therapeutic effects of behavior therapies. In the following chapters we will also see increased awareness among behavior therapists of the importance of including central psychological processes such as thinking, perceiving, and fantasizing in their conceptualization of human functioning. A simple conditioning model may be a basic beginning for a learning approach to behavior change, but it does not reflect the limitations of this approach in taking advantage of man's manifold potentialities.

The major risk in alienation of clinical techniques from their scientific origin lies in the danger that changes and advances of scientific knowledge may exert no influence toward improvement of clinical methods. The practitioner's model could remain fixed at an early stage of its development without benefit from continued growth in its fundamental science.

The Humanistic Issue

The accusation against behavior therapies from humanist quarters is simply an extension of the general repudiation of a behavioral approach to psychological phenomena. In the rejection of behavior therapy there is an alignment of numerous approaches which are divergent among themselves. What these critics share is a common concern that emphasis on behavior may run the risk of disregarding the value and dignity of human life itself. Koch (1964) has expressed this concern very succinctly:

"Modern society has provision for an ample margin of waste, especially of ideas. But nowhere can such 'give' in this system lead to less happy consequences than in psychology. For if psychology does not influence man's image of himself, what branch of the scholarly community does? That modern psychology has projected an image of man which is as demeaning as it is simplistic, few intelligent and sensitive non-psychologists would deny. . . . the mass dehumanization process which characterizes our time—the simplification of sensibility, homogenization of taste, attenuation of the capacity for experience—continues apace. Of all fields in the community of scholarship, it should be psychology which combats this trend. Instead, we have played no small part in augmenting and supporting it" (pp. 37–38).

The humanistic issue goes to the heart of the question about the sufficiency of scientific method for the study of man. The very objectivity and detachment which are the basis of a scientific approach seem a danger in their reduction of man's achievements and complexities to "nothing but" a set of relationships, perhaps even in mathematical terms. Once such functions are described, what is left of the qualities of man which distinguish him from other organisms? Can the richness of a man's feelings, his joys, ambitions, dreams, and agonies be reduced to a set of variables? The implicit assumption appears to be that knowledge of laws that govern behavior is incompatible with sensitivity to the variations in the expression of these lawful relationships. This assumption is parallel to the assumption that a knowledge of chemistry or natural processes reduces the aesthetic and utilitarian values of products, such as stained glass windows, or natural processes, such as the bloom of flowers.

There are undoubtedly behavior modification projects that, by their successes, have demonstrated that a simplistic direct translation from the animal level to human problems can accomplish behavioral changes without consideration of the nobler aspects of human life. Ultimately, it can increase the human dignity of a previously vegetative psychotic patient as much as any humane effort, when such a patient regains some of his earlier ability for independent living. Continued demonstration of the lawfulness of human behavior and parting of the curtain of mystery that has shrouded the human mind certainly run many risks. But any expansion of knowledge changes old ways and cherished beliefs. The conquest of space or a moon landing lowers the poetic importance of the moon in human romances. The glamorous aspects of the moon are lost as scientific data about its physical conditions become available. But, these data provide information for better understanding of the physical realities of our solar system. It may be deplorable that such increased understanding of the laws of nature, such as the laws of nuclear fission, creates problems that can profoundly alter entire societies, but the continued expansion of knowledge seems inevitable. Some contemporary scientists are seriously suggesting a moratorium on further progress in science until man is ready to master its control for society's benefit rather than society's doom.

The antibehavioristic attitudes, both within and without the social sciences, have been expressed on various grounds. Apart from the insufficiency of a peripheral S-R explanation, which is a scientific issue, the question of human values has been most frequently injected into the debate. In arguments against behavior therapy, one central issue revolves around the high degree of control exerted by the therapist. The inherently environmental approach has led to therapeutic methods in which patients are restricted in their social interaction, food consumption, or physical movements in order to enhance the utility of incentives. Use of computerized electronic equipment to provide precise contingent consequences for a set of patient responses produces a robotlike atmosphere. Similarly, use of aversive stimuli in conditioning and restriction of available choices of behaviors have led some to voice fears of dehumanization. The origin of conditioning methods in the animal laboratory and the rigorous or "regimented" nature of procedures further appear as alarming reductions of individuals to the status of animals, bereft of free choice and use of their rational faculties. These and many other considerations have resulted in lively discussions on the ethics of effective behavior control. This was not an earlier concern since behavior control has only recently become feasible by psychological instead of physical means (Kanfer, 1965a).

More recently, increased attention to individuality in behavior and to the moral, symbolic, and ethical features of the therapeutic process has appeared in the work of the behavior therapists. There also has been continuing pressure on psychologists to participate in mass modification of behaviors that are of national or cultural importance. The problems of cultural underdevelopment of minority groups, control of crime and delinquency, civil rights issues, inadequacies of educational systems have all represented problems for which broadscale simple solutions for large masses of people are sought, with little time and attention given to individuals within these target populations. While the pragmatic orientation of behavior modification techniques has expanded the scope of application of these techniques, the cost has often been a narrow problem-centered attack. In many situations the outcome of the application of behavior therapy methods has been an alleviation of a particular problem without the traditional concern about its basic causes or its accompanying behaviors. Whether this focused intervention is sufficient for a given problem depends on the particular situation. For example, symptom removal of a man's sexual impotence may solve marital problems for one couple, but only create additional problems for another. Training of severely retarded children to feed themselves can alleviate problems of the nursing staff, but does not solve the social problems of management of retarded persons. The final outcome of a behavior modification technique may seem to neglect the human value of total reconstruction because only one segment of the total problem is actually pursued. Case management, in which these techniques are imbedded, must take into account human values through the selection of targets for treatment and decisions about goals that are consistent with a given value system.

Since we will repeatedly encounter the choice of which problems to tackle, it seems sufficient here to point out that behavior modification technology is an instrument for accomplishing purposes set by society. Unlike certain personality theories (and the therapies based on them), behavior therapy and the learning paradigms are nonhumanistic instead of antihumanistic. They are also nonethical, in that they do not propose standards or values toward which man must aspire. In contrast, other psychotherapeutic schools provide criteria for normalcy and happiness. For example, nondirective therapy is based on the notion of self-actualization as a final human value or goal. Psychoanalysis, as a personality theory and method of therapy, similarly offers value judgments through its formulations about the origins of pathology and unconscious drives or conflicts. Developmental arrest at the anal stage or reliance on paranoid projection as a defense are inherently sick or abnormal, that is, detrimental to the individual and society. Universal criteria for adjustment of individuals and societies are widely discussed and evaluated in psychoanalytic writings.

Behavior modification, in contrast, is pragmatic in character—a technology without built-in goals or values. This fact does not demand that the behavioral approach be dehumanizing—its technology can be applied to achieve very humanistic values and goals. Political science can be considered the science of how *values* are attached to social behavior patterns; behavior theory is the study of how these *behavior patterns* are developed and changed. The values themselves originate in the society and its institutions. Values become attached to behavioral patterns through norms established by political and ethical organizations representing the people at large. It is not the therapist's task to select values for society or one of its members. As a private citizen and humanist the therapist tries to influence assignment of values; but in modifying behavior he acts as an instrument representing the goals of others, the patient, or a social agency.

The psychologist's knowledge of human behavior places him in a favorable position for participation in his social community in the shaping or changing of value systems because he can often offer methods to study or predict the consequences of a set of values or value changes (Krasner, 1965a; Kanfer, 1965a; Kelman, 1965; Rogers and Skinner, 1956). However, this is an educational or participatory role, not inherent in the therapist role itself. The scientist's responsibility in creating or supporting branches of special knowledge about an innovation or a problem area demands a more active role in assessing the problem's importance to society—be it knowledge about nuclear fission, natural resources, organ transplants, or behavior modification. Thus, it is less the ends than the means employed in behavior therapies that some humanists deplore.

CLINICAL AND LABORATORY MODELS COMPARED

Behavior modifiers alternately function as therapists and as researchers, and the methods of the two settings blend together. But differences exist in the settings and in the psychologist's *modus operandi* when he acts as experimenter and therapist. The area of clinical research combines features of both role models. It encompasses the basic scientific approach, but in field situations it often requires accommodations to fit the subject matter and the natural limitations on experimental manipulations and possible research methods. The greatest overlap occurs when the clinician is conducting research with patients and he is engaged in executing a portion of a preprogrammed treatment design. Even under these circumstances, however, the differences in settings, limitations on methods, expectations of certain beneficial outcomes, and ethical considerations affect the clinician to a different extent than the laboratory worker.

To understand the environment in which clinical research takes place we must first highlight the clinician's traditional activities. They can be characterized by these main features:

1. The clinician's task is to observe and treat a single individual. The behavior of the patient is subject to simultaneous influence by multitudinous uncontrolled variables. At best, only a small segment of behavior can be studied, yielding only limited and biased information as a basis for treatment.
2. The patient's plight demands immediate action although scientifically validated explanations or operations may not be available. The clinician's decisions rest on objective data and on his "educated guesses,"

and are goaded by consideration of the social forces which have brought the patient into treatment.

3. Relevant scientific knowledge is used side by side or in mixture with the clinician's personal experiences and information which have not been derived from or integrated with scientific psychology. The clinician's inquiry about emotional responses of a patient in particular interpersonal interactions is guided, for example, by casual awareness of his own and others' reactions to similar circumstances, as much as by awareness of personality research.

4. The clinician's decisions may have far-reaching and immediate impact on several people. Thus, he must have a high degree of social responsibility and must constantly evaluate his goals and methods in terms of their effectiveness and their social consequences.

These characteristics of clinical practice have a number of special consequences. Emphasis on practical resolution of problems in an everchanging social environment requires constant awareness of the many problems that people must cope with in their daily lives. Patients come from various walks of life and, except for brief periods of treatment, return to their roles as workers, teachers, salesmen or housewives. The clinician cannot isolate his intervention in the patient's life from the many other influences which also affect the patient. Frequently he must collaborate with members of other professions, adapt his predictions and solutions to the realities of the patient's world, and recognize the economic, political, social, medical, and legal forces which exert control over his patient's behavior.

These practical considerations often override technical conclusions derived from careful study of a patient. For instance, the ideal solution for changing the maladaptive behavior of a child may be to remove him from his parental home. The ideal solution for a neurotic adult may lie in providing him with freedom from anxiety over poverty, in separation from a marital partner, or in practice with a skillful heterosexual partner. Obviously, these ideal solutions are often unavailable because they are unattainable or unacceptable to others or to the patient himself. A practical approach to the resolution of a specific problem, therefore, demands that the clinician combine the results of his analysis for the specific case with the practical limitations imposed by society, patient, and therapist. The clinical decision-making process has much in common with the models which have been offered in the field of policy making in industry and politics. These situations all share the lack of a single best solution to please all interested parties. In these situations, constant consideration of the interests of different individuals or groups is required. A solution can only be achieved by "negotiation" or compromise between the rationally most desirable and practically most feasible alternatives (Bauer, 1966).

In contrast to the practical demands of the clinician's world, the scientific laboratory model requires systematic and empirical study of the relationship of observable phenomena under stringent control—without compromise due to social pressures. The laboratory researcher's activities can be characterized by these major steps:

1. Focus on a preselected class of events (dependent variables), defined and measured so as to be objectively described and publicly observable.
2. Planned manipulation of one or several similarly defined classes of other events (independent variables) by objective, measurable, public, repeatable operations, in order to assess their relationship to the phenomenon under examination.
3. Isolation of these manipulations and measurements from other sources of influence, in order that alternative explanations can be ruled out.
4. Attention to the sampling characteristics of subjects, events, definitions, measures, manipulations, in order that the generality of the results can be evaluated.

In comparing the clinical and scientific models, Maltzman's (1966) use of Reichenbach's distinction between the scientist's work within the context of *discovery* and the context of *justification* is helpful. The clinician operates on the basis of two separate sets of ground rules, depending on the role he is fulfilling. In formulating a picture of the patient's problems and their causal factors, the clinician operates within the context of discovery. The processes are those characteristic of hypothesis building by inductive thinking—procedurally vague and heavily dependent on individual creativity; but they are guided by knowledge of relevant behavioral dimensions and a working model of human functioning which suggest some factors likely to be pertinent in a functional analysis of behavior. Once the clinician has formulated a set of hypotheses for a given patient and has decided on a method of attack that is practical and sensible, he then works in the context of justification, under the ground rules of scientific procedure. The clinician shifts back and forth between the two attitudes more frequently and rapidly than the laboratory investigator, since new or contradictory information requires that he revise his formulation and begin part of the evaluation process anew. The scientist shifts mainly when his research plan is not working out. He then returns "to the drawing board" in a much more deliberate and clearly differentiated way. The sources of ideas for the scientist operating in the context of *discovery* are as difficult to pinpoint as for the clinician. Sidman (1960b) describes this dilemma:

"If one wishes to explore the conditions under which a phenomenon occurs, how does one determine the variables with which to work? There is no pat answer to this question. One may select those variables relevant to a given theory; or proceed on the basis of analogues from similar phenomena about which more is known; or select a variable for some reason of which one is completely unaware and cannot verbalize adequately. *Neither these nor any other methods of selection have any bearing upon the importance of the resulting data.* A variable may turn out to be relevant in contexts never suspected by the experimenter, or it may turn out to be minor and of minimal systematic importance" (p. 40, italics in text).

The distinction between operations during *discovery* and *justification* points to the impure nature of both clinical and scientific work, and to their similarity in relying heavily on the worker's judgment, albeit to a different degree and with differing frequency. Both scientist and clinician derive their first hunches from their own personal experiences and knowledge of their field. The kernel of ideas from which early speculations evolve, in the context of discovery, includes (for both scientist and clinician) values, favored assumptions, and other unknown features. However, once a set of testable hypotheses is established, be it a treatment plan or a research design, the behavioral clinician strives to operate within the strict rules of the context of justification, which he shares with the scientist. It is at this stage of the clinical enterprise, therefore, that the focus is shifted to observable responses, specifiable operations, and objective measures.

The general format of the behavioral clinician's plan of conduct can be compared with the steps usually described for the experimental psychologist. They consist of (1) formulation of the problem, (2) design of operational procedures that test the hypotheses stated in (1), (3) execution of the treatment, (4) analysis of the data, and (5) evaluation of the implications of the results for the problem. In clinical procedures, the steps in this process are less discrete. The last step may simply lead to a repetition of the cycle, if the results of a single treatment procedure do not resolve the original problem. Nevertheless, the formulation of a research problem and the design of a procedure in terms of available treatment methods (independent variables) and behaviors selected for modification (dependent variables) are parallel activities. Similarly, the analysis of experimental data is comparable to the clinician's evaluations of the effect of treatment. In both cases the relevance of the findings must be related to the original statement of the problem. The analogy between the two models is useful as a general guideline, but in practice it is far from perfect. The differences in goals for each procedure are obvious. The results of the different demands on the psychologist can be illustrated by considering differences between clinical and laboratory operations (see following).

Formulation of the Problem

The problem first presents itself to the scientist in the form of a vague idea and to the clinician in the form of a patient's ill-defined complaints. In refining his first impressions, the therapist attempts to develop hypotheses about the variables that may be responsible for a client's problematic behaviors and the particular behaviors that are, in fact, problematic. The researcher similarly attempts to forecast relationships among events in his experimental hypotheses. However, it is usually a concrete step for the laboratory worker when he "freezes" his problem and undertakes the experiment proper; whereas the clinician's hypotheses are constantly altered by new information. Since evaluative interviews or observations can also have therapeutic effects, the therapist's efforts to appraise the patient continuously merge with his function as an agent of behavior change. The patient's responses to various therapeutic interventions and the ongoing collection of data regarding target behaviors outside the therapeutic setting lead to further revisions of the clinician's formulations. This continues throughout therapy. The clinician's success often depends on the proper timing of a change in approach and on strategy changes *during* treatment—changes to an extent not acceptable for the scientist.

The clinician and laboratory investigator both attempt to predict behavioral changes that will occur as a function of their experimental or therapeutic manipulations. However, in the clinical situation, it is direction of effect which is predicted. For example, a desensitization procedure aims not to *change* fear reactions but to *reduce* their intensity or frequency. The double-ended statistical hypothesis that a variable will significantly affect a behavior—in an unspecified quantity or direction—is not appropriate for the clinician.

Behavior is Multiply Determined

The clinician usually cannot eliminate effects of extraneous variables. Many determinants contribute to the occurrence of a response. In clinical problems, isolation of each of these determinants is often not only impossible, but also unnecessary. Unlike the scientist, the clinician is interested only in finding *any* determinant that is sufficiently strong to control the problematic behavior and is sufficiently accessible to be used therapeutically. In his immediate therapeutic role, the clinician's goal is the attainment of effective change, not the comprehensive understanding of the variables influencing his patient. Favorable outcome of therapy is taken as support for the clinician's assessment of the problem and selection of appropriate therapy procedures. This parallels the support given an experimental hypothesis and theory or network of propositions by accurate prediction of experimental outcome. But the behavior modifier's task is not to isolate single causal factors of change within his interventions but to produce those changes crucial for his client's benefit. He is working for a certain threshold of change, by whatever means it may be produced. Testing his unique formulation and understanding the specific process of change in the single case is a secondary goal for the clinician. The reverse is true of the researcher. When a patient or client exhibits sufficient behavioral changes to function adequately, the therapeutic process stops, regardless of lack of clarity about the particular causes of improvement. The researcher's task is not completed when the data collected are favorable but when his research question is clearly answered. Since extraneous circumstances in a patient's life can also lead to failure or success, the clinician cannot validate his hypotheses on the basis of outcome alone. To the researcher, the effects of extraneous variables on his data are evidence of a poor research design.

Frequently clinicians feel rewarded in their work by the "insights" and "empathy" they achieve, mistaking private intellectual pleasures for accomplishments of actual goals and mistaking untested hypotheses for confirmed data. Such pleasures have their hazards. They may, for one thing, support the clinician in persisting on a false approach to the patient's difficulties. They may cause the clinician to regard *insight,* or understanding of the causes of his behavior by the patient, as a *sine qua non* of treatment, instead of seeking removal of symptoms. The argument for understanding and unraveling as a goal of therapy states, in effect, that to prevent future difficulties, all relevant determinants of the individual's complex behaviors must be explored. If such prolonged treatment were possible and effective, it would still be questionable whether the clinician's job should be extended to encompass a total evaluation and change of the patient's life pattern when the specific problem for which help is requested can be attacked more directly. The multiplicity of factors relating to a given problem, therefore, requires that the clinican limit his efforts toward some predetermined goal by manipulating whichever variables are practical and effective. Behavior change, not understanding, is the clinician's main goal.

The scientist, in testing the effects of one or several independent variables, controls the influence of all other variables. The clinician has greater difficulty in selecting the particular determinants which he should manipuate and test, because his initial formulation is more tentative and incomplete. Also, the clinician must give priority to outcome rather than to the examination of particular variables. The clinician, because of his concern with treatment outcome, is often uncertain which criterion measures to apply in order to test the relevance of multiple variables to his patient's behavior change. The researcher, even in exploratory studies, can systematically select isolated relationships for examination under experimental control. The clinician is faced with unknown and uncontrolled ramifications among response classes and with multiple and simultaneously active determinants that make it impossible for him to identify and measure all relevant dependent variables. Often quite unexpected and provocative relationships are accidentally discovered when, in clinical research, less promising criterion measures are included. For example, Gelder, Marks, and Wolff (1967) found quite unexpected relationships when measures of interpersonal adequacy were included among outcome criteria for behavior modification of phobias.

Treatment of the Single Case

Clinical practice deals with the individual case. In contrast, scientific laws are statements about probable relationships among classes of events. Application of psychological principles to individual behavior necessitates consideration of many individual parameters. Therefore, a high level of precision in prediction is impossible to obtain. The controversy over whether to study individual subjects in detail (the *idiographic* method) or to study limited behaviors in many subjects (the *nomothetic* method) has been raised not only in clinical practice but also in other areas of psychology. In discussing the problem of making inferences about individual behavior from group learning curves in rats, Estes (1956) has noted that group data have considerable value for summarization and theoretical analysis. But "no 'inductive' inference from mean curve to individual curve is possible, and the uncritical use of mean curves, even for such purposes as determining the effect of an experimental treatment upon rate of learning or rate of extinction is attended by considerable risk" (p. 134). Allport and Lewin have been among the many protagonists of the idiographic approach in personality research. When the single person is the object of study, consistencies and deviations within his own behavior permit establishment of norms for that individual. By this strategy, the richness of individual differences in therapy is preserved, and prediction for the single case can be improved. The nomothetic approach, championed by trait theorists and developers of actuarial prediction (among them Meehl, McClelland, and Eysenck), questions the utility of single case studies. These men assert that any person can be compared to others, at least with regard to particular classes of responses in order to arrive at meaningful statements that predict individual behavior from knowledge about other persons with the same characteristic. The nomothetists are not discouraged by the fact that it may take many test scores to determine an individual's position in a group. Nor do they deny that such scores may interact to form a unique pattern or profile for a single individual. The traditional case study represents the idiographic approach; the use of objective personality questionnaires or batteries of other tests represents the nomothetic approach. In actual scientific and clinical practice, both methods are often used in complementary ways.

Limitations of Observations

The practitioner, unlike the researcher, cannot choose the specific conditions under which he collects observations. Indeed, he may never observe the behavior which he is required to evaluate. This was even more true in the past, when clinicians restricted their activities to the office or hospital, thus missing collection of crucial behavioral observations during the patient's daily routine. Traditionally, therapists have relied almost exclusively on patient report, free association, or observations of symptoms in the office or hospital. They concentrate on reconstruction of a personality picture from inferences and test data. In contrast, behavior therapists focus on observable responses or, at a minimum, on multiple indices of less observable symptoms, such as subjective discomfort or disordered thinking. They may directly observe the patient in a hospital ward, in the patient's home, at work, or at school to obtain samples of pertinent behaviors in vivo.

In theory, automated, objective, reliable behavior records, comparable to the scientist's laboratory data, remain an ideal goal for the behavior therapist. In practice, the behavior therapist relies on far less adequate measures. The practical matters of arranging observations frequently prevent the behavior therapist from observing the situations in which the symptomatic responses occur and from controlling extraneous variables in these environments. Even when direct observation is arranged, the sample is still small. Such significant personal behaviors as intimacies and fantasy behaviors, or such discrete events as temper outbursts can easily be missed. The laboratory experiment includes provisions to elicit the behavior of interest and to exclude most irrelevant responses. Compare, for example, laboratory studies of communication in small groups, where subjects are isolated and their responses are recorded by means of button presses, with the recording of a family's natural interactions in their home. Sometimes even the standard clinical setting must be considered as a relevant variable in the interpretation of clinical data. For example, two-way mirrors are standard equipment in many clinic rooms. But the presence of a mirror can distract the patient and confound whatever the clinician is interested in. The problem is especially vexing because patients with various behavior disorders may react differently to their mirror-image and to the motivational and emotional overtones of the mirror (Gallup, 1968). Yet few clinicians are aware of these findings, nor can they be expected to have full knowledge of all the situational variables affecting their patient's behavior. Recent work on controlled environments or testing-booths (Elwood, 1969) represents attempts to control at least the physical environment in which observations are made.

The clinical setting is much less constant than the research laboratory. Consequently, the task of data collection under these differing circumstances requires different methods and yields measures of differing reliability. However, recent reports of clinical researchers have indicated that these obstacles are not insurmountable. They simply require a proper orientation, different equipment and greater patience. The distinction between the clinical and laboratory methods of data collection is in ease of accessibility of data, not in differences in the principles of their collection.

The Dual Role of the Clinician as a Participant-Observer

Sullivan (1954b) has described the ideal role of the clinician as one of concurrent objective observation and friendly participation. Isolation of the observer's activities from his actions as partner in a clinical interview is extremely difficult. But this problem is one that he shares with his experimental colleagues, probably to an extent much greater than was thought in the past. Although it is a major rule for the scientist to prevent uncontrolled contact with the object of his observations, even rigorously designed laboratory studies may introduce error by the act of observation or measurement alone.

The nature of clinical interactions can introduce biases due to the clinician's role in at least three ways: (1) by altering the "demand characteristics" of the situation, that is, the covert expectations and pressures for certain behaviors by the patient as a function of the clinician's individual style; (2) by varying the clinician's accuracy as an instrument of behavior measurement, due to his individual way of responding during observations; and (3) by affecting the subtle interactional "rapport" relationships, due to the relative comfort with which the therapist can work with a particular patient.

Establishing uniform demand characteristics, or at least, ascertaining what they are, has repeatedly been discussed as an important feature in accounting for a subject's or patient's behavior. In the clinic, patient expectations about the clinician's proper role behaviors and patient assumptions about the purposes and probable consequences of various procedures or drugs are salient determinants of patient reactions. One therapist's formal style, imposing office suite, and intellectual language present stimuli eliciting or "demanding" different patient expectations and responses than the clinician who speaks and moves casually in an informal relaxed setting. Orne (1962) and others have called attention to the marked effects of the demand characteristics of a situation. All the cues that convey a certain attitude or hypothesis to the person about the supposed purpose of an interaction—be it an experiment or an interview—potentially serve to modify the subject's behavior. However, perceived demand characteristics can affect the observer as well as the subject. From results of a series of studies, Rosenthal (1963) has suggested that preconceived biases by experimenters may seriously affect results of psychological experiments, even under stringently controlled and standardized conditions. Further, he found that personal characteristics (for example, sex, personality, and expectancies) of the two participants, experimenter and subject, interact to influence the extent to which experimenter bias is transmitted between them. While some of Rosenthal's conclusions have been disputed (Barber and Silver, 1968), his caution that experimenter bias can seriously distort research data is well taken.

The implications of these and similar studies for clinical as well as experimental interactions are quite clear. Unintentionally executed responses can serve as cues to the patient about the expectancies and values of a therapist. Even without any direct verbal cues, the clinician conveys information to his patient by differential listening and attention that serve as discriminative stimuli for the patient. The clinician also emits contingent reinforcement expressed either verbally or by more subtle modifications of posture, expression, tone, and verbal output. The whole formulation and treatment plan are likely to carry unstated expectancies and role information. On the other side, changes in a patient's report about his feelings or his plans would certainly be presumed to reflect not only lasting effects of the clinician's impact, but also the momentary change in perception of the demand characteristics of the situation by the patient.

The necessary interaction of clinician with client during assessment or treatment procedures tends to increase opportunities for a strong biasing effect in the clinician's observations and his measurement of behavior. Although it is possible to observe a patient's behavior during an interaction with some degree of objectivity, the clinician must constantly consider the extent to which his observations may be the result of his own biases.

The subtle interdependencies of the two members of a therapy dyad increase the contamination of the clinician as participant and as observer. Even at the physiological level, there is often a strong relationship between change in therapist and in patient as they interact, for example, in changes in heart rate (Coleman, Greenblatt, and Solomon, 1956). Apart from the heavy demands made on concentration, as the clinician works toward "rapport" (his effectiveness as a reinforcing agent), the clinician's response to the patient's behavior as potentially reinforcing for his professional and personal role affects his own and the patient's behavior in not too predictable ways. All important mutual influences are more prominent and less easily controlled in the clinic than in the laboratory, constituting another dimension in which experimental and clinical procedures differ greatly.

The Social Responsibility of the Clinician

The scientist is careful to avoid harm to any organism in experimentation. Most scientific professional organizations prescribe a code of ethics that strictly defines the experimenter's responsibilities toward his subjects, human or animal. The National Institute of Mental Health and other research-supporting agencies require that grantee institutions establish policies and regulations to safeguard experimental subjects and that individual investigators detail how such safeguards will be effected, including obtaining informed consent from human subjects. In most psychological research only limited areas of behavior are affected and temporary discomfort can be quickly dispelled after an experimental session. The experimental subject is ordinarily a volunteer who makes no special demands on the experimenter and expects no tangible beneficial results from the encounter.

When a clinician accepts a patient, it is assumed that he will not only avoid harmful effects, as does the scientist, but also contribute toward improving the patient's life. The medical concept of clinical responsibility may not be fully applicable to the psychological professions. However, in current practice it is presumed that the nonmedical clinician accepts some responsibility for the patient's behavior and that he takes appropriate action when the patient's well-being or that of others is threatened. Under such obligation and with only slight knowledge of how to predict individual behavior, the clinician is severely restricted in his methods. The behavior therapist, in accepting this responsibility, encounters a special difficulty because he does not always accept the popular distinctions between healthy and sick behaviors, nor the common assumptions of what is good for the patient. Society sanctions the use of therapy for sickness, punishment for illegal acts, and education as the remedy for ignorance. Sanctions are not so clear for changing behaviors that do not fit these categories precisely, acts that may be mildly annoying, embarrassing, expensive, or disgusting to the public. When the same behaviors are not defined as *sick*, but as socially unacceptable behaviors, the sanctions for their change are less clear-cut. As Ullmann (1967a), among others, has pointed out, this model of deviant behavior poses some ethical dilemmas for the therapist. Despite conflicting social values, the behavior therapist must decide which behaviors require change and which can be overlooked. By the nature of his work, the behavior therapist not only has to accept the onus of behavior control. Often he must also assume the burden of siding as an accomplice either on the side of the patient or on the side of society in determining what behaviors should be controlled. This issue is not easily resolved.

In his decision to undertake a program of behavior change, the clinician can be brought close to many problems of the individual's rights and civil liberties. For example, should antisocial behavior be changed only when an offender volunteers for help? What describes the limits of privacy, beyond which observational data should not be obtained (even with the patient's consent)? When consent cannot be obtained from a patient, due to his age or state of disorganization, should punishment or reward be used in treatment? What are the limits of confidentiality when a patient reveals a crime or his criminal intent? At what point does the arrangement of environmental contingencies become an infringement on the patient's civil liberties? The erroneous assumption underlying many of these questions is that the therapist is organizing environment-behavior-reinforcement relationships in situations in which there is complete absence of such systematic control. Actually, the social environment continuously exerts controls. The argument for therapeutic or preventive intervention is well presented by Baer (1968) for the case of child-rearing:

"To choose not to reinforce a child is simply to hand over his shaping to the rest of his environment; and there is no guarantee that the rest of the environment is programmed to reinforce desirable behaviors. The author, for example, might choose not to shape his 4-year-old daughter, but that would not allow her any freedom of development. It would simply leave her shaping largely in the hands of her peers (whose 4-year-old judgments and ambitions are not thoroughly admired by the author). If reinforcement works, in short, it cannot help but operate. The options are to analyze and use it systematically and therapeutically or to ignore it and leave behavior in the hands of whoever cares to program a contingency for it. Ethics would seem to favor the former" (p. 19).

The problem of confidential use of information is encountered in the clinic but rarely in the laboratory. Clinical interactions deal with personal material. A self-report may make the patient vulnerable to personal criticism. In some cases the information may be personally or financially damaging to the patient. It can be used to further other people's interests, to threaten, or to prosecute the patient. The clinician must therefore show restraint in the use of information, even if he wishes to use it to the patient's own advantage. It is not surprising that good clinical practice requires, for example, that a patient consent to release to an agency, a physician, or even to a spouse, of information that the clinician has collected about him. On the negative side, these constraints can limit the clinician's range of activities in testing hypotheses or validating patient reports.

The aura of mystery which has surrounded traditional therapy strategies has often been thought to help bring into the open the patient's unconscious thoughts. Even today, therapists do not discuss the basis of their procedures with their patients, presumably because such knowledge could result in influence-resisting behaviors. The concealment of the purpose of therapeutic techniques raises ethical issues shared with the laboratory experimenter. Kelman (1967) has reviewed the ethical implications of deception in social psychological experiments and suggests that ways of counteracting the negative effects of deception be explored, when it must be used, and that new techniques be developed that dispense with deception. The same positive steps seem equally appropriate for the clinical area.

The exact limits of the clinician's social responsibility are difficult to define. In fact, proper professional responsibilities require not only sufficient and meaningful care for a patient but also withdrawal from the patient's life when help is no longer needed. Termination of therapy presents an instance in which excessive caution can be to the patient's disadvantage. There is no definite criterion for ending treatment. An overly conservative approach can be confused with the clinician's financial motive when treatment is carried on beyond a point of sufficiently improved functioning. While the experimenter limits the design of his studies in advance to meet scientific standards, the clinician often finds it necessary to change his plan in midstream. His personal clinical standards can affect expectations for the patient's improvement. By contrast, the experimenter's adherence to a predetermined program requires no midstream decisions. Therefore, the distinction between the clinician's and experimenter's procedures once again is determined by the different conditions under which they operate.

The various difficulties in simultaneously maintaining a morally neutral attitude and a practical approach to clinical problems are well described by London (1964):

"It is impossible to overstate the importance of freedom from metaphysics and morals to the conduct of scientific research, especially to the objective analysis and interpretation of data. But the psychotherapist, in his actual practice, does not usually function as a researcher. He is a clinician. And much of the material with which he deals is neither understandable nor usable outside the context of a system of human values. This fact is unfortunate and embarrassing to one who would like to see himself as an impartial scientist and unprejudiced helper. It is a fact, none the less, and one which, for both technical and theoretical reasons, may be painfully important to students of human behavior in general and to psychotherapists in particular" (pp. 4–5).

Clinical Research Strategies and Deficiencies

The conduct of clinical research, with an experimental design using actual patients in a natural clinical setting, is necessary for answering the questions of which behavior therapy is most effective for which patients, and why. Yet clinical research must face the dilemma of serious compromises on both sides—scientific and clinical. Some of the solutions and their deficiencies will be briefly discussed here in preparation for evaluating research cited in later chapters.

If behavior therapies are considered a subcategory of the total field of behavior maintenance and change, then two broad areas of knowledge are relevant to their development. Most of the substance of psychology, dealing as it does with the functional parameters of behavior, is potentially relevant. From the opposite end, traditional clinical observations describing the natural history of common clinical problems are also relevant. Clinical case studies or clinical research can suggest correlations among classes of responses and events that may influence these behaviors. For example, clinical observation has provided the general picture of depression as a syndrome marked by frequent weeping, self-depreciation, self-preoccupation, a pessimistic outlook, and a low rate of emitted behavior. Often an immediately preceding loss of an important person, role, or status has been noted. This cluster of related behaviors has been theorized to be both a single disease entity and a final common pathway for multiple pathological processes, similar to the symptom of fever. Among the proposals for explaining depression as one process resulting from many different events is the behavioral formulation of depression as a relative lack of positive reinforcement. Loss of a loved person, of a work routine, or of physical capacities can all be construed as loss of important sources of positive reinforcement. This clinical hypothesis, built up from the observations made in case studies, has led in turn to propositions testable in the laboratory within the usual scientific paradigm. Similarly, clinical observation of the long-term adjustment of chronic schizophrenics has suggested that hospitalization, with the contingencies involved in a dependent institutionalized existence, might be responsible for many of the behavioral deficiencies of chronic patients. That is, hospitalization itself seems to expose patients to additional social isolation and behavioral deprivations, leading to increased deviancy, passivity, disordered communication, and withdrawal in the chronic patient. This hypothesis, in turn, has encouraged pioneering work in altering contingencies supplied by nursing staff in order to develop more self-reliant and acceptable behaviors in institutionalized persons (such as Ayllon and Michael, 1959), as well as a general skeptical reevaluation of usual institutional behavior shaping.

Between the extreme poles of laboratory research on general behavior influences and correlational or ecological clinical research lie studies of the effects and mechanisms of clinical behavior change techniques. These studies of therapeutic change may be controlled experiments using analogues of clinical symptoms, or they may be reports of uncontrolled clinical trials, but they all address the question of how effective a given therapy is for a specified set of behavioral complaints. Clearly, each of these three general sources of knowledge (behavior principles, clinical observations, and treatment research)—each with its own research strategy and goals—contributes to the progress of the behavior therapies and is enriched, as well, by feedback from applied settings.

There are several frames of reference within which current clinical research strategies can be viewed. One contrasts the nomothetic and idiographic approaches described earlier. This distinction appears again in the divergent research strategies of investigators of classical and of operant conditioning therapies. Or, from a different frame of reference, strategies relevant to the appraisal of therapeutic effectiveness can be compared with those used to discover the mechanisms underlying behavior changes. A third frame of reference compares the advantages and disadvantages of research in regular clinical settings with those using laboratory analogues of clinical problems and procedures.

An interesting additional feature of applied research has recently emerged in several social science projects. The collection of research data and the publication of results can, in turn, affect the same behaviors in the social group in which the study is conducted. For example, it has been suggested that the publication of the Kinsey reports on common sexual practices has affected subsequent sexual behavior and mores by serving as a guide to their readers. In hospital communities, the analysis and publication of staff attitudes have repeatedly been used to modify staff attitudes and hospital procedures. Even the decision to conduct research on a problem in a social or industrial organization can modify attitudes by directing attention to phenomena hitherto overlooked. The conduct of research, be it clinical or social, thus can itself become a significant instrument for behavior modification. The increased awareness of this use of research for social action is found in schools, government-sponsored community projects, and similar social projects. Proper utilization of this approach promises to accomplish not only expansion of knowledge but also a better integration of research methods into the social fabric.

Group Studies and Individual Replications

The distinction between idiographic and nomothetic approaches is characteristic of two different theoretical and experimental approaches to understanding the mechanisms of learning. It has also led to the development of divergent personality theories. Some learning theorists, such as Hull and Tolman, have used factorial research designs comparing mean performance of groups of animals on standardized tasks in order to construct general theories of learning. Skinner and his followers, on the other hand, build statements of empirical functional relationships on the basis of a few replications of highly controlled performances in single animals.

Clinical researchers, then, will differ in their idiographic or nomothetic emphasis, partly as a function of the paradigm of learning that each adopts for extrapolation to behavior change techniques. As a consequence, there is some disagreement among researchers as to what constitutes adequate evidence in evaluating the effectiveness of a given technique, or in testing hypotheses regarding the mechanisms responsible for effective techniques. Despite the insistence of adherents of both approaches that only their program can yield adequate data for construction of theories or principles, both approaches have demonstrated their usefulness, and both may be necessary to provide supportive data on different phenomena.

The advocates of the group data approach generally rely heavily on statistical hypotheses in the design of their experiments. Such designs in behavior therapy research usually deal with common symptoms in a fairly homogeneous population and contrast average improvement in experimental groups with untreated controls or groups treated by other means. One example of such research is a study by Paul (1966), designed to compare the effectiveness of a behavior therapy method with more traditional treatments. Paul selected college students with fears of public speaking and rested his conclusions on the mean changes (improvement) of the various groups on a series of measures, evaluated by sophisticated statistical tests.

Among those who use operant conditioning methods, the demonstration of behavior change in individual patients is common. Cumulative response curves present the changes in the rate of a symptomatic response, during pretreatment, on introduction of the critical treatment, and after withdrawal of the treatment variable. The effects of particular therapeutic procedures are compared from graphic presentations or by descriptive statistics, that is, by contrast of relative rates of responses under different conditions. Illustrations of this approach are found in Ullmann and Krasner (1965) and in the journal *Behavior Research and Therapy*. A single case is usually reported with specific description of the target symptom. Replication with several cases, independently described, serves to attest to the generality of the therapeutic effects of a procedure. Data collection and analysis are similar to the procedures described in animal research by Skinner and his students. General statements of relationships rest on the empirical findings from replicated individual case studies. The textbook by Sidman (1960b) discusses the research strategy of this approach. In stressing a functional analysis of behavior within an operant conditioning framework, Sidman emphasizes that "a group function may have no counterpart in the behavior of the individual. . . . individual and group curves simply cannot provide the same information, even if their forms should be identical" (p. 53). Sidman describes a number of techniques for replication of individual data, not for the purpose of assessing whether original observations are "real," but to examine the reliability and generality of a phenomenon. He argues, for example, that replication across successive individual subjects, each dealt with singly, is more powerful in testing reliability and generality than are replications of group data. In the latter, only the reliability of central tendency is tested, and group data cannot indicate the nature of exceptional cases. He argues that replication of observed functional relationships within the same individual is the most powerful investigative tool, and suggests procedures to use when irreversible effects or a changing base line pose difficulties for intrasubject replications.

A usual design for individual replication involves: (1) a base line or free operant measure of the dependent variable (A); (2) introduction of some experimental manipulation with a second measure of the response (B); and (3) a reversal or return to the base line, premanipulation conditions with a third measure of the dependent variable (A). A recent study by Ingram (1967) illustrates intrasubject replication studies of behavior modification and highlights the adaptation of such experimental designs to clinical problems. The disadvantage of the design lies in the fact that the scientific and therapeutic goals conflict with regard to the final outcome of the procedure. When a therapeutic intervention successfully changes a target behavior from its base line level and the behavior is returned to its basal level during the reversal condition, the scientific requirements for showing a causal link are met. But the therapeutic goal would optimally seek an *irreversible* effect that would *not* disappear when the reversal procedure is invoked. In fact, from a therapist's point of view, it is desirable not only that the new behavior is maintained by continued therapeutic intervention, but that it result in new behavior maintained in the patient's natural environment without continued therapeutic attention. In-gram (1967), working with Baer, altered the usual *A-B-A* design by making it into a series of successive manipulative probes and reversals, an *A-B-A-B-A-B* . . . design. The subject was a nursery school child deficient in certain desired social behaviors. Therapeutic intervention con-sisted of social reinforcement by his teachers contingent upon the desired behaviors. During reversal periods the teachers' attention was delivered noncontingently in a pattern and frequency matching that of the base line period. Each week the therapeutic intervention and the reversal proce-dure were alternated. With each successive reversal, less of the desired behaviors was lost, until after several weeks the reversal had *no* effect. Presumably the target social behaviors had come under the control of naturally occurring reinforcements in the environment and were no longer under the primary control of teacher attention. This procedure achieves, indeed, the therapeutic goal. This design of successive probes by reversals combines the advantages of scientific control and testing with the thera-peutic merits of eventual independence of the target behavior.

An alternate to the *A-B-A* design, suggested by Browning (1967b), eliminates the requirement of returning to the pretreatment condition and the problems created by this method. The design essentially employs the simultaneous availability of several treatment conditions (in phase B) by assigning each of these to different therapists for execution. For exam-ple, after the base line period (A), one staff member is assigned to give positive attention to the critical behavior, while another ignores it, and a third gives verbal admonishment. To eliminate person biases the assign-ment is then rotated over successive weeks. Finally, the most effective treatment condition is then programmed for all therapists in continuing treatment. This design is especially appropriate in residential treatment when many staff persons serve as behavior therapists.

Sidman (1960b) holds to the idiographic strategy adamantly: "A psy-chology that cannot describe, systematize, and control the primary source of all its data—the behaving individual—will forever be a weak sister among the sciences" (p. 107). Paul (1969a), in discussing *A-B-A* designs using single subjects, points to their utility in extending treatment evaluation across new classes of variables after a factorial study, or in testing hy-potheses about treatment procedures in a global fashion before using a factorial design. He grants that replications of such studies allow the re-searcher to reduce some confounding effects (for example, by using several different therapists). Thus this design may permit not only across-subjects cause-and-effect inferences, but also greater certainty regarding the nature of within-subject effects. However, Paul asserts that only factorial group studies can do this with assurance.

Strategies for Studying Outcome

A second distinction relevant to research strategy is the relative emphasis placed on evaluating effectiveness of a therapeutic "package," on dismantling the package to isolate the contributions of each part, or on testing hypothesized mechanisms of change. In part, which course is taken depends on whether one has a "package" to begin with. For example, the specific procedures described for Wolpe's systematic desensitization for phobias permit an overall comparison, at first, with other treatments. If the total method appears efficacious, one can go on to ask which components of the treatment are essential, and for which patients and symptoms the method is most useful. Lang (1969) has pointed out the hazards of the dismantling approach to streamlining a successful therapy package. He compared it to trying to learn the parts that make a car go by taking it apart and then reassembling it, one piece at a time, to discover which are the necessary and sufficient pieces. Given enough combinations of variables, however, this strategy has been fruitful in isolating effective variables, as Lang's review of desensitization research illustrates. It has led to improvement of the technique by dropping unessential procedures and sharpening those of known effectiveness.

When a specific laboratory procedure is adapted to therapy, the question of the relevance of separate components or underlying mechanisms to explain the change is no longer pertinent. Unlike the above approach, which investigates the *process* of change, studies of effectiveness of simple techniques have investigated the *outcome* of the method. For example, extinction, punishment, or reward of desirable alternative behaviors may be applied in the treatment of temper tantrums. The goal of comparing these methods lies in determining their economy and their power to achieve the end state of a near-zero frequency of tantrum occurrence. The processes involved are presumably the same as described in the general learning literature for these methods.

Outcome and process research in psychotherapy have a long history, with earlier experimental attention devoted to outcome. From a pragmatic viewpoint, it might appear that demonstration of favorable outcome is sufficient, since understanding the therapeutic process adds little practical value if the technique works well. In medicine there are numerous instances of the successful use of drugs, vaccines, and other therapeutic agents in the absence of a clear understanding of the effective process. There are, however, several problems in psychotherapy which counteract the argument for postponement of process research or its relegation to the area of pure academic interest. First, even outcome research is not a simple comparison of "cure-rates." Considerable argument exists about the proper criterion for improvement or cure of a behavior disorder. In fact, in this regard behavior therapists clearly differ from dynamic therapists in their specification of the behavior change which constitutes a desired outcome (for instance, in specifying removal of a given phobia or acquisition of the ability to assert oneself, as opposed to seeking conflict resolution or removal of a fixation as the therapeutic goal). Nevertheless, improvement produced by various techniques may occur in different behavioral segments, making a direct comparison of effectiveness meaningless. Many attempts to define uniform outcome-criteria have been made (for example, Luborsky and Strupp, 1962; Rubinstein and Parloff, 1959; Thorne, 1952). Their discussion would require consideration of the role of personality theory in molding goals and methods of treatment, of definitions of abnormal behavior, of measurement issues, and of other problems tangential to our present concern. It may therefore suffice here to call attention to the lack of agreement among clinical psychologists about criteria for successful therapy and to the consequent difficulties in outcome research in the absence of agreement of the relative advantages of one technique over another.

A second reason for the practical importance of the clinician's understanding of the therapy *process* lies in the need for momentary decisions and strategy changes during treatment, which we have previously discussed. Only with knowledge of the basic process can the clinician assess the partial effects of his separate therapy operations and introduce variations from a general or standardized procedure. Lack of this understanding would result in automatic and inflexible procedures with little room for adjustment for individual cases and, probably, little chance of success.

A final practical reason for process studies lies in the rudimentary stage of the development of therapy techniques. Only by understanding the process can innovations be produced. Therapy techniques and general psychology advance when clinicians can raise questions about the processes of behavior change and attempt to answer them by exploration of novel methods and careful laboratory study of the psychological phenomena observed in treatment.

Analogue Studies

Study of the process of psychotherapy is best conducted in its natural setting. However, there are methodical, practical, and ethical restrictions that have led investigators to create experimental analogues of psychotherapy. The laboratory situation overcomes three major obstacles of psychotherapy research. First, there are practical obstacles—the divergence of complaints by patients, differences in therapists' personalities and techniques, divergent goals of treatment, and the uniqueness of material make it difficult to replicate specific treatments and population characteristics. Secondly, there are ethical and moral obstacles, rooted in the cultural attitudes towards experimentation with human behavior. Use of control groups involves the risk that the untreated or pseudo-treated patient may get worse. The concept of ethical responsibility and confidentiality in the usual patient-therapist relationship also restricts the investigator. Finally, interaction patterns in therapy change rapidly and involve temporal sequences. Therefore, replication of a long series of treatment operations may be neither appropriate nor possible in any one case. By contrast, the laboratory setting can provide a slow-motion analysis of the therapeutic process and can focus on small aspects of the process (similar to the way in which the biologist works with his microscope to analyze larger phenomena).

The significant contributions that analogue research can make to the improvement of therapy techniques are well illustrated by research on the desensitization technique. The simple but ingenious notion that the therapeutic process can be examined with fairly homogeneous normal subjects, by application of desensitization to relatively mild behavioral problems, has resulted in many careful studies with college students and other normals who had snake phobias or fear of public speaking. Although this type of approach parallels the goals of treatment for more serious phobias or anxieties, it also permits study of groups relatively homogeneous with respect to such factors as age, general health, severity of symptom, and absence of other complicating symptoms. It runs none of the risks described above for similar research with patients who have asked for psychological services.

Analogue studies, however, do not completely serve as substitutes for in vivo clinical research. Zytowski (1966) has pointed out that analogue studies have often neglected the evaluation of some measures (such as changes in correlated nontarget behaviors, or in the target behavior in other settings) that may be desirable in clinical treatment, but irrelevant in the laboratory. A more serious criticism has come from those who suspect a discontinuity between response to mild stress, delivered in the laboratory analogue, and the intense pressures and tensions to which the seriously disturbed person is exposed. For example, the centrality to a subject's daily life, frequency of occurrence, and many other factors are different for a snake phobia in a normal person as contrasted with a fear of leaving one's home in a neurotic. Similarly, differences in personality variables of the neurotic and the normal person may represent additional serious limitations in extrapolating laboratory findings with college students to clinical populations.

The utilization of laboratory analogue data requires attention to the similarities and differences between the therapy analogue and the practical situation to which it is applied. Kanfer (1962) describes three types of analogue studies, each with a different assumed similarity to clinical behavior modification. The *analytic* analogue assumes that the laboratory and clinical settings share a common conceptual model that is logically applicable to both situations. Verbal conditioning studies as analogues of the interview interactions in therapy represent an analogue of this type. A *process* analogue focuses on a specific part of the total therapeutic enterprise. The researcher concentrates on a particular mechanism or hypothesized process, strips it of its clinical complexities, and studies it in a simplified and standardized version in the laboratory. In the process analogue, the similarity between the paradigm and the therapeutic interaction is much greater than in the analytic analogue, since the paradigm is abstracted from a model of the therapy process and dependent variables are selected directly from the clinical prototype. An example along the same dimension of verbal behavior is given by studies on the flow of dyadic communication in interviews. Such a process can be examined while control over the clinician's duration, rate, and content of speech is possible to a degree that cannot be achieved in the clinical setting. A third type of analogue is the *miniature* analogue. It bears the greatest resemblance to the therapy situation and consists of a limited sample of the process itself. Usually, the miniature situation preserves many of the originally relevant variables, much of the complexity of the therapy situation, and some of its divergence in influencing variables. Studies of desensitization using snake phobic college students, who are given a standardized version of the usual clinical treatment, illustrate this type of analogue.

Even though the degree of similarity increases as one goes from the first to the third type of analogue, none of the laboratory situations can be immediately extrapolated to the clinical behavior modification procedure without further validation at the clinical level. Heller and Marlatt (1969), in discussing the relevancy of research on verbal conditioning for therapeutic practice, similarly emphasized the necessity of careful consideration of the role of mediating variables before transposing research from the laboratory to applied settings. One illustration will clarify this point. There is evidence that the level of general anxiety and the pervasiveness of the patient's phobic reactions affect the outcome of treatment with Wolpe's systematic desensitization technique. College students, whose overall anxiety level is generally not as high as in clinic patients, may react differently to a desensitization procedure. Extrapolations from these findings would have to be modified to suit clinical populations. Further, when a target behavior is embedded in the context of other distressing behaviors, or is accompanied by detrimental influences in the patient's environment or personality or intellectual deficiencies, the effects of the technique may be quite different than when the target behavior represents a relatively isolated complaint in a well-functioning person. Changing a phobia in an anxious woman who is confined to her home, who has numerous fears about harmful situations, and whose entire life is changed by these fears represents quite a different problem from that posed by altering a fear of snakes in a sociable, active, and well-adjusted college girl.

Another limitation in extrapolation from analogue studies lies in the organization of behavior in different individuals. Buchwald and Young (1969) have pointed out that these organizational differences may also result in misleading extrapolations from laboratory findings to clinical applications. They point out that traditional clinical views have construed symptoms as interrelated behaviors and parts of a single "syndrome," whereas laboratory practice tends to isolate small behavioral classes and to view separate responses as independent. Presently, there are insufficient empirical data on the functional interrelationships of different responses for assuming either that such organizations of response classes are similar or different in individuals with varying degrees of psychological problems.

Laboratory analogues, then, present a convenient way for exploring clinical processes. They can facilitate innovation in clinical techniques and serve as a source of hypotheses about the therapeutic process. It is clear, however, that these studies serve as a point of departure and not as incontrovertible evidence for the nature of the therapeutic process.

SUMMARY

In this chapter, we have contrasted the setting of clinical practice, its goals, and its limitations with the activities of the laboratory researcher. Among numerous schools of psychotherapy, behavior therapy adheres most closely to the methodology and the philosophical and conceptual bases of scientific operations. Nevertheless, clinical and laboratory models for practicing psychologists show differences in interest, desired goals, degree of personal involvement, and social responsibility. Although the clinician of the last two decades has been trained to pursue the scientist-practitioner role, there are some changes as he shifts from one arena of activity to the other.

We have discussed some salient features of clinical research and the problems that arise in the conduct of this research. Although the clinician is aware of his potential for contributing to general psychological knowledge, he is mainly responsible for achieving improvement in his patient's behavior. Consequently, his research efforts are often carried out in artificial settings, although they originate from his observations of patient behaviors.

Despite the many distinctions between clinician and researcher, it has been noted that application of scientific methods can be practiced in the clinic during execution of a treatment procedure. It is primarily in the context of discovery and strategy decisions about a therapeutic program that the clinician relies heavily on his personal judgment and experience. In his execution of a program, observation of patient behaviors, and analysis of his own impact on the patient, the clinician works very much in the tradition of the scientist-researcher, albeit far less stringently.

CHAPTER 2

The Behavioral Learning Model in Clinical Psychology

The behavioral learning model of psychopathology and therapeutic change has only recently attracted widespread attention in clinical psychology. It competes with psychodynamic theories that for half a century have held center stage in psychiatry and other mental health professions without serious challengers. Based mainly on the work of Freud and his followers, psychodynamic theories have provided the scaffolding on which treatment procedures have rested until recently. The common goal of these methods of psychotherapy has been to alter the underlying personality of the patient. The manifestations of traits, impulses, and defenses against anxiety may appear in the person's momentary behavior, but less importance has been ascribed to the understanding of particular behaviors, than to their significance as indices of the organizing forces and stable personality structures characteristic of the individual.

Dynamic theories evolved from clinical observations of patients, from philosophical considerations of the nature and destiny of Man, and from conceptual formulations (concentrating on subjective experiences and inferred mental processes as the primary links in causal sequences resulting in deviant behavior). In contrast, models based on learning paradigms grew out of laboratory studies (often of animals) of behavior development and change, with emphasis on controlled manipulation of observable events, measurements, and resolution of complex events into simpler components. It is not surprising, therefore, that rules for observing human behavior, for making and verifying inferences from observations, and for designing techniques to change behavior are among the most characteristic contributions of the learning models to clinical psychology.

The behavioral model has its historic roots in American functionalism, American behaviorism, and Russian reflexology of the first few decades of this century. These three schools of psychology vigorously espoused

49

study of the determinants of simple behaviors in animal subjects, with special emphasis on scientific rigor in language and method and on the importance of learning in the development of behavior. In the United States the behavioral model which came to be called S-R psychology first focused on simple learning in animals. It was not seriously applied to human behavior until the late 1940s. Russian reflexology was applied to human behavior somewhat earlier, but its application was at first limited to simple motor acts or physiological functions. Several different theories of learning and extrapolations from isolated empirical findings then gradually were used as a base of operations for the practicing psychologist.

There is no single theory today that covers all learning phenomena. None, as yet, has been developed and experimentally supported at a level of complexity sufficient for handling social, perceptual, verbal, and intrapersonal processes. Recently, one particular theoretical orientation, developed by Skinner, has stimulated rapid expansion of experimental approaches to the analysis of many complex behaviors, human and animal. In the last two decades, research on human learning has progressed from analysis of simple responses in conditioning experiments or nonsense syllable learning to complex social and verbal interactions. An increasing number of studies deal directly with aggressive, sexual, or delinquent behaviors, mother-child interactions, acquisition of educational skills, and many other behaviors. This extension of the content of behavior under study partially was in response to social demands for help with clinical problems; and partially, it represented the attempts of clinicians to apply their knowledge directly to the behavior that they most frequently encounter in their daily work. As learning research begins to encompass the substantive or content aspects of development and maintenance of social behaviors, general learning principles are refined to take into account the special properties of particular response classes. At the same time, this accumulation of specific data enlarges our understanding of daily activities and variables that control the development of interpersonal skills, attitudes toward others and ourselves, complex motor skills, and innumerable verbal and nonverbal actions that are part of our daily lives.

At present, the substantive portion of learning approaches in clinical psychology has come essentially from earlier clinical practices or common experience. For example, we cannot yet specify essential elements in a patient's home environment, parental relationships, school experiences, or the interpersonal behaviors correlated with these settings that lead to the development of pathological subassertive behavior patterns. Nor do we have a clear understanding of the variables that produce similar social consequences whenever a patient shows excessive self-assertive behaviors. But the learning approaches have already contributed to understanding of conditions promoting other response patterns, such as aggressive behavior, social variables maintaining temper tantrums, hyperactive behavior and school phobias in children, and the relationship between symptom removal and changes in other behaviors not directly treated. Less work has been done on factors responsible for development of particular neurotic or ineffective behavior patterns than has been done on the effects which these symptomatic behaviors have on a patient's environment. In individual cases, therefore, selection of behavioral content for analysis still rests on fragments of traditional personality theories and the clinician's experiences. The main contributions of the behavioral learning models have been particular methods for analysis and treatment rather than identification of crucial content.

The methodological characteristics and assumptions about human behavior that are described in this chapter are shared to a large extent by most learning approaches and form the basis of clinical practice for the learning-oriented psychologist. In selecting from them we have favored the basic approach developed by Skinner and his students as a background for organizing material in this chapter. The Skinnerian model emphasizes the importance of reinforcing events in learning and minimizes the role of anxiety and other emotional states as primary features. Other learning models, including those dealing with cognitive aspects of behavior and the role of social and emotional factors in learning and personality development, have produced significant areas of research and are discussed in later chapters.

COMMON ASSUMPTIONS OF BEHAVIORAL LEARNING MODELS

1. The learning-based model focuses on *behavior*. Consequently, the content with which it deals is the activity of a person in relation to his environment. The data consist of empirical events described in a language that carefully separates these descriptions from theoretical constructs and from inferences about the significance or meaning that the events may be conjectured to have for the behaving individual. Thus concepts like defenses, impulses, unconscious conflicts, or character traits are rejected because they do not add knowledge about the person beyond the actual observations from which they are inferred. As will be seen later, this emphasis on observable events *does not deny* at the outset the importance of behaviors that may not be accessible to observation at a given moment; nor does it reject the utility of a person's self-descriptions or verbal narratives about events. However, it demands a clear and explicit understanding that these behaviors not be used as surrogates for observations of internal events and that

a theoretical construct, such as internalized hostility, not be accepted as an *explanation* of the very same behavior from which it is inferred.

2. The learning model attacks deviant behaviors directly. Emphasis on behavior in its environmental context orients the learning approaches toward changing a person's observable actions, instead of attempting modification of hypothesized personality structures, such as traits or impulses. This strategy results in an assault on deviant responses or *symptoms,* not underlying mental disease processes that are said to cause symptomatic behavior. The word "symptom" is used in this text for convenience; it simply indicates any target response selected for change. In our usage, it does not imply a surface indicant of underlying causes or a disease state. Recognition that the environment plays a crucial role in determining behavior implies that the appearance of symptoms may be restricted to an identifiable range of situations and is not invariantly characteristic of the person's behavior.

3. The learning model encompasses all behaviors as subject to the same psychological principles. Most dynamic theories distinguish between laws of learning, applicable to the acquisition of knowledge, and laws of personality integration, relevant to the development of social, emotional, and intrapersonal patterns of behavior. This distinction yields a concept of layers of personality, each subject to different laws of organization. For example, psychoanalytic writers have often distinguished *ego*-psychology as dealing with the former, while *depth*-psychology deals with the latter. This distinction is not made by learning approaches. The style and strength of a particular social response pattern, of responses to emotional stimuli, of appraisal of one's own behavior, or of skill learning are considered to result from operation of the same learning principles that, together with biological and social conditions, gradually shape any class of behavior.

4. The learning model shares its methods of inquiry into human behavior with all other sciences. Some dynamic theorists have proposed that the rules of theory construction and the methods and criteria common to science are inappropriate for collection of psychological data and verification of psychological principles. This methodological difference is most clearly demonstrated in the insistence by prominent leaders of the psychoanalytic school that criteria for validation of psychoanalytic propositions must be modified to accommodate unique features of the data. Psychological experiences, they insist, are not amenable to quantification and are recoverable only by an observer skilled in seeing special relationships due to objectivity gained by his own personal analysis. It is on these grounds that "critical" tests of some principles of psychoanalytic theory in the animal and human laboratory

have been rejected by analysts as inappropriate, and no significant rapprochement between psychoanalytic and behavioral approaches has been noted.

5. The learning model requires no special theory-related skills for observers, but it does require ability to make appropriate measurements. The admissibility of first-order constructs about observations as equivalent to the observations themselves has led dynamically oriented clinicians to impose on the observer the special requirement of familiarity with the underlying theory. Although training is necessary to enable any observer to recognize and reliably report the incidence of a specified behavior, no greater skill or theoretical knowledge is needed for learning approaches than for observation of any behavior—in man or animal, in naturalistic settings or in the laboratory. In fact, many observations can be automatically recorded. Precise definition of the observed (or treated) behavior, and the underlying requirement for dealing only with publicly observable responses, therefore permit use of observers with limited knowledge of psychological theory. However, a distinction must be made between persons who are responsible for specific observations or execution of a standardized treatment procedure and those who develop the treatment program and monitor its progress. For formulation of a behavioral analysis and evaluation of the adequacy of an initial treatment program, additional training and talent are required of the clinician.

6. Learning approaches recognize the importance of past events in the *formation* of learned behaviors. However, programs for behavior modification always deal with *current* behavior deviations. The behavior therapist directly attacks the problem response instead of a state that is assumed to be causally related to the symptom. He also begins with the present form of the problem response rather than a historically earlier form.

These features, which characteristically differ in dynamic and behavior modification approaches, are not exhaustive; nor do they reflect the many common sources of knowledge and observations that serve as the basis for decisions about the targets and methods in treating behavior problems. However, the basic difference should be clear. The relevance for the behavioral approaches of experimental techniques and empirical data from the body of psychology and the constant application of both method and theory of learning distinguish the behavioral from the dynamic approaches to clinical assessment and treatment.

In the remainder of this chapter we shall describe and outline implications of a schema for analysis of human behavior to which most learning models subscribe. We shall then present a brief summary of early efforts of applying the learning model to clinical phenomena.

THE BEHAVIORAL EQUATION AS THE UNIT OF ANALYSIS

The behavior of living organisms is continuous. A child's reaction in the classroom blends smoothly from attention to the teacher, to observation of the gardener outside the schoolroom window, to singing, writing his assignments, smiling at his neighbor, or tapping his foot. For convenience of analysis and abstraction, the flow of behavior has to be partitioned into segments that can be studied without losing the key elements of the behavior and the environmental conditions. Ordering of events is essential in all sciences for uniform observation and classification of independent and dependent variables. In the analysis of behavior this ordering process is complicated by the additional dimension of duration in time, which is a property of all psychological events.

The essential components for analysis of any behavior have been defined traditionally as *stimuli* and *responses*. An expansion of this paradigm includes representation of three other essential ingredients: the biological condition of the behaving organism, the consequence of the behavior for the organism's environment or for himself, and the contingency relationship between the behavior and its consequences. Lindsley (1964a) has suggested a four-component operant behavioral equation that includes stimulus, response, contingency relationship, and consequence. We have added one additional step to expand this formula:

S   Prior stimulation
O   Biological state of the organism
R   Response repertoire
K   Contingency relationship
C   Consequence

To indicate the relative temporal relationships and the centrality of the response, the formula may be written:

$$\text{Antecedent} \qquad \text{Consequent}$$
$$S \to O \to R \to K \to C$$

Complete description of any behavioral unit requires specification of each of these elements and their interaction with each other. In describing a man dialing a telephone number in a pay booth, one would specify the effective (discriminative) stimulus as the dial tone. The biological state includes the prerequisite physical skills for listening, looking, and dialing. The common contingency arrangement between the response and the consequence is one that is effective almost 100 percent of the time—correct dialing usually is followed by the ring in the home of the party called. In this example both the biological condition of the person and the contingency arrangement are relatively trivial because they commonly do not change the complex behavior of telephoning. When the effective stimulus, however, is an internal one, as in a call for help in an emergency, the person may not wait for the dial tone. The discriminative stimulus may be activated by the person's own preceding response (that is, lifting the receiver), and the internal state of emotional arousal may interrupt the orderly behavior sequence. If the illumination in the booth is inadequate for dialing or if the person is temporarily blinded, the response will also be quite different. If a person calls someone with the assurance that he will receive bad news, the aversive consequences predictable from past occasions or as a result of knowledge of the outcome of his behavior by vicarious experience affect the response. Finally, when environmental contingencies are significantly altered, the entire behavior chain is disrupted, and considerable new learning is required. The American who has experienced use of telephones in Europe—where speaking but not listening requires a coin deposit, and the coin button must be pushed *after* the called party answers—can easily attest to the importance of the interrelationship between S, R, and C, even in a simple task such as telephoning. Under these conditions the well-practiced chain of responses quickly falls apart when it brings no results.

An analysis of many common everyday behavior chains offers an instructive lesson in gauging the requirements of a task for skillful execution. For example, operating an electric typewriter, a small computer, steering a motor boat, or driving a car would have been regarded as formidable feats by our forefathers. Mastery of the operation of these and other machines is possible today, even for persons with limited intellectual capacity. The interrelations between stimulus changes and the immediacy of consequences of each separate response in the behavioral chain may facilitate acquisition of activities that combine simple, separate behavior elements into an impressive complex chain. When situational cues or response consequences are less distinct or immediate, such as in operating a camera or flying with navigational aids, the task may not be learned as quickly. Leonard (1968) gives an excellent description of the relevance of various components of the behavioral equation for human learning potential in relation to an important cultural product, the motorcar.

"Brain Research Institute researchers have compared the brain-wave patterns of subjects driving along the Los Angeles freeways with those of jet pilots flying practice air-defense interception missions. The automobile drivers showed up with more complex and stressful patterns. And there are millions of them. As a matter of fact, mankind's universal response to the motorcar provides a good example of human potential and how it is best elicited. The automobile makes a perfect teacher. It is a highly interactive learning environment, providing quick feedback for the student driver's every action. Anything that can be verbalized by an instructor about this process is trivial compared with what the car in motion tells the learner. The interaction between environment (car in motion) and learner is frequent, intense and often novel. The learner's behavior is changed during the process. And, at best, learning to drive is ecstatic. (Ask any sixteen-year-old.)" (Leonard, 1968, pp. 37–38.)

The utility of the behavioral equation lies in its requirement of detailed analysis of each element which can affect the learning and execution of an act—be it driving, hiding from mother, or avoiding a crowded elevator. The behavioral equation thus serves to summarize all the conditions acting *at the time of the response,* which may have relevance to the probability of response occurrence. The equation also indicates that all behavior is considered a function of specific and limited determinants, and that these determinants can be fully represented by the elements in the equation.

The Response—R

Learning theorists have often differentiated responses into two classes. Responses that are elicited by a particular stimulus without training and with little regard for the response consequences have been called *respondents* by Skinner. These are characterized by Mowrer as involuntary acts. Establishment of new connections between a new stimulus and the original response follow the principles of classical conditioning or sign learning. The well-known Pavlovian experiment for conditioning salivary responses in a dog illustrates the means by which such an innate or unconditioned response can be coupled to a new environmental cue by contiguity of an originally neutral stimulus and the unconditioned stimulus. A second class of responses, called *operants,* are conditioned by their consequences that is, by reinforcement. In this case, the particular eliciting stimuli that occasion the response need not be known. Rearrangement of response occurrence is carried out by providing a reinforcing event after the response is made. Since an operant procures a reward or punishment, it has also been called an *instrumental response.*

There is considerable disagreement regarding the necessity or value of this distinction between two types of response mechanisms with two different principles of learning governing their acquisition. (See Kimble,

1961, and Rescorla and Solomon, 1967, for comparisons of classical and instrumental conditioning.) From a pragmatic view, the most significant difference between respondents and operants in human behavior is the difference in the locus of control prior to or subsequent to occurrence of the response. While respondents are modified by variations in prior stimulus conditions, operants are modified by changing subsequent reinforcing consequences. However, the distinction remains superficial because a simple operant rarely is encountered in the human after early infancy. Most responses are embedded in a sequence of events that includes some signal, cue, or discriminative stimulus preceding the response. Therefore, both stimulus and reinforcement control can be (and usually is) applied to discriminated operants. For example, an operant, such as a child's call for mother, quickly comes under control not only of the probability of mother's subsequent appearance but also discriminative stimuli, such as her presence in the room.

Modification and Control of Responses. For the psychologist who is interested in modifying human behavior, the most important characteristic of the respondent is the fact that it cannot be modified by reinforcing contingencies alone. As Ferster (1963) has indicated: "The reflex (respondent behavior) represents involuntary control in the sense that full control of the behavior is in the eliciting stimulus which in turn derives its effect almost completely from the phylogenetic rather than the ontogenetic history of the organism. When the unconditioned stimulus is specified, the unconditioned response is almost completely determined" (p. 207).

Practically, then, respondent behavior is difficult to interrupt, and its management requires knowledge of the specific unconditioned stimulus that elicits it. Since numerous human activities involve both respondent and operant components, some methods of behavior modification have been developed by which respondent behavior can be brought under operant control. As a general rule, it is helpful to distinguish between respondents and operants as differing with regard to the bodily systems involved. Emotional behaviors—responses that involve autonomic activity—are generally considered to be respondents. Behaviors that involve the skeletal system, motor movements, and verbal responses are generally considered to be operants. Behavior modification methods that have emotional responses as their target, including physiological arousal to sexual or fear stimuli, usually focus on stimulus control of the respondent components. The majority of responses that are attacked in clinical behavior modification are, however, operants.

Whether the clinician is dealing with presumed operants or respondents, his most important assumption about undesired responses is that most specific behavior patterns are learned. Despite the immense richness of the adult behavioral repertoire, a great many actions carried out by an adult could also be performed by an average six-year-old with some additional training. During World War II, European children of grade school age learned to barter, fight, engage in sexual behavior, and protect their siblings at an age at which the American child is heavily dependent on adults and highly restricted in his activities. Recent research in educational psychology (Moore, 1966) suggests that a carefully programmed responsive environment can extend the repertoire of behaviors at any age far beyond common expectations. For example, children can be taught to read or do arithmetic below kindergarten age, contrary to earlier assumptions that reading "readiness" does not develop until a later age. Similarly, other assumptions about the range of human potentials are destroyed as the human environment is radically altered. Space travelers can learn to perform basic functions in a gravity-free environment, and men can remain physically and mentally active for seven or eight decades, achieving feats previously considered impossible. Thus the building blocks of behavior may be present in the repertoire of an individual but biological and environmental conditions dictate the degree to which *patterns* of responses are learned so that they form an effective behavioral act. There is probably no single "innate" pattern of any great complexity or importance in human behavior that is maintained throughout life without continuing modification. Cultural progress results in continuous expansion of the utilization of man's potential.

Personal experiences and controlling social events continually change the arrangement of response elements and shape behavioral acts, which eventually become differentiated in individuals in a manner that is described as a person's "style of behavior." These individual idiosyncrasies make up a portion of the content that is studied in the psychology of personality because they characterize the noninstrumental aspects of operant human behaviors. Herrnstein (1966) suggests that stylistic characteristics may be based on conditioning of special features of an act when accidental contingencies are operating. For example, the gait of an individual, his vocal inflexions, or his handwriting may be distinctive because particular forms of the response have been gradually conditioned by accidental reinforcement of both the essential and trivial components of the instrumental response of walking, speaking, or writing.

Response Classification. Responses can be classified either on the basis of their topographic similarity from the observer's point of view, or on the basis of functional relationships among the class members in terms of common consequences. In simple situations these two types of rules for classification may overlap. For example, in the laboratory an experimental subject may be required to respond to a discriminative stimulus by moving a lever until a light is turned on. Observations of hand movements, the tracings of the lever, and the flashes of the light will yield highly correlated response measures. If the subject tires and decides to move the lever with his elbow or shoulders, the topographic classification would yield no observations of hand movement for that period. A classification based on the common consequences of the acts would continue to accumulate measures of instrumental responses that turn on the light. The distinction between bodily movements or responses with similar structure or content and behavioral acts that differ in topography but produce the same consequences has been urged by learning and personality theorists of varied persuasions (for example, Murray, 1938).

In the analysis of complex response patterns, classification according to the functional properties of a response is generally preferred. This choice permits a more comprehensive description for subdividing behavioral units into components that can be modified by similar consequences. Decisions regarding which basis of classification to use in therapeutic modification schemes depend in part on whether the topography or consequence of the target act is defined as objectionable, a matter that is subject to cultural and social definitions. Differences in response topography (for example, the manner of holding one's fork, pronouncing a word, or asserting an opinion) may be targets for modification even when the consequence is the same (for example, food in mouth, word understood, opinion transmitted). On the other hand, discrimination of different consequences for topologically similar responses may be the therapeutic target, as, for example, when a hammer is held and moved identically in striking a nail and a valuable vase.

What Are Responses? The behavioral definition of a response has often been confused with a purely physicalistic definition of a body movement. Contemporary behaviorists include the full range of human motor and verbal responses as the legitimate object of study for psychology. However, two important methodological limitations are observed. First, social and verbal responses are considered responses in their own right, not as substitutes for mental events, descriptions of internal states, or expressions of other inferred processes. For example, a man's report of some inaccessible event within his skin, such as his state of hunger or anxiety, is considered to be multiply determined. It may be under control of some physiological events or it may be under control of the audience to whom the subject addresses these remarks. At any rate, it remains a verbal response regardless of the actual congruence with other events that it purports to describe.

Second, behavioral processes that are normally covert, such as thinking, perceiving, controlling oneself, or deciding, are events that are subject to experimental analysis only when the responses can be brought under experimental control, *at least* under special conditions in the laboratory. Skinner (1953) discussed the difficulties of dealing with private events of this type in a natural science, but recent research has demonstrated the feasibility of exploring such phenomena with the tools of modern psychology. Since many social and clinical behaviors involve normally covert responses, additional care must be taken to deal with these responses only when they can be directly measured, observed, or defined in such a way that there need be no recourse to hypothetical intervening events that are not demonstrable.

Whether the behaviors examined are ordinarily overt or covert, responses are defined by the experimental operations performed to measure and manipulate them. From the totality of a naturalistic act the experimenter abstracts one property to record as the indicant of the response in question. The response is entirely defined by this measurement operation in experimental research. The difficulty posed for clinical behavior modification is in achieving similar clarity of response specification.

Even in laboratory experimentation the process of abstraction obscures the nature of the actual phenomena, and therefore needs attention. In classical conditioning the conditioned response (CR) only partially replicates the unconditioned response (UCR), even when the latter is selected because of a close correspondence between CR and UCR. Conditioned eye blinks, for example, have a somewhat different form and can be differentiated from unconditioned eye blinks by their latencies, intensities, and other manifestations.

In clinical practice, target responses usually have been denoted only as very general classes, such as enuresis, phobia, depression, without operations for measuring and identifying precise response classes or series of responses. When the behavior modifier applies abstracting and operationalizing procedures to one of these target classes, he arrives at new formulations of the symptom and designs new methods for symptom control. For example, Lovibond's (1964) analysis of enuresis and urinary retention into a number of related component responses (for example, rectus abdominus and levator ani muscle responses, inhibition of micturition reflex, escape and avoidance responses) led him to suggest an operant avoidance instead of a classical conditioning paradigm for establishing control of enuresis, with improved therapeutic outcome. The problem of achieving the objectivity and precision implied by the use of the laboratory concept "response" is a major and continuing one in the theory and practice of behavior modification.

Responses as Dependent or Independent Variables. In observing human behaviors, it becomes apparent that responses can have multiple functions. For example, in normal social intercourse the behavior of striking another person can be treated as a dependent variable. The psychologist's interest then lies in ascertaining the variables that control the frequency or specific conditions of occurrence of such a response. The behavior may also be regarded as an independent variable, shifting the focus of analysis to ascertaining the consequences of this response for the person who is struck, for bystanders in a social environment, or for the striking person's own subsequent behavior.

In clinical psychology this differentiation is especially pertinent because traditional analyses have dealt mainly with a patient's responses as dependent variables, endeavoring to find the "causes" of the behavior. Of course, problematic behaviors are, by definition, always dependent variables when being attacked by modification procedures. However, current behavioral formulations also examine the patient's behavior as an independent variable. In etiological and descriptive formulations this difference in traditional and behavioral approaches occurs as a corollary of their differences in attention, either *only* to the person, or to the person *and* his effects on his environment. When a child chronically wets his bed, a traditional clinical formulation would take up the historical interpersonal and unconscious emotional variables producing the emotional disturbance (dependent variable). A behavioral formulation also considers the here-and-now consequences of micturition. In examining the mother's response to the child, for example, the enuresis is an independent variable in the behavioral equation. In either case, of course, the enuresis is an independent variable with respect to the mother's chagrin (and laundry washing), which initiates the clinical investigation in the first place.

External and Internal Environments—S

The response component describes the action of the individual, while the stimulus component of the behavioral equation is concerned with specifying the environmental conditions that have a functional relationship to his behavior. Psychologists have repeatedly emphasized that, of the total complex of stimuli impinging on the organism from its environment and its internal milieu, only the particular components that affect some property of the ongoing behavior are of relevance. Care must be taken to define the stimulus components from the viewpoint of the behaving organism rather than from the observer's position.

The Discriminative Stimulus. In Skinner's two-factor theory of learning, the role of the stimulus is explicitly different in respondent and operant behavior. Although the unconditioned stimulus in classical or respondent conditioning is inherently related to the response that it elicits, stimulus control of operant responses is built up by a gradual process of discrimination. In this process an organism is differentially reinforced only in the presence of a specified set of signals or discriminative stimuli (S^D) while reinforcement is omitted in the presence of another set of specified signals (S^Δ). Thus the role of discriminative stimuli in the control of operants is to specify that reinforcement will or will not follow a response. Food (UCS) and, after conditioning, a bell (CS) elicited respondent salivation in Pavlov's dog. Bounding over to his keeper was a discriminated operant built up through a history of positive consequences (feeding, petting) following this response to the keeper (S^D).

Reinforcing stimuli that follow a response eventually take on discriminative properties on subsequent occasions (Dinsmoor, 1950; Reynolds, 1968). Although operant behavior can be described completely in terms of the components O-R-K and C of the behavioral equation, after infancy the stimulus events that provide information about the probability of reinforcement for a potential response become increasingly important as behavior determinants. Therefore, the operant encountered in the observation of a clinical phenomenon is generally a *discriminated operant*. A discriminated operant is a response that occurs only in the presence of some environmental signal and is not randomly emitted at all times or under any conditions. This signal, an S^D, has accompanied situations in the person's past history in which there was a high probability of reinforcement for the response. A child may engage in begging behavior in front of the candy rack (S^D) in a supermarket when mother is in a cheerful mood (S^D) but not when she has already been cross (S^Δ) with the child.

Behavior Chains and Response-Produced Cues. Discriminative stimuli may consist of stimuli produced by other persons and stimuli produced by responses of the individual himself. In the latter case, a complex sequence may involve self-presentation of cues, which then affect the person's subsequent behavior. Most effective human behavior is composed of series or chains of responses. These chains are formed when one response serves as a discriminative stimulus for the following response. Each of the links, as well as the entire chain, is affected by the terminal consequences. Thus one response produces a stimulus for the next and signals the potentialities for reinforcement at the end of the sequence. For example, in solving a mathematical problem, a man's response to some element of the problem may serve as an S^D for verbalizing a series of steps for solving equations. These verbal responses then result in a complex chain of responses as the problem-solver attempts to apply a previously learned set of mathematical operations to the specific problem. Ultimate reinforcement of the entire "attack on the problem" follows correct solution and strengthens this mode of attack.

The capacity of the human organism to present himself with response-produced discriminative cues is essential in maintaining social behavior. Many S^Ds and S^Δs are not continuously physically present in the environment but are so well conditioned into each citizen's repertoire that they serve to guide individual behavior. For example, the existence of a legal code, law enforcement agencies, and numerous signals for the high probability of aversive consequences when a person behaves in illegal ways provide a complex net of controls by which society can affect the probability of illegal behaviors prior to their occurrence. It is an obvious corollary that any failure to experience aversive consequences under numerous conditions that are said to describe a high probability of punishment would tend to weaken such social controls for individual behavior. The resultant "antisocial" behavior is often the target of clinical attack in the delinquent person.

The Guiding Role of Social Stimulation. A person's behavioral repertoire is constantly modified through learning and exposure to new experiences. Society guides and directs the individual toward some learning experiences and excludes him from others. These social influences are mediated by the parents who serve as S^Ds and S^Δs for behaviors that the child can expect to lead to reinforcement or nonreinforcement. The child's teachers, his playmates, and the entire social fabric around him guide and shape development of his response repertoire by these cues. In addition, by providing observational learning and demanding imitation, the social enviroment establishes the conditions under which the child can expect to affect his environment successfully and achieve satisfactions.

It is through this guiding and controlling function that social subunits can produce differences in the content of behavior in children from rural or urban areas, in children who live in economically underdeveloped countries or technologically advanced countries, or in children who are reared in institutions. These social influences not only determine the skills and knowledge of the developing person; they also affect his reactions toward himself (self-observations and self-descriptions) and the way in which the individual's hierarchy of reinforcing stimuli is arranged. A cultural environment that emphasizes the importance of immediate satisfaction of biological needs at the expense of long-range social reinforcing stimuli is likely to develop a repertoire that lacks self-controlling behaviors. For example, in a slum area the emphasis is often on immediate obtainment of food or physical comforts to alleviate some bodily need. The adults' stress on satisfaction of bodily needs tends to become the focus of the child's attention. For persons in this environment the social variables become less powerful determinants of satisfaction-seeking behaviors than for people who live in a society in which reinforcing events of a biological nature are continually ranked low in the order of desirability or are supplied amply on a relatively noncontingent basis.

The Organism—O

The study of man and his physical environment is sufficiently complex to require some division of labor among scientists in the investigation of living organisms. Despite some practical convenience in the division of the subject matter of science into diverse fields like chemistry, physics, biology, psychology, or sociology, so much knowledge has accumulated in each of the areas and about the interrelationship among areas that the earlier boundaries of each field now appear arbitrary. Scientists in various fields recognize that many of the answers to their questions depend upon explorations of variables outside the immediate subject matter of their field. It is especially true in the application of science to human affairs that collaboration of men from different scientific disciplines is required. For example, full understanding (and hence control) of the regulation of food intake and obesity requires knowledge not only of the complex response chains, stimulus controls, and reinforcers involved in eating behaviors and exercise levels but also of the genetic, physiological, neurological, biochemical, and mechanical variables that enter into food consumption and the conversion of food into energy expenditure or fatty deposits (Mayer and Thomas, 1967; Schachter, 1968).

Some authors have expressed the view that the genesis of behavioral disturbances can be linked directly to damage or malfunction of biological systems or structures, particularly in the brain. Others hold that interactional effects between biological or genetic insufficiencies and social learning combine to create behavior deviations. A third group denies the relevance of organismic factors in all but a very few cases of behavioral aberrations. The wide variety of patterns of behavior disturbances has enabled each group to offer some evidence for their hypothesis. For example, brain lesions and cerebral deficiencies in concentration of biochemical substances are encountered in some patients but they are absent in others with similar behavior patterns. Substances like glutamic acid have been credited with a central role in intellectual functioning. Benzedrine, LSD, and other chemical substances have been shown to produce hallucinatory and other deviant behaviors. On the other hand, the same substances differ in their effects on individuals and similar effects can be produced by social-psychological factors alone. In psychology, two opposing viewpoints regarding disciplinary boundaries have long been expressed. Some psychologists believe that ultimately all behavioral phenomena should be explained in terms of the biological, physiological, and bioelectrical characteristics of organisms. Others consider biological factors of secondary interest. The former group, characterized as *reductionists*, have concentrated their research efforts on physiological and anatomical variables affecting behavior.

Interaction of Social and Biological Variables. There can be no question of the importance of biological factors in human functioning. In clinical psychology there are numerous examples of behavior problems in which biological factors constitute the single most important controlling variables. For instance, the presence of toxic substances can result in transient or permanent disorganization of behavior. Toxic psychoses, disturbances following serious damage to brain structures or to their blood-supplying system, or behavioral changes associated with glandular disturbances offer ample evidence of the significant role of biological processes in the maintenance of behavior. However, some authors have contended that all extreme behavior deviations can be traced back to biological variables. Schizophrenia, alcohol and drug addictions, sexual deviations, and antisocial behavior have been particularly singled out for attention by investigators holding the biogenic hypothesis of behavior deviation.

Recent genetic studies of the chromosomal constitution of delinquents illustrate the complexity of relationships between biological and psychological variables. Montagu (1968) reports a series of studies that point to the unexpectedly high frequency of an XYY chromosome pattern in criminals. This aberration occurs when the paternal germ cells undergo abnormal cell division, producing sperm cells with a double Y complement. The sperm's Y chromosome, on union with a normal ovum (carrying the X chromosome), produces a male offspring. Montagu hypothesizes: "It appears probable that the ordinary quantum of aggressiveness of a normal XY male is derived from his Y chromosome, and that the addition of another Y chromosome presents a double dose of those potencies that may under certain conditions facilitate the development of aggressive behavior" (Montagu, 1968, p. 46). It is estimated that the frequency of XYY males at birth ranges from 0.5 to 3.5 per 1000. Several investigators have reported higher incidence of this type in prison populations. Does this mean that the fate of the XYY male is inevitable? The answer to this question is not clear. The XYY constitution does not always produce antisocial behavior; nor do even a sizable minority of criminals show this aberration. Investigators of this phenomenon suggest that the prophylactic solution lies in early identification of these persons and in helping their parents to institute a preventive program early in the child's life.

The reader of these studies is impressed by the ramifications of these findings for social attitudes toward delinquency. Is the XYY male "responsible" for his aggressive action, or is he an unfortunate product of nature, like the retarded or congenitally deformed? Are there clear limits to the modifiability of aggressive behavior in XYY persons by social-psychological means? Is the antisocial behavior a result of a long history of conflict that increasingly intensified and refined an early, mild but consistent deviation into a vicious antisocial pattern? Many similar research findings from the study of the biological and constitutional correlates of behavior disorders leave unanswered, at this time, the tantalizing question of the biogenic hypothesis of behavior pathology concerning the extent of biological determinants and their mechanisms. Yet there can be little doubt that no behavioral analysis is complete without consideration of the biological characteristics of the person.

Another instructive illustration of the rich interdependence and inseparability of social, behavioral, and biological factors is given in recent work on the role of biological factors in the maintenance of population density in mammals (Christian, Lloyd and Davis, 1965; Snyder, 1962). Experiments with rats, mice, dogs, woodchucks, and rabbits, in natural settings and the laboratory, examined the influence of fluctuations in population density on biological and social functions and their ultimate outcome on population growth. Increased population density eventuated in increased mortality due to suppression of normal biological defense mechanisms—presumably as a result of increased corticoid secretion and increased renal glomerular disease. These endocrinological changes were observed to affect young and subordinate animals to a greater extent than dominant and old ones. A second set of endocrine responses, serving to decrease birth rates, involved inhibition of maturation, diminished fertility, increased intrauterine mortality, increased developmental abnormalities, and inadequate lactation. Taken together, these two sets of biological changes, through a variety of biochemical mechanisms, tend to slow the growth of a population and eventually to maintain the population at a level below that which would exhaust the environmental resources. Increased crowding in living cages and similar social environmental conditions also led to distinguishable changes in the animals' sexual response and in numerous other biological mechanisms essential to reproduction of the species. In a review of the literature on the social and biological factors in population control Thiessen and Rodgers (1961) conclude that "the endocrine response, triggered by both social and sociophysiological conditions, appears to undergo changes so as to provide a self-limiting control of population size." Thiessen and Rodgers further conclude that "learning ability, emotionality, and other behavior may also be altered by variations in density of population" (p. 450).

A more immediate influence of biological factors on behavior is illustrated in the study of responses to punishment. Ulrich and Azrin (1962) found that exposure to electric shock caused a rat to attack other rats or other small animals. The authors characterize this behavior as "reflex fighting" and report that this elicited aggression has been found in several species and under different types of painful stimulation (Azrin and Holz, 1966). The observed behavior was independent of any favorable consequences, thus suggesting an unconditioned response. Here we see another set of biological factors that can significantly influence the same behavior as that which can also be obtained through manipulation of appropriate stimulus conditions or response consequences.

Research findings like these make it clear that biological characteristics must always be considered in the behavioral equation to the extent that they affect the particular behavioral unit under consideration.

Contributions of Biological Factors to Learning. Somewhat less spectacular but more commonly encountered organismic conditions which need to be remembered in observation or control of behavior are the biochemical states that affect response to common reinforcing contingencies. For example, various organic diseases, nutritional deficiencies, age, genetically determined characteristics, or physical deformities all may specify the parameters for the individual organism's response to environmental stimulation or consequences of his behavior. These variables also determine the individual's capacity to change responses. Individual differences in anatomical structures, physical capacities, or emotional responsiveness affect the response system and its viability in the face of attempted behavior changes.

In the study of clinical behaviors, the effects of drugs on organismic functions are of special interest. Drug-induced inhibition or acceleration of physiological activities affect complex behavior patterns characterized as psychological deviations. For example, ingestion of tranquilizers or psychotomimetics (drugs that produce intensified emotional states, usually accompanied by behavior disorganization) may bear a direct relationship to the intensity or frequency of responses that constitute the original complaint of the patient. Drug effects may be temporary or they may cause secondary alterations in the person's biologic systems. Drugs can also modify the operant links in a behavior chain by changing the organism's reception of sensory inputs or stimulation from his own functioning. While drug effects do not themselves result in establishment of new and more effective social behaviors, they can improve the effectiveness of behavioral intervention. Many behavioral deviations, such as social withdrawal or temper outbursts, are maintained by consequences in the immediate social environment of the person. Disruption of these pathological behaviors by drug intervention often leads the people in the patient's environment to respond more favorably, thus creating the opportunity for learning more adequate interpersonal behaviors.

Social Attitudes Toward Biological Factors in Individuals. Finally, we wish to call attention to attitude differences among various cultures or social groups toward biologically deficient conditions. These attitudes partially determine the importance of a particular biological defect in the person's ability to function effectively in a given social setting. Hence a psychologically oriented definition of the biological adequacy of an organism must take into account the social milieu. Consider, for example, the differential social consequences to a person who may have been a stroke victim or have suffered mild residuals of poliomyelitis in childhood. In a primitive nomadic culture even a minor paralysis of a limb may have disastrous consequences. In the United States this type of physical incapacity may alter the vocational behavior pattern of an office worker very little, but it would completely disrupt the life of a logger or athlete, and may handicap an office worker's sexual and social behaviors because of reactions of others and of self to physical deformity. Variations in eyesight or hearing are now compensated by prosthetic devices to the extent that even severe deficiencies can be corrected. Technologically advanced cultures generally tend to attach less instrumental importance to individual biological differences than less advanced cultures. Within the United States the importance of such biological variables, however, varies from one subculture to another, and social-interpersonal consequences may be great even when instrumental effects are slight. Influence of social consequences and self-reactions even on direct manifestations of a biological defect is illustrated by the gross increase in tremor in persons with Parkinson's disease (caused by a brain lesion) when they are aware of being observed or are attending to their tremor. When absorbed in a task and not attending to the symptomatic response, Parkinson patients may show relatively little tremor.

The Consequence—C

All learning theories recognize the relevance of a response's consequence for the subsequent probability of that response. The best known statement of the relation of consequence to response occurrence was given by Thorndike's *Law of Effect.* This principle asserted that satisfactory consequences tend to increase response strength while unsatisfactory consequences tend to decrease it. Contemporary learning theorists, however, have rejected Thorndike's inherently subjective frame of reference in which the consequence of a response must be registered by the organism as pleasant or unpleasant.

Explanations of Learning. Hull, a major contributor to clarification of the functional relationships of consequence and response, reformulated the Law of Effect in terms of physiological referents that define the state of affairs created by the consequence. His *drive reduction principle* postulates the drive states underlying behavioral motives to be either of a biological nature, such as hunger or thirst, or of a secondary (learned, social) nature, such as anxiety. Stimuli following a given response that have the capacity for reducing an existing drive state are designated as reinforcing stimuli and are said to increase the strength of the preceding response. Hull and his followers introduced many refinements to the original statement in order to avoid the necessity of postulating a separate drive corresponding to each (reinforcing) stimulus that appears to affect behavior. This theoretical approach generally accepts the notion that reinforcing stimuli possess properties that transcend their idiosyncratic characteristics. Reinforcing stimuli have in common a capacity for bringing the acting organism to a more stable equilibrium with external and internal environments and to a lower level of activity by eliminating the drive stimuli that originated the instrumental behavior.

Exponents of *contiguity* theories of learning hold that the essential condition of learning is the simultaneous occurrence of a set of stimulating events and a set of responses with which the stimuli become associated. However, contiguity theories also recognize the importance of the events following a response, because of the special position of the last response of a series of responses performed under similar conditions. Responses that have some impact on their environment tend to change the stimulus conditions or remove the organism from exposure to them. Therefore it is the bond between the last response and the stimuli that is strengthened. Guthrie, the foremost exponent of contiguity learning theory, recognized the importance of events that other theorists have called reinforcing stimuli, without subscribing to the motivational explanations of their effect on learning.

Skinner gave central importance to the consequence by his emphasis on reinforcement in operant conditioning. However, in order to avoid the circularity implicit in the Law of Effect and its later reformulations, Skinner has defined consequence purely in terms of an empirical relationship. Any immediately consequent event that has the effect of changing the probability of the preceding response is defined as a reinforcing stimulus for that response. This definition resolves the dilemma of establishing long lists of needs and drives in human organisms. But its problems lie in the opposite direction. The effectiveness of a reinforcing stimulus for a given response varies as a function of all of the components in the behavioral equation. For instance, a parental kiss may serve to reinforce behavior of a four-year-old but may have the opposite effect when bestowed upon a teenager in front of his friends. Even a reinforcing stimulus that appears to have a fairly constant physical relationship to an organism's activity may produce opposing effects under changing conditions. It has been found, for example, that rats will increase their rate of bar pressing in a Skinner box when such behavior results in lighting a dark cage. Rats will also increase bar pressing that turns off a light of similar intensity in an illuminated cage. Thus Skinner's empirical definition faces the investigator with the task of constructing lists of reinforcing stimuli appropriate only for highly specific conditions for individual organisms. In fact, in application of operant learning methods to behavior modification it must constantly be remembered that a particular event selected as a potential reinforcing stimulus can be so defined with certainty only *after* it succeeds in changing the probability of the preceding response. Although such reinforcers as food, money, and social approval may be durable in effect over a long time and across many people and situations, their effects can be radically changed by altered environmental features. Since it is also not always possible to eliminate the presence of other factors that may have affected response probabilities, a post hoc definition that depends only on response-probability changes is not completely satisfactory.

Within Skinner's framework, Premack (1959) has suggested that the relationship between a response and the subsequent event be treated purely on the basis of *relative* response probabilities. Briefly, Premack asserts that a *behavior* serves as a reinforcing stimulus if its probability of occurrence is greater than that of the behavior to be reinforced, when both responses are freely available. Behavior modification simply involves a rearrangement of responses so that opportunity for making the high probability response is always contingent upon prior execution of the desired response of somewhat lower probability.

Conjugate and Episodic Reinforcement. As we have previously emphasized, conceptual treatment of human behavior as static is a matter of convenience and not a reflection of fact. In the smooth operation of daily activities, response sequences, reinforcing events, and stimulus events continuously interact in an intricate ongoing process. In order to accommodate this temporal dimension within a definition of reinforcing events, Lindsley (1963a) has suggested the term *conjugate reinforcement* to denote a continuous interdependence between response, response consequences, and subsequent behavior. The intensity or availability of a continuously present reinforcer can be made a direct function of the rate or sequence of the person's response. For example, viewing a projected movie cartoon may require activation of a switch at a certain rate to assure that sound volume or brightness of the picture is maintained. This laboratory example parallels the everyday continuities encountered in the support of a speaker by a listener's small reinforcing cues, or of the advances of a lover by the small signs of approval from his beloved.

In conjugate reinforcement, continued exposure to a reinforcing event requires continuous behavior. In the experimental situation, the movie projector is programmed so that the film and sound fade away when the minimal response requirements are not met. In natural social interactions, conjugate reinforcement is the rule. Maintenance of social contacts requires that the person continuously emit sequences of socially effective responses, which a partner reciprocates. The progressive and piecemeal nature of most social reinforcement defines the continuity of personal "relationships" in courtship, friendship, business interactions, and psychotherapy. In all of these, a continuing adjustment to the partner's behavior and the accumulation of small but important consequences over time characterize the interactional system. Lindsley (1964b) believes that conjugate reinforcement requires only very basic and simple processes and can therefore maintain complex behaviors much more effectively than episodic reinforcement. The advantages of conjugate reinforcement for training of social behaviors clearly appear in the fact that long behavioral sequences can be taught and maintained by adding new elements to the same general procedures.

Similar to the concept of conjugate reinforcement is the concept of *chaining*, which we have briefly discussed before. Most effective human behaviors consist of chains of responses, linked by small reinforcing events and by the discriminative stimuli provided by the preceding response. When a person opens a door he first inserts the key in the lock. Its fit serves to reinforce that bit of behavior and signals the response of turning. If the lock gives way, the turning response is reinforced and the occasion is set for the next step of moving the other hand on the door knob. These chained behaviors are quickly interrupted when a particular consequence does not occur. A broken lock, a bad key, or any event interrupting the well-learned behavioral sequence results in changes and emission of a new set of responses. The sequence that we have just described in regard to opening a door serves as a simplified model of the type of stimulus-response-consequence interrelationships encountered in complex behaviors, such as social interactions, courtship, or other human interactions. A response consequence is the basic requirement in all of these situations in order to maintain smooth behavior.

In *episodic reinforcement* the person is rewarded only after completing a long sequence of behaviors. This arrangement describes most learning and problem-solving experiments. School grades and salaries also represent episodic reinforcement. In everyday activities episodic reinforcement generally follows the execution of a complex and extended series of behavior. The reinforcing effects are usually not specific for the detailed manner of completing the job but for the achievement of the product or terminal response. Therefore, episodic reinforcement tends to reward the end instead of the means in a task.

The Response-Consequence Contingency Relationship—K

The final component of the behavioral equation concerns the particular arrangement between behavior and its consequences. In the natural environment, many behaviors inevitably result in specified consequences because of the characteristics of our physical world. For example, the law of gravity specifies that there are inevitable consequences for every occasion when a person lets go of an object in midair. The laws of physics also point to consistent consequences for behaviors such as pulling, kicking, or pushing small objects. The response-consequence arrangement for these physical events remains relatively constant in a wide range of situations. In most activities, including almost all social behaviors, this contingency arrangement is far less reliable. The probability that an infant's cry will be followed by mother's approach depends on many factors that vary from moment to moment. The mother's general attentiveness to her child's behavior, her momentary engagement in other activities, or her physical distance from the child may be among the variables that determine the probability of her responding to the child's cry. In many social situations contingencies are intentionally withheld for many occurrences of the same response. For instance, teachers do not reward a child for each accurate response in the classroom. They tend to distribute reinforcements on a schedule that may be based on the frequency of the behaviors, on the time elapsed since the last reinforcement for a response, or some other undefined basis.

Schedules of Reinforcement. The most common systematic arrangements of response-reinforcement contingencies have been carried out in the laboratory under schedules that vary the proportion of reinforced responses or the time intervals after which reinforcement can be obtained. These schedules have been shown to modify the probability of the occurrence of a given response and the characteristic sequence and form of the selected behavior. Ferster and Skinner (1957) provide an extensive description of effects of various reinforcement schedules on the speed of acquisition of a response, the strength at which it is maintained, and the decrease or decay of an established response. Discriminative stimuli often signal which specific schedule is in effect for a given response. In social behavior such discriminations are often associated with the characteristics of the persons controlling the reinforcing event. Children will respond at different rates for a father who is known to be conservative in rewarding behavioral output than for a mother whose praise and approval flows generously for each small accomplishment of her child. The predominance of *intermittent* reinforcement schedules, with less than 100% reinforcement, and of constant shifts in schedules introduces considerable variablity in social behaviors. Often a person acts inappropriately because he may not know the particular schedule on which other people base reinforcement of his behavior.

Schedules of reinforcement may overlap in complicated ways. *Multiple schedules* may be determined not only by the person's momentary behavior but also by the output and nature of the preceding responses. In animal research it has been clearly demonstrated that discriminative stimuli signalling which alternative schedule is in effect immediately modify a laboratory animal's rate of response. Shift in schedules or concurrent existence of multiple schedules usually are not directly signaled in ordinary human interactions. The numerous experiments on the effects of reinforcement schedules provide a basis for regulation of response rates in human behavior modification and also serve as a reminder of the changeability and complexity of the response-reinforcement relationship in the assessment of human behavior. Maintenance of a given response rate not only is determined by its consequence but also by the particular schedule under which the consequence is administered.

Changes in K. In addition to the schedule under which the reinforcing event occurs, arrangements of the response-reinforcement relationship may also involve a gradual shift of reinforcing events from one class of behavior to another overlapping but slightly different response class. This procedure, called *shaping*, is a technique by which increasing demands for precision of response are made on the organism. The experimenter at first reinforces a class of responses that is only distantly similar to the ultimately desired response. Gradually he reinforces only the responses more closely approximating the desirable one. The same gradual change in arrangement between response and reinforcement by shaping has been used clinically to bring about an increasing similarity of vocal patterning in nonverbal children until their noises accurately copy speech sounds.

Although the goal in programmed learning is to utilize R-C relationships that lead to most effective and efficient behavior, natural circumstances often provide arrangements that encourage less effective development. For example, parental failure to gradually withdraw positive consequences for dependent behavior may lead to persistence of "immature" responses in adulthood. The response-reinforcement arrangement can be intentionally programmed on a random basis in order to maximize response variability. These simple methods of controlling behavior can often be observed in children's play when rules for behavior are changed frequently, permitting the person who dispenses the reinforcing events to maintain control over the responder by exposing him to an unpredictable reinforcement schedule.

For similar reasons, a precise statement of the requirements for dispensation of the reinforcer are often withheld from the behaving person by the social agent controlling the reinforcement. Under these conditions a person will then engage in behavior directed at testing the reinforcement schedule in effect. These activities appear as variations in behavior that are often described as hypothesis testing, testing the limits, or discovering the rules. When a person discovers the effective response-consequence arrangements, he can change his behavior to suit the schedule in effect, thereby achieving optimal payoff with minimal effort. Students, employees, and others whose behavior is directly controlled by another person can easily detect the habitual reinforcement schedules of that person, such as those implicit in the teacher's pattern of spot-checking homework by alphabetical order, or the employer's tendency to examine work output at the end of the week, or at the beginning of the day.

IMPLICATIONS OF THE BEHAVIORAL EQUATION IN CLINICAL USE

In addition to the analysis of the various components of the behavioral equation that the learning-oriented clinician undertakes in examining clinical cases, the behavioral equation highlights several other assumptions of behavior therapies that differ from traditional clinical methods and that have already been introduced in Chapter 1. They can now be elaborated on in terms of the components of the equation.

Stress on Current Influences

If maladjustment is viewed as a condition brought about by faulty learning, the major task of the clinican is to change the socially deviant behavior by manipulating whatever variables are found to exercise control over these behaviors. Knowledge of the original controlling variables may be obtained from a thorough investigation of the patient's history. But this information rarely suggests to the clinician how to gain control over the current occurrence of the symptomatic response. Present problematic behavior can be affected only by variables acting in the present. Whether these variables are S (Stimulus), O (Organism), or C (Contingency) features, the clinician must look for them in the present social environment, the biological condition, and the supporting environment of the patient. Consequently, the behavioral approach dictates collection of historical material about the patient's life only if such knowledge has relevance to discovery of variables that may still influence the patient's behavior, and if it suggests a method of therapy in which these variables are used to change the patient's deviant behavior. Thus, behavioral assessment rests on the functional analysis of current conditions. This analysis considers not only the stimulus environment but also the different consequences attached to the range of behaviors in which the patient can engage, his repertoire of available responses, the arrangements for reinforcing events that are provided by the patient's social environment and by persons close to him, and similar events.

Symptoms Are Learned

The assumption that all problematic behavior is learned suggests two possible methods for therapeutic change: (1) unlearning or replacement of the undesired response by any of the procedures based on laboratory learning paradigms, and (2) modification of the environment so that the symptom, a discriminated operant or a stimulus-controlled respondent, no longer occurs, due to the absence of the antecedent conditions that control it. Application of various learning procedures and the underlying principles and methods for changing environmental cues are discussed in the following chapters.

Subjective Experiences

Many clinical complaints deal with phenomena representing inaccessible internal events and reactions of the organism toward his own functioning. These events cannot be dealt with directly by means of a learning approach since they cannot be brought under the therapist's control. But a patient's report about his subjective discomforts must be treated as a behavior that has the dual function of affecting the listener to whom the report is made and serving as a cue-producing response to whatever internal stimuli may be acting. After helping the patient to discriminate between these two sources of stimulation and to recognize early cues in these sequences, the therapist can teach the patient to control his own behavior. For example, a wife's report of anxiety may be discovered to be the end of a chain that begins with the husband's query "What's for dinner?" The chain continues with her thoughts of his past criticisms of her cooking, to reexperiencing anger and frustration occasioned by those criticisms, to recall of inability or abortive attempts to assert herself, to internal physical cues associated with the self-label of "anxious." The wife may be taught to identify food-related remarks by her husband as a crucial early event in this chain and to attach new behaviors (humor, ignoring, assertion) to it. Alternatively, she may condition her husband to dispense more positive comments about food. By either tactic, she can circumvent her own reported anxiety. Thus analysis of a patient's verbal reports can bring some of his self-reactions under control in therapy. Subjective experiences are assumed to have their origin in some earlier social experience and can be influenced through therapeutic operations. By altering the behavior which they initiate, the consequences to the patient are thereby improved.

Continuity of Behavioral Principles Across Species

The behavioral model has been built on the basis of principles and procedures developed in the animal laboratory. Increased complexity in the behavior of higher species is assumed to result from increasing complexity in biological structure, capabilities, and richness of experience. But the basic principles of learning are expected to remain unchanged for all living organisms and no special psychological principles are required for the understanding of human behavior. It is necessary to supplement the more general principles with special relationships due to the unique features of human life. Many distinctly human functions arise from the capacity for language and transmission of culture during human development. These features are presumed to be subject to analysis by the same methodological approach as used for animal behavior, even though they present additional problems (such as accessibility to observation and manipulation) to the researcher and theorist.

Although the above features characterize the methodological approaches and underlying assumptions of the behavioristic model, selection of particular behavioral contents for clinical behavior modification is deeply entrenched in observations made over centuries by men with totally different theoretical viewpoints. In the following section we shall examine some earlier attempts to combine the conceptual learning model with traditional psychotherapeutic approaches. These writers often accepted the traditional characterization of the disturbed individual as a person whose early emotional experiences are the root of pathological behavior. These traditional approaches tend to consider behavior deviations as fairly universal patterns of response to physiological or emotional stress. In the early days of learning approaches to clinical psychology, the role of anxiety was especially singled out as the causative factor in the disruption of normal behavioral organization. Some contemporary learning approaches focus on the reduction of anxiety as the major target of behavior modification— but this factor is no longer seen as the single most important etiological agent in the development of behavioral disturbances.

Early Learning Models

ATTEMPTS TO REFORMULATE PSYCHOANALYSIS

It may seem surprising that learning theories of behavior pathology should have developed from research on animal instead of human learning.

The reason lies in the orientation of early learning experimenters toward the discovery of the laws of mental associations and their quest for the fundamental laws of learning and forgetting. Investigators seeking the basic rules of acquisition and memory for simple verbal items carefully isolated the subject from his life experiences, eliminated variations in motivation, and selected tasks that bore little relationship to everyday life. In contrast, animal research grew out of a pragmatically oriented tradition that included from the very outset the animal's adjustment to his environment. Though both the learning task and the laboratory environment were quite dissimilar from the animal's natural environment, the controlled laboratory experiences and quantified behavioral observations permitted study of controlled environmental influences and a wide range of motivational variables. Opportunities for a rapprochement between the psychology of learning and personality arose only when learning experimenters began to develop conceptual schemas to account for experiential and motivational effects on performance.

Early efforts to encompass the phenomena of behavior disorders and psychotherapy within a learning framework were made up of two distinct approaches. The first, based on Hullian theory, remained closely associated with the methods and observations provided by psychoanalysis. Attempts to establish a parallel between Hull's drive reduction hypothesis and Freud's pleasure principle provided a convenient starting point for translation of data and concepts from one system into the other. The second approach is represented by application of the classical conditioning paradigm to neurotic behavior. Disordered behavior observed in animals subjected to difficult discrimination tasks seemed to Pavlov, Watson, and others to be similar to the behavior observed in breakdown of effective functioning in human neuroses. While Watson regarded the conditioning theory of neurosis as being in direct contrast to the psychodynamic theories of his day, Pavlov and his students made efforts to integrate conditioning theory into neurology and psychiatry. In contrast to the Hullian group, neither Pavlovians nor Watsonians attempted to reinterpret contemporary treatment procedures in terms of their learning theories. Instead, they were among the first to suggest new treatments for neurotic symptoms on the basis of their theory.

A further distinction between the two approaches lies in the fact that the Hullian group accepted the underlying concept of neuroses as a defense against anxiety. Consequently, therapy was directed at reducing the anxiety that had caused the symptom. On the other hand, the early conditioning experimenters viewed neuroses mainly as a "bad habit." The therapeutic goal was removal of the undesired response by extinction, without attention to the underlying causes.

Mowrer

Among the earliest papers joining learning theory to the Freudian anxiety theory of neurosis was Mowrer's (1939) S-R analysis of anxiety as a reinforcing agent. He proposed that anxiety is a conditioned pain reaction, a learned response associated with conditioned stimuli or signals that had previously been experienced in conjunction with pain or injury. Mowrer assigned two properties to anxiety: (1) motivation characteristics in arousing the organism for action, and (2) reinforcing properties associated with any behavior capable of reducing the anxiety state. He proposed that anxiety has adaptive value—it is evoked in the presence of stimuli signaling the proximity of danger and motivates actions that avoid the danger and its associated stimuli. Reduction of anxiety then strengthens the relief-bringing behavior. Experimental support for this formulation was provided in an animal study (Mowrer, 1940) in which one group was given trials pairing a neutral tone and an electric shock at constant intervals; a second group was given tone-shock delivery at randomly varied intervals; and a third group was given irregularly interpolated shocks between the tone-shock pairings. The animals in the constant interval group learned a locomotor escape response most quickly, with the irregular interval group and the interpolated shock group following in that order. Mowrer interpreted the results as indicating that regular recurrence of the danger signal (tone) leads to formation of an expectancy or preparatory set as the time approaches for the occurrence of the next stimulus presentation. When this preparatory tension (anxiety) is sufficiently strong to be "uncomfortable," it takes on motivational properties. Its reduction should therefore reinforce accompanying behavior. Mowrer argued that regular presentation of a preshock stimulus results in a greater drop in tension when followed by escape than does irregular presentation, because of the anxiety build-up preceding the expected shock. The escape response, reinforced by tension reduction, should be learned less quickly when variations in intertrial intervals yield no clear anticipatory signal and the escape response may alternately follow weak or strong tension.

Mowrer (1950) also distinguished two types of learning that have different functions in everyday life. *Classical conditioning* or *sign-learning* is based on temporal contiguity between an originally neutral stimulus and an unconditioned stimulus. It is largely involuntary and, for Mowrer, sets up the first step in the anxiety sequence, creating a state of heightened physiological tension in response to the previously neutral tone. *Instrumental conditioning* or *problem solving* refers to the process by which a response is learned as a function of the consequences that follow it.

The escape response to the tone signal represents trial and error learning with the response reinforced if it reduces the existing tension.

According to Mowrer, both learning processes occur in the development of a behavior disorder. A child may be exposed during socialization to painful events resulting in frequent anxiety in situations that require the sign-learning of social attitudes necessary for normal development. A neurosis is formed when the child then develops instrumental behaviors to escape further anxiety and to cope with the additional problems created by *not* learning. This description of the learning of neurotic behavior suggests that a neurotic has managed to avoid learning important instrumental acts early in life and suffers from a *learning deficit* that can be remedied only by freeing him for additional opportunities for learning during his adult life. In this regard, Mowrer differs from Freud by arguing that it is not overlearning but underlearning during childhood that is responsible for neurotic behavior. Treatment therefore requires that the socializing education be continued, helping the patient to achieve increased maturity and social responsibility. Mowrer also calls attention to the importance of the time relationships between the neurotic response and reinforcement. Although a symptom may have immediate positive effects in anxiety reduction, its larger negative consequences may occur much later. The apparent paradox of explaining why a neurotic engages in self-defeating actions and, even in therapy, resists abandonment of his neurotic behavior which creates more problems than it solves, is resolved by taking into account the timing of the reinforcing events.

The other contributions of Mowrer to analyses of personality processes in S-R terms are too numerous to mention here. Especially important is that his work represents a pioneering combination of research from the animal laboratory with psychological theory in order to revise the basic conceptualization of the etiology of behavior disorders proposed by Freudian theory. Together with other learning theorists of his era, Mowrer has helped to provide a learning language for the etiology and maintenance of human pathology and to set the stage for eventual independent development of a learning theory basis for clinical psychology—independent not of the observations but of the theoretical framework of earlier nonbehavioral models.

Dollard and Miller

The publication of Dollard and Miller's *Personality and Psychotherapy* (1950) represents the high point of the movement to recast dynamic personality theory into a learning framework. It is unquestionably the most complete systematic effort toward an encompassing learning theory of the development and treatment of neurosis. Dollard and Miller had no quarrel with psychoanalytic theory. They took as their task the translation of psychiatric theory into a learning language in order to achieve viability and broadened foundations for an essentially psychoanalytic treatment theory. For example, careful analysis in Hullian terminology of transference, of repression, of the critical stages in child training, of free association, and of classical defense mechanisms put into new focus events that had long been singled out by psychoanalysis as having fundamental significance. Dollard and Miller's schema is characterized by use of the common units of all learning theories: innate and learned drives, cues, and reinforcement, with special emphasis on the influence of learning processes by the primary drives, especially pain and sex. They apply learning principles to language with the aid of a mediation hypothesis in order to account descriptively for higher mental processes. Verbal responses are cue-producing responses mediating further behaviors that ultimately serve as cues for action or instrumental responses. Verbal responses can thereby not only control other behaviors but also can order a person's experiences and can extend his repertoire from old to new situations. Neurotic patterns are learned early in childhood, with aggression and sex as the main underlying primary drives. Dollard and Miller present a schematic diagram that summarizes the factors involved in neurotic behavior (Figure 2-1). Their schema illustrates the circularity and self-perpetuation of neurotic behavior. Conflict between learned fear and the basic drive, which would normally be reduced by execution of the uninhibited response, results in an unreduced (high) drive state as the neurotic vacillates or finds a symptom. Thus the anxiety is reduced but not the conflicting drive. Fear also motivates "stopping thinking" or the repression of verbal or other cue-producing behavior. As a result, the neurotic is "stupid," for he is blocked in using his mentality to solve his conflicts and is incapable of making verbal discriminations that could help in extinction of unrealistic fears. The chronically high drive state may also produce physiological effects and psychosomatic symptoms, which further increase the drive state. In all these processes, social factors play a crucial role in determining the conditions for fear and conflict arousal, the relative utility of symptoms, and the availability of socially accepted fear-reducing behaviors.

Dollard and Miller view therapy as a special situation in which all conditions are designed to help the patient to learn better solutions for his conflicts. Some of the main features of this favorable situation are:

Free Association. This procedure is the reverse of the condition under which the patient has learned repression of unpleasant thoughts. It motivates the patient to talk. Gradual anxiety reduction by extinction during

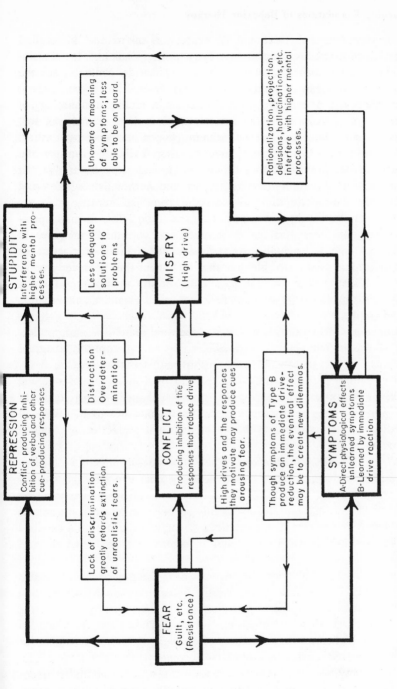

Figure 2-1 Schematic diagram of some basic factors involved in neuroses. Arrows indicate "produces" or "tend to contribute to." Heavy arrows indicate major causal sequences; lighter arrows, subsidiary ones (from Dollard and Miller, 1950, pp. 223).

free association eventually removes the repression and allows articulation of feelings and verbal responses associated with the problem. This reversal of the childhood conditions for learning to evade the conflict frees the patient to cope with it in an intelligent way.

Permissiveness. The therapist's calm nonjudgmental acceptance of the patient's communication serves as a model for reducing the patient's own anxieties. In due time fear of free communication is also extinguished. Rewarding talk by attention and understanding further encourages the therapeutic interchange. Freedom of thought is not achieved at once. It is important that the patient recite the forbidden thoughts while being afraid. As the patient timidly and reluctantly produces sentences, in the face of his fear, the permissive therapist makes certain that no punishment occurs. Thus the fear attached to the formerly forbidden sentences is not reinforced and is gradually extinguished. The extinction effects generalize from talking aloud to thinking and the patient thus achieves greater freedom of thought. But only if it actually occurs during therapy can the fear be extinguished. If the patient is not at all afraid, no therapeutic result can occur.

Transference. Responses that originally were attached to significant persons in the patient's life are transferred to the therapist because of the similarity of the therapeutic relationship to the patient's earlier relationship to authoritarian figures—his parents and teachers. Weakening of inhibition through permissiveness further enhances transference of strong emotions. This transference offers an opportunity to identify and label earlier reaction patterns so that they can be integrated in the patient's mental activities.

Labeling and Discrimination. When new cue-producing verbal responses are provided for vague experiences, the cues can be related easily to instrumental behaviors appropriate for the class of events carrying the given label. Discrimination between events of long ago and current stimuli reduces fears. New verbal discriminations strengthen the patient's capacity for differentiating between real and neurotic sources of fear and satisfaction.

Control of patient behaviors by regulation of the approach and avoidance components of conflicts and of the balance between anxiety and relief experienced during therapy sessions enables the therapist to set the maximum speed at which treatment can progress. The balance must always be somewhat higher for continuation of therapy than for avoidance of the anxiety created during sessions. To accomplish this balance, careful dosing of anxiety-producing interventions is carried out and the patient's motivation to continue must be kept high on the basis of realistic hopes and expectations.

This brief summary of Dollard and Miller's views should suffice to illustrate their major accomplishments in reinterpreting dynamic therapy operations in learning terms. However, it is equally noteworthy that this reformulation had little impact on therapeutic practices. The new vocabulary promoted some research on learning in neurotics and psychotics. It did not yield experimental evidence from human studies that could provide the foundation for an extension of S-R learning theory to human behavior. Dollard and Miller's view also led to a more molecular approach in personality research and in the analysis of therapy interactions than espoused by psychoanalysis. But no radically new methods of treatment can be traced directly to the theoretical reformulations by Dollard and Miller. More radically behavioristically and environmentally oriented clinicians have made little use in the newer forms of behavior modification of the reformulations offered by Dollard and Miller, Mowrer, and their colleagues.

The work of Dollard and Miller has not escaped criticism from the psychoanalytic side. Even those who are willing to accept animal data as relevant to the study of personality view their reformulation as an oversimplification, and perhaps even as dangerous because it substitutes pretension of scientific respectability for clinical sophistication. Rapaport (1953) expressed his belief that the subject matter is just too complex for examination by usual experimental methods:

"Under such handicaps, not even scientists equipped with the methodology of operationalism and with experimental know-how, as Dollard and Miller certainly are, can develop a neat and simple theory for us. Indeed, the more they try to make it neat and pat, the more cavalier they become in their disregard of clinical fact" (p. 207).

Other Contributors

Shoben (1949) offered a detailed analysis of psychotherapy as a problem in learning theory. Beginning with a review of psychotherapy practiced at that time, Shoben called attention to four features common to all treatments: (1) all schools of therapy claim some cures; (2) most patients present symptomatic behaviors that are maintained on the basis of anxiety-reduction, and anxiety is their main and common motive; (3) the common goal of psychotherapists is the diminution of anxiety; and (4) most clinicians employ the two-person interactional relationship and conversational exchanges as their main tool. Shoben's argument is summarized:

"The common problem characterizing clinical patients is anxiety and the behavioral defenses built up against it. The goal of psychotherapy, regardless of the therapist's theoretical leanings, is to eliminate the anxiety and thereby to do away with the symptomatic persistent non-integrative behavior. To accomplish this goal, all therapists use the devices of conversing with the patient about his anxiety and the situations calling it forth both currently and historically and forming a unique therapeutic relationship. Since all psychotherapies seem to have successes to their credit and since psychotherapy seems to be a process whereby a patient learns to modify his emotional reactions and his overt behavior, it is hypothesized that therapy may be conceptualized from the point of view of general psychology as a problem in learning theory. Such a conceptualization must account for the changes that occur in counselees in terms of these factors that are apparently common to all forms of counseling" (pp. 375–376).

Shoben proposed that three steps in the therapy process can be discerned (each representing a particular learning problem), amenable to analysis in a learning framework. The first step is lifting repression and developing insight through symbolic reinstatement of the stimuli for anxiety. The situation that had originally resulted in punishment and the cues associated with it that have become danger signals are now revealed in conversation with the therapist. The clinician's permissive (anxiety-reducing) and nonpunishing attitudes not only facilitate reinstatement of the anxiety-arousing cues but also set the stage for the second step in therapy, anxiety-reduction by counter-conditioning. In this step the pairing of the anxiety-provoking stimuli with the positive cues of the counseling relationship results in gradual reduction of the anxiety. Shoben's stress on attacking generalized anxiety underlying many different situations and related in complex ways, instead of counter-conditioning a single symptomatic response, distinguishes his approach from counter-conditioning techniques to be discussed in later chapters. Shoben believed that single symptom elimination might result only in learning new anxiety-reducing instrumental responses, and that anxiety might be attached to too many elements to eliminate singly each of numerous symptomatic responses. The third and final step of therapy, in Shoben's view, is reeducating the patient to establish healthy goals and to acquire effective behaviors for achieving them. During this terminal stage, the therapist helps the patient anticipate behavioral consequences and select plans that have long-range adjustive value.

Shoben's formulation, developed in the Hullian tradition and under Mowrer's influence, differed from the previously described view in that it took as its starting point the prevailing therapy practices instead of the theory underlying them. Although Shoben accepts anxiety as a major etiological factor, he goes further than Dollard and Miller in analyzing both the patient's and the therapist's behaviors from a pragmatic point of view.

The key role of repression removal in psychotherapy had been accepted by early learning-oriented therapists without much debate. However, the analysis of this process in S-R terms presented some difficulty. Shaw (1946) pursued Mowrer's observation that the neurotic's inability to use symbolic behavior is the major obstacle to effective adjustment. Shaw then set as his central task the analysis of repression and insight from a learning point of view. He proposed the suppression of punished bar-pressing behavior observed in animals by Estes (1944) as an analogue to repression. In addition, he suggested that cues from the initial stages of an anxiety-arousing impulse also might produce nonperception of the impulse, since this would prevent a further build-up of anxiety. Only when the neurotic can recognize that the immediately satisfying consequences of his behavior are also accompanied by more important disadvantageous results at a later time is he able to modify his behavior. Shaffer (1947) suggested a similar explanation, stressing that self-control can be effectively exercised only when symbolic behavior is available.

EARLY CONDITIONING TREATMENTS

Initial reports of application of conditioning principles to psychiatric problems came from two separate groups, headed by Pavlov in Russia and Watson in the United States. Neither group attempted to relate their work closely to the psychoanalytic model. A *direct* use of learning principles in symptom-removal characterized these approaches.

Pavlov

Pavlov's basic experimentation with the conditional food reflex was supplemented from its very outset by observations and recordings of other reactions of the animals in the laboratory and their home cages. As complexity of experimental conditions increased, observations of individual differences and extraexperimental reactions were related more closely to the conditioning paradigm. Eventually Pavlov formulated a comprehensive model of neurophysiology that served as his foundation for understanding neurotic disturbances. The model states that the formation of the conditional reflex is affected by structural features of the organism as well as environmental conditions. Cortical excitation, inhibition, and other changes in brain processes correspond to the observed behavior changes. The constitutional character of the nervous system determines degree of response and tolerance for stress. In Pavlov's later theorizing he postulated personality types to explain individual differences among animals in reactions to conflicting stimuli. This postulate was based on investigations of experimental neuroses, in which animals were exposed to difficult discriminations, excessively powerful stimuli, or changes in the signal function of a stimulus. The animals showed behavioral disorganization similar to the human neurotic condition, which Pavlov explained as a result of excessive strain on the nervous system from traumatic conflict. Numerous animal experiments on conflict were conducted for the purpose of understanding the etiology of human neuroses and the effectiveness of therapeutic procedures in removing the neurosis.

Pavlov defined neurosis as a chronic deviation of higher nervous activity, expressed "in a weakening of both processes (conditioned positive and negative reflexes) separately or together, in chaotic nervous activity, and in various phases of the hypnotic state. Different combinations of these symptoms give entirely distinct pictures. Whether or not the animal breaks down and in what form depends upon the type of nervous system" (Pavlov, 1941, p. 73). Treatments effective for neurotic animals were rest and retaining, drug medication, and sleep or hypnosis. Pavlov cautioned that his observations of dogs should not be taken to presume that human neuroses and their treatment proceed in identical ways, but he was confident that a similar approach is applicable to the study of human higher nervous activity. He noted that in extending animal work to the human level it is important to consider the differences between infrahuman species and men. The main distinction was in the availability to man of the *second signal system*. All organisms adapt to the environment by unconditioned reflexes or by connections between conditional external stimuli and responses. These transactions constitute the *first signal system*. In humans, verbal responses are available for the formation of new links between signal and response. The language system, the *second signal system,* permits abstraction and generalization of the welter of input information and makes possible the development of a complex self-regulatory system, unequaled in lower animals. Words serve as units in a higher-order conditioning process, extending the basic paradigm of the conditioned reflex to all human behavior. The mediating function of language (the crucial property of the second signal system) admits thought, self-control, and other higher mental processes into Pavlov's conditioning model.

Use of the "classical" conditioning paradigm underlies most of the later Russian work on *semantic conditioning* (Razran, 1961), and on the regulatory function of speech (Luria, 1961), distinguishing it from most American work in this field, which has usually been within an instrumental or operant conditioning framework (see Creelman, 1966, for a review). Under Pavlov's influence many developmental studies on meaning were conducted. The procedure is illustrated by studies in which external signals, for example colored lights, are paired with simple motor responses. The color names then serve as test stimuli for their power to evoke responses in children of different ages, thus examining development of generalization of the conditioned response to verbal cues as a function of age. In adults, semantic generalization to synonyms, antonyms, and other verbal classes has been tested by using salivary responses, blink responses, or motor responses. These and other experiments helped demonstrate the role of compound conditioning in the development of concepts and language. Pavlovian conditioning methods and theory have continued to dominate Russian research in child development and education, neurosis, and language, and have influenced American and British investigators by providing a schema of neurophysiological and behavioral functioning within which normal and abnormal behavior can be studied and explained.

Watson

As the father of behaviorism in America, Watson contributed significantly to the methods and philosophical basis of psychology as well as to its content. His conceptualization of personality incorporated the main tenets of his general psychological theory without additional assumptions or integrative principles. Watson defined personality as a complex reaction system built up by training from birth on, and including habits, instincts, emotions, the capacity for altering habits or forming new ones, and the capacity for retention. This view describes human functioning as a progressively expanding system of learned habits, in which simple S–R connections learned in early infancy serve as basic building blocks for more complex and larger units of behavior acquired throughout the person's life.

Watson's stress on the all-important role of environmental influences is reflected in his suggestion that "the only way thoroughly to change personality is by changing the environment in such a way that new habits have to form" (Watson, 1924). Analysis of human behavior requires study of the stimulus functions of the environment to which specific responses have become attached. Control over behavior by careful manipulation of the environment to which the person is exposed is illustrated in Watson's advice to parents in his book on child-rearing (Watson, 1928). Mothers are cautioned to organize day and night care routines in such a way that appropriate behaviors are evoked by arrangements of the environment that minimize the opportunity for the formation of bad habits. For example, prevention of thumb-sucking involves keeping the baby's hands away from his mouth and tucked under the covers at night. If the habit develops despite these precautions, "sew loose white cotton flannel mitts with no finger or thumb divisions to the sleeves of the nightgown and on all the *day dresses, and leave them on for two weeks or more—day and night"* (Watson, 1928, p. 138, italics in Watson). Similarly, Watson warned parents that exposure to companionship of only the child's own sex may start the dangerous path toward homosexuality, since necessary social and heterosexual behavior cannot occur in the absence of the stimulus conditions necessary for learning these skills and habits.

Fears are removed by gradual reexposure of the child to weak dosages of the fear-arousing stimulus (an unconditioning technique that is the forerunner of currently practiced desensitization therapies), or by counter-conditioning through gradual substitution of an incompatible response under the same stimulus conditions (an element used in current reciprocal inhibition therapy). The first method was illustrated by the example of a child who has slipped in the bathtub and is now afraid of his bath water. Watson advised that the child not be taken to the bathroom for a time. Instead, he is to be given sponge baths in the nursery for a few days. A wash basin with a little water is then used and the amount of water increased until the child can be taken to the bathtub again.

The second procedure is seen in two classical experiments that illustrate the experimental establishment and removal of a conditioned fear response. Watson and Rayner (1920) reported conditioning an 11-month-old child, Albert, to fear a while rat by striking a steel bar behind the child's head simultaneously with the presentation of the rat. The sound, an uncondi-tioned stimulus, evoked an unconditioned fear response consisting of violent movement and crying. After a few paired presentations, the rat alone evoked the fear response, and the response generalized to other furry objects. The elimination of such a conditioned fear response was reported by Jones (1924) in children who were afraid of rabbits. A rabbit was introduced into the room while the child was eating. Each day the animal was moved a little closer until a disturbance in the child was barely noticed. Several repetitions of this procedure eventually eliminated the child's fear reaction. In describing one child, Peter, who was given this treatment, Watson notes that Peter's fears of other furry objects also disappeared after the unconditioning procedure.

Watson believed that all emotional reactions develop out of three innate sets of emotional stimuli and reactions: (1) fear, elicited by loud sound and loss of support; (2) rage, elicited by restraint of body movement; and (3) love, elicited by rocking, stroking of the skin, and similar stimula-tion. The complexity and richness of adult emotional behavior develop from these basic situations by conditioning. The classical conditioning of love-responses can, according to Watson, result in excessive dependency and immaturity if the mother's presence is too frequently associated with hugging, kissing, and other close contact. The mere sight of mother then evokes these cuddling behaviors and disrupts the child's constructive and independent activities.

Another complex behavior system, language and thought, Watson handled by tracing complex behavior right back to simple rudiments. Thinking is subvocal talking with associated bodily and visceral reactions. In turn, language is based first on conditioning of words to objects, then on imitation and conditioning of word combinations, phrase patterns, and sentences. Words become stimuli for other words as language learning progresses. Eventually the child has conditioned word responses for most objects and events. Watson noted, incidentally, that internal processes, due to their unobservable nature, remain largely unverbalized. He considered these responses to be the equivalent of the Freudian unconscious.

The radical mechanistic environmentalism of Watson, his recourse to a biological basis of behavior, and the simplistic nature of a theory encompassing all human behavior on the basic of habits and conditioned reflexes have resulted in sharp criticisms of Watson's theory. Yet, his influence on American psychology has extended beyond the study of conditioning and learning because of his pioneer attempts at direct application of simple conditioning principles to child-rearing and the study of language, personality, and abnormal behavior. Watson's view of human behavior and of the nature of personality and behavior disorders differed from that of the Hullian group (as does Pavlov's) in that the analysis of complex behaviors is developed directly out of psychological and neurophysiological work instead of by fitting psychological concepts to psychodynamic theory. Both Pavlov and Watson shared a relative lack of emphasis on the consequences of a response, although the classical conditioning paradigm provides for reinforcing stimuli in the form of the unconditioned stimulus. Watson further mentioned use of attention and affection following performance of a desired behavior, although he did not detail the underlying mechanism. Watson and Pavlov prepared the ground for current learning approaches to clinical phenomena. A full-scale attack on clinical problems with learning methods became possible only after two decades of further integration and research in the areas of social and learning psychology.

Our brief review of the pioneer attempts to formulate psychotherapy in behavioral terms suggests that learning approaches in clinical psychology did not suddenly emerge in the last two decades. Both the Hullian and Watson-Pavlov explorations served as the classical foundations on which current conditioning methods and modification techniques by interviews were developed. From a historical point of view, many factors may have combined to postpone a broad-scale effort to apply learning principles extensively in clinical psychology. Among the most significant factors was the lack of dissatisfaction with psychodynamic methods until post-World

War II demonstrations of the ineffectiveness of these methods. Only after the psychoanalytic system had reached its peak in popularity and had begun its decline were serious questions admitted about the possibility of other approaches.

The Hullian approach, as we have noted, essentially attempted only to appropriate the analytic techniques for learning theory, offering no springboard for new theoretical formulations nor for new techniques. The Pavlovian approach was kept alive in Russia but its development was closely tied to political philosophy. Too little cooperation among scientists from the United States and Russia existed prior to World War II to permit mutual influence or joint investigations. It was Skinner's revival and reformulation of Watson's behaviorism that set the stage for a fresh attempt to introduce conditioning methods into clinical psychology, facilitated by the many sociocultural changes that made a behavioral point of view more acceptable, and by the increased number of research-trained clinicians who were sufficiently interested to pursue these new directions in clinical practice.

SUMMARY

The behavioral therapy model originated in the learning laboratories, combining the methodology of psychological research with the content of personality theory and clinical psychology. Despite some differences in their explanations of the learning process and in therapeutic techniques, the several behavioral models all share a focus on behavior in its environmental contexts, that is, the belief that a science of behavior must deal with the interchange resulting from action and subsequent reaction between persons and their environment. This emphasis is further contrasted with traditional dynamic therapies in that the approach centers mainly on measurable events as targets for therapy. These events, characterized as "symptoms" because of their undesirable role in the person's life, are first examined to find the variables that maintain them, and then altered by changing the controlling variables. There is no attempt to modify hypothesized personality structures; nor is behavior change sought primarily by helping the patient to gain insights into the historical causes of his problems. The behavioral approach deliberately separates psychological data and interpretations based on these data. It stresses not the genesis of a problem but the conditions which are currently maintaining it—be they in the patient's environment (social or biological) or in the relationship between these factors.

A behavioral equation was suggested as the basic unit of analysis, both for assessment of behavioral problems, and development of a program for their treatment. The five essential components proposed in this equation concern the nature of the stimulational environment, both external and internal (S); the biological state of the person (O); the availability and characteristics of the response under examination (R); the relationship between the response and the timing, magnitude, or frequency of the consequences that it produces (K); and the change in the environment or the consequence produced by the response (C). The simplicity of the behavioral equation, however, does not reflect the many considerations and specifications that go into establishing each of the elements of the entire equation and their interaction with each other.

In clinical application, the behavioral equation highlights several assumptions that differ from traditional clinical methods. The behavioral model stresses the effects of the response on the person and his environment, rather than the antecedents or causes of the behavior. It is assumed that problematic behavior is learned and that it can be changed either by unlearning (brought about through procedures adapted from laboratory learning paradigms) or by modification of the environment so that stimulus control of the symptomatic behavior is changed. The patient's subjective experiences, including reports of his discomforts, his thoughts, feelings, and other covert activities are treated as behaviors that have the dual function of affecting the listener to whom the report is made and serving as a response to whatever internal stimulation has occurred. This approach also assumes a continuity of behavioral principles across species and rests heavily on methodology and findings from animal research.

The chapter briefly reviewed several pioneering attempts at formulation of abnormal behavior and its treatment in terms of learning principles. The most important early developments arose out of attempts to reformulate psychoanalytic principles in the language of the learning laboratory. Efforts were made to wed the two approaches by arguing the similarity of the basic principles of modification and of therapy, and by experiments on animals and humans to bolster the theoretical merger with empirical evidence. The integration of psychoanalysis and learning analysis was never fully accomplished. Instead, the early conditioning work of Watson and Pavlov on the one hand, and Hull's approach to anxiety as a drive on the other hand, served as the twin anchor point for current models of behavior modification.

Part II

The Basic Learning Paradigms for Behavior Therapy

CHAPTER 3

Behavior Modification by Control of Stimulus-Response Arrangements

In this chapter we shall consider behavior modification techniques that are derived mostly from the classical conditioning paradigm. This model offers control of an undesired response through control of the stimuli that elicit it. Novel stimuli, usually noxious, are paired with those stimuli that elicit or set the condition for the symptomatic response. Techniques included in this chapter concentrate on reorganization of the environmental and internal stimuli to which the person responds. They characteristically place primary emphasis on arrangement of the S (prior stimulation), O (biological state of organism), and R (response repertoire) elements of the behavioral equation, with much less attention to response consequences (C).

Pavlov's primacy in the development of learning theory, and the early date at which attempts were made to apply explicitly his empirically well-integrated and well-instrumented model, make this a most suitable place to begin. Consideration of therapeutic techniques styled as Pavlovian in character will serve to plunge us into some of the complexities involved when theoretical models, or even controlled laboratory procedures, are used to provide, describe, or explain procedures for modifying naturally occurring symptom behaviors. It can raise questions not only about the extent and manner in which therapies have actually been deduced from learning principles, but also about the interaction of incomplete principles and impure techniques to produce the uncertainty still remaining as to which techniques are more effective, and why.

One of the earliest direct extrapolations of a learning model to modify problematic behaviors was that by Kantorovich (1929). Using the Pavlovian model, Kantorovich attempted to condition sight and thoughts of alcohol—the presumed eliciting stimuli for the response of drinking in his alcoholic patient—to the novel aversive stimulus of electric shock,

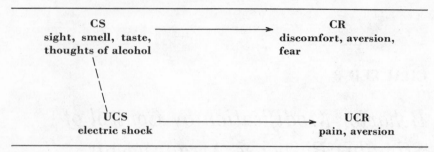

Figure 3-1   Classical conditioning paradigm as applied to treatment of alcoholism.

as shown in Figure 3-1. The cues associated with alcohol (CS), once giving rise to drinking and pleasant effects, now are paired with the shock (UCS), a stimulus that is innately tied to a pain reaction. Eventually, the CS takes on a similar stimulus function as the shock. The person now responds with aversion and fear (CR) to the sight or taste of alcohol.

CLASSICAL AND INSTRUMENTAL CONDITIONING—SEPARATE PROCESSES OR TWO FACETS OF THE SAME PROCESS?

The classical conditioning paradigm in its pure case is defined by operations in which an experimenter pairs a conditioned stimulus (CS) with an unconditioned stimulus (UCS) until a conditioned response (CR) follows administration of the CS alone. However, the UCS usually has reinforcing characteristics not only for the conditioned response (CR) and unconditioned response (UCR), but also for other behaviors that occur immediately prior to the CS and during the CS–UCS interval. Consequently, classical conditioning operations often permit operant or instrumental conditioning to intrude. For example, the CS in Figure 3-1 usually consists of a group of S–R chains that includes raising the glass of alcohol to the lips, taking a sip, and tasting it. These instrumental acts are followed by contingent electric shock, that is, by punishment for these operant chains.

The purity of the instrumental or operant conditioning paradigm is similarly a fiction. A repeated response-reinforcement sequence usually takes place in the presence of fairly stable situational cues that may function as a CS, thus permitting classical conditioning to occur on the basis of pairing between the CS and the subsequent reinforcing stimulus or UCS. Consequently, if the straight punishment model was invoked in treating alcoholism, with every consummatory response followed by an immediate inescapable noxious stimulus (for example, shock), the discriminative stimuli (S^D's, such as smell and sight of alcohol) for the positive consequences that usually follow the instrumental act would become discriminative stimuli for shock instead. They then may lose their own secondary positive reinforcement value and come to elicit the CR (aversion, fear) through classical conditioning.

The difficulty in distinguishing between precise laboratory operations that follow the classical and the instrumental conditioning paradigms has been the subject of extensive research and discussion. A practical distinction would appear to be the difference in the locus of control over the subject's fate when he responds. In pure classical conditioning the CS–UCS sequence is *noncontingent*. Regardless of the nature or the intensity of the subject's response to the CS, the experimenter administers the UCS in acquisition and withholds the UCS in extinction. In instrumental or operant conditioning, stimulus properties usually are not emphasized or are unknown. Instead, the focus is on maintaining a strict contingency between a specified form, magnitude, or latency of response and an experimenter-delivered reinforcing stimulus subsequent to the critical response. In our alcoholism example, if only sight or smell of alcohol is used as the CS, and if preceding approach responses are ignored, then shock (UCS) is controlled by the experimenter and is delivered in a noncontingent fashion. If the subject's response of raising the glass and sipping from it is the critical response for shock delivery, and if spitting out the alcohol is immediately followed by termination of the shock, then the reinforcing stimulus is contingent and controlled by the subject's own behavior. He can avoid the UCS by not engaging in the target response. Figure 3-2 schematically depicts a hypothetical S-O-R-C chain involved in naturalistic alcohol consumption, and classical and operant (punishment, escape, and avoidance) conditioning paradigms for its modification. The mixture of respondents and operants, the concurrent social setting for drinking, the multiplicity of cues associated with the entire sequence make it quite obvious that a simple laboratory analogue, be it of classical conditioning to the sight of alcohol or an operant punishment for sipping, only deals with a small sample of the behaviors involved. Each model tends to ignore key elements, as shown in Figure 3-2. Particularly, the stimulus substitution formulation of classical conditioning tends to ignore the usual prior responses to the CS and the differences between CR and UCR and omits the avoidance response to the CS, which is presumably the final therapeutic target. The operant model tends to ignore the O and S variables that precede the punished response and may contribute to the nature of the usual positive consequences (C+). In fact, effective treatment may depend on both conditioning processes, thereby changing the discriminative (or eliciting) and secondary reinforcing values of the

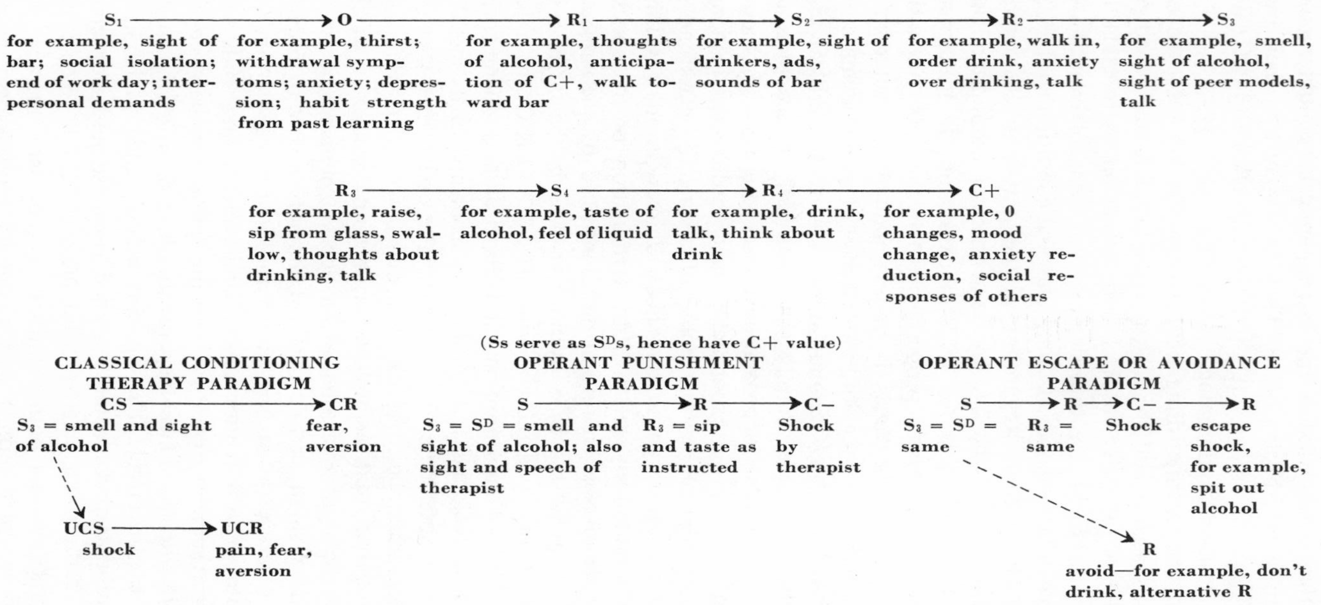

$S_1 \longrightarrow O \longrightarrow R_1 \longrightarrow S_2 \longrightarrow R_2 \longrightarrow S_3$

S_1 for example, sight of bar; social isolation; end of work day; interpersonal demands

O for example, thirst; withdrawal symptoms; anxiety; depression; habit strength from past learning

R_1 for example, thoughts of alcohol, anticipation of C+, walk toward bar

S_2 for example, sight of drinkers, ads, sounds of bar

R_2 for example, walk in, order drink, anxiety over drinking, talk

S_3 for example, smell, sight of alcohol, sight of peer models, talk

$R_3 \longrightarrow S_4 \longrightarrow R_4 \longrightarrow C+$

R_3 for example, raise, sip from glass, swallow, thoughts about drinking, talk

S_4 for example, taste of alcohol, feel of liquid

R_4 for example, drink, talk, think about drink

$C+$ for example, 0 changes, mood change, anxiety reduction, social responses of others

(Ss serve as S^Ds, hence have C+ value)

CLASSICAL CONDITIONING THERAPY PARADIGM

CS $\longrightarrow$ CR

S_3 = smell and sight of alcohol

CR fear, aversion

UCS $\longrightarrow$ UCR

UCS shock

UCR pain, fear, aversion

OPERANT PUNISHMENT PARADIGM

S $\longrightarrow$ R $\longrightarrow$ C−

S_3 = S^D = smell and sight of alcohol; also sight and speech of therapist

R = sip and taste as R_3 instructed

C− Shock by therapist

OPERANT ESCAPE OR AVOIDANCE PARADIGM

S $\longrightarrow$ R $\longrightarrow$ C− $\longrightarrow$ R

S_3 = S^D = same

R_3 = same

C− Shock same

R escape shock, for example, spit out alcohol

R avoid—for example, don't drink, alternative R

Figure 3-2 Schematic representation of alcohol consumption and of classical and operant conditioning paradigms applied to its sequence of events in modification.

CS (by classical conditioning) and suppressing the target response (R) while reinforcing an alternative response (by operant conditioning).

Comparisons of Underlying Mechanisms and Response Systems

Some authors have differentiated between these two types of learning not only on the basis of experimental operations but on the assumption that different fundamental psychological and biological mechanisms are involved. The most significant differentiation has been made on the basis of the response systems of the organism for which each type of learning can be employed. Classical conditioning has been considered the *only* type of learning that can modify autonomic or involuntary responses. These responses have generally been characterized as emitted, reflexive, or emotional and as having special adaptive consequences for the organism. Instrumental conditioning has been viewed not only as the preferred but as the only appropriate method for modification of voluntary and skeletal-muscular behaviors. These responses enable the organism to affect its environment and constitute the basis for interaction with the world.

An entire body of literature has been devoted to the comparison of classical and instrumental conditioning procedures in different response systems (see Kimble, 1961 and Beecroft, 1966, for description and discussion of these studies); yet clear distinctions have not been established even for simple behaviors. Careful studies on the conditioning of the eye blink with a light stimulus or air puff as a UCS have demonstrated that even this simple response is subject both to voluntary and involuntary control. The CR in eyelid conditioning has been shown to differ somewhat in form from the UCR, permitting speculation that attempts to modify the eye blink response classically and instrumentally actually result in conditioning of different responses by differing processes. Conflicting and confounding reports also come from attempts to condition heart rate, GSR, and EEG response by instrumental procedures. These and other reflexes, such as salivation, knee-jerk reflex, nausea, vasomotor reactions, gastrointestinal secretions, and similar essentially biological reactions of the organism would be expected to be conditionable by classical procedures only. The achievement of operant control over autonomic responses has also been reported (see, for example, Grings and Carlin, 1966; Helmer and Furedy, 1968; Kimmel and Hill, 1960). A recent report by Shapiro, Tursky, Gershon, and Stern (1969) provides evidence of the possibility of operant control over systolic blood pressure. Male adults were given auditory feedback via an automatic device that measured blood pressure at each successive heart beat. Depending on their group assignment, subjects were instructed either to lower or increase their blood pressure. Success on each trial was indicated by a brief light flash and tone. The reinforcer was a slide of a nude female projected on a screen for every 20 flashes of light. Subjects were told to try to make the light and sound come on as often as possible. The results indicated that subjects markedly lowered their blood pressure by an average of nearly 5 mm of mercury pressure in 25 trials. The men who were instructed to increase their pressure tended to maintain the same pressure. The results have important implications for the possible treatment of patients with essential hypertension by use of external feedback and operant reinforcement.

In a review of earlier studies, Katkin and Murray (1968) critically examine the experimental designs and suggest a modification of the conclusions about instrumental conditioning of autonomic responses. They believe that it has not been clearly demonstrated that autonomic responses can be *directly* conditioned instrumentally without the mediation of cognitive or somatic processes (factors that can never be fully ruled out in awake humans). Therefore, the data are best interpreted to show that autonomic responses can be brought under control by learning. The theoretical question—whether this represents pure instrumental conditioning or a more complex learning process—is best held in abeyance until more definite evidence is available.

The problem of distinguishing the means by which autonomic responses can be modified is of special interest to us because it reflects the complex interactions of several possible mechanisms in many learning tasks encountered in clinical problems. The close articulation of autonomic and muscular behaviors, voluntary and involuntary responses, and biologically determined and socially trained reactions represents one of the realities of human behavior. The resistance of the phenomenon to dissection into simple units of learning, even in highly controlled laboratory situations, prepares us to expect even greater difficulty in an attempt to analyze clinical cases on the basis of pure paradigms. The interrelationship between the two types of learning can be demonstrated quickly by experiments from the conditioning laboratory. In eyelid conditioning, subjects instructed to blink to the CS easily give more responses than uninstructed subjects. However, when subjects are instructed *not* to respond to the CS, the results are more variable. While some investigators have reported marked decrease in CR performance, others have found that their subjects could not inhibit the eye blink in response to an air puff (CS). Similar interactional effects were found by Lindley and Moyer (1961) in a study of a classically conditioned finger withdrawal CR, when they instructed their subjects that shock would no longer be given. These investigators and Wickens (1939), in an earlier study, found that the CR did not come under immediate control of the verbal instructions and continued to occur during the early extinction trials.

On the other side of the picture we find divergent reports about the conditionability of autonomic responses. One study will suffice to illustrate the overlap between instrumental and classical conditioning procedures in human situations. Shapiro, Crider, and Tursky (1964) asked subjects to "think emotional thoughts." Experimental and control subjects heard a tone when the experimenter allegedly was able to detect "emotional responses" by means of a physiological monitor. Each subject was paid a nickel for each tone occurrence. The experimental subjects were given the tone immediately following a GSR, but for the control subjects a tone never followed a GSR in less than ten seconds. The GSR frequency declined in the control group while the experimental group maintained its rate of GSRs. Contingent reinforcement clearly affected the autonomic responses.

Interpretation of the many experiments investigating separateness of classical and instrumental conditioning processes is difficult, due to the unavailability of adequate controls. When an experimenter is interested only in studying one process and measures only a particular response, other mediators established by the alternate process are often overlooked. For example, in an attempt to establish leg flexion in an animal by use of shock as a UCS, the animal may position his leg in a flexed manner or he may flex during the shock, if such behavior reduces the aversiveness of the shock. The possibility of such a mediating instrumental response negates the interpretation of flexion as pure classical conditioning, since a mediating response may produce the same learning by the avoidance or escape paradigm. Experimenters have made numerous efforts to control such unnoticed operants. One approach lies in administration of curare, a drug that temporarily immobilizes the skeletal system. Birk, Crider, Shapiro, and Tursky (1966) were able to produce GSR changes in an instrumental avoidance situation with a partially curarized human subject. Even this method is subject to criticism. Rescorla and Solomon (1967) point out that:

". . . there is the disturbing possibility that even the use of curare agents may not permit us to rule out operant mediators. Curare only precludes peripheral skeletal mediators and allows central responses to occur. Thus, even while paralyzed, a human can think of emotional events which will reflexly produce peripheral respondent events. It is not at all clear whether such 'thoughts,' or brain events which are clearly subject to response-contingent reinforcement, should be considered to be 'skeletal' or not" (p. 158).

A better strategy for differentiating the two types of conditioning lies in concurrent measurement of the development and maintenance of both classical and instrumental learning in the same subject. For example, a dog can be trained to lift its paw when a tone sounds, in order to obtain food. Muscular movement and salivation can then be concurrently measured. Several investigators have found that the operant component of the response develops prior to the conditioned salivation. These results are somewhat contradictory to the hypothesis proposed by some clinicians that the classical UCR in a combined classical-operant sequence serves as a reinforcing stimulus for the instrumental response. This temporal sequence is especially important for the general interpretation of anxiety (see Chapter 4) in which the autonomic fear responses are seen as cues for subsequent instrumental responses and the latter are strengthened by reduction of the autonomic state. These results, however, are further complicated by the findings of Shapiro (1961). When dogs were trained to press a panel to obtain food on a low rate of reinforcement, salivation regularly *preceded* the operant, although intensified salivation was also observed *after* the occurrence of the operant.

Changes in heart rate have been widely used as an index of classical conditioning during instrumental avoidance training. The evidence in this area is also conflicting. Black (1959) and other investigators have found general increases in heart rate early in instrumental avoidance training of dogs. Typically, classical heart rate conditioning occurred prior to acquisition of the avoidance response. Schoenfeld, Bersh, and Notterman (1954) observed human subjects who were exposed to tone-shock sequences. They found that the heart rate depression observed during acquisition of the avoidance response diminished after successful avoidance. These results conform with the hypothesis that the acquisition of the instrumental avoidance response weakens the classical response established during early training stages. Similar contradictory results have been found in extinction, with loss of the cardiac CR and avoidance response showing no consistent relationships across experiments. Although none of the numerous experiments conducted in this area have shown clear-cut support for a uniform theoretical description of the learning process, all have pointed to the very subtle interactions between various bodily systems and among large numbers of separate responses that may participate in the acquisition and extinction of a new behavioral act.

PROCEDURES LEADING TO MIXED MODELS

The purity of the classical conditioning model can be easily destroyed when minor modifications in the operations are introduced. In fact, one modification that appeared to be relatively insignificant when it was first introduced became the base for the entire body of research on avoidance conditioning and helped to establish the differentiation between instrumental and classical conditioning. In an early study, Brogden, Lipman, and Culler (1938) introduced the opportunity for guinea pigs to avoid a noxious UCS by running prior to shock delivery while housed in a running wheel. According to the custom of previous studies, these animals had first been exposed to the CS–UCS pairing for many trials and only feeble learning had occurred. Eventually, the animals made the critical running response and avoided the UCS. The omission of shock on subsequent trials would have been expected to result in classical extinction. However, the guinea pigs showed excellent retention. This type of avoidance conditioning has been classified under instrumental or operant learning. Yet it is obvious that the initial experience of the CS and the UCS (shock) necessary to establish the avoidance response occurred in conformity with the rules for classical conditioning. Avoidance learning has been of special interest to clinical psychologists because of the early supposition that this type of conditioning underlies the formation of many neurotic symptoms, including phobias, hysterias, and other avoidance behaviors considered abnormal in our society. The theoretical dilemma lies in description of the precise motivational factors that maintain such avoidance behavior when the organism fails to experience the UCS for hundreds or even thousands of trials.

Another slight alteration of the avoidance paradigm permits the organism to *escape* the UCS shortly after its onset. Although this modification poses a less serious problem in interpreting the maintaining conditions, it is another instance in which classical and operant procedures are practically indistinguishable in the overall execution of the experimental design. Escape always implies the delivery of the UCS, thus taking the operations right back to the classical model.

A third modification of the classical conditioning procedure also leads to overlap between methods. If the UCS is omitted on some trials in classical conditioning, development of the characteristic features of the CR depends on the particular schedule for administration of the UCS. This procedure becomes nearly indistinguishable from operant avoidance conditioning under the control of partial reinforcement. As in the previous examples, maintenance of a response under intermittent administration of the UCS usually requires initial training under the traditional classical procedure with one hundred percent administration of the UCS. Thus training paradigms shift from a clear classical conditioning procedure to one resembling the operant method.

In the present chapter we discuss some examples of clinical methods grouped under *aversion therapy* that utilize noxious stimuli either for changing the affective value of a well-established CS (stimulus substitution) or for activation of a new instrumental escape or avoidance response. Although the latter methods are not examples of the pure classical paradigm, behavior therapists tend to emphasize the CS–UCS sequence, often classifying these methods loosely as classical conditioning techniques. A more valid reason for combining these methods lies in the clinician's use of aversive stimuli for behavior control, even though the subject has control over reception of the UCS in some procedures but not in others.

Another problem in differentiating learning models that use aversive stimuli is frequently encountered in clinical application of response suppression by punishment. The effects of administering a punishing aversive stimulus can be altered when the person has available an escape response that terminates the aversive stimulus. In child-rearing practices such behaviors as running away or promising not to repeat the punished act provide children with well-established escape responses. The underlying mechanism was clearly demonstrated in an animal study by Leitenberg (1967). His results indicated that punishment was most effective when escape was prevented. Presence of an escape response reduced the suppressive effect of punishment, and response frequency was more resistant to recovery following removal of punishment in the no-escape condition than in the escape condition.

In punishment situations several operant procedures with noxious stimuli are combined. Since punishment is usually administered as a response-contingent consequence, many procedures that employ punishment are discussed in Chapter 7, even though they often rely on control by aversive stimuli as well. As already noted, whether a therapeutic method is termed "punishment" or "aversive conditioning" often depends more on the theoretical affinity of the author than on any analysis of the operations used. Treatments of sexual and addictive or compulsive disorders by aversive stimuli usually are discussed together as "aversive conditioning" since the experimenter-therapists most active in this area came from the Pavlovian tradition. Methods of control of self-destructive or asocial acts by aversive stimuli have been termed "punishment" by their operant-oriented originators. Note, too, that the term "aversive conditioning" tends to be applied when the responses—whether autonomic or skeletal—are less easily observed. We follow this general practice in assigning material to this chapter and Chapter 7, but need to stress repeatedly the impurity of operations and paradigms and the uncertainty regarding effective variables.

In sum, uses of aversive stimulation in therapy can be separated, at least conceptually, into three classes: (1) *punishment*—the aversive stimulus is intended to suppress an undesirable behavior; (2) *escape and avoidance learning:* the aversive stimulus serves to establish new responses that terminate or prevent the noxious stimulation; and (3) *classical conditioning* (or related discrimination learning procedures)—the aversive stimulus serves to build up a new stimulus function for an object or event by its coinciding with a stimulus that has established aversive properties. The last procedure is the major focus in this chapter, although the lack of "pure" cases results in considerable difficulties when attempting to isolate this process in a complex clinical procedure. The punishment and escape-avoidance models are discussed in Chapter 7, since operants usually play a large role in their clinical application.

This brief review of the experimental literature makes it clear that currently available laboratory studies do not permit the classification of learning situations into separate processes following the Pavlovian or Thorndikian models for learning. A brief glance at these problems, however, should also demonstrate that any learning procedure in a living organism, even under highly controlled laboratory conditions, involves numerous response systems. Emphasis may be placed on one or another of these systems, but their interaction seems inevitable. Any behavioral act, especially at the level of complex human functioning, involves parameters of each of the interrelated factors discussed in our behavioral equation. Changes in the organism affect other response systems, which in turn modify both receptivity to stimulation and the effects on the person's environment. In our analysis of learning paradigms in clinical psychology we must constantly be aware of these interrelationships and must recognize that separation of specific techniques by learning models is a matter of convenience for didactic purposes. In each case, the paradigms may describe the most critical aspect of the procedure without denying the presence of many other influences that would modify the predicted effects.

SUBSTITUTION METHODS

Let us now consider some of the learning components in behavior modification treatments. The practitioner is usually faced with a patient who cannot present a circumscribed and particular response as a target of therapeutic attack. Frequently, identification of the response pattern to be changed, of the available controlling stimuli, and of the patient's resources requires extensive assessment procedures. Furthermore in the clinical setting, establishment of a positive therapist-patient relationship is often necessary to insure cooperation and enhance treatment effectiveness. Wilson, Hannon, and Evans (1968) have noted both a tendency to ignore this relationship in descriptions of behavior therapies, and the potentials of the latter for clearer definition and testing of relationship variables. Marks and Gelder (1966) have listed some of the components of psychological treatments that are found in both psychodynamic and behavior therapy methods (see Table 3-1). As this list suggests, any clinical treatment usually encompasses a large number of therapeutic efforts. In discussing therapy techniques we are focusing only on a small portion of the total clinical enterprise. Treatment is always carried out in combination with assessment, reassessment, and comprehensive analysis of the patient's total living pattern.

The above considerations should make it clear that the customary division of behavior modification techniques into Pavlovian or classical meth-

Table 3-1   Components in Psychological Treatments—A Comparison of Behavior Therapy and Psychodynamic Methods (adapted from Marks and Gelder, 1966, p. 19)

A. **Components present in most treatments including some psychodynamic methods**
  1. Nonspecific: a. Placebo
                   b. Patient expectations
                   c. Suggestion
  2. More specific: a. Encouragement, advice, reassurance
                    b. Environmental manipulation
                    c. Pointing out current sources of stress
                    d. Pointing out repetitive patterns of behavior
B. **Components present in most psychodynamic methods but usually not important in behavior therapy**
  1. Pointing out unrecognized feelings
  2. Understanding relationship with therapist
  3. Encouraging expression of feeling about therapist
  4. Relating present behavior to past patterns
  5. Interpreting fantasy and dream material
  6. Pointing out symbolic meanings
  7. Attempting modification of present personality
C. **Components present in behavior therapies but usually not in psychodynamic methods**
  1. Emphasis on direct symptom modification
  2. Use of a hierarchy in practical retraining
  3. Use of a hierarchy in fantasy retraining
  4. Aversion techniques
  5. Positive conditioning
  6. Negative practice
  7. Other special techniques
D. **Components present in several treatments but not necessarily psychodynamic**
  1. Relaxation and hypnosis
  2. Anxiety reducing drugs
  3. Abreaction

ods and instrumental or operant methods reflects a convenient division of specific procedures. In actual operation the methods often bear only a distant resemblance to the pure learning model from which they have been derived. Furthermore, the methods are complemented by other clinical procedures that aim at the collection of data prior to treatment, not at behavior modification.

The most direct demonstration of the classical conditioning paradigm in clinical problems lies in two experimental analogues to the development of behaviors usually classified as symptoms of psychopathology. As early as 1920, Watson and Rayner demonstrated the production of a phobia by classical conditioning. As described in Chapter 2, the authors presented a white rat to an eleven-month-old boy, Albert, who showed no aversive reaction. After presentation of the animal was paired with a disturbing loud sound, Albert began showing signs of fear whenever the rat was presented. This fear was also observed in response to other similar stimuli, such as furry animals. Albert's behavior can be characterized as a phobic reaction to furry objects. The learning process involved pairing of an originally neutral CS, the white rat, with a fear-arousing UCS, the loud noise. As acquisition proceeded, the fear response occurred in the presence of the CS even when the UCS was no longer given. Although this demonstration and one reported below support the general model of the acquisition of a symptom by learning, it should not be assumed that they rule out the possibility that similar symptoms can be formed in other ways. Eysenck and Rachman (1965) summarize the essential features of the theory underlying the classical conditioning hypothesis of phobia development by the following nine points. Each point is based on experimental evidence and clinical experiences cited by the authors.

"**1.** Phobias are learned responses.

2. Stimuli develop phobic qualities when they are associated temporally and spatially with a fear-producing state of affairs.

3. Neutral stimuli which are of relevance in the fear-producing situation and/or make an impact on the person in the situation, are more likely to develop phobic qualities than weak or irrelevant stimuli.

4. Repetition of the association between the fear situation and the new phobic stimuli will strengthen the phobia.

5. Associations between high intensity fear situations and neutral stimuli are more likely to produce phobic reactions.

6. Generalization from the original phobic stimulus to stimuli of a similar nature will occur.

7. Noxious experiences which occur under conditions of excessive confinement are more likely to produce phobic reactions.

8. Neutral stimuli which are associated with a noxious experience(s) may develop (secondary) motivating properties. This acquired drive is termed the fear-drive.

9. Responses (such as avoidance) which reduce the fear-drive are reinforced" (pp. 81–82).

A more recent demonstration of the development of a symptom is reported by Rachman (1966a). The author had previously treated sexual fetishists by means of aversion therapy and wanted to demonstrate a possible analogy of the etiology of these disorders. Three young unmarried male volunteers were exposed to the following procedure. A colored slide of a pair of black, knee-length woman's boots (a common fetishistic object) constituted the CS. The slide was presented for fifteen seconds and was followed one second later by a thirty-second exposure of colored slides of attractive naked girls. Occurrence of sexual arousal manifested by penis volume changes was measured by a modified plethysmograph, an instrument developed by Freund (1963) for the study of sexual responses. The CR was defined as a set of five successive plethysmograph reactions to the originally neutral CS. After the series of acquisition trials, each subject was exposed to a test for stimulus generalization. For this purpose, Rachman presented slides of shoes of different color and appearance. After this test, extinction was continued until no sexual responses occurred. The experimental procedure was carried out in daily sessions during which eighteen conditioning trials were given, with five-minute rest periods interposed after each block of six trials. The three subjects required between 24 and 65 trials before reaching the criterion of acquisition. Each subject showed generalization to one or two test stimuli. Spontaneous recovery was noted in all subjects one week after extinction, necessitating further extinction trials at that time. In a replication study (Rachman and Hodgson, 1968) a control procedure was introduced to eliminate the possibility that the earlier results were due to pseudoconditioning. Successful replication with all five subjects confirmed the earlier findings.

These studies essentially support Watson and Rayner's earlier findings that an originally neutral object can become a CS for behaviors that are considered socially undesirable or disadvantageous to the individual. The one point at which the analogue differs from clinical cases is that fetishists fail to show such rapid extinction, possibly because their experience often includes repeated fulfillment of the sexual sequence to orgasm, which may serve to reinforce the deviant behavior.

Counter-Conditioning

The technique of *counter-conditioning* involves the introduction of a CS for a symptom-antagonistic response with the goal of changing the effects of the stimulus complex (or, in vernacular terms, its meaning), so that the total situation no longer evokes the previous nonadaptive response. This technique has been most widely used with anxiety-related responses, and has been described by Wolpe (1958) under the *reciprocal inhibition principle*. The methods in which stimuli are substituted to effect response changes have been most frequently reported for cases in which the newly introduced stimulus is aversive. The aversive stimulus reduces the symptom by means of a competing response of discomfort, pain, or disgust. Wolpe's use of counter-conditioning is a notable exception in its utilization of a positive new stimulus, for example, one inducing relaxation. However, Wolpe's procedure has included other therapeutic elements that complicate the simple classical conditioning model. Wolpe's and related procedures that use the counter-conditioning model are discussed in detail in Chapter 4. Our present attention turns to the use of substitution methods in which strong and undesirable approach responses are the target of treatment.

AVERSION THERAPY OF SEXUAL DEVIATIONS

The removal of an established sexual deviation can be undertaken by several different conditioning methods. Conditioned aversion therapy has been applied in a wide variety of situations. The type of aversion therapy that parallels the classical conditioning model most closely is characterized by the pairing of a noxious UCS with some stimulus object associated with the undesirable behavior. When the stimulus that presumably had aroused the symptomatic response is coupled with close temporal proximity to an unpleasant event, it is assumed that the stimulus function of the CS becomes predominantly one of signaling the onset of an unpleasant, fear-arousing, or anxiety-producing event. Consequently, the CS, for example the sight of a fetishistic object, now evokes fear, nausea, or another response incompatible with the original pleasurable consequence. Its effects may serve to interrupt the objectionable behavior sequence. New and more appropriate responses can then be developed.

The aversion therapy method is illustrated in a study by Raymond (1956). The patient was a man who had spent time in a mental hospital and had repeatedly been apprehended by the police and jailed for willful destruction of perambulators and handbags. The patient was sexually aroused by these objects. In attempting to change this behavior, Raymond chose to attach a noxious UCS to the fetishistic objects. The patient was given injections of apomorphine, a nausea-producing drug, prior to each session. At a point when it could be expected that the subjective experience of nausea was reaching its peak, the patient was shown handbags, perambulators, and pictures of these objects. Through repeated pairings, the originally sexually arousing objects would become a CS for the feeling of nausea (UCS) and would therefore release an antagonistic response to the earlier sexual feelings. Raymond reported that, after intensive treatment, the patient's pathological behavior no longer occurred. In fact, after the second course of treatment the patient showed a strong aversion to the fetishistic objects. It is reported that the patient remained well for three years. When he began to find control more difficult, he received a further course of treatment. Two years later, he was still reported to be doing well. Raymond's discussion focused on the classical conditioning feature of his technique. However, the full clinical treatment included deprivation of food and sleep during the initial treatment phase, and the patient was also seen at a psychiatric clinic for a six month follow-up. But this patient had previously undergone prolonged psychotherapy without benefit. Since the fetishistic behavior had resulted in several arrests, the suppression of the fetishism immediately alleviated one major source of difficulties in his life. He also reported improved sexual relationships with his wife. Although these consequences cannot be directly ascribed to the conditioning treatment, it is clear that the removal of a major problematic behavior in a person's life may tend to cause many other changes, most of which are probably beneficial.

Selection of Appropriate UCS and CS

Raymond's use of the effects of apomorphine can serve to introduce some of the issues in selecting and defining an appropriate UCS. There are special problems inherent in the use of drugs of this purpose, despite their almost exclusive use by investigators as aversive stimuli until recent years (except for Kantorovich's salutory example of the early use of electric shock). Animal and human studies of conditioned avoidance responses mediated by CR's of conditioned fear demonstrate that drugs such as reserpine, chlorpromazine, morphine, emetine, and other depressant drugs block acquisition and the performance of already-acquired conditioned avoidance responses (see, for example, Herz, 1960). Morphine and several other drugs also attentuate the response-suppression effects of punishment. Some stimulant drugs can, on the other hand, facilitate acquisition of avoidance responses and hence are potentially useful as adjuncts to aversive conditioning. Clearly, then, a drug used as UCS may, in fact, act against the effectiveness of the conditioning procedure. Since apomorphine is a derivative of morphine, the same objection applies to its widespread use. The process involved in the action of any UCS must be carefully considered, along with the character of the resultant UCR and CR, in designing an aversion therapy.

A further difficulty with drugs such as apomorphine has to do with the need in classical conditioning to control *precisely* the temporal relationships of CS and UCS. Individuals differ greatly and unpredictably in the speed and intensity of their reaction to the nausea-producing drugs, and intraindividual differences from one occasion to the next also are usual. Even if the CS–UCS interval can be precisely controlled, some recent evidence suggests that the nature of the CR is different when short or long (0.5 or 5 seconds) intervals are used. When conditioning involves autonomic responses as the CR, presumably the case in aversion therapy, the longer interval may be more efficient, which is contrary to the usual rules about 0.5 optimal intervals (Grings, Lockhart, and Dameron, 1962). Until CR parameters are directly measured and CS–UCS time intervals systematically varied in controlled trials of aversion therapy, the relevance of such laboratory findings for improved therapeutic effectiveness is uncertain.

Early practitioners often inadvertently used procedures involving backward conditioning, with UCS preceding CS, because of the difficulties in accurately timing a drug-induced UCS of nausea (Franks, 1963). Uncertainty is a related problem regarding the particular stimuli that should be or are being used as the UCS. Raymond (1964) indicates that the feeling of nausea, and not the act of vomiting, is the relevant event for acquisition of an avoidance CR. Both events have been described as the UCS by other investigators. Determination of the relative effectiveness of various stimulus components and measurement of the appropriate UCS events is, at best, difficult with apomorphine and related drugs. Rachman (1965a) has discussed the advantages and disadvantages of drugs, electric shock, and other aversive stimuli for conditioning therapies and notes added disadvantages of emetic drugs such as their possible harmful side effects and distastefulness to the therapy staff.

Concerning the character of the CS, the "reconditioning" procedure can be applied either to stimulus objects associated with the pathological behavior or to some component of the pathological behavior itself. Cooper (1963) used emetine, another nausea-producing drug, as the UCS in treating a female-clothes fetishist, and the CS was the actual carrying out of his cross-dressing fetishistic behaviors. In this case, the contribution of the conditioning treatment becomes more difficult to evaluate. In addition to conditioning sessions, the patient was given "intensive moral suggestion" and was not allowed to discard his female clothes. He was instructed to observe himself and to reenact in his mind his "disgusting perversion." He was also kept awake at night and was not allowed to eat or sleep for six days. Every two hours a tape recording with moral suggestions was played for twenty minutes. The same patient had complained of impotence in his marriage and this problem was separately treated. Nine months after termination of aversion treatment he continued to feel a revulsion toward his transvestism. Cooper's work highlights the difficulties in teasing out the specific effects of various fragments of treatment that are woven into one integrated procedure. Punishment, moral persuasion, physical deprivation, and organismic changes due to the drugs are all supplementary variables in the basic conditioning procedure.

Most other case histories reporting successful cessation of symptoms in fetishes and transvestism pair the unusual arousal stimulus (CS) with chemical or electrical aversive stimuli (UCS). Variations in technique of interest to us mainly concern the utilization of a wide range of behaviors or stimuli as CS. Tape-recorded descriptions of the patient's sexual perversions, pictures of fetishistic objects, actual execution of deviant responses, masturbation to deviant fantasies, presentation of words representing sexual stimuli, and similar events have been used as CS.

The assumption that classical conditioning represents the underlying learning mechanism is most doubtful when the symptom itself (that is, the cue properties of the deviant response) is used as a CS. Under these conditions, for example, when a male patient is asked to dress in female clothes or to masturbate with instructions to engage in perverted fantasies, the target responses are identical to the behaviors to be eliminated. When they are followed by shock or drug-induced nausea, the consequences are more accurately described as aversive reinforcing stimuli following the symptomatic behavior. This situation is most clearly illustrated by the use of the patient's increase of penis volume as the signal for the therapist to deliver a shock. This procedure fits the operant conditioning model since the focus is on the response rather than its cue, and delivery of the aversive stimulus is contingent on the patient's response. But isolation of eliciting cues from overt or covert responses is nearly impossible for naturally occurring complex behaviors (such as sexual arousal) where (1) long S-R chains are likely; (2) each S would probably have secondary reinforcement value; and (3) each R is likely to have acquired cue properties for the next R. It is difficult to choose an element to be termed the CS or elements to be designated as the critical response. Therefore, it is indeed a dilemma to decide which learning model is actually represented by the therapy operations.

The ultimate difficulty is to determine the extent to which therapy operations can be defined and measured by the standards of the laboratory and the most effective extrapolation of laboratory findings to therapy when these standards of clarity cannot be met. Figure 3-3 depicts a hypothetical chain of S-R events that might be entailed in fetishism. An early point of therapeutic intervention may be the patient's initial sexual fantasies

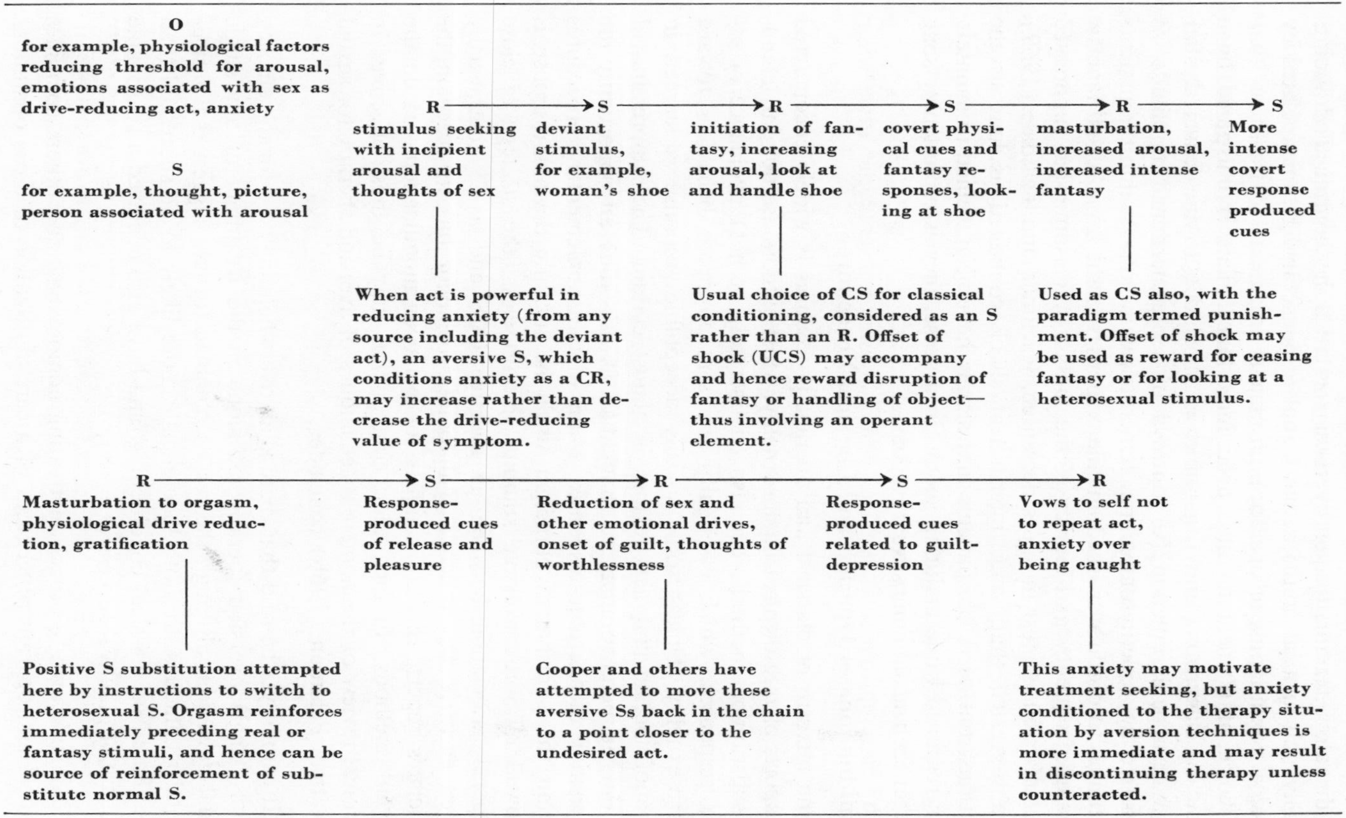

O
for example, physiological factors reducing threshold for arousal, emotions associated with act as drive-reducing cues, anxiety

S
for example, thought, picture, person associated with arousal

R → stimulus seeking with incipient arousal and thoughts of sex

S → deviant stimulus, for example, woman's shoe

R → initiation of fantasy, increasing arousal, look at and handle shoe

S → covert physical cues and fantasy responses, looking at shoe

R → masturbation, increased arousal, increased intense fantasy

S → More intense covert response produced cues

When act is powerful in reducing anxiety (from any source including the deviant act), an aversive S, which conditions anxiety as a CR, may increase rather than decrease the drive-reducing value of symptom.

Usual choice of CS for classical conditioning, considered as an S rather than an R. Offset of shock (UCS) may accompany and hence reward disruption of fantasy or handling of object—thus involving an operant element.

Used as CS also, with the paradigm termed punishment. Offset of shock may be used as reward for ceasing fantasy or for looking at a heterosexual stimulus.

R → Masturbation to orgasm, physiological drive reduction, gratification

S → Response-produced cues of release and pleasure

R → Reduction of sex and other emotional drives, onset of guilt, thoughts of worthlessness

S → Response-produced cues related to guilt-depression

R → Vows to self not to repeat act, anxiety over being caught

Positive S substitution attempted here by instructions to switch to heterosexual S. Orgasm reinforces immediately preceding real or fantasy stimuli, and hence can be source of reinforcement of substitute normal S.

Cooper and others have attempted to move these aversive Ss back in the chain to a point closer to the undesired act.

This anxiety may motivate treatment seeking, but anxiety conditioned to the therapy situation by aversion techniques is more immediate and may result in discontinuing therapy unless counteracted.

Figure 3-3 Hypothetical chain of S-R events in fetish behavior and points of therapeutic attack.

113

or his efforts toward gratification. A second point is the beginning of the deviant behavior, frequently chosen as a CS in classical conditioning. Finally, full arousal or the active sexual response may be manipulated by classical conditioning or operant punishment.

Choice of CS can be of crucial importance. This is illustrated by a study by Bancroft (1966) in which a shock UCS was delivered after a CS of a penis erection (to fantasy) of a predetermined amplitude, as measured by a plethysomograph. Bancroft's data indicate that the patients continued to produce marked erectile responses to the homosexual fantasy, although frequency and latency of the fantasy were somewhat suppressed and self-rated interest in males decreased. Rachman and Teasdale (1969) have suggested that, since intermittent shock continued as long as the erections continued, the patients may simply have been trained to maintain their response while enduring shock. In a sense, they were just practicing further their usual homosexual responses.

Combinations of Operant and Classical Procedures

The mixture of classical and operant procedures is widely encountered in reports of treatment of homosexuality. Most authors use not only stimulus substitution methods, but also (deliberately or not) avoidance or escape responses, which essentially represent approach behaviors toward heterosexuality. Unless some socially acceptable response is learned in place of the deviant act, relapse is almost certain. The suppression of the deviant behavior may be thought of as providing an opportunity for acquisition of alternate responses. Many of the supplementary procedures also fit the punishment paradigm since the sexually deviant response is followed by some aversive stimulus. Nevertheless, the strategy of close temporal association between an aversive UCS and a CS that usually occurs early in the patient's symptomatic behavior has its place in the clinician's repertoire of techniques for behavior modification—as do the operant methods. In fact, their combination may be most effective. In a critical review of the numerous techniques of aversion therapy for sexual deviation, Feldman (1966) concludes:

"It cannot yet be said that there is an overwhelming case for the efficacy of any single aversion therapy technique in the treatment of any single sexual deviation, although the results obtained to date suggest that instrumental techniques are both theoretically more likely to be successful than those based on classical conditioning, and have also achieved a reasonable measure of practical success" (p. 78).

Feldman's own approach in treating homosexuals and others combines classical and operant procedures with careful attention to those operations likely to promote resistance to extinction and generalization (Feldman and MacCulloch, 1965; MacCulloch, Feldman, and Pinschof, 1965; Feldman, 1966). Citing the evidence that instrumental avoidance responses are more resistant to extinction than are effects of classical conditioning, and the evidence of Morgenstern, Pearce, and Rees (1965) that operant conditioning tests (verbal conditioning) predict outcome of aversion therapy whereas trials of classical conditioning (eye blink) do not, Feldman concludes that sexual behavior is primarily operant in character and should be so treated. This conclusion is supported by evidence that deviant sexual responses are gradually learned and then maintained by the reinforcement obtained from masturbation to a memory involving in part the deviant stimulus element (McGuire, Carlisle, and Young, 1965; Evans, 1968). For the reasons already cited, Feldman uses electric shock as the UCS. Because of possible difficulty in developing and attending to fantasy (although many other experimenters report no difficulty with this and indeed use latency of fantasy development as a criterion of therapeutic progress), Feldman uses projected pictures of arousing deviant stimuli. It should be noted that these slides are less likely to reproduce accurately the patient's usual arousal situation than is his own usual fantasy, although the procedure permits better stimulus control by the therapist.

To promote resistance to extinction of the newly acquired response in therapy, trials are distributed rather than massed, partial reinforcement on variable ratio-interval schedules is used, habituation to shock is avoided by using initially high levels rather than gradual increases, and some avoidance responses are delayed. The fact that use of partial reinforcement had not been the typical case is reminiscent of Eysenck's (1965b) comment that the theoretical and experimental advances in learning and conditioning might as well have been nonexistent for all the attention paid to them by practitioners. However, we also note that Holz and Azrin (1966) advocate one hundred percent reinforcement delivery whenever possible if the aversive stimulus is being used as a punishment. Since the CS and deviant act cannot be prevented from occurring outside the therapy, however, one hundred percent punishment is not possible. Indeed, this feature and the fact that a clear discrimination of the occurrence of the UCS can be formed since it cannot occur outside treatment sessions, are major objections to aversion therapies and present a paradox to the extent that they actually do work. General problems in the use of avoidance, escape, and punishment paradigms are discussed again in Chapter 7.

Feldman, in using an operant model, seeks to enhance aquisition of an alternative response, replacing deviant with normal heterosexual responses. Since direct routes to the practice of normal sexual behaviors are not sanctioned in most therapy settings, Feldman and others pair images (real or fantasied) of females with termination of the CS and UCS. This procedure should change the initially neutral female images into positive reinforcers because stimuli accompanying offset of shock become secondary reinforcers (Kimble, 1961). Davison (1968a) and others have moved even farther in this direction, pairing client-produced masturbatory orgasm with attention to or fantasy of female stimuli. The patients used deviant fantasy to maintain arousal but always switched to fantasy of females as orgasm approached, and gradully were able to move this normal fantasy back in time until the deviant fantasy could be given up. However, both Davison (1968a) and Thorpe, Schmidt and Castell (1963) found it necessary to combine this positive conditioning approach with an aversive procedure for altering the CR to the deviant CS. The long overlearning of the deviant pattern presumably makes it dominant over any alternative new response unless it is directly interrupted. Feldman warns that this positive conditioning technique could involve backwards conditioning and could enhance avoidance of females should the switch to female stimuli result in detumescence. Even after heterosexual stimuli have been successfully substituted for deviant ones, a patient is likely to require help in learning to engage in courtship behaviors with females. He also may need treatment to reduce his past anxieties associated with social and sexual contacts with women. This last point emphasizes again the need for careful individual behavioral assessment and a comprehensive therapeutic approach that takes into account all the relevant elements involved in complex social behaviors.

The final special element in Feldman's technique is the use of an anticipatory avoidance response. A homosexual patient, for example, views a slide-projected picture of a nude male "for as long as he finds it attractive." After eight seconds, a painful electric shock is delivered until the patient closes a switch that removes the male slide and projects a female one. If the patient closes the switch before the eight seconds elapse, he avoids shock. Shock delivery and female slides both are put on a random partial reinforcement schedule. Rachman and Teasdale (1969) have criticized Feldman's conditioned avoidance response as quite artificial and unrelated to the instrumental acts even potentially available for avoiding naturalistic homosexual behavior, just as slides of males and females are remote from the real and fantasy stimuli that usually elicit the patient's arousal. Despite such reservations, Feldman's procedures apparently yield promising success.

It should also be considered that performance of perverted sexual responses in the clinic or laboratory is carried on in the presence of the treatment staff. This type of public performance surely must be accompanied by some anxiety, which further complicates our understanding of the particular process underlying reports of therapeutic success. The anxiety may be reduced when the noxious UCS finally occurs, similar to when the UCS in the animal laboratory terminates anxiety observed during the CS–UCS interval (Estes and Skinner, 1941; Schoenfeld, 1950). Thus an aversive UCS has the potential of maintaining the preceding behavior if it becomes a signal for subsequent administration of positive reinforcement. Such rewards may be inherent in the relief of terminating a trial or in approval from the therapist. "Masochistic" behavior could interfere with the reduction of the symptom attacked by aversion therapy, as may have been the case in the above-mentioned attempt by Bancroft (1966) to eliminate homosexual behavior. Therefore, care is taken in clinical procedures to terminate the UCS only when the patient no longer performs the perverted response, thus eliminating the possibility of avoidance conditioning.

In general, the aversive conditioning treatments in combination with supplementary procedures have had very promising success in treatment of sexual deviations, particularly when one considers the poor results of other therapies. Feldman and MacCulloch (1965) report (at 1 to 14 months follow-up) complete cessation of homosexual fantasy and behavior in 10 out of 16 patients treated in the manner described above. These 10 patients at follow-up were actively practicing heterosexual behavior and/or fantasy. A later report (Feldman, 1966) on 26 patients (3 months to 2 year follow-up) indicates 18 patients with this level of "cure," and 8 patients unimproved.

Marks and Gelder (1967) treated five men with fetishism and/or transvestism with twice-daily aversive conditioning for two weeks, followed by booster treatments weekly and then monthly. Treatment consisted of intermittent shock delivered when the patient signaled that he was vividly imagining himself in a customary deviant sexual situation and later when the patient was actually carrying out deviant behavior. The following criteria were used to indicate successful treatment: (1) by the end of treatment the latency for conjuring up the perverse situation was greatly increased; (2) penile plethysmograph measures indicated either much longer latency or inability of the deviant stimuli to produce erectile responses (this change was very specific to the particular stimulus object selected for shock, so that each stimulus—such as skirt, slip, and panties—had to be treated individually); (3) semantic differential ratings showed devaluation to a neutral point of the deviant sexual stimuli; (4) all deviant behavior outside of the therapy sessions ceased. At one year follow-up, two of the five patients showed some measure of relapse. These two studies, with 60 percent to 70 percent rates of "cure" at follow-up, represent surprising success in patients with very long histories (average of

20 years) of deviant sexual behavior. It is difficult to surmise the degree to which the patients represent a favorable selected sample in respect to general pathology, motivation to change, overall anxiety level, history of existence of some normal sexual fantasy and behavior, available hetero-sexual outlets, and environmental reinforcement of these outlets. Future work would do well to follow the example of Marks and Gelder in taking multidimensional criterion measures as therapy proceeds, with the addition of autonomic measures to get at the course of the presumed conditioned fear and with attention to other variables of presumed prognostic value.

Criteria of Change and Generalization of Effects

Two points are especially worthy of attention, as we try to untangle the behaviors involved and the therapeutic effects obtained in these treatments. When multiple criteria are used, it appears that various aspects of sexual behavior are relatively independent. Thus the changes in fantasy, attitudes, and physical arousal were found by Marks and Gelder to proceed at different rates. Mees (1966b) found in one case study that deviant fantasies, normal heterosexual fantasies, and normal heterosexual behavior occurred independently. Aversive conditioning did not affect the frequency of his patient's use of deviant fantasy for masturbation, even when the patient was carrying out normal heterosexual intercourse, until normal fantasy was deliberately strengthened. Similarly, Marks and Gelder found the semantic ratings of the aversively conditioned deviant stimuli became only neutral, not negative—a neutralization that would have little to do with positive changes in normal sexual stimuli. Some of the theoretical background of aversive conditioning has assumed a reciprocal relationship between abnormal and normal sexual patterns and a positive correlation between fantasy and practice. We have cited work suggesting that habitual fantasy reinforces practice. But until the interrelationships among these behaviors are clarified by further research, the proper target of conditioning will not be clear, and multitarget therapies will remain preferred. The importance of initiating changes in sociosexual and fantasy behaviors is underlined by Bancroft and Marks (1968) in a report of treatment of male homosexuals by electric shock aversion therapy. Although most patients showed some changes immediately after treatment, these therapeutic effects were not sustained. Bancroft suggests that the procedure may best be viewed "as a method of changing attitudes comparable to methods investigated by social psychologists in a nonclinical setting. The stability of such attitude change will depend on its translation into behavioral change." Bancroft and his colleagues at Maudsley Hospital in London, who have done extensive and carefully controlled work in this area, all warn that a comprehensive therapeutic program is needed for effectiveness.

In our own experience, behavior patterns of criminal sex offenders suggest that many persons who engage in perverse sexual behaviors lack the repertoire and skill not only for engaging in but also for thinking about (planning and anticipating) normal heterosexual courting and fulfillment. Since sexual fantasy is often accompanied by arousal and self-stimulation, reinforcement for the dominant themes in the patient's fantasy may be central for a sustained behavior change. In fact, building up of a verbal and visual fantasy repertoire and the skills for interactions with socially acceptable sexual partners seems a basic precondition for treatment of patients who lack prior successes (that is, effective instrumental behaviors) in normal relationships. The specific behaviors and the incentive function of normally arousing sex stimuli may have to be built up. Depending on the patient's particular status, therefore, desensitization of anxiety about heterosexual contacts, reinforcement of heterosexual fantasies, aversive conditioning of deviant fantasies and behaviors, discrimination training, and practice with reinforcement of heterosexual social skills add up to a comprehensive therapeutic package. However, a multi-barreled approach permits no evaluation of the relevance and contribution of each component unless cast in rigorous research designs.

A second related point deals with the generalization of effects. Marks and Gelder found great specificity in aversive conditioning of each CS. Furthermore normal sexual stimuli were not adversely affected: it was not "sex" that was aversively conditioned. And yet the effects of therapy generalized from the treatment setting—surely a place of artificial stimuli and unique attributes—to the patient's behaviors in the privacy of his home where no electrodes, staff, and instructions were present. The issue of generalization is one to which we will return again. For the moment, it is enough to note with Rachman and Teasdale (1969) that the most amazing thing about aversive conditioning is that it works despite the precise stimulus discriminations of which humans are capable. Elucidation of the interrelationships of the various response systems, as discussed above, and of the relative contributions of classical and operant conditioning effects, should go far in explaining this empirically gratifying but theoretically puzzling outcome.

ALCOHOLISM

A second area of pathological behavior to which the stimulus substitution or the aversion therapy paradigm has been applied is alcoholism. In a review of this field, Franks (1966) has indicated the inadequacy of a large number of studies, which were conducted in the United States and the Soviet Union during the 1920s. In the earlier attempts the most widely used UCS was apomorphine, the unsuitability of which was discussed earlier. Aside from the backward conditioning, impairment of conditionability through sedation, and other problems imposed by the use of drugs as UCS, other defects in these early studies included inaccurate reporting, limited follow-up, and inconsistent procedures. Conditioning therapies for alcoholism were largely abandoned because of the poor success rates of these studies, until several well-done studies in the late 1940s and early 1950s renewed interest in the potential of this technique. Meanwhile antabuse, a drug that leads to nausea and vomiting if followed by alcohol consumption, came to be widely used as a treatment and prevention agent. But its action is a direct physical one in reaction to alcohol and hence it is not a conditioning procedure. To the extent that learning enters into its effects, treatment with antabuse is a punishment paradigm with nausea following the response of alcohol consumption. Easy discrimination is possible, since the patient can obviously remember whether or not he had recently taken the antabuse. Some mild conditioned aversion to alcohol as a consequence of antabuse therapy has been reported, but this method is not a conditioning procedure in the usual sense. The person who has taken antabuse experiences severely unpleasant reactions upon drinking alcohol. However, the process is primarily physiological instead of a matter of established associations between stimuli and responses where none existed before (Franks, 1966).

Among the best studies using an emetic drug (emetine) as UCS is that of Lemere and Voegtlin (1950). In their procedure the patient was given drugs to control serious side effects, oral saline to provide easily vomited stomach contents, and both injected and oral emetine. Just before the moment of expected onset of nausea and vomiting, various forms of alcohol were smelled and tasted by the patient. Most experimenters have also given large quantities of nonalcoholic beverages and bottled soft drinks between sessions in order to maximize differentiation between the conditioned response to alcohol and its containers and the response to other liquids. Lemere and Voegtlin (1950) report that 60 percent of over 4000 treated patients were abstinent for at least one year, 51 percent for at least two years, 38 percent at least 5 years, with an overall 51 percent total abstinence rate for the 13 years covered by their follow-up survey. Miller, Dvorak, and Turner (1964) used the Voegtlin technique in a group procedure and obtained 50 percent total abstinence at 8 months.

A more drastic procedure has employed scoline or anectine, a curarizing drug that momentarily produces complete paralysis, including sudden cessation of the patient's respiratory function, without affecting the patient's state of consciousness. Administration of scoline requires careful medical supervision and has intensely terrorizing effects on the patient, who is presented with the taste and smell of alcohol just prior to the onset of paralysis. When this dramatic method was compared (Madill, Campbell, Laverty, Sanderson, and Vanderwater, 1966) with a pseudoconditioning group receiving only the UCS not paired with the sight, taste, or smell of alcohol, and a placebo group receiving only the CS but not the aversive stimulus, no significant differences in days of abstinence among the three treatments were observed in a three-month follow-up.

Only two of the twelve patients treated were abstinent at a one-year follow-up. Despite the ethical cautions that are involved in the use of such as an extreme UCS, the patients were unaware of the nature of the "frightening but harmless" experience that they were told they would undergo. Since only limited use of this procedure in research is demanded by its severe effects, experimental designs to maximize the informative value of the study should be employed. No adequate controls nor multiple measures were reported in this study. The common failure of experimenters to inform patients in advance of the use of curarizing drugs as a UCS is puzzling because it is ethically unsound and because the patient's awareness of the drug's action may have additional positive effects on the results.

More recently, as in the treatment of sexual deviation, electric shock has been used as a UCS in preference to emetic drugs. Drugs are used as aversive stimuli with alcoholism more often than with sexual problems—perhaps because of the longer history of usage and natural association of nausea and vomiting with oral consumption. Most of the same difficulties and perplexities hold for the aversion treatments of both conditions. Alcoholism, as compared to sexual deviation, involves more theories about its origins and maintenance (such as anxiety reduction as the maintaining reinforcer), less certainty about the endogenous and exogenous cues likely to elicit the target response in real life, and more variability in the circumstances, methods, and other acts likely to accompany the target response. For example, while most persons with deviant sexual behavior masturbate in private to fantasies that contain most of the stimuli crucial in eliciting their sexual arousal, alcoholics vary tremendously from each other and individually from time to time in what, how, when, and why they drink. Similarly, arriving at a competing alternative response for alcoholism is much more difficult. The sought-after reinforcement of orgasm is clear, and alternative socially acceptable means of achieving it are equally clear. Neither classically conditioned cues nor universal operant reinforcers present appropriate alternatives for the response of drinking alcohol. Hence, arriving at a substitute for drinking is difficult or impossible until one can state for *which* aspect of the chain of behaviors and consequences in alcohol consumption the substitution is made. The same difficulties beset conditioning treatments of other consummatory responses, such as overeating, use of narcotics, or cigarette smoking. If extinction of a conditioned aversion to the primary CS (provided it can be identified) is usually relatively rapid, prevention of recurrence must take the form of providing alternative responses during the aversive-conditioning grace period. Herein lies the practical problem.

Rachman and Teasdale (1969) point out that, at first glance, sexual arousal is probably an elicited response attached to learned cues. They suggest that generalization of aversion therapy effects to events outside of the treatment setting is mediated by the anxiety attached to the CS. Drinking alcohol is hardly likely to be elicited primarily by smell and sight of alcohol; therefore, aversion is not likely to be dealing with the eliciting cues but rather with classical conditioning of some cue properties of the response or with punishment of the response itself. Solomon (1964) has indicated that punishment is especially effective in suppressing consummatory responses (as opposed to nonconsummatory instrumental acts) but the generalization and persistence of these effects are less certain. There is evidence that aversive classical conditioning of food stimuli does not reduce feeding behaviors in animals despite the fact that the conditioned fear is established. Punishment of the act of eating is more successful in suppressing the behavior (Lichtenstein, 1950). If this would prove to be the case in humans, a punishment model would seem to be preferred in treating alcoholics.

In this connection, an attempt by MacCulloch, Feldman, Orford, and MacCulloch (1966) to apply their anticipatory avoidance conditioning technique to alcoholics is of interest. The alcoholic patients developed neither a consistent avoidance response nor a conditioned cardiac response to the CS, both of which did occur in homosexuals successfully treated by their method and which would appear to be essential evidence for the establishment of a conditioned aversion. A further difference in suitability of aversive conditioning for sexual deviancy and alcoholism is that the alcoholics are often assumed to be reinforced in their symptom, alcohol consumption, by reduction of anxiety. If this is the case, anxiety conditioned to the sight and smell of alcohol might readily increase the drinking response, since this act would reduce the anxiety (Gwinn, 1949; Eysenck and Rachman, 1965).

Despite these reservations, aversive conditioning of alcoholism using either shock or drugs as a UCS has, as already noted, shown great promise. Blake (1965, 1967) for example, using a combination of verbal motivation, relaxation, and aversion (shock as UCS), has reported 46 percent total abstinence after a one-year follow-up. A series of controlled studies comparing treatments within defined patient populations and with physiological, attitudinal, and behavioral measures before, during, and after treatment (similar to the work of Marks and Gelder with sexual disorders and phobias) is badly needed for evaluation of aversion therapy in alcoholics. At the same time, clinical practice needs to be as comprehensive as possible, with behavioral therapy of anxiety symptoms, development of social and vocational skills as needed, provision of necessary environmental reinforcers, and conditioned aversion to alcohol. Lazarus (1965b) and others have initiated broadly based treatment programs of this sort, backing up aversive conditioning with other techniques.

Successful use of avoidance conditioning has also been reported in a few cases of obesity. Although the nature of food and alcohol consumption differs in biological significance, immediate effects, and long-range consequences, both consummatory behaviors share socially facilitating settings in which they can occur and some features of the actual consummatory responses. A report by Meyer and Crisp (1964) describes the use of electric shock for approaching a tempting food during the treatment sessions with two obese patients. Although successful weight reduction was maintained in one patient until two years after treatment, the second patient failed to respond to treatment. Kennedy and Foreyt (1968) paired the smell of a favorite food (CS) with the highly noxious odor of butyric acid (UCS). At the end of a 22-week period, the patient lost approximately 10 percent of her body weight. The additional use of diet-controls, training in computing calories for food, and a "take-home" bottle of the noxious smelling gas for control of eating urges at home confound the evaluation of the effects of avoidance conditioning per se. However, as in treatment of sexual deviations, alcoholism, and other conditions, it is almost impossible to limit a treatment procedure to a specific technique without introducing other changes in the person's life, even if only the contact with the therapist. Control procedures therefore remain essential in evaluating a given procedure, even if the spectacular successes of the procedure appear to be convincing evidence of its effectiveness. The use of avoidance conditioning in obesity adds no new insights to the therapeutic mechanism, but attests to the spreading usage of the underlying paradigm.

ENURESIS

Bed-wetting is a third clinical problem to which stimulus substitution methods have been widely applied. Enuresis has been attributed to an underlying emotional disturbance. Dynamic personality theories have regarded the failure to establish control over urinary function variously as a manifestation of passive-aggressive behaviors toward the parents, as deep-seated emotional conflicts, or as substitute forms of gratifying repressed sexuality. Despite the prevalence of this view at the beginning of the twentieth century, Lovibond (1964) reports that, as early as 1830, J. Nye proposed a method for the treatment of enuresis resembling in many regards contemporary learning-based methods. Nye suggested attaching one pole of an electric battery to a moist sponge fastened between the shoulders of the patient and the other pole to a dry sponge attached to the urinary canal. The child slumbers undisturbed until the latter sponge is moistened and becomes a conductor of electricity. Once the circuit is completed the patient is aroused by the mild electric shock, awakened, and "caught in the very act and thus caveat is entered by the will as well as by the electricity against further proceeding at least for this time" (Quoted in Lovibond, p. 8).

In 1938, Mowrer proposed a more refined apparatus to accomplish the same purpose. Mowrer viewed stimuli from the child's full bladder as a CS that could be paired with the sound of a bell (UCS). Since the bell leads to awakening and sphincter contraction, the stimuli of bladder distention eventually would serve as a CS for awakening and sphincter contraction (CR). In principle, the proposed mechanism for conditioning treatment of enuresis is the same as that encountered in the classical conditioning treatment of the sexual and alcoholic problems described above. Cues that usually result in the patient's undesirable behavior are paired with a UCS that inevitably results in an antagonistic response. That this process is indeed involved in the successful conditioned control of enuresis has been questioned. Lovibond (1964) suggests instead that the paradigm is one of avoidance conditioning. He considers the occurrence of bell, electric shock, or loud noise to be contemporaneous with the initial reflexes associated with urination. In other words, the CS is considered to be the pattern of stimuli arising directly from the act of micturition, which closely precedes the aversive UCS. Contraction of the sphincter and continence, developed by repeated pairing of CS and UCS, represent an avoidance response to the UCS. If Lovibond's analysis is correct, the aversive reinforcing stimulus represents the consequence of the act of urination and leads to reduction in the probability of the preceding response (that is, the various behaviors associating with voiding)—and thus urine is withheld as an avoidance response. The major flaw in this interpretation is one that is shared with many other situations relying on an avoidance paradigm—how does one justify maintenance of the newly conditioned response, in the absence of further reinforcing stimuli?

Lovibond's analysis suggests that the most efficient therapeutic instrument would be one that terminates the CS associated with sphincter relaxation and urination. In actual operation this analysis led Lovibond to design an apparatus that uses two auditory stimuli. The first is a warning signal lasting approximately one second. It is followed by a silent interval of one minute. The second signal is a buzzer, which operates continuously until switched off. The first warning signal serves as the aversive stimulus, which can be terminated by sphincter contraction. Thus the child can either terminate the warning signal or avoid the second buzzer by sphincter contraction. Lovibond's procedure diverges from previous emphasis on the wakefulness of the child as a critical factor in treatment. If sphincter inhibition occurs in response to the first signal, representing an escape learning situation, the child might then return to sleep without awakening. The only drawback to this procedure is associated with findings in the animal learning literature that the opportunity to escape the aversive stimulus early during training reduces the possibility for building up strong aversive reactions to the conditioned stimulus.

The literature on enuresis represents an excellent example of the utilization of laboratory learning principles in the engineering of practical methods for changing behavior. There have been extensive studies in which large numbers of children have been given comparable treatments so that evaluation of the effectiveness of the technique rests on firmer data than for most other methods. Nevertheless, even in this area, the practical problems in obtaining parental cooperation in the procedure, minor apparatus variations, and other differences between studies have yielded variations in the reported proportion of successful cases. Lovibond's own cases yielded a 45 percent relapse on a two-year follow-up; standard conditioning treatment generally shows a relapse rate of about one third in five-year follow-ups.

The basic conceptualization of enuresis as a problem in faulty conditioning was used by Turner and Young (1966) to test an hypothesis proposed in Eysenck's personality theory—that drugs that stimulate the central nervous system should have a facilitation effect by increasing the rate of conditioning. The investigators used dexedrine and methedrine in conjunction with the conditioning treatment, both of which tend to increase activity level. A comparison control group was conditioned without drugs. In two thirds of the unsuccessful treatment cases, failure was attributed to the fact that the child had not been aroused by the buzzer. The adjunctive use of the stimulant drugs resulted in a significant increase in the speed of treatment. Fewer cases dropped out due to parental uncooperativeness in comparison to the control group. However, at a one-year follow-up the dexedrine group was found to have a much higher relapse rate. At longer follow-up intervals (up to five years), both drug groups had significantly higher relapse rates, the dexedrine group again showing worse results. The follow-up period was longest for the conditioning-only-group and only 32 percent had relapsed. The conditioning-and-dexedrine group had 76 percent relapse, and the conditioning-and-methedrine group, 43 percent. As Turner and Young point out, the studies that successfully speeded up acquisition of continence resulted in much higher relapse rates than occurred with the standard conditioning technique. It may be that overlearning during training strengthens resistance to extinction, just as Lovibond found that intermittent reinforcement with his twin-signal technique helped to reduce relapses.

A more basic issue concerns the conceptualization of the normal development of nocturnal continence and the physiological correlates of abnormality in this process. Broughton (1968) has proposed that enuresis is one of four classical sleep disorders (including also somnambulism, nightmare, and sleep terror), which occur at the time of arousal from a nondreaming phase of sleep, characterized by EEG slow waves. His data indicate that persons with these disorders show various physiological deviations throughout the night, independent of the enuretic episode. These abnormal autonomic and other physiological changes during sleep predispose the person to micturition. The enuretic episode seems to be merely an increase in these changes to an intense level. Any arousal from slow-wave sleep was found to provoke bladder contractions, analogous to stress incontinence; indeed, the autonomic responses at arousal indicate that the experience is very intense. Cyclic arousal from slow-wave sleep is a normal event during sleep and is accompanied by confusion and disorientation, automatic behavior, relatively low reactivity to stimuli, resistance to being awakened, and retrograde amnesia. As Broughton points out, procedures that rely upon conditioning at the time of the enuretic response, when the confusional state and the autonomic reaction are at their height, would seem less than optimally timed in regard to the person's amenability to conditioning. Perhaps failures attributed to the inability to arouse the child (by bell, parents, or shock) reflect the persistence of this confusional state. Since stimulant drugs affect midbrain sensitivity, the more rapid conditioning due to use of these drugs seems to support Broughton's proposal. In this regard, it is interesting to note that Browning (1967a) used positive reinforcement to establish the response of waking after the bell, a procedure that may alleviate some of the sleeper's resistance to wakefulness.

The management of the behavior therapy program for enuresis requires not only contact with a therapist but also focuses the attention of the entire family on the child's nightly performance. The effectiveness of the technique can be ascribed to the conditioning procedure alone, or to the social intervention effects of the treatment procedure (and *not* to conditioning), or to an interaction between both. Since the effects of placebo treatment and the general, nonspecific effects of the mere context and ritual of psychotherapy have repeatedly been shown to effect some behavior changes, it is necessary to demonstrate that the specific elements of the conditioning method and not its accompanying (secondary) effects are responsible for improvements. Baker (1969) examined this question in a study that compared a conditioning group with a "wake-up" group in which all the features of the treatment were duplicated, except for the conditioning. A third group of children was placed on a waiting list and treated at a later time. Baker found the conditioning procedure to be greatly superior to the wake-up method, indicating that the treatment effects are, in fact, attributable to the specific learning-based method and not to relationship or nonspecific effects. Baker had taken a number of pre- and posttreatment measures of the children's general adjustment. Contrary to the fears of some that removal of the bed-wetting symptom might create new symptoms caused by the underlying (and untreated) emotional conflict, the children showed some improvement in reported behavior, self-reports, and test scores.

AVERSIVE IMAGERY AS UCS

In all of the aversive conditioning techniques that have been considered, the persistent difficulties in categorizing ongoing real-life behavior into definite and identifiable S and R components and in selecting one component as "the" CS and another as "the" antagonistic CR have been noted. In the animal laboratory one can precisely control the history, environment, and response latitude permitted of the subjects and can often afford to ignore stimulus and response elements that are not of primary interest. The matter is quite different when one tries to intervene in the daily behavior of patients. We will return often in this text to the propensity of humans to provide themselves with unobservable cues or thoughts that, no matter how lawful, ultimately add to the difficulty in identifying the relevant behavioral segments. A relatively recent development in aversive conditioning can illustrate this point further, and can demonstrate, as well, problems in defining the UCS that are comparable to the CS definitional problems encountered in the treatment of sexual deviancy, alcoholism, and enuresis.

For reasons of ethics and convenience, a number of investigators have used imagined aversive events as the UCS in place of shock and drugs—a technique variously termed "covert sensitization" or "aversive imagery." The substitution of imagined for real stimulus events has already been discussed in the section dealing with treatment of sexual deviations. Indeed, fantasy recapitulation of a patient's usual masturbatory imagery often has been viewed as more "realistic" than slides or pictures used as CS. Gold and Neufeld (1965) went one step further and combined imagined

CS and UCS. They instructed a homosexual patient to imagine sexually arousing stimuli in aversive surroundings, with level of attraction and aversiveness of the elements so graded that there was an advantage for the aversive elements. For example, the patient imagined himself in a toilet, either next to an ugly man, or next to a more attractive man with a policeman nearby. They also used imagined scenes of attractive women in pleasant contexts to counter-condition heterosexual attraction. Cautela (1966) successfully treated cases of alcoholism and obesity with a procedure involving relaxation, imagined contact with the CS (for example, alcohol), and imagined aversive events accompanying the CS (for instance, vomiting on himself and his companions as the glass touched his lips). The patients practice imagining this sequence at home between therapy sessions, an obvious advantage of a technique that does not require elaborate apparatus.

Although controlled outcome studies have yet to be performed, success with this technique has been reported with alcoholism, obesity, drug addiction, sexual deviations, and compulsive behaviors. Anant (1968) has reported total abstinence in 25 out of 26 alcoholic patients treated by Cautela's approach, at fourteen and twenty-one month follow-ups. Ashem and Donner (1968) found 40 percent abstinence for patients treated by Cautela's technique (but including patients for whom a backward conditioning procedure was used) in comparison with zero abstinence in a matched control group.

These very promising results are both encouraging and perplexing. When the CS and UCS are imaginary, the difficulties of identifying, monitoring, and measuring CS and UCS, of elucidating the processes involved, and of relating the results to experimental laboratory findings are magnified beyond our present technical capacities. The understanding and precise control of these covert behaviors seem a rather difficult feat at present. On the other hand, the opportunities for direct use of the patient's own experiences, obviating the requirement for generalization from the laboratory or clinic, the potentials for use of wide varieties of CS conditions replicating real-life events, the reduction of the apparatus-specific nature of the UCS, and the possibility of frequent trials without the presence of the therapist are great advantages in this technique. Continued reports of success would establish this approach on pragmatic grounds though its mechanisms may not be fully understood.

SUMMARY

The classical conditioning model has served as a basis for several behavior modification techniques. The model is an abstraction from an ongoing segment of behavior in which the relationship between a response and its eliciting stimuli is taken as the focus. In clinical application, control of undesirable behavior is most frequently obtained by substitution methods. An aversive stimulus, usually with strong known noxious effects, is paired with the stimuli that usually precede the symptomatic response. With repetition, the unconditioned response to the aversive stimulus eventually dominates over the antagonistic symptomatic response. Finally, the previous conditions for execution of the symptom become conditioned aversive stimuli themselves. These methods are especially appropriate for behaviors in which the patient shows an excessive reaction to stimuli for which only minimal or moderate approach responses are tolerated, such as responses to homosexual stimuli or to alcohol. In common parlance, the results of treatment would be described as having brought about a change in the meaning of the stimulus.

The application of the pure classical conditioning model in treatment is complicated by the difficulty of separating this mechanism from operant conditioning. Since the UCS usually has reinforcing characteristics not only for the CR and UCR, but also for other behaviors that occur immediately prior to the CS and during the CS–UCS interval, operant or instrumental conditioning can easily intrude during the procedure. Furthermore, either extrinsic or implicit reinforcement often follows any substitutive behavior that the patient originates and that is more consistent with social norms.

Some authors have attempted to differentiate between the two types of conditioning processes by suggesting that different learning models are required for two different types of responses—skeletal or autonomic—and that different fundamental psychological and biological mechanisms operate for involuntary or reflexive responses and for voluntary or skeletal-muscular behaviors. Conflicting reports of attempts to condition autonomic responses by instrumental procedures, however, and the clear evidence of successful use of this procedure suggests that autonomic responses can also be directly conditioned instrumentally. Therefore, the proposed distinction offers little aid in separating the two models.

In surveying current behavior therapy practices the conceptual model of classical conditioning is encountered most frequently in the aversion therapies for use with sexual deviations, alcoholism, and enuresis. Treatment of phobias and other anxiety-related behaviors by counter-conditioning or stimulus substitution methods forms part of a behavior modification technique named "systematic desensitization," which is discussed in detail in Chapter 4. The classical conditioning model has also been used in demonstrations of the acquisition process of symptoms, such as phobias or sexual fetishes. In these speculations about the etiology of neurotic symptoms, the coincidental temporal association between an originally neutral stimulus and a UCS is viewed as the main mechanism by which the patient's response, be it anxiety or sexual arousal, is associated with an unusual stimulus event.

In the treatment of sexual perversions, the classical conditioning model has usually been applied by presentation of a signal for the symptom, such as the picture of the arousing CS, simultaneously with the administration of electric shock or a similar aversive stimulus as the UCS. In aversion relief the therapist provides, in addition, an escape or avoidance response, which represents the socially desirable counterpart (for example, an approach response to a heterosexual picture for homosexuals) with the intent of pairing this new stimulus with the termination or avoidance of shock. In essence, the second part of this procedure represents the use of operant conditioning methods by which an escape or avoidance response is strengthened in the presence of the original symptomatic situation.

The classical conditioning paradigm has a long history of use in treating alcoholics. In its original application the use of nausea-producing drugs as aversive stimuli probably carried with it the attempt to associate aversive or unpleasant experiences with the entire episode of drinking. Since the effects of an ingested drug may vary in the time of peak effectiveness, these techniques often fail to take advantage of the optimal temporal relationships required for effective classical conditioning. In fact, in some cases it is conceivable that the maximum effect of a nausea-producing drug, for example, may occur subsequent to the behavior of alcohol ingestion, thus following a backward conditioning paradigm. More recent work in alcohol treatment with classical conditioning has employed electric shock as an aversive stimulus, increasing the therapist's control over the temporal onset of the aversive UCS.

A third clinical problem to which stimulus substitution methods have been widely applied is bedwetting. As early as 1938 Mowrer proposed the bell and pad method. In this procedure the sound of a bell represents the UCS for waking, paired with the child's full bladder as the CS. Since awakening and sphincter contraction are expected to follow the bell, the stimuli of bladder distention eventually should serve as a CS for awakening and sphincter contraction. In more recent work, Lovibond has suggested that the pattern of stimuli arising from the onset of urination acts as a CS that closely precedes the UCS of voiding. Sphincter contraction then serves as an avoidance response for voiding. Lovibond's procedure therefore uses a warning signal at first, terminable by sphincter contraction. If sphincter inhibition does not occur, a second continuous buzzer is given. Further complications in understanding enuresis are introduced by the suggestion of some authors that physiological abnormalities in sleep disorders might predispose the person to involuntary micturition during sleep.

The administration of the UCS need not necessarily be carried out by a therapist or experimenter. In recent studies investigators have used imagined aversive events as the UCS in place of shock, drugs, or similar stimuli. This technique has variously been termed "covert sensitization" or "aversive imagery." The patient is instructed to present himself with images of aversive events whenever the cues for the socially undesirable behavior are present. The success of these new approaches promises utilization of the classical conditioning model without the difficulties of elaborate laboratory arrangements. To date, classical conditioning methods have been used alone only in relatively few clinical situations other than those mentioned above. Yet, the presence of respondents in most behavior segments that contain emotional responses makes it essential to consider this paradigm in devising treatment procedures.

CHAPTER 4

Mixed Models of Stimulus and Response Control

The preceding chapter summarized clinical treatment methods that attempt to parallel closely the classical conditioning model. It has been noted that impurities of the stimulus substitution paradigm in the clinical case are inevitable consequences of the difficulty in isolating response units in human behavior. Discussions about alcoholism, enuresis, and sexual perversion illustrated the point that classically conditioned responses represent only a small portion in the behavioral sequence. Many operants, mediating verbal behaviors, and complex physiological experiences are components of the pathological act.

In the present chapter we discuss applications of learning principles to situations in which complexity is contributed by two major considerations: (1) the presence of emotional responses surrounding the target instrumental response, and (2) the advantages and disadvantages associated with the power of a person's own covert and overt verbal responses to serve as controlling stimuli for his behavior. Before taking up treatment methods that deal with emotional responses as pathological behavior, however, we shall consider some of the available data on the nature and effects of anxiety and on the relationship between physiological and operant responses.

ANXIETY

Behavior disorders are frequently characterized as *emotional* disorders. In the layman's language this adjective suggests a causal relationship. Some mental or physiological states, crudely called emotions, are assumed to result in deviant or unacceptable behavior. The psychologist cannot accept this definition, for it fails to contribute useful information about the observed behaviors or their antecedents. The scientific worker can measure properties of the observed behavior in terms of stimulus condi-

133

tions, organismic state, response characteristics, or consequences. He can then assign a special name to a group of stimulus situations, physiological conditions, or response classes which share common features or result in similar consequences for the environment or the behaving organism. By far the greatest number of studies of emotional states has been devoted to examination of *anxiety*.

Definition of Anxiety

The construct of anxiety has been anchored to many different observations. First, anxiety has often been defined on the basis of a person's verbal description of an internal state. These verbal responses are measured by means of inventories or interviews or are inferred from projective personality tests. Some inventories are so constructed that the content of specific items can be considered irrelevant, since the scores correlate well with other behavioral measures of anxiety. The validity of these tests rests on the congruence between patterns of answers on the verbal items and patterns obtained in the standardization sample of patients with known diagnoses or behavior characteristics. In the Minnesota Multiphasic Personality Inventory (MMPI) test, for example, the main emphasis is on correspondence of the patient's pattern of True and False answers with the patterns given by individuals with known behavior disorders. An analysis of the patient's self-descriptive statements is secondary and rarely done. Other inventories, interview procedures, and personality tests give full credence to the person's description of his internal state as if it were a directly observed event. A second approach to the definition of anxiety is by assessment of physiological and behavioral patterns. The magnitude, duration, threshold, or variation in these responses to standardized stimuli yields a pattern that is characterized as an indicant of anxiety. A third approach anchors the definition of anxiety in experimental operations. For example, Skinner and his collaborators define anxiety as the behavior pattern observed during the interval between a warning signal and an unavoidable strong aversive stimulus.

Although animal experimenters have been able to retain clarity by relying on only one of these definitions—usually that of experimental operations—in the clinical literature it is a different matter. Consider a patient who presents herself for behavior therapy with the complaint that for several years she has been "housebound," unable to leave her home without experiencing great tension, rapid heart beat, hyperventilation, and thoughts of panic by the time she reaches the garden gate. The behaviorist wants to measure the target response; but is it the self-report of panic, the observable behaviors of escaping by reentering the house and avoidance by not leaving again, or the physiological changes, that should be electronically monitored? As Lacey (1959) and Lang (1968), among others, have pointed out, there is little correspondence between concurrent measures of autonomic, verbal, or overt motor measures of anxiety. Despite our phenomenal experience of fear as unitary, its measured intensity depends upon the response definition we use; just as the definition used will determine which other variables can be shown to affect the response. Discrepancies between physiological responses and verbal reports are common, and measures of particular physiological responses (for example, heart rate, GSR and respiration) do not always show similar patterns for different individuals under the same experimental conditions. For example, Lang, Lazovik, and Reynolds (1965) found that closeness of approach to a phobic object did not correlate significantly with the subject's self-report of anxiety or his rating of the general intensity level of his fear. This leaves the investigator of human anxiety with no single "true" index of anxiety for different persons, but rather with several equally valid, rather independent indices. Which of the multiple responses related to the anxiety construct are to be the therapeutic targets is a crucial problem to which we will return.

Theories of Anxiety and Symptom Formation

The construct of anxiety has a central role in almost all theories of psychopathology. The theories have in common the assumption that the aberrant behaviors, which mark the neurotic and psychotic patient, are basically adjustive reactions that avoid or terminate an overwhelming and intensely terrifying emotional state, anxiety. Attributed to anxiety are the properties of augmented biological activity, reduced behavioral efficiency, and stereotyped and fixated "defensive" avoidance reactions. If anxiety does not subside, these reactions increase in frequency, vigor, and stereotypy until they are no longer consistent with social norms. Such excessive reactions characterize a psychopathological syndrome and include both instrumental and emotional components. When a person manifests an array of symptomatic responses, as illustrated in Figure 4-1, the therapist can decide to attack any of these separately. For instance, unconditioning of the physiological responses may reduce the symptoms of rapid heart beat, sweating, and hyperventilation. Changes in the other behaviors (for example, the content of the patient's conversation) may or may not occur.

The construct of anxiety is pivotal not only in psychoanalytic and dynamic theories, in which symptoms are seen as defenses aiding repression of unconscious anxiety, but also in explanations of clinical problems in terms of the data of experimental psychology. In the laboratory, the behavioral patterns termed anxiety have been attached to previously neutral cues through classical conditioning and, once established, have been found

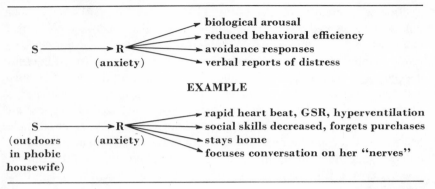

Figure 4-1   Behavioral properties of anxiety: which is the therapeutic target?

to be remarkably resistant to extinction. Escape and avoidance responses, which are seen as analogues to symptomatic behaviors, can be attached to the conditioned stimulus that elicits anxiety. Escape is readily seen to be reinforced by termination of the UCS (anxiety reduction), but the explanation of the avoidance response is more difficult. Successful avoidance, by definition, means that the UCS never occurs. Then what reinforces the avoidance response?

Avoidance responses are extraordinarily persistent in the face of many unreinforced trials. The crucial question, for experimental and clinical investigators alike, is: if a neurotic symptom, such as a phobia, represents conditioned anxiety and learned anxiety-avoidance responses, why do not both of these aspects of the symptom gradually weaken in the absence of the UCS that had initially begun the sequence? Figure 4-2 illustrates the development of anxiety and avoidance responses as it occurs in the laboratory and the parallel that is proposed to account for the case of a human neurosis. The progression from classical conditioning of the anxiety to the development of escape and avoidance responses is shown in successive diagrams. In either case, the puzzle remains: what maintains the anxiety and avoidance responses, and why don't they extinguish in the absence of reinforcement?

Biological Reactions to Stress

Two major competing explanations have been offered to explain this paradox. Since several variants of each interpretation have been proposed, we shall summarize the underlying reasoning in only a general way. The first approach emphasizes the membership of anxiety patterns in the family of biological reactions to stress. The best known proponent of the underly-

Laboratory

UCS (shock) ——→ UCR (pain, fear)
CS (tone) - - -→ CR (fear or anxiety)

Real life

UCS (interpersonal failure, rebuff) ——→ UCR (fear, pain)
CS (shopping center, generalizes to all outdoors) ——→ CR (anxiety)

Anxiety is classically conditioned and then may persist for many unreinforced trials and over long time periods.

UCS (shock) ——→ UCR (pain, fear)
CS (tone) ——→ CR (anxiety)
CR (anxiety) ——→ UCR (escape, e.g., by jumping on shelf)

Instrumental escape responses to the UCS may be attached to and initiated by onset of the CS. Escape extinguishes unless maintained by reinforced trials in which UCS occurs.

UCS (failure, rebuff) ——→ UCR (fear, pain) (escape by return home)
CS (outdoors) ——→ CR (anxiety) (escape by return home)

UCS (shock) ——→ UCR (pain, fear)
CS (tone) - - -→ CR (anxiety)
CR (anxiety) ——→ UCR (escape)
CR (avoidance, e.g., by jumping on shelf)

Avoidance responses may be associated with the CR. By definition, the UCS does not occur on successful avoidance trials, yet the response persists without that source of reinforcement.

Thus appears a "sick" rat, or a "sick" housewife.

UCS (failure, rebuff) ——→ UCR (pain, fear) (escape)
CS (outdoors) ——→ CR (avoid by staying in)
CS (outdoors) ——→ CR (anxiety)

and

CS (outdoors) ——→ CR (stay inside)

Figure 4-2 Laboratory paradigms for conditioning of anxiety and avoidance responses. Note UCR is general arousal; escape is a learned response but termed UCR here to indicate acquisition in past.

ing theory is Hans Selye (1950), who has described three consecutive stages of biological reactions to continuing stress in the organism. The entire process is termed the *general adaptation syndrome*. Each of these stages, known as the alarm reaction, the stage of resistance, and the stage of exhaustion, has its own characteristic endocrinological and other physiological changes. During the initial alarm reaction there is a general increase in biological activities and biochemical substances that counter the effects of stressors (for example, adrenalin release). In the second resistance reaction, the body's defensive activity is intensified and confined to the particular site of the body affected by the stressor. Finally, if the stressor continues, these defensive reactions wane until progressive damage and even death may result.

The activation or arousal theory of emotions is a similar formulation, the essence of which is the postulation of a continuum from complete rest to intense excitement. All behavior can be placed somewhere along this continuum, with emotional patterns near the higher end of the activity dimension. Considerable research has provided evidence that experimental operations producing behaviors defined as emotion (fear, anger, frustration) also produce numerous increases in delicately balanced physiological functions or arousal. Changes in the vascular system, hormonal secretions, and respiratory and gastrointestinal functions have been reported. These changes mutually affect each other but tend to differ for the same situation among individuals. Malmo (1957) has suggested that increases in level of arousal normally activate inhibitory mechanisms, which tend to redress the imbalance. Prolonged exposure to arousal stimulation, such as the continued evocation of frustration, fear, or other intense emotional responses, may lead to loss of effectiveness of the inhibitory mechanisms. As a result, neurotic patients, who are assumed to have undergone prolonged periods of heightened emotional responsiveness, would be expected to show greater responsiveness to minimal stress situations, a slower return to a resting state, and other differences in their response to stress. Numerous studies comparing neurotic and normal populations have reported these differences. These permanent changes would explain ready evocations of anxiety, as a pattern of physiological arousal, without continued exposure to an original aversive UCS. At the same time, however, the absence of this anxiety pattern in many psychotic patients also must be noted. In fact, clinical experience has led many to characterize the psychotic patient as one whose *lack* of heightened anxiety distinguishes him from neurotics. The most important consequence of Malmo's thesis for behavior therapy lies in the suggestion that the formation of particular behavioral disorders may have been accompanied by irreversible biological changes. Although this approach does not contradict a learning formulation for the particular behaviors that are acquired and maintained as symptoms, it does suggest that the concomitant biological changes may limit the extent to which emotional disturbances can be reversed by learning.

Conditioned Reactions to Stress

A second general experimental interpretation of neurotic behaviors regards anxiety as a conditioned response to painful stimulation. It is this interpretation that is diagramed in Figure 4-2 and that we have briefly discussed in our review of the translation from psychonanalysis to learning theory proposed by Mowrer, and later by Dollard and Miller. Several variations of this hypothesis have been proposed. Essentially they share the view that a conditioned emotional response (CER) is established, by classical conditioning, when a CS is paired with a painful stimulus. Mowrer (1950) and Schoenfeld (1950), although using slightly different learning models, both have proposed that this CER, the anxiety response, includes autonomic components associated with the aversive properties of the original pain stimulus. In turn, this conditioned emotional response (CER) serves as a cue or drive stimulus that persists until some instrumental response removes the organism from the original environment. Miller (1951), following Hull's drive reduction hypothesis, further suggests that the autonomic components of the CER, acquired through association with the original pain response, which itself has drive properties, come to act as an acquired drive that can be reduced by appropriate avoidance or escape responses. When applied to human phobias, the analogy has been used to presume that a conditional fear drive is established in a traumatic learning situation and that the CER or acquired anxiety drive then sustains phobic responses that avoid the now anxiety-provoking situation on subsequent occasions. Miller has demonstrated with laboratory animals that a variety of instrumental responses will be learned if the animal is permitted to escape from a confined compartment in which it had previously been shocked. Congruent observations were also made in humans and animals indicating that any blocking of the habitual avoidance response, either the phobic response in the human or the instrumental jumping or wheel-turning response in the rat, results in increases in noticeable physiological concomitants of the conditioned fear response.

Skinner and his co-workers provide a variant of the conditioned response approach to anxiety. They have mainly emphasized changes in rate of well-established operants when a new CS aversive-UCS sequence is imposed. The basic experimental paradigm of Estes and Skinner (1941) illustrates the procedure. The authors conditioned rats to press a bar for food reinforcement on a fixed interval schedule. After this response was well-established, a tone was sounded continuously for five minutes, terminating with presentation of a brief electric charge to the grid floor of the cage. Rate of bar-pressing was depressed during the interval between the onset of tone and shock. In addition, after shock terminated, rate of bar-pressing for food increased. Extinction of the conditioned suppression was relatively slow.

This model has been used to examine the particular suppressive effects of conditioned anxiety on a number of instrumental and autonomic responses. The specific change in rate of the operant response during the anxiety interval may, it appears, be a function of the compatibility between the operant response and the unconditioned response to the aversive UCS. In some cases, the established operant actually increases, rather than being suppressed, during the anxiety interval. For example, Kanfer (1958), measuring rate of verbal output and heart rate during the conditioned anxiety interval, found an increase in verbal output during this interval, which was maintained one week after the initial conditioned anxiety acquisition session. Application of conditioned anxiety as a therapeutic method, for example, to reduce the rate of an undesirable response, clearly would require exploration of the suppressing or enhancing effects for each class of operant.

Extinction in Avoidance Conditioning

Of particular importance for modification of deviant behaviors are understanding of and control over the acquisition and extinction of avoidance responses, as the theories of anxiety sketched out above make clear. Anxiety is often presumed to mediate both acquisition and maintenance of these responses. The well-developed avoidance behavior, however, either is the symptom or presumably plays a vital role in preventing rapid extinction of the disturbing symptom of anxiety. The anxiety responses themselves, acquired through classical conditioning, do not always constitute the target for modification.

A series of studies by Solomon and Wynne (1953) investigated avoidance responses in dogs, using high intensity shock as the UCS, with a shuttle box divided into two compartments by a removable barrier used to control the CS and UCR. A dog was placed in one compartment, the CS was presented, the upper part of the barrier was removed, and ten seconds later shock was administered. Solomon and Wynne found that for the first few trials, the animals attempted to escape (UCR) only when shocked, but that soon the dogs were executing avoidance responses (CR), and with increasing speed. It is significant that response latency continued to decrease even after the animal managed to avoid shocks. Even with as many as six hundred trials, animals showed no sign of extinction. If a dog was prevented from jumping across the barrier, it showed intense emotional reactions.

The investigators accepted the basic arguments of the two-step acquired fear theory which we have described above. However, the remarkable resistance to extinction of the avoidance response led them to propose two additional principles for learning under highly traumatic conditions. The first, the *anxiety conservation* principle, suggests that the rapidity with which an avoidance response can be made prevents full-scale arousal of anxiety. That is, the very effectiveness of the avoidance response prevents extinction of the acquired drive that maintains it. The second principle, that of *partial irreversibility*, proposes that a relatively permanent linkage may be established when a highly intense UCS is used to condition a fear reaction. Solomon's interpretation thus represents a combination of the two approaches to anxiety as a biological stress reaction.

More recent data suggest that the reinforcement operations maintaining avoidance responses are far from settled. Bolles (1968), for example, notes that neither initial escape learning nor termination of the CS upon avoidance is necessary for avoidance learning, although both are usually called upon as required operations relating the anxiety attached to the CS to the avoidance response. As shown in Figure 4-2, both have been viewed as the steps leading to the onset of the avoidance response. Bolles also suggests that the rate of extinction of an avoidance response is a function of availability of a feedback stimulus or safety-signal, a role that CS termination can play. He points out that the CS does not always come to function as an aversive stimulus. For example, rats do not act to prevent a CS that signals shock when escape or avoidance are not possible. They seemingly prefer signaled to unsignaled shock (Lockard, 1963). These findings raise questions about the role of the CS as either a conditioned aversive event or as a cue for conditioned anxiety. Bolles offers a punishment hypothesis to explain acquisition and maintenance of avoidance responses. He proposes that the UCS acts as a punishment to suppress all behavior other than the avoidance response, which itself is not directly reinforced. While this hypothesis perhaps does not adequately explain acquisition of new behaviors to escape the CS alone, nor the resistance to extinction of the CER, it does indicate that even in animal laboratory work there remain unsettled crucial questions about conditioned anxiety and the functional interrelationships of UCS (pain), CS, CER (anxiety), and CR (avoidance).

Acquisition of and Responses to Anxiety in Humans

Most of the research supporting the anxiety relief hypothesis of abnormal behavior has come from the animal laboratory. This fact limits in a number of ways our ability to generalize to normal and abnormal human behavior. In animal experiments the UCS is almost invariably a painful stimulus, specific in its source and its elicitation of physiological mechanisms. In the case of the neurotic patient, the hypothesized traumatic UCS events usually do not involve painful stimulation or physical insults. Kessen and Mandler (1961) have attacked the narrowness of sources of conditioned anxiety implied by pain as the UCS, noting that the anxiety response may occur in conjunction with numerous human situations that threaten the individual's comfort or ability to predict or achieve goals. These situations may involve any condition in which the organism's basic needs are not met, be they social or biological.

Finally, most of the animal studies have used a model in which escape or avoidance responses are available. In a unique laboratory study with humans, Campbell, Sanderson, and Laverty (1964) examined the characteristics of a human CER acquired under extreme stress. The traumatic UCS was not itself painful, and no escape or avoidance response was available. The authors used scoline, a drug that produces nearly complete paralysis of the skeletal musculature and temporary interruption of respiration (lasting about two minutes). The subject, who remains conscious throughout the paralysis, undergoes no pain, but describes the experience as extremely horrifying because of the inability to control breathing or to do anything about it. The subjects were presented with a tone CS before and during the paralysis. Each subject was given only a single traumatic conditioning trial during which there was continuous monitoring of the galvanic skin resistance, respiration, heart activity, and muscle tension. After a five-minute recovery period, the subjects were exposed to thirty extinction trials. The extinction sessions were repeated one week and three weeks following the conditioning trial. Control subjects were given either the UCS or the CS alone. In contrast to the controls, the experimental subjects failed to show extinction of any of the conditioned autonomic responses. In fact, the galvanic skin response decreased in latency and increased in magnitude as extinction progressed. A similar tendency was noted for the cardiac response, while the respiratory and muscular components of the CR tended to develop longer latencies and to level off during later extinction trials. These findings are consistent with the results reported by Solomon and Wynne for a conditioned avoidance response, as described above. The difference, however, lies in the fact that in the Campbell et al. experiment, no instrumental avoidance behaviors were possible. It is noteworthy that in this experiment the respiratory and muscular responses, which are generally considered to be voluntary, and the "involuntary" GSR and cardiac responses all showed a similar fate in failing to extinguish. The results of this study, though requiring replication for full acceptance, cast doubt on the tenability of anxiety reduction as an explanation for the continuation of avoidance responses following a severe trauma. They fit more adequately any interpretation that presumes some partial irreversibility of the response pattern acquired in the presence of the CS.

A recent study by Katzev (1967) raises a methodological point about the conditions under which avoidance responses are difficult to extinguish. In most procedures the UCS is omitted in extinction but the warning signal (CS) is terminated after a response. This procedure, Katzev maintains, is indistinguishable from the training trials. When Katzev compared a conventional extinction procedure with one in which the termination of the CS was delayed until well after completion of the response, the avoidance response extinguished very rapidly. These findings suggest that efforts to eliminate an avoidance response in clinical subjects would be most effective if close temporal contiguity between the response and the CS were carefully eschewed—a point not unlike the implication of Bolles (1968) and others that presentation of a safety signal would enhance extinction or retard acquisition of avoidance behaviors.

Verbal Mediators in Anxiety

So far we have primarily discussed animal research in which knowledge is limited about other essential controlling factors that may modify the progress of anxiety. In human subjects, the availability of language provides potential controlling stimuli, which may modify the course of an acquired fear reaction. The importance of self-instructions and similar verbal behaviors has already been pointed out in connection with eye blink conditioning research. Similar findings in other situations have shown that human subjects who are instructed about the CS–UCS relationship or about omission of the UCS in extinction will rapidly alter their response pattern. A study by Silverman (1960) illustrates the powerful effects of instructions in effecting extinction rate of the GSR in a classical conditioning experiment. Silverman conditioned a GSR response to a two-second tone by means of a six-second UCS shock to the subject's left arm. The CS–UCS interval was at an optimal value, 0.5 seconds, in one group, but at six seconds in another group. A third group received randomly interspersed CS and UCS administrations, which were not paired. Half of the subjects in each group were instructed prior to extinction that the UCS would no longer be administered. The conditioned GSR was markedly reduced by instructions in the 0.5 second group. However, the six-second group was not affected by the instructions. These findings are difficult to explain. One speculation is that the delay between CS and UCS permits the intrusion of other subject behaviors that maintain S's anxiety pattern. Silverman suggests that "in other words, the six-second CS and UCS interval may act as a potent anxiety-arousing technique" (p. 125). Acquisition of a conditioned GSR with a backwards conditioning procedure (UCS preceding CS) has also been shown to be a function of the way a human subject structures or perceives the experimental procedure. Only subjects who attribute causal or signaling significance to the delayed CS show the backward conditioning effect (Zeiner and Grings, 1968). Many other recent studies report the modifying effects of instructions in the acquisition and extinction of GSR responses (see, for example, Hill, 1967), eyelid conditioning (Gormezano and Moore, 1962) and finger withdrawal (see, for example, Lindley and Moyer, 1961).

The probable role of verbal behaviors in evaluating the regularity of the UCS and in causing the subject's avoidance is apparent in a study by D'Amato and Gumenik (1960). College students were required to guess whether a light on the right or left would go on, indicating their guess by pressing a lever below the appropriate light. After an initial series of training trials, the subject received an immediate shock every time he pressed one lever and a randomly delayed shock every time he pressed the other lever, irrespective of whether he guessed correctly or incorrectly. The delays varied from zero to 20 seconds. After the experiment, subjects were asked to rate the relative pleasantness of the two types of shocks and to estimate the percentage of trials on which the left or right light went on. The subjects showed an avoidance of the randomly delayed shock; on questioning, sixteen out of twenty subjects judged the randomly delayed shock as more unpleasant. Further, their recall of the stimulus events and their behavior during the shock trials was markedly poorer than for nonshock trials.

The contribution of a person's verbal behavior to the control of an anxiety response is especially crucial to behavior therapists, since many techniques are based almost entirely on manipulation of verbal responses that are believed to affect other behaviors. It is common sense that a person cannot stop being anxious simply because he tells himself not to be. Yet both the designation of one's state as emotional arousal and the behavioral consequences of having labeled such arousal in a particular way may have some bearing on a person's maladaptive behavior. In a series of studies on the labeling of emotional patterns attached to aroused body states, Schachter and his co-workers (1964a) have demonstrated that a person's interpretation of the nature of his bodily state of arousal can be modified by the explanations provided him by instructions or other experimental procedures, if he has no good immediate explanation himself. "To the extent that cognitive factors are potent determiners of emotional states, it could be anticipated that precisely the same state of physiological arousal could be labeled 'joy' or 'fury' or 'jealousy' or any of a great diversity of emotional labels depending on the cognitive aspects of the situation" (Schachter and Singer, 1962, p. 381).

In a study by Nisbett and Schachter (1966), subjects were given a placebo before painful electric shock. Half were told that the drug would cause arousal symptoms such as palpitation and tremors. The other half expected no such symptoms as a result of the placebo pill. It was found that subjects who believed themselves to be in an artificial state of arousal found the shock less painful, were willing to tolerate more of it, and tended to attribute the shock-produced autonomic symptoms to the pill rather than the shock. In several other studies Schachter and his co-workers have shown that the particular emotional label (for example, fear and anger) attached to a drug-induced state of arousal depends on environmental cues rather than on actual internal physiological stimulation. Other research suggests different arousal patterns for various emotional and motivational circumstances (Ax, 1953; Lacey and Lacey, 1958). Gellhorn (1964) has proposed that feedback from specific autonomic patterns may exert subtle control over cognitive events. The person's acceptance of a preferred label would thus seem to depend on the degree of ambiguity in the situation, his past history, and perhaps, the intensity or specificity of the arousal pattern.

From the viewpoint of the clinical psychologist who deals with anxiety responses in a continually thinking and actively interpreting human, the verbal component or "cognitive" aspect of the anxiety response represents an important consideration. The preceding studies suggest that modification of human behaviors occurring in association with a CER can be brought about by providing a more effective alternative to the avoidance response and by putting under verbal control both the emotional response and the behavior contingent upon it. The crucial role of these "cognitive" factors in a person's regulation of his own behavior are discussed in detail in Chapter 9. It should be noted here, however, that the flexibility of labels for physiological arousal carries the important implication for clinicians that a person's prior disposition toward a particular label (such as fear or anger) or overlearning of that label can bias his interpretation of ambiguous situations in the direction of his characteristic affective experiences (Goldstein, Heller, and Sechrest, 1966).

Lazarus and his co-workers (Lazarus, 1966) have focused on the effects of what they call cognitive reappraisal in reducing reactions to stress. In contrast to studies of methods for reduction of already conditioned anxiety responses, their work has followed a prophylactic strategy, comparing the effectiveness of various training procedures in producing reductions in heart rate, GSR, and self-report measures of reaction to a subsequently imposed laboratory stress. Subjects are induced to reappraise a threatening event (such as a gory movie) by rehearsal in imagination of its occurrence and of their own defensive reactions to it (for example, denial, intellectualization and reassurance). This anticipatory practice at "coping" has been found to significantly reduce subsequent stress indicators in comparison to untreated or relaxation-training controls (Folkins, Lawson, Opton, and Lazarus, 1968).

The hypothesis that cognitive set can influence the subjective and physiological components of anxiety is supported not only by Lazarus' work, but by studies that indicate that many instructional or set and modeling variables will modulate the effects of aversive stimuli. Hart (1966), for example, found that snake phobic subjects decreased in snake avoidance behavior after they made up a speech to teach others not to fear snakes. Subjects' autonomic responses to a drug or verbal reports about electric shock are in part a function of what they are instructed to expect from the stimulus (Sternbach, 1964; 1966). Generalization from these analogue studies to anxiety complaints in the clinic is hazardous. Laboratory stresses are mild, temporary, and understandable as part of an experimental procedure, and the effects of the cognitive variables are likewise short in duration. Furthermore, as Lang (1969) and others have noted, incipient anxiety symptoms often seem to be the most potent cues for an increase in anxiety in persons seen clinically. "Thinking about being anxious during a test" and "beginning to feel butterflies in the stomach" are frequently reported as the most potent stimuli for anxiety attacks by students suffering from severe test anxiety.

It is partly because of the apparent admixture in the therapies taken up in this chapter, of manipulations of stimulus events, autonomic and motor responses, and mediating or cognitive responses, that this chapter is titled "mixed models." If, as we have noted before, classical and operant components apparently occur together in daily behavior in ways impossible to sort out, this is even more true in the case of techniques intended to modify anxiety.

Anxiety and Arousal

The literature dealing with anxiety inventories, sources of anxiety, and effects of anxiety on learning, perception, and performance is too extensive to be covered here. It should at least be noted, however, that anxiety patterns of autonomic arousal have been reported during avoidance conditioning and in many other conflict situations. Consistent with Pavlov's original finding of "neurotic" behavior in dogs exposed to difficult or impossible discriminations, physiological arousal patterns have been found in humans faced with a difficult discrimination in a complex avoidance learning situation. Similar patterns have been encountered in the few studies of natural situations often associated with anxiety.

Beam (1955), for instance, tested subjects immediately before they presented an oral report as a college course requirement, prior to appearing in a play before a large audience, and prior to taking a preliminary examination for a graduate degree. Although we have spoken of anxiety as an arousal pattern without reference to the specific environmental features associated with it, distinctions have been made between this pattern as a chronic state and as a response to a particular transitory event, such as a college examination. The many results attempting to correlate inventory scores on anxiety scales and performance on learning tasks suggest that the effects differ for simple and complicated demands.

BEHAVIOR THERAPIES FOR ANXIETY

The preceding section has given us a better understanding of the reason for the central position of anxiety in the treatment of behavior disturbances. We must agree with Martin (1961) who states, after a thorough review of the assessment of anxiety by behavioral and physiological measures, that: "One cannot conclude on the basis of the researches reviewed in this paper, despite many suggestive leads, that any clear-cut pattern of physiological-behavioral responses associated with anxiety arousal, distinguishable from other arousal patterns has been demonstrated" (p. 251). Nevertheless, the available research points to complex interrelationships between classical and instrumental conditioning in producing symptoms associated with a conditioned emotional response. The available studies also suggest intimate interplay of verbal, physiological, and other behavioral events in the formation and weakening of avoidance responses that are associated with anxiety. If one accepts the partial irreversibility principle for severe anxiety, it appears likely that a discontinuity exists between the effects and durability of responses associated with mild anxiety arousal states and with intense life-threatening experiences. In regard to what follows we must keep in mind the underlying theoretical uncertainty about the conditions that produce anxiety responses, even though the pragmatic evidence may lead us to accept therapeutic techniques based on any of the proposed theories and laboratory findings, not because of their truth but because of their effectiveness in reducing human misery and suffering.

Wolpe's Reciprocal Inhibition

One widely used method of behavior therapy was first proposed as a total package by Wolpe (1958). Dissatisfaction with psychoanalytic methods of treating neurotic anxiety led Wolpe to search for more effective techniques in the experimental work of Pavlov, Jones, Watson, and Masserman on "experimental neuroses" in animals. During 1947 and 1948 Wolpe carried out a series of experiments that produced persistent "neurotic" behavior in cats by confining the animals in small cages and delivering shocks preceded by a CS. As part of the response to this procedure, the cats would no longer eat in the cage. Wolpe found that he could eliminate these reactions and restore normal cage behaviors by feeding the cats in places that were distinctly dissimilar from the original experimental cage. As the animal appeared less anxious and behaved more efficiently, Wolpe gradually approximated the original traumatic situation more and more closely, until the cage itself could be used without behavioral disruption.

Wolpe's technique with neurotic patients parallels this early procedure. Two essential ingredients are contained in the method. First, the subject is exposed to a weaker form of the same CS that is presumed to have originally been conditioned to anxiety through association with some potent UCS. Because of this stimulus grading, the conditioned emotional response itself is produced, if at all, at only a very low level of intensity. This feature characterizes the *desensitization* aspect of Wolpe's method. Second, a response is introduced that is antagonistic to the anxiety response, as eating was in the cats. This feature is termed *reciprocal inhibition* by Wolpe and is equivalent to conditioning a more probable competing response to the CS, leading to conditioned inhibition, which minimizes the anxiety reaction.

Wolpe has stated his reciprocal inhibition principle in a formal way: *"If a response inhibitory of anxiety can be made to occur in the presence of anxiety-evoking stimuli it will weaken the bond between these stimuli and the anxiety"* (Wolpe and Lazarus, 1966, p. 12). In his original presentation (Wolpe, 1958) the theoretical explanation of the reciprocal inhibition phenomenon was based heavily on Hull's concept of conditioned inhibition, supplemented by further neurophysiological explanations. Current utilization of this technique, however, discards the underlying speculations in favor of emphasis on the therapeutic operations themselves.

Wolpe's incompatible response hypothesis has some similarity to Guthrie's learning theory. A pure contiguity principle of learning would suggest that the juxtaposition of an incompatible response, which already has high strength, with stimulus elements previously associated with some portion of the undesirable response would eventually result in extinction of the old response and learning of a new association. Further, Pavlov suggested an experimental procedure in which one response is substituted for another by presentation of the original UCS at low intensity while simultaneously enhancing opportunities for an incompatible response to occur in its presence. The term *counter-conditioning* has been applied to this general procedure and is therefore often used to characterize Wolpe's technique. The essential feature of reciprocal inhibition, then, is selection of anxiety as the target for attack. As we have previously seen, anxiety is at least partially classically conditioned and in turn gives rise to other behavioral symptoms. For this reason Wolpe's method has frequently been classified under the classical conditioning rubric. The method demands, however, that an antagonistic response, toned with positive affect, also be elicited and maintained. Since such responses are usually operants, the actual operations in desensitization include elements of both learning processes. It is for this reason that the methods in this chapter are termed "mixed models."

When the anxiety response is associated with inability to express appropriate feeling or to carry out adaptive acts in interpersonal relationships, the patient's expression of his feelings and attitudes can function as the competing response for counter-conditioning. Thus *assertive* behavior represents a particular vehicle for use in desensitization. Wolpe and Lazarus (1966) recognize that the subassertive neurotic patient who is finally able to hold his own with other people usually experiences rewarding consequences for his assertive behavior. *"The counterconditioning of anxiety is thus intertwined on each occasion with the operant conditioning of the instrumental response* and each facilitates the other" (Wolpe and Lazarus, 1966, p. 40). Wolpe first used this approach with many patients but found that this response was inadequate for patients whose anxiety responses were associated with nonsocial stimuli (as in the classic phobias) or whose anxiety was aroused by the mere presence of certain groups of people, by being the center of attention, by a feeling of rejection, and so on. A more appropriate antagonistic response would be one in which no new behaviors need to be formed that would be at the mercy of reinforcement by other people.

Eventually Wolpe turned to relaxation as a widely applicable response antagonistic to anxiety. Although deep muscle relaxation has become an intrinsic feature of most systematic desensitization treatments, it is important to note that in principle Wolpe's theory permits use of any other antagonistic response. In fact, sexual behaviors, eating, or similar behaviors have been so employed, in addition to assertion and relaxation.

Before examining the theoretical and empirical issues of Wolpe's treatment, we shall consider in more detail the steps in the actual therapeutic procedure. Essentially, the technique involves three separate sets of operations: (1) training in deep muscle relaxation; (2) the construction of hierarchies of anxiety-eliciting stimuli; and (3) counterposing relaxation with the stimuli from the hierarchies.

The first two steps in systematic desensitization, relaxation training and hierarchy construction, are carried out in three to six initial sessions. Deep muscle relaxation, thought by Wolpe to be a response competitive to or inhibitory of anxiety, is usually an abbreviated version of Jacobson's (1938) training method. Jacobson's method involves alternate tensing and relaxing of successive gross muscle groups, on cue from the therapist, along with suggestions of pleasant affect and calmness. The second half of these early sessions is devoted to interviews in which the therapist acquaints himself with the patient's problems and, jointly with the patient, establishes the central stimulus complex currently provoking the patient's most intense anxiety reponses. Situations related (presumably along a generalization gradient) to this stimulus complex are ranked according to the degree of anxiety they elicit and are ordered at equal-appearing intervals into a stimulus hierarchy. Hierarchy items typically have in common a single theme (for example, snakes, assertion) or an approach gradient in time and space to one fixed target stimulus, or a combination of both. The items serve to provide anxiety-eliciting stimuli and are later presented to the patient when he is relaxed.

A mixed hierarchy dealing with test anxiety, in which type of test and proximity in time are both varied, is shown in Table 4-1. One advantage of imaginal over in vivo presentations is evident in this list—several items deal with internal events not available for in vivo presentation, such as thinking about being anxious. The numbers in the table are the patient's ratings, on two occasions, of the intensity of anxiety elicited by each item on a scale from 0 ("Totally relaxed") to 100 ("As tense as you ever are"). Similar ratings, often on a ten-point scale termed a Fear Thermometer, have been used in controlled studies of desensitization (Lang and Lazovik, 1963). As Table 4-1 demonstrates, equal-appearing intervals may be difficult to achieve, and in any case the ratings and hence item order may change during therapy. Considerable clinical skill is required for constructing adequate individual hierarchies, a task not yet as amenable to automation as are other steps in the desensitization process (Lang, 1968). This point is related to the earlier-mentioned low correlation among anxiety indices so that, for example, scores on the Fear Survey Schedule (Wolpe and Lang, 1964) showed low correlations with self-rating ($r = -0.04$), with overt avoidance ($r = -0.26$), and with observer's rating ($r = -0.14$) (Lang, 1968). Clearly, a patient's failure to describe adequately the degree to which situations actually arouse his fears would yield misleading hierarchies and reduce treatment efficacy. Similarly, case studies often note initial *failures,* which are ascribed to inadequate hierarchy construction. Wolpe (1966) describes a lawyer whose anxiety when speaking to an audience did not benefit from desensitization on a hierarchy involving speaking to groups of increasing size,

Table 4-1 A Mixed Desensitization Hierarchy for Test Anxiety[a]

Fear Ratings

First Ratings	Second Ratings	Hierarchy Items
0	0	Beginning a new course
15	10	Hearing an instructor announce a small quiz two weeks hence
20	25	Having a professor urge you personally to do well on an exam
35	40	Trying to decide how to study for an exam
40	45	Reviewing the material I know should be studied—listing study to do
60	50	Hearing an instructor remind the class of a quiz one week hence
60	65	Hearing an instructor announce a major exam in three weeks and its importance
75	75	Hearing an instructor announce a major exam in one week
80	70	Standing alone in the hall before an exam
80	80	Getting an exam back in class
80	80	Anticipating getting back a graded exam later that day
80	85	Talking to several students about an exam right before taking it
85	80	Thinking about being scared and anxious regarding a specific exam
90	85	Studying with fellow students several days before an exam
90	90	Hearing some "pearls" from another student which you doubt you'll remember, while studying in a group
90	90	Cramming while alone in the library right before an exam
90	95	Thinking about not keeping up in other subjects while preparing for an exam
95	90	Thinking about being anxious over schoolwork in general
95	95	Talking with several students about an exam immediately after
100	100	Thinking about being generally inadequately prepared
100	100	Thinking about not being adequately prepared for a particular exam
100	100	Studying the night before a big exam

[a] Ratings: 0 = Totally relaxed;
            100 = As tense as you ever are

but did respond to the use of a hierarchy dealing with humiliation in front of others, especially strangers.

In contrast to the clinical skill required for this step, relaxation training can be carried out by use of prerecorded tapes. Hypnosis, initially used for inducing relaxation, apparently contributes no special effect and is rarely used now. The nonspecific effects of a therapist-patient relationship at this stage in treatment also do not seem crucial for success. Drugs are sometimes used when relaxation is otherwise difficult to achieve, with apparent success and without the anticipated difficulties in generalization from drug to nondrug state, at least in the case of methohexitone sodium (Friedman, 1966; Friedman and Silverstone, 1967).

The third step is the desensitization proper. This begins with practice and evaluation of the patient's ability to imagine the hierarchy items vividly enough to provoke anxiety when relaxation is not present. Then the patient is induced to relax deeply, to imagine the lowest hierarchy item, and to signal the therapist the moment any slight cue of tension or discomfort is noted. If the patient signals, he is instructed to stop visualizing that item and to focus on relaxation or perhaps to imagine a pleasant scene. If the patient does not signal, the visualization continues for 10–15 seconds, is stopped, and relaxation alone is continued for 15–30 seconds. Then the item is presented a second or third time, after which the next item in the hierarchy is attempted. When an item evokes signaled tension, an item lower on the hierarchy may be repeated, or the distressing item is repeated until it evokes no tension for two or three presentations.

In vivo presentations may be used after items have been imaginally presented (Meyer and Gelder, 1963) or in place of imaginal presentations (for example, Wolpe, 1966). Slide projection has also been used as an alternative (Goldberg and D'Zurilla, 1968). Paul (1969a) has summarized many of the procedural variations and made recommendations for choice among them. According to Lazarus (1964), the most frequent procedural pitfalls leading to negative outcomes are in handling repeated signaling of tension on one item, adequate relaxation intervals between imagined scenes, the number of scenes presented per session, and the duration and spacing of sessions.

Controlled Experiments on Systematic Desensitization

Demonstration of the efficacy of most methods of psychotherapy has suffered from several disadvantages. Until the advent of the behavior therapies, the underlying theoretical framework of therapy was so complicated and often so logically inconsistent that it did not lend itself to specific predictions that could be put to experimental tests. Since the multiple facets of interactional behaviors in traditional verbal psychotherapy require of the therapist that he adjust his own behavior from moment to moment to match the patient's behavioral fluctuations, exact specifications for therapist activities were difficult to establish. Further, most dynamic therapies avow as their goal in treatment the restructure of the patient's personality. Such a complex construct provides little opportunity for quantitative measurement. Since it is often not the symptom that is attacked in dynamic therapies but some broader and often poorly specified characteristic of the patient's behavior, progress cannot be assessed by simple comparison of pre- and posttherapy performances on specified tasks, inventories, or behavioral situations. Most dynamic treatment methods suggest that changes occurring in the patient's behavior outside the treatment room are brought about by indirect efforts at modifying the patient's verbal and interpersonal behavior in the office. Since the specific behaviors to which treatment manipulations may show a generalized effect are usually not stated, neither a record nor an analysis of the effects of treatment can be obtained in a way that permits comparison of techniques across many patients. Despite these obstacles, largely due to the influence of Carl Rogers and other experimentally oriented clinicians, research on psychotherapeutic methods has been undertaken at a growing rate during the last two decades. Many experiments required use of analogue situations or analysis of small portions of the natural treatment sequence.

Wolpe's technique is especially well-suited for analysis by common experimental methods. The desensitization procedure is relatively standardized; the underlying theoretical assumptions can be fairly well described; the treatment goal is specified in advance of therapy; and the less ambitious piecemeal approach to reduction of symptomatic behaviors provides easy criteria for evaluating success of the treatment. All these factors have contributed to the availability of many excellent studies with this technique. On the following pages, selected studies will be reviewed in relation to the particular questions raised about the desensitization method. First, can the reputed effectiveness of systematic desensitization be demonstrated in the objective laboratory environment? Secondly, if such effectiveness is demonstrated, it still leaves the question of differentiating among the various features that make up the total treatment procedure. Therefore, which of the features of Wolpian therapy are necessary and sufficient for effectiveness? Finally, research of broader scope is needed to test the theoretical assumptions made about both the formation of the undesirable behavior *and* the means by which it is removed. The last point is of crucial importance because the effectiveness of a therapeutic method does not necessarily substantiate the theory about why it works nor the manner in which the symptom originates. As we have noted in Chapter 3, the demonstration, in Albert's fear of rabbits and Rachman's creation of shoe fetishists, of one possible way in which symptoms may develop does not suffice to guarantee the exclusiveness of the underlying model; nor can one deduce from it the sole treatment method. This logical inconsistency has also been pointed out by Davison (1967) in a well-needed reminder that knowledge about changing a phenomemon is not tantamount to knowledge about the process by which it is created. We must therefore be cautious in interpreting the following findings as supportive of a *treatment* effect and not of a theory about the genesis of human neuroses.

Treatment Effectiveness. Lang provided an ingenious vehicle for meeting most of the criteria for a laboratory test of the effectiveness of systematic desensitization. Although fear of snakes presents no urgent problem to most people, this fear is commonly encountered. In one to three out of a hundred college students, behavior associated with snakes meets all the criteria of a phobia. Lang and Lazovik (1963) set out to remove this phobia under experimental conditions. Their experiment had two purposes: to evaluate the effectiveness of systematic desensitization therapy in removing the phobia, and to determine whether the accoutrements of the reciprocal inhibition technique, that is, training in deep muscle relaxation, hypnosis, and good rapport with the therapist, alone would produce such changes. Twenty-four snake-phobic students were selected on the basis of a classroom questionnaire. These students reported such somatic disturbances as tenseness, sweaty palms, and stomach upsets in the presence of snakes. They reported avoidance of the reptile section of the zoo and upset reactions at the sight of snakes, even when viewed on television or in the movies. The authors tested the phobic behavior both by questionnaires and by directly confronting the subject with a nonpoisonous snake confined in a glass case in the laboratory. The subject was asked to approach the snake when he was at a distance of fifteen feet from the glass case. The actual distance at which the subject refused to proceed was recorded, as well as his ratings of his fear at that point.

The experimental groups then participated in a series of sessions during which an anxiety-hierarchy was constructed, the subjects were trained in deep muscle relaxation, and finally were introduced to hypnosis and were taught to visualize vividly. The control groups went through the same procedure. At the completion of this training both experimental and control groups were again tested on inventories and with the approach test in the laboratory. The experimental groups then were given a series of systematic desensitization sessions. In the final test, the written inventory and the laboratory test with the live snake were supplemented by extensive interviews. A follow-up test was conducted six months after termination of the "treatment." The effectiveness of the desensitization treatment was clearly shown by the significant difference in number of subjects who held or touched a snake during the avoidance test period. Over half of the experimental group subjects now handled the snake, while in the control group less than 25 percent passed this test. At the six months posttest, the experimental group continued to show gains on the avoidance test, although two subjects relapsed. On the self-report measures the experimental groups showed a decrease in reported fear when compared with the control subjects, but the difference between groups did not attain statistical significance. After the six-month interval, however, a significantly greater decrease in self-reported fears was found in the experimental groups than in the control groups.

The identification of the desensitization procedure as the essential ingredient in Wolpe's reciprocal inhibition technique was shown by the fact that no significant effects were obtained from relaxation and hypnosis alone. Since all experimental subjects were restricted to a standard eleven therapy sessions, some did not complete the 20-item hierarchy. When Lang and Lazovik further analysed their data, they found that those subjects who had completed over 15 items showed significant improvement on nearly all measures employed in the experiment, while subjects who completed less than 15 items differed little from controls.

In a second study, Lang, Lazovik, and Reynolds (1965) repeated essentially the same design except that they included a "pseudotherapy" group. This group was relaxed during the therapy interviews and their hierarchy items were discussed. But the therapist avoided presentation of anxiety-provoking stimuli and guided conversation toward pleasant experiences. The pseudotherapy group was under the impression that they were undergoing a form of dynamic or interpretive therapy. The results of the second study were clear-cut. Neither the controls nor the pseudotherapy subjects showed any significant reduction in phobic behavior. These results suggest that fear reduction after desensitization cannot be attributed to a common placebo factor associated with participation in therapy. Hypnosis, muscle relaxation training, hierarchy building, and the general therapeutic context also did not alone produce changes in the phobic behavior. These studies substantiate the pragmatic utility of Wolpe's procedure. Beyond that, they also stand as clear-cut demonstrations that circumscribed phobic responses can be reduced without knowledge of the presumed causes, and that treatment of a specific pathological behavior pattern does not require elaborate probing into the subjects' attitudes and life experiences. Indeed, to the contrary, a *generalized* reduction of anxiety and an improvement in overall adjustment apparently follows this seemingly narrow treatment approach (Paul and Shannon, 1966). Later work by Lang and his colleagues showed that concurrent reduction of other fears not directly treated by desensitization occurs as a function of their similarity to or correlation with the stimuli that are treated (Lang, 1969).

Paul (1966) investigated the effectiveness of systematic desensitization with another fear commonly encountered in college students, the fear of public speaking. Paul's experiment is of note because it stands among the best controlled studies yet to appear in the area of psychotherapy. Five groups of carefully matched students were exposed to (1) systematic desensitization, (2) traditional insight therapy, (3) a pseudotherapy procedure, (4) a no-treatment control, and (5) a no-contact control. The comparison therapies were carried out by experienced psychotherapists who conducted their customary type of insight therapy in that group, followed a program of suggestion and support in the pseudotherapy group, and conducted desensitization sessions after training by the experimenter. Each student received five therapeutic sessions. The results represented an independent verification of the Lang and Lazovik data. The desensitization group made greater progress in reduction of their phobia, as indicated by subjective reports, measures of physiological arousal, and ratings of their behavior in a class of public speaking.

Paul's major contribution lies not only in replication of previously reported findings with a different phobia but also in the demonstration of the greater effectiveness of this procedure in comparison to traditionally practiced insight therapy. Despite the elaborate care in Paul's design, some questions still remain. For example, the experienced therapists had probably not followed a carefully outlined stepwise procedure in practicing their own therapeutic style, while their training in desensitization was recent and highly specific. Also, traditional psychotherapy is usually conducted over many sessions and the initial establishment of rapport has been considered a vital though time-consuming prerequisite. In five sessions these techniques may not have been put to a fair test. Despite these and other questions raised by the experiment, there is no doubt that the findings of Lang and his colleagues and of Paul demonstrate the usefulness of systematic desensitization. They do so strictly by empirical demonstration of the therapeutic power of desensitization. Neither the underlying assumptions about the development of neurotic behavior, which go with Wolpe's theory, nor the particular learning mechanisms said to occur in desensitization were tested by these studies, although relaxation and hierarchy construction were shown to be insufficient in themselves to produce the effect.

The conduct of analogue studies on effectiveness of therapy in healthy college student volunteers always runs the risk that the positive results may not be generalizable to different populations and different symptom targets, for example, patients who have intense fears and poor psychological adjustment. Desensitization effects, however, have been demonstrated in psychiatric populations in a series of studies by Gelder, Marks, and their collaborators (Cooper, Gelder, and Marks, 1965; Gelder and Marks,

1966; Marks and Gelder. 1965). In comparison with traditional individual and group psychotherapy methods using insight, interpretations, transference, and similar techniques, desensitization achieved earlier and greater reduction of anxiety and other improvements in behavioral efficiency. Extent of positive outcome was related to the severity of the initial complaints. No appearance of new, "substituted" symptoms was encountered. These clinical studies suggest complex interactions between symptom-relief and other aspects of the patient's behavioral history and his adjustment. For example, greater and more rapid improvement in work and leisure adjustment was found with desensitization. Desensitization and group therapy both produced improvements in interpersonal relationships, but in the former this occurred after symptom change, while in the latter it took place without symptom change (Gelder, Marks, Wolff, and Clarke, 1967).

Why Does Systematic Desensitization Work? Once the clinical effectiveness of desensitization therapy had been demonstrated, investigators turned to examination of the process involved in desensitization. The nonspecific factors of therapy, that is, effects of the therapeutic relationship, suggestions, and therapist's personality were shown to be insufficient to produce the therapeutic benefits, by the studies described above. In fact, patients can be trained to administer hierarchies at home from tape recordings (Migler and Wolpe, 1967) and automation of this procedure is under way. Lang (1968) has reported use of a Device for Automated Desensitization, fondly known as DAD, which stores hierarchy and relaxation instructions on magnetic tape. It automatically presents instructions in hypnosis, relaxation, and the items of the prerecorded hierarchy in sequence. The items can be presented a given number of times and terminated by indicants of the subject's distress. The procedure closely duplicates all procedural features of desensitization without the presence of a therapist. Accumulating research with this device suggests that the interpersonal relationship is not necessary for effective treatment.

Kahn and Baker (1968) assigned volunteer college students with mild phobias to a conventional desensitization or to a "do-it-yourself" group. The experimental group received one interview in which a hierarchy was constructed. They were then given a do-it-yourself kit to take home. For the next six weeks, the only contact with the therapist was once weekly by phone. The students' kit, consisting of a manual and an LP phonograph record, was sufficiently complete to permit an average of two weekly sessions during the experiment, at home and without the experimenter's aid. The conventional desensitization group met for 12 thirty-minute sessions. Although the procedure is interesting, the results are difficult to interpret. Three months after the end of treatment all subjects were interviewed by telephone. On the basis of this conversation, the subjects' status and improvement were rated. The authors report that all of the six subjects in the experimental group improved, while five of the seven students in the conventional group showed improvement. Since these data are based on the therapist's rating of phone reports of students with phobias of varying severity and types, there are so many possible variables that could affect the results that they are practically useless. Experimenter bias, untruthful reports, or verbal influence in the interview are a few of the uncontrolled variables. Nevertheless, the study serves to describe the trend toward increased detachment of the procedure from the relationship to the therapist. In later sections we see that the independence of the treatment from the therapist's role is not accepted by many investigators.

On the other side of the picture, there have been many suggestions that the role of the therapist cannot be disregarded. In addition to the facilitative effects of the presence of a nonjudgmental professional person, the subtle effects of encouragement, praise, or other guiding comments may constitute the therapeutic elements of verbal reinforcement for the patient's fear-conquering behavior. Leitenberg, Agras, Barlow, and Oliveau (1969) compared three groups of snake-phobic female college students. The groups were divided into (1) those who received the standard desensitization treatment (including instructions suggesting the effectiveness of the treatment and praise for successful completion of hierarchy items); (2) those who received relaxation and graded hierarchy presentation, but without indication in the instructions that therapeutic benefits may occur, and without reinforcement for progress; and (3) those who did not receive treatment between testing sessions. The same 27 items containing snake scenes were used for all subjects. The actual approach behavior to a live snake was measured before and after treatment. During the treatment, GSR measures were also taken. The authors reported a greater magnitude of increase for the snake approach behavior in group (1) than group (2), although both groups showed reduction in snake-phobic behavior. For group (2) this change was not much superior than for the control group (3). The authors argue that, if selective reinforcement and therapeutically oriented instructions are customarily part of the desensitization procedure, then the theoretical explanations of the mechanisms underlying the technique are brought into question. We will return to this point later in the chapter, after examination of other studies testing the theoretical model of desensitization. At this time, the study is noted for the evidence that the therapist, deliberately or not, can affect treatment success, even if the preceding studies suggest that his presence may not be critical.

An incidental finding of Leitenberg et al. is also of interest. During desensitization it was found that verbal reports by the patient (such as stating that he feels anxious) occurred on a greater percentage of hierarchy items than did GSR responses. These findings are consistent with our earlier discussion of the lack of a high correspondence between verbal and physiological indicants of anxiety. They also confirm the results reported in several other investigations which are reviewed in this chapter, that verbal reports tend to change more slowly during desensitization than physiological or behavioral measures.

What of the specific steps in systematic desensitization? A number of investigators have assessed the contribution of relaxation to outcome, with the general conclusion that it enhances positive results and hence is, for the present, a desirable part of the desensitization package, but that its physiological role as a competitor to anxiety is less well established as yet. The technique of placing a phobic person at a distant point from the object of his fear has been reported in the clinical literature for many years. Dorcus and Shaffer (1945) describe this technique under the term *desensitization* and suggest that repeated exposure to the phobic object in gradually increasing doses may be therapeutically effective. In some cases, clinicians have reported success with this technique when they accompanied the patient to the site of his phobia and gradually increased the duration of his presence amidst the fear-arousing stimuli. This clinical procedure, however, does not require or deliberately utilize the clinician's presence to serve the antianxiety function of Wolpe's relaxation response.

Rachman (1965b) assigned psychiatric subjects with known spider phobias to four groups: desensitization with relaxation, desensitization without relaxation, relaxation only, and no treatment controls. We have already seen from Lang's research that relaxation alone does not produce significant changes in the phobic behavior. Rachman's procedure explored the question whether desensitization alone might be effective. There are good reasons for expecting some effectiveness for desensitization alone, since the essential ingredient could well be simple extinction. Rachman's spider-phobic subjects showed marked reductions on avoidance tests and subjective reports only when desensitization was accompanied by relaxation. The author concludes that "neither relaxation nor desensitization is effective in its own right. The catalytic effect of the two procedures is greater than their separate actions. It means also that the learning process involved is probably conditioned inhibition rather than extinction. This is not meant to imply that extinction is never responsible for a reduction of fear. In the present context, however, inhibition is a more effective process" (Rachman, 1965b, p. 250). Subsequent studies, reviewed by Rachman (1968), showed that muscular relaxation training was not always required for therapeutic effects. Further, experimenters who gave a few or only a single muscular relaxation training session (compared with six sessions recommended by Wolpe) also reported successes (see, for example, Cooke, 1966). When actual phobic objects are used (in vivo desensitization), the presence of the feared object surely keeps the patient physically active and makes it quite unlikely that muscular relaxation is maintained. Finally, observations of muscle action by electrical recordings during desensitization indicate that subjects may report calmness and relaxation while their recorded muscle tension shows no decline. These lines of evidence have led Rachman (1968) to reconsider the problem in a later paper. He proposed that *muscular* relaxation may not be a necessary part of systematic desensitization, although it probably facilitates the treatment. Instead, a feeling of calmness or relaxation may constitute the main active therapeutic ingredient. A similar view, based on observation of the continued anxiety in subjects whose muscles are "relaxed" by the drug *curare,* is reviewed later in this chapter. Davison (1966) also suggested that a pleasant affective state, rather than muscle relaxation, can be incompatible with anxiety. Rachman's later paper thus proposes that the *muscular* relaxation technique is only one method for achieving the necessary state of "mental relaxation" antagonistic to anxiety, and that many *cognitive* procedures could accomplish the same goal. This change in method would not affect Wolpe's basic theoretical proposition concerning the inhibition of anxiety by an incompatible response.

The role of relaxation can also be explored by asking whether it is a *sufficient* instead of necessary condition for therapeutic success. Johnson and Sechrest (1968) compared the effects of desensitization and relaxation training in test-anxious college students. It was hypothesized that the beneficial effects due to counter-conditioning would be found only in the desensitization group. The investigators found that final examination grades (in a psychology course from which all subjects were drawn) of the students who had previously suffered from debilitating anxiety on examinations, significantly improved in the desensitization group. The relaxation group did not differ from a no-treatment control group.

Relaxation without pairing with a hierarchy has been found to be as effective as systematic desensitization in reducing interview anxiety in schizophrenic patients (Zeisset, 1968). This study is of special interest since it is one of the few involving psychotic subjects and confirms the superiority of desensitization over placebo-attention and no treatment with this patient group. Zeisset not only trained his relaxation-without-desensitization subjects in progressive relaxation but also instructed them in how to use relaxation in vivo when in stressful situations. Thus, as the author himself notes, Zeisset's results do not seem incompatible with a counter-conditioning role for the relaxation, since the relaxation-only subjects may have had in vivo practice equivalent to the relaxation-CS pairing experienced by the desensitization subjects.

In a different vein, competing responses other than relaxation have been often advocated (such as sex and assertion, by Wolpe and Lazarus) and less often tested. In an uncontrolled case study of seven phobics, Solyom and Miller (1967) used relief from aversive shock in place of relaxation, pairing presentations of stimuli via photographs and tape recordings with the termination of shock. Six of the seven patients were symptom-free at follow-up.

Davison (1968b) tested the hypothesis that systematic desensitization involves a counter-conditioning process, with the rationale that such a process is sufficiently described by the contiguous association of a graded anxiety-provoking stimuli and incompatible relaxation responses. The further assumption made by Wolpe, that the antagonistic response *suppressed* the anxiety responses, appeared to be unnecessary since the counter-conditioning hypothesis is by far the simpler one and directly derived from Guthrie's learning theory. Instead of presuming the reduction or suppression of the anxiety responses, the counter-conditioning hypothesis directly ascribes the obtained effects to the process of substitution of the stronger incompatible positive response for the weaker anxiety reaction.

Female college students with a snake phobia were assigned to one of four groups. One group received systematic desensitization. In a second, "pseudodesensitization," group, treatment was identical to the desensitization procedure except that the content of the imagined stimuli paired with relaxation was essentially neutral and irrelevant to snakes. A third "exposure" group was presented the same series of graded aversive items but in the absence of deep relaxation. This condition served as a control for extinction effects from repeated exposure to the conditioned aversive stimuli. A no-treatment control group participated only in the pre- and posttherapy tests of their fear behavior. Davison further controlled progress in the pseudodesensitization and exposure groups during treatment by yoking them to partners in the desensitization group. By this design the number of treatment sessions, the duration of each session, the number of stimulus exposures per session, and the duration of each exposure were equated for the three main comparison groups. While this seems an admirable control, it also raises difficulties in interpretation of the results, since only the systematic desensitization group proceeded according to each individual's idosyncratic pace. The members of the pseudodesensitization group may have found the procedure, to which they signaled more anxiety than did the experimental group, especially aversive since their pace was externally controlled. The posttherapy test was carried out three days after completion of treatment. If temporal conjunction of relaxation and anxiety-provoking stimuli are sufficient for the attachment of new and less disturbing responses to the snake-related stimuli, Davison argued, then only the desensitization subjects should show improvement.

Table 4-2 summarizes Davison's findings. Matched cluster refers to each yoked set of subjects and the data are the change scores for each subject on a 13-item behavioral test.

It is clear that in each replication, except cluster 5, the subject in the desensitization group made greater improvements. In cluster 6 this improvement was exceeded by the pseudodesensitization subject. The statistical analyses showed significantly more snake-approach behavior in the systematic desensitization group than in any other group.

Of theoretical interest is Davison's observation that the desensitization subjects were able to handle snakes after treatment but that their reported anxiety remained high, although reduced from pretreatment levels, the decrement in reported anxiety being significantly correlated with amount of overt behavioral improvement. This finding, also mentioned by other investigators, raises interesting questions about the role of the subject's self-instructions and the correlation between motor activity and intensity of emotional arousal as well as about the independence or mediation role of anxiety with respect to avoidance behavior. Although it is commonly assumed that a person's action is determined by his subjective experiences, recent behavioral formulations of self-reactions have suggested an alternate possibility. The overt actions of a person may affect his subsequent feelings and reports about his emotional arousal, as well. In the previously cited study by Leitenberg et al. (1969), the authors speculate

Table 4-2   Changes in Snake-Approach Behavior Displayed by
Subjects in Each of the Treatment Conditions
(from Davison, 1968b)

Matched Cluster of Yoked Subjects	Treatment Condition			
	Desensitization	Pseudo-Desensitization	Exposure	No Treatment
Cluster 1	3	2	2	0
Cluster 2	3	−1	0	—
Cluster 3	6	0	−1	−1
Cluster 4	5	1	−5	0
Cluster 5	0	1	2	—
Cluster 6	6	8	1	0
Cluster 7	12	0	0	—
Cluster 8	7	1	1	—
Mean	5.25	1.50	0.0	−0.25

that the reinforcement group may have benefited from the feedback contained in the instructions and verbal reinforcement. These sources of information enable the patient to observe his own behavior more adequately. In turn "such *self-observed* signs of improvement may account for much of the success of all graded behavioral therapies, not only systematic desensitization" (p. 118). We shall consider this issue in greater detail in connection with our discussion of self-regulation in Chapter 9. In our appraisal of the relevance of this issue to systematic desensitization, however, we must remember that the correlation between a person's description of his attitudes or emotional state and his actual execution of the behavior may vary as a function of the specific conditions under which each of these two behaviors take place.

Although many studies have compared groups in which some element of the common desensitization procedure was removed from the standard treatment, few have attempted to test the role of several components at once. Cooke (1968) examined changes in behavior toward laboratory rats in female college students, who showed high fear of rats. He also selected subjects who had a high general anxiety score, thus reducing the variable effects of one important personality factor that had been generally disregarded in previous studies. Five groups were formed, (1) desensitization (standard), (2) desensitization without relaxation, (3) relaxation, (4) hierarchy construction, and (5) no-treatment control. The results indicated that neither hierarchy construction nor relaxation alone produced reduction in fear. Both desensitization groups, (1) and (2), showed less fear in the approach test (looking, holding, and touching a rat) after treatment. This finding is consistent with Rachman's hypothesis, described above, concerning the role of muscular relaxation. However, Cooke found no therapeutic effects on responses to the Fear Survey Schedule and judgments by observers of the subjects' behavior in the fear situation, in any of the groups. Consistent with other investigators, Cooke found that subjects who completed the full hierarchy showed less fear on the approach test than those who failed to complete all items.

The Role of the Stimulus

Wolpe originally utilized actual stimulus objects to represent hierarchy items. In present practice, instruction to the patient to imagine a scene is employed most widely. The use of the patient's imagery as an inferred stimulus event creates great theoretical problems. After all, once the therapist relinquishes control over the presentation of stimulational events, he cannot be sure what stimuli occur in conjunction with the relaxation response, nor can he ascertain whether his intended therapeutic operations are carried out. It is not inconceivable that a subject might imagine a pleasant and restful landscape when instructed to visualize an embarrassing social situation or a bloody automobile accident. On the other hand, a patient who is inclined to be overzealous might well visualize a more intensely arousing scene, thus skipping items in the prepared hierarchy. Further, there are obvious individual differences with regard to a patient's readiness to indicate an unpleasant state of arousal by signaling this state to the therapist with a raised finger. Broad patterns in the subject's tendency to conform with behaviors that he may regard as socially desirable for the given situation may lead him to raise his finger too soon or too late. While the theoretical problems are not resolved by empirical evidence of the equivalent effectiveness of visualized and actual stimulus objects, such demonstrations do aid in reassuring the therapist that his clinical operations are probably conforming to the systematic desensitization paradigm with most patients.

Some partial answers to the thorny question of the nature of the stimulus in systematic desensitization have been offered by studies that compare imaginal and in vivo presentation of anxiety-arousing items. Cooke (1966) used female college students with a well-established intense fear of laboratory rats as his subjects. After assessment of intensity of the specific phobia, Cooke selected subjects with the highest phobic scores and further divided them into high and low general anxiety groups on the basis of the Bendig emotionality scale. This selection reduced the subject population to twelve students. The six subjects with high anxiety scores and the six with low anxiety scores were randomly assigned to each of three treatment conditions, leaving two subjects in each cell: direct deconditioning (rat present), imaginal deconditioning (rat absent), and control. The experimental subjects were seen for four consecutive therapy sessions at three-day intervals. The control group received no treatment. The two experimental groups went through a relaxation phase and the usual desensitization procedure, except that for the direct deconditioning subjects a live rat was used in an actual execution of the appropriate anxiety hierarchy item. Posttreatment measures were given five days after the last therapy session and consisted of readministration of questionnaires and laboratory presentation of a rat.

Both experimental groups showed comparable improvement on all of the measures, in contrast to lack of change in the control subjects. The method of stimulus presentation did not significantly affect the magnitude of fear decrement. Cooke further reports an interaction between the treatment method and general anxiety level. Although the groups did not differ under in vivo treatment, the high anxiety subjects showed a significantly greater decrease in fear on two measures under imaginal treatment. This finding is of interest because it alerts the researcher to the possibility that personality variables may interact with treatment effectiveness. The finding also adds a note of caution regarding generalization from analogue studies to clinical populations whose general anxiety level will be higher on the average. However, the small numbers of subjects used in this study permit only guarded interpretation of this finding. Further, Eysenck and Rachman (1965) and others indicate that high general anxiety impedes or prevents systematic desensitization. In this light the relationship of this variable is as yet quite unclear, although clearly important in clinical practice. A further artifact is introduced in Cooke's procedure by the fact that subjects were standing in the in vivo group and sitting in the imaginal group. Since muscle relaxation is the presumed competing response, difference in position would affect the nature and extent of accomplished muscle relaxation, and hence of treatment outcome.

A slightly different approach to the problem can be made by establishing the degree of arousal during instructed visualization. When hierarchy items are presented in random order, while a spider phobic subject is relaxed, changes in heart rate are correlated with the hierarchy level of the item (Lang, 1969). Grossberg and Wilson (1967) also tested the assumption implicit in Wolpe's reciprocal inhibition hypothesis that imagining an item from the anxiety hierarchy should be accompanied by physiological reactions characteristically associated with anxiety. The investigators compared changes in heart rate, skin conductance, and forehead muscle activity in female college students who had not been relaxed and were instructed to imagine fearful or neutral situations. Neutral and disturbing items were selected from the Fear Survey Schedule and scenes composed by the experimental subject for both sets of items. After an initial adaptation interval, the subject was asked to visualize a scene that was read to her. Neutral and fear scenes were presented four times with 25 seconds allowed for each visualization. To control for any cues conveyed by the experimenter's voice in reading the fear scenes in a more exciting or arousing way, tape recordings of the experimenter's delivery were played to an additional group of subjects who had previously indicated no fear on either scene on their questionnaires. While the experimenter's reading of the fear scene was no more arousing than his reading of a neutral scene, the instructions to imagine fear scenes produced significantly more physiological arousal than instructions to imagine neutral scenes. It would seem that self-produced stimulation, occasioned by instructions to imagine fear scenes, produced more activation than similar stimulation presented by the experimenter's voice.

Of further interest is the finding of an adaptation effect in heart rate and skin conductance over repeated reading trials, and for skin conductance during successive imagining. These results suggest that repeated presentation of the fear scenes results in a decrease in their arousal potential, that is, that repeated presentations alone lead to some extinction of the physiological responses. The control groups also showed significant conductance differences between fearful and neutral scenes during reading and for skin conductance and heart rate during imagining. These findings suggest that the content or the mode of presentation of fear scenes could have produced differential arousal and is confounded with the subject's estimate of the fearfulness of the scenes. However, it also suggests confirmation of the hypothesis that instructions to imagine tend to generate measurable and reliable increases in tension.

In spite of some inconsistencies in the results, the study generally supports the conclusion that visualization does have some measurable effects on subjects. The study illustrates the type of research necessary to understand what specific effects, if any, instructions to imagine may have on the subjects, a question crucial to an understanding of the processes operating in systematic desensitization. Grossberg and Wilson's findings remain tentative because of the reported inconsistencies.

Work done by Wilson (1966) suggests that a major difficulty might lie in the selection of normal students for assessment of arousal. Wilson selected "apparently normal" young adults who were instructed to watch a series of colored slides of landscapes, spiders, and snakes. The scenes were exposed for one second with a 15-second interval between slides. Skin resistance was continuously monitored. Wilson reports no significant difference in GSR magnitude for responses to the three picture types, and concludes that normal subjects do not give differential GSRs to different stimulus categories in this situation. However, Wilson then selected two phobic patients. A 32-year-old woman with a cat phobia was shown a series of assorted animal pictures, including one of a white cat. GSR responses to the cat picture were consistently in a considerably higher range of magnitude than responses to other pictures. Wilson notes that the woman's ratings of pictures of tigers, rats, and snakes as "very disturbing" did not correlate with a comparable GSR response, another example of the low correlation between physiological and self-report measures. A 21-year-old woman with a spider phobia was similarly tested by presentation of pictures of landscapes and spiders. The GSR was again quite high in response to the spider pictures. However, with this subject the effects on the GSR of repeated exposure of the fear stimuli were noticeable. The response decrement over successive sessions was so great that at the end of the fourth session, the GSR to spider and landscape responses were almost identical. These findings are consistent with the observations of Grossberg and Wilson in the previously cited study.

The meager evidence of the fate of physiological indices of the anxiety state does not appear to match the behavioral findings reviewed earlier.

While several studies have indicated that behavioral measures do not show a decrement in response to the phobic stimulus simply as a function of repeated exposure, the physiological indices do seem to show adaptation after repeated exposure. It is obvious that further clarification of the course of physiological arousal during desensitization is required in order to confirm the reciprocal inhibition hypothesis that anxiety weakens only when antagonistic responses are simultaneously carried out.

Is Gradual "Dosing" of Anxiety Necessary? Two lines of evidence can be called upon in debating the merits of a gradually progressive approach to full strength of symptomatic anxiety. Animal experiments have varied extinction procedures either by massing extinction trials or by introducing the CS at a lower intensity than originally present in acquisition and gradually increasing it in strength. The net results of these two techniques are the same. Rats who are extinguished with the CS initially at low strength and then increased gradually until the CS reaches its original intensity extinguish more completely than animals to whom the CS is immediately presented at full strength (Kimble and Kendall. 1953). The term "flooding" is used by Polin (1959) for the opposite technique of long-lasting continuous CS stimulation in extinction, in which the avoidance response could occur. Compared to a group that had briefer exposure to the CS on extinction trials and was not permitted to make the avoidance response, the flooding group showed the greatest amount of extinction.

The fundamental importance of *gradual* desensitization in Wolpe's technique similarly contrasts with a group of clinical techniques involving immediate full exposure to the anxiety stimuli or to as severely arousing a situation as the patient can tolerate. These procedures are based on the assumption that the greatest efficacy of extinction procedures in humans is obtained when the original traumatic situation is reinstated in full intensity, or in concentrated periods of ascending intensity. Unfortunately, many of the early clinical reports of these techniques are not controlled studies and involve very few subjects. More recently, Ramsey, Barends, Breuker, and Kruseman (1966) desensitized college students with phobias for various animals, reptiles, or insects. In one group 20 items from the fear hierarchy were submitted to subjects in a 20-minute period. In the massed-practice group a 40-minute session was used to cover 40 items. The results suggest the superiority of the spaced group but are very equivocal because of the inadequate statistical analyses and because actual trials per minute did not differ in the two groups. Although the authors themselves qualify their conclusions, this study has been cited by others as indicating the greater efficiency of distributive practice.

In a study of several variations on desensitization procedures, Wolpin and Raines (1966) reported successful extinction of an avoidance response without use of graded stimuli or relaxation in two snake-phobic women. The clinical observations of these authors are of interest because they repeat the observations that we have previously made concerning the discrepancy between the patient's description of his own fear attitude and his actions. Wolpin and Raines describe the behavior of one snake-phobic patient as follows: "She proceeded to take the snake and play with it. She was rapidly proceeding to pet it and clearly seemed to enjoy it. All the while she expressed amazement at her behavior, saying things like 'I'm holding a snake—I don't believe it.' She let it crawl on her lap and in her arms with no signs of discomfort at all. She wondered that maybe her other fears, which she experienced as tremendous, were really small, as had apparently been demonstrated by the speed with which she conquered the seemingly huge fear of snakes" (p. 34).

Rachman (1966b) used the flooding technique with three spider-phobic female students. In contrast to the results of Wolpin and Raines and others, subjects in the flooding group showed no improvement, while a comparison group undergoing usual desensitization treatment showed considerable improvement. Wilson (1967) notes that the discrepancy between the findings of Rachman, and Wolpin and Raines can be due to differences in experimental procedure. While Wolpin and Raines instructed their subjects to consider their practice as training for overcoming their fear of snakes, Rachman encouraged full emotional arousal. Wilson believes that Rachman's subjects were imagining frightening situations and *rehearsing fear responses* in these situations. On the other hand, Wolpin and Raines' subjects were prepared to rehearse coping behaviors, overcoming their revulsion during the imagined scenes, in a fashion parallel to the work of Lazarus and his associates described earlier.

Avoidance in Phobias and Its Extinction. As we saw earlier in this chapter, the reinforcement mechanisms that maintain avoidance responses are by no means clear even in the case of the laboratory rat, nor are the differences in extinction strategies. Of special relevance, then, for systematic desensitization is the issue of the nature of any avoidance response by the patient, and of the reinforcement process that maintains his phobic anxiety. Certainly, until the evidence is clearer in controlled laboratory studies, we cannot expect to answer these questions in clinical cases. But we have seen that the analogue and clinical studies of the contribution of relaxation to desensitization do shed light on whether the technique acts as an extinction or a counter-conditioning procedure. Related animal studies, constructed as partial analogues, suggest that an instrumental avoidance response is rapidly extinguished when the avoidance response is *prevented* in the presence of the CS prior to initiation of extinction trials (see for example, Baum, 1966). These studies also suggest that traditional extinction is as effective or even more effective than counter-conditioning procedures in eliminating avoidance responses, but that the more a response competitive to the avoidance is evoked and reinforced, the more *rapidly* the avoidance behavior is eliminated (Gambrill, 1967). However, as Gambrill notes, both punishment and counter-conditioning produce an immediate response suppression, but when they are removed (for example, when the competing response is no longer available), the rate of avoidance responding increases again. Hence, unlike flooding or the gradual "dosing" procedures of Wolpe, and Kimble and Kendall, counter-conditioning and punishment do not increase susceptibility to extinction. Gambrill concludes, as have others, that extinction aided by gradual exposure to the CS is the effective ingredient in reduction of avoidance responding, a conclusion counter to that of the clinical studies showing more favorable outcomes when relaxation is used in conjunction with the graded hierarchy.

Lomont and Edwards (1967) investigated the relative efficacy of systematic desensitization and extinction in snake-phobic college students. Lomont and Edwards carefully equated the two experimental groups so that they differed only in that the desensitization group was required to engage in muscle relaxation in the presence of the imagined anxiety hierarchy items while the extinction group tensed their muscles during this time. Lomont and Edwards found that contiguity of relaxation and anxiety hierarchy item presentation resulted in significantly greater reduction on all measures of the snake fear. The study is of interest, however, for another reason. In contrast to research reported by other investigators, the extinction group showed no decrement in the snake fear at all. In fact, there was a slight increase on two of the measures. Since muscle tension induced during imagining of the snake-related items might actually have duplicated or facilitated some degree of emotional arousal, subjects in this group may have actually undergone additional fear acquisition trials. Lomont and Edwards interpreted their results as evidence that relaxation is crucial to systematic desensitization, thereby supporting the basic assumptions of the reciprocal inhibition paradigm.

Lomont (1965), in reviewing animal studies of counter-conditioning versus extinction in reducing avoidance behaviors, decided that there was no evidence conclusively favoring counter-conditioning, but that at least one study, by Sollod and Sturmfels (1965), did favor counter-conditioning over extinction in the elimination of *fear* (as opposed to avoidance). Interestingly, then, the area in which animal evidence is clearest, that is, the value of gradual emergence or graded CS exposure, is least well examined in clinical studies of desensitization. Whereas for the issue of counter-conditioning versus extinction, the basic animal findings are more equivocal than are the clinical studies, though both are not finally settled.

The studies of the contribution of relaxation and of a graded stimulus hierarchy ultimately confront us with the question raised at the beginning of this section. Why doesn't phobic behavior extinguish in the patients at least at the same slow rate as it does in animals? Perhaps patients are not, in their daily life, in a true extinction situation: merely the occasional occurrence of the UCS could maintain the symptom. In the laboratory, it has been shown that as many as 70 percent of the UCS presentations can be omitted without decrement in the CR (Boren and Sidman, 1957). Or the avoidance response may occur at the very earliest indication of any potentially anxiety-arousing situation so that exposure to the CS may rarely occur. For example, in the case of the house-bound housewife the occasion for interpersonal stress is minimized, and the snake-phobic person, who avoids even walking in the woods, is unlikely to encounter snakes. Or random UCS presentations, unconnected with the CS, may maintain the avoidance CR (Sidman, Herrnstein, and Conrad, 1957).

However, some conditioned anxieties appear not to extinguish even though no avoidance response is apparent. At least this would appear to be the case, for example, with some of the fears that have been favored targets for researchers. In test and public speaking phobias, the victims may go right on taking exams or answering in class, receiving no apparent UCS and yet continuing to experience severe anxiety. Persons with fear of snakes, spiders, or rats usually complain of escape, not avoidance responses, the former maintained despite the absence of any clear aversive consequences other than the fear itself when the creature appears.

It would appear that the conflicting evidence regarding the effective mechanisms in desensitization may reflect differences in the nature and availability and timing of any avoidance response, a facet more often presumed than directly studied in clinical investigations. Table 4-3 sums up the most common situations that have been treated by desensitization. It is apparent from this table that the consequences about which the subject complains can be quite different. The CR ranges from outright avoidance to reduced efficiency due to a number of competing responses, often not obviously connected with the CS. Although in animals it is the avoidance response that is most often measured, in humans one or several criteria of fear (not always well correlated with each other, and therefore giving conflicting results) are frequently used as measures of the effect of the CS. Lang, Paul, and others do include measures of approach behavior to the fear-arousing object. Thus their research can be more easily described by the avoidance paradigm. A further obscuring variable sometimes is the UCS intensity, since there are suggestions that counter-conditioning, or extinction plus punishment of avoidance, may be more effective than extinction alone when a very intense UCS is involved.

Table 4-3 Speculations About Fears Investigated in Analogue and Clinical Studies

CS	Context Stimuli	CR	UCS	Contact Frequency	Life effects and Anxiety Level	Symptom Complained of
Snakes, spiders, bugs in "normals"	Appearance un- expected, movement unpredictable, naturalistic surroundings	Escape	Difficult to guess, maybe R of model	Relatively rare in vivo or in imagination	Usually mini- mal, general anxiety low	Escape and fear
Classic phobias	Stimuli broadly generalized usually	Avoid all CS and situations with risk of CS	Presumed trauma	Very frequent in vivo and in imagination, but avoidance often eludes anxiety	Greatly re- stricting, gen- eral anxiety high	Avoidance responses
Test or per- formance	Stimuli are spe- cific but may occur in many contexts, for example, any written test	Anxiety with reduced effec- tiveness— often avoid- ance is mini- mal in vivo, but may be great as R to symbolic S, for example, avoid or escape studying for test	Possibly failure, humiliation— but this is often delayed	Frequent in vivo and more frequent in imagination. Avoidance rarely eludes anxiety.	Medium to severe	Performance decrement and physio- logical dis- tress
Evaluative- social	Stimuli vague and general- ized, include situation calling for R even when no R is given	Escape or avoid, performance decrement	Possibly fail- ure, humilia- tion	Frequent es- cape and avoidance only moderately successful in eluding anxiety	Moderate to severe	Performance decrement, avoidance, physiological discomfort

Still another source of confusion may reside in the possible presence in humans of a self-delivered aversive UCS, at least in those instances in which overt avoidance does not seem to be involved. For example, in test anxiety, recall of past severe anxiety, with reduced efficiency and all the rest, may itself be an aversive UCS, involving physiological feedback, which the test-phobic person repeatedly administers to himself whenever he thinks of the CS, an upcoming test. No outside UCS may be required; in humans the experience of anxiety may in a sense reinforce itself. If these factors can be shown to be sufficient to explain the continuance of the phobia, the classical conditioning model will have to be expanded to include these cognitive processes.

Finally, in assessing the uncertainty regarding these issues, we need to recollect that there are large individual differences, the determinants of which are unknown, in most of the animal studies of reduction of avoidance responding, whether by extinction plus punishment (Solomon, Kamin, and Wynne, 1953), by traditional extinction, or by counter-conditioning (Gambrill, 1967). Even greater variability would be expected with humans, whether in analogue or clinical studies, the challenge lying in investigation of its determinants, some of which may reside in the factors we have been discussing.

Implosion Therapy

Another line of investigation relevant to the contribution to desensitization of graded stimuli is the work of Stampfl and his colleagues (1967) in their use of an intensive extinction procedure called *implosion therapy*. Stampfl, like Wolpe, assumes that neurotic symptoms are learned avoidance responses maintained by anxiety reduction. Stampfl, however, interweaves this assumption and his extinction procedure with traditional psychodynamic formulations. The contents of scenes to be imagined contain many psychoanalytic interpretations of the symptoms. But the most important difference between implosion and desensitization lies in the fact that counter-conditioning of relaxation and a graded hierarchy are not used. In fact, the most intense level of a fear-arousing situation is immediately presented. Stampfl rests the implosion model on the original Pavlovian extinction principle, which describes the reduction in response (CR) as a result of presentations of the CS without the UCS. The extinction of an emotional response is expected to proceed most quickly when the stimulus conditions in extinction are most similar to those associated with the original acquisition situation (Stampfl and Levis, 1967). Therefore, the patient is presented with scenes designed to evoke a maximal level of anxiety and is asked to experience them with genuine emotion and affect. The procedure is repeated until a diminution of anxiety is noted.

Hogan's (1966) description of a typical session implies some grading of CS, but not to the degree involved in desensitization. The intensity of the CS is portrayed well beyond the level reached in any desensitization hierarchy.

"A person afraid of a snake would be requested to view himself picking up and handling a snake. Attempts would be made to have him become aware of his reactions to the animal. He would be instructed to feel how slimy the snake was. Next, he would be asked to experience the snake crawling over his body and biting and ripping his flesh. Scenes of snakes crushing or swallowing him, or perhaps his falling into a pit of snakes would be appropriate implosions.

"Similarly, an acrophobic would be requested to imagine himself falling off a high building or cliff, or perhaps be instructed to picture himself falling through space and in complete darkness. Ideally, the person should be made aware of his feelings and sensations while falling. Then he should feel the impact of his body with the ground and view his crushed, broken body. It is important that the therapist emphasize how the person looks and feels throughout the scenes. If the client should recall an actual traumatic experience, the clinician should center succeeding imagery around that experience" (p. 26).

An experimental test of this procedure is provided by Hogan and Kirchner (1967) in a study with rat-phobic female college students. Subjects were seen for one session—the time of the session varied in duration with each subject. The average time was 39 minutes for the experimental subjects and 30 minutes for the controls. The experimental subjects were exposed to immediate and intense cues evoking such scenes as rats running over their bodies, biting them, destroying their internal organs, and so on. The content of the presentations was changed with each subject, on the rationale that "the therapist knew what scenes generated the most anxiety, and he elaborated upon them" (p. 108). The controls were exposed to neutral imagery, with relaxation rather than anxiety cues emphasized. Thus the comparison was not with systematic desensitization, but with mild relaxation. At the end of the single session, 14 of the 21 experimental subjects picked up a white rat in the behavioral test, as compared with two out of 22 control subjects. The authors concluded that "the implosive idea of experiencing intense anxiety without primary reinforcement in order to extinguish fear has been supported" (p. 109).

Hogan (1966) also reported success in the use of implosive therapy with a sample of hospitalized psychotics. Compared to controls, 26 patients treated with implosion showed significant improvement on five scales of the MMPI and a statistically significant higher rate of discharge. Incidentally, it is interesting to note this difference in acceptable criteria for clinical improvement to substantiate therapeutic effectiveness. As we have seen, criteria for evaluation of systematic desensitization have generally been specifically behavioral or have been at least in terms of a predicted change on a symptom-specific self-report instrument. It is further worthy of note that Wolpe and Lazarus (1966) express reluctance to use implosive techniques because in their experience cases have been made worse by exposure to situations provoking great anxiety, either in imagination or in reality. The differential effectiveness of the same technique in the hands of different therapists raises the interesting question that other factors may be at work, which modify the efficacy of the technique as a function of the patient's response to the therapist or the setting. However, a study of implosion therapy with clinic patients, in which its effectiveness was demonstrated rather weakly (by significantly greater change scores over combined controls on two out of ten MMPI scales), found no difference between a novice and an experienced implosion therapist (Levis and Carrera, 1967).

The Role of Verbal Mediating Processes. Recent studies have shown increased interest in expanding the original Wolpean model to include a number of cognitive factors. Two separate research trends can be differentiated, although separation is more convenient than real. The first problem relates to our discussion in a previous section of this chapter of the role of the therapist, that is, his influence via interpersonal channels on treatment progress in desensitization. If the interpersonal relationship in therapy is scrutinized, it is noted that the skillful therapist controls his own behaviors so that his comments are selective. They pinpoint the behaviors on which treatment focuses. In this way the therapist's remarks or gestures may serve discriminative functions. In addition, the therapist's comments or attitudes of support or disappointment give the patient information about his evaluation of progress. Therefore, the therapist's actions can assume reinforcing functions, much like praise or blame in a laboratory learning task. On closer look, however, these same properties of the therapist's or experimenter's operations are also characteristic of operant conditioning methods (Chapter 6). If such subtle conditioning influences operate in desensitization procedures, then their role must be explored to determine whether these are necessary or, indeed, sufficient conditions for behavior modification of the phobic response. The finding that the clinical procedure can be partially automated reduces the likelihood that operant conditioning *alone* is a determining factor. Yet, even in studies using some automated devices the overall setting and the attitude of the therapist cannot be ruled out as important factors for facilitating the treatment.

The second series of studies have emphasized the role of verbal mediating processes by which a patient may change his own behavior once he has clear information about his own actions and their impact on the environment. The overlap between these two areas is mainly due to the fact that the actual experimental operations tend to utilize feedback that includes response-contingent information about several dimensions of the person's behavior. This feedback can have both informational and motivational characteristics and may thus serve to change behavior either via (cognitive) verbal control, or via its functions as a facilitating social stimulus (reward), or an aversive social stimulus (punishment), or both.

So far we have reviewed research that essentially has regarded the patient as a nonparticipating passive battleground on which anxiety, avoidance, and relaxation responses compete for superiority. Nevertheless, the reader will have noted indications in several of the studies already reviewed that the patient's evaluation of his own behavior and his verbal activities may play a role in mediating the obtained changes. Recent studies of self-persuasion (Bem, 1965) and self-regulation (Kanfer, 1967b) have amassed evidence that a subject's evaluation of his own response, both autonomic and motor, may affect his subsequent behavior. It is quite conceivable that the effectiveness of the desensitization procedure may lie not only in the opposition of emotional arousal and relaxation responses, but in the subject's interpretations of his own behavior in the presence of fear-arousing stimuli and the shift of his subsequent behavior toward the phobic object to a new set of controlling verbal stimuli that have arisen during the treatment procedure.

Lang proposes a similar hypothesis (1969):

"The subject's control of the imagined fear stimulus, its length, frequency, and sequence of presentation, is another important cognitive element in the desensitization procedure. When this control element was eliminated in Davison's experiment, positive reduction in fear was not obtained. It may be that the aversiveness of phobic stimuli lies in the helplessness of the subject, the fact that he has no organized response except flight and avoidance. Hebb (1949) has suggested that the essence of fear is a cerebral disorganization evoked by stimuli for which no adequate response is available. These stimuli elicit partial responses which are either incompatible with each other or with the reactive properties of the stimulus. Thus, behavioral sequences cannot be smoothly completed. The central processor becomes disorganized, energy is mobilized which cannot be appropriately discharged, and the result is the uncoordinated, helpless behavior we associate with fear.

"In desensitization the subject learns to control the presentations of stimuli, and perhaps in turn to control the responses that they evoke. He is encouraged to make discriminations in degree of threat within a stimulus class, that previously only generated a generalized avoidance. The individual thus develops a controlled transaction with the environment, in which behavior is modulated according to stimulus intensity and a variety of other associated semantic or structural factors. It is not clear that the development of such a control system is best conceptualized as exclusively cognitive (Hebb, for example, stated his theory in neurophysiological terms). In any event, this conception of fearful and fearless behavior deserves attention as it applies to densensitization therapy" (p. 188).

It is the fate of a clearly specified theoretical formulation to give rise to new research areas and to raise new questions, even if new findings require modification of the theory. Desensitization therapy is an example par excellence of a set of operations for which the presumed underlying processes have been clearly spelled out. Paradoxically, such clarity places a heavier burden of proof on the defenders of the formulation because they must defend against all newcomers whose research evidence points toward different directions.

Weitzman (1967), in a critique of behavior therapy, has offered interpretations of the effectiveness of systematic desensitization from a number of nonbehavioral points of view, ranging from decision therapy to psychoanalysis. He challenges nonbehavioral clinicians to test these alternate explanations and to accommodate this procedure in their own respective models. As an illustration of technical innovations within desensitization which might be derived from dynamic but not behavioral models, Weitzman describes Gendlin's (1962) procedure. Patients were given the most intensely disturbing scene in a hierarchy series and continuously instructed: "Attend to the way you feel. Don't talk! Don't think! If thoughts come, let them pass through your mind. Don't attach yourself to them. Keep watching your feelings." Fifteen minutes were given to each presentation and equal time was later spent in discussing the content of the patient's experiences. Both of Gendlin's patients who were treated this way, after conventional desensitization, reported initial intensification of anxiety, followed by their understanding of what they were feeling and, finally, by disappearance of anxiety. The reader will note the similarity of this procedure to *flooding,* which we described earlier. The effects are quoted by Weitzman, from Gendlin, as follows:

"Both patients felt that, *in contrast to their experience with systematic desensitization,* they 'made sense to themselves,' felt good about themselves and 'in touch with themselves' after each session. In addition, while the *effects* of desensitization were experienced as 'real,' the procedure seemed magical and mysterious. By contrast, in this new procedure, the patients felt that they had healed themselves" (pp. 311–312).

Weitzman suggests that the systematic desensitization procedure, giving only 10 to 15 seconds to each presentation, may actually prevent the type of therapeutic introspection that provides anxiety relief in the Gendlin procedure in one long presentation. This time limitation may not permit the patient's feelings to pass the peak of anxiety; thus it appears possible that "the necessity of multiple, hierarchical presentations was an artifact of the technique itself" (Weitzman, 1967).

Weitzman's criticism calls attention to the incomplete considerations of all processes during desensitization and submits reinterpretation of the process from a dynamic frame of reference. However, even within the behavioristic framework, research is accumulating that points to the necessity of incorporating the subject's self-regulatory processes in a full account of systematic desensitization. Valins and Ray (1967) raise the possibility that it is not the relaxation but the subject's cognitive response to his internal reactions that may facilitate reduction of the avoidance response. Their hypothesis is anchored in work by Schachter and others whose research on the importance of the subject's labeling of his own state of arousal we have discussed earlier. Valins and Ray conducted two experiments that used essentially the same procedure. They differed only in that the replication used subjects who had scored high on a snake-fear test, while the first experiment was conducted with unselected college undergraduates. The latter were only moderately frightened of snakes. In the second study, the experimental subjects were exposed to observation of a live snake in a glass cage, while slides of snakes were used in the first study. All subjects were shown, in random alternation, ten slides of the word "shock" with contiguous administration of electric shock, and ten slides or in vivo exposure of snakes. The experimental subjects also believed that they were hearing their own amplified heart sounds, which ostensibly increased in rate during the shock trials but not during presentation of the snakes. Control groups differed only in that the extraneous sounds were not identified as the subject's own heartbeat. In this way, the experimental subjects were led to believe that the sight of snakes did not affect them internally. It was found that the experimental subjects showed significant increases over the control group in the approach and handling of a live snake after the experimental sessions. These subjects had been led to believe that they observed heart rate increases following shock, but that no such increases occurred during exposure to the snake stimuli. The results suggested that avoidance behavior can be modified by changing the subject's cognitive information about his internal reactions to the originally fear-arousing stimuli, even when this information does not actually correspond to the person's autonomic responses. The authors point out the similarity between the false heart rate feedback procedure and the usual muscle relaxation procedure in desensitization; both lead subjects to believe that phobic stimuli are having few internal effects. The rationale for the effectiveness of these two procedures, however, is quite different. While Valins and Ray assume that changes in the subject's appraisal of his own behavior are important in bringing about other behavioral changes—whether these assessments are correct or not—advocates of desensitization therapy ascribe the effects directly to the presence of the antagonistic relaxation response.

The effects of feedback in a procedure that resembles desensitization were experimentally tested by Leitenberg, Agras, Thompson, and Wright (1968). In this study two cases are described in which the patients received graduated practice in facing their phobic stimuli (small enclosed rooms in one case and knives in the second). In some trial blocks the patients were required to record their tolerance of exposure to the phobic situation on each trial, while no such record of their behavior was made on other blocks. Contingent verbal praise for the patient's behavioral improvement was also given in one case. The authors report that the introduction of precise feedback of trial-by-trial performance facilitated behavioral change. When feedback was omitted, a decline in progress was noted in both patients; reinstatement of feedback resulted in renewed improvement. Addition or removal of selective praise for the second patient did not change his progress. The strength of the argument for the effects reported by the authors in only two cases is limited by the small sample size. However, the results are consistent with other reports (discussed in Chapter 9 under self-controlling procedures) that require a patient to attend to his own behavior and to record its frequency and its relationship to environmental events may have beneficial effects. Whether these effects operate through direct alteration of the patient's state of arousal or through reinterpretation of this affective state remains in question.

A somewhat similar point is made by Davison (1966). The contradiction he sought to resolve lies in the finding that curare-induced relaxation, which blocks transmission of neural messages to the muscle fibers, does not inhibit anxiety; whereas relaxation induced by instructions is antagonistic to anxiety. Davison suggests that relaxation in desensitizaiton may, in fact, inhibit anxiety only because self-induced relaxation generates strong positive affective states that are incompatible with anxiety. Secondly, he suggests that the significant features in the inhibitory power of relaxation over anxiety might not lie so much in a muscle state as at a higher cortical level. In other words, the effects of the subject's beliefs and attitudes about his physiological state, be they correct or not, may serve as the more important determinant of the patient's response than his actual bodily state. It should be pointed out that these questions do not imply a simple "suggestion" effect in desensitization techniques. Although the directive conduct of the desensitization procedure certainly contains elements of strong persuasion, the case made for the importance of verbally mediated responses in the reduction of avoidance behavior rests on the assumption that all of these external variables simply play their part in affecting the patient's own pattern of appraising himself and his behavior in relation to his environment.

Several studies in which relaxing drugs have been used to enhance desensitization may appear to contradict the preceding argument. For example, Brady (1966) reported use of Brevital to induce relaxation in order to hasten desensitization. Friedman (1966) has successfully used a related drug with 25 phobic anxiety cases. Closer examination of the procedure, however, does not resolve the puzzle. Brady actually instructed his patient to expect the relaxing effects of the drug. He asks the patient's participation: "You must facilitate this effect by letting yourself relax as much as possible." Although Friedman's report is rather brief it suggests the patient has knowledge of the desired drug effect since the injection of the solution continues "until he (the patient) admits to feeling calm and relaxed." These procedural complexities leave unexplained the many potential processes by which the relaxation procedure may operate. It may initially induce a bodily state which commonly signals a "good feeling" to the patient, and second, lead the patient to label his newly relaxed bodily state, thus modifying the patient's self-description of his reactions to the presented fear-arousing stimulus.

One puzzling bit of contradiction comes from a study by Sherman (1967) with laboratory animals. This research established a conditioned emotional response by training animals to press a lever for food and then introducing a shock for lever-pressing. After the last shock (punishment) session, Sherman injected some animals with saline solution to control for the effects of the injections. These animals also were injected with amobarbital sodium *after* the first reconditioning session to control for any long-lasting general effects of the drug. The "drug group" was injected with amobarbital sodium *prior* to the first reconditioning session and with saline following the session. A "gradual withdrawal group"—consisting of half the drug group animals—was continued on reduced dosages of the anxiety-reducing drug for three more deconditioning sessions. In the "abrupt withdrawal group"—consisting of the remaining drug group animals—and the control group, isotonic saline injections were substituted.

The relearning of the adaptive bar-pressing behavior was facilitated by the gradual withdrawal treatment, in comparison to both the abrupt withdrawal and control groups. At the completion of the gradual drug withdrawal, the lever pressing continued in the nondrug state without decrement. The abrupt withdrawal group showed a clear decrement after cessation of drug injections, with slow performance-recovery in later sessions, similar to that found in the control group. In this study the similarity to the gradual desensitization procedure is only inferential. However, gradual withdrawal and desensitization methods share the technique of maintaining the threatening effects at a level below that necessary for triggering an avoidance response. Conceptually, this should permit extinction of the residual anxiety and counter-conditioning of adaptive behavior. Sherman states the difference as one of emphasis: "Whereas in systematic desensitization the emphasis is on the stimulus control of anxiety with concomitant direct control by the anxiety-inhibiting relaxation, in gradual withdrawal the emphasis is on the direct physiological control by the drug with concomitant stimulus-change control" (p. 128).

An important aspect of Sherman's findings is that in animal research it is only by inference that the physiological variable, the drug injection, can be assumed to have graduated anxiety-reducing effects. In humans the same inference is drawn from the subject's verbal report. However, central or verbal-mediational factors cannot be assumed to be operating in the rat (though they well might) and the subject's verbal evaluation of the stimulus situation or his feelings cannot account for the treatment effects. These experimental findings encourage further efforts to ascertain the extent to which human and animal studies can be interchangeably utilized without consideration of parameters peculiar to each of these species. They also suggest that the treatment effects may differ for anxiety-related problems in which the stimulus events are physically threatening, as in the animals, or imaginary or social, as in many patients.

In the work reported more recently we have clearly seen a tendency toward a breakdown of the strict procedural rules for desensitization methods originally laid down by Wolpe. An interesting example of the merging of different techniques is given in a pilot study by Wilson and Smith (1968), which is somewhat similar to Gendlin's method, described above. The authors argue that in cases in which specific hierarchies are not easily established because the anxiety-arousing situations are pervasive, Freudian "free association" techniques could be used. Since it is assumed that the patients' associations at first deal with material that is of lesser threat and only gradually approach areas of more intense anxiety, it was hypothesized that free association, used in conjunction with muscular relaxation, would be an efficient means simultaneously to define and to counter-condition complexes of anxiety-mediating stimuli. The procedure utilized relaxation training. However, instead of a presentation of hierarchy items the patient was requested to talk about situations that related to his problems. As in desensitization, the therapist asked the patient to stop and to relax when increasing anxiety or muscle tension was noted. In both clinical cases the rate of improvement during counter-conditioning by this procedure, according to the authors, "was at least as rapid as that reported for counter-conditioning using hierarchies of scenes." At the end of the counter-conditioning procedure, the patients were given additional training. In one case, practice in self-assertion and family therapy followed counter-conditioning. In the second case, conversational therapy and verbal exploration were continued with the patient in a series of sessions. Although the limited number of cases precludes full evaluation of this technique, the successful treatment is another illustration of the current attempts to extend the counter-conditioning model of therapy by combination with previously practiced therapeutic methods.

The Role of Verbal Conditioning in Desensitization Procedures

The integration of various therapy models is also illustrated by several recent studies on the effects of deliberate therapist control of patient behaviors by operant reinforcement. This technique will be discussed in detail in a following chapter. At the moment it will suffice to recall that operant conditioning techniques are clearly distinguished from the stimulus-substitution model by their emphasis on changing the consequences of a selected response class instead of their antecedent stimuli. Several earlier studies had shown that most patient-therapist relationships contain some elements of operant conditioning, as we have previously noted, through the selective and motivational characteristic of the therapist's response to his patient. The importance of suggestion and verbal conditioning in desensitization therapy is illustrated in a recent study of Leitenberg, Agras, Barlow, and Oliveau (1969) who examined the role of therapeutic instructions and positive reinforcement in the desensitization procedure. Female snake-phobic college students were either assigned to the common desensitization procedure or to a second group in which therapeutic instructions and positive reinforcement for completion of a hierarchy item or for reports of progress were withheld. A third group (control) was given no treatment. The results clearly show that the effects of desensitization are markedly enhanced when the nonspecific reinforcement of signs of progress and the instructional sets toward positive outcome are part of the therapeutic procedure. The authors interpret their findings in congruence with the previously described studies, to suggest that the desensitization procedure may include verbal and mediational responses whose pivotal role cannot be overlooked as one source of the beneficial results of the procedure.

Bergin (1969) presented a case study in which a desensitization approach was integrated with procedures used in traditional verbal therapy. The patient was a young homosexual woman who presented her problem as inability to relate effectively to men and as being in conflict over a recent homosexual relationship. She was seen for 14 sessions that were devoted to self-exploration with empathy, warmth, and questioning by the therapist. This series of traditional interviews enhanced her relationship with the therapist and her understanding of her problems but did not materially change them. It was therefore decided to treat her fear of men by means of desensitization. Bergin found that his client could not even construct a hierarchy because of her intense anxiety. He therefore relaxed the patient first and then asked the client not only to imagine but also to explore and discuss the memories, thoughts, and feelings connected with the items under discussion. The process of hierarchy construction and the discussion of items under relaxation thus proceeded simultaneously. Whenever the patient became very upset, discussion of the material was terminated, relaxation instructions were reintroduced, and discussion returned to a less upsetting level. Good treatment progress was observed both on personality tests and in her greater efficiency in everyday relationships with men. In fact, after a two-and-a-half-month follow-up she had maintained her gains and was engaged to be married.

Bergin recognizes the limitations of the case study as a demonstration of a technique rather than as evidence of its efficacy. However, he suggests that "the range of events experienced during desensitization of a hierarchy item can be significantly broadened and intensified by virtue of these procedures because they, along with questioning and moderate interpretation, elicit a variety of cognitive and emotional responses which have been and are in the present consistently associated with the event structurally described by the item itself" (p. 16). After prior demonstration, within a framework of client-centered therapy, that the therapist's attitudes of warmth and empathy may serve as powerful reinforcers for positive behaviors in interview therapy, Truax and Carkhuff (1967) suggest that such operant conditioning techniques may be used in a theoretical framework distinct from behavior therapy but within the methodological procedures suggested by desensitization techniques. Such integrations and recombinations of techniques currently stand as isolated reports in the clinical literature. In principle, however, they illustrate the potential fruitfulness of a flexible approach that examines and clarifies not only specific features of a total therapeutic approach but also attempts to recombine various elements to suit ᴜne need of individual patients and to produce the most powerful effects that prediction from a conceptual framework will permit.

Despite the relative simplicity of the original model suggested by Wolpe, it is clear that the actual operations are not confined simply to manipulation of stimulus variables by grading anxiety arousing stimuli and manipulation of the response variables by juxtaposition of two opposing responses. Representation of organismic variables in terms of the bodily arousal of the patient, and a large number of possible consequence variables, including consequences of the patient's own evaluation of his response, have been discussed. Some research data point to the probability that the patient's coping behavior is explicitly or implicitly reinforced by the therapist and by other people in his natural environment. Wolpe's assertive training presents an especially clear case of a combined utilization of a desensitization technique with operant reinforcement.

Perhaps the most important distinction between this technique and clinical methods discussed in the preceding and following chapters lies in the fact that the greatest emphasis both for research and clinical practice is *not* on the behavioral changes that are actually obtained but on the inferred bodily state, the anxiety reaction, which is the target of attack and which is postulated to be a causal factor of the symptom. Because clinical observers can most readily document the concurrence of emotional arousal and phobic avoidance behavior, it is with these disorders that most experiments have dealt. Once the desensitization procedure is modified to suit the particular problems encountered with other behavior disorders, the very elegance and clarity of the systematic desensitization operations are lost. The restricted applicability of the desensitization paradigm to particular problems and the success obtained when this technique is fitted into the patient's total therapeutic program remind us once again to guard against the false hope that all the richness and complexity of human behavior may be encompassed by one simple model. We must also keep in mind that it is naive to expect a single standardized procedure to be effective for all instances of a particular class of problems or to believe that only one therapeutic procedure may be applicable to each class of behavior problems.   ♦

SUMMARY

In this chapter we have discussed applications of learning principles to complex symptom patterns which include the presence of anxiety as a dominant feature. In these cases the classical conditioning paradigm is often supplemented by operations that fit the operant conditioning model. Although it is commonly used to characterize neuroses, anxiety is a construct that is difficult to define. The empirical referents have variously been a person's verbal description of his own internal state, his responses on an inventory, interview, or personality test, or the record of his physiological responses. Despite the ambiguity of the term, the anxiety construct has played a central role in most theories of psychopathology. Specifically, many symptomatic responses have been considered as adjustive reactions that avoid or terminate an overwhelming or intensely terrifying emotional state, called anxiety. The symptomatic responses, then, can be examined as avoidance responses or escape responses and the focus of attention shifts to the question concerning the variables prominent in the acquisition, maintenance, and extinction of these responses. The continued occurrence of these avoidance responses has raised a puzzling question about the factors that maintain the anxiety and avoidance responses. While some theoretists suggest that repeated experiences with anxiety-arousing stimuli result in permanent changes lowering the threshold for an anxiety response, purely psychologically oriented theories view the conditioned emotional response as a drive stimulus that persists until some instrumental response removes the organism from the original environment. A combination of both the biological and psychological approaches is found in the work of Solomon and Wynne. They account for the remarkable resistance to extinction of the avoidance response by the twin principles of anxiety conservation and partial irreversibility.

In human subjects the acquisition and maintenance of anxiety responses are affected by the person's verbal characterization of the environment and of his internal emotional state. It is because of this apparent admixture of stimulus, instrumental, and autonomic response components, and supplementary verbal mediating responses that the treatment techniques described in this chapter have been classified as fitting under mixed models.

The most widely used techniques for dealing with anxiety-related symptoms have evolved from Wolpe's reciprocal inhibition method. In Wolpe's approach, anxiety is selected as the target for therapy, and is reduced by presentation of an inhibitory response in the presence of the anxiety-evoking stimuli. The term *desensitization* has been applied to the method of presenting the CS for the anxiety response at a very low level of intensity at first, and gradually increasing the intensity according to a hierarchy of anxiety-eliciting stimuli. The term *reciprocal inhibition* describes the conditioned inhibition that minimizes the anxiety reaction. Wolpe originally utilized muscle relaxation as the primary antagonistic response to anxiety and presented the anxiety-arousing stimulus items either in vivo or through instructions that the patient imagine their presence.

Wolpe's careful description of his underlying theoretical rationale and of the components of his treatment procedure has permitted experimental tests of both.

Much of the work supporting both the rationale and claims of success for this technique has come from laboratory analogues in which relatively well-adjusted individuals were treated for such phobias as fear of snakes, spiders, or public speaking. Laboratory studies, as well as clinical reports, have demonstrated the effectiveness of the systematic desensitization technique. Discrepant findings, however, are reported about many of the separate procedural steps. For example, some authors find that relaxation is a necessary ingredient of the desensitization procedure, while others suggest that a receptive psychological state, rather than muscle relaxation, may be sufficient to serve as an antagonistic response to anxiety. Other experiments have questioned the necessity of Wolpe's reciprocal inhibition component, claiming that the procedure is basically rooted in counter-conditioning of anxiety-incompatible behaviors.

Among other variables investigated in the desensitization model are the effects of in vivo and imaginal presentation of anxiety-arousing items, the number of hierarchy items completed during treatment, the general anxiety level of the subject, and the role of extinction. Some researchers have also tested the hypothesis that operant reinforcement for the patient's progress during treatment and for his compliance with both his and the therapists's expectations for improvement plays an important role in successful treatment.

When the desensitization technique is used without the attempt to introduce the CS for anxiety gradually, the result is a procedure that follows Pavlovian extinction principles, with presentation of a CS in full strength but without the prior UCS. This technique, advocated by Stampfl, has been called *implosion therapy* and has also been reported to reduce anxiety and phobic responses effectively.

Although the therapeutic effectiveness of the treatment models presented in this chapter has been widely documented, the precise range of effective variables and the minimal necessary elements of the therapeutic paradigm have not yet been clearly established. Meanwhile, the mixed models discussed in this chapter have been widely adopted on pragmatic grounds.

CHAPTER 5

Social Learning and Behavior Rehearsal

In the preceding chapters we have seen how basic conditioning principles may be applied to the description and modification of clinical problems. Such extrapolations of these principles have often been criticized, both as treatment operations and as modes of understanding human behavior. They are said to be overly simplistic and mechanistic, too restricted in relying on animal laboratory paradigms, and too narrow in the behaviors and independent variables they examine. In this and the next two chapters, we will take up recent developments that attempt to broaden behavioral learning principles by extension to characteristically human aspects of individuals and their social environment.

The material discussed in the present chapter is variously termed social learning, vicarious learning, imitation, and observational learning. The usage of these terms has been quite arbitrary and no distinction among them will be made in this chapter. The main problem to be considered is the analysis of the effects on the development of novel attitudes or skills of an individual's exposure to the behavior of others. Specifically, the task of the learning theorist is to relate the process of observation of another's actions to the changes in the observer's performance when he is presented with a similar situation. At the empirical level, these tasks consist of studying the particular relationships between the extent to which the observer's behavior changes and parameters of three conditions: (1) observation, (2) memory or storage, and (3) test for reproduction of observed behaviors. Study of the interplay between these conditions and the personality of the observer provides further clues for understanding the selective nature of the socialization process. Social learning thus determines the content of a person's repertoire and is determined by his previous experiences and personal characteristics.

Although the experimental and theoretical roots of social learning can readily be traced back to modern psychology's beginnings (see, for example, Baldwin, 1895), and these roots are part of the developments in S-R learning models in the thirties and forties (Miller and Dollard, 1941),

187

social learning has been relatively neglected as an area of inquiry. The recent upsurge of work in this field probably reflects several influences: (1) dissatisfaction with therapeutic applications of the conditioning models we have so far considered; (2) aspirations to include more complex social phenomena within the explanatory systems of behavioral learning theories in competition with other models; (3) recognition that uniquely human capacities require special consideration; and (4) the confluence of streams of interest in related phenomena within social, developmental, clinical, and learning psychology.

An example may help to elaborate on the nature of the dissatisfactions with simple S-R learning explanations. Consider a person who finds himself, with a group of friends, at a table in a Japanese restaurant for the first time. A conditioning account might run as follows. Our novice diner finds none of the implements he has long been accustomed to use in transferring food from plate to mouth. He is hungry and were he alone he might readily resort to earlier learned behaviors—now weak but still in his repertoire—and eat rice and vegetables with his fingers. However, the presence of an audience has become an S^Δ for such behaviors, a signal that social reinforcement would be withdrawn. Through stimulus generalization he responds to the chopsticks and begins a trial-and-error process of learning a novel behavior, using components of dominant responses in his hierarchy for handling eating tools. Since none of these available eating responses include holding two implements in one hand, his behavior is only gradually shaped toward more efficient food transport by the natural contingencies of food-in-mouth and food-in-lap. Since food-in-lap has become, from past experiences, a conditioned aversive stimulus, our hero experiences conditioned autonomic responses of acute embarrassment and annoyance. These response-produced cues ultimately lead him to call the waiter, a previously reinforced response to restaurant discomfort, and to ask for a fork.

Alternatively, our naive diner might be described in social learning terms: he might notice his companions' initial responses to the chopsticks and thereby fasten his attention on them, or he might ask: "Are these what you eat with?" Once he is responding to the proper stimuli, he is still faced with acquiring a set of novel responses in their use. Observing his date spill wet vegetables down her dress front, he experiences a vicariously conditioned response of anxiety that mediates an instrumental avoidance response—he moves his chopstick away from his plate.

But then a generalized tendency to imitate in novel social situations, reinforced on many past occasions, comes to his rescue. Noting the suave competence of the chap seated next to him, our hero selects him as a model and proceeds to imitate his chopstick technique. The same food-to-mouth and food-in-lap consequences help to arouse our novice and to focus his attention on the ways his responses do and do not match those of his model. He verbalizes to himself the salient features of his model's chopstick grip, modifies his own behavior accordingly, but finally asks for instruction. The model then demonstrates in stepwise fashion the proper grip and manipulative movements, while verbalizing such rules as "keep this one steady; don't squeeze too tightly." The model exemplifies his technique by transferring a good sized portion of food to his mouth. Our diner, having witnessed the reinforcement of the model's performance, repeats the verbal instructions to himself, carries them out, and enjoys success and greater improvement with each attempt. The process of learning by observation that he has exemplified is, however, by no means clear; in fact, the explanation of this learning process constitutes the subject matter of this chapter.

The example embodies a number of the features commonly cited as shortcomings when classical and operant animal learning models are applied to modification of human behavior. Repeated efforts to apply learning theory to the modification of human behavior in education, psychotherapy, and child-rearing have highlighted limitations that are inevitable because of the narrowness of the laboratory data from which S-R learning models have evolved. The human capacity for language and thought provides behavioral capacities to bypass simple conditioning arrangements. These same verbal and social skills also enable the individual to benefit from the learning experiences of his fellow men even when he is not formally placed in a "learning situation." Acquisition of intellectual, social, and moral behaviors, and in fact of most behaviors that turn the human infant into a member of his society, is not easily explained in learning terms. These complex social learning situations cannot be described as exclusively under control of CS-UCS pairings in early childhood; nor can contingent consequences be held totally responsible for the billions of responses that are executed during early development.

S-R theories have been criticized frequently for their inability to handle adequately the acquisition of novel responses, language and social development, the role of language and thinking in behavior control, and recent data indicating observational learning by an inactive, unreinforced witness. The counter argument has been that insufficiencies of strict S-R models lie not in the models themselves but in the narrow range of phenomena to which they have been applied. Early research in learning concerned itself not so much with parameters of acquisition of radically novel behaviors as with changes in rate, latency, or topography in the execution of fairly well-established simple responses in animals, such as running and jumping. More recently, behavioral field and laboratory studies have attempted, in the face of severe methodological obstacles, to examine the functional relationships involved in more complex, subtle, continually changing, and often not directly observable events. Although by their nature these processes most often require humans as research subjects, animal studies have continued to play an important role in developing generalizations regarding social learning. The few available accounts of the development of complex social behaviors in animals, both in their natural habitat and artificial environments, are among the most fascinating observational studies in psychology. These accounts and laboratory studies with many species suggest that the young animal is an active, curious, exploring learner who searches the environment for new stimulation and constantly shows new variations in behavior patterns. We must therefore guard against the assumption that "learning" means passive exposure to environmental stimuli, experimental manipulations, or response-reinforcement contingencies.

Two basic features appear to form a basis for the organism's search for new experiences. First, living organisms respond to novel stimuli in their environment and engage in behavior that procures changes in environmental stimulation. Whether this phenomenon is explained on the basis of curiosity, exploratory drive, stimulus hunger, or similar concepts, it is a well-accepted characteristic of living organisms. The second feature concerns the finding, documented for rats, monkeys, and humans, that the behavior of a peer model tends to result in *imitation* by the observing animal when placed under similar conditions. Observational learning has been demonstrated not only by anecdotal evidence but also repeatedly in the laboratory. For example, Darby and Riopelle (1959) exposed monkeys to observation of successful solution of discrimination problems by another monkey who was rewarded on half of the trials; the observing monkeys were never rewarded. The observer monkeys were then exposed to the same problems and rewarded for making the same choices as had the models. Their performance in acquiring the discriminations was significantly superior to that of control animals not exposed to the model.

However, the extent to which observational or vicarious learning plays a role in an organism's total life probably differs across species. The greater the complexity of the behavioral repertoire needed for survival, and the availability of sensory, motor, and intellectual capabilities to observe, recall, and execute modeled behaviors, the larger is the role played by observational learning. In addition, the human capacity for language enhances observational learning. For example, in a study by Bandura, Grusec, and Menlove (1966), children observed a film of an adult model engaging in a series of novel responses. Those children who were asked to verbalize the modeling stimuli during their presentation showed a significantly greater tendency to execute the responses than did children who observed passively.

In clinical work it often appears that a patient's neurotic behavior patterns are related to similar nonadaptive behaviors he has observed in parents or other models. Many a child has been admonished by a teacher for exhibiting language or manners acquired by observation of a father's behavior in the privacy of his home. More serious disruption occurs when a child adapts an ineffectual, "sick" method of coping with stress, such as pleading illness or using assaultive violence, after observing successes with this method in siblings or parents. The problem often is first defined as such outside the home. The family may tolerate, and thus sustain, these behaviors, but other social groups may punish them. Clinicians also note that many actions, originally learned by peer group observation, turn into nonadjustive behavior when they are no longer acceptable in a broader social community. The acquisition of delinquent behaviors in institutions, clubs, or in any situation that permits observation of these skills and that rewards their performance is an excellent example of the opposite consequences for the same behaviors in different circumstances. Yet the frequency of exposure and personal importance of the group make a juvenile a better imitator of behaviors of his friends than of the standards of conformity vaguely provided by adult society. Many personality theorists have put basic importance on learning by example, but have asserted that early identification with parents and other models influences lifelong behavior by molding the nature of relatively permanent personality structures in the individual. A behavioral view suggests that development of these response patterns can better be understood within the context of observational learning and conditioning, and can be influenced at any time during the person's life. In fact, extensive change can even be brought about by deliberately programmed observational learning in psychotherapy. The present chapter deals with this area of learning as a fundamental process in human development and in behavior modification methods.

OBSERVATIONAL LEARNING: RESEARCH PARADIGMS

A clear differentiation of types of studies in this area is difficult due to incomplete control of variables that are now known to be relevant. For instance, some studies choose, as behaviors to be imitated, responses with special properties (for example, aggressive responses). In other studies the sources of direct and vicarious reinforcement cannot be isolated. Still others permit no distinction between effects due to learning and to motivation to perform. Gilmore (1968) has suggested that lack of operational specificity in referring to particular behaviors and in identifying what particular questions are being addressed about these concrete behaviors has added to theoretical and empirical confusion. His own recommendation for research strategy is to "explain a behavior, not a concept," and to "attend closely to the particular question(s) that theory of imitation actually is directed toward answering, for these may be neither those claimed nor those assumed" (p. 219). Bandura (1962) similarly has pointed out the confusion that results from a failure to distinguish between imitative performance, or the observer's use of knowledge acquired by observation, and imitative acquisition, or the achievement of knowledge through observation. In the former case, the emphasis is on the conditions under which a person will make maximal use in a test situation of *prior* observations. In the latter case, the process of learning *during* observation is under scrutiny. Each of these behavioral dispositions is affected by different variables. Yet this distinction is often ignored.

In the interests of clarity, a number of organizational schemes have been used to classify types of behaviors, mechanisms, and paradigms within observational learning (Flanders, 1968; Tolman, 1968; Berger, 1968). The major operational variables that commonly are used to define these categories include presence, source, and nature of the reinforcement conditions for the subject (S) and model (M) during training, the model's instrumental and expressive responses, and the subject's cue, response, and drive or arousal state, including the incentive conditions for the subject during testing. Table 5-1 lists a number of these parameters included in different types of observational learning research. The table suggests that not only the subject's own characteristics but his relationship to the model, and the situational aspects of the test conditions also affect the obtained evidence of vicarious learning.

Gilmore (1968), in emphasizing the importance of attending to the specifics of the behaviors studied, has divided instances of imitation into those that do and do not require that the subject attend to similarities and differences between the model's response and his own. Within these two broad classes, he distinguishes several subtypes. To focus attention from the start on the differences among behaviors all termed "imitative," Gilmore's classification is shown in Table 5-2. As Gilmore himself asserts, his types rarely are to be found in "pure" form in nature or research. Instead, recognition of these types, made up of various combinations of the variables in Table 5-1, may help us to look for different factors governing different types of imitation, and to parcel out their relative contributions to the complex experimental paradigms usually at hand. The organization of the rest of this chapter reflects an attempt to order experiments by procedural similarities for ease of presentation. From time to time,

Table 5-1   Some of the Major Variables Manipulated in
Observational Learning Research

Training Conditions

Model's	Expressive response
	Instrumental or reflex response
	Presumed stimuli associated with response
	Reinforcement
	Status, sex, and other enduring personal characteristics
Subject's	Arousal
	Response
	Covert or verbal rehearsal of instrumental or reflex response
	History of inhibition or general response tendency for emitting the response
	Reinforcement
	History of imitation training
	History with model or figures similar to model
	Age, sex, and other enduring personal characteristics

Testing Conditions

Status of incentives for subject
Presence or absence of model and/or other audience
Reinforcement
Degree of Task Structure (ambiguity)

---

however, we will return to the variables and behavior types listed in Tables 5-1 and 5-2, in order to inquire how they enter into the more complex designs under discussion.

Experiments on vicarious learning encompass all situations in which some relationship can be shown to exist between an observer's later behavior and the behavior of a model. These studies can be divided into five categories on the basis of their underlying operational paradigms. In addition, each category tends to have different implications for the theoretical explanation of the many-faceted processes in observational learning. The five categories we will discuss follow.

1. *Matched-dependent* designs require the subject to follow the example of a leader, with rewarding consequences for the subject. The subject is rewarded either directly for copying or by the achievement of a reward for which the imitative behavior is essential.

2. *Identification* studies deal with the acquisition of noninstrumental idiosyncratic behaviors of a model by an observing subject. In the context of the subject's performance some specific instrumental responses

Table 5-2   Classification of Imitative Behaviors
(Adapted from Gilmore, 1968, p. 230) (M-model, S-subject)

Nonfunctionally Imitative Behaviors: All those behaviors where S does not need to attend to cues of similarity and difference between M's behavior and his own.

Type I   Coincidental type. M's behavior is not necessary for the occurrence of S's similar behavior.

Example: S walks into dining room right behind M, who happens to precede him.

Type II   Reflexive type. S's behavior is a reflexive or classically conditioned response to a stimulus from M, which happens to be similar.

Example: S shows a startle response when M jumps in startle as a fallen ice cube touches him.

Type III   Cue-resembling or matched-dependent type. M's behavior has been instrumentally learned to be a discriminative stimulus that indicates when S's response (which happens to be similar) may bring reward.

Example: S, seeing M with a rather lascivious facial expression, turns to look at the same female entertainer with the expectation he'll find her appearance rewarding.

Type IV   Altered-inhibition type. Observation of M's behavior leads S to anticipate consequences and alter the inhibitions connected to his responses in such a way that a response (which happens to be similar to M's behavior) is then performed.

Example: S sees that M is using his fingers to eat some meat chunks without receiving criticism from their table mates, and so decides he too will risk it.

Type V   Attention-facilitated type. M's behavior increases the reaction potential of a similar, inhibited response of S, through the directing of attention to this response.

Example: S picks up his chopsticks after M's reaching for his own called S's attention to the pair by his plate.

Functionally Imitative Behaviors: All those behaviors where S must attend to cues of similarity and difference between M's behavior and his own.

Type VI   Generalized learning type. S seeks a reward, which is contingent upon a judgment that M's behavior has been matched, irrespective of any consequences to M.

Example: S, chopsticks in hand, selects M as a model of proper Japanese table manners.

Table 5-2   (Continued)

Type VII	Modeling type. M's behavior achieves a goal state that S also seeks, and thus informs S which of his reponses will achieve the goal.
	Example: S sees M manipulate his chopsticks deftly to break apart a large chunk of fish, and faced with a similar larger-than-bite-sized morsel, copies his act.
Type VIII	Avoidance-of-differing type. S imitates M because of the expected punishment for not doing so.
	Example: S voices positive opinions about the fun of using chopsticks, after all his friends voice strong positive opinions.
Type IX	Information-seeking type. S imitates M to achieve understanding, comprehension, or other gain in information concerning M, his behavior, or his viewpoint.
	Example: S observes M eating raw fish, wonders what it would be like, and tries some.

may be rewarded, but imitation of the model's *style* is the target of direct reinforcement. Thus the term is used here to refer to the subject's response, not, as by other authors, to designate a person's identification or empathy *with* a model.

3. *No-trial learning* paradigms examine subject behaviors following observation of a model, without apparent practice or contingent reinforcement for the observer's performance. The observer is given the opportunity to perform the same task as the model and the occurrence of instrumental as well as stylistic imitative responses can be measured.

4. *Co-learning* designs study the effects of observation of the performance of a model engaged in the same learning task as the subject, usually with alternate opportunities for watching and doing. Influence of social motivation and utilization of observed information are evaluated in the observer's performance increments.

5. *Vicarious classical conditioning* experiments study the responses of a subject witnessing the administration of an unconditioned stimulus for an emotional response, or the response itself. The impact of observation of conditioned emotional states in others on the subject's further observation, his learning, and his performance can be measured.

Many studies combine paradigms to yield different combinations of instrumental responses and reinforcing events in the model, in the observing subject, or in both.

The Matched-Dependent Paradigm: Learning to Imitate

In this experimental procedure the subject observes the action of a model and then is rewarded for executing the same response as did the model. This paradigm represents the simplest case because all that is required of the subject is imitation of the model's response, without knowledge of the particular cues to which the model responded and without observation of any positive consequences for the model. Gilmore's Type III, or cue-resembling imitative behaviors, falls within this paradigm. His classification calls attention to the fact that the model's response serves only as a discriminative stimulus for a particular class of subject responses. Any other S^D presumably would serve a comparable role. Continued trials of rewarded matched-dependent behaviors would, however, promote acquisition of Gilmore's Type VI imitation, a generalized tendency to imitate in similar situations.

Some reliance on imitation for acquisition of effective behaviors is basic to most social institutions. Conformity and compliance are obtained from the school child by the teacher's encouragement of imitation of model peers, and by subsequent reinforcement for correct performance. A drill sergeant "socializes" the new recruit by similar methods, and table manners are taught by demonstration and reinforcement for imitation. These procedures are most effective when the response is one that the learner can easily imitate and one that does not require practice for its actual execution.

A study by McDavid (1959) illustrates this design. Preschool children were asked to make a simple discrimination in choosing one of two differently colored compartments in a wooden box. An adult experimenter served as model and took turns with the child on alternate trials. When a child made the same choice as had the model on the preceding trial, he found a small piece of candy on the floor of the compartment. McDavid found an increase in imitative responses as trials progressed, confirming earlier reports by Miller and Dollard (1941) about children learning to imitate. In a later study using a similar task, McDavid (1964) altered the design by making reinforcement contingent on cues other than M's behavior alone. He thus was able to compare the matched-dependent procedures with other paradigms. Groups of children were rewarded either for following the model (matched-dependent learning) or for responding to a color cue (direct learning). Children learned the correct response equally well whether the discriminative cue was the model's behavior or the color of the goal box. In a third group, cues from color and the model's behavior were variably inconsistent as S^D's (combined direct and matched-dependent learning). The children in this group showed poor discrimination learning. McDavid's analysis of this third group suggests that partial association between social (imitative) and nonsocial (goalbox color) cues tends to result in development of blind imitation of the model.

A matched-dependent learning procedure was carried out by Stimbert, Schaeffer, and Grimsley (1966) with laboratory rats. The authors trained eight *leader* rats, who were on 22-hour water deprivation, to run to one of four goal boxes. Two leader rats were trained to go to each goal box. The goal boxes were partitioned to allow two animals access to water. *Follower* rats then received training trials in which they attained access to water only if they ran to the same goal box as their leader. The followers were paired with different leaders in order to avoid the establishment of a preference for a particular goal box. All animals learned to follow the leader animals when access to water was contingent on their following. These results expanded the findings of earlier studies with rats in which the follower animals were faced with a much simple two-choice discrimination problem.

Training to imitate has been used in preference to laborious shaping of emitted operants for establishing speech and other complex useful behaviors in autistic and schizophrenic children. For example, Lovaas, Freitas, Nelson, and Whalen (1967) trained schizophrenic children to imitate nonverbal responses on the part of an adult model by reinforcing (with food) increasingly close approximations to the model's behavior. Once generalized imitation was established, socially and intellectually useful behaviors (hygiene, drawing, games, smiling) were taught through imitation procedures. It was considered that generalized imitative behavior was established when the child responded with imitation upon the first presentation of a novel behavior by the model. Figure 5-1 shows the acquisition of nonverbal imitation by one of the children. The tasks were both simple and complex discriminations. The figure shows that the child learned to solve the tasks after six or fewer modeled trials, by the end of imitation training. A reversal procedure was employed by Lovaas et al. during initial training to demonstrate that reinforcement delivery was required to maintain imitative behavior, at least in those children early in their training. However, Baer and Sherman (1964) and others have demonstrated that imitative responses, never themselves reinforced, may be maintained as long as other contemporaneous imitations are being reinforced. In using imitation to develop speech in autistic children, Lovaas has found that social reinforcers, and later presumably self-generated reinforcers, may gradually replace food as reinforcers of imitative verbal responses (Lovaas, 1967).

The relationship between model and learner often represents a critical variable in the rate at which imitation learning progresses. For example, McDavid (1959) and others report differences in imitation by children

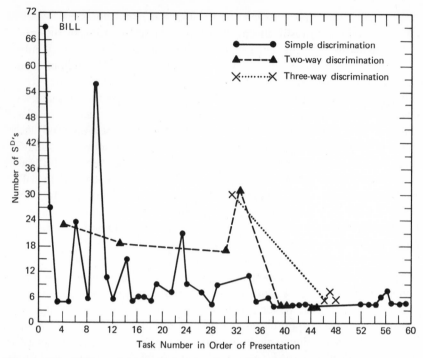

Figure 5-1 Bill's acquisition of nonverbal imitation. The ordinate shows the number of trials (S^Ds adult responses) required for the child's mastery. The abscissa shows the tasks in order of their presentation. The three lines correspond to one-, two-, and three-way discrimination tasks (from Lovaas et al., 1967, p. 175).

of male and female adults. Greater model competence tends to facilitate matched-dependent learning, whether such competence is attributable to age, demonstrated skill of the model, or to other factors. Rosenbaum and Tucker (1962) asked college students to guess the outcome of an imaginary horse race after they were given the results of another subject who ostensibly was also guessing at the outcome. The bogus information was varied so that the model was correct on 80 percent, 50 percent, or 20 percent of the trials. Model competence was thus communicated by his alleged success. Observers imitated the model's responses earlier and more often, the more successful the model. Control subjects who were reinforced for nonimitation were not affected by the differences in the model's success.

The matched-dependent paradigm for imitation learning is most appropriate for the production of blind obedience by the observer. As long as he is reinforced for copying the model, he needs to learn no further skills. The imitative response also generalizes to new situations with the same model and to other models. As we have seen from McDavid's (1964) experiment, however, the imitative response is most easily learned when no other contradictory cues are available.

The Identification Paradigm

Freudian theory has suggested that the value system of the parent becomes the foundation of the child's conscience. The process by which this is accomplished has been characterized as an internalization of parental values during the child's Oedipal stage of development. Similarly, other clinicians have used the term identification to characterize a special relationship between a person and a model that involves not only specific response imitation but also incorporation of emotional reactions, broad meaning systems, and moral values. The asumption of a unitary identification process, that is, the patterning after a parental model of the child's behavioral dispositions toward moral regulation and social behavior, is contradicted by the findings of Lazowick (1955), who reported that people showed no greater similarity to their actual parents than to randomly matched parental figures. Recent work on identification learning also casts doubt on the earlier assumption that response patterns associated with moral judgments are acquired early in life and remain fixed through life. For example, evaluation of one's own behavior, development of criteria for self-rewards, and similar value related responses have been shown to change systematically with exposure to models. Studies of the influence of group membership on conforming behaviors also suggests the modifiability of many attitudes and belief statements by exposure to individual models or group standards.

Hill (1960) and Bandura (1965b) have suggested that the picturesque terms, identification, internalization, and introjection, be abandoned in favor of a more precise technical analysis of the mechanisms underlying transmission of various social behaviors from a model to an observer. According to Hill, since the underlying relationships between behavior of a model and an observer can be analyzed in learning terms, acquisition of complex social behaviors simply represents a special case of common learning processes. Despite these objections, it may be useful to retain the term identification to refer to acquisition of nonessential, idiosyncratic, or stylistic properties of behavior, incidental to the transmission of instrumental responses from a model to a learner. This usage of "identification" differs from the Freudian concept by its reference to S's responses, instead of to the entire process of personality development by personal involvement with another.

A good experimental demonstration of the acquisiton of nonessential responses in imitation learning is provided by Bandura and Huston

(1961). Nursery school children observed a model solving a two-choice discrimination problem, similar to the one employed by McDavid in the previously described experiment. In this study, however, the adult model exhibited certain rehearsed behaviors that were totally irrelevant to the performance of the discrimination task. For example, at the beginning of a trial the model remarked "here I go" and verbalized "march, march, march" as he approached the box containing the toy reward. It was found that the children imitated not only the discrimination behavior but also the programmed incidental behavior of the model. Bandura and Huston introduced an additional variable into the study by exposing the children, prior to the discrimination task, either to a nurturant session in which the model fostered a warm and rewarding interaction, or to a nonnurturant condition in which the model avoided interaction with the children. Subjects who had experienced the nurturant interaction later exhibited more of the model's stylistic behaviors than did the children treated in a nonnurturant way. An interesting exception to this finding was the high rate of imitation of aggressive responses, regardless of the quality of the prior experience with the model. This high imitation rate suggests that the level of the initial probability of a modeled response in the observer's repertoire may have an overriding influence on the tendency to imitate. The results of this study demonstrate that observational learning can extend beyond specific instrumental responses to incorporate the model's personal style, such as the particular mannerisms shown by Bandura's and Huston's models. Training of idiosyncratic behaviors can, of course, also be accomplished by matched-dependent learning or by arranging contingencies so that unique *stylistic* properties of a response are required for reinforcement. However, these other procedures result in acquisition of stylistic properties by requiring their occurrence for reward, while in identification learning their acquisition is incidental from the point of view of the experimenter's contingency arrangements.

An explanation of acquisition of distinctive noninstrumental aspects of human behavior has been proposed within an operant conditioning framework, based on the mechanisms of "superstitious conditioning" discussed in Chapter 6. Herrnstein (1966) regards stylistic features as the result of response variability in operant conditioning. When reinforcement is given, random individual response properties may be accidentally reinforced and their probability increased. A dominant response style then would be maintained until the incidental feature goes unreinforced on many trials. Differential reinforcement for the simpler act eventually results in streamlining and stereotyping the instrumental response alone. The everyday observation of a group of recruits on the drill field contrasted with the performance by a crack drill team illustrates the intentional shaping of uniform motor behaviors. When individuality of behaviors has reward-ing consequences, as in painting, writing, dancing, dress designing, or public speaking, stylistic variations among performers are likely to be maintained by reinforcement from the social community. Comparison of the writings of novelists and scientific experimenters nicely demon-strates the results of social reinforcement for either individuality or con-formity in different activities. Similarly, the products of identification learn-ing can undergo different fates, depending on the subsequent tolerance of the individualistic response by the reinforcing environment.

The two views presented above represent a difference in focus, rather than a divergence of learning principles. The study by Bandura and Huston reflects the concern of some investigators about the origin of novel re-sponses, emitted in a particular form for the *first* time in the person's history. Research on stylistic changes during operant conditioning, on the other hand, deals with the mechanisms that maintain idiosyncratic response variations during repeated executions of the act. This difference in emphasis should be remembered, since our discussion of the applicabil-ity of vicarious learning procedures to clinical problems will attempt to clarify the importance of the distinction between methods for eliciting new response forms and methods for maintaining them in a person's social environment.

The No-Trial Learning Paradigm

Bandura (1965b) has applied this term to a group of studies in which an observer acquires new S-R associations even though there is no explicit opportunity for rehearsal of the behavior or any obvious reinforcing con-sequence of the imitative behavior. These studies differ from those classi-fied as identification learning only in that the imitated behavior is spe-cifically an instrumental response, often followed by reward for the model. Evidence for imitative learning is obtained if previously existing responses are increased or decreased in frequency as a result of the observation trials. Once imitation of the particular model-behavior is established, gen-eralization of the vicarious learning effects can be tested by examining the change in other behaviors not directly demonstrated by the model (response generalization), or by exposure of the subject to slightly different situations (stimulus generalization).

Bandura and his co-workers have carried out many studies with children that examine the effects of specific parameters on the magnitude of imita-tive behaviors. Among the variables studied were: prior model-observer in-teraction, reinforcement of model, filmed or live model presentation, model characteristics, sex and age of the observer, and sex and age of the model. Description of one study can illustrate the general paradigm. Bandura,

Ross, and Ross (1963b) tested the hypothesis that exposure of children to models engaging in aggressive behavior would increase aggressive behavior under subsequent mild frustration. One group of nursery school children observed an adult model play with children's toys. The model first played constructively but then exhibited specific aggressive acts, such as sitting on a Bobo doll, pommeling it on the head with a mallet, tossing the doll in the air and kicking it. These acts were accompanied by aggressive verbal statements. A second group viewed the same models perform on a film, and a third group watched a cartoon film, produced to' parallel the model behaviors but executed by a cartoon cat in a fantasyland setting. The control group had no exposure to models. To induce mild frustration in all the children they were shown some highly attractive toys but were not permitted to play with them. They were led into a testing room that contained the same toys as those available to the model. Imitative and nonimitative responses were then recorded during a 20-minute free play session. Children who viewed live models, film models, or cartoon models did not differ in displayed aggressiveness. All three groups showed more aggressive behavior in general than did the control group. The experimental groups also manifested more of the specific forms of aggressive behavior demonstrated by the model. The results of this study were replicated by Hicks (1965) who also found small residual effects on a retest after six months. These residual effects were greatest when an adult male had served as model. The use of mild frustration in the test situation illustrates the general view that manifestation of behaviors learned by imitation is most likely when the conditions for performing the imitated response are most favorable.

The results of Bandura's experiments suggest that observation may affect both the quantity and quality of behaviors in situations that resemble the observed ones. Observation facilitates some behaviors, and provides cues for execution of specific responses, which otherwise may not occur. In these experiments, witnessing an adult's aggressive behavior probably also was an indication to the child that such normally inhibited behavior was acceptable in the experimental situation, that is, that anticipated punishment would not occur in this setting.

In the preceding study the children observed no reinforcing consequences of the model's aggressive behaviors. In another study with nursery school children, Bandura, Ross and Ross (1963c) exposed some groups to aggressive models who were either punished or rewarded for their behavior. Children who had witnessed the rewarded aggressive model showed more imitative aggression than children who had witnessed a punished aggressive model. Thus, just as observation of rewarded behavior tends to enhance imitation, observation of aversive consequences tends to inhibit it.

In social institutions, the concept of punishment of offenders as deterrent to the population who witness the punishment has a related rationale. The closer analogy lies in the schoolroom where demonstration of the aversive consequences of aggression is frequently used by teachers as a means of control by vicarious learning. Bandura, Ross, and Ross (1963a) also demonstrated that imitation of nonrelevant stylistic model behaviors, described in the Bandura and Huston study above, occurred more frequently when the adult model had previously revealed that he controlled positive reinforcers, such as toys, cookies, or juice, then when the model had previously competed with the child for attractive toys. The model's power status is a significant variable in imitation.

Learning of Self-reinforcement Standards by Observation. The potential of modeling for transmission of behavior is especially important in the development of children's standards for evaluation of their own achievements and establishment of moral judgments. In adults, faulty self-reactions are frequently hypothesized to be the crux of a neurotic patient's problems; clinical interactions often aim at their modification. The use of vicarious learning procedures for changing self-reactions is therefore of great interest to the clinician. The bulk of research on the influence of modeling on modification of self-reinforcement has been carried out with children. Although these studies deal with innocuous situations and the consequences to the child are not nearly as far-reaching as in the home or school environment, demonstration of observation effects on self-regulating behaviors lends credence to the hypothesis that these behavior patterns are not fixed character traits but behaviors accessible to change. Recent applications of these methods in the clinic support their therapeutic value and are discussed later in this chapter.

In one paradigm used by Bandura and his co-workers to study imitation of self-reinforcement and self-punishment, a child observes a model playing a miniature bowling game. Upon attainment of a prearranged score, the model can reward himself by taking candy or tokens from a freely available supply. The score contingency and criteria for self-reward are made explicit by the model's comments. Verbal self-praise or self-criticism accompany the model's self-reinforcements. The child then plays the same game and his scores are manipulated so that they are similar to those of the model, eliminating the effects of the child's skill. The dependent variable is generally the number of self-rewards, self-criticisms, or the number of trials on which rewards are taken. Bandura and Kupers (1964) found that children imitated both the material self-reinforcement patterns and the self-evaluative verbalizations of adult models. Peer models were less effective in setting standards for nonreinforcement of low-level performances. More of the children exceeded the magnitude of candy rewards taken by the model on each occasion when the model was a peer rather than an adult.

A model's criteria for self-reward has an interesting influence not only on the observing subject's evaluation of his own performance but also on his evaluation of others. Marston (1965) found that adult subjects reinforced other persons at a higher rate after observation of a high self-reinforcement rate model than after a low self-reinforcement rate model. Mischel and Liebert (1966) similarly found that criteria that observing subjects imposed on another children tended to be identical with those they imposed on themselves.

The selection of criteria for self-reward does not depend simply on a model's performance. Bandura and Whalen (1966) exposed children to success or failure experiences on games appearing to measure physical strength, problem solving ability, and psychomotor dexterity. The children then observed models set high, moderately high, or low criteria for self-rewards on a miniature bowling game. The prior experience of success or failure did not influence self-reinforcement rates in children whose own scores were manipulated to be at a high level. However, when their performance was set at a low level, children who had previously failed, rewarded themselves less often after observation of inferior models; children in a prior success condition took more rewards than those who observed equally competent superior models. The results point to a complex interaction between modeling cues, prior history, and current performance as joint determinants of the adoption of criteria for reward self-administration.

The effects of combinations of prior nurturant interactions with an adult model, observation of reinforcement to the model contingent on strict self-reinforcement criteria, and additional observation of a peer model with low criteria for self-rewards were examined by Bandura, Grusec, and Menlove (1966). The authors expected model nurturance and vicarious reinforcement to increase imitation of stringent criteria for self-rewards, and peer modeling to reduce that imitation. It was found that observation of model reinforcement resulted in adoption of more stringent criteria, while model nurturance and exposure to lenient peer models led the subjects to adopt more lenient criteria for self-rewards.

When the model explicitly verbalizes the rules for self-reward, children engage in fewer rule violations than children who observe a model engaging in the same behavior without verbalization of the rules. However, high structure of rules was found to increase self-rewarding verbalizations, with verbal behavior that closely paralleled that of the observed model (Liebert and Allen, 1967). The interesting implications of the last study lie in the fact that the pairing of rules for appropriate self-rewards with observation of such behavior in a model tended to affect verbal and material self-rewards differently. Although increased structure increased the children's self-administration of verbal praise and criticism, it decreased the self-administration of tokens that were exchangeable for packaged prizes. In Liebert's and Allen's study the magnitude of the available reward did not affect the frequency of the child's rule violation (that is, taking undeserved self-rewards).

The experimental demonstration of the modifiability of self-imposed criteria for reinforcement invites reexamination of earlier theories about the development of behavior standards in the child's moral and social growth. The effectiveness of model observation appears to extend beyond imitation in relatively isolated play situations. Bandura and McDonald (1963) presented children with a series of items testing moral judgments. It was found that observation of an adult model, who expressed judgments that were either congruent or opposite to the children's altered the children's judgments on a series of additional items presented by a second experimenter. Evidence from studies such as these tends to contrast with the frequently expressed clinical opinion that the nature of a person's characteristic self-evaluative mode and his moral standards are relatively inflexible. Continued findings of this kind would suggest that even those disturbed persons whose clinical picture reveals distortions in their self-regulatory behaviors or in their moral judgment might be amenable to behavior modification, by exposure to behavioral sequences in which a model's criteria for rewards or for moral judgments are closer to the usual social norms.

The Co-Learning Paradigm

In the preceding sections we have discussed situations in which imitative responses are acquired by an observer who does not have explicit knowledge that he will have the opportunity to repeat the observed behavior or that he will be rewarded for such imitation. Many observations among animals and humans have led to the assumption that the mere presence of another organism increases individual activity. When this increase in response frequency occurs in the presence of an organism that is not engaging in the same behavior as the observer or is not engaging in any activity at all, the phenomenon has been called an "audience effect." Audience effects have been observed in feeding situations of many animals, including fish, birds, rats, dogs, and monkeys. In these experiments the difference between the amount of food ingested by a food-deprived animal in the presence and in the absence of a second animal has been taken as a measure of the effect. When the second animal is engaged in the same behavior as is the subject, the effect on the subject's behavior is termed "social facilitation." For example, introduction of a second feeding animal can restore the normal eating behavior of satiated subjects. The social facilitation phenomenon has also been demonstrated in the restoration of key-pecking responses in pigeons after suppression of these responses during a CS-shock interval. Introduction of a second pigeon who continued to key peck for food resulted in resumption of the subject's key-pecking behavior (Hake and Laws, 1967). Several reports of a fear-reducing effect from the presence of another animal have attested to the potential benefits of a second animal in reducing behavioral suppression produced by aversive stimulation (Davitz and Mason, 1955; Harlow and Zimmerman, 1959).

Facilitation due to the presence of another individual who is actively engaged in the same task as the experimental subject is characterized as a *co-learning* situation. Investigators' interests usually concern the facilitating effect of particular parameters in the behavior of the modeling individual on the ease of acquisition of a topographically similar response in the learner. In contrast to the studies discussed in the *no-trial learning* paradigm, human subjects are instructed to direct their attention to the learning task. In animals, reinforcement of a critical response sequence for both model and observer or training in a group, constitute parallel operations. This experimental paradigm differs somewhat from the matched-dependent imitation learning model in that the learner may be exposed to both correct and incorrect model responses and is not explicitly rewarded for copying the precise form of the observed response. This paradigm represents the situation commonly encountered in social learning in which a person who is confronted with a task gains some advantage from the opportunity to observe another. Current educational practices of classroom learning through exposure to the performance of other children, with subsequent examinations of all individuals, illustrates the co-learning situation in everyday behavior.

Panman, Arenson, and Rosenbaum (1962) investigated the effect of demonstrations on maze performance by college students. Subjects who witnessed a demonstration were more successful in their performance than control subjects. However, two demonstrations were sufficient to obtain maximum effects. A third demonstration showed no significant increment in the observer's performance. The authors also found that an initial errorless demonstration did not facilitate learning more than a demonstration containing errors. On the other hand, an additional demonstration with errors resulted in significantly better performance than an additional error-free trial. These results suggest that vicarious learning in the co-learning paradigm does not depend on strict imitation of the model's response.

The observer appears to benefit from information available through observation of the model's behavior, both the model's errors and his correct responses.

Kanfer, Marston, and their co-workers have compared vicarious learning with direct learning and have examined the effect of several related parameters on performance. In one study (Kanfer and Marston, 1963c), college subjects were required to respond alternately with another subject on a verbal learning task. The co-learner was actually a tape-recorded confederate whose responses were experimentally programmed. Following an appropriate response by either the model or the subject, correct responses were verbally reinforced by the experimenter according to the treatment condition. It was found that listening to a tape of a reinforced model was sufficient to produce significant learning; in fact, the further addition of reinforcement for the subject did not significantly enhance learning. On the other hand, when the model gave the same verbal response but was not reinforced, subjects did not imitate the model's verbal behavior. In a second study, Marston and Kanfer (1963a) investigated the relationship between the size of the observed group of models and the amount of learning in the observer. The same verbal conditioning task was used as in the previous study, that is, subjects said words alternately with tape-recorded voices. It was found that decreasing the proportion of reinforced vicarious responses by adding group members resulted in significantly lower learning. As in the previous study, the addition of direct reinforcement to vicarious reinforcement did not significantly increase learning.

The effects of the behavior of a co-learner may be manifested both during the acquisition procedure and during extinction. Differential effects of vicarious reinforcement on acquisition and extinction can be expected. In acquisition the subject requires considerable information about the nature of the task and the appropriateness of certain responses. However, once the subject has learned to perform a task, continued execution of the response during extinction may only require information regarding whether to continue or to change his responses. Marston (1966) found that instructions to continue emitting critical responses were effective in retarding extinction, a result similar to findings reported in other verbal learning experiments. The observation that continuation of vicarious reinforcement during extinction trials has no significant effect on the slope of the learner's extinction curves further strengthens the hypothesis that the main effect of observing the response and contingent reinforcement of another person is on acquisition rather than on maintenance (Marston, 1964).

In most tests of the effect of vicarious learning parameters in co-learning paradigms, the model exhibits a progressively increasing frequency of critical responses during acquisition. Ditrichs, Simon, and Greene (1967) varied the distribution of critical responses over the model's acquisition trials. Some groups heard the model give increasing frequencies of reinforced correct responses; others heard a decreasing or a constant frequency over all trial blocks. Exposure to the natural pattern of improvement in the model was found most effective. When a person is exposed to a series of trials in which the model gives progressively fewer correct responses and obtains progressively fewer reinforcements, acquisition by the learner is not facilitated.

Smith and Marston (1965) hypothesized that vicarious learning of verbal responses would be a function of the size of the response class reinforced in the model and of the word frequency of the responses within this class. They found that the use of high frequency words resulted in better learning than the use of low frequency words. Use of common words provided greater clarity of the response-reinforcement contingency and, in turn, enhanced the benefits of observation by providing information more quickly to the observer. The ease of conditioning by vicarious reinforcement was also found to be greater when the critical response class included many class members already in the subject's repertoire. A similar suggestion that lessened cue ambiguity in observational learning results in faster improvement comes from McDavid's (1962) findings. An observer who is exposed to a model appears to benefit most when the information presented by the model is explicit, when it occurs during acquisition, and when the model increases his own effectiveness over trial blocks. The utility of information based on the model's performance can be varied experimentally by changing the percentage of reinforced trials for the model, the complexity of the learning task, the instructions to the subject, and similar variables.

We have noted in a previous section that the effectiveness of vicarious learning can be modified by varying the model-subject relationship. Several studies have demonstrated that the competence of the model as perceived by the subject substantially influences the observer's learning. Rosenbaum and Tucker (1962) trained subjects to make predictions of the outcome of a series of fictitious horse races, after exposure to the predictions and correctness of these predictions made by a simulated partner. The subjects imitated most when the model's competence in predicting was highest. In a later study (Rosenbaum, Chalmers, and Horne, 1962), the subjects were first exposed to a trial with either success or failure conditions on the same task. By thus providing some criteria for the subject's evaluation of his own skill, the authors could investigate the interaction between observation of a competent or incompetent model and the subject's evaluation of his own performance relative to the model. Prior failure, in contrast to prior success, led to faster acquisition of imitation. The more competent the model's performance appeared, the greater was the tendency of subjects to match the model's behavior. In this study no interaction between the two variables was found. The same group of experimenters also found some relationship between the general level of self-esteem of a subject and his tendency to match the behavior of a model instrumental for success. However, this tendency did not seem to relate to a broad predisposition to match others (Rosenbaum, Horne, and Chalmers, 1962).

A subject's disposition to attend to a model's behavior is crucial to his reception and utilization of information. From the learner's viewpoint, however, such attention may be most effective at the beginning stages of learning when the learner's own competence is lowest. Later, the increased skill of the learner can be expected to decrease the impact of observation on the subject's own performance. If a learner further notes incompetence of the model, he would be expected to use available time for rehearsal of already acquired responses rather than for attending to the model's performance. In fact, continued attention to a model who makes predominantly incorrect responses should disrupt the performance of a subject who has already acquired some degree of efficiency. Kanfer and Duerfeldt (1967b) varied model competence, subject competence, and number of vicarious learning trials in a paired-associate nonsense syllable task. Subjects at the beginning or near the end of their own course of learning listened to a model who was in an early or late stage of learning. The results indicated that model competence alone did not affect learning significantly. However, vicarious trials late in the subject's own acquisition had a disruptive effect, while early exposure to the model yielded benefits similar to those obtained in direct reinforcement trials. The results suggest that a model would influence a beginning learner more than an "experienced" learner.

The experimental work that we have summarized points to many possibilities for modification of individual behavior by observation of a model or by joint participation in a learning task with other subjects. The experimental data so far have had only limited application to complex social learning phenomena encountered in the clinic. The few examples will be summarized at the end of this chapter. However, it should be noted at this point that all of the preceding methods for producing new social learning have some bearing on clinical processes in which a therapist serves as a model for interpersonal behaviors, or in an institutional setting where group behavior is constantly open to observation by the patient. Before discussing clinical applications, however, we shall turn to a summary of laboratory studies concerned with the facilitation of emotional or classically conditioned responses by observation.

Paradigms for Vicarious Conditioning of Arousal

Transmission of emotional experiences by observation is of special interest to clinical psychologists because many patients manifest emotional behaviors that are detrimental to their social effectiveness. Thorough investigation of patients' past histories often fails to reveal particular traumatic experiences in which these emotional responses were strongly reinforced on their first occurrence. Instead, some pattern of emotional response may have become established at first by observation of someone and may have been only subsequently reinforced in the patient's own experience. Arousal of emotional responses by observation of another person is a basic ingredient in the dramatic arts. Free-flowing tears among watchers of tender romantic movies, expressions of anxiety, fear, and erotic stimulation during TV and filmed dramas attest to the impact of emotional behavior on the observer. Berger (1962) terms this process *vicarious instigation.* The definition of this phenomenon requires that the observer respond emotionally to the witnessing of an unconditioned emotional response in another. The particular form of the emotional response in the observer may be identical or dissimilar to the model's response. In the former case, the process has been called *empathy,* while in the latter, it is commonly described as *sympathy.* Berger characterizes four possible combinations of pleasant and unpleasant emotional responses in a model and observer in terms of *concordant* or *discordant* reactions. For example, empathy is defined by a pain response of an observer who watches pain in another, or by a joyful response in the presence of such a response in a model. On the other hand, sadism is defined by discordant joy in the observer when the model is experiencing pain.

Vicarious emotional conditioning can take the form of classical or instrumental conditioning. In vicarious classical conditioning, the observer's vicariously elicited emotional response becomes conditioned, through temporal contiguity, to formerly neutral stimuli. In human experiments, a model is typically exposed to a painful experience in the presence of a neutral stimulus (CS). An observer who exhibits emotional responses to the conditioned stimulus alone, even though he has never experienced the UCS himself, is said to have acquired the response by vicarious classical conditioning.

Berger (1962) conducted a study that illustrates this procedure. Observers witnessed alleged administration of shock, indicated by a CS of a buzzer and dimming of a light. The model also reacted with an arm movement when apparently shocked. The observer's GSR responses were recorded. During observation of the model's conditioning trials and on test trials, observers showed a significantly higher number of GSR responses than subjects who were not told that the model had been shocked. In a control group, which believed that the model had been shocked but could not observe an arm movement, the frequency of GSR responses was lower.

Whether the prior experience of the observed emotional reaction by the subject is a necessary precondition for obtaining the effect was examined by Church (1959). One group of rats was pretrained by suffering brief shocks simultaneous with observation of shock delivery to another rat. One control group received the same number of shocks but they were not associated with observation of stimulation to another rat. A third group received no aversive stimulation during training. The effect of pretraining on response to observation of shock delivery to another rat in an adjacent cage was examined by measuring the rate of suppression of bar-pressing for food. The animals that had been shocked simultaneously with observation of shock to another rat showed the greatest decrement in responding. Animals that had experienced shocks not associated with concurrent stimulation to another rat showed some decrement in responding, and the control group showed little change in their bar-pressing behavior. In humans, inferences about the effects of a pain-evoking stimulus on another person, or inferences about the stimulus conditions that may have brought about an apparent pain reaction in a model, may suffice to mediate establishment of a vicariously conditioned respondent on the basis of the subject's own past experiences in similar situations. Often the observer's inferences may be erroneous, since either the aversive stimulus or the obtained response may not be directly observable. The basis for such conditioning need not necessarily lie in the emphatic emotional experience but can, instead, lie in the interpretation of the situation by the observer, perhaps (as in animals) based on some prior conditioning experience in which pain had been associated with pain cues in the behavior of other animals.

Several studies suggest that communication of emotionality among individuals may proceed in a very subtle way. An interesting example of these findings comes from a series of studies by Malmo and his co-workers (Malmo, Boag, and Smith, 1957) on the interrelationship between the physiological states of two adults in clinical interactions. These studies of "interpersonal physiology" revealed correspondences in various physiological measures in patient and interviewer. In one study, 19 female neurotics were given a Thematic Apperception Test and interview. One striking finding was the correspondence between recorded notes by the examiner about his own subjective state and the patients' mean heart rate. As shown in Figure 5-2, the patient's mean heart rate during the psychological test rose significantly more on the examiner's "bad" days than on his "good"

Patient's Heart Rate

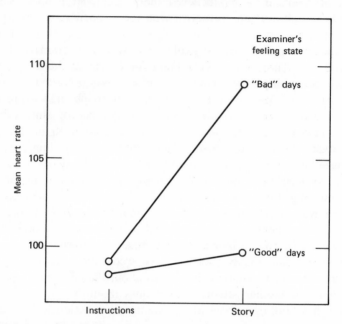

Figure 5-2   TAT. Mean rise in patients' heart rates as a function of examiner's feeling state. Note greater rise in patients' mean heart rate on examiner's "bad" days (from Malmo et al., 1957, p. 114).

days. It is obvious that such subtle mutual modifiability of emotional responses could have profound influence on the course of psychotherapeutic interaction. A series of studies by Miller and his co-workers (Miller, Banks, and Ogawa, 1962; Murphy, Miller, and Mirsky, 1955) have also shown that subtle communication of emotions occurs in animals and can become the basis for learning instrumental behaviors.

The demonstration of a vicariously conditioned respondent requires several steps. First, it must be demonstrated that the stimulus context of the observed situation is sufficient to elicit an emotional response in the observer. Second, the vicarious affective arousal thus instigated must then be shown to be conditionable to a CS. And finally, the emotional response must show other properties of learned behavior, such as the continuation of its strength for some time after removal of the reinforcing stimulus until extinction progresses, or the generalization of the emotional response to other situations. It would also be of interest to discover whether such emotional responses facilitate the vicarious learning of instru-mental behaviors in a model with whom the subject shares emotional responding.

The degree of psychological stress due to observation of motion pictures has been examined in several studies. For example, Lazarus, Speisman, Mordkoff, and Davidson (1962) had college students observe a film of a crude operation performed as part of a primitive puberty ritual in an Australian tribe. Scenes of the operation, which included expressions of pain and cries from a young boy, were accompanied by increases in au-tonomic responses of the observing students. Modifications of the sound track's expressions of pain and commentaries about the operation altered the degree of autonomic arousal. Alfert (1966) compared the effects of observation and direct experience of painful stimulation on heart rate, skin resistance, and respiration in college students. Some subjects watched a film of an accident. Others were exposed to a stressful shock threat situation. In both groups, changes were found in heart rate and skin resis-tance that were similar in direction of change but differed somewhat in magnitude of change. The respiration measure did not change significantly in the shock threat situation and decreased during the film observation. Individual subjects also showed significant correlations in their response to the two forms of threat.

Changes in autonomic functioning can be produced by considerably less threatening experiences than watching the blood and gore associated with operations or accidents. Craig and Weinstein (1965) monitored skin resistance in subjects who observed a model failing or succeeding in the performance of an ostensibly difficult motor task. Groups observing failure consistently responded with more GSR responses than groups observing success. However, subjects were no more responsive when told that shock would be administered to the model if he failed than were subjects who did not receive this information. Parallel findings were obtained by Koba-sigawa (1965) who used an indirect method of measuring emotional arousal. First grade boys observed an adult ostensibly guessing the location of a marble in one of two blocks. The model was successful on some trials, completely failed on others, and failed on the remaining trials when close to reaching criterion. The observing child was required to depress a plunger that turned off a buzzer at the end of each trial. The magnitude of observationally aroused emotions was inferred from the child's reaction time and amplitude of the response. The children responded with signifi-cantly greater amplitudes and greater speeds following observation of the model's failure just before reaching the criterion. The author concludes that situations that are differentially frustrating to the model elicit cor-respondingly different magnitudes of response in the observer.

If the arousal level of the observer is a major factor in vicarious classical conditioning, then variations in this arousal level by experimental manipulations should result in differences in vicarious learning. Bandura and Rosenthal (1966) tested this hypothesis by varying the degree of psychological arousal, using injections of epinephrine in three dosages, a placebo injection, a placebo injection plus threat of shock, and a neutral condition. The subjects observed a model who ostensibly received shock and exhibited pain cues following a buzzer (CS) during his performance of a pursuit rotor task. The frequency of GSRs served as a measure of emotional responsiveness in the observer. The study confirmed that arousal could be induced by observation of punishment of another. The placebo injection plus shock threat increased the frequency of conditioned GSR responses. The high dosages of epinephrine, however, did not yield the expected results. In the highly aroused groups, many subjects attempted to divert their attention from the model's pain by generating competing responses, such as thinking about something else; this may have added to the complexity of the findings.

Equivalence of physiological responding during observed experience and imagined emotional scenes is of special interest to the clinician because many therapeutic methods attempt to short-circuit direct behavior modification in vivo by use of verbal recall, observation of the experiences of others, or pictures of emotional situations. Craig (1968) compared the magnitude and quality of physiological arousal as a function of imagined, observed, and experienced pain. Naive subjects served as both models and observers. Each subject was requested to undergo the cold pressor test, in which the hand is immersed in ice water. All subjects underwent this experience directly, observed their partner, and imagined the experience. The sequence of these conditions was balanced for the experimental groups. The direct experience resulted in significantly greater arousal than the other conditions. Respiration rate increased during the vicarious and imagined conditions, but decreased during the actual experience. Heart rate increased considerably for the direct stress and imagined stress conditions but not for the vicarious condition. In fact, a qualitative difference was noted, with acceleration of heart rate during direct and imagined stress and deceleration during vicarious stress. Skin conductance measures showed greater increases with direct experience than with vicarious experience, but the imagined stress did not differ significantly from either the direct or vicarious condition. Direct arousal also produced changes that lasted over a longer period of time. Similar results were obtained by Craig and Wood (1969). Both direct and vicarious experience with the cold pressor test produced increases in skin conductance. Heart rate, however, accelerated with the direct experience and decelerated with vicarious experience. When the direct preceded the vicarious experience, the deceleration was more pronounced. Craig and Wood interpret their findings according to Lacey's hypotheses (Lacey, Kagan, Lacey, and Moss, 1963) that situations requiring sustained attention to environmental input (for example, empathic observation) should produce heart rate deceleration while situations calling for avoidance of external input (such as cold pressor) should produce heart rate acceleration.

Although these studies do not involve vicarious conditioning, they do have important implications for work on vicariously instigated conditioned emotional responses. The qualitative differences in arousal pattern from direct, imagined, and vicarious experiences suggest different emotional arousal patterns, involving divergent changes in different autonomic components, which may affect central learning processes and behavioral consequences. Prediction of the variables affecting vicarious respondent conditioning solely by extrapolation from studies on direct conditioning would thus appear to be invalid.

Increment in emotional arousal in an observer would suggest a change in his motivational dispositions, if one views emotional states as drive states with directive and potential reinforcing properties. The consequences of emotionally arousing observation for an instrumental response have been described in the previously cited study by Kobasigawa. A further test of the effects of emotional arousal on an instrumental response has been provided by Di Lollo and Berger (1965). Female college students observed a model who was supposedly shocked during a series of trials in an alleged reaction time experiment. For some subjects the model manifested pain cues by moving her arm, while other subjects only observed the alleged administration of shock but no movement by the model. Control subjects observed movement or no movement by the model but without instructions that the model was shocked. Reaction time of the subjects on the same task was considerably shorter when both shock and movement has been vicariously experienced. When the model gave no pain cues, the observer's reaction time was not affected. The importance of the observer's interpretation of the witnessed event was highlighted in this study. When the model gave no evidence of the presumed shock by arm movement, 23 of the 25 subjects on postexperimental questioning expressed their belief that the performer received only a mild shock or was not shocked at all. Thus subjective interpretation by the observer may have been sufficient to reduce vicarious arousal in the presence of a scene in which aversive stimulation was allegedly given to the model.

In the preceding studies, which used the no-trial paradigm, the subject is commonly reassured that he will not receive painful stimulation subsequent to observation of such aversive treatment of the model. Vicarious learning, however, may also occur when the model's behavior has direct consequences to the observer. Craig (1967) had subjects observe the performance of a model on a temporal maze. Whenever the model made an error, both the model and the observer were shocked. Compared with other subjects who received no shock but only observed the model being shocked, the punished subjects differed in their subsequent learning of the same task. Shocked male subjects performed more efficiently, but shocked female subjects learned more poorly than the nonshocked groups. Since the females rated the shocks as more painful than did the males, the effect may be related to the subjective intensity of the aversive stimulus during observation. Craig also found that naive models required many more trials to master the task than did the observing subjects on their later test. These findings substantiate earlier reports of the facilitative effect of observation. The studies reviewed in this section suggest that the observation of painful or frustrating experiences in a model does not always result in as intense an emotional arousal as a direct or imagined experience, but that the observation does produce some arousal. The subject's interpretation of the observation affects his response. In turn, vicarious arousal modifies the observer's later performance on the same task, but vicarious learning is not necessarily the same in magnitude or kind as learning predicted if the subject were in the model's position.

Subject and Model Characteristics Influencing Vicarious Effects

We have already alluded to evidence that relatively enduring characteristics of models influence observers' imitation. When a model is powerful, that is, in the past or present has controlled the observer's access to resources he values, imitation is increased. If the model loses this control, imitation decreases (see, for example, Mischel and Liebert, 1967). Miller and Dollard proposed in their initial writing that model status, as conferred by age, skill, or social prestige, would increase observer imitation. A number of studies have verified this prediction. Conclusions regarding the effects on imitation of the quality of past interaction between model and observer are uncertain since the evidence is conflictual. There is some support that model nurturance (noncontingent affection) enhances observer imitation, and that the observer's affection for a model may do likewise, but the conditions under which these variables do and do not increase imitation are as yet not clear (Hetherington and Frankie, 1967; Sampson and Insko, 1964).

Of special interest are the effects of the observer's relatively enduring personality characteristics on his acquisition of new behaviors. These exemplify the advantages of knowing the role of individual differences in the planning of treatment. However, at this stage, the behavior therapies have not yet given much attention to this set of variables. What patient characteristics increase or reduce the probability of his utilizing models to acquire new useful behaviors? This question, in general form, requires study in connection with all of the operations of behavior modification and we will discuss it briefly in Chapter 10. In the area of social learning, a study by Patterson, Littman, and Brown (1968) illustrates the role of personal traits in moderating the effects of a model's behavior. Negativism or "negative set" was assessed in first grade boys by counting the number of times the child altered his initial choice on a picture preference task after an adult model made the same choice. Children with high negative sets were also found to show little effect of modeling. When and to what extent negative set affects acquisition or matching behaviors, and what model, task, incentive, and other situation characteristics may influence the extent of negative set are questions yet to be explored. Other observer characteristics of a more temporary nature that have been found to influence degree or quality of imitation include level of physiological arousal, dependency, self-esteem, immediately prior experiences with failure and social isolation, and an affective state (anger) consonant with the model's responses (aggression).

Until the mechanisms involved in imitation and vicarious learning are better understood, the accumulation of isolated findings of the effects of moderating situational and personality variables can have a crude sort of usefulness in clinical applications. But they do not permit the planned utilization of these variables in enhancing imitation effects for therapeutic purposes. They also suggest the necessity of including some constructs of central processes to account for the imitation process, since subjects appear to respond not by simple imitation of rewarded behavior alone. Their imitative behavior also depends on their attention to the model, their interpretation of the witnessed behavior, their attitudes, and similar complex variables. Indeed, some investigators hold that observational learning has particular value in studying mediational processes within S-R theory because of the dilemmas posed for S-R formulations by such data as Bandura's "no-trial learning" (Greenwald and Albert, 1968).

THEORETICAL ISSUES IN VICARIOUS LEARNING

Our review of laboratory experiments in vicarious learning has given ample evidence of the richness of data on variables affecting observational learning. Despite the multitude of studies, however, the theoretical explanation of observational learning is still vague and incomplete. The lack of a clearer conceptualization of the vicarious learning process may be responsible for the failure of clinical psychologists to make more extensive use of the vicarious learning paradigm in their daily clinical activities. Several alternate theories have been advanced to explain the principal dilemma of the nature of reinforcement in vicarious learning, when the observer is clearly not exposed to direct reinforcement. Among these are five major approaches.

Theories of Matched-Dependent Behavior (Miller and Dollard; Skinner)

Two theoretical analyses of matched-dependent behavior have been proposed. Miller and Dollard (1941) hypothesized that the model's actions serve as a cue for matching responses in a motivated subject. In copying behavior, the critical requirement for reinforcement of the follower is a progressively closer match to the model. In matched-dependent behavior, the observer's imitative performance leads to direct reward, usually similar to that obtained by the model at the end of the behavior sequence exposed for imitation. Drive reduction accounts for strengthening of the imitative response.

The operant analysis of imitation (Skinner, 1953) is based on the assumption that, through a history of discrimination training, a repertoire of matching responses is established in every child. Repeated reinforcement for imitating the behavior of the adults, peers, and animals who populate the child's world eventually results in selective imitation due to differential reinforcement for imitating such diverse behaviors as a peer's eating habits, mother's household activities, or a sibling's play patterns. The model whose behavior the child gainfully copies becomes an S^D in whose presence copying can be expected to increase.

Neither Hullian nor Skinnerian interpretations appear sufficiently comprehensive to account alone for socialization by imitative learning. The high dependence on the relationship between model and learner and on the reinforcement of the instrumental response that is copied, and the restriction of imitation to responses that the learner can execute without difficulty tend to limit somewhat the wide use of these techniques for clinical purposes. However, the experimental data on imitation clearly demonstrate that conformity behavior can be established by reinforcement of imitation responses, at least when simple behaviors are involved and reward is directly given for performance of discrete imitative behaviors. In the clinical case, research on the conditions that modify a person's motivation to follow a leader and research on other verbal-mediational factors influencing the probability that an adult will blindly perform an observed response suggest that careful attention to such parameters as the therapy relationship and the skill of the patient in execution of the modeled response is required before imitative learning methods can be used for therapeutic purposes.

Mowrer's Theory of Imitation

Mowrer (1960a) proposed two possible explanations for observational learning. In the case of immediate reinforcement of the observer, contemporaneous with the model's performance, the observed response becomes associated with positive reinforcement until it gradually acquires secondary reward characteristics. When no direct reinforcement to the observer is given, learning is assumed to occur because the observer experiences both the response-correlated stimuli and, vicariously, through the mediation of his own instigated conditioned emotional responses, the reinforcing consequences of the model's behavior. This experience produces positive sensory feedback and the observer will therefore tend to imitate the model's responses.

Bandura's Imitation Theory

Bandura (1965b) proposes a contiguity theory of observational learning. The perceptual, symbolic, and sensory events possess cue properties that later serve as discriminative stimuli for the same overt responses as those that have been observed. The observer thus learns to associate certain responses with the observed conditions. These associations, without execution of the actual behavior, provide the basis for imitation when the observer is now in a similar position as the model had been, and he is motivated sufficiently to act. Bandura states that "thus, in this mode of response acquisition, imaginal and verbal representations of modeling stimuli constitute the enduring learning products of observational experiences" (1965b, p. 47).

This conceptualization treats acquisition of matching responses on the basis of stimulus contiguity. Since most experiments deal with responses that are already in the observer's repertoire, the question of how the observer acquires skill in execution of the imitated response is not a critical one. Bandura further distinguishes between the learning process during observation and the performance of the imitated response in test situations. It is in the latter situation that availability of reinforcement to the learner may modify his performance of the previously learned behavior. An experiment by Bandura (1965a) supported his hypothesis that reinforcements administered to a model influence the performance but not the acquisition of matching responses by the observer. Children watched films of aggressive adult models who were rewarded, punished, or suffered no consequence for their responses. In a subsequent test, the children in the three groups produced differential amounts of imitative behavior, as predicted. However, when attractive reinforcers were then offered to the children in all groups for reproducing the model's aggressive behavior, the previously observed performance differences were eliminated and all children demonstrated similar learning effects. From an experimental viewpoint, Bandura's study is significant in calling attention to the need for a careful separation of the variables that affect learning during observation, and the conditions that enhance or inhibit the reproduction of such learned behaviors in later tests.

Bandura's mediational hypothesis is further supported in a study by Greenwald and Albert (1968). Observers watched a model perform a visual discrimination avoidance task. The observers were later tested on the same task, but for some groups their position with respect to the apparatus was rotated, or the instrumental response was shifted from one hand to the other. It was found that only the group for whom both the orientation and hand were changed performed slightly more poorly than their model. For the other groups, learning by observation was shown to be as efficient as learning by practice. The demonstration of a positive transfer, even when specific response requirements were changed from observation to performance conditions, tends to support Bandura's suggestion that what is learned during observation is not a set of highly specific single responses but a general set of "imaginal and verbal representations" that can be altered to suit slightly different stimulus conditions.

Gewirtz's Conditional Discrimination-Learning Model

In a recent paper Gewirtz and Stingle (1968) propose a simple mechanism for acquisition and maintenance of generalized imitation, representing a more detailed analysis derived from an operant conditioning framework. The authors view imitation as a particular type of learned stimulus control over a class of functionally related (imitative) responses that are acquired, as other behaviors, by extrinsic reinforcement. Gewirtz and Stingle trace the origin of imitation to the early reinforcement of an infant's imitative responses. After the infant has imitated an adult model in many instances—even though they vary in content—he will have experienced repeated successes for imitation. Thus, a class of functionally equivalent behaviors are acquired—a generalized tendency to imitate—since all share the common fate of reinforcement in the context of particular stimuli (model cues).

Development of this class is analogous to training subjects in matching-to-sample tasks. In this laboratory task, animal or human subjects learn to respond only to the identity between a set of comparison stimuli and a standard stimulus, with the specific character of the matching set of shapes or objects varying from trial to trial. "On each trial, S's response to the comparison stimulus from the finite number in the array that matches the standard stimulus (the sample) is analogous to his selecting from a large set of alternatives (i.e., from his own repertoire) the response that matches the cues provided by the model's response, that is, the imitative response" (Gewirtz and Stingle, 1968, p. 380). This formulation overcomes the major criticism of the response-for-response matching required by other S-R formulations, since copying is a generalized process and not response-specific in this model.

Maintenance of imitation is presumed to occur because in daily life innumerable copying behaviors are extrinsically reinforced, at least on an intermittent schedule. The paradigm therefore can relinquish the concept of intrinsic and vicarious reinforcement in the acquisition of imitation. Gewirtz and Stingle call attention to the ubiquitous overlap in early socialization between a child's behaviors, viewed by adults as progress toward more competent and mature behaviors, and behaviors that he has observed older models perform. Thus reinforcement for progress toward increasing competence can at the same time be reinforcement for generalized imitation. Although the content, models, and reinforcement schedules may change as he grows up, the general response class of imitation continues to be reinforced throughout the child's development.

The imitation model is extended by the authors to the acquisition of general attitudes, values, or motives of others, thus providing a parsimonious basis for describing the development of identification. The imitation of adult behaviors in children's play, the assumption of large behavior segments (roles) of the models and eventually the performance of complex repertoires that are similar to those of one or many models are events that depend upon (as in the simple case) the amount of extrinsic reinforcement available for these behaviors during their acquisition. This view opens the way for exploration of changes in identification content, since extinction for a particular model or response class would be expected if differential nonreinforcement follows imitative behavior under special conditions. Gewirtz's and Stingle's view thus stresses the role of direct reinforcement to the observer in learning to imitate, rejects mediating or stimulus-contiguity mechanisms as basic processes in imitation, and proposes instead a model in which the social conditions of early development combine with learning processes to give rise to a special type of social learning mechanism. The proposed model has interesting implications for new research approaches in developmental psychology, and is an example, par excellence, of the use of the simple S-R model for analysis and explanation of complex social processes. Its viability will depend upon verification of the large assumptions made by the authors about the distribution of copying behaviors and their common fate during infancy and childhood.

Berger's Vicarious Instigation Hypothesis

Berger (1961, 1962) has emphasized the importance of isolating vicarious learning processes from the effects of direct reinforcement to the performer. He argues that any demonstration of vicarious reinforcement must eliminate all potential sources of direct reinforcement of the observer. This requirement is difficult to meet, since experimental subjects who are exposed to modeled behavior often assume that such demonstrations are only a prelude to their own later execution of similar responses. Berger mentions as the most common sources of contaminating direct reinforcement in the study of vicarious processes: direct reinforcement to the observer for imitation; the possibility that the model's responses may serve as discriminative stimuli for subsequent direct reinforcement to the observer; and the condition in which the performance of the model may itself have direct reinforcing effects on the observer because of the nature of the performer's responses. Berger's definition of *vicarious instigation* restricts the term to behavior in which the observer experiences an emotional response in conjunction with the unconditioned emotional response of the performer. Experimental situations in which other cues serve to elicit the observer's response are described as instances of *pseudovicarious instigation*.

Berger's emphasis on the importance of controlling observer rehearsal and its potential reinforcing consequences during observation is illustrated in several experiments that examined the role of the observer's practice. A theoretical position admitting the possibility of learning without response rehearsal demands that any test for such learning be free of direct reinforcement. The opportunity for an observer to engage in covert or symbolic responses would introduce possible sources for some reinforcement to the observer through his execution of the response. Berger (1966) found that the majority of his observers practiced the critical responses during exposure to the model's behavior. He also showed that retention of observed responses was a function of the magnitude of this rehearsal. Practice occurred even when the observers were instructed that they would not participate in the experiment and had little basis for anticipation of later reinforcement. These experiments led Berger to conclude that observational learning may be the result of an ongoing tendency for observers to practice modeled behaviors during the exposure period.

RELATION OF VICARIOUS LEARNING TO SOCIAL PSYCHOLOGY AND RESEARCH TRENDS

Our review of imitation learning has stressed *learning by imitation* rather than *learning to imitate,* and the S and C variables rather than the O and R variables of our behavioral equation. The personal and emotional conditions and the behavioral content that determine a person's tendency to imitate are of central interest to social psychologists. All of these features are embodied in the summary in Table 5-2, but are also relevant to the study of attitude development, the dynamics of persuasion, and social conformity. Table 5-2 includes in Types I to V situations in which the model's behavior serves mainly as a cue for the observer's independent actions. The facilitating effects of the presence of another person or of observation alone must be differentiated from imitation, as described in Types VI through IX of Table 5-2. An observation having an effect is not sufficient for inferring imitation. The specific effect must be a performance by the observer highly similar to that of the model.

To illustrate the continuity of vicarious learning with other work in social psychology, two examples will suffice. It has been hypothesized that *mere presence* of another organism increases general arousal level, and hence acts as an energizer of all response tendencies (Zajonc, 1965). Differential predictions for observational learning could be derived from this hypothesis for vicarious learning situations in which initial drive level and competition among response tendencies is varied. Further predictions for individual behavior in social groups are also possible on the basis of social facilitation alone, for example, the increase of eating, drinking, or copulating behavior when animals in moderate drive-states are exposed to the presence of others (Zajonc, 1968). The proposition that a model may exercise a disinhibiting or constraining influence on the subject's performance falls under Gilmore's Type IV classification of imitative behaviors (see Table 5-2). Yet anyone interested in the study of leadership or emotional contagion in social groups must understand the directing influence of a model in channeling instrumental behaviors toward a specified goal, and its interaction with the prevailing response disposition of the group.

The contribution of the subject's past history has been touched upon only in a few studies, even though experiments in social psychology have shown the continuing influence of personality variables on the perception of others, on the susceptibility of influence to social pressures, and other behavior dispositions of importance in vicarious learning. In summarizing a symposium devoted to the topic of social facilitation and imitation, Hoppe (1968) expressed this trend toward rapprochement of social psychology and imitation research.

"Since the study of social facilitation may involve investigating any type of behavior which is effected by the presence of others (no matter what they may be doing), it is basic to the study of imitation. Indeed, the study of social facilitation is basic to social psychology. Imitative behavior is very widespread, and the understanding of it is crucial for the understanding of many types of social behavior. The investigation of imitation can, of course, be aided by understanding social facilitation" (Hoppe, 1968, p. 244).

Present theoretical analyses of vicarious learning processes leave open several important questions concerning underlying mechanisms. Imitation of a model could be determined by an early developmental pattern in which a general set to imitate has been continuously reinforced. Imitation per se may thus be a strong secondary reinforcer in older individuals. The Greenwald and Albert study is almost alone in examining the specificity of the learned imitative behavior. Although their experimental work suggests that imitative behavior is not exact in duplicating the observed response, experimental evidence of the degree of generalization or transfer of modeled behavior to new situations is still needed. This evidence is especially crucial since vicarious learning in clinical situations would primarily be directed toward learning general rules about behavior, instead of acquisition of situation-specific responses. Theoretically, it would aid in differentiating between the cue function of model responses for execution of one set of observer behaviors or another, and the function of model responses as prototypes for their precise adoption by the observer.

Experimental data have dealt mainly with acquisition by imitation. There is as yet little evidence about the durability of the imitated response. Although the response may be imitated during an initial test, many other factors may determine whether the imitative behavior is maintained over a long period of time. A further experimental problem lies in determining the exact probability of the imitated response in the observer's repertoire prior to observation. Modeling may gain much of its effect by directing an observer's attention to potentially effective behaviors in a social environment. The role of modeling experiences in offering discriminative control would be especially useful in modifying the behavior of individuals who are relatively competent in their performance of the necessary response but for whom differentiated stimulus control has failed to produce such behaviors at the appropriate time. Further clarification of these and other points would substantially facilitate the utilization of vicarious learning techniques in practical situations.

THE EFFECTS OF MODELING IN FIELD SITUATIONS AND ON CLINICAL PROBLEMS

The beneficial effects of modeling on altruistic behavior were studied in a series of experiments by Bryan and Test (1967). The naturalistic setting of one experiment was that of a young lady in distress with a flat tire on the side of a highway. In the experimental condition another automobile approximately a quarter of a mile before the experimental car was raised by a jack under the bumper and a girl was watching a man change a flat tire. The dependent variable consisted of the number of cars that stopped and offered to help the young lady whose car was incapacitated. In three other experiments models donated coins in a Salvation Army kettle in a busy shopping center. The results in all four situations were quite consistent. The presence of a helping model significantly increased helping behavior. The particular mechanisms in the observer's altruistic behaviors under these natural conditions are much more complex and cannot easily be described in terms of a pure modeling effect. Nevertheless, the studies demonstrated the global facilitative effect of a model in complex social behaviors. Their experimental situation parallels the widespread selling practice of exhibiting a consumer using a product in order to decrease the observer's resistance to buying that product. Probably the most deliberate use of such modeling is that of the proverbial "shill" who is the first in the crowd to step up to a lottery, a card game, or a similar venture.

Modeling Treatment of Phobias

A direct test of the effectiveness of modeling positive behaviors in the reduction of fear and avoidance behavior was carried out by Bandura, Grusec, and Menlove (1967). Nursery school children who displayed fearful behavior toward dogs observed a fearless peer model approach a cocker spaniel in the context of an enjoyable party atmosphere. On four consecutive days the dog-avoidant children observed the peer model in petting, feeding, and other positive interactions with the dog. This episode was introduced while the children were enjoying a party accompanied by the usual paraphenalia of treats, colored hats, and balloons. The demonstrated approach responses were graduated, with progressively stronger behaviors displayed in successive sessions. Control groups of other children equally afraid of dogs were exposed to (1) the same graduated modeling stimuli but in a neutral context; (2) observation of the dog alone in a positive context without model; and (3) participation in the positive party activities without exposure to either dog or model. The children who had observed the peer model in fearless play with the dog showed significantly greater reduction of avoidance behavior on subsequent behavioral tests. This fear reduction was maintained at a follow-up evaluation one month after the posttreatment test. The addition of a positive context to the modeling behavior did not prove to be especially beneficial. Later studies using similar procedures by the same group of investigators indicated that live demonstrations are more powerful than symbolic modeling (films) in reducing the children's fear, but this difference can be offset when the movies include a broader range of models and aversive stimuli (Bandura and Menlove, 1968). If the differences between direct versus symbolic experience with a model are replicated, they have important implications for desensitization (and perhaps aversive conditioning) therapies, which usually rely on symbolic stimuli.

The efficacy of modeling and desensitization treatments have been compared, *in toto,* using criteria of affective, behavioral, and attitudinal changes in snake-phobic adolescents and adults (Bandura, Blanchard, and Ritter, 1968). Four conditions were used. (1) Subjects instructed in anxiety-inhibiting relaxation watched films of models engaged in progressively more fear-inducing interactions with a snake. The subjects controlled their own rate of exposure to the films and were instructed to restore relaxation and to start the films over any time they became anxious. (2) Subjects repeatedly observed a live model interacting with a snake in progressively more intimate steps. At each step, the subjects themselves carried out the behavior they had observed in the model. Again, progress through the graded approach behaviors was controlled by the subjects' reported fear. Only when they were fearless with one approach response was the next step begun. (3) The third group received standard Wolpian systematic desensitization (see Chapter 4). Therapy continued until all snake-connected fears had been extinguished, or for six hours of treatment, which was the maximum time for all groups. (4) A control group took all pre- and posttests but received no treatment. When the groups were compared on a behavioral avoidance test, the controls were unchanged. The symbolic modeling with relaxation group and the desensitization group showed substantial gains in approach behaviors. The live modeling and guided practice group achieved total elimination of avoidance in 92 percent of the subjects. Both of the modeling treatments also significantly reduced reported anticipatory anxiety before the behavioral test, and reported anxiety during the test.

An unusual feature of this study was the inclusion of attitudinal measures (rating scales and semantic differential). Social learning and experimental social psychology studies have provided evidence that lasting attitudinal changes are most effectively induced by getting a person to emit new behaviors, without untoward consequences toward the attitude object. As hypothesized, Bandura and his associates found that this "behavior-oriented strategy" produced the greatest attitudinal changes in the live modeling and practice group. Desensitization and symbolic modeling, which involved extinction of negative affect and thus can be termed an affect-oriented approach to attitude change, also showed favorable attitude change results but to a lesser extent than in those subjects who had gained experiential feedback. Generalization of reduced anxiety to other stimuli than snakes also was most widespread in the live modeling and practice group. The symbolic modeling group showed reduction both in animal fears and in other areas of functioning, whereas subjects treated by desensitization showed generalization of fear reduction only to other animals. At a one-month follow-up all of the improvements had been maintained.

One further feature of this study deserves special mention. The investigators noted that when a given therapy exercises only weak control over behavior, other variables (such as personality of patient and characteristics of therapists) are likely to strongly influence the outcome. To demonstrate that treatment rather than personal characteristics were involved when subjects failed to lose all snake-phobic behavior, the control, desensitization, and symbolic modeling subjects were subsequently given the live modeling and guided experience treatment. All of these subjects then lost all of their snake-phobic behavior within a few brief sessions, and showed the same generalization of fear reduction and attitudinal changes as had the initial live modeling group.

Snake-phobic children treated in groups by live modeling or by live modeling plus guided experience showed similar outcomes (Ritter, 1968). Snake phobia was completely extinguished by modeling alone in 53 percent of the children and in 80 percent of the children by modeling plus guided experience, in only two sessions of 35 minutes.

We have described the Bandura, Blanchard and Ritter study at some length because it is one of the few that addresses itself to relative efficacy and efficiency of several behavior modification therapies, and because it attends to several important different criteria of change. Especially important to clinical application in the future will be research clarifying the mechanisms through which modeling and guided experience operate. The comments concerning the importance of understanding the theoretical as well as the engineering aspects of a technique, made earlier in connection with analogue studies and "dismantling" studies of desensitization, apply here also.

Bandura (1968) explains the power of modeling combined with guided participation in producing extinction according to the dual process theory of avoidance behavior (Rescorla and Solomon, 1967) discussed in an earlier chapter. According to this paradigm, repeated modeling of approach responses reduces in the observer the arousal potential of the aversive stimulus to a level below that necessary to activate avoidance responses. The observer can then engage in approach behaviors, even if somewhat anxiously, thereby experiencing positive consequences for this new behavior. These favorable consequences compete with any residual anxiety and avoidance tendencies to produce attitudinal changes and anxiety-free approach behaviors. It is interesting to recall that Wolpe, Salter, and others began their extinction of anxiety with in vivo procedures, Wolpe switching to symbolic (imagined scenes) stimuli as a matter of convenience. Other workers have more recently tried in vivo graded approach experiences without prior modeled or symbolic desensitization, with only mild success. Bandura's combination of indirect and direct experience is more like that of Meyer (1966) who has his patients immediately experience each hierarchy item after it has been desensitized by Wolpe's procedure. One provocative question then has to do with the similarity and differences in efficacy and mechanism between Wolpian imagined scenes in which one engages in nonavoidance behaviors, and exposure to symbolic models in similar circumstances. Similarly, Bandura et al. in the above study used relaxation as a competing response during exposure to symbolic models. Humphery (1966) uses candy rather than relaxation to elicit responses competitive to anxiety in phobic children in a procedure otherwise very similar to the symbolic modeling in this study (for example, patient control of rate of progress through hierarchy and use of projected stimuli). Finally, the superiority of live over symbolic models suggests that use of actual experiences may enhance the effects of the standard systematic desensitization procedure. Judicious combinations of imaginal modification in interviews with systematic use of live modeling situations may also provide a treatment program in which various levels of behavior, verbal and active, are used to achieve more rapid and wider changes in inefficient behaviors.

Modeling Approaches to Interview Behaviors

The vicarious learning model has been applied directly to interview therapy. Traux, Wargo, Carkhuff, Kodman, and Moles (1966) used a co-learning design in which groups of hospitalized mental patients and institutionalized juvenile delinquents received pretraining by listening to a modeling tape that contained several segments of preselected group therapy interactions demonstrating "good" patient behavior. The investigators hypothesized that such pretraining would facilitate learning by providing information about the "proper" patient role of self-exploration in psychotherapy. In client-centered group psychotherapy, a major goal of treatment is to achieve a change in the patient's self-concept, manifested by a changed relationship between self and ideal concept measures. The effects of the vicarious pretraining session, therefore, were evaluated by means of a series of measures commonly used to evaluate adjustment changes within this theoretical framework. The introduction of a vicarious pretraining session resulted in greater positive change on several of the measures, indicating that the vicarious pretraining facilitated therapeutic progress. If gains through the traditional interview method of psychotherapy are achieved when the patient can freely describe his problems, explore his feelings and attitudes, and respond to the therapist's comments, then pretraining for these patient role behaviors should expedite therapeutic progress. For example, Dollard and Miller (1950) and other learning theorists have proposed that patients may resist discussion of personal problems during interviews because of their past experiences of punishment for admission of weaknesses or discussion of conflicts and fears. Observation of a model who discloses his problems and of a therapist who responds with encouraging or accepting comments should enhance the patient's freedom and spontaneity in talking about himself.

Marlatt, Jacobson, Johnson, and Morrice (1966) conducted a study in which college student subjects in a waiting room were exposed to a programmed interchange (consisting of problem statements by the model) between a model patient and a therapist. Three experimental groups were used, differing in the quality of experimenter's comments. The therapist was either discouraging, encouraging, or passively accepting of the model-patient's statements. Control subjects did not overhear any discussion. The experimental manipulations resulted in significant differences in the frequency of problems admitted by subjects in their own later interviews. The encouraging and passively accepting groups showed an increase in problem admission, while the discouraging and control groups showed a decline, when each subject's scores were compared with his own performance in a premodel interview. In other studies, Marlatt and his associates also showed that the model may be presented in person or on tape, or the subject may simply read the model's responses in a written script, without apparent loss of effectiveness. They also found that ambiguity of instructions regarding their own interviews significantly affected the extent to which subjects imitated the model patient (Marlatt, 1968).

This effort to partial out effects of differing task characteristics represents the sort of research strategy necessary to explicate both mechanisms involved in vicarious influences on performance and the features that will govern its value in clinical application. Thus Marlatt's study supports the role of attention-focusing aspects of a model's behavior, that is, a discrimination theory approach to observational effects on behavior. It also indicates that clear instructions as to the behaviors wanted may sometimes achieve similar results in clinical interviews. Whether instructions can duplicate modeling effects when the target behavior is, for example, level of affect in therapy group members (Schwartz and Hawkins, 1965), instead of the number of problems admitted, remains to be discovered. This underlines again the necessity of studying different target behaviors that may differ in important and defined ways, prior to their attack by a technology of behavior modification. Comparisons of vicarious and direct reinforcement therapies for behaviors that have already been independently subjected to both types of approach is also a high priority research need, both for selection of clinical tools and for clarification of theoretical disputes. Marlatt, in following a discrimination theory of observational effects, emphasizes the disruptive and distracting effects on performance of direct reinforcement (as have Hillix and Marx, 1960). He stresses the need for separation of acquisition and performance in studies of vicarious processes, in order to explicate the informational and motivational-incentive components of reinforcement.

Duke, Frankel, Sipes, and Stewart (1965) also demonstrated that subjects who had heard tapes or read scripts of interviews in which interviewees talked about topics on which the subjects had spoken least during an earlier interview, later talked significantly more on these topics than did control subjects who did not hear the tapes or read the scripts. The results point to the critical role of information in this use of vicarious learning, since the transcripts provided no direct observation of the model's actual interview behavior. These recent studies strongly suggest that modeling, or perhaps even a very explicit briefing session, may contribute to short-circuiting the cumbersome process of teaching patients what is expected of them in psychotherapy. While it has been traditionally held that considerable ambiguity in the structure of psychotherapeutic interactions may be an essential ingredient of the therapy process, more recent findings demand a reexamination of this hypothesis. If it can be demonstrated that a brief instructional period or observation of the behavior of another person in psychotherapy can help the patient know what is expected of him, and that the therapeutic effects of interview sessions are not destroyed by these procedures, then pretraining by vicarious learning would represent a large step toward greater economy in interview therapy.

The effectiveness of videotape observation of counseling sessions on the information-seeking behavior of observers was examined by Krumboltz, Varenhorst, and Toresen (1967). High school students who had requested special counseling about their future educational and vocational plans were shown videotape of counseling sessions. The counselors' attentiveness to the modeled counselee was varied by portraying the counselor as supportive and interested or as indifferent and distracted. The experimenters also varied the apparent prestige of the videotaped counselor by using different introductions to the tape. The dependent variable was the frequency and variety of student information-seeking behaviors in the interval between observation of the videotape and a later counseling interview with the same subject. For example, it was noted how often each student had engaged in such behaviors as writing to colleges or other agencies for catalogs or pamphlets, talking to people working in an occupation being considered, or visiting schools that were being considered. Subjects who had seen the videotape produced a greater frequency and variety of information-seeking behaviors than did control subjects. Observation of the taped interview also resulted in more of this sort of activity on the part of the students than did a verbal summary of the content of the tape or the direct suggestion that the students seek information on their own at first and then contact the counselor. The attentiveness and prestige of the model counselor did not affect the observer's information-seeking activities.

Although the few available studies on the use of modeling procedures in counseling give overwhelming evidence of the facilitating effect of such procedures, their application is not yet commonplace in clinical practice. Numerous traditional techniques, however, haphazardly involve provision of information by exposing the patient to a behavioral model. In interview therapy, the therapist may serve as a model of interpersonal behaviors or of problem-solving approaches. Evidence for the modeling effects in interview therapy comes also from studies showing that patients tend to approach the therapist's characteristics and personal attitudes after prolonged and successful treatment. In fact, the skillful therapist has often been described as a person who is able to model, by his comments and his actions, the way in which a patient ought to view himself, consider his problems, and arrive at an effective plan for action.

In the next section we will briefly discuss several clinical techniques in which manipulation of stimulus conditions is used to achieve behavioral changes in the patient. The following techniques are not clearly definable as applications of vicarious learning. However, they share with the vicarious learning methods the use of information input by the therapist as stimulus control for the purpose of therapeutic accomplishments.

REPLICATION TECHNIQUES

A number of well-established treatment methods use procedures in which significant parts of the patient's extratherapeutic environment are replicated or simulated for observation and manipulation in the therapist's presence. These techniques provide the patient with an opportunity to evaluate his own problematic behaviors and to try out new behaviors without the fear of traumatic consequences. In these techniques two major changes can be fostered—the elimination of behavioral deficits by rehearsal or observational learning, and the reduction of anxiety or other undesirable autonomic correlates of behavior. The features shared by all of these methods are the therapist's arrangement of contrived situations, his use of verbal instructions, his deliberate control of the stimulus conditions to modulate intensity of evoked anxiety responses, and the opportunity for the patient to rehearse novel responses. In individual psychotherapy, as well as in family therapy, the patient is often requested to participate in role playing of a significant incident and is then helped to evaluate his behavior and its effects on others in realistic terms. Recent use of tape recordings and videotapes has made it easier to present a patient with a sample of his own behaviors. Confronted with a verbal or visual reproduction of himself, the patient can discover and try out behaviors that will improve his social effectiveness.

Utilization of relatively nonthreatening stimulus materials in miniature therapy situations is illustrated in a study by Patterson (1965c). A school-phobic child was encouraged to enact in doll play the conditions that were associated with his phobic response. The child's reaction to separation from his mother had maintained his fear of leaving home and going to school. In doll play the child was given opportunities to rehearse new behaviors for which he received immediate candy reinforcement. In these sessions the doll play gradually replicated longer and more complicated episodes, such as going to school, staying in school, playing with peers, and handling aggression from peers. With therapy methods such as these, the patient's capacity to cope with environmental stimuli and with his own behaviors can be increased in the artificial environment. Generalization of these behaviors to naturalistic situations can be further enhanced by planned graded shifts from the simulated to the daily life setting.

Variants of a therapeutic technique called *psychodrama* have been employed for over fifty years. Moreno and his students have developed role playing and other action techniques since 1911. Patients are encouraged to act out some personal problem in front of a group of patient observers. Moment to moment feedback, directions from the therapist, and discussion of the patient's behavior provide him with information and behavioral practice, as well as an opportunity to express the extremes of his affect without untoward consequences. In psychodrama, spontaneity in social affairs is encouraged through assumption of numerous roles that are characteristic both of one's own behavior and of other people's behavior. The more roles one learns to play, the greater flexibility one has in dealing with others. Moreno further holds that role playing, be it of imaginary or real events, decreases distance between individuals and permits more effective social behavior.

A different utilization of role playing is encountered in Kelly (1955). In a method that he calls *fixed-role* therapy, the patient is invited to explore behaviors that sharply contrast with his own, or to act "as if" he were a different person, the kind of person he might like to be. Practice of such behaviors is demanded of the patient during everyday situations. The rationale of this technique lies in the assumption that the patient can practice new behaviors more comfortably when these are portrayed as only temporary "make-believe" actions that the patient is free to reject at any time. He thereby is able to perceive how the world appears and reacts when he himself behaves in different ways. Actual increased skill in interpersonal behavior is supplemented by new experiences of social feedback, as the patient's social environment alters its response to his new role.

Among the behavior therapists, related techniques have been termed behavior-rehearsal (Lazarus, 1966), role playing, or behavioristic psychodrama (Wolpe, 1958; Sturm, 1965). Behavior rehearsal has been reported most often in case studies where it was an adjunct to desensitization in treating deficits of self-assertion that presumably were the basis for generalized anxiety and phobic avoidance of close social interactions. The therapist may enact the role of a person who usually stimulates anxiety in the patient, while the patient attempts to act out increasingly assertive and forthright behaviors. Both the situations enacted and the degree of patient assertiveness are graded along a hierarchy of anxiety-producing items. Verbal approval by the therapist and enacted positive consequences, as well as elicited self-appraisal are presumed reinforcers for the new behaviors. This procedure clearly resembles Bandura's technique using a live model with guided practice, discussed earlier, except that a modeled person rather than a live snake is involved. Lazarus (1966) compared the effectiveness of behavior rehearsal, direct advice, and nondirective reflection-interpretation in changing specific social or interpersonal complaints of 75 patients who had received no previous therapy. After four 30-minute sessions, information was sought from the patients regarding changes in objective behaviors in their daily lives. Lazarus reports that 92 percent of the behavior rehearsal group reported such changes, in comparison to 44 percent of the advice group, and 32 percent of the reflection-interpretation group. This study does not provide independent objective assessment of outcome, nor control for therapist, patient, and target response effects. Nonetheless, it points to a needed area of research, and like Bandura's work, suggests superiority of procedures in which the patient actively engages in the desired new behaviors.

As we have noted, the mechanisms in modeling and role playing that produce attitudinal and behavioral change have yet to be clarified. As in the case of desensitization, analogue studies that involve a precisely defined target behavior present in all subjects may help to sort out the relative contributions of various components. Janis and his co-workers have examined the effects of role playing on a significant behavior, cigarette smoking, in normal subjects. Janis refers to his procedures as "emotional role playing" because the subject's enactment is of emotional rather than new instrumental behaviors. For example, heavy smokers play the role of patients being told by a "doctor" (the experimenter) that they had developed lung cancer (Janis and Mann, 1965). The subjects were guided to include emotional expressions associated with threat of pain, hospitalization, and early death. A comparison group listened to tape recordings of one of these sessions, but did not play the role themselves, and an untreated control group simply gave the same reports on smoking behaviors and attitudes. Even at an 18-month follow-up, those subjects who had engaged in the emotional role playing showed significantly less cigarette consumption than the other groups of subjects (Mann and Janis, 1968). A cognitive role-playing procedure, in which subjects enacted a debate and argued against smoking, was also less effective in changing smoking habits than was the emotional role-playing procedure (Mann, 1967). Information alone about the dangers of smoking produced only a temporary decrease in untreated controls, but enhanced the effects of vicarious and live emotional role playing (Mann and Janis, 1968). Note again that while symbolic or vicarious experiences had some beneficial effect, live participation had a greater effect, as in the case of Bandura's study.

In contrast to the Janis and Mann findings a recent replication by Lichtenstein, Keutzer, and Himes (1969) failed to show clear-cut advantages of role-playing over passive listening to a taped role-playing session. Some attitude changes were found for subjects in both groups. The authors of the replication suggested several differences between the studies to account for the discrepancies. Among them is the interesting speculation that the appearance of the Surgeon General's report in 1963, after the Janis and Mann data were collected, altered the situation. Today's smoker is more aware of the health hazards associated with smoking. Thus, "the fact that she smokes in the face of such evidence leads one to infer that she is better immunized or defended against fear manipulations than was the female smoker of 1963" (Lichtenstein, Keutzer, and Himes 1969, p. 387). The findings of other recent studies with significant but less dramatic effects of role-playing than reported by Janis and Mann further emphasize the relevance of the role-player's attitudes, skills, and prior knowledge in producing behavior changes by this technique.

A wide variety of specific techniques has been used in psychotherapy to entice the patient to engage in novel behaviors, sometimes by arranging stimulus situations for him. These arrangements may be necessary in order to reduce anxiety associated with acting out any behaviors about which the patient feels uncertain or anticipates negative consequences. These enactment techniques can be employed in individual therapy as well as in groups. Unfortunately, there is little research that sheds light on the learning process occurring in role rehearsals. Effectiveness of the techniques is also more frequently established by testimonials than by empirical evidence. A study by Rothaus, Johnson, and Lyle (1964) illustrates one approach to the investigation of the consequences of various role-playing behaviors. The authors compared two role-playing techniques for changing typical behavior patterns in psychiatric patients. Active and passive patients were assigned group discussion roles, either similar to their usual behavior (role repetition) or opposite to their usual behavior (role reversal). After the group discussions, the patients filled out rating and reaction scales. The patients tended to exaggerate their typical behavior during role repetition. Under the role reversal condition, typically passive individuals experienced more difficulties in carrying out their role assignments than did the typically active patients. Passive patients who played a passive role reported no frustration, while active members playing passive roles felt highly frustrated. The role-reversal technique was found to result in greater feelings of satisfaction for all participants than the role-repetition technique.

Interaction among group members within a therapy group can itself be used for analysis and as a basis for learning experiences. Sensitivity training groups, often called T (training) groups, utilize this principle. Most commonly, these methods use a combination of cognitive, emotional, and behavioral elements (Schutz, 1967). Modeling enters as an important facet in all of these procedures. The model may be the therapist, another group member, or a sketch of an imaginary event or person. Since any intimate encounter in psychotherapy involves the juxtaposition of the personal experiences, beliefs, and behaviors of a therapist and a patient, and in some cases, a group of individuals who function effectively at least in some aspects of their life, the sessions almost always provide some cues to a learner for elicitation of new behavior on the basis of modeling.

The subtle changes that result from the therapist's modeling have been illustrated in several studies. For example, Rosenthal (1955) studied twelve patients who presented a wide variety of diagnoses. Prior to therapy, the patients and their therapists were given several tests of moral values. At the conclusion of treatment, the patient's scores on the moral values tests changed in the direction of greater similarity to their therapist for those patients who were rated as improved. Similar findings were reported by Pentony (1966). Others have found that not only test scores but also the content of discussion in therapy, the terminology appropriate to the theoretical framework of the particular therapist, and other complex behaviors seem to be modified during successful psychotherapy so that the patients become more similar to their therapist. In addition to modeling, other learning mechanisms, for example, the continued reinforcement of patient behaviors and statements that the therapist finds acceptable, may serve to strengthen the patient's patterning of his own behavior after that of his therapist.

In this chapter we have attempted to survey studies in vicarious learning that may eventually become the basis for deliberate therapeutic procedures to ameliorate behavioral deficits or to change pathological behaviors in patients. Our review should make it clear that the precise mechanisms of vicarious learning are not yet fully understood. Although occasional reports are available of deliberate efforts to utilize these principles in psychotherapy, the majority of current clinical techniques resort to modeling procedures rather loosely and with little attention to parameters derived from laboratory experiments which might facilitate such procedures in the clinic.

SUMMARY

In addition to direct behavior modification by classical and instrumental conditioning, human learning often is accomplished by observation of another person. This type of learning has been variously discussed under social learning, vicarious learning, imitation, or observational learning. Experimental work in this area has dealt mainly with the parameters related to the observation, the memory of the observed event, and the conditions under which the observer's behavior is tested. Observational learning is relevant to behavior therapy for a better understanding of the development of some symptomatic behaviors and as a vehicle for behavior modification.

Five categories of observational learning can be differentiated on the basis of the experimental operations: (1) matched-dependent behavior, (2) identification, (3) no-trial learning, (4) co-learning, and (5) vicarious classical conditioning. The five categories are differentiated by the relationship between the subject and the model during observation, by the availability of consequences to the subject during observation or afterwards, by the degree of overlap between the observed and tested behavior, and by the operant or respondent nature of the observed response. Matched-dependent behavior can be obtained when a subject is reinforced for copying a model and the imitated behavior also generalizes to new situations. However, in training for matched-dependent behavior strong reliance is placed on the presence of a model or a leader, and the procedure is more appropriate for obedience training than skill building. In identification learning, exposure to the behavioral model is found to result not only in imitation of the instrumental behavior but also of the incidental behavior of the model. In the no-trial learning paradigm the emphasis is on the change in the observer's behavior as a result of model observation, without apparent rehearsal or practice. In co-learning situations, two individuals are actively engaged in the same task. In the experimental design the model is usually a subject whose behavior is preprogrammed and attention centers on the effects of particular model strategies or successes on the learning of the observer. This situation differs from the identification and no-trial learning paradigms in that the learner is given a learning task with inherent or explicit reinforcement for his accomplishments. In vicarious conditioning of arousal, attention focuses on the conditions that lead an observer to show a pattern of emotional response similar to that of his model.

The main theoretical issues in the area of vicarious learning revolve around the question of what is learned during observation (since no overt rehearsing of responses by the observer is noted) and what elements of the situation serve as reinforcing stimuli for observation and for later replication of the observed behavior. Some theorists hold that a stimulus-stimulus association during observation is the basis for learning, and reinforcement of the imitated behavior plays a role only in the reproduction of the observed material. Others have suggested that imitation of a model is determined by an early developmental pattern in which a general set to imitate has been continuously reinforced. Imitation per se thus may be a sufficiently strong secondary reinforcer in older individuals to maintain imitated behaviors in numerous situations. Another theoretical question concerns the function of the model responses. As stimuli to the observer, model responses can have cue functions indicating permissibility or desirability of execution of the observed behavior in similar circumstances, especially when the response is already at high strength in the observer's repertoire. The model responses can also serve as discriminative stimuli for attending and rehearsing the observed response.

Several experiments have demonstrated the facilitative effects of model observation on an observer's execution of similar complex social behaviors. Modeling has also been used to extinguish phobic behavior, and to help patients in learning proper role behavior for various social situations, such as job interviews, social interactions, or therapy interviews.

Although not directly derived from vicarious learning research, techniques that are related, in principle, to observational learning methods have collectively been subsumed under the term *replication therapy*. Most of these methods share the following common features: the therapist's arrangement of contrived situations, his use of verbal instructions, his deliberate control of the stimulus conditions to modulate intensity of evoked anxiety responses, and the opportunity for the patient to rehearse modeled responses. By partly or completely replicating problematic life situations in the clinical setting, the therapist helps the patient to discover and try out new behaviors to improve his effectiveness. These new responses are open to selective reinforcement by the therapist or by a patient group. Many traditional techniques, such as psychodrama and fixed role therapy, as well as new approaches, such as behavior rehearsal techniques, utilize the mechanisms of vicarious learning for therapeutic purposes. The potential of deliberate application of vicarious learning methods for training patients in improving their effective social interactions has barely been tapped. Even though the precise mechanisms of vicarious learning are not yet fully understood, the pragmatic utility inherent in modeling and shaping of imitative responses for removal of psychological difficulties promises to provide yet another important tool in the clinician's storehouse of therapeutic operations.

Part III

Behavior Modification Paradigms with Emphasis on Response—Contingent Consequences

CHAPTER 6

Behavior Modification by Manipulation of Consequences

The preceding chapters reviewed therapeutic approaches that mainly rely upon manipulation of stimulus properties anchored in the classical conditioning paradigm. In this chapter and the next we review the operant conditioning model and methods of behavior modification and control based upon it. Differential emphasis on components of the behavioral equation, S-O-R-K-C, characterizes the main differences between these two paradigms. Classical conditioning entails study of the first two terms of the formula, environmental and internal conditions *preceding* a response, and of their relationships to the following responses. The operant model concentrates on the relationship of R to the *subsequent* two elements, K and C. Therapeutic interventions based on the operant model primarily rearrange contingent behavioral consequences, including rewards and punishments, in order to alter undesired behaviors or to remedy behavioral deficiencies. The operant paradigm, since it does not require specification of antecedent stimulus conditions, is more convenient for conceptualizing and manipulating a wide range of responses in natural settings that do not permit clear identification of eliciting stimuli. Consequences that have effects on both the surrounding world and the behaving individual are the major objects of observation because they largely control the probability that the behavior that produced them will occur again (Skinner, 1953). Antecedent stimuli, because they indicate availability of reinforcing consequences, may also control behavior and be used in therapeutic discrimination training.

Operant conditioning differs in a number of other respects from the paradigms already considered. These differences are reflected in research strategy and design, in the nature of the variables examined, in the choice of subjects and target behaviors for research and therapy, and in the nature of investigative questions raised. The view of operants as preeminent in human behavior also leads to formulations about the nature,

241

etiology, and treatment of disordered behaviors that stress the importance of the social environment. Consequently, analysis of the interaction between the behaving organism and the environment in which the behavior occurs is central to operant-based therapy. Modification of this *interaction*, either through direct manipulation of the organism's response or indirectly through changing environmental feedback (contingent consequences), is the chief goal of strategic planning for therapeutic intervention.

CHARACTERISTICS OF THE OPERANT PARADIGM

Among the characteristics of the operant approach that have particular relevance to its application to therapeutic behavior change are the following interrelated points:

1. *It is empirical, it eschews mediational constructs.* The formulations and research strategy of Skinner and his students epitomize the empiricist tradition of American psychology. Operant behavior therapists do not usually have recourse to constructs such as "anxiety" or "psychosis" in explaining or modifying deviant behavior. The Skinnerian model does not make reference to inner systems or inner "causes" because they are difficult to observe and are likely to imply mechanisms or forces whose existence can be neither confirmed nor denied. The inner events themselves are often of little significance in attempts to alter behavior.

"The practice of looking inside the organism for an explanation of behavior has tended to obscure the variables which are immediately available for a scientific analysis. These variables lie outside the organism, in its immediate environment and in its environmental history. . . . The objection to inner states is not that they do not exist, but that they are not relevant. . . . " (Skinner, 1953, p. 31, 35).

2. *It is a practical engineering approach.* Despite the atheoretical bias, operant methods can be used to test theoretical issues and hypotheses through skillful experimental arrangements. For example, questions concerning the contribution of environmental factors to maintaining autistic behaviors in children or to stuttering can be evaluated by careful engineering of experiments that vary the consequences of such behaviors. Similar systematic variation of environmental feedback to patients in interviews or to disruptive children in classrooms has contributed to better understanding of conditions that nurture problematic behaviors and has contributed remediation of these conditions.

The engineering aspect is also illustrated by emphasis on precision of measurement. In fact, most research on operant behaviors has focused on response rate as the single behavioral datum. Demonstration of experimental control over a behavior is taken as sufficient evidence that the relevant independent variables have been discovered and no further conceptual explanation is sought. To the operant conditioner, then, residual variation in an organism's behavior poses a challenge for discovery of those determinants that have been overlooked.

"Much of traditional behavior theory has been encouraged by the inexact and often complex relationships between stimulus and response variables. When these relationships are made more precise, the need for terms referring to unobservable states or responses diminishes. . . . When the independent variables which determine . . . variability are discovered, the need to postulate an unobservable process will disappear" (Honig, 1966, p. 9).

The operant model thus tends to equate knowledge of variables controlling a behavior with understanding of the behavior. It is not surprising that this model has led its protagonists in clinical psychology to search more diligently for practical, precisely designed remedial methods rather than for causal relationships.

3. *Emphasizes analysis of the single case.* Precisely engineered behavioral control requires that individual differences among organisms be taken into account by adjusting techniques to the parameters characteristic of the single organism. We have already pointed out in Chapter 1 that the single case analysis approach to experimentation is especially attractive for work with clinical populations because of the wide variations in individual characteristics among patients. Operant research, from its very outset, has utilized single animals for laboratory study. Cumulative records of response rates of individual animals and graphic presentation of the effects associated with changes in environmental consequences (C) or reinforcement schedules (K) have been preferred to statistical group designs and quantitative data analysis based on group trends. It is by replication of an observed phenomena rather than by demonstration of average trends that operant conditioners gain support for hypothesized relationships between independent and dependent variables. In clinical application, a functional analysis of an individual case entails the examination of the relationships between behavior and controlling environmental events.

Although operant methodology emphasizes intensive and controlled study of one individual, replication of therapeutic effects in a series of different individuals with similar behavior problems permits some general statement about the utility of given procedures under specified conditions. The operant approach, then, in keeping with its engineering emphasis, ultimately aims to provide an organized collection of techniques and general principles from which the therapist might choose one or a combination of several techniques for use with one patient.

4. *Its emphasis on present determinants does not deny the importance of historical variables.* As we have already indicated in Chapter 1, the achievement of control over behavior through variables acting in the present situation does not necessarily indicate that the same variables have contributed to the development of the behavior. Human behavior is frequently the result of the interaction of many shifting independent variables. For example, a youngster's temper tantrums may originate in emotional arousal and frustration, be maintained at first by consequent material rewards, and persist later in the face of occasional punishment because no alternative behavior achieves as much parental attention. The unknown past history of various problematic behaviors presents formidable obstacles in a functional analysis. If the present disturbing behavior can be modified without regard to its original determinants, however, the task of the behavior therapist is accomplished. Thus, a patient's avoidance of social contact may indeed be traced to his early humiliation for inept social behavior by his mother. Restoration of social skills by gradual training of social approach behaviors and by arranging for rewarding consequences of his initial attempts can resolve the psychiatric problem more easily than attempts to extinguish the entire avoidance complex associated with mother and his early social training.

EARLY USE OF OPERANT CONDITIONING IN BEHAVIOR THERAPY

Prior to discussion of relevant laboratory data and of issues pertinent to their clinical application, it seems useful to illustrate the operant approach by describing early attempts to apply its technology directly to clinical problems. To the extent that all behavioral changes are in part an effect of consequence on preceding response, operant principles are involved, deliberately or not, in any therapeutic attack. Thus, even in the classical study by Mary Cover Jones (1924) in which a child's fears were modified and which has been used as an illustration par excellence of classical conditioning, features are encountered that involve not only systematic desensitization, but also modeling and imitation, and contingent social and primary (food) reinforcement. Jones also predicted that later reinforcement of avoidance and other immature behaviors by the child's mother was likely to undo the therapeutic benefits that he had experienced. This early study anticipated many of the issues that are still cogent for today's behavior therapies.

It was not until the 1950s, however, that deliberate efforts were made to apply the methods of a functional analysis of behavior to clinical problems. Fuller (1949) reported an early trial of operant conditioning in an 18-year-old feebleminded patient. The response selected for conditioning was a movement of the patient's right arm to a vertical or nearly vertical position. For a reinforcing consequence, a small amount of sugar milk solution was delivered contingent upon execution of the critical response. Fuller reported that rate of responding during the fourth training session was more than three times as great as during the first. His experiment demonstrated the conditionability of a human vegetative subject by operant methods. However, it should be noted that this early experiment with a clinical subject was not intended to produce therapeutic changes but simply to demonstrate the possibility of application of operant principles to human behavior.

Direct application of programmed positive reinforcement was used therapeutically by Peters (1952, 1955), although he did not explicitly draw upon the Skinnerian model. In order to enhance the incentive value of sweets, Peters administered subshock dosages of insulin to chronic schizophrenic patients and deprived them of breakfast. He then dispensed bites of fudge for correct solution of a series of graded problems such as pencil mazes, choice discrimination problems, and cooperative discrimination tasks that two patients could solve only by joint efforts. Ratings of work output and other behaviors in daily occupational therapy sessions revealed improvement after treatment in comparison to controls. Although Peters formulated his "learning treatment" in terms of "developing the functioning of the patients' cortex," his operations are identical to a procedure for improving operant performance by positive reinforcement in patients with behavior deficits.

Lindsley (1956) probably deserves the credit for the first systematic exploration of operant conditioning principles in a clinical population. He used small experimental rooms as "Skinner boxes" to study the effects of various reinforcers, contingency schedules, and discriminative stimuli on the rate of lever pulling in chronic schizophrenics. Figure 6-1 shows a patient seated in such an operant conditioning room, facing a panel that contains the levers he operates, slots for display of discriminative stimuli, and an opening through which reinforcers are delivered by automatic programmed control. Among Lindsley's ingenious experiments were tests of the reinforcing properties of various picture stimuli (for example, nudes of either sex), or of "altruism" when the subjects' lever pulls were followed by delivery of milk to a hungry kitten. Lindsley's work not only illustrated the relevance of the model for psychotic patients but also from the start introduced into clinical application the methodological features

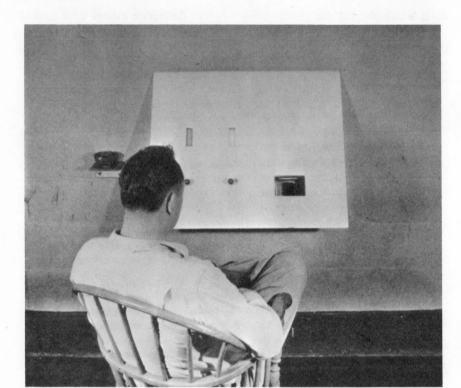

Figure 6-1   Interior of operant-conditioning room for human subjects. Subject is facing the panel containing plungers which he pulls to receive reinforcements (courtesy of Dr. Ogden Lindsley, from Maher, 1966, p. 380).

of operant technology. Response rate as the dependent variable was recorded for a precisely defined response class with the same precision and instrumentation as in the animal laboratory. In order to introduce as few changes as possible in extrapolating from animal laboratory to hospital setting, Lindsley instituted strict stimulus control and a minimum of verbal instructions. His initial work paved the way for later, more complex therapeutic uses of the operant model.

Another illustration of early direct utilization of operant laboratory procedures for therapeutic purposes is a study by Tilton (1956) who employed candy rewards to train motor responses in schizophrenic patients. He went on to develop with his colleagues (King, Armitage, and Tilton, 1960) a procedure for treating severe chronic schizophrenics. Initially, simple operant responses (lever pressing) were reinforced in the presence of the therapist with candy, cigarettes, and colored slides. Gradually more complex discriminative verbal and interpersonal response components were systematically incorporated into the procedure, in accordance with the patient's progress. Eventually, groups of as many as six patients had to cooperate and communicate with one another in order to succeed on the tasks and receive their rewards. The authors found that their procedure, which they called an "operant-interpersonal method," was more effective in promoting clinical improvement than were verbal or recreational therapy given to control groups, as assessed by ward observation and interview.

These early experiments were rapidly followed by widespread reports of clinical applications of operant methods. It is not surprising that the first applications of operant conditioning to psychiatric patients were carried out with chronic, regressed schizophrenics when we consider the inclination of many lay people and clinicians alike to view these techniques as akin to brainwashing or Orwellian control. Only in the case of persons already rejected from free society, already sanctioned as targets of unusual restraints and regimentation, were operant procedures initially acceptable. By and large the development of operant-based behavior therapies in the 1950's continued for some time to deal with severe mental defectives, psychotics, prisoners. That is, they dealt in general with persons showing extreme behavioral deviations, whom others had, with frustration and lack of success, already sought to control in concrete daily activities, and whose placement in an institution resulted not so much from their own complaints but from the complaints of others. The empirical nature of trials of operant therapies and the apparent simplistic nature of the target behaviors and therapeutic operations led professionals to limit their early applications to "hopeless cases" unlikely to suffer harm from clinical trials of this new approach.

THE OPERANT PARADIGM

The major operations in the operant paradigm are presented schematically in Figure 6-2. The horizontal arrows (read as "followed contingently by") plus the symbol for the stimulus or response event represent a given operation. The use of symbols such as C+ in Figure 6-2 to represent a positively reinforcing consequence demands a reminder that such symbols denote *functions* of events, not objects alone. The consequence (C+) is defined by its effects. Thus, a piece of candy may have reinforcing properties for a hungry child but not for a diabetic patient.

The operant paradigm uses as its primary dependent variable the probability of response. As suggested in Figure 6-2, this variable is most often

	Reinforcement		Result
	Assumed	Operation	
Positive	$R > 0$ rate $C+$	$R \rightarrow C+$	Rate and intensity of R increase and topography of R narrows.
Negative	$C-$	$R \rightarrow (\downarrow C-)$	
	Punishment		
Aversive	$R > 0$ rate $C-$	$R \rightarrow C-$	Rate of R decreases; escape and avoidance Rs develop. (See next chapter.)
Response cost	$C+$	$R \rightarrow (\downarrow C+)$	Rate of R decreases. (See next chapter.)
Extinction	$R > 0$ rate and history of $R \rightarrow C+$ or $R \rightarrow (\downarrow C-)$	$R \rightarrow 0$	Rate of R decreases; topography of R becomes more variable.
	Reinforcement and extinction combined		
Response differentiation or shaping	Class of R at > 0 rate and $C+$	$R_1 \rightarrow C+$ $R_2 \rightarrow 0$	Subclass R_1 increases and subclass R_2 decreases in rate.
Discrimination	$R > 0$ and $S_1, S_2, C+$	$S_1 \rightarrow R \rightarrow C+$ $S_2 \rightarrow R \rightarrow 0$	S_1 becomes S^D, S_2 becomes S^Δ; R occurs with S^D but not with S^Δ.

Figure 6-2　Major operations of operant conditioning

measured experimentally by the frequency per unit time or rate at which a given response is emitted. An *operant* is a response that effects a consequent, contingent change in the environment, or is instrumental in bringing about the change. Skinner rejected the term "instrumental response" because of its purposive connotation, just as he preferred to denote the subsequent consequence as *reinforcement* rather than to use the poorly defined and subjective term, reward. The advantage of response rate as a dependent variable lies in its sensitivity to programmed environmental changes. The basic paradigm, however, can be expanded for examination of complex behavioral chains. In clinical application the size of the response unit has often been defined functionally by its relevance to the desired effects, thus sometimes encompassing a series of smaller response units. The basis for delimiting a response class, therefore, depends on the particular problem at hand and the functional relationships between the observed class and the environmental consequences. Current clinical studies using the operant paradigm have utilized such relatively large response classes as a child's "disruptive behavior." This class includes many subclasses of long and complex chains of behavior, for example, all the sequences of acts involved in physical attack on other children. "Sick talk" during interviews by schizophrenics, stuttering, or approach responses to another person have been selected as response classes for modification. Duration, intensity, and periodicity of a response have also been used as the dependent variable. For instance, duration of sustained work effort or the intervals between aggressive outbursts have been derived measures of very complex response classes.

Each of the operations schematically described in Figure 6-2 (reinforcement, punishment, extinction, response differentiation or shaping, and discrimination) plays a role in the tactics of therapeutic behavior change. Once a response class has been selected as a target for treatment, choice of which technical procedures to use depends upon: (1) availability of controlling stimuli (for instance, environmental cues commonly associated with a desired response), (2) the limits of the individual's repertoire for acquiring new constellations of simpler response components, and (3) the availability of reinforcing stimuli for the therapeutic purpose. No assumption is made in the operant model about the intrinsic character of the disordered behavior other than viewing it as a response pattern that is inconsistent with the demands of the social environment or ultimately detrimental to the patient's survival or social adjustment. A particular target response is selected on the basis of an analysis of the total behavior under scrutiny, and not solely on the basis of the patient's complaint or the effects of the behavior on a complaining person in the environment. For example, when a child interrupts progress in a classroom, operant conditioning methods might be applied to increase his attending behaviors, his academic skills, the time he sits still in his seat, or socially approved behaviors by which he could more appropriately gain attention. Because the operant paradigm requires relatively precise specification of a response class, behavior therapists often single out response components of a total symptom for separate therapeutic intervention.

As indicated in Figure 6-2, the basic elements of the operant paradigm include, in addition to the response and consequence, the stimulus elements in the situation and the contingency relationship between reinforcement and response. Detailed accounts of the various operations by which these elements can be modified to bring about behavioral changes are available in several introductory books on operant conditioning (see, for example, Millenson, 1967; Reynolds, 1968). Our brief review here will attempt only to highlight those features of the operant conditioning paradigm that are of special relevance to behavior therapy operations.

Reinforcement Operations

Any response, even if it has a very low probability of occurrence, is subject to the operation of reinforcement. Reinforcement basically involves an environmental event or stimulus consequence (C) that is contingent upon the particular response (R) and whose occurrence increases the probability that the response will occur again. Some authors would reserve the term "reward" for this effect, using "reinforcement" in a more general way to include the UCS of classical conditioning and the less well-defined events that produce verbal-cognitive learning. Some of these authors would also apply the term "reinforcement" only to events that increase response probability, that is, to the acquisition of responses but not to their asymptotic performance (Berlyne, 1967). In this chapter, however, we will follow the terminology of Skinner and his students. Similarly, we touch hardly at all upon two major questions concerning reinforcement: How do reinforcing events work? For example, do they work through expectancy mechanisms, positive feedback mechanisms, contiguity mechanisms? What do reinforcing events have in common that determines their reinforcing power? For instance, do they have in common drive reduction, change in hedonic state, production of central arousal? These are issues that, like others dealing with organismic influences, are not essential for our consideration of the empirical operations of operant conditioning.

At the simplest level, there are four possibilities for administration of contingent reinforcing consequences: positive stimuli (C+) can be presented or removed, or negative stimuli (C−) can be presented or removed. In addition, both types of consequences can be withheld after a period of presentation. These six possibilities are shown in Figure 6-3, labeled by the terms commonly associated with these operations. *Positive reinforcement* and *extinction* denote contingent presentation or withholding of positive stimuli.

When an aversive stimulus is presented after a particular act, this operation is usually termed *punishment*. When aversive stimuli are removed after a particular act, the operation is a case of *negative reinforcement,* and fits the escape training paradigm in the language of instrumental conditioning. In therapeutic settings, this is sometimes termed aversion relief. Utilization of aversive stimuli has been previously discussed in connection with the classical conditioning model. Use of aversive stimuli with operants is treated in the next chapter. The aversion-relief operation has been illustrated in the mixed model paradigm for the treatment of homosexuality (Chapter 3). Thorpe, Schmidt, Brown, and Castell (1964), for example, used this term to describe their procedure of rewarding desired competing behaviors with removal of an aversive stimulus. For example,

Operation	Positive Consequence: C+	Aversive Consequence: C−
Contingent Delivery	Positive reinforcement R → C+ Child obeys request → adult's friendly approval	Punishment R → C− Child refuses request → adult scolds
Contingent removal	Response cost R →↓ C+ Child disobeys request → adult removes attention	Negative reinforcement (escape or aversion-relief) R →↓ C− Child apologizes → adult stops scolding
Withheld after series of presentations	Extinction R → 0 Child yells demand → adult ignores	Avoidance R → 0 Child obeys when first requested → adult withholds scolding

Figure 6-3 Reinforcement operations

the patient read aloud words relating to his symptoms (for example, "homosexual") upon visual presentation, and was immediately given a painful electric shock. The shock was terminated when the patient said the "relief" word (such as "heterosexual") that then remained in the patient's view after shock termination. The use of single words to represent such complex behavior chains as homosexual or heterosexual interactions, the relative value of removal of shock as a reinforcer, and the relationship of this approach to respondent aversive conditioning and reciprocal inhibition await controlled studies. However, as described in Chapter 3, laboratory studies have demonstrated that neutral stimuli associated with termination of an aversive stimulus, such as electric shock, do acquire conditioned reinforcing properties sufficient to produce acquisition of a new response. Further, the conditioned reinforcing value is not dependent upon any necessary discriminative function of the stimulus (Kinsman and Bixenstine, 1968). Thus there is utility in a general strategy of removal of aversive stimuli to promote the reinforcing value of stimuli associated with weak responses, at least until other ecological reinforcers can support their occurrence. This may be carried out in an instrumental escape-avoidance paradigm (see next chapter) or in a respondent conditioning paradigm (see Chapter 3). In either case, removal of aversive stimuli is a reinforcing operation that can produce symptoms or be used to alter them. The matter does not remain as simple as Figure 6-3 may suggest, however. Stimuli may be manipulated noncontingently as well as contingently, simultaneously with other events as well as singly. Furthermore, absence of a class of stimuli has different effects than its removal; as every mother knows, an absent toy has less effect on a child than her efforts to remove it. Figure 6-4 outlines the possible manipulations when some of these complexities are taken into account. Most, but not all, of the manipulations of positive stimuli (C+) are discussed in this chapter. The remainder, which generally result in response decrements, are taken up in the next chapter because they are functionally similar to aversive events.

We have noted that the reinforcing properties of a stimulus are established by demonstration of its effects on response probability. Considerable criticism at the theoretical level and difficulty at the practical level have resulted from this type of definition. Both researchers and clinicians, for the sake of expediency as well as to escape circularity, have often presumed that a reinforcing stimulus, for example, a bite of food, a spanking, social approval, or an electric shock, will have the same effect for many individuals and under different circumstances. Were this true, the stimulus could be characterized as a "reinforcer" and defined as such in advance. A classical example is the general acceptance of food pellets as reinforcers for laboratory animals, providing certain deprivation operations are carried out. Attention, candy, or verbal statements such as "good" have similarly been assumed to be ubiquitous reinforcers in behavior modification studies with humans. However, a number of studies, as well as daily experience, have demonstrated that the reinforcing effects of a given stimulus cannot be assumed to be similar for different individuals, nor, indeed, for the same person at different times. In the animal laboratory, for example, one contingent pellet of food may increase lever pressing if the food box has been empty in the past; it may reduce responding if, in the past, 100 pellets were always delivered per press (see, for example, Perkins, 1968). Junior high school students completed more correct difficult discrimination problems when their solutions produced photographs of a peer whom they liked than when a disliked peer was pictured (Lott and Lott, 1969). Mild electric shocks have often been described as pleasant by human subjects and have been noted to increase a response. Lindsley (1968) has spoken of "chocolate punishers" because he has found that some children in his behavior modification programs decrease rather than increase the rate of desired behavior when contingently given M&M candies.

Premack (1959, 1965) has offered one solution to the implied circularity of the definition of reinforcement and has demonstrated the relativity of reinforcement operations by showing that children could be reinforced

	Noncontingent Provision	Noncontingent Removal	Response-Contingent Provision	Response-Contingent Removal or Absence	Noncontingent Provision Paired with S	Noncontingent or Contingent Removal Paired with S
C+	Satiation Adventitious (superstitious) conditioning	Deprivation	Positive reinforcement Discrimination training if paired with S^D Conditioning of secondary positive stimuli	Extinction Time-out Response cost Discrimination training if paired with S^Δ	Classical conditioning (Classical conditioning of secondary positive stimuli)	Classical conditioning of secondary aversive stimuli
C−	Arousal Adventitious (superstitious) conditioning	Adventitious (superstitious) escape conditioning	Punishment Discrimination training if paired with S^Δ Conditioning of secondary aversive stimuli	Negative reinforcement of escape-avoidance training Discrimination training if paired with S^D	Classical aversion conditioning (Classical conditioning of secondary aversive stimuli and conditioned emotional reaction)	Classical conditioning of secondary positive stimuli ("relief"; S: aversion relief)

Figure 6-4   Possible manipulations of positive and aversive stimuli

253

for eating when this response provided contingent opportunities to press levers. He had predicted this finding from his reinforcement hypothesis that, for any pair of responses, the one that has a higher probability of occurrence will reinforce a preceding one with lower frequency of occurrence. Premack (1965) puts it this way:

"Reinforcement is a relative property. The most probable response of a set of responses will reinforce all members of the set; the least probable will reinforce no member of the set. However, responses of intermediate probability will reinforce those less probable than themselves but not those more probable than themselves. Intermediate members of the set thus both are and are not reinforcers, depending upon the relative probability of the base response. . . . The reinforcement relation is reversible. If the probability of occurrence of two responses can be reversed in order, so can the reinforcement relation between the two responses" (Premack, 1965, pp. 132–133).

The reinforcement effect of more probable on less probable responses in the contingency situation apparently requires, as the necessary and sufficient condition, that the organism be compelled to increase his instrumental response in order to maintain opportunity for the contingent behavior at its free-performance level (Eisenberger, Karpman, and Trattner, 1967). These investigators found that the more probable response reinforced the less probable response only when the contingently available behavior was suppressed beneath its free-performance level. On the other hand, the less probable response reinforced the more probable one when the latter was suppressed below free-operant level.

It is clear, then, that in any experimental design or clinical application, the effectiveness of a particular stimulus as a reinforcer must first be demonstrated for the given situation and a given subject. In the clinical situation, in which conditioning may proceed over a long period of time, it is even necessary to reevaluate the effectiveness of a reinforcing stimulus a few days or weeks after its initial introduction. A further difficulty in assuming generality for the effects of a reinforcing stimulus, even for a given person, is the dependence of the reinforcing stimulus on the organismic condition of the subject. Thus, food pellets may serve as effective reinforcers for a hungry animal until his intake of pellets is sufficient to satiate him; a child may increase responding in order to be able to play with a novel and unfamiliar toy but not for the same toy with which he has become familiar. In clinical application, a further problem lies in the fact that as a patient improves clinically and enlarges his behavioral repertoire, the reinforcing stimuli that may have been attractive to him in a simple and restricted hospital environment may not have sufficient reinforcing properties to maintain his behavior in normal daily life.

A stimulus may further vary in effectiveness as a reinforcer as a function of the rate of reinforcement, that is, the reinforcement schedule (K). Experiments with laboratory animals have clearly shown that a small pellet of food will maintain behavior over a long period of time and for many responses under certain schedules. The magnitude of the reinforcing stimulus or its reinforcing value may be sufficient to produce behavior acquisition or maintenance under one schedule but not another. In the gambling casinos, this interaction between reinforcer and schedule is well known. Machines that have a small payoff are usually programmed to reinforce the guest's gambling behavior at a different schedule than machines that have a large payoff. A long string of responding, which feeds a one-armed Bandit, may be maintained by the small cost required (for example, feeding in pennies) or by the size of the anticipated jackpot (for instance, silver dollars). Similarly, the size of a piece of chocolate or of a bank check will interact with the frequency and schedule of its delivery in determining its control over the work output of a person.

Reinforcement and Motivation

With the specification of the conditions under which a given event is reinforcing, the practitioner of operant conditioning has little need for motivational constructs. Skinner (1953) states that the phenomena generally covered under the term "motivation" can be described in terms of the effect of deprivation and satiation operations. Since the emphasis is on the effects of reinforcement, motivational conditions are accounted for when the probability of a child's working for a piece of candy is shown to be a function of the child's earlier experiences with candy, the time since his last meal, the difficulty of the task, and similar variables. These precisely describable variables cover exactly the same event as the broad statement that "the child is highly motivated for candy." They have the additional advantage of permitting the investigator to vary any of the several variables when the child ceases responding, in order to bring the behavior under control again.

It is obviously impractical and scientifically unsatisfying to be forced into an analysis of effective reinforcers for each individual case. Therefore, researchers are continuing to investigate the conditions and processes that determine the reinforcing effects of a stimulus. A number of stimuli can be relied upon to retain a reinforcing effect under a wide range of circumstances. Often called *primary* reinforcers, these are reinforcing stimuli that are not dependent on the individual's past history of conditioning and are encountered in most members of a species. Food, water, stimuli that reduce discomfort or pain, and sexual stimuli are among those that are generally attractive to most people at most times. Changes in the environment after prolonged monotony, opportunities to interact with other human beings, verbal statements of approval or affection and praise are among the stimuli that are less reliable but appear, nevertheless, to maintain their reinforcing properties for a wide range of conditions and persons.

Situations that are often described by complex social motivational constructs can themselves be investigated by operant procedures. For example, Lindsley (1962) assessed "motives" of psychotic patients by projecting pictures of religious content, male and female nudes, and other objects, contingent on the subject's continuous lever pressing. With somewhat more complicated equipment, social events or materials that maintain operants can be investigated. Nathan, Schneller, and Lindsley (1964) have presented a laboratory method for the analysis of changes in interpersonal influences by measuring the rate at which a person will continuously push a switch to see or hear material presented on a television screen. Various dimensions of the presented material, for example, content, familiarity, intensity, or redundancy, can be investigated as to their reinforcing properties by measuring their potential for maintaining a high rate of switch pushes.

Conditioned Reinforcement and Social Reinforcers

Unlike primary reinforcers, most contingencies in everyday life have acquired their potency from repeated associations with other reinforcing events in the previous experience of the person; they are termed *conditioned reinforcers*. The click associated with delivery of a pellet in a food magazine is commonly used in animal work as a conditioned reinforcer. Eventually, the animal continues to bar press even when food is no longer delivered, so long as the click follows the response. New responses can also be acquired when the click is contingently delivered, further demonstrating the conditioned reinforcing effect of the click.

Skinner (1938) early demonstrated that a discriminative stimulus (S^D), which by definition is a stimulus associated with reinforcement, can also acquire reinforcing properties. Presumably the *conditioned* reinforcement value of an S^D is relatively resistant to extinction because it is acquired and used on an intermittent schedule of reinforcement. Zimmerman (1959), Kelleher (1961), and others have demonstrated that behavior maintained by S^Ds as reinforcers in indistinguishable from that maintained by primary reinforcers when intermittent schedules are utilized. Although discriminative stimuli usually function as conditioned reinforcers, establishing a stimulus as an S^D is neither necessary nor sufficient for making it a conditioned reinforcer (Kelleher and Gollub, 1962). That is, not all conditioned reinforcers are discriminative stimuli, and not all discriminative stimuli are conditioned reinforcers. Simple pairing of a stimulus with a contingent reinforcing stimulus may establish it as a conditioned reinforcer, since conditioned reinforcers apparently depend upon classical respondent conditioning for their establishment (Wittenborn, Adler, Lukacs, Sharrock, and Simmons, 1963). Indeed, some theorists have proposed that all behavior change consists of "transmission of differential attractiveness" to antecedent stimuli, that is, by the mechanism of conditioning secondary reinforcement (Perkins, 1968). In any case, the power of a stimulus as a conditioned reinforcer is a function of the frequency with which it has been paired with another established reinforcer, as would be expected if it is classically conditioned. Since conditioned reinforcers control rates and patterns of responding as do primary reinforcers, they are important in maintaining long chains of responses when primary reinforcement is available only for the terminal response, and they act to retard extinction when primary reinforcement is not forthcoming.

In human behavior, conditioned reinforcers generally occur within long chains of responses and stimuli. A chain is composed of responses joined together by stimuli that act both as conditioned reinforcers and discriminative stimuli. Reynolds (1968) gives a good example of the overlapping function of these two properties of a stimulus in human behavior.

"We do not try to get into our car until the door is open. Nor do we attempt to order food unless there is a waiter at our table. Each of these discriminative stimuli is, in addition, a conditioned reinforcer. The opening of a door, for example, is reinforcing because the open door is a stimulus in whose presence the response is reinforced. The entire chain of behavior is maintained by the food we finally ingest; we simply do not go to restaurants which furnish either bad food or no food at all" (p. 53).

When a conditioned reinforcer is established by pairing a stimulus with many different primary and secondary reinforcers, it is called a *generalized reinforcer*. Money, attention, or credit cards and green stamps are examples of the many generalized reinforcers widely used in our culture. Generalized reinforcers are especially useful in clinical application because they depend so much less on the momentary condition of the person for their effectiveness. Thus, fairly continuous consequence control of behavior is possible even when the individual is neither hungry, nor thirsty, nor concerned about social approval. It is by use of such generalized reinforcers as money that behavior uniformity can be obtained even as the person's interests, deprivations, and personal requirements change.

The superiority of generalized reinforcers over discrete conditioned reinforcers in facilitating human learning and their higher incentive properties have been demonstrated by Kanfer and Matarazzo (1959), Kanfer (1960) and others.

Tokens, points, or other symbols (poker chips, play money, etc.) exchangeable for a variety of objects and activities are not only convenient generalized reinforcers in shaping individual behaviors, but their utility has also been established repeatedly when entire institutional settings are placed on an "economy" using a token exchange system (Ayllon and Azrin, 1968). The reinforcing value of tokens is easily acquired by most individuals, even severely defective or psychotic persons. Sidman (1965), for example, has described successful conditioning of tokens as generalized reinforcers in very severely retarded children. The therapist first gave candy to a child, then a token that was instantly traded for candy. Subsequently, tokens were exchanged for candy with gradually increasing delays. Eventually a "store" was set up at which a large number of items (toys, food, clothing) were available for token exchange once or twice a day.

Social Reinforcement

Among all available reinforcing stimuli, the verbal and nonverbal responses of other persons are perhaps of greatest relevance for shaping human behavior. Between the subtle smile or wink and the outright verbal statement of love or rejection lies a large range of cues that shape, guide, and control our behavior in everyday interactions. Much remains to be learned about the functional characteristics of social reinforcers, despite their presumed fundamental importance. Several interesting research directions promise to facilitate a functional analysis of the operations by which social stimuli come to exert varying degrees of control, as reinforcers, over behavior. Stevenson (1965), Lindsley (1963a), and others have pointed out that the same social stimuli can have eliciting, discriminative, facilitative, suppressive, or reinforcing functions. Lindsley (1963a) has developed a device for assessing conjugate reinforcement, which should facilitate laboratory study of continuous social reinforcers and related phenomena while avoiding confounding by other variables of social behavior. Figure 6-5 depicts one version of Lindsley's experimental arrangement by which silent movies of the mother smiling can be presented to an infant in his crib. A panel that the infant presses with his foot is linked through a control mechanism ("conjugate reinforcer" in the figure) to the projector lamp in such a way that rate of panel pushing is directly related to the intensity of the projected picture. Using this device, Lindsley has found that the smile of a female stranger is reinforcing to a five-

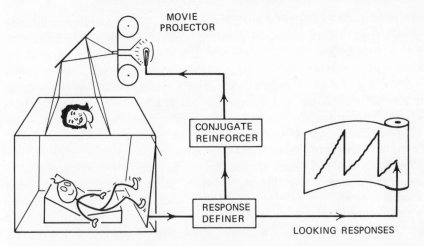

Figure 6-5   Schema of apparatus for measuring reinforcing value of silent movies for a human infant. The continuously available moving picture is presented on a conjugate reinforcement contingency. This contingency appears most suitable for social reinforcers (from Lindsley, 1963a p. 631).

month-old infant. Similar conjugate reinforcement devices have been used to study the reinforcing properties of a therapist's televised voice and image for his patient during regular psychotherapy sessions (Lindsley, 1963b).

Stevenson (1965) has measured the effectiveness of social reinforcers by using a simple tedious task involving minimal prior learning. When children are given positive comments for dropping marbles through holes into a bin, their rate of marble-dropping has been found to be related to (1) their own and the experimenter's sex (girls respond more to a man's comments, boys to a woman's); (2) the interaction of the child's age and the experimenter's sex and other characteristics (for example, individual men who are especially effective as reinforcers with young children are also effective with older children, while those women who are especially effective with young children are less effective with older ones); (3) the interpersonal relationship and presumed history of reinforcement with the reinforcing agent (parents were less effective reinforcers than strangers); and (4) the age of the child (older children responded equally well to praise or to a signal light). A long series of laboratory studies on social reinforcement of children has underscored the complexity of these operations. Popularity, aggressiveness, friendship ties, age, and other features of a peer interact in complex ways both with the task and with subject characteristics in determining the effects of peers as social reinforcers

(Hartup, 1967). A child's tendency to attend to, be reinforced by, and in turn reinforce other people's emission of social stimuli may be influenced by congenital factors. The child may then, by his degree of responsivity, shape the social behavior of his parents, so that a closed cycle is established (Bell, 1968). A child's deficient behavior repertoire may thus result in further limitations and compound his difficulties in interacting with his social environment.

More recently, investigations of social reinforcement have been extended from the laboratory into the natural environment. Hartup, Glazer, and Charlesworth (1967) have studied the relationship between peer reinforcement and sociometric status in groups of nursery school children. Their results suggest that positive sociometric status is significantly correlated with frequency of giving positive reinforcement but unrelated to the amount of negative reinforcement a child gives. Negative choices on the sociogram were correlated with the amount of negative reinforcement the child gave, but unrelated to his delivery of positive reinforcement. The children received more positive reinforcement from the peers they liked than from those they disliked. However, they did not receive more negative reinforcement from peers they disliked.

While ecological investigations often suffer from the weakness of a priori definitions of positive and aversive reinforcers, their data usually support the facilitative role ascribed to classes of social stimuli. That is, naturalistic studies provide an opportunity to test assumptions about which social events function as reinforcers. In some cases, earlier hypotheses about constitutional or psychodynamic origins of a disturbing behavior pattern have been weakened or replaced by demonstrations that social reinforcement may maintain the behavior. In studying aggression, for example, Patterson, Littman, and Bricker (1967) hypothesized that aggressive and assertive behaviors in young children are operants. The consequences provided by the victim, such as compliance, crying, defensive postures, or counterattack or retaliation can either weaken or maintain the aggressive behavior. The authors point out that a number of laboratory studies have demonstrated that aggressive acts can be brought under the control of social or material reinforcing stimuli (see, for example, Hinsey, Patterson, and Sonoda, 1961; Lovaas, Baer, and Bijou, 1963; Walters and Brown, 1964) and that these same studies had demonstrated a significant relationship between laboratory-shaped aggressive behaviors and those occurring in a natural setting. At the same time, they also point out:

"It is unlikely, however, that the culture is programmed to dispense these classes of reinforcers for assertive behaviors or that the reinforcers are on the same kind of regular schedules used in laboratory studies, e.g., continuous or fixed ratio. An adequate understanding of the child's acquisition of aggressive behavior requires identification of the actual consequences and schedules provided by the social culture for his assertive-aggressive behaviors" (Patterson, Littman, and Bricker, 1967, pp. 6–7).

When observers coded episodes of aggressive acts and their consequences during ordinary nursery school play, the events predicted a priori to function as reinforcers were indeed found to have the predicted effect. Rate of aggression, its type, and selected victim all varied according to the positively or negatively reinforcing reaction of the victim. Further, initially passive children, if they were frequently victimized by aggressive peers and if they experienced some tentative successful counterattacks, were rapidly conditioned to accelerate their own rate of aggressive behaviors.

When reinforcement operations in natural units of socialization are studied, it becomes possible to discover the mechanisms by which the young child learns the rules of the social game through trial and error and social feedback. Patterson and his co-workers, as one illustration, have formulated a general process to explain how social agents in a child's environment often maintain the child's deviant behaviors even though these same agents complain vigorously about that same behavior. Patterson and Reid (1967) propose two mechanisms, reciprocity and coercion, as primary in social reinforcement operations of dyads and of more complex social systems, such as a hospital ward or family. Reciprocity exists when two persons, A and B, dispense social reinforcements to each other at an equitable rate. Coercion refers to the situation in which person A demands or forces a disproportionate share of positive social reinforcement from B, while maintaining B's compliant behavior by removal of the aversive demanding stimuli. Their observations suggest that families, as well as parent-child dyads, have stable and systematically different ratios of social reinforcement delivery (degree of reciprocity). They have made quantitative observations of the operation of coercive exchanges in parent-child dyads that apparently maintain the child's symptomatic behavior (Patterson, Ray, and Shaw, 1968). In one family the mother and the problem child were each involved in coercive, nonreciprocal relationships with the other family members, and the ratio of positive to aversive consequences for the family was quite small. When the amount and balance of mutual positive reinforcement were altered by therapeutic intervention, the family went from "bedlam" to a relatively low rate of disruptive behaviors (Patterson and Reid, 1967).

Studies on the occurrence, effects, and modifiability of social reinforcement in natural settings exemplify an approach to three related issues in behavior modification. First, greater knowledge of ecological reinforcement operations is necessary for extrapolation of results from laboratory to therapeutic settings. Second, as Patterson and Reid put it:

". . . the social environment must be the primary focus of the behavior modifier who is interested in the development of intervention programs for the noninstitutionalized child. It is necessary to develop not only a conceptual framework for investigating the parameters governing the dispensing of reinforcers in target social environments, but it is also crucial to develop a technology which will effectively alter these parameters" (p. 2).

Thus therapeutic modification of coercive child-parent interactions is part of Patterson's programatic research. Third, these studies represent the few efforts to investigate seriously the role of social stimuli in the development of deviant behaviors. The potential contribution of such work is thus basic in understanding the *origins* of problematic behavior, in *preventing* its more severe forms, and in more *efficient application* of modification therapies.

Another source of increased understanding of social reinforcement lies in studies of conformity, imitation, and social evaluation, which are increasingly being cast in the language and operations of social learning. Hill (1968), for example, has reviewed various hypotheses about the effects on an individual's behavior of positive and negative evaluations (praise, ridicule, success, criticisms, etc.) by himself or by others. Evaluations as social feedback operations may be hypothesized to operate as reinforcers. Hill concludes that evaluative expressions function as discriminative stimuli for primary reinforcers. He argues that the interpretation of evaluative statements as conditioned reinforcers is contrary to experimental evidence. Evaluative statements apparently are far more resistant to extinction than are other conditioned reinforcers, and often are more powerful in affecting behavior than are any primary reinforcers upon which they might be based. However, in these comparisons, the character of evaluation as a *generalized* reinforcer, in contrast to *specific* primary reinforcers, may not have been given sufficient weight. The social sanctions attached to cowardice that may lead a soldier to risk death perhaps act as prepotent generalized conditioned reinforcers, just as does money for the starving miser—another example of a generalized conditioned reinforcer having greater potency than a specific primary one. Hill suggests, therefore, that evaluative stimuli are associated with a variety of primary reinforcers in childhood, and thereby become generalized S^Ds, and hence conditioned reinforcers. The intermittency of the original pairing and later pairings throughout life maintains their reinforcing power and resistance to extinction.

Whether Hill's evaluative stimuli are a special subclass of social reinforcement by others, or whether the two classes are equivalent seems an issue deserving further exploration. For example, is "attention" *ever* nonevaluative, as responded to by its recipient? Clinical novices are taught specific attending behaviors (eye contact, postural orientation) on the assumption that attention acts as a reinforcer to maintain client talk in interviews (Ivey, Normington, Miller, Morrill, and Hasse, 1968). A related and more general issue has to do with the need to be able to determine any functional difference between the informational and motivational aspects of social feedback. Does response-relevant information from others always function as reinforcement? If not, what conditions determine its reinforcing function? Do evaluations by others of an individual's behavior (such as grades, praise, criticism) constitute a reinforcing operation different from informational feedback from them? Stevenson (1965), as noted earlier, found that for older children, a signal light is as effective as praise in maintaining the boring work of marble dropping. In Chapter 9 we will encounter a number of studies of self-regulation in which real difficulty is encountered in composing subject groups that do not seek some external reinforcement. Any response-related information may operate as reinforcement in the usual experimental setting and with achievement-oriented college students. Blind-folding dart players illustrates the extreme procedure that researchers have been forced to use in order to by-pass the effects of evaluative components of information from others.

Hill's formulations underscore several points important for behavior therapy. First, many patient complaints center around interpersonal interactions and social evaluations. The ubiquity of social reinforcers, their presumed centrality to daily behavior, and their availability in the environment make them a prime tool in behavior modification. Just as others' evaluations may guide and reinforce behavior, self-evaluations may also have the same function. However, the rate and nature of evaluations by others and by oneself may be discrepant. Many neurotic patients show negative self-evaluations as a prime symptom. These often seem unaffected by positive external evaluations. Indeed, negative self-evaluations often come to function as cues for negative evaluations from others, who tire of the "I'm no good" refrain. Children's behavior problems have been found to vary as a function of the child's differential responsivity to various sources of social reinforcement, for example, mother, father, and peers (Patterson and Fagot, 1967). Empirical advances in understanding and controlling social reinforcement should have immense payoffs in therapeutic application as Krasner (1962a) predicted when he called the psychotherapist a "social reinforcement machine."

Second, social reinforcement operations may serve as a major bridge between traditional operant paradigms, social learning, and mediating variables proposed as mechanisms in self-reactions. Hill, for example, jointly considers evaluations by others and by the self, and connects these with operant and social learning formulations. Baron (1966) describes the effects of social reinforcement in terms of internalized norms, developed from prior history of social reinforcement, against which the individual judges current contingencies. Direction and magnitude of discrepancies between evaluations by others and self-judgments produce affective responses, which in turn can influence motor performance. In this view social reinforcement again serves as a theoretical bridge.

Chaining of Responses

Response chains and conditioned reinforcers are related phenomena, and both are of great importance in maintaining complex and continuous human behavior. An operant chain is a sequence of responses and discriminative stimuli, with each response producing the S^D for the succeeding response. Each S^D may act as a reinforcer maintaining the preceding responses. Skinner (1938) termed the (S^D–R) element in a chain a "reflex" and hypothesized: "a discriminative stimulus . . . used as a reinforcement in the absence of ultimate reinforcement creates in another reflex a reserve just equal to that of the reflex to which it belongs" and that "in a chain of reflexes not ultimately reinforced, only the members actually elicited undergo extinction" (p. 105). His hypotheses have been supported by later research (see, for example, Dinsmoor, 1950).

These related principles mean that in therapeutic modification, chains should be built backwards from the response most immediately preceding the final reinforcement, that is, the last element in the chain should be established first. Also, each element must maintain its S^D functions or else the elements (reflexes) preceding it will undergo extinction. If the final reinforcement is inadvertently omitted, all elements of the chain that actually occur suffer extinction equally, but the later elements extinguish later. Great care must be taken in building a response chain to insure that competing responses don't break it before the reinforcement is delivered, that the conditioned reinforcing value of each S^D is well established before another element is added, and that reinforcement eventuates. These procedures can be used to teach and maintain in a rat such a long and complex chain of behaviors as: climb a spiral stair, cross a bridge, climb a ladder, pull a chain that brings a toy car, climb into the car, pedal it to another stair, descend, squeeze through a small tube, enter an elevator that descends to the start box, press a lever—and obtain a food pellet (Pierrel and Sherman, 1963). (See Figure 6-6.)

Although a chain is composed of a number of elements, it may sometimes be treated as a single operant by defining it in terms of the common

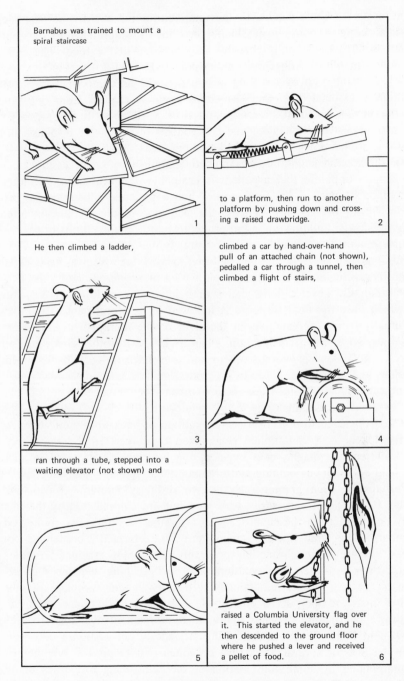

Barnabus was trained to mount a spiral staircase

to a platform, then run to another platform by pushing down and crossing a raised drawbridge.

He then climbed a ladder,

climbed a car by hand-over-hand pull of an attached chain (not shown), pedalled a car through a tunnel, then climbed a flight of stairs,

ran through a tube, stepped into a waiting elevator (not shown) and

raised a Columbia University flag over it. This started the elevator, and he then descended to the ground floor where he pushed a lever and received a pellet of food.

Figure 6-6   Building a complex response chain (from Pierrel and Sherman, 1963, as adapted by Ferster and Perrott, 1968, p. 183).

relationship of the elements to the final reinforcing event. For example, a rat's eating response in a Skinner box involves approach to the food pellet, sniffing, and finally chewing and ingestion of the food. The entire sequence is often defined as one response. If the larger response unit has been reinforced over a long period of time, its component links can be tightly associated so that the entire chain is run off from one time to the next with great precision and little variability. It is only when we are interested in changing the components of the larger response unit that it is broken down into the smaller components.

In therapeutic situations, this refined analysis is often necessary when it becomes apparent that a patient is incapable or untrained in executing a component part of the total unit. When a patient's difficulties are primarily those of response deficits, the behavior modifier's task is often that of slowly building up appropriate response chains through positive reinforcement. For example, we have already mentioned Sidman's (1965) conditioning of severely retarded children to work for tokens as generalized reinforcers. Beginning with the simple eating of proffered candy, the children gradually develop long chains of behavior by addition of elements of which only the final response is followed by reinforcement. Thus they eventually learn, for example, at the sight of the therapist, to stop other activities, go to a certain location, sit in a circle with other children, wait quietly until a ball is rolled to them and they have rolled it back, accept a token and save it for three to six hours, go to the ward "store," select an object they want, and trade in their tokens for the selected object. The toy or food is the final "back-up" reinforcer. "Back-up" refers to the fact that the selected object serves to maintain or back-up the effectiveness of the token as a conditioned generalized reinforcer. In the same way, the children are taught, step by step, the long chains involved in such self-help behaviors as bathing and dressing, table manners, and toileting.

Perhaps of even greater relevance to ordinary human behavior are chains that are not necessarily very long but are complicated by the fact that each element in the chain leads to a number of alternative reinforced elements. Such multioperant chains are often termed "branching" or "trees," as are similar branching programs in teaching machines. Findley (1962) has indicated that multioperant or branching sequences of responses are more easily maintained and brought under complex stimulus control than are long serial chains. He hypothesizes that in a serial sequence, each operant depends upon the reinforcement available from its subsequent link, whereas in branching sequences, one response may produce the S^Ds for several alternative or concurrent responses and thereby be maintained by some combination of the reinforcing properties of all of them. As Findley suggests, further investigation of multioperant sequences should clarify reinforcement operations such as those of intermittent reinforcement. Branching chains would seem to closely represent much of the behavior all people carry out in daily living, and hence would have particular relevance to establishing normal response repertoires. With few other procedures are we as strongly reminded of the applied technological nature of therapeutic operant behavior modification; success in building repertoires of response chains in behavior-deficient patients is mainly a matter of careful engineering.

Schedules of Reinforcement—K

A schedule of reinforcement defines the formal relationship between reinforcement delivery and response occurrence in terms of time *intervals* (t) that must lapse before reinforcement, or the number of responses (n) per reinforcer, defined as a ratio of these values. Figure 6-7 summarizes a few of the schedules commonly used. Many lawful relationships for simple schedules have been demonstrated; some of these are summarized in the figure. For example, fixed-ratio schedules, in which a reinforcer is delivered following a fixed number of responses since the last reinforcement, produce high rather uniform response rates, with brief pauses occurring only immediately after reinforcement. Combinations of the basic ratio or time interval schedules can produce immense numbers of compound, second-order, or concurrent schedules. These complex schedules are under investigation but their effects are less well known. There is some evidence that the characteristic patterns produced by different schedules can occur even when reinforcement is delivered in a noncontingent fashion (Zeiler, 1968). The interested student can pursue these matters in Ferster and Skinner (1957), the chapters by Herrnstein, Morse, Kelleher, and Catania in Honig (1966), and other specialized texts. It suffices here to introduce the main terminology of schedules in Figure 6-7 and to acknowledge the potency of schedules for generating and maintaining very complex behaviors. Morse (1966) emphasizes this point:

"The experiments pertaining to schedules have additional general significance in showing the tremendous range of behaviors that can be produced by schedules, the power of behavioral control induced by schedules, and the intricate relations that exist among the variables controlling behavior. The range and the complexity of behaviors that can be produced by intermittently reinforcing responses in time is incredible. That these scheduling procedures are the most powerful techniques known for generating behavior is of course, of fundamental significance: it emphasizes that histories of reinforcement are the primary determinants of behavior" (Morse, 1966, pp. 57–58).

Schedule	Operations	Some Usual Effects on R Patterns
Ratio schedules	C+ delivered contingently only after emission of n number of Rs since last reinforced R (or some other event).	Reinforcement is independent of inter-response time. Generates high rates of responding.
Fixed ratio (FR)	Value of n is fixed, for example, FR 10 means reinforce only 10th R after last reinforced R.	High, uniform rate with slight pause after C+; pause duration and R rate are functionally related to n. Very high values of n possible by gradual increases of n. Resistance to extinction varies inversely with n, and during extinction pauses lengthen while responding continues at high rate between pauses.
Variable ratio (VR)	Value of n changes from trial to trial. For example, VR 10 means on the average 1 R in 10 is reinforced, but n varies from trial to trial, usually by a random program. Numeral (for example, 10) indicates mean value of n; range is arbitrarily set.	Produces stable very high rates and high resistance to extinction.
Interval schedules	C+ delivered contingently only after an interval, t, of time has elapsed since last reinforced R (or some other event). No specifications for R between start of t and end of t (when C+ becomes available).	Reinforcement can be related to interresponse time but has only an indirect relation to rate.
Fixed interval (FI)	Value of t is fixed and C+ delivered for next R after fixed t has elapsed. For example, FI 10 means reinforce only for R after 10 seconds lapse since some event, most often the last C+.	Very low or zero rate after C+, then abrupt or gradual acceleration to moderate rate as end of t approaches. Generally, indirect reinforcement of lower rates, in contrast to FR which indirectly reinforces higher rates.
Variable interval (VI)	Value of t is variable; for example VI 100 means on the average t = 100, but elapsed time between some event and next availability of C+ will vary from trial to trial, usually by a random program.	Stable and uniform moderate rate. Rate increases as average value of t required decreases. Very high resistance to extinction. Duration and amplitude of R more variable.
Alternative or concurrent schedules	Either of two independent simultaneous schedules determines C+ availability, whichever is satisfied first.	Schedule competition or preference, and cross-schedule effects may be studied.
Multiple schedules	A type of concurrent scheduling in which SDs are used to identify which schedule is operative; usually schedules alternate randomly.	Performances under the two schedules are quite independent, permitting use of one of the schedules, for example, to function as a "control" index for the other.
Chained schedules	R1, initially itself reinforced, acts as eliciting or discriminative S for R2 which is followed by C+. That is, R1 produces a stimulus, which acts as an SD since R2 is reinforced in its presence.	Long behavior chains can be built up with only one final C+ maintaining all of the Rs of the sequence. Probably some chaining occurs in stable FR schedules.

Figure 6-7 Summary of reinforcement schedules. Notational system is that of Ferster and Skinner (1957).

The behavior modifier thus may have at his disposal control of the timing, frequency, or magnitude of reinforcement. Some schedules are inherent in the nature of the situation; for example, aversive consequences follow one's touching a hot stove on a 100 percent FR schedule. Often schedules are especially important not so much when ongoing responses are being maintained but when a *change* in the schedule disrupts ongoing behavior or produces inappropriate behavior. An instructor accustomed to teaching in the classroom with continuous live feedback from his audience (eye contact, restlessness, laughter, questions) may find his delivery disrupted when he suddenly shifts to lecturing in a TV studio where live feedback occurs only at the end of his lecture. In many situations, persons in interaction adjust their behaviors to provide mutually satisfying schedules, as in the case of conversation or sexual interactions. Close interdependence of the two individuals in maintaining each other's behavior by suitable schedules is most dramatically illustrated when it fails, as in the families studied by Patterson, or as in the case of the cocktail party conversational partner whose long periods of inattention while he looks for a more prestigeful person may rapidly leave one speechless.

Among the various scheduling effects, the advantages of intermittent over constant reinforcement have received the most attention from behavior therapists. Intermittent schedules produce greater resistance to extinction, are more efficient in terms of reinforcement cost per response, and reduce the likelihood of satiation during training. As described in Chapter 3, early aversion therapy of sexual deviation was criticized by Feldman (1966) because shock had been delivered on a 100 percent schedule; his own work indicated, as expected, more durable results when a variable ratio or variable interval schedule was used. A common procedure for developing a new response is to initiate a program with a 100 percent schedule and then gradually to *thin* the schedule, first on a variable ratio and then on a variable interval schedule, until relatively few reinforcing operations are required to maintain the desired new behavior. The nature of the reinforcer, the subject's past history with different schedules, and various organismic variables all affect the rate at which these transitions can be carried out without disrupting the desired performance. Figure 6-8 illustrates such a transition over a period of 40 hours spent in reading on the part of educationally retarded school children (Staats, Minke, Goodwin, and Landeen, 1967). The amount of reading material required per unit of reinforcement (money) was gradually increased without performance decrement, regardless of the ability level (high, middle, low) of the children. Reinforcement per response was cut to one-fourth while the children continued to increase the rate and difficulty level at which they read. As this example suggests, the ability to operate on various

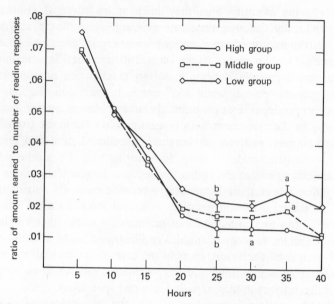

Figure 6-8 Ratio of the monetary value of the tokens received divided by the number of reading responses made as a function of time in reading. The letter (a) on each ability group curve represents the last point in which all Ss are represented and the letter (b) indicates the time block in which the bonus was introduced for most Ss (from Staats, Minke, Goodwin, and Landeen, 1967, p. 11).

schedules may be important as a therapeutic goal in itself. One goal of treatment may be to enable patients to respond on complex schedules that they have not yet mastered. Retarded children have been trained to perform on multiple schedules initially beyond their ability. The assumption was that individual differences in performing on multiple schedules were part of the general performance deficits in such children (Bijou and Orlando, 1961). Similarly, a salesman often needs to learn to be tolerant of a very "thin" (high VR) schedule if he is to maintain his sales-seeking behaviors and avoid depression or escape behaviors (golf, drinking, sleeping late).

Untoward schedules of reinforcement have been suggested as causes of problematic behavior, as well. For example, depressions have been ascribed to insufficient positive reinforcement from the environment. Insufficient work output in students may result from their usually very thin schedules of reinforcement, a large amount of work being required for each reinforcement. A low disposition to engage in behaviors that are readily available in an individual's repertoire suggests a defective schedule of reinforcements as the difficulty. Figure 6-9 (Patterson, McNeal, Hawkins, and Phelps, 1967) illustrates a very thin schedule of mutual reinforcement between a problem youngster and his mother, in terms of their rates of speaking to one another. A major complaint about the boy was that he was seclusive and withdrawn. The observational data, collected in the home, suggest that mother did not positively reinforce the patient for interacting with her, but neither did the boy reinforce mother's attempts at conversation. The steeper curves in the figure represent the improvement in their interactions after an operant conditioning treatment program was instituted.

Schedule effects can lead to problematic behaviors in a number of ways. If schedules are suddenly or drastically changed (for instance, "straining the ratio" by rapid transitions from one ratio to another), responding is likely to drop sharply or stop altogether. A child used to constant praise from his mother may refuse to perform at school where he has suddenly been placed on a much thinner schedule of attention. Behaviors learned under one schedule may become self-defeating, inefficient, even

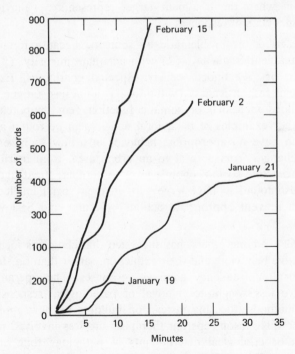

Figure 6-9 Cumulative curve: rate of words per minute of interactions between a mother and child at home (from Patterson, McNeal, Hawkins and Phelps, 1967, p. 189.

bizarre when they persist under a new schedule. The person who continues to feed dimes to the soft drink vending machine when no drinks are forthcoming is likely to appear foolish to his companions. Finally, when a person fails to encounter an expected schedule, his behavior may be disrupted. The high school honor student who expects many A's at the University often suffers disruption of his study and test-taking behaviors when poorer grades are obtained. All of these schedule effects have important clinical implications. The behavior therapist must look for schedule changes as possible precipitating factors for his client's problems. In training new behaviors and in providing for transition from clinic or hospital to the client's usual daily world, the therapist must engineer appropriate schedule effects. He may elect to use changes in schedule as a treatment *method,* or he may develop in the client an ability to operate on new schedules as a treatment *target.*

THERAPEUTIC USE OF REINFORCEMENT OPERATIONS

Operant strengthening through positive reinforcement is most useful in the clinic when the treatment target represents a behavioral deficit, that is, when a class of responses is:

". . . described as problematic by someone because it fails to occur (1) with sufficient frequency, (2) with adequate intensity, (3) in appropriate form, or (4) under socially expected conditions. Examples are reduced social responsiveness (withdrawal), amnesias, fatigue syndromes, and restrictions in sexual or somatic function (e.g., impotence, writer's cramp). Other examples of behavioral deficits can be found in depressed patients who have no appropriate behavior in a new social environment, e.g., after changes from a rural to an urban area, from marital to single status, or from one socio-economic level to another. 'Inadequate' persons often are also found to have large gaps in their social intellectual repertoires which prevent appropriate actions" (Kanfer and Saslow, 1969, p. 431).

Meehl (1962), among others, has suggested that clinicians focus too often on maladaptive behaviors and their extinction, rather than on strengthening of absent or low frequency adaptive responses. The operant approach tends to give less weight to removal of pathological responses than do traditional methods, focusing instead on building up new appropriate responses. For this reason, operant therapists are less involved in searching for elicitors or etiological determinants of pathology than are dynamic or classical conditioning therapists. Although "stamping out pathology" is frequently the therapeutic goal of behavioral approaches, maximizing and building on a patient's assets is an equally viable and efficient strategy.

Experimental Designs to Assess Clinical Operations

Many clinical studies combine an extinction procedure with strengthening of desirable but deficient behaviors. In applied work, it is often difficult to demonstrate the reinforcing function of the manipulated events. Naturalistic observations are often made of the ongoing flow of behaviors and consequent events in an effort to discover possible reinforcement effects for later therapeutic use. It is tempting in such circumstances to describe the observed sequence of events as a reinforcement operation without any controlled demonstration of the fact that the succeeding event is contingent and does indeed operate as a reinforcer. Observational procedures may be interesting and suggestive and are often sufficient as guides for clinical trials, but they do not yield clear evidence that a reinforcing operation has taken place. Research designs and use of controls are therefore often needed in clinical settings in order to combine therapeutic intervention with a secure knowledge of the mechanisms to which behavior changes can be attributed. Once the operation of reinforcement mechanisms has been demonstrated in the maintenance of a symptomatic response, it is tempting to blame these same operations for the acquisition of the response. This attempt to infer from treatment to development of a problem is fraught with dangers, since behaviors can be acquired under one set of conditions and later be maintained by a totally different set of factors.

Compare, for example, the conclusions that can be drawn from two studies of patients whose problematic behaviors were assumed to be maintained by the attention of their attendants. Gelfand, Gelfand, and Dobson (1967) observed hospital staff responses to various classes of behavior on the part of six severely psychotic patients. Observers rated every patient behavior on a five-point scale of appropriateness and simultaneously recorded subsequent staff responses as positive attention, negative attention, or ignore. The data revealed that staff nurses attended positively to 39 percent of the psychotic behaviors, and nursing assistants to 30 percent. Desirable prosocial behaviors were ignored 66 percent of the time by nursing assistants and 32 percent of the time by staff nurses. Thus prosocial behaviors often were not given positive attention while inappropriate behaviors were followed by positive attention at a high rate on an intermittent schedule. Further, the more psychotic the patient, the larger the proportion of his inappropriate behaviors that received positive attention. These data were suggestive enough both of lost therapeutic opportunities and of possible antitherapeutic effects to lead the investigators to instruct their staff in the principles of operant conditioning. The data do not, however, establish any causal connection (in either direction) between patient and staff behavior. Therefore, there is no basis for asserting that staff attention was positively reinforcing (causing or maintaining) patient symptoms.

In contrast, a study by Allen, Hart, Buell, Harris, and Wolf (1964) manipulated the presumed reinforcer of a child's undesired nursery school behaviors in order to collect empirical support for its functional role. The authors describe the child, Ann, as readily adapting to teachers and other adults but as not playing freely and spontaneously with other children. Ann's advanced language and conceptual skills, long attention span for creative teacher-initiated projects, and slow halting speech appeared to elicit and reinforce considerably more teacher attention than peer attention. As in the Gelfand, Gelfand, and Dobson study, time sampling observations were carried out, revealing that Ann spent 10 percent of her time interacting with other children, 10 percent in noninteractional proximity to children, 35 percent interacting with adults, and 45 percent alone. Most adult attention appeared to be contingent on behaviors incompatible with peer play. After base line data were obtained, the teachers made their attention to Ann contingent on play with other children, minimizing attention when she was alone or approached an adult.

Figure 6-10 shows the change from the base line, in percent time spent in interacting with peers and adults, when these new contingencies were applied. To test whether Ann's interactional behavior was indeed under the control of contingent teacher attention, the procedures were then reversed. Attention was made contingent upon solitary play or adult interaction, while play with children was ignored. As predicted, the percent of time spent with children and adults returned to base line levels. The contingencies were then again shifted in the therapeutic direction and Ann's social behavior with other children again improved. From these results the authors concluded that teacher attention was a powerful reinforcer for Ann, that it could be used to strengthen desired behaviors, and that it had in the past been maintaining her undesirable behaviors. Their observations of the quality of Ann's interactions also suggested that her skills with peers (including presumably her ability to reinforce them) improved as she spent more time with the other children; such skills did not have to be manipulated directly by the teachers. Note also that the authors apparently implicitly assumed that Ann's responsivity to peer reinforcement would gradually change so that adult attention would no longer be required to maintain peer play. However, this shift in sensitivity to peers as reinforcers had not occurred by the time the reversal was introduced (see Figure (6-10), hence the immediate drop in Ann's peer play when it no longer produced adult attention. It would be of interest for diagnostic purposes to know what would happen to her peer play if adult attention were not made contingent upon a competing response (approach to

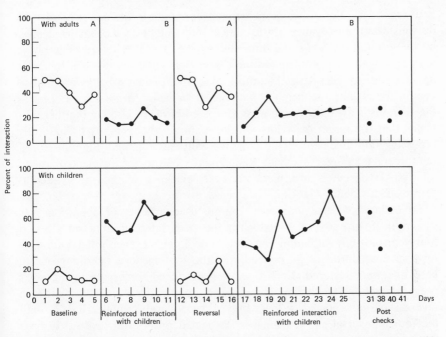

Figure 6-10 Ann's interaction with adults and children (from Allen et al., 1964, p. 514).

adults), but rather were simply withdrawn. Since Ann initially spent 50 percent of her time alone, it is not clear whether, as the authors state, adult attention caused her peer-avoidance by competing with it, or whether peer behaviors were simply not reinforcing Ann's interactions with them. In the latter case, the same therapeutic change would have occurred if adult attention had remained on the same contingency basis as in the base line period, but candy or some other nonsocial reinforcer had been used to shape Ann's peer approach behavior and to maintain it until she learned to respond to peers as conditioned reinforcers. Clearly such considerations were not necessary once the desired therapeutic outcome was achieved. They are relevant, however, to inquiries into the etiology of problematic behaviors and serve to caution us against making inferences about symptom etiology from the fact that one particular therapy technique works. Nonetheless, the ABAB same-subject design allows at least the formulation of some tentative hypotheses about the origin and presumed sources of reinforcement of the problem behavior.

Two other designs have been used to assess the therapeutic effects of contingency manipulation. Ingram (1967) was interested in another issue raised in the Allen et al. study. The ABAB design, necessary to demonstrate the relevance of the clinical intervention to a behavior change, by its very nature *denies* the durability of the effects. If the reversal phase increases again the problem response and thus confirms that the therapist has established the desired control over the patient's behavior, it also demonstrates that the newly strengthened behavior decreases as soon as the therapist's systematic reinforcement is withdrawn. Usually the therapist hopes that the target behaviors will be maintained eventually by naturally occurring reinforcement in the patient's daily environment. Should natural reinforcers take over behavior maintenance before the reversal phase of the ABAB design is instituted, however, evidence of the specific therapeutic effect would be lacking.

Following base line measures, Ingram used a series of operations (as shown in Figure 6-11) to increase the peer interaction of an isolated four-year-old boy attending nursery school. After each intervention, a reversal procedure was introduced, and the contingencies operating during base line were restored. Each operation produced some gain in the boy's peer interactions, including increases in cooperation and sharing. Each reversal period showed a loss, but of successively smaller levels, until the fourth reversal showed no loss. Repeated probes, by reversal to base line contingency operations, were able to assess the gradual development of this independence, as shown by the equal lengths of the final two bars in Figure 6-11. At this point, the boy's peer interactions had become independent of the teacher's interventions. This independence represents the true goal of therapy, since it is hoped that the patient can eventually live without the aids of therapeutic reinforcements.

Baer and Wolf (1967) use the term "behavioral trap" to refer to an environment in which naturally occurring positive reinforcement will take over and maintain desired new behaviors once these have been therapeutically established. They propose that usually only certain responses are crucial for gaining access to an environment that then shapes other desired behaviors as well as maintaining newly established "entry" ones. In the Allen et al. study, we noted that Ann's behavior with other children changed not only in absolute quantity, but also in topography—she talked more fluently and loudly and complained less of trivial injuries once her increased contact with peers made possible their further shaping of her interactions. The nursery school was a "behavioral trap" for Ann and for Ingram's boy; their needed entry behaviors were increased peer interaction.

Ingram's design is essentially an extended ABAB design. An alternate design, which copes with irreversible changes during the first therapeutic intervention, with unstable base line data, and with problems in pro-

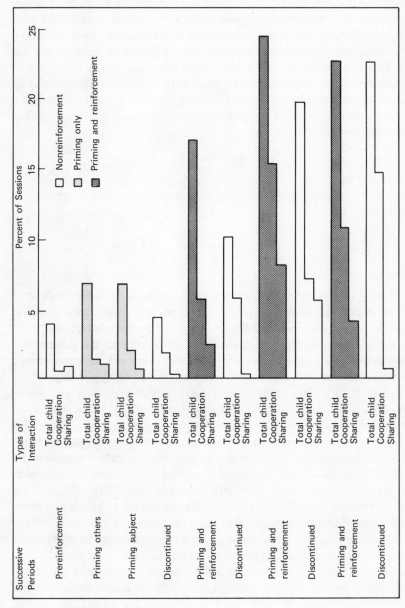

Figure 6-11 Gradual development of response independence of therapeutic reinforcement contingencies (from Ingram, 1967, in Baer and Wolf, 1967).

gramming staff reversal to "usual" (base line) contingencies is illustrated by Browning (1967b). This design was used by Browning to test the hypothesis that the "grandiose bragging" of a nine-year-old boy, under residential psychiatric care, was an operant maintained by staff attention. During base line observations, the staff was observed to react to the patient's symptomatic behavior by positive interest and praise (A), verbal admonishment (B), or purposeful ignoring (C). These were selected as the three experimental contingencies. Each of three groups of staff was assigned to use exclusively one of the contingencies for a one-week period. The design, over three weeks, was:

Staff Group	Week		
	1	2	3
1	A	B	C
2	B	C	A
3	C	A	B

Frequency and duration of bragging incidents were recorded while staff members responded according to this program. The hypothesis was that the patient would seek out and brag to the staff group who reacted positively to that act. During the three weeks of treatment, the patient did indeed consistently brag significantly more (in duration) to some groups of staff than to others. Surprisingly, however, the data suggest that verbal admonishment was more effective as a positive reinforcer than was praise and positive attention; the patient bragged most to the "admonishment" group of staff. Analysis of interaction effects also demonstrated differential effectiveness of the different staff groups in employing the various contingencies, a side benefit for selection of later therapists from among the staff. This study illustrates the utility of testing assumptions about which events may be functioning as reinforcers, the possibility of designing studies of operant therapies in which the patient serves as his own control, and the value of including comparisons across operations and across therapists. The latter controls, common in group designs of therapeutic effectiveness, are unusual in studies of operant behavior therapy.

The sections that follow illustrate clinical use of a number of particular operant operations and tactics. A number of the examples entail designs similar to those discussed here, used to monitor the effects, if any, of presumed reinforcing operations. Others involve no such controlled assessment but rely on more circumstantial evidence to analyze what is going on within the therapeutic operations. The nature of the complaint may make a reversal design inadvisable, for instance in the case of violent aggression or depressive episodes. Or environmental controls may be difficult to reverse, as when parents have little inclination to restore their previous (presumed) reinforcement of a child's temper tantrums just to satisfy the clinician in knowing what in particular led to their child's new and delightful mild-manneredness. Teaching families new patterns of mutual reinforcement may be difficult but fruitful in ridding them of problems. The clinician, therefore, is loath to tamper further, by temporarily undoing his teaching, in instituting a reversal period. Innovations in application of social learning principles may be ill-suited to the reversal designs usually used with operant procedures. Although all behavior therapists probably agree that controlled demonstration of effective variables is generally desirable and that new designs or modes of analysis are needed to supplement reversal and group comparison designs, many would also assert that innovative exploration of clinical use of the operant-social learning paradigm would be stultified by demands for rigid adherence to traditional experimental controls.

In summary, the nature and consequences of the target problem, the degree and direction of control of the environment exercised by the clinician, the complexity of the stimuli being manipulated, the cooperation environmental agents are willing to give, and similar factors will govern the extent to which controlled tests can be made of the mechanisms producing change in any given clinical investigation. In general, the conflicts that may at times exist between the primary responsibilities of the clinician and the laboratory scientists, as discussed in Chapter 1, will determine to what extent a controlled investigation is built into a clinical intervention. The clinician, for example, is primarily expected to produce a beneficial result, and only secondarily to ascertain how he did so. If the secondary goal jeopardizes the primary one, or if patients and important persons in their lives do not agree with the relevance of the secondary goal, more stringent examination of the mechanisms of therapeutic effect will usually not be possible.

Strengthening Incompatible Responses

The examples of therapeutic application of reinforcement and schedule effects discussed thus far have focused on strengthening behaviors that are deficient in the patient's repertoire. When problematic responses instead represent a behavioral excess, a different treatment strategy is needed. One effective device is to strengthen a different, desirable response that is incompatible with the symptomatic behavior. If the two response classes are competitive and cannot occur at the same time, strengthening the more desirable class should reduce the probability of the symptomatic one. This tactic, often termed "counter-conditioning," is a parallel within instrumental conditioning of Wolpe's substitution of relaxation for anxiety as classically conditioned responses to particular stimuli (see Chapter 5).

Strengthening incompatible responses has certain advantages over the alternative techniques of punishing the undesirable behavior or extinguishing it by removal of the maintaining reinforcers. When a problematic response is simply removed, by punishment or by extinction, which behaviors will increase in frequency to fill the gap is left to chance. If a patient has gained important reinforcers mainly through his symptomatic behavior, and if he does not have acceptable alternative responses available to produce the same consequences, then extinction or punishment is likely to fail or to lead to general behavioral deficits and other problems associated with insufficient reinforcement. Strengthening of incompatible responses avoids therapeutic complications (such as replacement of one symptom with another equally undesirable act, or return of the symptom after temporary improvement from punishment or extinction) and the possible undesirable effects if aversive procedures are used.

Another advantage of the technique of strengthening incompatible behaviors is that it does not require the difficult task of identifying and controlling the reinforcing events maintaining the symptomatic behaviors. Incompatible desirable behaviors that are maintained by reinforcers other than those maintaining the excessive problematic behavior can be used when it is difficult or impossible to control the reinforcers of the symptom. For example, Lovaas (1967) has noted that occurrence of self-stimulation (for example, rocking, spinning, and arm flapping), which is by far the most frequent behavior in autistic children, seems to be inversely related to the frequency of other behaviors. The presumed intrinsic reinforcement of self-stimulation is not accessible to therapist intervention, but occurrence of competing behaviors that reduce self-stimulation can be increased by therapeutic procedures.

Becker, Madsen, Arnold, and Thomas (1967) observed that their efforts to extinguish problem classroom behavior simply by withdrawal of teacher attention led to an increase in the children's misbehaving. Presumably, peer reinforcement or intrinsic reinforcers were involved in maintaining the mischief; hence ignoring by the teacher was ineffective. In fact it only removed her verbal punishment that had inhibited the behaviors somewhat. On the other hand, combining ignoring of deviant behaviors with reinforcement of incompatible study and work responses was especially effective. These results were obtained even when the reinforcer was dispensed to another child (for instance, praise for reading quietly) at a time when the target child was misbehaving and being ignored. Presumably this latter procedure both reduced peer reinforcement of the misbehavior (since the peers were reinforced for reading quietly, which is incompatible with giggling at the mischief-maker) and provided vicarious reinforcement for the target child for behaviors incompatible with misbehaving.

Problems can arise unless the incompatible response is one that is desired and likely to be maintained later in the natural environment. Ayllon and Michael (1959) illustrated the difficulties that may arise when the incompatible response is not in itself desirable. They treated violent behavior in a psychotic woman by reinforcing an incompatible response, her low-frequency behavior of sitting quietly on the dayroom floor. Unfortunately, the latter behavior was also incompatible with polite approach behaviors, which they wished to reinforce at the same time. When floor-sitting was extinguished in order to make approach behaviors possible, the violent behaviors increased over base line before the patient had the opportunity to obtain reinforcers for polite approach. At that point, the staff put her back under physical restraints. Similarly, distracting a toddler may often be only a temporary expedient in reducing undesired acts (for example, exploring a hostess's knick-knacks) because the response involved in the distraction may itself become a nuisance; the toddler may insist that mother continue to play the silly game she initiated to distract him.

Rather than relying on contingent delivery of positive reinforcement, which has been the principal operation in the work described so far, the clinician may withhold the positive reinforcement maintaining problematic behaviors. The operations involved in this procedure, which is termed extinction, were indicated in Figure 6-2. Extinction operations require the presence of a previously acquired response, the occurrence of which is currently maintained by identifiable reinforcement. When the response occurs but is no longer reinforced, a gradual reduction in its rate (extinction) occurs. Unless responses are actually emitted and go unreinforced, they are not weakened. It is therefore not sufficient to withhold reinforcement or to keep a patient out of situations in which the troublesome response occurs. Response curves obtained from rats show only a small difference between extinction trials run one day and 45 days after the original strengthening (Skinner, 1938). The weakening effects of extinction are very large and rapid in comparison with those of forgetting.

Extinction may be implicated in the production and maintenance of problematic behavior as well as in its treatment. Social institutions and people often seem to act as if reinforcement is important for acquisition of particular behaviors but is unnecessary for maintaining previously acquired behaviors. A mother may expect her children to behave appropriately without giving them any rewards for doing so. Since reinforcement on an effective schedule is required to maintain any operant, no matter what its strength, extinction ensues and the disappointed mother nags and scolds. On the other hand, extinction accompanied by reinforcement of new responses is a natural part of a child's maturation; when this process is slow or omitted, complaints about the child's behavior are likely. A child who has been heavily reinforced for "cute" baby talk may persist in it long after his parents have tired of his prattle and scold him in an effort to elicit adult speech. If adult speech patterns occur at a low rate and are not reinforced strongly (as behavior incompatible with baby talk), baby talk may not extinguish as long as it is reinforced even very infrequently, or as long as it is vicariously reinforced when the child sees that a younger sibling is reinforced for the same infantile speech.

Several characteristics of a response undergoing extinction and of the parameters affecting rate of extinction have particular relevance for therapeutic applications. The cumulative curve of a response undergoing extinction is usually a very irregular one. Rate at first rises and the response becomes more variable and intense. Gradually, response rate decreases to its base level while simultaneously other behaviors that had been suppressed by the target response gradually return to their previous rates. Extinction does not show a smooth response decrease. Instead, extinction consists of a gradual increase over time in the number of periods in which the response does not occur; in periods when it does occur, it occurs at the same high rate (see Hurwitz, 1957). The early rise in response rate, intensity, and variability, when reinforcement is first withheld, can be useful therapeutically. If a more intense or frequent response is desired, the new extinction-produced rate or intensity can be reinforced. This process of alternate extinction of one level of a response and reinforcement of a new higher level is discussed in the section on response shaping.

The degree of persistence of a response during extinction is another characteristic of importance for both theory and practice. Response persistence, or *resistance to extinction,* is measured by the number of unreinforced trials required to return the response to its operant level or to some low criterion rate. When resistance to extinction has been studied as a dependent variable, it has been found to be a function of the number of preceding reinforcements up to a certain maximum, of the effortfulness of the response, and of the number of preceding cycles of extinction and restrengthening. These variables must be taken into account in treatment. For example, a patient may be deficient in a certain desirable behavior that has in the past undergone repeated cycles of strengthening and extinction because of the vagaries of the patient's environment. After the therapist again strengthens the behavior, only one unreinforced trial may be enough to undo all of the therapeutic gains. The response may be extinguished in one trial and return to the patient's operant rate. In effect, the patient had previously learned a discriminated operant in which one unreinforced response functions as an S^Δ. Much everyday behavior is under similar discriminative control. Through past experience with broken vending machines, most people extinguish after the first dime is lost. Resistance to extinction may often underlie durability of maladaptive behavior. A behavior, adaptive at one time in a person's life and very widely and frequently reinforced, may extinguish so slowly at a different time, when it has become maladaptive, that it is viewed as a symptom. Individual differences in general resistance to extinction due to different organismic or reinforcement histories may be important sources of variability in the extent to which people show maladaptive behavior.

Extinction as a Therapeutic Tactic. Extinction is a useful therapeutic technique when behavioral excesses comprise the intervention target. In a classic example, Ayllon and Michael (1959) instructed nurses in how to extinguish the numerous disruptive visits of a psychotic patient to the nurses' office. On the assumption that nurses' attention (including their scolding the patient, leading her away, etc.) was a reinforcing consequence maintaining this behavior, they instructed the nurses to withhold *all* attention when the patient entered the office. From a base line average of 16 entries a day, the patient was down to two entries per day after seven weeks of extinction. Similar extinction operations have successfully reduced delusional speech (Rickard, Dignam, and Horner, 1960; Ayllon and Michael, 1959), hypochrondriacal complaints (Ayllon and Haughton, 1964), various dependent behaviors (Ayllon and Haughton, 1962) and many other behavior excesses.

Often extinction of undesired behaviors is a necessary preliminary to positive reinforcement of weak but desired behaviors. For example, Blake and Moss (1967) found that they could not initiate speech acquisition training of a four-year-old mute girl because frequent intense crying and tantrums disrupted all other activities. To extinguish the crying and tantrums, all access to possible reinforcement of them was removed. A shutter in the training booth that closed off access to light, the therapist, food, and other reinforcers, was dropped whenever crying or tantrum behavior began. Later in training, after eye contact had been trained as a necessary prerequisite for reinforcement of other responses, mildly disruptive behaviors were quickly extinguished by removing this conditioned reinforcer—the therapist looked away and avoided eye contact when the patient began to behave disruptively. The procedures used by Blake and Moss go beyond the operations of extinction since more is removed than simply access to whatever reinforcers were maintaining the disruptive behaviors. Access to all reinforcement for any *other* behaviors was removed as well. This latter procedure is termed "time out" from positive reinforcement (a time interval when reinforcement is unavailable) and is discussed further in Chapter 7. "Time out" is considered to be a form of punishment because it is applied *contingent* upon a particular response and has the characteristics of an aversive event. Although extinction and time out procedures differ, they both involve withholding reinforcement following a given undesirable response; in application they often overlap. When attention from the therapist is presumed to be the reinforcer maintaining an undesired behavior, such as crying, and when the therapist's attention also is an S^D for reinforcement of desired behaviors, extinction necessarily involves some brief periods of a time out type of punishment when attention is removed. When all reinforcement maintaining an undesired behavior cannot otherwise be removed, for example, peer support for a child's mischief in class, a more complete use of this time out procedure may be necessary. The child may be removed without further attention to another room where social and other reinforcers are not available. Return to the reinforcing environment is contingent upon a lapse of time without further disruptive behavior. Potent reinforcers, such as food for a hungry child, may be necessary to maintain the conditioned reinforcing value of the therapy room when a time out procedure has to be invoked often, early in treatment.

Several characteristics of extinction make it an undesirable therapeutic technique under certain conditions. Among these is the problem just exemplified in the preceding paragraph, the identification and removal of all reinforcement maintaining the problematic behavior. Many behaviors may be maintained by intrinsic effects, by self-reinforcement, or by subtle contingencies on complex schedules, making client observation and testing of maintaining reinforcement events impossible. Patient report can help at times with the identification difficulties but with these classes of reinforcers as well as with those dispensed by many different social agents in the patient's environment, the clinician is left with the severe difficulties of trying to control occurrence of reinforcement in order to apply extinction. In such instances, other techniques either from the operant paradigm (punishment, reinforcement of competing responses) or from other paradigms (self-regulation—see Chapter 9; vicarious learning—see Chapter 5) must be applied. The challenge posed to the therapist who needs to identify and remove the reinforcers maintaining a symptom can be illustrated by a partial list of potential reinforcers that have been implicated in alcoholism (Mertens and Fuller, 1964): removal of aversive stimuli (for instance, anxiety, responsibility), social reinforcers available in the drinking environment (such as tavern buddies), nurturant behavior from wife or others when drunk, reduction of inhibition of other behaviors (for example, sexual approach, boasting, enhancement of self-responses such as "I can lick the world"), tolerance or encouragement by others of otherwise unacceptable behaviors, drugs effects (sedative, hypnotic, analgesic), and access to social reinforcers (for example, bartender) in an otherwise interpersonally barren life.

Extinction clearly requires complete environmental control since other agents may unwittingly reinforce the behaviors the therapist has under extinction. If equally accessible environmental agents systematically differ in reinforcement delivery, they simply come to function as S^D or S^Δ without reducing the overall rate of the response at all. If this discrimination does not occur, the intermittent reinforcement provided by one agent will simply make the response more resistant to the extinction efforts of others. When dispensers of the relevant reinforcers in the patient's natural setting are willing to cooperate, extinction becomes a much more feasible approach. Extinction of alcoholic drinking is possible by enlisting the aid of the patient's drinking companions. Friends have been instructed to emit, at a high rate, all of their usual social behaviors (talking, joking, attending to the patient) in the local tavern but only so long as the patient drank soft drinks. They would immediately withdraw all social reinforcers (ignore him and leave) the moment he began to drink an alcoholic beverage.

The initial brief rise in rate and intensity of a response undergoing extinction can pose a different sort of obstacle. The reinforcing agents may not be able to tolerate this brief increase long enough for the subsequent decrease to begin, and so may abandon the procedure since it not only seems not to work immediately but even seems to make the problem worse. Alternatively, they may begin to reinforce the response intermittently when it is particularly noxious, and maintain their planned extinction at other times. The reinforcing agents thereby simply shape higher rates and intensities of the undesirable behavior. This pattern is probably the cause of parental complaints that ignoring makes temper tantrums worse. Sometimes the nature of the troublesome behavior is such that extinction cannot humanely be used. Lovaas (1967) has pointed out that since self-destructive behaviors of autistic children (head banging, biting own hands or arms) are maintained in part by attendant attention, they are amenable to extinction. However, most often these behaviors must be dealt with by punishment because of the physical dangers consequent to any initial *increase* under extinction.

In the discussion of strengthening incompatible responses, we pointed out another disadvantage of extinction: it permits neither control nor prediction of which new responses will substitute for the one being extinguished. When acceptable alternate responses for procuring reinforcement are already readily available, this need not be a problem, since they will increase as the probability of the symptomatic response is reduced. In other situations, concurrent positive reinforcement of an acceptable alternative behavior may have to accompany extinction.

Finally, the extinction procedure has aversive properties. Since reinforcement has cue functions, its removal leads to ambiguity as well as to frustration until other responses are successful in producing reinforcement. A number of studies have shown that extinction produces emotional, aggressive, and other behaviors similar to those produced by pain and other aversive stimuli (Mowrer and Jones, 1943). Extinction has been successfully used as a punisher for other responses, thereby clearly demonstrating its aversive properties (see, for example, Ferster, 1958a; Zimmerman and Ferster, 1964). Physical attack on other nearby animals has been elicited by extinction procedures with pigeons (Azrin, Hutchinson, and Hake, 1966). In therapy, particularly when a patient's aggressive behaviors are already at high strength, the side effects of extinction as an aversive event may be too great to tolerate. The ready availability of alternative behaviors for achieving the same reinforcement would, of course, greatly reduce the frustration effects of extinction of a particular response.

There are other characteristics of behavior under extinction that have not yet been explored for their relevance to behavior therapy, but that may prove to be useful. Contrast phenomena, for example, involve an increase in one response component of a multiple schedule when the other component is put on extinction. Whether and to what extent symptomatic behaviors are under control of multiple schedules and show contrast effects is unknown, but contrast may be a source of difficulty when extinction is used. There is also evidence (D'Amato, Etkin, and Fazzaro, 1968) that cue-producing responses or observing behaviors that supply only redundant information (beyond that normally necessary to identify discriminative stimuli) increase during extinction of an operant. A wife whose dependent behaviors with her husband are being extinguished may increase her rate of asking "Do you love me?" or of reading his mail when he withholds attention and concern following her dependent behaviors. Investigators in this area have viewed reinforcement as uncertainty reduction, thus emphasizing the aversive ambiguity caused by extinction. Again, the potential relevance of this line of work to patient behavior both in symptom formation (for example, a neurotic's endless requests for reassurance) and in side effects during extinction therapy seems intriguing.

Response Differentiation or Shaping

When a child uses words that are unacceptable to the adults around him, the behavior therapist can put the bad language on an extinction schedule while reinforcing more acceptable expressions until the offensive behavior disappears. The problem is different, however, for a child who has never acquired intelligible speech. In such an instance, the principles of reinforcement and extinction may be combined into a technology that reorganizes elements of available behaviors into what appear to be new responses, either by molding complex new behaviors from simple elements or by building complex chains of simpler responses. This procedure is termed *shaping, response differentiation,* or *successive approximation.*

Rather than straightforward use of reinforcement or extinction to change the probability of an existing response, shaping employs differential reinforcement and differential extinction to gradually shift the topography and organization of a response into a new constellation of components. By applying differential reinforcement to one extreme subclass of a set of responses and extinction to all the other responses in the set, the more extreme subclass is differentially strengthened and becomes dominant. By successive applications of this procedure, complex behaviors can be established. The extreme features of a response on which differential reinforcement of members of a set is based may be intensity, effort, topography, rate, or duration. Differential extinction also plays an important role in this procedure since it produces wide response variability, and hence makes available more extreme responses for differential reinforcement. For example, a pigeon may be shaped to turn in complete circles by making food reinforcement contingent, first upon any slight turn of the head or body in one direction, then requiring a slightly greater turn. On each occasion, a greater turn in the right direction is reinforced while small turns or movements in the opposite direction are extinguished. Finally, through the increasingly stringent requirements for reinforcement, all body shifts except a complete turn remain nonreinforced and only a complete turn is reinforced. New components can be added in the same fashion; the pigeon might be required to move toward a bell, lift the head toward it, and finally to peck the bell after making its circle turn. In this way, long chains of responses can be built through successive approximations from small elements of the organism's repertoire of free operants. Skinner (1962) taught pigeons to play "ping-pong" by such a procedure, as illustrated in Figure 6-12.

Shaping is a critical procedure in the practical application of reinforcement techniques, since criteria for reinforcement during acquisition of new complex responses must always be graded to fit current response probabilities. Criteria that are too stringent mean too infrequent reinforcement and little behavior control, while shifting criteria can strengthen and control behavior rapidly. Failure to use realistically graded criteria for reinforcement is a prominent cause of failure in behavior therapy. Shift-

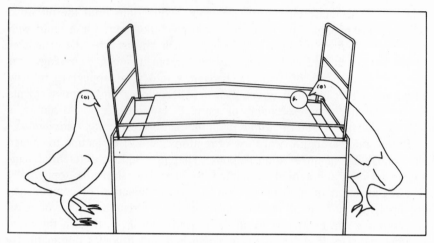

Figure 6-12 Two pigeons "playing Ping-Pong" (from Skinner, 1962, p. 531).

ing the requirements for reinforcement is especially important when a patient is given "assignments" to perform outside of the therapy session. In
this treatment approach (see Chapter 9), direct observational data are not
available to guide the therapist in pacing progress. Only careful inquiry
or self-monitoring can reveal whether responses are appropriately graded
and reinforced. For example, Stuart (1967) and Ferster, Nurnberger,
and Levitt (1962) have described programs in which patients carry out
a series of graded steps in learning to control overeating. Stuart's patients
begin by keeping written records of the timing, context, and quantity
of their food intake. They then progress to brief interruptions of eating
during meals, go on to establish set places and times for preparing foods,
to establish slow rates of ingestion, and to develop alternate responses
for occasions when the probability of eating is high (for instance, responses
to compete with popcorn-eating in movies or with the refrigerator raid
at midnight). The program is designed to shape new eating habits gradually by verbal assignments of a series of behavioral changes, each slightly
more demanding than the previous task. Use of small steps insures adequate reinforcement throughout the treatment.

Because of its relevance to producing novel arrangements and sequences
of behavior, shaping has a prominent place in therapy when behavior
deficits are to be remedied. The preliminary steps necessary for other
modification procedures may be initially "shaped up," for example, getting
a hyperactive autistic child to enter the therapy room, to sit still in a
chair, and to attend to the therapist's face and voice. Were one to wait

for this whole chain to occur as an operant in order to reinforce it, one might wait forever, whereas each component of the chain can be rapidly shaped separately and then combined in a behavior chain that is maintained by continued differential reinforcement. The major treatment goals may also be achieved entirely by shaping. For example, Isaacs, Thomas, and Goldiamond (1960) have described a painstaking procedure used to reinstate verbal behavior in a mute chronic psychotic. At first, they reinforced the patient simply for moving his eyes toward the offered reinforcer (chewing gum), then for small lip movements while looking at the gum. Next the gum was withheld until lip movements produced a sound, then until the patient vocalized a sound, and finally until the vocalization became a closer and closer approximation of the word "gum," which was cued by the therapist. Unless the response class is a sufficiently general one, shaping can be very laborious. The slow rate at which change is produced by this procedure represents an occupational hazard for the therapist, since his own therapeutic behavior is usually maintained by seeing the patient improve. Should the therapist attempt to speed up attainment of his own reinforcement by shifting the patient's criteria too rapidly, he risks losing the gains already achieved.

The time and labor involved in shaping often can be reduced by training a general response class which then can be used to initiate other new sequences of behavior. Imitation, or the matching of a response to an S^D provided by the therapist, is one example of such a general response class. Risley and Wolf (1967) shaped imitation behavior as the initial step in developing speech in autistic children. A first goal was to develop reliable and correct imitation by the child so that his utterance of a new word in an appropriate context could be brought under the control of the therapist's speech. The therapist said a given word every four or five seconds. The child was reinforced at first for immediately emitting *any* sound, and then for sounds that more and more closely approximated the desired terminal behavior, the immediate and exact imitation of the utterance. By varying tone, intensity, and pitch of word presentation, the therapist increased the probability of imitation early in the training, but as the imitation process was shaped, these cues were omitted. When the child was reliably responding to two words presented alternately, more words were interspersed with the original ones until a general imitative response had been established. While successive approximations of imitation of the desired word were being reinforced, other nonimitative, irrelevant, and inappropriate verbalizations were extinguished; the stimulus word was presented only when the child was silent. As reliable imitation increased, other extraneous behaviors were also extinguished; the stimulus word (which is an S^D and thus acts also as a conditioned reinforcer) was presented only when the child was sitting still, attentive, and looking at the therapist.

Figure 6-13 graphs the rapid acquisition of reliable word repetition by an echolalic child. The child gradually increased his rate of acquisition until only one trial is required for each new word when imitation has been well established. In shaping this child's responses, particular care was taken to find an effective reinforcer. As is often the case with severely disturbed patients, this child initially required powerful extrinsic primary reinforcers to control his behaviors, such as food after withholding a meal. To increase the precision of the reinforcement contingencies and to begin conditioning of more convenient social reinforcers, the therapist usually says something like "good" immediately after the child's response and when he puts a bite of food in the child's mouth.

Risley and Wolf's study also illustrates the difficulty in distinguishing between shaping of free operant responses by sheer differential reinforcement (as in the example of the pigeon's turning), and simultaneously developing stimulus control of a given response (as in training imitative

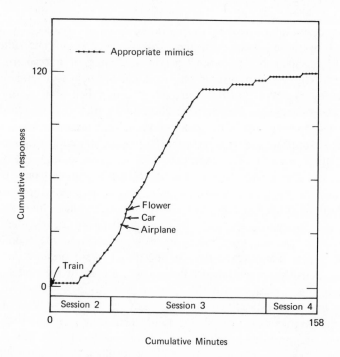

Figure 6-13   A record of the initial rate of appropriate imitations (mimics) by Carey. Each dot represents two minutes of session time (from Risley and Wolf, 1967, p. 79).

behavior). Similarly, building response chains and shaping new patterns of response are often carried out together so that the two procedures become blurred, even though they represent separate techniques.

Shaping procedures play a prominent role in other therapies involving vicarious and imitation learning paradigms (see Chapter 5). Replication techniques, such as role playing and psychodrama, that are used with adult neurotics usually include provision for acquisition of new social skills by a shaping method. A patient may be taught to be more assertive by role playing a series of interactions that gradually require more elements of assertion in order to produce therapist reinforcement.

When behavioral deficits are presumed to be based on insufficient past reinforcement but the response is known to be available in the patient's repertoire, although only at low strength, elaborate shaping and systematic extrinsic reinforcement may not be required at all. Verbal instructions to perform the behavior may be sufficient. For example, Ayllon and Azrin (1964) compared instructions, positive reinforcement, and instructions plus reinforcement in their effects on psychotic patients who usually did not pick up eating utensils when entering the dining room for meals. Instructions alone produced a utensil-collecting behavior in 25 percent of the patients, reinforcement (extra dessert) alone produced it in only 10 percent of the patients. With instructions plus reinforcement, all patients collected their utensils.

Discrimination and Stimulus Control

Skinner (1938) distinguished four roles in which a stimulus may function: elicitation, reinforcement, discrimination, and emotion. Thus far this chapter has emphasized the reinforcing properties of stimuli. However, in behavior therapies, as in daily life, a tremendous amount of behavior control is exerted by the environment through eliciting and discriminative stimuli. As we noted in earlier chapters, stimulus manipulation therapies deal mainly with eliciting stimuli. Operant behavior therapies make extensive use of discriminative stimuli. The distinction between these two roles is recalled by the empirical generalizations describing respondents and operants. While the former tend to be elicited on each occasion by the appropriate stimulus, the function of the discriminative stimulus in operant conditioning is merely to set the stage for responding. Variables other than the discriminative stimulus play a strong role in determining the probability of occurrence of the response.

Stimulus control plays a vital role in most behavior modification, as one would expect from the statement that most behavior consists of discriminated operants. Many of the clinical studies described earlier involved response strengthening under discriminative stimulus control. For example, to increase peer play, Allen et al. (1964) reinforced Ann with teacher attention in the presence of peers (S^D) but not when alone or with teachers (S$^\Delta$) (see Figure 6-10). Nursery school children have been trained to react to certain classroom-oriented teacher behaviors as an S$^\Delta$ for noisy play. The children were provided with clear S^D's for noisy play, which was a potent reinforcer, contingent upon nonresponse to the teacher's S$^\Delta$. That is, the S^D and following noisy play reinforced appropriate use of the S$^\Delta$ (Homme, de Baca, Devine, Steinhorst, and Rickert, 1963). Behaviors are often presented to a therapist as problems needing change, not because the behavior is universally undesirable, but because it occurs under inappropriate circumstances. Indeed, therapy is sometimes described as being primarily a matter of discrimination training. Aggressive behaviors in children are not always undesirable; rather, a child needs to discriminate between the attack of a bully and the presence of a desired toy in another child's hands as stimuli signaling that his aggression will be rewarded. The whole range of neurotic and psychotic symptoms often exemplifies specific stimulus control problems instead of inappropriate rates of response. For the exhibitionist, it is where he undresses rather than the rate of undressing that leads to complaints. Similarly, patients may often need training in delivering clear discriminative stimuli to others, in order to develop more satisfying interpersonal interactions. Subassertive persons, for example, not only tend to reward demands on them by others, but also fail to signal, until much too late, when they will and will not reward such demands. The other person is left bewildered by an ultimate temper outburst since there has been no earlier indication that a request would not be happily accepted this time as similar ones had been in the past.

An interesting example of discrimination training in behavior therapy involved training mothers to react differentially to different behaviors emitted by their problem children (Wahler, Winkel, Peterson, and Morrison, 1965). Each mother was prompted by instructions and a signal light to guide her in selecting appropriate responses to the child and in turn was reinforced for correct responses by a signal light and praise. She was trained to react to the child's dependent behaviors as an S$^\Delta$, to his independence as an S^D. That is, she did not receive reinforcement herself if she reinforced the child for dependent behaviors. She was praised, however, when she gave attention and praise to the child for his independent acts. Her responses of attention and praise for the desired behaviors were both reinforced by the experimenters and were reinforcing to the child. In this way each mother was taught to discriminate different aspects of her child's behavior as cues for different actions on her part. A reversal design was used to demonstrate that the reinforcement contingencies exercised control over mother's and child's behavior.

Several techniques are closely related to stimulus control and are often combined with it in treatment. *Fading* is a technique that facilitates forming new discriminations. One stimulus that initally exerts powerful discriminative control is gradually "faded out" as another stimulus acquires greater power of control. Fading is illustrated in studies in which echolalic children are taught a labeling vocabulary. Such children can be trained, through shaping and positive reinforcement, to repeat a word immediately after the therapist utters it. For such a child, saying "ear" is under the stimulus control of the word "ear" spoken by the therapist. Functional speech requires a different sort of stimulus control. A first step toward independent speech is to train the child to attach the word to the object or pictures of the object, that is, to acquire a labeling vocabulary. The trainer points to a selected stimulus (for example, his own ear). When the child visually fixates on it, the trainer says "What is this?" and then speaks the appropriate noun label ("ear"). If the child imitates the sound, he is reinforced. This procedure is repeated on each trial, but the prompt (saying "ear") is gradually faded. The trainer speaks more and more softly and/or pronounces less of the word ("ea–") until the child says the word upon presentation of only the training stimulus and the question "What is this?" More and more words are introduced in this fashion, and previously mastered stimuli are interspersed with new ones to insure that only the object or picture itself is the potent S^D. Figure 6-14 presents data for one echolalic child's acquisition of a labeling vocabulary (Lovaas, 1967). The data indicate that the child gradually acquired a learning set under the fading procedure so that in later training he required only one prompt, or labeling of an object by the trainer, to acquire the correct response.

In the next stage of the training procedure, various representations of each object are gradually introduced as discriminative stimuli to insure a generalized response class (for example, child's nose, doll's nose, picture of a nose). Words for common activities (walking, laughing, etc.) are trained in similar fashion, and shaping and fading techniques are also used to train abstract speech, and finally, conversation. At each step, care is taken that discriminations are not conditioned to adventitious stimuli such as time lapse or schedule effects.

Similar fading procedures have been successfully used with adults. To retrain aphasics who are unable to match their own motor responses with self-instructions to move in a given way, technicians state the desired self-instruction aloud, the patient imitates it aloud while the technician physically guides the patient through the motion, but over trials gradually fades out both the verbal and physical prompts.

Sidman and Stoddard (1967) compared several discrimination training procedures for teaching retarded children to make form discriminations.

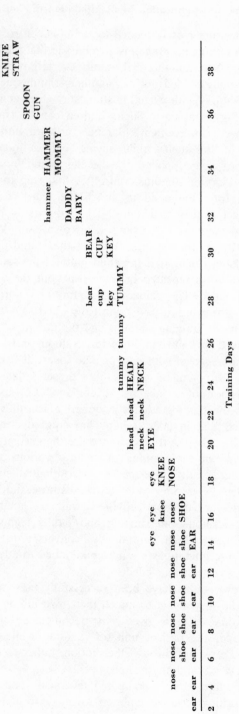

Figure 6-14 Acquisition of a labeling vocabulary by Taylor, a previously mute boy. The abscissa denotes training days. The objects are printed in lower case letters on the days they were introduced and trained, and in capital letters on the days they were mastered (Lovaas, 1967).

They found a fading procedure to be superior to training without fading, in terms of number of errors and level of final acquisition of the correct solution. Half of the children who were unable to acquire a discriminated response between a circle and ellipse under reinforcement and extinction alone were able to do so under a fading program. Those who failed to acquire the discrimination at all were found to have adopted response patterns (for example, position alternations incompatible with appropriate stimulus control), an outcome that can be avoided if errorless training procedures are used.

Fading and other discrimination training procedures often are accompanied by some of the "side effects" of any extinction process. Risley and Wolf (1967) note that temper tantrums and other emotional outbursts initially occurred when S^Δ was presented in their speech training of echolalic children. The children also showed these behaviors when there was an increasing delay between presentation of the training object (S^D) and the therapist's verbal prompt. These outbursts were extinguished relatively rapidly. A positive benefit accrues from the therapist's role as dispenser of reinforcement. Because it is a necessary precondition for reinforcement, the therapist's attention in turn becomes an S^D and acquires reinforcing value, an important consequence in these disturbed children for whom other persons often have had no S^D or reinforcing value or have served as S^Ds for symptomatic behaviors because of their tendency to reinforce such symptoms.

Stimulus facilitation, which was discussed in Chapter 5, is closely related to stimulus control; often the effects and mechanisms of the two cannot be differentiated. Social facilitation occurs when response rate increases in the presence of another individual, such as an audience or a co-actor engaged in parallel behavior. For example, it has often been observed that an animal whose rate of eating has dropped because of satiation or aversive conditioning will begin to eat more when another eating animal is introduced into the situation (Masserman, 1943). The results of such experiments have often been interpreted as illustrating discriminative control. The second feeding animal may serve to change the situation from S^Δ to S^D by signaling in his own behavior that aversive stimuli are no longer forthcoming. However, recent studies (Hake and Laws, 1967) have demonstrated social facilitation effects even when aversive stimulation continues. The work of Berkowitz and his associates (Berkowitz, 1962, 1964; Berkowitz and LePage, 1967) has also demonstrated facilitative effects on aggressive behaviors by stimuli that do not signal differential reinforcement. For example, subjects were given an opportunity to deliver electric shock to a peer who had apparently shocked them. They delivered significantly more shocks when a gun was in the room than did subjects in a room with a badminton racket. Thus facilitation effects do not appear to require that a facilitating stimulus function as an S^D. Since the effect of observing the stimulus as a guide for action is the same whether it is simply a facilitator or is an S^D, the distinction is less important in promoting behavior change than it is in theory.

Another issue that arises in assessing the role of particular stimuli in behavioral treatments is distinguishing between a reinforcer and an S^D. Since it is common for an S^D to acquire conditioned reinforcing value, this distinction may seem unnecessary. However, at times a behavioral diagnosis may presume that a given S is acting as a reinforcer to maintain symptomatic behavior, whereas experimental manipulation would show it to be an S^D signaling access to another more potent reinforcer. The treatment program design would be different in each case. Studies in which, for example, teacher attention is postulated to reinforce a nursery school-child's crying, often infer that a cure by extinction is evidence for this postulation. To test the accuracy of this inference, however, teacher attention would have to be delivered during the experimental phase at the same rate as during base line but randomly rather than contingently. Otherwise, teacher attention could be either an S^D or a reinforcer, and have the same effect during the extinction procedure. That is, witholding attention would reduce crying whether attention was a positive reinforcer or an S^D. This may be of some importance for understanding the origins and maintenance of problematic behaviors in the natural ecology.

Stimulus Control as a Therapeutic Obstacle. In contrast to the contributions of stimulus control to therapeutic goals which we so far have been reviewing, overly specific stimulus control can also pose serious obstacles in therapy. When generalization of behavior changes is desired from the treatment setting to the patient's ordinary environment, stimulus control may subvert any therapeutic gains. For example, in treating a nine-year-old boy for hyperactivity and lack of attending behavior, Patterson (1965a) sought to promote generality of behavioral improvement by positively reinforcing the boy while he worked at his desk on normal classroom materials. Despite the precautions of conducting treatment in the normal school environment, reduction of hyperactivity and increased attending behavior came under the discriminative control of the therapist's presence and did not generalize to the rest of the class day. As a remedy, Patterson suggested randomizing the therapy sessions throughout the day and removing the therapist from sight by using devices remotely controlled from an observation booth. In later work these changes were helpful in promoting generalization of desired behaviors. Many other examples have been reported in which the therapy setting exerted unwanted stimulus control over behavior changes. As one illustration, Hingtgen, Sanders, and DeMyer (1965) found that social cooperation, reinforced in six schizophrenic children, generalized to similar behaviors within the treatment room but did not change in frequency on the ward where the children lived. Other examples of unwanted stimulus control were given in Chapter 3, for example, the tiqueur whose symptoms ceased when shock apparatus was set up, but at no other time.

The degree to which undesired stimulus control by the treatment setting occurs may be a function of multiple factors including the range of stimuli available and their similarity to the natural environment, the scheduling and obtrusiveness of therapy sessions, the nature of the reinforcers used, and the nature of the responses being modified.

In general, in thinking about stimulus control of behavior, it is useful to recall the point made in the discussion of the S component in the S-O-R-K-C formula: the S component may refer to large and complex aspects of the environment and is far more encompassing than the sort of precisely defined narrow stimuli manipulated in many experiments. All behavior takes place in some setting. If the setting, which may involve a complex constellation of stimuli, is systematically related to particular behaviors and reinforcement, it acquires a controlling function. If the setting is associated with many variations in behavior and does not indicate which acts will be reinforced, it does not exert stimulus control. It is in this broad sense that the behavior therapist needs to manipulate stimulus control as it occurs in the complex settings of daily life.

ENVIRONMENTAL ENGINEERING

The engineering character of operant-based therapy and its requirement of strict environmental control have been emphasized throughout this chapter. These characteristics have encouraged the application of operant therapies to problems with which clinical psychologists have not dealt previously, and by persons who have not been trained in the full range of skills provided in university clinical training programs. Several current developments are likely to enhance further the expansion of operant technology in nontraditional applications of environmental control.

For one, innovations and improvements in instrumentation should in the future offer far more in the way of standardization, reduction of variability by automation and increased efficiency, and cost reduction. Electromechanical devices should bring into existence types of data collection and therapeutic interventions not now feasible. Schwitzgebel (1968) surveyed devices available for monitoring and recording behavior, transforming stimuli, scheduling consequences, prompting and teaching, and effecting neurological alterations. He concluded that many devices are experimental or of dubious value, that safe and effective parameters of equipment remain to be established, but that research and application in behavior modification will be substantially improved as more sophisticated instrumentation systems are developed. Lang's (1969) Device for Automated Desensitization (see Chapter 4) is one example of how therapeutic procedures can be instrumented with consequent gains in standardized control and personnel savings. Miniaturized radio devices are in use to monitor, transmit, and record all interaction of a subject, doing away with the need for live observation and apparently reducing the distortions produced by an observer's presence (Purcell and Brady, 1966). Automated devices used to program and record conjugate reinforcement permit exploration of continuous delivery of a wide variety of reinforcers, from mother's face (Lindsley, 1963a, see Figure 6-5) to the utterances of a psychotherapist (Nathan, Schneller, and Lindsley, 1964). In contrast to dynamic therapies, where the therapist is his own recorder and measurement device, the behavior therapies, in particular those using the operant paradigm, require measurement precision which can be significantly aided by advances in instrumentation.

A second area of development likely to enhance the utility of operant techniques stems from their specificity, which permits training of technicians who, in turn, apply them to problematic behaviors of patients. The relative ease with which operant technology can be mastered by hospital orderlies, nursery teachers, parents, and others who work in the natural environment has already been demonstrated (Walder, Breiter, Cohen, Daston, Forbe, and McIntire, 1966; Baer and Wolf, 1968; Ayllon and Michael, 1959). Improved training technology should increase the efficiency and competence with which these agents are trained, and in turn improve their own therapeutic effectiveness. As one example, Patterson and Gullion (1968) have developed a brief programmed text for parents that presents basic operant principles in terms of parental influence on child behavior. Parents are required to complete the program and to graph the rate of problematic behaviors before they and their child obtain help by more direct behavioral interventions from a research-treatment team. This approach facilitates generalization and long-term maintenance of improvement since the parents cooperate in a very systematic way in assessing target behaviors and bringing about their change. Their regular collection of quantitative data illustrates the use of research methods and goals as therapeutic devices per se, in operant therapies.

Still another area whose development should contribute greatly to the utility of operant behavior modification is that of training the patient in self-regulatory behaviors. Engineered environments or programmed technicians in the patient's ecology may be required for control and change of symptomatic responses in many patients. For others, it is the patient himself who can be programmed to apply operant technology to his own behavior. When this is possible, the therapist's role becomes that of *instigating* behavioral change in the patient's own daily living, rather than directly *intervening* in the patient's ongoing behavior or creating some replication of the patient's environment in which to shape and practice desirable responses (Kanfer and Phillips, 1969). The gains in efficiency from this approach are obvious. Self-regulation is taken up as a separate topic in Chapter 9 because of its importance, but it forms a background development relevant to the present discussion since it represents an innovation in a direction opposite but complementary to that of engineered environments, one equally well suited to operant procedures.

These and other developments in society at large (see Chapter 11) are likely to expand present applications of the technology of behavior control in the natural environment. We will consider in turn the use of individual agents in a patient's daily life setting, the engineering of token systems as therapeutic environments in hospitals and schools, and the concept of prosthetic environments. These applications are dealt with in some detail because of their innovative character within clinical psychology and the peculiar suitability of the operant paradigm for their development. It must be remembered, however, that operant procedures are equally well suited to individual behavior modification, even within verbal therapies, with the neurotic, and with other clinic patients.

Therapeutic Agents in the Natural Environment

We have already mentioned the pioneering work of Ayllon and his associates at Anna State Hospital, and of Baer and Wolf in nursery school settings, in teaching operant technology to the indigenous caretaking personnel in order to facilitate therapeutic effects through the many interactions of nurses or teachers with their charges. Ayllon and Michael (1959) pointed out that the duties of nursing personnel bring them into constant contact with hospitalized patients. Nurses and aides are therefore in an excellent position to act as "behavioral engineers" by substituting systematic behavior modification for their traditional efforts to control or pacify patients.

Training of indigenous personnel in the application of operant principles for behavior modification offers a number of advantages. First, behavioral engineering in the natural environment is convenient because it provides more direct and constant access to symptomatic behavior as it naturally occurs. Many behaviors cannot readily be brought into the traditional treatment settings of an office or clinic, but are easily accessible to agents in the patient's own environment. Second, maintenance of desired behaviors and their generalization across settings is enhanced when treatment is done in the home, or school, or in the institution in which the patient lives. A responsive social environment provides for control of a larger proportion and range of target behaviors and supports the changed behaviors in various forms and under many different circumstances. Baer and Wolf (1967) have particularly stressed this point, indicating that when behavior changes are brought about directly in the natural environment, the opportunities are increased for programming the changes in such a way that others in the environment, in the natural course of events, will take over the cueing and reinforcing operations of the behavior modifiers. Prevention of new symptoms is also achieved more readily through corrective actions of therapeutic agents who monitor and act on naturally occurring behaviors.

Finally, use of nonprofessionals as effective therapeutic agents offers some hope of more adequately meeting the mental health needs of the community despite perpetual shortages of trained professional personnel. As discussed more fully in Chapter 11, expansion of the use and responsibility of nonprofessional mental health workers is continuously advocated (see, for example, Ellsworth, 1968; Frederick, 1969a). The present trend toward changing the definition of psychopathology from mental disease to problems in living has made not only acceptable but also urgent the opening up of therapeutic roles to the nonmedically, nonpsychologically trained, and especially to those in the natural environment who are most likely to first encounter problematic behaviors and remain most closely in contact with them.

Parents were among the first nonprofessional groups to be trained as *in situ* therapists. They had obvious practical advantages for obtaining and maintaining change in problem behaviors in their children. Initially, the child and a parent were brought into the clinic. There, their interactions were observed and recorded and the parent was trained, often by means of instructions, light signals, and reinforcement by the therapist, to apply operant technology to the child's deviant behaviors (Wolf, Risley, and Mees, 1964; Wahler, Winkel, Peterson, and Morrison, 1965; Straughan, 1964). Allen and Harris (1966), for example, hypothesized that the excessive self-scratching of a five-year-old girl was an operant rather than respondent behavior, and that it was maintained by maternal attention. The symptom was so severe that it threatened permanent disfiguration. All parental disciplinary efforts had failed to reduce the scratching. Laboratory observation indicated that the mother spoke to the child only in a critical or directive fashion and did not positively reinforce the child's large repertoire of social and intellectual skills. The mother was asked to keep daily records of the frequency of the child's scratching, other behaviors, and her own spankings and scoldings. The mother's records revealed that during constructive play the child did not scratch. The records also showed that most maternal behaviors were aversive. The mother was instructed in the use of behavior techniques including extinction, positive reinforcement, and ignoring the trivial behaviors she usually had criticized. She was instructed to give food or gold stars and warm approval for every half hour in which the girl did not scratch and to award toys for nights without scratching. After 5 weeks, all symptomatic behavior had ceased, the sores had healed, and most importantly, the mother had changed her customary pattern of interacting with the child from aversive to positive control, with accompanying changes in her feelings toward her daughter.

In this study and similar ones, it is usual for the course of behavior change to be erratic because of the parent's initial "poor technology." For this reason, and to assure greater representativeness of the mother-child interactions which are observed and shaped, many investigators have trained the mother within the home (see, for example, Hawkins, Peterson, Schweid, and Bijou, 1966). Patterson and his associates have carried out a series of studies to develop and evaluate a program for training families to alter their mutual reinforcement contingencies so that desired behaviors are strengthened and undesirable ones are weakened. The program includes instruction in learning principles through a programmed text and in observing and recording the frequency of a child's target behaviors and the usual consequences. A team of experimenters then joins the parents in designing a modification program, models its operation in the home, supervises the family in carrying it out, and finally monitors the data that the family continues to collect on symptomatic responses and their consequences. Particular attention is given to increasing the parents' effectiveness as social reinforcers. Backup primary reinforcers, initial use of a very heavy schedule, and reduced aversive control are used for this purpose. Figure 6-15 shows the changes obtained in rate of deviant behaviors on the part of the identified child patient in six families in which parents were trained to act as therapeutic technicians (Patterson, Ray, and Shaw, 1968). The data provided a number of promising observations for further research. For example, the initial parental recording of deviant child responses sometimes resulted in a decline in their frequency, presumably in part because each recording act was mildly aversive to the child. The parents may also alter their own reactions to the deviant behaviors simply as a consequence of recording them because for the first time they may become aware of circumstances under which the problems occur.

One of the major investigative efforts of this group has been toward systematic identification of the reinforcers necessary to maintain the altered behaviors of *all* family members, including the parents. Otherwise, the

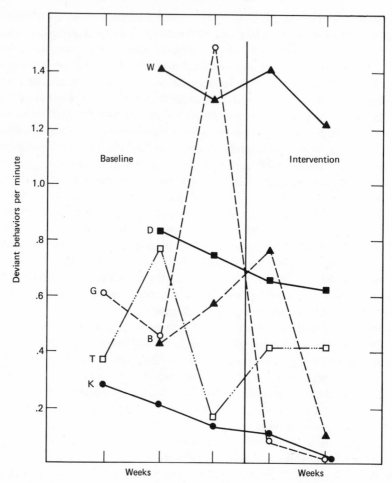

Figure 6-15   Rate of deviant behavior in the home for six subjects (from Patterson, Ray, and Shaw, 1968, unnumbered).

family's previous reinforcement patterns that had strengthened problematic instead of desirable behaviors are likely to return. The coercion hypothesis of Patterson and Reid (1970), described earlier in this chapter, suggests that when, after therapeutic intervention, parents are reinforced by a child's constructive play rather than by cessation of a temper tantrum or other aversive act upon their giving in to a demand, they in turn will reinforce the child's play by their attention, rather than to reinforce tantrums by their compliance. Thus, the child would no longer exercise coercive control over the parents. The reciprocity hypothesis, on the other hand, points to one source of difficulty in maintaining effective parental behavioral engineering. When a family system is characterized by nonreciprocal reinforcement interactions, such that some members provide many but receive few reinforcements from other members, it seems likely that a change toward reciprocity *within* the system is necessary for long-term maintenance of new parental patterns. That is, the family has to learn to provide a more equitable distribution of positive reinforcement for all of its members. Experimenter reinforcement of new parental behavior toward the deviant child alone would not suffice. In one family, Patterson and his colleagues had to train all of the children to reinforce the mother in order to rectify the balance of mutual reinforcement.

Teachers are another large group who have been trained as behavioral technicians. Unlike most studies in which parents act as therapists for their own children, studies within school settings typically employ the ABAB experimental design described earlier. The control over the adult's contingencies necessary for this design is easier to achieve with teachers than with parents, whose own contingencies are so much more dependent on the child patient and the rest of the family and whose goals are focused entirely on a symptom loss. Among the questions under investigation in classroom operant management is one concerning the effects of various contingencies typically used by teachers. Madsen, Becker, and Thomas (1968) systematically varied the behavior of two elementary school teachers to discover the effects on children's behavior of specifying explicit rules, ignoring inappropriate behaviors, and showing approval for appropriate behaviors. The responses of teachers and children were recorded for base line and experimental phases. In the experimental periods, each lasting several weeks, the three classes of teacher behaviors were introduced, one at a time. Rules alone were found to exert little influence, and ignoring inappropriate behavior alone resulted in unchanged or worse behavior. Both teachers found it difficult to adhere to this condition. The combined condition of ignoring plus approval for appropriate behaviors achieved significant improvement in classroom behavior and was demonstrated in a reversal to be exerting the effective influence. In other studies the same investigators demonstrated that disruptive classroom behaviors are inversely related to the use of approval as a controlling contingency by the teacher (Thomas, Becker, and Armstrong, 1968).

Because of the number of comparable children, teachers, and situations available, the classroom situation lends itself more easily to research designs that can yield information beyond the simple change of a target behavior, that is, to factorial or control group designs. This has made possible experimental studies of the effects of specific teacher operations on pupil behaviors. Goodwin (1966), for example, trained seven experimental teachers to reinforce task attention and not to reinforce inattentive behavior of second grade pupils. Two inattentive children in each class were observed, one as a control unknown to the teachers, and one child who was the target of the teacher's modification efforts. A second group of seven teachers and their pairs of inattentive pupils served as a control group. The data revealed that the experimental teachers tended to make more use of appropriate reinforcements than did control teachers, but used them inconsistently. Presumably because of the teachers' inconsistency, the experimental and control group children did not differ in attentiveness at the end of the study. However, *both* groups of pupils showed an increase in task-oriented behaviors. Such findings underscore the need for controlled experiments and for recording of the actual application of the prescribed procedures (that is, teacher reinforcements). Without a control group, the changes in the experimental group would have been misinterpreted as evidence of the program's effectiveness. This study also points to the need for giving as much attention to the technology of training therapeutic technicians as is given to the therapeutic techniques themselves. As Goodwin noted, instructions without actual rewarded practice can be insufficient to alter the teachers' behaviors, despite their expressions of interest in the program.

When teachers are trained as behavior therapists by a program that includes cuing, rehearsal, and reinforcement, success in changing children's classroom behavior is usually much greater. Hall, Lund, and Jackson (1968), for example, trained teachers in an urban poverty-area school to reinforce study behavior. Instructors prompted the teacher by a signal whenever a child was oriented toward the proper person or materials. The teacher then moved to the child and reinforced him with praise. Inattentive behaviors were ignored. The children's study behaviors improved markedly under this procedure. When a reversal phase was instituted, the teachers deliberately returning to their previous contingencies, the children's study behaviors decreased.

The wards of psychiatric hospitals and institutions for the retarded and delinquent represent a third environment in which nonprofessional persons are potential behavioral engineers. Although these settings are for many patients only a short-term "natural environment," many remain for long periods. In any case, behavior modification is desirable for all residents whether for therapeutic benefits eventuating in discharge or for more rewarding and normal lives within the institution. Whichever the goal, the methods used may be very similar, but the behavioral targets selected for change may be much more individualized for therapeutic goals and more standardized over a group of patients when mainly a caretaking function is involved. Registered nurses, therapeutic camp counselors, hospital aides, and volunteer college students have all been successfully employed in studies of modification and control of patient behaviors (Kreitzer, 1966; Rickard and Dinoff, in press; Ayllon and Michael, 1959). Studies of the usual contingencies operating in institutions indicate that often deviant behaviors are maintained by staff and peer reinforcement (Gelfand, Gelfand, and Dobson, 1967; Buehler, Patterson, and Furniss, 1966). Findings of this sort emphasize the important role of staff in affecting the behavior of those for whom they care, whether for good or ill. Most of the recent studies involving beneficial behavior control by institutional staff utilize token systems to provide some uniformity in procedures.

Token Systems as Therapeutic Environments

Institutional settings offer special advantages for programmed engineering of behavior change. They provide the opportunity to manipulate target behaviors in vivo, thereby obviating difficulties in obtaining generalization from treatment to natural settings. They have available personnel who can be trained to apply an operant technology systematically and consistently to a wide range of target behaviors. Because they provide the daily necessities of their residents and control the residents' daily routines and environments, institutions permit more immediate control over discriminative and reinforcing stimuli than is the case in most environments. Goffman (1962) has vividly described how inmates in "total institutions" rapidly learn to "make out," that is, to find ways to obtain irregular privileges and reinforcers and to exercise some control over their routine. Nonetheless, such institutions can be engineered to control, change, and maintain behavior far more than can other settings.

Because of the advantages of generalized reinforcers, a number of institutional settings have recently experimented with their use in providing immediate reinforcement on a heavy schedule for desired patient behaviors. Use of poker chips, tokens, check marks, gold stars, and other items established as generalized reinforcers is common in other behavior modification settings as well. However, an institutional ward often includes a number of patients who have many problems in common and for whom the institutionally-demanded behaviors and responsibilities are likely to be very similar. These communalities make possible and desirable the application of generalized reinforcers on a larger and more systematic scale. Such systems are often termed "token economies" (Ayllon and Azrin, 1968) because, as in a cash economy, patients earn tokens by performing desired behaviors and they can spend the tokens for goods, services, or privileges that they select. These "back up reinforcers" maintain the conditioned reinforcing value of the tokens.

In a relatively brief span of time, the use of token systems has become widespread, especially in large public hospitals and penal institutions.

Ayllon and Azrin (1965) initiated the use of tokens in their early work with individual hospitalized psychotics. Their methods were expanded by large-scale application to all patients on a ward by Atthowe and Krasner (1965) and many others. Many studies have supported the conclusion that an operational token program can lead to significant behavior change and maintenance in institutionalized patients.

A token system benefits not only from the potency of generalized reinforcers discussed earlier but also from the ease with which reinforcement can be carried out. Tokens can be dispensed with varying delays and on different schedules without disrupting ongoing performance by their delivery. They can be exchanged for any or all backup reinforcers that the environment allows. They may vary in value, and can be changed in value over time. Since tokens are spent as the patient chooses, they go far toward solving the problem of providing reinforcers appropriate for each individual. Tokens may be charged for such necessities as a bed, food, or daytime clothing and thus have considerable incentive value. Further, a ward-wide token system permits many of the required contingencies to be standardized across all patients. For example, all patients may be given tokens if they are dressed appropriately at a specified time, or if they are engaged in social interaction at the time of an unannounced observation period, or at the end of each period of work. Standardization of contingencies reduces the burden on staff and increases the probability that staff will operate according to the agreed-upon contingency system. Indeed, patients themselves can often be made responsible for parts of token delivery and collection, for example, awarding "points" to a peer who initiates a social conversation as required by his therapy program.

Token systems have certain disadvantages as well, usually because of practical or technical problems rather than weakness in underlying principles. The value of the token as a generalized reinforcer must be carefully established and maintained. The token is dependent for its potency upon the value and variability of the backup reinforcers. Unless the payments and collections of tokens are consistently adhered to, the contingencies will not be effective. Tokens are open to all of the abuses that occur with money and other generalized reinforcers: stealing, forgery, and hoarding. Therefore, development of a "balanced economy" requires the same considerations that are encountered in handling the economics of any social group. Supply and demand must be brought into optimal relationship, necessitating a great deal of preparatory work and later adjustments. Frequency of prescribed behaviors, tokens earned, and tokens spent must be in relative equilibrium.

Liberman (1968), in reviewing token systems in four mental health facilities in California, found that the major operational difficulties encountered included not only the problem of incongruence between the token system and the natural environment, but also escape from contingencies, poor training and motivation on the part of the nursing staff who administered the program, and difficulty in strengthening behaviors that were at very low operant rates. Some of the mechanics used to overcome these problems (for example, periodic "devaluations" to combat hoarding) are described by Liberman (1968), Schaefer and Martin (1969), Atthowe and Krasner (1968), and others. For example, paralleling solutions to manpower problems in the natural monetary system, complex automated behavior shaping devices are being used to dispense tokens for behaviors even as specific and elaborate as toileting technique. Other vending machines exchange tokens for reinforcers ranging from food and magazines to music and movies (see, for example, Watson, 1967). Ayllon and Azrin (1968) have presented a number of valuable rules to guide the design and conduct of token economies, together with the laboratory and clinical research on which they are based. Schaefer and Martin (1969) similarly cover many of the practical aspects of token systems.

A frequent objection raised to token systems, as well as to the use of other material reinforcers, is that for most persons, behavior must ultimately come under the control of social and other reinforcers which occur naturally in daily living. However, when the system is used as a means, not an end, this ultimate goal can be taken into account satisfactorily. Most token systems provide for social reinforcement paired with each token and for "weaning" patients from the tokens as their behavior improves. When the behaviors shaped are those that the natural environment is likely to reinforce in the ordinary course of events, difficulty in transition to more natural contingencies rarely materializes.

That transition from material tokens to social reinforcement can readily be accomplished, and indeed may enhance the desired behavior, is illustrated by one of a number of studies carried out in a token system at Parsons State Hospital (1967). Figure 6-16 depicts a cumulative record of the daily frequencies with which a mentally retarded girl brought soiled clothing for laundering instead of wearing it or hoarding it as she had customarily done. Upon delivering her clothes for laundering, the girl received both praise and tokens exchangeable for money to be spent during a special trip into town after 15 days. Immediately after the trip, she stopped bringing in her clothing. However, after six days she began to do so again and continued the desired target behavior although reinforced only by praise.

The transition from tokens to social reinforcement is especially important in trying to provide continuity from institution to home upon discharge. Other measures that are used to facilitate this transfer include shifting toward community-oriented jobs as the tasks to be reinforced, using real money and a banking system in place of tokens, requiring

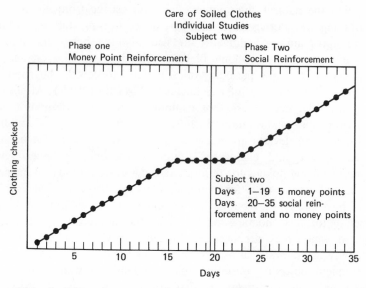

Figure 6-16   In Phase One this subject received points exchangeable for money for bringing her soiled clothing to the Cottage Aide to be checked for placing it into a laundry bag. During Phase Two only praise was given as a reinforcer (from Parsons State Hospital Progress Report, 1967, p. 36).

more complex social behaviors for reinforcement, and gradual release from the formal contingency program. This potential problem with the use of token systems is a specific case of the more general need for any artificial treatment environment to manage the transfer and maintenance of new behaviors in the patient's natural daily environment. This problem is just as acute for traditional psychotherapy interviews as it is for traditional hospital wards or token systems. When an artificial treatment setting can gradually incorporate more and more segments of the larger, more natural environment, and fade out the prosthetic devices (for example, tokens, therapist reinforcement), patients are gradually forced to deal more with the persons and events they will later encounter in society outside of the artificial community in which treatment occurs.

The pioneering work of Fairweather and his associates (1967) exemplifies how a hospital program can gradually be extended into the community. Fairweather's treatment approach incorporates social learning principles and specific behavioral targets with a system of levels to define expectations and available rewards as the patients progress. Tokens per se are not used. Chronic schizophrenic patients are rewarded by the level system in the hospital for development of social, work, and personal care skills, for group cohesiveness, and for cooperation. Later the patients move out and live together in an ordinary house in the community, gradually taking over full management of the home. They are provided with their own service business, such as janitorial service, that they are trained to operate and manage. As increasing independence and responsibility on the part of the patients are shaped, staff supervision is decreased, until the patients are independent of professional care in every way, but dependent on their own group.

A system of levels similar to Fairweather's has often been used in combination with a token system to help the transition from token to more natural consequences as well as to tailor the specific contingencies to individual patient needs. Each level comprises a different set of target responses, available reinforcers, and requirements in terms of stringency, contingencies, and behavioral monitoring. Tokens may be charged for moving up from one level to another. Figure 6-17 depicts a level system used in a token economy for alcoholics (Narrol, 1964). The levels provide an initial deprivation and a series of increasingly attractive reinforcers with which to back up the tokens, thereby avoiding satiation or premature leveling off of behavior. Movement through the levels is contingent on behavioral change and payment of tokens is earned by constructive behavior.

Level systems illustrate the fact that token systems and other behavioral engineering environments are miniature social systems that allow experimentation with a wide variety of social and psychological parameters. They provide a special opportunity to examine and manipulate psychopathology within its broad social-psychological context, which can be only indirectly included in other therapeutic approaches. Generalized reinforcers are often used with individual patients in outpatient treatment, as when the therapist returns a portion of his fee for each pound lost by an obese patient, or a husband and wife contract through the therapist's suggestion to fine each other for unfair fighting tactics. It is the direct inclusion of the miniature but whole social system in therapeutic study and planning that makes institutional token systems different from these individualized applications, and of special interest to behavior modifiers.

Educational Environments

A number of projects in special schools, educational laboratories, and institutions for the retarded have involved behavioral analysis, programmed contingencies, and stimulus control as an educational package. This contrasts with the more piecemeal use of teaching machines or programmed materials for isolated parts of the curriculum in ordinary school settings. Teaching machines and programmed instruction represent, of

V

Open ward of
choice, con-
tinued off
ward employ-
ment, pro-
gressively
longer passes
become avail-
able.

IV

Open ward,
continued off
ward employ-
ment, short
passes avail-
able.

III

Closed ward
but ground
privileges and
off ward em-
ployment
available, still
better mate-
rial and social
environment.

II

Closed ward,
on ward work,
more pleasant
material and
social environ-
ment.

I

Closed ward,
on ward work,
drab material
and social en-
vironment.

Figure 6-17 Progress levels of pay-as-you-go project. Patients stayed on each level at least one week. (From Narrol, 1964).

course, one of the most widespread deliberate and systematic uses of operant principles to modify behavior, in this case, cognitive skills in educational settings. A number of reviews of research on these methods are available (see, for example, Brown and L'Abate, 1969; Morrill, 1961; Lumsdaine and Glaser, 1960). Here we will only briefly describe some of the broader applications of operant technology to educational goals, particularly in connection with special learning problems.

As the principles and technology of the more comprehensive approaches are further developed, they are likely to penetrate increasingly into teacher training and school curricula in general. A number of investigators have already developed instructional methods to be used to train teachers in behavior modification techniques for managing day-to-day classroom activities. Programmed and regular texts are beginning to appear that are intended to instruct teachers in the principles and techniques of functional behavioral analysis (Woody, 1969; Ferster and Perrott, 1968). Since modification and control of verbal, social, and motor behaviors within the classroom are likely to have preventive values, these developments have potentially great significance not only for skill acquisition but for adjustment in general. Several factors place the classroom teacher in a crucial position for prevention or early detection and modification of behavior problems. There is increasing insistence on prevention as the primary solution to the nation's mental health problems and hence a great increase in consultation, training, and support is made available to classroom teachers for these activities. The teacher is often the first adult who has close contact with a child and who is also competent to evaluate the significance of a deviant behavior pattern. In addition, a teacher contributes to the development or modification of any child's social behaviors. The classroom is often the first and major arena in which the child develops peer social skills, self-control, and behaviors oriented toward competition and achievement, and the reinforcements they bring. The teacher, as the behavior-manager in this crucial setting, can utilize behavioral engineering of classroom activities in general and the actions of individual children in particular in order to prevent behavior disorders and to modify problems early in their development.

Most investigators who apply operant paradigms in special educational settings assume that problem learners require remedial development and strengthening of such behaviors as attention and concentration, perseverance, and cooperation that are prerequisites for effective studying. They further assume that the scheduling, rapidity, quantity, and quality of reinforcement in the ordinary classroom are insufficient for these pupils. Frequently, generalized reinforcers, such as points or tokens, are awarded immediately and on a heavy schedule, often in conjunction with shaping procedures, to develop task-relevant behaviors and sustained work with instructional materials. A wide variety of backup reinforcers are made available frequently to insure the continued attractiveness of tokens. Programmed instructional materials are made freely available for the child's use to earn tokens. Extinction and time-out (removal from the classroom and hence from access to reinforcement) procedures are used to eliminate any disruptive behaviors, although these are as a rule quickly reduced as the pupils become involved in earning tokens through their work.

Early case study evaluations revealed improved study behaviors and skill acquisition for children in such experimental classrooms. Birnbrauer, Bijou, Wolf, and Kidder (1965) established a Programmed Learning Classroom for severely mentally retarded boys, using procedures roughly like those described above. Their pupils showed significant improvement in time spent in productive work, rate of finishing tasks, and amount of correctly performed work.

Other experiments compared the effects of contingent and noncontingent token awards on performance. Tyler and Brown (1968), for example, found significant differences in performance by delinquent boys on tests of current events under contingent and noncontingent conditions. Correlational studies have also supported the inference that contingent tokens control study behavior. Cohen, Filipczak, and Bis (1967) described a comprehensive token economy for institutionalized delinquent boys, all of whom were educationally retarded. Each boy could earn points by performing school work, including independent work on teaching machines. Interestingly, included in the items students could "buy" with their points were tutoring, additional classroom time, and admission to advanced academic courses. The sensitivity of performance to contingent reinforcement is suggested by the drop in work each Friday. Friday morning was payday, and typically on that day the collected points and boys' time were spent in recreational and consumer activities, as shown in Figure 6-18. The authors found that the boys formed roughly two groups with respect to the control exerted on their study behaviors by the reinforcers available from earned points. Curve (b) in the Figure illustrates the performance of a boy who was very responsive to the number of points he had available to spend from one payday to the next. Curve (c) shows the more nearly constant behavior of a boy from the other group, who maintained a stable high level of work throughout the week, presumably reflecting a higher level of intrinsic reinforcement for the school work. The latter students are those who more often purchased access to the more advanced, higher status, courses.

Another group of studies manipulated the value of tokens, compared performances on reinforced and nonreinforced tasks, and used untreated control groups to evaluate program effectiveness. For example, Wolf, Giles, and Hall (1968) reported a series of experiments in an after-school remedial education token program for low-achieving fifth- to sixth-grade children. Achievement tests and report card grades of the treated remedial group and of an untreated control group provided pre- and postprogram evaluation. The control group made only half the gain of the remedial group on the achievement tests. Report card grades showed an average 1.1 grade point gain by the remedial group compared with an average 0.2 grade point gain for the controls. In other experiments using only the remedial

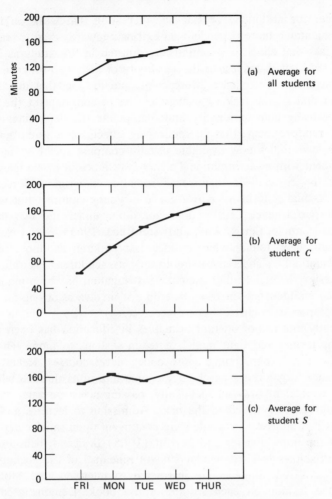

Figure 6-18   Changes in educational work time in relation to collection of C+
(from Cohen, Filipczak, and Bis, 1967, pp. 85, 86, 87).

group, it was found that manipulation of the number of points that could
be earned drastically influenced reading rates. When points for reading
were reduced, rates fell; when points were doubled, rates rose—even
when the initial rate was already high. Similarly, students shifted from
preferred to nonpreferred (judged from base line rates) workbooks
when differentiated rates of pay were instituted. For some students,
after increased points had shifted their reading rates to high levels, return to base line levels of point payments did not result in a return
to base line reading rate. This partial independence of rate of pay did

not occur for arithmetic or English, suggesting that work on the latter subjects is much more dependent on extrinsic rewards than is reading.

The fact that students systematically differed in this study as in Cohen et al. (1967) with respect to the sensitivity of their performance to short-term fluctuations in token reinforcement, and the fact that this sensitivity is a function of the task as well as of the person, suggest the potential value of being able to identify and manipulate the determinants of "intrinsic" reinforcement, that is, reinforcing effects of a given activity per se. The few studies now available usually compare social or material reinforcement with an informational signal that indicates that a learning-task response is "correct" or "incorrect." Social or material reinforcement accompanies higher levels of performance in young children, but with older children performance usually does not differ under the two conditions (see, for example, Lewis, Wall, and Aronfreed, 1963). Social class differences have been found; white middle-class children are more responsive to informational signals than are lower-class children (Terrell, Durkin, and Wiesley, 1959). Little systematic investigation has been made of performance maintenance on tasks that do not involve as strong an informational component of correct versus incorrect.

Recently, the use of operant principles in education has been extended from the formal and tight model of token systems to more general programs such as programming entire college-level courses. Keller (1968), for instance, organized a psychology course into units through which each student worked his way independently, passing a test on each unit before being allowed to proceed to the next. Admission to lectures and demonstrations as well as course grade were contingent upon satisfactory progress through the units. Ferster and Perrott (1968) designed their text on behavior principles to elicit regular student rehearsal of the vocabulary and concepts covered. Students are instructed to interview one another in a prescribed fashion on each section of the book. Demonstrated fluency with the material is required before the student is allowed to advance to the next section. Just as a functional analysis approach is beginning to be applied more broadly in the classroom to problematic behaviors in order to prevent serious later adjustment difficulties, instead of being restricted to clinical applications to "disturbed" children, so is its influence on educational practice moving from highly specific technologies for use with special learning deficits to the development of a "technology of teaching" (Skinner, 1968) applicable to all of education.

Prosthetic Environments

A development more embryonic at present but potentially more encompassing is the design of behavior controlling environments, not only in formal education but for all aspects of living. Skinner's *Walden Two* (1948) perhaps represents the epitome of a social utopia based on behavioral principles. But we need not go to fiction. The Mississippi Research and Development Center has proposed a Human Resource Development Center that would place 100 lower-class families, victims of their own "culture of poverty," into a controlled environment to erase their cultural deficits. Similar proposals have been made for "Urban Learning Villages" (Segal, 1968). Segal suggests that a total programmed physical, social, and economic environment is required to equip slum dwellers with the behavioral skills to attain and sustain a rewarding life pattern. Behavior modification techniques including encounter groups, modeling, and programmed instruction with powerful incentives would be coupled with physical and cultural facilities designed to promote new interests and new opportunities.

Less ambitious projects of environmental enrichment are conducted and evaluated in connection with stimulation of infants and preschool children in culturally deprived homes. Mothers are trained in a training center and at home in modeling and reinforcement procedures. At the same time they are helped to devise "play" objects (from common materials) that stimulate a wide range of perceptual and motor behaviors of the child (Schaefer and Furfey, 1967). Language development, intellectual functioning, concept formation, cognitive style, and achievement orientation are among the target dependent variables. Results of interim evaluation of these projects are encouraging, showing, for example, an average gain of 15 points in the children's IQ over a year, educational and vocational upgrading in over half the mothers, and more subtle changes in the families' life styles (Miller, undated).

Environmental behavioral engineering schemes fall into two general types: instructional-therapeutic and prosthetic. "Urban learning villages" are an example of the former, since their intent is to rapidly and permanently alter the behaviors of transient inhabitants. Prosthetic environments, as the term has been used by Lindsley (1964a and b) are contrived to maintain behavior that would occur at a low rate or not at all in the ordinary environment. Should research continue to indicate that certain groups of children require the reinforcement characteristics of a token system to sustain their academic learning, they might remain in such a special classroom, as a prosthetic environment, for the duration of their education. A prosthetic environment thus fills a relatively permanent remedial role for a small group of persons whose behavior is handicapped in a similar way. In contrast, utopias such as *Walden Two* are designed to control the behavior of much larger groups or entire populations, also on a relatively permanent basis.

Whether the contingent reinforcers associated with an activity are inherent in or extraneous to the activity itself is a second distinction made among behavioral engineering environments. The latter are exemplified by token systems. Moore (1966) holds that intrinsic reinforcement is optimal for acquisition of complex symbolic skills. He uses the term *autotelic responsive environment* to denote a setting in which intrinsic reinforcement predominates and in which the learner explores the responses of his environment freely, experiences its consequences immediately, sets his own pace, and is encouraged to make interconnected discoveries about relationships in his physical, cultural, and social surroundings. The particular responsive environment with which Moore is experimenting is best known as "the talking typewriter," but actually involves a computer input and read-out device (Edison Responsive Environment) within a laboratory devised to be "simple, distinct, and separate" and managed by a carefully programmed instructional staff. The curriculum concentrates on language acquisition (written, spoken, read) and apparently has had remarkable success with very young, retarded, and gifted children, although empirical data as yet are unavailable.

Behavioral control is increasingly being considered in designing the consequences and stimuli provided by the physical environment. Architects are increasingly concerned with the behavioral effects of their buildings (Cohen, 1964; Fuller, 1962; Sommer, 1969). Empirical data on behavior patterns (traffic and work flow, communication patterns, temporal patterns) guide their city planning, allocation of vehicular and pedestrian traffic, school and hospital floor plans, and so on.

Despite the potential for the future that programmed prosthetic, preventive, and therapeutic environments seem to hold, knowledge and technology are not yet sufficiently advanced to guarantee achievement of the desired results from large-scale social engineering. Some of the ethical and humanistic concerns about behavior control and about large-scale behavioral engineering are discussed in Chapter 11. Research that makes the long-range consequences more predictable is one partial solution to these concerns. Means to test effects must be found in analogue or miniature situations which preserve the essential features of the larger environment without carrying the hazards of large-scale intervention. The research required to strengthen the foundations of environmental behavioral engineering programs is implicit in their content. Greater knowledge of natural functional classes of responses and of their typical naturalistic interrelationships is required. The ramifications of change in one response or dimension for other parts of a person's behavioral repertoire must be clarified before large-scale social-behavioral engineering can be undertaken without serious risk.

SUMMARY

Behavior therapies that apply the principles and technology of the operant learning paradigm are more widely used for a greater diversity of target symptoms and within more varied social contexts, than are any of the other behavior therapy models. The operant paradigm concentrates on the final three components (R-K-C) of the behavioral equation, describing the probability of a response as a function of its contingent effects or consequences. Since most significant human acts come under discriminative control early in their acquisition, the stimulus component of the equation plays an important discriminative (but not eliciting) role in controlling operant behavior.

The empiricism and pragmatism of operant principles make them peculiarly suited to the construction of therapeutic technologies that are content-free in the sense of being independent of any particular preference for therapeutic targets or of particular formulations regarding the etiology of problematic behavior. Thus while anxiety is a central construct in theories of neuroses and its treatment based on classical conditioning, the operant model of pathology relies on no such central construct. Rather, behavioral excesses and deficits are viewed as products of the same learning variables as are any other behaviors. Operant therapies therefore employ the same general principles and technology to reduce the avoidance behaviors of a housebound phobic housewife, to increase play with peers by a preschooler, to alter a couple's interactions in the interests of greater marital harmony, to decrease psychotic talk and increase constructive behaviors in a hospitalized psychotic, or to improve the accuracy and rate of acquisition of scholastic skills by students at all levels. Large-scale standardized interventions to modify and control the behavior of large groups of "normal" people (for example, students in a college course, slum dwellers) differ in scope but not in type from individually tailored, highly specific therapy programs to alter a given patient's particular behavioral complaint.

Reinforcement, as the key operation in operant conditioning, is therapeutically manipulated to strengthen or extinguish behavior, to gradually shape new constellations of responses through rewarding successive approximations, to build long and complex response chains, or to bring behavior under more appropriate discriminative stimulus control. Increasing the potency or variety of reinforcers effective for a given patient, or altering the contingency schedules under which he is able to operate effectively are therapeutic goals involving the reinforcement operation itself. Since conditioned reinforcers, particularly social ones, are especially crucial in the development and maintenance of most human behaviors, behavior modifiers are concentrating particularly on (1) understanding better how social reinforcement operates in the natural environment to produce desired and undesired behavior, (2) how to increase the potency of social reinforcers in persons for whom they are not effective consequences, and (3) on their use to control behavior in a wide variety of settings beyond the usual clinical treatment environment. Generalized reinforcers, such as money or tokens that can be exchanged for a wide variety of material backup reinforcers, are more likely to be used when standardized intervention programs are applied to a group of persons. But even here provision is usually made for transition from tokens to more ordinary social reinforcers for behavioral maintenance.

Its character as a content-free technology makes the operant model unusually well suited to the design of special environments for particular behavioral goals. Thus while reinforcement and related operations have been readily applied to the usual sorts of complaints of neurotic and other traditional clinic patients, they have also formed the basis for construction of special therapeutic-educational or prosthetic environments in hospitals, schools, penal institutions, and other settings. In the same fashion, parents can be taught to revise reinforcement contingencies to make the home a more constructive environment, that is, less likely to promote problematic behaviors in family members. In both institutional and family settings, nonprofessional persons can be readily trained in applying operant principles to modify behavior. Not only does this amenability to technician-level application suggest that operant therapies are relevant to manpower shortages in the mental health field, but also that they can be used by persons who are natural agents of behavior influence (for example, parents and teachers) to prevent more serious problems.

Evaluation of the effectiveness of operant behavior modification typically uses single-case own control designs, although more traditional group comparisons are at times feasible and appropriate. Evaluation is made somewhat more difficult because therapeutic programs are likely to be pragmatic and improvisational in their conduct. Criticisms of operant therapies point not only to this on-the-spot engineering as a limitation of prediction and evaluation of change, but also to humanistic-moral questions regarding control, to seeming neglect of internal self-regulatory processes, and to logical or empirical weaknesses in formulations about reinforcement and other key operant variables. Sections in later chapters deal with some of these criticisms at greater length, including discussion of issues in assessment, ethics, self-regulation and subjective experiences, and verbal behavior.

CHAPTER 7

Behavior Control By Aversive Consequences

Positive reinforcement and its withdrawal are powerful events involved in behavior control. However, the presentation in the preceding chapter of the operant model of learning and behavior maintenance paid little attention to another class of events that presumably is equally prevalent in behavior control, namely *aversive consequences*. This chapter considers and discusses the paradigms in which aversive consequences are applied and the parameters governing their effects. It also illustrates their potential use for therapeutic purposes. One important topic in this consideration is the comparison of the role of aversive stimuli in the operant model and in the classical aversive conditioning model which was presented in Chapter 3.

Much of everyday behavior is undoubtedly governed by painful or unpleasant stimuli provided by natural forces and by other people after particular acts. As a child learns to walk, the naturally occurring consequences of imbalance rapidly shape responses that keep him upright. Only a very few experiences with a hot stove or radiator are sufficient to train both child and pet to avoid further contact with it. The child who cries or the adult who manifests symptoms of anxiety when entering the dentist's office are showing emotional responses conditioned by previous painful experiences in that setting; both may avoid the dentist's office until a decaying tooth is more painful than the dentist's drill. Parents and teachers rely heavily on punishment and threats of punishment to socialize and to maintain control over children. Although little is known about the common frequencies in home or school of positive reinforcement and aversive consequences, the latter seem to be used more explicitly and deliberately. A parent is likely to be much more able to describe his approach to "discipline" and even the stimuli controlling his unplanned punishments (for example losing temper, irritability) than to describe how and when he provides interest and attention, affection, and other social positively reinforcing consequences. "Discipline" in home and school often connotes only punishment, rather than positive reinforcement as well. Delivery of aversive consequences is often much more immediate, discrete, and contingent on particular behaviors than is planned delivery of positive stimuli. For example, a parent may provide a child's weekly allowance noncontingently but fines against it may be levied immediately and explicitly following a specific bit of mischief. Observational data of low socioeconomic status mothers training their own children in new language skills has confirmed that they use little and erratic positive reinforcement and do not break down complicated tasks into manageable units. They present a difficult problem and then punish errors and nag their child to sit up, pay attention, and give the right answer, but they rarely praise desired behavior or correct answers. Only after elaborate training do the mothers shift from generalized aversive to specific positive control (Risley, 1968a).

Similarly, society's most clearly defined and structured methods of behavior control largely involve legally prescribed aversive consequences for undesirable behaviors. For certain classes of behaviors (such as criminal, psychotic, and addictive acts) public discussion, legal codes, and penal practices give preference to aversive control of undesired behavior instead of using positive reinforcement to shape and maintain more desirable behaviors. Consider, for example, in the case of prisons the controversy that often accompanies introduction of educational programs, or daytime release from prison for job experiences, or conjugal visits. Use of positive reinforcements as a motivational retraining technique is often seen as "coddling" or encouraging criminality. On the other hand, making positive consequences contingent upon desired behaviors is protested in other environments, where positive consequences are frequently viewed not as privileges but as inherent "rights" that should be provided freely and noncontingently. Families and administrators will protest if meals or beds are given only contingently to reward healthy responses by hospitalized patients. Nurses may insist that their tender loving care must be freely (not contingently) dispensed to institutionalized patients. Teachers may deplore the contingent delivery of "points," candies, or attention as "bribery."

In their use of positive and aversive consequences, social agents often seem to assume that they are better able to predict and control the effects of aversive consequences than the effects of potential positive reinforcers. Thus, despite the controversy of experts, legal fines and imprisonment are generally accepted as effective deterrents to misdeeds, whereas social welfare schemes arouse fears that they will lead to inadvertent positive reinforcement of unwanted behaviors. Programs of aid to dependent children are sometimes called "rewards for sexual promiscuity;" guaranteed annual income and subsidized health care plans are attacked for rewarding laziness and malingering.

Interestingly, despite society's apparent preference for aversive control, the general climate of public opinion currently tends to deplore aversive control. At least at the level of intellectual discussion, positive incentives are favored. Teachers seek pupil-directed and interesting materials to insure studious involvement; parents strive for acceptance and communication with their children in order to maximize their own influence; and welfare workers talk of changing the values and attitudes of the poor so that prevailing middle-class behaviors can be shaped by prevailing middle-class incentives.

In theories about development of personality disorders, a prominent role is given to the untoward effects of aversive stimulation. Skinner (1953) views anxiety as an emotional reaction associated with a signal characteristically preceding an aversive stimulus. Punishment contingencies are especially likely to generate anxiety, since strong emotional predispositions are aroused by the beginning of severely punished behavior. "These are the main ingredient of what we speak of as guilt, shame, or a sense of sin" (p. 187). Control by social agents (parents, teachers, employers) or social agencies (government, law religion) may be inconsistent or excessive in their use of punishment. The harmful by-products of such control can result in deviant or damaging behaviors, constituting the behavior pathologies of neurosis and psychosis. According to Skinner, "the principal technique of [traditional] psychotherapy is thus designed to reverse behavioral changes which have come about as the result of punishment. There is, therefore, a certain opposition between psychotherapy and religious and governmental control" (Skinner, 1953, p. 371). Some personality theorists have stressed the role of conflict between pleasure-seeking and internalized social taboos as the core of neurotic development. Early infantile traumas, excessive punishment, aversive stimulation, and defenses against real or imaginary personal threats are among the numerous constructs used to explain behavioral deviations. Each contains the general idea that avoidance of personal threat is the basis of symptomatic behavior. This pervasive concept of anxiety reduction, threat avoidance, or escape as the critical factor in the etiology of behavior disorders indicates the common belief that the many varieties of human misery and deviations are mainly the consequence of aversive social control. The recent trend toward exploration of new methods of social control by positive reinforcement is therefore not surprising, in the wake of increased public psychological sophistication.

Even in experimental psychology, research on aversive control has been shunned until the past decade or so. Solomon (1964), in an influential paper, deplores the relative neglect of the functions of aversive stimulation as an area of research and the contemporary tendency to underestimate its potential for behavior control. Solomon ascribed to the influence of Thorndike, Skinner, and Freud the origins of what he called "unscientific legends" held by psychologists about presumed inadequacies and undesirable effects of aversive control. With respect to punishment in particular, these "legends" state that punishment is less effective than positive reinforcement because it does not weaken response strength but only indirectly and temporarily suppresses responses; that punishment is pragmatically a poor and unreliable determinant of behavior; and that it results in undesirable side effects including pathological anxiety, inhibition, and neurosis. The bulk of this chapter is devoted to experimental and clinical investigations providing evidence by which to assess these beliefs, and to frame questions about the effects and utility of aversive control in a more precise and scientifically testable form.

Before taking up substantive research findings, it seems useful to consider the various paradigms within which aversive stimuli occur, and then to confront some of the difficulties in defining the variables within these paradigms, especially the term "aversive stimulus" itself.

PARADIGMS FOR AVERSIVE CONTROL OF BEHAVIOR

In a later section we will take up the problems of defining aversive events, just as the nature of positive reinforcement was considered in terms of functional operations and behavioral effects. Meanwhile, we adopt the naive assumption that environmental events can be classified as involving either positive or aversive stimuli, comparable to Thorndike (1913) speaking of satisfying and annoying states of affairs, so that we can consider the possible manipulations of aversive stimuli. The situation when an aversive stimulus is presented after a particular act, and cannot be escaped or avoided, is termed *punishment*. When aversive stimuli are contingently removed following a specified response, it is a case of *negative reinforcement,* and fits the escape training paradigm in the language of instrumental conditioning. From the person's point of view, escape responses produce relief from aversive stimuli; this procedure is often termed *aversion relief.* Stimuli may be manipulated noncontingently as well as contingently, simultaneously with other events as well as singly. Figure 6-4 summarized the available operations on aversive stimuli and the terms by which they are designated. The manipulations of positive stimuli that produce response decrement are covered in this chapter because they are functionally similar to aversive events.

Aversive Manipulations of Positive Stimuli

Under special conditions, *satiation,* the excessive consumption of positive stimuli, can be an aversive state. The effect of forced food-intake is an example of this situation. In clinical use, Ayllon (1963) found satiation successful in eliminating a disturbing symptom, towel-hoarding, in an institutionalized schizophrenic by what amounted to stuffing her room full of towels. *Extinction* can be considered aversive if omission of reward is an effective stimulus in attenuating behavior. *Time-out* is a parallel operation; in this procedure, access to *all* positive reinforcement is blocked for a given period of time, contingent upon the occurrence of some undesired behavior. The difference between extinction and time-out is mainly that in the latter reinforcement is also withheld for all competing responses. Consider a child who displays frequent temper tantrums at the grocery store toy counter. An extinction procedure would focus on discovering and eliminating the positive reinforcers maintaining this behavior. A time-out procedure, on the other hand, not only eliminates the positive reinforcement maintaining the tantrums (for example, mother's attention or purchase of a toy) but temporarily also removes the opportunity to obtain *any* other positive reinforcers. Mother might isolate the child for a brief time in the car outside, removing *all* opportunities for him to gain her attention and praise as well as to engage in other pleasant activities in the store. In Table 7-1 extinction and time-out are contingent upon temper tantrums and tend to reduce their frequency. Both are aversive for the child in the sense that positive reinforcers are removed. But time-out is like a generalized reinforcer: it removes not only the toy and attention that tantrums formerly earned, but all other positive reinforcement as well.

Response cost involves not just the absence of positive reinforcement but its direct removal, and thus is most easily done with secondary reinforcers such as money, points, and so on. Here a response is followed by removal of reinforcers previously held by the person. For example, a mother might impose a fine on her child by taking away the nickel she had given him earlier. Response cost can also be manipulated by escalating the cost or effort required to obtain a given quantity of reward. The "price" of a food pellet for an animal may be increased by requiring a larger number of responses, greater pressure on a lever, or raising the quality criteria of a discrimination. This procedure has different effects than the first ("fining") method, although both ultimately result in severe response decrements.

Finally, as was indicated in Table 6-4, if removal of positive reinforce-

Table 7-1 Comparison of Extinction and Time-Out Paradigms

EXTINCTION

Behavioral Description	Child sees toy display $\xrightarrow{S^D}$	Child yells, kicks, bangs head $\xrightarrow{R_1}$	Mother scolds, restrains, gives toy $\xrightarrow{C_1^+}$	Probability of temper tantrum (R_1) in future is increased

Extinction	Child sees toy display $\xrightarrow{S^D}$	Child yells, kicks, bangs head $\xrightarrow{R_1}$	Mother ignores $\xrightarrow{\quad}$ 0	Probability of temper tantrum (R_1) in future is reduced

TIME-OUT

Behavioral Description	Child sees toy display $\xrightarrow{S^D}$	Child chats, pushes cart $\xrightarrow{R_2}$	Mother praises, jokes, chats $\xrightarrow{C_2^+}$	Probability of child's cooperative acts (R_2) is increased
	Child sees toy display $\xrightarrow{S^D}$	Child yells, kicks, etc. $\xrightarrow{R_1}$	Mother scolds, restrains, gives toy $\xrightarrow{C_1^+}$	Probability of child's temper tantrums (R_1) is increased

Time-out	Child sees toy display $\xrightarrow{S^D}$	Child yells, kicks, etc. $\xrightarrow{R_1}$	Mother briefly isolates child in car without otherwise attending to tantrum $\xrightarrow{TO}$	Child loses access to C_2^+ as well as not experiencing C_1^+. Probability of tantrums reduced

ment is paired with some neutral stimulus in a *classical conditioning* paradigm, the neutral stimulus may come to act as a secondary aversive stimulus. For example, if a particular room in the home is regularly and exclusively associated with a time-out procedure, the room itself may come to be an aversive stimulus to the child.

In all of these models, positive reinforcers are manipulated in such a way that the result is aversive stimulation. When the aversive event is presented in a punishment paradigm, the frequency of the preceding response will decrease. Thus the time-out procedure can operate as a punishment of the response on which it is contingent. However, aversive stimuli can also operate to *increase* the frequency of a response, as can aversive manipulations of positive stimuli, yielding a paradoxical outcome. For example, removal of access to positive reinforcers (time-out) can act as an aversive event, punishing the preceding response. Any behavior that successfully *avoids* an impending time-out will thereby be reinforced and increase in frequency. If a youngster's begging and whining leads mother to relent in imposing a time-out, its avoidance will positively reinforce whining and begging. Then the threat of a time-out will become an S^D for these whining and begging behaviors. Needless to say, as a punishment, the time-out would become quite ineffective, establishing more troublesome behavior instead.

Paradigms Involving Aversive Stimuli

As shown in Table 6-4, noncontingent delivery of aversive stimuli is usually followed by behavioral and physiological indications of *arousal,* especially if the stimuli are sudden, novel, or intense. When the stimuli are repeatedly administered, the arousal responses to them tend to disappear, unless the stimuli are very intense.

Aversive stimuli can lead to *superstitious conditioning* just as positive stimuli sometimes do, if their noncontingent occurrence adventitiously follows some particular response. It is on this basis that a neurotic may learn to avoid places in which he has felt anxious, received bad news, or suffered personal setbacks. In dynamic therapies, the recognition of the adventitious nature of the pairing of a thought and reinforcing event is encouraged, in order to reduce the effects of the conditioning history by insight. Noncontingent removal of aversive stimuli can act in the same fashion as noncontingent positive stimuli, producing *superstitious negative reinforcement.* Presumably, accidental association of symptom loss with the response of taking patent medicines illustrates the consumer economics of superstitious conditioning through removal of aversive stimuli.

Punishment is operationally defined as the delivery of an aversive stimulus contingent upon the occurrence of a particular response. The punishment operation is usually expected to decrease response frequency. Under certain circumstances it can result in response *increase* as well: as, for example, when it increases the frequency of respondents such as anxiety or of behaviors that have previously terminated the punishment such as whining or lying. Punishment can have many effects, depending on concurrent conditions, the procedures used, parametric values, and previous history. Because of its theoretical and practical importance, punishment will be given a large share of attention in this chapter.

The other paradigms involving aversive stimuli which are central to this chapter and have been extensively studied in the laboratory are *escape* and *avoidance*. An organism that is under noxious stimulation is reinforced in any (escape) act that terminates the stimulus. Any act that avoids the noxious stimulus similarly will be increased on later occasions. The cat avoids touching a hot stove, the child covers his ears when being scolded, everyone tells fibs to avoid censure.

Many theories about the processes involved in punishment and escape-avoidance training rely upon the model shown in Table 6-4 as *classical aversive conditioning* to explain genesis of the avoidance or escape response. Therefore, although this chapter focuses on aversive consequences within the operant model, the discussion of classical conditioning initiated in Chapter 3 is also relevant here. Finally, when aversive stimuli are removed in the presence of a neutral stimulus, the neutral stimulus may come to function as a positive reinforcer. Through classical conditioning, the positive effects of escape from noxious stimuli can become associated with a neutral stimulus, which is then termed a *"relief"* stimulus and acts as a secondary positive reinforcer. An example of this *aversion relief* paradigm was presented in Chapter 3: pairing the shock termination with presentation of pictures of females in treating male homosexuals.

All of the above models for aversive behavior control are depicted symbolically in their simplest forms in Table 7-2. Although symbolic diagrams require some effort to follow, they highlight procedural differences and will be useful in considering the paradigms in more detail.

DEFINITIONAL PROBLEMS

For convenience in introducing the various paradigms, the term "aversive stimulus" has been used without concern for its definition. Yet this definition is the key in theories and research on aversive control; the operations within the models are relatively easy to specify, but the defining characteristics of their central variable, the aversive event, are not.

Thorndike's (1913, 1932) Law of Effect speaks of "an annoying state of affairs" or of "annoyers" to denote aversive stimuli. Other writers refer

Table 7-2 Symbolic Representations of Aversive Control Paradigms Using Rat in Skinner Box as Prototype

Symbols:		
R_1 = lever press	C^+_1 = food in tray
R_2 = approach water tube	C^+_2 = water in tube
R_3 = approach food tray	C^+_3 = removal of shock
R_x = any chance act	C^+_4 = absence of shock
CER = conditioned emotional reaction	C^-_1 = shock
ER = emotional response	C^-_2 = absence of water
S^0 = neutral tone	C^-_3 = absence of food
S^{0L} = lever	C^-_4 = removal of food from tray

Satiation	$R_1 \rightarrow 0$ $R_3 \rightarrow C^+_1$ $R_2 \rightarrow C^+_2$	**Deprivation**	$R_1 \rightarrow 0$ $R_3 \rightarrow C^-_3$ $R_2 \rightarrow C^+_2$

Extinction   *Build response   then   extinction*

$R_1 \rightarrow C^+_1$	$R_1 \rightarrow C^-_3$
$R_2 \rightarrow C^+_2$	$R_2 \rightarrow C^+_2$
$R_3 \rightarrow C^+_1$	$R_3 \rightarrow C^-_3$

Time-out   *Build response   then   time-out*

$R_1 \rightarrow C^+_1$	$R_1 \rightarrow C^-_3$
$R_2 \rightarrow C_2^+$	$R_2 \rightarrow C^-_2$
$R_3 \rightarrow C^+_1$	$R_3 \rightarrow C^-_3$

Response-cost $R_1 \rightarrow C^-_4$

Secondary Aversive Stimulus $R_3 \rightarrow S^0 + C^-_1$ *then* $S^0 \rightarrow$ CER

Arousal $C^-_1 \rightarrow$ ER

Superstitious Aversive Conditioning $R_x \rightarrow C^-_1$ *then* $R_x \rightarrow$ CER

Superstitious Escape Conditioning $R_x \rightarrow C^+_3$

Punishment   *Build response   then   Punishment*

$R_1 \rightarrow C^+_1$ $R_1 \rightarrow C^+_1 + C^-_1$

Punishment Conditioning of Secondary Aversive Stimulus   (same) $S^{0L} \rightarrow$ CER

Negative Reinforcement of Escape C^-_1, *then* $C^-_1 \rightarrow R_1 \rightarrow C^+_3$

Negative Reinforcement of Avoidance $S^0 + C^-_1$, *then* $S^0 \rightarrow R_1 \rightarrow C^+_4$

Classical Aversion Conditioning $S^0 \rightarrow C^-_1 \rightarrow$ ER, *then* $S^0 \rightarrow$ CER

Aversion Relief C^-_1, *then* $C^-_1 \rightarrow R_1 \rightarrow C^+_3 + S^0$

to "noxious stimuli," to a "sudden and painful increase of stimulation" (Mowrer, 1947), or they use the word "punishment" to denote the stimulus as well as the procedure of the punishment paradigm. Clearly the difficulty with these definitions lies in their subjective nature and the circularity of using the same term for an entire class of events even though only those events that have a particular effect are properly defined as punishers. As in the case of "positive stimuli" or Thorndike's "satisfying state of affairs," a definition is needed that rests upon a functional behavioral base and is fully described by effects on behavior.

Among the available choices, the most frequently used definition of "aversive stimulus" has relied on escape procedures. Thorndike defined an annoying state of affairs as "one which the animal does nothing to preserve, often doing things which put an end to it" (1913, p. 2). Many experimenters have followed Thorndike in defining an aversive stimulus as any stimulus that, when applied according to the escape paradigm, maintains stable escape responses. In studies of punishment, some investigators use the escape definition to describe the stimulus as a punisher, even though in practice the stimulus had never been tested in an escape procedure or may be one that cannot be escaped at all.

The difficulty with the escape definition of an aversive stimulus is that the parameters that affect the success of escape training have different values when the same stimulus is used in some other model, for example, punishment. As Church (1963) has stated:

"The use of the single concept of noxious stimulus to embrace the procedures of aversive classical conditioning, escape training, avoidance training, punishment, and preservation may be a costly parsimony. In a particular situation there will be a measurable threshold of intensity of the punishment necessary to obtain some response suppression. Is this also the threshold of fear? Is it the weakest aversive stimulus that will elicit competing responses? Is it the threshold for escape or for avoidance? . . . . Similarly, there are many factors other than the severity of the stimulus that determine the effectiveness of the procedures of aversive classical conditioning, preservation, escape training and avoidance training. For these reasons, no indirect definition of a noxious stimulus can be made with confidence" (p. 371).

In the operant tradition, Azrin and Holz (1966) abandon the escape definition and use a definition derived from their procedure in punishment research: a punishing stimulus is "a consequence of behavior that reduces the future probability of that behavior" (p. 381). This definition avoids both subjectivism and the problems indicated by Church. Yet it requires cumbersome language to describe the operational specifics, and limits comparison among paradigms.

In animal experiments, researchers prefer to use electric shock as the aversive stimulus since it is readily controlled and measured. By relying on the known aversive properties of shock in all procedures, they simply avoid the definitional problems altogether. In studies with humans, particularly when aversive control is examined in naturalistic settings, the definitional obstacles are more difficult to surmount. Even when electric shock can be used, cognitive mediational events and differences in personal histories make the definition of "aversive" much more complex. For example, some people report that shock has a pleasant "tingling" effect and they act accordingly. More natural aversive stimuli are likely to be difficult to quantify. Aversive stimuli may also depend on their prior history for their reinforcing value, as we will see later. On the one hand, these complexities offer fruitful ground for clinical and laboratory research with humans; but on the other hand they obstruct specification of variables and probably promote imprecise language in research and clinical reports. In the preceding chapter, we noted the tendency of psychologists to speak of "positive reinforcers" in nonbehavioral terms. When the stimulus has a history of positive properties for the experimenter, it is called reinforcing. In the case of aversive stimuli, this loose language usage is even more common. For the case of positive reinforcement, Premack (1959) defines the positive reinforcing potential of an event by its relatively higher probability of occurrence in relation to the preceding response. However, no related probabilistic concept of aversive events (other than the escape definition) can offer the same simplifying advantages that it provides in the area of positive reinforcement.

A third way to define aversive events is independent of both specific stimulus properties and specific response changes, relying instead on biological state variables. Olds and Olds (1965), Grastyán, Karmos, Vereczkey and Kellényi (1966), and others have proposed separate positive and aversive reinforcement systems in the brain, both activated by changes in the organism's arousal level. Berlyne (1967) has summarized a number of suggestions that the degree of change in arousal determines which system is activated, and that the two systems are mutually inhibitory. Moderate increases in arousal are said to activate the reward reinforcement system, whereas more extreme changes in arousal cause the aversive reinforcement system to become active and to inhibit the effects of the reward system. Both individual differences and the organism's background arousal level would determine the threshold for the aversion system.

A biological definition based on brain functions is impractical in clinical work because it cannot be applied by observation of the intact organism. Nevertheless, the biological definition can have important implications for psychopathological clinical studies and for clinical strategies using aversive stimulation. For example, sociopaths have been found to be slower in acquiring avoidance responses to painful stimuli than normal people. Under the arousing influence of injected adrenalin, sociopaths improve their avoidance learning while normals do not (Schachter and Latané, 1964). Since aversive stimuli are typically used in efforts to control socio-pathic behavior, clarification of the role of arousal in sociopaths' response to different classes of stimuli is obviously of importance in preventing or modifying sociopathic behavior patterns.

As another illustration of the implications of the research on interactions of arousal and reinforcement, Eysenck's (1967) work suggests that intro-verts and extroverts differ in preferred level of stimulation or arousal. Extroverts tend to experience "stimulus hunger" while introverts tend toward "stimulus avoidance." Levels of stimulation that would be aversive to introverts could not be used to achieve similar behavior control with extroverts. Eysenck's hypotheses, like Schachter's, are based on inferred biological differences (particularly those about cortical excitation and auto-nomic reactivity) that are consistent with Berlyne's general theory of arousal as the basis of positive and aversive reinforcement.

Since there is no adequate universal definition of aversive control, we will be using a variety of definitions of aversive stimuli in this chapter, depending upon the work that is described. But we will attempt to point out the implications of the respective definition when it seems to affect the conclusions.

RESPONDENT AND OPERANT ELEMENTS
IN AVERSIVE CONTROL

Another central definitional issue involves the distinction between aver-sive control of operants and respondents, that is, between classical and operant conditioning models using aversive stimuli. In Chapter 3 we dis-cussed the theoretical and procedural implications of the mixture of the two models. In this chapter we therefore only briefly review these distinc-tions and the ultimate arbitrariness of attempted separation of the two models in most experiments. Later we emphasize the role of mixed re-spondent and operant components in theories of punishment, avoidance, and other paradigms involving aversive consequences.

As was discussed in Chapter 3, aversive stimuli can be used to *build stimulus functions*, that is, to create conditioned aversions and conditioned positive reinforcers by pairing neutral stimuli with onset or termination of an aversive stimulus in a classical conditioning paradigm. In the operant conditioning paradigm, aversive stimuli can be used to suppress a response by making the stimuli *contingent* on the occurrence of the response. Or aversive stimuli can be used to maintain a response by making their removal contingent upon the response. At the level of theoretical description, the distinction between the stimulus-building function of classical conditioning and the response-contingency function of the operant conditioning model seems clear. In actual practice, however, the two models cannot be made completely mutually exclusive. Observed effects can usually be ascribed to either model only by arbitrary decision, or by attending only to certain elements in the behavioral equation. Furthermore, the various operant paradigms for application of aversive stimuli that are clearly distinguished at the level of pure description (as in Table 7-2) are not easily distinguishable in actual practice.

Theories attempting to account for the processes by which aversive consequences achieve their effects reflect these difficulties in procedurally separating classical and operant conditioning models and the various paradigms within the operant model. For example, some theories of punishment rely on classically conditioned skeletal or emotional responses elicited by the punishing stimulus to explain its effect on the punished act. Other theories of punishment use the operant avoidance paradigm to explain suppression of a punished act. These theories are discussed further in connection with the topic of punishment. The point emphasized here is simply that the overlap of models and paradigms produces not only uncertainty with respect to which variables bring about a desired effect in the practice of aversive behavior modification, but also produces competing theories which at present cannot be differentially favored on the basis of empirical data.

To illustrate the difficulty of separating aversive paradigms in practice, we may examine an example of clinical behavior modification using aversive control. Lang and Melamed (1969) state that they used an aversive conditioning paradigm to treat a nine-month-old male infant whose life was threatened by persistent vomiting and rechewing of the vomitus (ruminative vomiting). No organic basis for the vomiting could be discovered, and various medical and other therapies yielded no benefits. Since several studies had previously demonstrated that vomiting can be a conditioned response (see, for example, Pavlov, 1927), and since behavior modification has been successful with other alimentary symptoms (see, for example, Bachrach, Erwin and Mohr, 1965) as well as with ruminative vomiting (White and Taylor, 1967), Lang and Melamed decided to try aversive conditioning to save the infant's life.

Initial observations and electromyograph (EMG) recordings indicated that the infant vomited most of his food within ten minutes of intake and continued to regurgitate small amounts all day. Onset of vomiting was always accompanied by vigorous throat movements of a distinctive pattern which occurred at no other time. Fortunately, vomiting did not occur during feeding, nor did sucking occur at the same time as the vomiting, although it usually preceded vomiting. Elimination of vomiting through aversive control therefore was not expected to disrupt vital feeding and sucking behaviors.

The treatment procedure consisted of one-second electric shocks to the leg (at an intensity judged by the therapists to be painful and sufficient to elicit distress behaviors in the infant), delivered at one-second intervals from the start of vomiting until the end of vomiting. The onset of vomiting was determined by EMG records and a nurse's observations. By the end of the first session, frequency and duration of vomiting had markedly decreased. By the end of the second session, the infant was anticipating the shock; after beginning the usual sucking behavior, he cried loudly. He also began to avoid shock by curling his foot, so that the electrodes had to be moved from the plantar surface of the foot to the calf; vomiting again quickly decreased. Vomiting no longer occurred in the sixth session, and the infant's vigorous thumb-sucking had been replaced with more passive thumb-in-mouth behavior. Slight spontaneous recovery after two nontreatment days was reduced by three additional sessions. Six months later the infant was still free of symptoms and had regained his normal weight. Concurrent with the treatment sessions, the infant's smiling, playing with toys, and responsiveness to others had increased. These positive changes were maintained at follow-up.

Although Lang and Melamed refer to the therapy as aversive conditioning, they also mention punishment and counter-conditioning and discuss at some length the various alternative models that could be used to explain the therapeutic procedures. If we consider vomiting to be a conditioned or unconditioned respondent, the EMG monitoring which indicates onset of stomach motility can be used to define a neutral stimulus (CS) preceding the actual response. Thus classical conditioning of this CS with the shock (the UCS) can be carried out. Even if the major components of vomiting were operant responses, classical aversive conditioning to these early links (stomach motility) in the response chain is still a possible explanation. The therapists noted that "the sequence of vomiting, chewing and sucking, and vomiting again suggests a strong self-reinforced behavioral loop" whose stimulus components could acquire secondary aversive functions by pairing with shock.

On the other hand, the interpretation that direct operant suppression was obtained through shock punishment of the vomiting response is equally plausible. Since the unconditioned response to shock was crying, a behavior incompatible with vomiting, it might have enhanced the punishment effect. However, several features of the infant's reactions to treatment also suggest that avoidance training, including escape and later reinforcement of competing avoidance responses, was involved. The competing crying behavior coincided with termination of vomiting and of shock on most conditioning trials. In the middle stage of treatment, sucking was followed by crying rather than vomiting, and shock was thereby avoided. When an alternate avoidance response was possible (foot flexion when the electrode was attached to sole of foot), vomiting was not inhibited. During the session, when foot flexion reduced or avoided shock on some trials but was not successful on all trials, delivery of shock apparently was accompanied by *increased* vomiting, a result not unusual when an avoidance response is itself punished. Finally, the authors note that although positive reinforcement of social behaviors competitive with vomiting could not alone explain the outcome, these behaviors may well have supplemented other factors in producing success. The infant's social responses, which increased as vomiting decreased, were met with warmth and attention from his nurse and may have replaced his previous nonsocial behavior.

As an analysis of this case illustrates, the effective variables in clinical and laboratory studies cannot always be isolated. Nonetheless, each operant aversive paradigm has certain features which, at least in pure form, serve to distinguish it and to commend it for particular therapeutic applications. Overlapping and ambiguity of paradigms will be noted in the following sections that discuss the use of inescapable aversive stimulation, escape and avoidance training, and punishment precedures.

INESCAPABLE AVERSIVE STIMULATION

The effects of contingent aversive stimuli need to be viewed against the background of the behavioral effects of inescapable aversive stimuli, applied on a random, noncontingent schedule over a period of time. The unconditioned responses to sudden, intense aversive stimulation vary from one species to another but typically they include certain motor and autonomic responses. These are usually called emotional reactions, and trial and error efforts at escape are noted. Thus, a dog in a shuttle box (from which he can escape) begins to howl, defecate, urinate, and run about frantically upon onset of intense electric shock. He finally climbs over the barrier and escapes shock. Freezing and reflexive fighting or elicited aggression are other frequently observed reflex responses upon shock delivery (Ulrich and Azrin, 1962). Noncontingent aversive stimulation does not permit discrimination learning; therefore noncontingently delivered shock results in more general behavioral suppression than does contingent shock, or punishment (see, for example, Hunt and Brady, 1955). Not only general behavioral suppression but also enduring disruption of behaviors such as trained discrimination, can result from noncontingent aversive stimulation; in contrast punishment produces only temporary disruption (Hearst, 1965). Church (1963) has pointed out that the differences between contingent and noncontingent aversive stimulation are likely to be greatest when the intensity of the noxious stimuli is low. At high intensity, all responding is likely to cease regardless of any contingency relationship; whereas at low intensities the discriminative properties of the aversive stimuli are likely to have an effect under contingent delivery even though the intensity is too low to cause emotional responses (see, for example, Annau and Kamin, 1961).

Because of the problems in the use of noxious stimuli with human subjects, relatively little is known about stimulus intensity as a parameter in human escape and avoidance learning. In several recent studies of autistic children, Lovaas and his associates (Bucher and Lovaas, 1968; Stahelski and Lovaas, 1967) have found that noncontingent stimuli (a loud "no" or slap) reduced smiling and babbling but increased echolalic speech and looking at the adult's face. Pleasant stimuli (for instance, placement in a warm bath) had opposite effects. These investigators also found that the suppressive effects of the noxious stimuli were relatively short-lived; spontaneous speech, for example, was suppressed for less than 13 minutes after a slap. As the investigators point out, whether these changes are unlearned affective responses or represent learned responses associated with aversive events acting as discriminative stimuli, their immediacy and affective quality point to the importance of including consideration of affective variables in behavior modification designs.

An interesting application of noncontingent shock has been reported in a case of urinary retention. Barnard, Flesher, and Steinbook (1966) hypothesized that the symptom was due to overstimulation of sympathetic control of the bladder, and that a strong parasympathetic impulse would cause sphincter relaxation. Parasympathetic discharge can occur as a "rebound" effect after relief from a sudden stress. The therapeutic procedure, based on these hypotheses, involved shock application until the patient reported that it had become intolerable. When it was suddenly terminated, voiding occurred. The patient administered further trials to herself until voiding was under voluntary control (other behavioral therapies were given simultaneously, for example, assertion training).

The role of accidental classical aversive conditioning has often been emphasized in discussions of the etiology of neuroses. Adventitious pairing of some neutral event with noxious stimulation can serve as a basis for long-lasting avoidance behaviors. In everyday life, avoidance of a restaurant in which a meal was later followed by gastric discomfort, without evidence of any causal relationship, and avoidance of the company of people present at an unpleasant experience, are examples of the effects of the temporal proximity of events that may have had no causal connections. The experiments on the development of phobias, discussed in Chapter 3, illustrate the results of such contiguity of events in clinical problems.

A fascinating and still unexplored question concerns the nature of biologically based avoidance responses. Although research has shown that many apparently instinctive harm-avoidance behaviors are, in fact, learned by observation or experience, animals and men often do show a "wisdom of the body" in avoiding foods, dangerous situations, and other harmful experiences with little or no demonstrated learning. Theories of motivation have postulated some mechanisms for such behaviors (Cofer and Appley, 1964). But "unlearned avoidance" responses range from complex behaviors in man to even the simplest (and probably most biochemically or mechanically determined) avoidance patterns in amoeba or bacteria in the face of new man-made drugs or such other lethal agents as X-ray irradiation. At some future point, a full catalog of man's repertoire of innate avoidance-eliciting stimuli and their underlying mechanisms would add considerably to the clinician's skill in assessing behavior problems and programming their treatment.

A final feature to be discussed in the use of noncontingent aversive stimulation is the extent to which such experiences may "sensitize" or "immunize" the individual to later experiences with the same aversive stimuli, including when they are response-contingent. As far as the classical conditioning model is concerned, the consequence is clear: neutral stimuli (CS) repeatedly associated with the onset of a noxious stimulus (UCS), whether the latter is response-contingent or not, become aversive in themselves and later elicit the same emotional reactions and other responses that followed the original noxious stimulus (UCS). Since the emotional reaction then becomes conditioned to a larger complex of stimuli, the individual is in one sense "sensitized" by his experience. The child who, after undergoing a prior similar experience, shows a conditioned emotional reaction (CER) of fear, crying, and trying to escape as he approaches and enters the doctor's office, sees the hypodermic and receives a shot, emits more emotional behavior and over a longer time than on his first experience when crying occurred only after the shot. Since many more stimuli elicit his emotional response now, it is more intense and prolonged, and in this sense shows sensitization.

What are the effects of initial exposure to noxious stimulation that is both noncontingent and not associated with the same set of contextual stimuli as later occurrences? Does prior isolated exposure make aversive stimuli more or less potent as reinforcers of instrumental acts? Apparently several different aspects of the initial experience influence the later effects of the aversive consequence. When rats are exposed to weak electric shock, subsequent punishment by electric shock is less effective; whereas prior exposure to intense shock produces an increase in the effects of subsequent punishment. Thus, either adaptation or sensitization can result from exposure to an aversive stimulus that is later used as an operant reinforcer. However, when the initial exposure environment differs greatly from the later test environment, adaptation may not occur (Miller 1960; Walters and Rogers, 1963; Karsh, 1963; Church, 1969).

A different line of investigation suggests that the organism's opportunity to make an instrumental response to the initial noncontingent aversive stimulus will determine its later effects. In a series of studies Seligman, Maier, and their co-workers have investigated what they term "learned helplessness" in dogs (Seligman, Maier, and Geer, 1968; Seligman and Maier, 1967). When dogs are exposed to inescapable, noncontingent intense shock and are then placed in an escape-avoidance training apparatus within approximately 24 hours, they fail to learn to escape or avoid shock although control animals readily learn to do so. Seligman and Maier (1967) propose that the animals have learned a relationship of *independence* between their responses and the aversive shock, just as animals can learn the relationships of contiguity (positive reinforcement) and of dissociation (extinction) between an instrumental response and environmental events. The dogs act as if they have learned not to expect their own behavior to affect shock delivery. When placed in a new situation, the shock mediates generalization of their passive behavior.

The "helpless" behavior (failure to learn to escape or avoid) does not occur if there is a 48-hour delay between initial shock exposure and the escape training. However, the "helplessness" becomes chronic if the animals are given several trials of shock in the escape apparatus within 24 hours of the initial shock exposure. Apparently, generalization of the passive response or the learned independence relationship from one environment to another must occur rather early, but once made, the generalization is very durable. Another important feature of the "helpless" behavior of the dogs is that even if they did make successful escape or avoidance responses, they later passively took the shock. Apparently, learning that its responses are independent of shock termination not only reduces the probability of the dog's initiation of later escape behaviors but also inhibits his later association of any response with relief from shock.

Dogs with "chronic helplessness" can be given "therapy" by forcing them to make normal avoidance responses. The amount of force needed (measured by pull on a leash) to move them to a "safe" area of the cage decreases over trials, but a large number of trials is required before reliable avoidance behavior is established. This supports the notion that the animals had been inhibited in associating a response with aversion relief (Seligman, Maier, and Geer, 1968). The dogs could also be given "preventive therapy" that prevents the formation of chronic helplessness. If they were given prior experience with *escapable* shock, later exposure to inescapable shock had no effect on new escape learning (Seligman and Maier, 1967).

The concept of "learned helplessness," or more precisely of learned independence of response and aversive stimulation, may be useful in understanding the pathology of passive behavior in the face of threat. Previous experiences of patients, in situations analogous to the dog experiments, could also account for the large individual differences noted in people's responses to particular aversive stimuli. For example, a child may show no reaction at all to hard slaps but alter his behavior when given a new noxious stimulus, such as an electric shock. His past history with slaps from adults has taught him that they are inescapable and independent of his own behavior, while shock delivery can be controlled by his own actions. The therapeutic strategy of forcing the individual to experience the behavioral contingency in operation is similar to the procedure for speeding up extinction of an avoidance response, namely by restraining the animal in the place where aversive stimuli had previously been administered. The reader will recognize the similarity of these procedures to the methods of implosion therapy, discussed in Chapter 3. Systematic desensitization achieves the same goal by a more gradual reintroduction of the original situation. The preventive use of experience with response-contingent aversion relief before exposure to noncontingent aversive stimulation seems related also to preventive relaxation training or to Lazarus' (1968) use of practice in reappraisal of anticipated aversive stimuli to reduce their effect when actually presented.

Other authors have construed the ability to learn from aversion-relief as equivalent to "hope," the opposite of "helplessness" (Mowrer, 1960b). Berlyne (1967) has suggested an aversion-reducing system in the brain that inhibits the action of the aversion center and that is energized by stimuli associated with relief or "hope." Mandler's (1964) theory of anxiety similarly involves helplessness and the absence of an appropriate response: "free floating anxiety does not stem from the generalization of the anxiety response to a variety of stimuli from some initial traumatic association, but rather the anxiety phenomenon is seen as conditional upon the *absence* of appropriate environmental stimuli and associated responses" (Mandler, 1964, pp. 184–185).

Preventive and therapeutic procedures modeled on those of Seligman and Maier have not yet been applied systematically in clinical cases. However, it is clear that the usefulness of particular aversive stimuli for behavior modification depends upon the individual's prior experiences with these stimuli and his history of ability to escape or avoid their impact. Noncontingent aversive stimulation has been used to a limited extent for therapeutic purposes. For example, some autistic children appear to be lethargic, insensitive to social contingencies and to their own failures, and lacking in normal anxiety. Lovaas and his associates (Perloff and Lovaas, 1967; Bucher and Lovaas, 1968) have hypothesized that aversive stimulation could help such children to achieve the anxiety feelings that normal children experience and use in learning. One autistic child, Jimmy, was progressing well in an imitation training program as long as food reinforcers were used, but gave many fewer correct responses with social reinforcement. Noncontingent aversive stimului (a slap on the buttocks) restored his performance with social reinforcers to the level at which he had been with food reinforcement. After a series of alternate training and extinction trials, Jimmy maintained a high proportion of correct responses for as many as seven days; an aversion trial restored his high performance when the effects of the preceding slap diminished after extinction trials. The aversive slap, since it was not contingent upon any response, did not carry cue information. At one point, after Jimmy had dropped to only 10 percent correct responses and aversion was again applied, his incorrect rather than correct responses rose. Use of contingent food reinforcers was necessary to restore Jimmy's discrimination of correct from incorrect responses, after which the slap again led to correct performance. As the investigators note, "noncontingent aversive stimulation, or anxiety, which it probably would be called in a more clinical sense, is likely to be helpful to a patient insofar as he knows what he is supposed to do. Otherwise, the aversive stimulation is discriminative for an increase in behavior in general, including incorrect behavior" (Bucher and Lovaas. 1968, p. 106).

Noncontingent aversive stimuli may function as discriminative cues because of the history of their use in a contingency relationship. Thus schizophrenic children trained in social responsiveness, initially through an escape-avoidance paradigm using shock, suddenly increased their partially extinguished social responses after only one *noncontingent* shock. Similarly, after response-contingent shock had been used to punish autistic self-stimulation, the behavior had gradually returned. One *noncontingent* shock was sufficient, however, to restore the suppression (Bucher and Lovaas, 1968). Such findings may explain why aversive stimuli can produce unexpected effects when used therapeutically, whether contingently or not. An unknown past history with the stimuli may have endowed them with unsuspected discriminative properties.

ESCAPE AND AVOIDANCE TRAINING

Escape and avoidance responses are trained by use of what Skinner terms *negative reinforcement,* that is, termination or avoidance of aversive stimuli. In a typical laboratory experiment, shock can be delivered through the floor of the animal's cage; the animal can terminate or escape from the shock by pressing a lever. The onset of shock may be signaled several seconds in advance, so that by pressing the lever the animal learns to avoid delivery of shock altogether. Both of these paradigms are outlined in Table 7-2. As the table indicates, the response under examination in these procedures is the one that is followed by *relief* from aversive stimulation. Any other behavior in which the animal engages prior to stimulation is irrelevant within this model. Thus escape and avoidance training build *new* behaviors, affecting old behaviors only by competing with them or by involving them in superstitious behavior chains.

"Pathological" Escape and Avoidance

In Chapter 3, escape and avoidance responses often represented therapeutically desirable behaviors. The introduction of an aversive stimulus in association with a homosexual picture or the sight of alcohol is intended to establish avoidance and escape behaviors in place of socially unacceptable responses. However, we have previously noted the common assumption that behavioral deviations represent avoidance or "defensive" reactions that reduce anxiety or remove the neurotic from a conflict or threat. In daily life, some escape or avoidance responses have contradictory immediate and long-range effects. A catalog of common symptoms has been described in the hypochondriac, the hysteric, the sexual pervert, and in other patients for which the immediate relief consequences of the symptoms are devious. The excessive concern over infections can aid the hypochondriac in avoiding socially stressful gatherings, and the child molester is hypothesized to avoid dreaded contact with sexually mature partners by his symptoms. Expectation of failure, social isolation, or an attitude toward the self as inadequate forestall exposure to situations with high risk for failure, as phobias avoid contact with feared objects. Thus escape or avoidance behavior may be unacceptable from society's viewpoint, but it may have relief consequences just the same. The secondary beneficial consequences of a pathological avoidance response often appear only after the symptomatic behavior has been well established. Reactions from the social milieu, such as sympathy, support, or privileges granted by society to its "sick" members may serve to maintain the avoidance behavior at high strength. This effect has long been noted by clinicians, under the term "secondary gain," as an obstacle to symptom removal.

The particular features that affect the development of "self-defeating" avoidance reactions have been studied extensively in the animal laboratory. Sidman (1960a) has described several studies with monkeys that illustrate the complexities of avoidance learning. The animals had been trained to obtain food by a stable bar-pressing operant. When a tone signal was introduced that always ended with a brief, unavoidable shock, the animals showed the usual *conditioned suppression* (Estes and Skinner, 1941) that is, they stopped bar pressing during the tone interval. These results have been widely demonstrated and are presumed to be based on aversive conditioning. When Sidman put his monkeys on a partial reinforcement schedule, associating tone and shock only 25 percent of the time, the stable conditioned suppression gradually broke down and was replaced by a variety of behavioral anomalies. Further studies showed that duration of the warning tone and duration of its absence were the main controlling variables. When periods of silence were relatively long, suppression of responding was maintained for relatively longer durations than when periods of silence were short. This relationship, it turned out, minimized loss of positive reinforcers; the animals maintained a relatively constant overall rate of positive reinforcement, about 90 percent of base line, regardless of the varied durations of tone and silence. If conditioned suppression resulted in greater loss of positive reinforcement than this, the suppression disappeared. As Sidman puts it: "The animals manifest anxiety only to the extent that they can afford to do so in terms of reinforcement cost" (p. 64).

This finding seems particularly relevant to understanding conditioned anxiety in humans and the responses presumed to be reinforced by avoidance of this anxiety. It is reminiscent of the earlier suggestions that phobic and compulsive behaviors may be reduced by insuring that their total cost in terms of positive reinforcement is great (Meyer, 1966). Particularly, this finding is a warning that effective behavior therapy programming must also account for other positively reinforced behaviors, even though the escape and avoidance paradigms per se do not require these considerations.

Sidman's further experiments illustrate how behaviors unrelated to successful avoidance can become paradoxically involved when aversive stimuli are applied. He first trained monkeys to lever-press to avoid shock; each press delayed a shock for 20 seconds. Then the usual conditioned suppression paradigm was introduced: a tone was followed by an unavoidable shock. The animals showed a paradoxical behavior change—they pressed normally during the silent period, thereby avoiding all avoidable shocks, but pressed at a much higher rate during the tone, when pressing had no actual consequence at all, since the shock at the end of the tone was unavoidable. This *conditioned facilitation* ultimately extinguishes but is relatively durable and represents nonadaptive behavior based on a particular history combining negative reinforcement with current adventitious contingencies (the successful avoidance responses associated with the spurious ones).

When two different responses were available, one with a food contingency and one with a shock avoidance contingency, similar adventitious conditioning occurred. During a period of tone signaling an unavoidable shock, *both* responses increased. The food-reinforced responses came under the control of the shock-avoidance contingency despite its irrelevance under the experimental conditions. It had become part of a behavior chain, even though only one response was relevant to shock avoidance. The entire chain increased in frequency during a period when it was entirely irrelevant, when no shocks were forthcoming except an unavoidable one at the end.

This latter phase, termed "second-order superstition," Sidman suggests, is a possible model of "sick" behavior that is produced and maintained by lawful, orderly processes. No evidence is available to support directly the suspicion that many clinical behavior problems are the consequence of subtle histories of aversive stimulation. As in the case of symptoms presumed to be based on classical aversive conditioning, it is difficult to test hypotheses regarding the origin of behaviors possibly maintained by avoidance, except by animal analogue research like Sidman's. Clinically, relevant aversive stimuli are often obscure and identified only *post hoc*. Their original occurrence is difficult to ascertain. Nonetheless, as a general model, animal investigations such as Sidman's have clinical as well as scientific utility. They stress the importance of the many unplanned positive consequences that may affect a person's response to aversive stimulation in the natural environment.

Parameters of Escape-Avoidance Learning

Single parameters that affect escape and avoidance learning can be described rather easily, although their detailed interactions can be quite complex. As indicated in Table 7-3, the intensity of the aversive stimulus, the durations of warning signals and aversive stimuli, their temporal relationships, their relationship to the response, and the nature of the response are all important determinants of the speed, reliability, and durability with which escape and avoidance responses are learned. Fuller descriptions of the relationships between values of these parameters and response acquisition and rate are available in a number of reviews (see, for example,

Table 7-3   Some Parameters Affecting Escape-Avoidance Learning

	Nature	Timing
Aversive stimulus (UCS)	"Surprising" or "unexpected" UCS is necessary for association with warning stimulus (CS). Intensity and density of UCS are positively related to acquisition reliability and response rate; thresholds tend to be lower than for punishing UCS. Prior exposure to UCS may increase or decrease rate of acquisition and affects initial responses especially.	Quicker termination enhances acquisition for less reflexive responses. Optimal R-UCS interval is a function of the UCS-UCS interval. Longer durations of escape (removal of UCS) produce more reliable acquisition.
Response upon which escape avoidance is contingent	Rs similar to unconditioned Rs to the aversive stimulus are acquired more rapidly. Less "reflexive" responses are slower to appear as escape but faster and more persistent as avoidance.	Responses with longer latencies are acquired as avoidance more rapidly and durably. Intertrial interval is curvilinearly related to speed of acquisition. Intersession interval is inversely related to speed of acquisition.
Warning stimulus (CS)	The less redundant the information given by CS, the more rapid is acquisition. Termination of CS by avoidance response enhances acquisition. When competing Rs are maintained by C^+, potency of CS for avoidance acquisition is directly proportional to its potency for conditioned suppression.	Longer CS-UCS intervals impede acquisition.

Dinsmoor, 1968; Hoffman, 1966; Kamin, 1968; Sidman, 1966; Solomon and Brush, 1956; Turner and Solomon, 1962).

Theoretical description of escape learning is also relatively straightforward. Onset of the aversive stimulus comes to serve as a discriminative cue for the response that terminates it; termination of the aversive event functions as a positive reinforcer. Patterns of behavior obtained under various conditions and schedules of reinforcement by aversion termination are similar to those obtained by conventional positive reinforcement and can be relatively easily established.

The matter is quite different in the case of acquisition and maintenance of avoidance responses. Successful avoidance *prevents* the occurrence of the aversive stimulus. Thus the dilemma lies in explaining what is reinforcing the avoidance behavior. The *absence* of an environmental consequence is not a satisfactory "event" unless appeal is made to some intervening or mediating events. This seeming paradox has resulted in a number of competing theories to explain avoidance learning. However, as yet, no entirely satisfactory basis for choosing between them has been offered.

Even though no good theoretical explanation of the development of avoidance responses is available, some empirical generalizations can be made about procedures that enhance the acquisition of avoidance responses. Avoidance behaviors are extremely resistant to extinction, and a single reinforced trial can reinstate them to a high level after extinction has occurred. Presumably this is due to the discriminative stimulus function of the aversive event. A single shock can inform the animal that the aversive contingency is still in effect; it indicates the difference between successful avoidance and the environmental absence of aversive stimuli. A schedule that is progressively more intermittent and variable, provision of "booster" aversive stimuli, and prevention of clear discriminative control enhance resistance to extinction.

Alternative escape-avoidance responses must be prevented. Just as rats may learn to lie on their backs, using their fur as an insulator to avoid shock from a floor grid, so too patients may make unwanted but successful avoidance responses. The infant whose vomiting was suppressed by shock at first avoided the shock by arching his foot. Loud sound as an aversive stimulus poses difficulty if covering the ears, moving away, or turning the head can reduce it. And patients, of course, may simply leave therapy in ultimate avoidance of therapeutic aversive conditioning.

The timing of the CS and UCS can be significant factors, as can the level of development of conditioned emotional reactions to the CS. Prior escape training, which firmly establishes conditioned fear to the CS, usually enhances avoidance acquisition. Turner and Solomon (1962) note that short CS–UCS intervals promote conditioning of the fear reactions, but longer intervals are required for a slow skeletal avoidance response to be reinforced by CS and UCS termination. They therefore suggest that training of a highly emotional person, a description fitting many patients, should begin with a short CS–UCS interval that is gradually lengthened. Similarly, Turner and Solomon suggest beginning with an intense UCS, then gradually reducing it to produce long-latency escape responses, which in turn enhance avoidance learning. Usual clinical procedure is the reverse, increasing intensity as the patient adapts to the UCS.

The nature of the escape or avoidance response seems particularly crucial to successful training. If the response has a low initial probability of occurrence when the person is experiencing fear, its training may be very difficult or impossible to achieve except with verbal instructions. Turner and Solomon (1962) state that the more reflexive the avoidance response is in character (the more respondent or visceral), the more difficult it is to train. If a fearful person's behavior contains large components of the avoidance response to be trained, it is likely to be respondent or reflexive in nature and hence difficult to train even though its probability is very high. Lower levels of aversive stimulation may reduce the intensity of the skeletal behaviors associated with fear, and hence make them easier to condition as avoidance responses.

Clinical Application of Escape-Avoidance Training

It should be clear to the reader that the examples given in illustration of aversion therapy in Chapter 3 included many instances of escape and avoidance training as well. For instance, Feldman's (1966) aversion treatment of homosexuals permitted patients to escape or avoid shock by changing the CS, a picture of a nude male, to one of a nude female. Similarly, shock during sipping alcohol could be avoided or escaped by alcoholic patients by spitting out the alcohol. The method of an aversion-relief combination thus offers an incompatible response as an alternative to the UCS. The "relief" portion of treatment utilizes a desirable response as a potential positive reinforcing stimulus, deriving its positive qualities from its contiguity with aversion-escape. Theoretically, either the anxiety associated with the CS–UCS interval is reduced (Estes and Skinner, 1941) or positive emotional responses are conditioned to termination of the noxious UCS (Mowrer, 1960a). The relief stimulus thus is intended to accomplish two functions: (1) it serves to provide an avoidance or escape response, and (2) it increases the potential reinforcing property of the associated stimulus event. Since the role of relief-stimuli in escape-avoidance training is not yet clear in experimental work, their benefits in behavior modification are mainly conjectural. Yet the practice of the desirable response, coupled with the probable explicit or implicit social approval from the experimenter and the provision of an alternate response, may suffice to yield important practical benefits in therapy.

Aversion-relief to produce secondary positive reinforcement has been successfully used as a principal therapeutic procedure in a number of uncontrolled clinical cases. For example, Solyom and Miller (1967) altered the quality of phobic stimuli from aversive to positive by pairing them with termination of shock. Six of their seven patients were symptom free after six months. Thorpe, Schmidt, Brown, and Castell (1964) describe a procedure combining aversive conditioning and aversion-relief conditioning, but focus on the latter aspect in their discussion. Using words related to symptoms as CS, and shock as UCS, they reported therapeutic success in six of eight patients with a variety of complaints (for example, obesity, homosexuality, transvestism, and phobia).

Other therapeutic applications of escape-avoidance training have aimed primarily at increase of the response associated with relief. Lovaas and his co-workers, for example, wanted to increase the social behavior of two autistic children (Lovaas, Schaeffer, and Simmons, 1965). The children were placed in an area of a room that had an electric shock grid in the floor. They were asked to approach the experimenter. If the child did not approach, shock was delivered and continued until an approach was made. In later sessions, shock could be avoided by approaching within 5 seconds of the request. The avoidance response, approach toward an adult, was rapidly acquired and did not extinguish after nine months without further shock. When a sudden decrease in approach then occurred, one *noncontingent* shock was sufficient to restore the avoidance. Furthermore, untrained compliance with other requests occurred in the experimental room, although not elsewhere. Again, one shock avoidance experience in other rooms was sufficient to establish generalization of compliance at full strength.

A combination of punishment and escape-avoidance has been used to treat aphonia, torticollis, functional eye closing, and similar behaviors. Often it is difficult to distinguish punishment and escape-avoidance in these therapies. For example, Jones (1967) attached electrically conductive metal false eyelashes to the eyes of a man who was incapacitated for work because, after a period of eye trauma, he could not keep his eyes open. Eye closure completed an electrical circuit and delivered a shock terminated by eye opening. This is a good example of the practical utility of combining elements of punishment and escape-avoidance. When a symptomatic target behavior has a directly antagonistic behavior that can be strengthened, all elements are likely to be present in aversive control. In this instance, eye closing was punished and the stimuli associated with eye closing were aversively conditioned. The competing behavior of keeping the eyes open was reinforced by escape and avoidance. Aversive therapy for writer's cramp offers a similar example (Liversedge and Sylvester, 1955). A metal stylus, used by the patient to trace a pattern on a metal plate, closes an electrical circuit and produces shock when the patient deviates from the outlined pattern. Or a pen may be modified so that excessive thumb pressure produces a shock terminated by reduced pressure. Elements of punishment, aversive conditioning, and escape-avoidance training are simultaneously present. However, investigators frequently focus only on one component in describing the theoretical rationale for these mixed procedures.

Some terminological confusion, however, seems to be due to mislabeling or incomplete description of procedures rather than the complexity of the model. As an example, Kennedy and Foreyt (1968) state:

"An avoidance conditioning paradigm was used. While S was wearing the oxygen mask, the CS (food smell) was presented. When S signalled by nodding her head that she smelled the food, the stopcock was switched and the UCS (noxious gas) was blown up to S" (p. 574).

In this case, the description suggests a straight classical conditioning paradigm, since no avoidance response is described.

The mixed model procedures may be most effective in some cases because several mutually supportive models are applied to produce additive therapeutic effects, while application of a single paradigm provides insufficient control over the symptom to yield results. In any case, the greater the instrumental importance of the escape-avoidance response, and the wider the range of environments in which the training is carried out, the more successful behavior modification is likely to be. The effectiveness of multiple-paradigm procedures may also relate to the difficulty of aversion methods in obtaining generalization from the therapy setting to the social environment. When a therapeutic strategy employs positive reinforcement to strengthen a desirable response, the patient's everyday environment can often be relied upon to continue the administration of positive reinforcement. For example, improved study behavior, increased assertive responses, or skilled heterosexual patterns often result in a natural increase in reinforcement to the patient. In the case of aversive control, contingent aversive stimulation or reward of an avoidance response (for example, for homosexual behavior or for withdrawal from delinquent social contacts) is much less likely to occur. Furthermore, the special equipment and make-believe nature of procedures using such artificial noxious stimuli as electric shock or drug-produced nausea clearly set off the laboratory situations from the patient's daily environment. Stimulus discrimination may then serve to narrow the range of situations in which the newly acquired behavior occurs, unless deliberate efforts are made to bridge the transition to the natural world. Undoubtedly, the patient's verbal and thought proceses can serve to mediate or to limit the effects of the therapeutic procedure. The additional use of interviews and association of the patient's daily experiences with the therapeutic procedure are commonly described as ancillary procedures in aversion therapy and would serve to enhance the therapy effects. The various uses of self-monitoring, recordkeeping, and reports of related experiences between sessions (discussed in Chapter 9) can complement the aversion techniques for nonhospitalized patients.

An interesting study by Carlin and Armstrong (1968) was based on the hypothesis that the favorable results of aversive conditioning therapies may be based, not on a learning model, but on the incongruence between the patient's behavior and his beliefs, once he is committed to a behavior change. Three groups of men, interested in treatment to stop smoking, were assigned the following treatments: (1) conditioning—shocks were administered on a variable interval schedule during smoking; (2) pseudo-conditioning—subjects were shown slides, of which a third were relevant to smoking, and shocked during the viewing; (3) control—the same treatment was administered as in the conditioning group, except that shocks were omitted and subjects were told they would receive "subliminal shocks." Carlin and Armstrong report significant reduction in smoking during the four-day treatment series in all groups, but the groups did not differ in magnitude of smoking decrease. The study raises many questions, despite its limited range and lack of follow-up data. At least *during* treatment, participation in the experiment resulted in a considerable reduction of smoking, regardless of the treatment method. The authors state that their intent was not to compare the efficacies of different treatment methods in this study; "rather [the experiment] attempted to demonstrate that all behavior change occurring in conditioning therapies should not be assumed a function of conditioning" (p. 677). The results leave no doubt that similar behavior changes during treatments can be achieved by a combination of techniques.

Avoidance Training and Anxiety

The central role assigned to anxiety in the development of behavior pathologies has been discussed previously and is detailed in most textbooks on abnormal psychology. Several researchers have examined differences in avoidance learning as a function of anxiety level and traditional diagnostic classification. This research area is of interest not only for its clinical content but also for its theoretical approach. Interpretation of these studies is based on the assumption that anxiety serves to mediate the acquisition of an avoidance response, and that anxiety reduction maintains this response. The best-known formulation of this hypothesis is Mowrer's two-stage theory (1947). Briefly, he proposed that classical conditioning represents the first step of the process, with emotional responses (anxiety) aroused during the CS–UCS interval. These serve as cues for instrumental escape responses which, if successful, are reinforced by anxiety reduction. The hypothesis is difficult to verify and has caused such skeptical comments as the following by Sidman (1966): "Whenever a challenge [to the theory] does arise, the properties of anxiety are simply revised to fit the new facts" (p. 448).

The anxiety hypothesis suggests, nevertheless, that some emotional behaviors are needed to mediate avoidance learning. Animal studies have demonstrated that rats injected with epinephrine, a drug that mimics the arousal of the sympathetic nervous system, acquire an avoidance response much more readily than control animals (Latané and Schachter, 1962). Lykken (1957) showed that criminal sociopaths are relatively anxiety free and virtually incapable of learning to avoid a painful stimulus although matched normal controls learned readily. Schachter applied to Lykken's work his own general proposition that an emotion is a joint function of physiological arousal and of cognitions appropriate to the arousal so that, for example, sympathetic arousal mimicked by epinephrine injection heightens self-reports of and behavior related to euphoria, amusement, or anger depending on the context and cognitive conditions (see, for example, Schachter and Singer, 1962). By injecting controls and sociopaths with epinephrine and comparing their learning before and after injection, Schachter and Latané (1964) in the study described earlier, showed that sociopaths and normals learn equally well under positive reinforcement but that normals readily learn to avoid pain while sociopaths do not. When injected with a sympathomimetic drug, sociopaths improve markedly in avoidance learning while normals perform more poorly under this condition. Sociopaths were further found to be more sensitive to sympathomimetic drugs and autonomically *more* responsive to a variety of stresses than normals. Schachter and Latané interpret these seemingly contradictory results as suggesting that only intense autonomic reactions that can be readily differentiated from their usual high arousal state will be labeled as an emotion (such as anxiety) by the sociopath and will successfully mediate avoidance learning.

To the extent that anxiety-mediated avoidance responses are the basis of many socially conforming behaviors, treatment of criminality in sociopaths is likely to require either training in labeling of their emotional responses, or avoidance learning under very high levels of anxiety or arousal. Their ready acquisition of positively reinforced behaviors supports programs such as token economies that can build desirable behaviors, competitive with antisocial behaviors. However, these results also suggest that sociopaths will not learn to avoid painful consequences without special training procedures; thus, the usual methods of administering noxious events to violators of social regulations are quite unlikely to affect the sociopath.

In a different line of investigation, again based on Mowrer's two-factor theory, Sloane, Davison, Staples and Payne (1965) studied avoidance learning in neurotic patients. Neurotics are generally characterized as autonomically hyper-reactive and emotionally volatile (see, for example, Duffy, 1962). Schachter and Latané (1964) suggest that this reactivity of the anxiety neurotic is cognitively determined and unrelated to adrenalin sensitivity. Thus his hyper-reactivity would be opposite in character though quantitatively similar to that of the sociopath. Their hypothesis is that the neurotic always interprets the environment in threatening, emotional terms, thus triggering autonomic activity. The sociopath rarely labels his autonomic arousal as emotion; the neutrotic always does. Sloane et al. (1965) again found their neurotic subjects to show heightened autonomic reactivity. The patients were impaired in learning an avoidance response, but they classically conditioned to unavoidable shock more readily than normals. When highly anxious, introverted patients were compared with extroverted, acting-out patients, the former showed slower instrumental learning reinforced by social approval while the latter responded more easily to approval and less to punishment or pain in an avoidance paradigm. Their results, like Schachter's, suggest that anxiety increase is necessary to teach avoidance responses to acting-out patients, while the reverse is true of highly anxious neurotics. The latter, in Schachter's theory, might best be helped by learning new nonarousing labels for their physiological state, a proposal discussed in the earlier chapter on systematic desensitization.

The role of avoidance behavior in the natural world, and the long-range effects of a high proportion of avoidance on other behaviors in a person's repertoire are not known. Despite demonstrations that laboratory animals can maintain high rates of avoidance responses for long periods of time, there are suggestions that this contingency exacts a toll in stress reactions, even though aversive stimuli are successfully avoided. The conditioned emotional reaction presumed to mediate avoidance may lead to illness and even death. The famous studies of "executive monkeys" (Brady, Porter, Conrad, and Mason, 1958; Brady, 1958) showed that monkeys, pressing a lever at a high rate to avoid shock, developed duodenal ulcers from which they died within a few weeks. Yoked controls, who received the same shocks but had no avoidance contingency available, showed no ulcers at all. Apparently the critical factor was the program used;

only with alternate six hours of avoidance and six hours of rest was the damaging effect noted. Other cycles did not produce ulceration. In view of the stringency of the required program, there seems little danger that avoidance responses trained in therapeutic operations risk psychosomatic side effects. Avoidance-related anxiety may, however, play an important role in psychosomatic complaints of neurotic patients. According to Schachter's notion, neurotics label a large proportion of environmental stimuli as noxious, and could be on an alternate avoidance-rest cycle that approximates the density of Brady's schedule in the monkeys with ulcers.

PUNISHMENT

Punishment is much used, often maligned, and little understood as a method of behavior control. As we discussed earlier in this chapter, for many years theorists deplored the use of punishment as unpredictable and likely to produce undesirable side effects. Researchers largely ignored it and clinicians urged reliance on positive reinforcement in place of punishment. More recent research has clarified parameters governing the diverse effects of punishment, and resulted in a reexamination of its supposed harmful side effects. Reviews, such as those of Church (1963), Solomon (1964), Azrin and Holz (1966), Boe and Church (1968), and Campbell and Church (1969) have fostered renewed investigative and clinical work with punishment.

The basic paradigm for contingent punishment is simple and straightforward: a specific response, previously acquired and maintained by positive reinforcement, is followed by a noxious stimulus. In practice, however, the behavior being punished, such as a child's stealing a cookie or a patient's homosexual response, is rarely only under aversive control. If it were, extinction of the response through repeated omission of positive reinforcement would be expected. In fact, the same behavior is often maintained under concurrent schedules of aversive and positive control. This state of affairs, in the laboratory as in daily life, is commonly designated as conflict. A considerable research literature has been developed about behavior in such situations, with frequent reference to its relevance to the etiology of neuroses. Since behavior therapy methods have not made much use of these findings, they will not be discussed further here. What is of interest to us is the fact that punishment is rarely a sole consequence of the behaviors with which the clinician deals, nor is the situation usually free of alternate responses that can avoid, escape, or minimize punishment effects. When administered by mother, employer, experimenter, or therapist, however, punishment does have the potentiality for increasing variability in behavior. Similar to extinction, it alters the strength of the response on which it is contingent.

Solomon (1964) underscores the similarity of response-contingent punishment and avoidance-training procedures when he refers to punishment as *passive avoidance learning.* He notes that the two procedures differ mainly in the relative specificity of the behaviors *producing* and *terminating* the noxious stimulation. In the case of avoidance training, the behaviors leading to onset of the aversive stimulus are unspecified, although the particular response terminating the noxious stimulation is precisely defined. The opposite holds for punishment. The behaviors producing the punishing stimulus are clearly specified, but those terminating the noxious stimulation are undefined. While avoidance teaches the individual "what to do," punishment teaches him "what not to do." In both cases the training goal is achieved when aversive stimulation is no longer suffered. The practical difference is that passive "not-responding" is sufficient for evasion of punishment. No new behaviors are substituted unless they are positively reinforced. In avoidance training, the avoidance of the impending aversive stimulus alone is sufficient to build new behaviors, as we have noted in our discussion of the use of relief-stimuli in therapy. In both situations, discriminations can easily occur or avoidance can spread. The child quickly learns to wait until mother is out of sight before hitting his baby brother, or he runs away from home, lies or hides to avoid aversive consequences of his behavior.

Theories of Punishment

The basic similarity of avoidance and punishment plays a central role in many theories explaining the means by which punishment affects behavior. Woodworth and Schlosberg (1954) distinguished the two paradigms as punishment for *action* and punishment for *inaction,* a distinction complementary to Solomon's *active* versus *passive* avoidance learning. Church's (1963) review of theories of punishment categorizes punishment theories into two broad types: those that do not require any correlation of response and punishment, and those that do involve correlation of response and punishment. Table 7-4 outlines some of the theories of each type. Most of the theories in Table 7-4 that rely on discriminative stimuli independent of the punished response deal with fear mechanisms commonly used to explain escape-avoidance by the two-factor theory. Among the theories that involve *response-produced* discriminative stimuli and thus require some correlation of response and punishment to explain the effects, the hypothesis that avoidance learning underlies all punishment is the chief contender. Thus most theories involve some parallels between escape-avoidance and punishment.

Table 7-4   Theories of Punishment as Classified by Church (1963)

Theories not requiring correlation of response and punishment:

Fear Hypothesis: Unconditioned fear response to C⁻ is classically conditioned to discriminative stimuli controlling target response (or to response-produced stimuli).

Competing Response Hypothesis: Unconditioned motor response to C⁻ are classically conditioned to discriminative (or response-produced) stimuli.

Escape Hypothesis: Response terminating C⁻ generalizes to preceding discriminative stimuli.

Discrimination Hypothesis: Punishment decreases responding when it changes conditions from those of training, facilitates responding when it restores training conditions.

Theories requiring correlation of response and punishment:

Suppression Hypothesis: Some form of inhibition of responding results from C⁻.

Avoidance Hypothesis: Some form of reinforcement for not responding (avoiding) results from C⁻, mediated by classically conditioned anxiety or fear.

The challenge for all theories of punishment is to explain its seeming paradoxical results; punishment may completely, partially, or temporarily suppress responses, or it may facilitate them. Church's (1963) conclusion is that both types of theories, those emphasizing response-contingent discriminative functions of punishment and those emphasizing the generalized emotional effects of punishment, are in part correct or necessary. Response-contingent aversive stimulation results in greater response suppression (or less facilitation), but aversive stimulation contingent only upon discriminative stimuli will also suppress responding. The *suppression* hypothesis and the *avoidance* hypothesis (see Table 7-4) both account for these findings. Church, from his review of empirical studies, concludes that there is little choice between the two theories as yet, but that effects of conditioned and unconditioned emotional reactions (for example, as used in the avoidance hypothesis) must be included in any explanation of both suppressive and facilitating effects of punishment.

Solomon (1964), in favoring the *avoidance theory* of punishment, points out some of its practical implications. For example, he suggests that effects of punishment will be more durable to the extent that the response that terminates the punishing stimulus and competes with the punished response is more specific. In this case, the terminating behaviors are positively reinforced, while the punished behaviors are suppressed by their association with conditioned fear reactions. Extinction of punishment effects would then require two extinction processes, one of the classically conditioned fear, and one of the operant terminating (competing) behavior.

Parameters Influencing Punishment Effects

Although theories about punishment still are not adequate for a clear description of its mechanisms, the body of accumulated research in this area permits a reasonable guide for its utilization and an indication of the parameters affecting its power. Azrin and Holz (1966) have summarized the implications of some of the most relevant variables, in prescribing arrangements that will maximize elimination of a response by punishment:

"(1) The punishing stimulus should be arranged in such a manner that no unauthorized escape is possible. (2) The punishing stimulus should be as intense as possible. (3) The frequency of punishment should be as high as possible; ideally the punishing stimulus should be given for every response. (4) The punishing stimulus should be delivered immediately after the response. (5) The punishing stimulus should not be increased gradually but introduced at maximum intensity. (6) Extended periods of punishment should be avoided, especially where low intensities of punishment are concerned, since the recovery effect may thereby occur. Where mild intensities of punishment are used, it is best to use them for only a brief period of time. (7) Great care should be taken to see that the delivery of the punishing stimulus is not differentially associated with the delivery of reinforcement. Otherwise the punishing stimulus may acquire conditioned reinforcing properties. (8) The delivery of the punishing stimulus should be made a signal or discriminative stimulus that a period of extinction is in progress. (9) The degree of motivation to emit the punished response should be reduced. (10) The frequency of positive reinforcement for the punished response should similarly be reduced. (11) An alternative response should be available which will not be punished but which will produce the same or greater reinforcement as the punished response. . . . (12) If no alternative response is available, the subject should have access to a different situation in which he obtains the same reinforcement without being punished. (13) If it is not possible to deliver the punishing stimulus itself after a response, then an effective method of punishment is still available. A conditioned stimulus may be associated with the aversive stimulus, and this conditioned stimulus may be delivered following a response to achieve conditioned punishment" (Azrin and Holz, 1966, pp. 426–427).

This list of practical guidelines abstracts the crux of many parametric studies of punishment. Table 7-5 outlines some of these relationships with reference to the main variables. The chief influences we might single out for discussion, however, are similar to those emphasized in avoidance training: the nature of the response to be suppressed, the past history of the individual with the aversive event, and the reinforcement schedule maintaining the punished response and the behaviors competing with it.

The Nature of the Punished Response

Selection of the punished response is critical in the use of punishment for behavior modification. First of all, as noted in the table, punishment of an escape or avoidance response tends to increase rather than suppress the punished behavior (see, for example, Black and Morse, 1961). For example, the child whose crying has been reinforced by termination of a parent's scolding or spanking and who thereby has been trained to cry to escape, will increase its crying when spanked *for* crying, an observation common to onlookers in public places.

Punishment is often the procedure of choice because the reinforcement history and current maintenance of the undesired behavior is unknown, making difficult the use of extinction or of the same reinforcer with an acceptable alternative behavior. But this lack of knowledge may also lead to punishment of functionally useful escape-avoidance behaviors and achieve exactly the opposite results in treatment. For example, Bucher and Lovaas (1968) describe the use of punishment after four months of making no progress in food-reinforced imitation training of an autistic boy. The patient, Kevin, covered his ears and left his chair when spoken to or whenever training was attempted. They postulated that Kevin was strongly reinforced for negativism, rendering the positive reinforcement for correct behaviors ineffective. For five days, three hours per day, Kevin was slapped on the thigh and yelled at when he either covered his ears or left his chair. The adult therapist became exhausted but Kevin only *increased* the frequency of the punished acts. At this point, electric shock was substituted for the slap. Within ten minutes, Kevin showed fear, initiated eye contact with the adult, and ceased the punished responses. Within two hours he was imitating correctly 100 percent of the time on tasks he had been failing for the prior four months. This example can be used to illustrate a number of factors affecting the outcome of punishment, since any one of them might be relevant to the differential effects of slapping and shock. Table 7-6 summarizes the factors possibly responsible for Kevin's sequence of behaviors.

Table 7-5   Some Parameters Affecting Punishment

Variable	Relationship
C^- Intensity	R suppression is a monotonic function of C^- intensity. As intensity increases, there ensues detection, temporary, partial, or finally complete suppression. Very intense C^- produces complete and durable suppression; mild C^- results in R recovery. R suppression can occur with levels of C^- too low to produce CER or avoidance.
C^- Delay	R suppression is less, the greater the delay of C^- following R.
C^- Frequency & Schedule	R suppression is greater, the greater the proportion of Rs followed by C^-. Intensity of C^- interacts with its frequency; weak C^- may be effective on a high schedule. R recovery after suppression is more rapid if C^- was on continuous schedule.
C^+ Schedule	Continuous C^+ and C^- schedules make C^- discriminative for C^+. Consummatory acts may be suppressed, or C^- may be ineffective, or may facilitate R, depending on C^- intensity. C^+ schedule used determines temporal pattern of R during punishment, e.g., C^- during FR, C^+ affects total rate but not terminal rate of R. Only ratio C^+ schedules consistently reduce C^+ under punishment.
C^+ Frequency	R suppression greater by C^-, the less frequent is C^+. C^- during extinction reduces R faster than extinction alone.
Motivation	R suppression is less if motivation to R is increased.
R alternatives	When alternative R receives C^+, suppression of R is greater. When escape to unpunished use of R is possible, R suppression is greater even at low intensities of C^- which usually are ineffective.
Nature of R	C^- for negative instrumental R (escape-avoidance) restores training conditions and thus, at least initially, facilitates R. If C^- same in punishment and avoidance training, extinction of avoidance is delayed.

Table 7-6   Possible Reasons for Ineffective Aversive Stimuli:
The Case of Kevin (Bucher and Lovaas, 1968)

Nature of R	R was "negativism": covering ears and leaving chair. R could easily be escape behaviors, hence initially facilitated by C⁻.
Nature of C⁻	If R was an escape-avoidance act, and the yell-slap C⁻ was similar to those under which R was acquired, facilitation would result. The shock C⁻, very dissimilar to escape acquisition, would suppress R.
Nature of R	If R was instinctive response to aversive stimuli, C⁻ might increase and then fixate it.
Previous exposure to C⁻	Adaptation to C⁻ may have occurred, especially if intensity was gradually increased and presentation was not sudden. Previous pairing of C⁻ with ensuing C⁺ may have made it a positive discriminative stimulus.

In the context of the present discussion, it seems plausible to hypothesize that Kevin's negativistic behaviors were escape-avoidance responses previously reinforced by termination of yells and slaps from adults. The topography of the behaviors and the frequency with which adults favor these aversive stimuli over others would seem to make this a reasonable assumption. The effect of using the same aversive events to punish the escape-avoidance behaviors would be, at least initially, to increase them, as indeed happened. Since this facilitative function gradually fades and the avoidance response is suppressed, the effectiveness of the shock may have been due in part to its timing. However, when the punishing aversive stimulus differs from that in effect during escape-avoidance acquisition, suppression of the response is much more rapid (Carlsmith, 1961)—a more probable explanation of the effectiveness of electric shock.

Another aspect of the nature of the response that may influence effectiveness of punishment has to do with instrumental versus consummatory or instinctive behaviors. Solomon (1964) hypothesizes that behavioral fixations and inhibitions and other phenomena of "experimental neurosis" (see, for example, Masserman and Pechtel, 1953) result when instinctive or consummatory responses are punished. Lichtenstein (1950), for example, produced long-lasting eating inhibitions by punishing the act of eating, and Masserman's (1943) "neurotic" cats were similarly punished in the act of eating. Noncontingent aversive stimulation associated with an instrumental act, when it is not signaled, can produce similar results, however. Klee (1944), for example, found that rats may starve to death rather than jump from a Lashley apparatus when half of the trials were punished, half rewarded by food, and the discrimination problem was insoluble. Solomon suggests two major parameters that may enhance the effects of punishment associated with consummatory behaviors. The availability of behavioral alternatives culminating in a consummatory response and a high degree of discriminative control over onset of punishment can increase punishment effects. Solomon speculates that because of the intimate association of drive incentive with punishment when consummatory responses are punished, it may be that drive stimuli or incentives become conditioned stimuli for conditioned emotional reactions. In the case of Kevin, had his negativism been an instinctive act in response to noxious stimuli, punishment might be expected to fixate it. The topography of the behavior and its susceptibility to shock punishment indicates this was probably not the case.

In general, the availability of a discriminative stimulus (S^D) prior to punishment of a consummatory response leads to avoidance behaviors, while the lack of an S^D leads to disorganized responses. In clinical cases, the latter situation, paradoxically, may be more easily treated, since any newly established avoidance response can be paired with an S^D on the basis of deliberate selection. When an avoidance response is already well established, as in the case of the starving rats, its haphazard development can fixate a response that has serious long-range consequences, even though it avoids the aversive event. It is on the basis of this consideration that care must be taken, when using punishment, to provide avoidance responses that are socially desirable, or to offer alternatives for the consummatory behavior.

Prior Experience with the Aversive Event

Previous exposure to the punishing stimulus may increase the individual's later resistance to disruption by it (see, for example, Miller, 1960). Gradual presentation or use of gradually increasing intensities, are likely to enhance this adaptation or resistance, although the use of the procedure of gradually increasing intensities is often intended to counteract any adaptation effects. Since slaps and loud "no's" are frequent punishers used by adults, adaptation to prolonged, low intensity use of these in the past is another potential explanation for Kevin's lack of response to them.

Past exposure to the punishing event can drastically alter its effects if its onset has customarily preceded positive reinforcement. Shock delivered while an animal eats leads to severe behavioral disruption, but shock *prior* to eating can act as an S^D and actually decrease response latency (see, for example, Holz and Azrin, 1962). Thus the discriminative properties of punishment may often be sufficient to explain its effects, without appeal to its aversive properties. It seems likely that parents often fall into the trap of making punishments discriminative stimuli for positive reinforcement. For example, when a parent yells or slaps a child at first, then presents a fascinating new toy to distract him, or hugs and kisses him to make amends, he is using punishment as a signal of a reward. If Kevin had had such a history, punishment would at first *increase* the frequency of the undesirable responses, as Kevin worked harder to produce a reward. Only after repeated trials without positive reinforcement would this effect gradually extinguish. On the other hand, since a prior history with shock is quite unlikely, it would act immediately to suppress Kevin's punished acts.

The discriminative properties of punishment are important in another way, less applicable to Kevin's particular circumstance. An aversive event is a signal that the punishment contingency is in effect. Fixed ratio and temporal schedules quickly permit discrimination of punishment periods. Similarly, when punishment is paired with extinction, it serves as an S^Δ, signaling that positive reinforcement is not forthcoming. In both of these instances, delivery of a punishment may rapidly suppress responding because of its discriminative properties. Omission of punishment will be followed by a rapid return to a high rate of responding. Data demonstrating these "pseudopunishment" or discriminative effects of aversive stimuli (Holz and Azrin, 1962) have clear relevance to clinical application. They are also important theoretically since they delineate the conditions under which punishment appears not to weaken a response, since the response returns at high strength as soon as punishment is omitted. In these cases, simple discrimination learning is the better process model.

Positive Reinforcement and Competing Responses

We have already mentioned that the concurrent schedule of positive reinforcement maintaining a behavior will interact with the punishment schedule for the same response to produce a variety of patterns of response rate, even when the overall rate of responding is suppressed (Azrin and Holz, 1966). Also, it was pointed out that availability of alternative responses that procure positive reinforcement without punishment enhances response suppression in the punishment situation.

In practical settings use of punishment is complicated most by the opportunity for many escape or avoidance responses that terminate the aversive stimulus by their effect on the punisher. A child who can think of a bright remark during punishment often is well rewarded for this escape response and the intended disciplinary effect is subverted. Or the use of whining, promising, or pleading may be sufficiently aversive to a parent to serve as choice escape-from-punishment behaviors. Finally, "escape" into fantasy, covert verbal behavior, or other escape behaviors over which the parent has no control can serve to reduce the intended suppressive effects of punishment.

Punishment suppresses old behaviors whereas positive reinforcement strengthens new ones. By breaking up an old behavior pattern, punishment can provide the occasion for the positive reinforcement of new operants that are of greater value to the person. The combination of positive reinforcement with punishment appears most effective. When punishment alone was compared with other methods for eliminating behavior, and maximally effective parameters were used for each method, punishment proved to be more complete and irreversible than extinction, satiation, stimulus change, and restraint, and just as rapid and enduring (Holz, Azrin, and Ayllon, 1963; Azrin and Holz, 1966).

A final feature of punishment in behavior modification is the relationship between punisher and punished. Punishment is often simply the aggressive response of one person toward another, and is often determined more by the emotional state of the punisher than the immediately preceding behavior of the punished. The recipient of punishment, in turn, can often reciprocate by aggression or delivery of aversive stimulation toward the punisher. Studies with children in the family setting (Patterson and Reid, 1970) have suggested that such mutually coercive relationships often are maintained by the effects of relative control (and noxiousness) that each partner can exert on the other. The ultimately undesirable aspects of such means of relating to another person are clear to the clinician, but these patterns are easily established and difficult to break in social settings that tolerate or even encourage use of such psychological (or physical) power in social contacts. In fact, the habitual pattern of dealing with people by subtle aversive control has been considered characteristic of passive-aggressive personalties and other neurotic patients.

Special Punishment Paradigms: Time-Out and Response Cost

We have discussed three possible contingencies thus far: presentation of a positive or a negative reinforcer, and removal of a negative reinforcer. The fourth possible contingency, removal of a positive reinforcer, has been termed *time-out* by Ferster, who has investigated it at some length (Ferster, 1957, 1958a). As Verhave (1962) has pointed out, since presentation of a reinforcer is very brief in temporal duration, removal of positive reinforcement mainly involves removal of stimuli associated with its presence, that is, of conditioned positive reinforcers. Usually, a time-out period, when the organism can no longer obtain any positive reinforcement contingent on his responding, is signaled by a time-out (TO) discriminative stimulus. In daily life, the departure of a lover after a quarrel, the "cooling-off" period for children overly excited in a game, the interruption in mother's storytelling for a misbehaving child, the refusal to serve a boisterous drunk at a bar, are among the many examples of time-out. In these situations, the contingent withholding of positive reinforcement, often preceded by threats (S^D), is used to put the behavior under control of the rewarding agent.

Ferster (1958a) demonstrated that signaled time-out has many of the properties of conventional aversive events for the ongoing response. A number of other studies employing time-out procedures support the general conclusion that it acts as an aversive event. Leitenberg (1965), in reviewing this research, points out that "the most convincing evidence that TO is aversive comes from those studies demonstrating escape from stimuli which previously set the occasion for nonreinforcement" (p. 439). Leitenberg notes also that time-out at times produces different effects than electric shock in a punishment paradigm and that shock is a more effective suppressor.

The time-out procedure in humans permits the occurrence of avoidance or escape responses, when used in a punishment design. For example, a child who is sent to his room for his misbehavior during a party can indulge in fantasy or other substitutive behavior that reduces the aversive consequences of the procedure. Similar to the case of punishment, the effects of the control procedure are weakened when other positive reinforcement is available. The similarity to punishment also holds with regard to the relationship of the magnitude of "lost" reward and the effectiveness of the technique. That is, the overall frequency or magnitude of positive reinforcement under a particular schedule for correct responding will influence the effectiveness of time-out in suppressing incorrect responses (Ferster and Appel, 1961; Baron, Kaufman and Rakauskas, 1967). The time-out procedure differs from extinction in that the former is contingent on *undesirable* responses, while the latter follows previously reinforced behavior. Yet, both techniques suppress responding at least temporarily.

In practical situations, the time-out procedure also has the advantage of interrupting an interaction that has explosive potentials for escalation. The dispenser as well as the recipient of reinforcers can use the time-out interval to consider his own behavior, to review alternate strategy, and to calm down. Since a child's aversive behavior has its effects on the teacher, for example, imposition of a time-out interval can prevent her from overreacting emotionally to the child. In many instances of clinical application punishment is also impractical or inadvisable. Extinction may not be possible because a patient's disruptive behavior is often dependent on reinforcers that are hard to identify or impossible to control. The time-out procedure offers a convenient alternate technique.

Time-out procedures are frequently used as mild punishment to eliminate disruptive behaviors. Their use presupposes that the person is under relatively high reward conditions, since the termination of positive reinforcement must have aversive impact and must be readily discriminable. The husband who threatens to leave home unless his wife stops nagging him will have little effect on these behaviors, if she is eagerly looking forward to being rid of him. Nor will a child stop yelling under threat of time-out if class attendance is aversive to him and time-out promises to bring some relief. In fact, under conditions of low positive or high aversive reinforcement, the contingent time-out procedure for the disturbing response serves as a relief-stimulus, strengthening the noxious response according to the escape paradigm. Thus, the reluctant child learns that destructive behavior in an unpleasant situation can lead to escape into time-out; the apparent ineffectiveness of this procedure is often due to its inept utilization.

A frequent suggestion to parents for handling behavior problems of a child in the home is the use of physical isolation, equivalent to time-out contingent upon undesirable behaviors. This procedure, however, is likely to involve more features of behavior control than just time-out. Isolation, for example, being confined alone in a room for a specified period, may in itself be aversive aside from its properties as time-out. (This assumes, as the time-out procedure must, of course, that the room is not full of alternative attractive reinforcement opportunities, such as a color TV set or telephone.) Time-out removes positive reinforcement for the undesired behavior (for example, attention from parents or siblings) and reduces the total amount of positive reinforcement for all responding. And finally, since release from time-out (from the room) is usually made contingent upon both lapse of time and cessation of the target response, release may positively reinforce behaviors competitive with the target behavior. In application of time-out, as with other techniques, it is difficult to distinguish the sole effective variable that may be producing therapeutic changes.

Similarly, when time-out fails to suppress the target behavior, it may be difficult to be certain of the reasons for the failure. For example, Risley (1968b) reports inability to suppress an autistic child's dangerous climbing behaviors by use of a time-out procedure in the laboratory and at home. But electric shock as a punishment rapidly eliminated the behavior in the laboratory. Later, time-out was supplemented in the home by shock, and was partially successful in controlling climbing there. However, time-out was effective in reducing less disruptive behaviors, such as emptying cupboards of their contents or getting into the refrigerator.

It may be that the child was receiving little reinforcement at the times when she was climbing, so that little more than pleasure intrinsic in the climbing itself was lost during time-out. Since deprivation of attention for climbing and reinforcement for incompatible behaviors also had no effect on climbing, it is probable that social reinforcement was not maintaining this behavior and that the intrinsic reinforcing value of climbing outweighed other competitive reinforcers offered her.

In a survey of reports on experiments and clinical reports of time-out, Patterson and White (1969) believe that the following conclusions about the use of this technique are warranted:

"(1) In a variety of situations, especially the classroom, TO has been more efficient and effective than what might be termed "passive ignoring." (2) Although TO of long duration has been used . . . short periods have the added advantage of allowing for an increase in the time available for positive reinforcement of acts representative of social skills. (3) Size of TO rooms needn't be restricted to cramped quarters. Studies reporting effective use of TO have used rooms about the size of a small bedroom. (4) Maintaining supervision of TO while in use is desirable. It is necessary in studies where the child is to be returned to class immediately following cessation of tantrum behavior. . . . In addition, several investigators subscribe to the notion that high amplitude destructive or verbal behavior in TO should be mildly punished by telling the child that, "That cost you two more minutes. Every time you kick the door, it is two more minutes." There are however, no data which demonstrate the outcome of this procedure. (5) TO procedures avoid some of the problems associated with the use of direct physically painful punishment. . . . For example, use of TO, contrasted with physically aggressive punishment methods, does not provide the child with an aggressive model for imitation. . . . That is, 'no models displaying methods of counter aggression which could be used against parents, teachers, or peers" (p. 3).

Response cost is a related conditioned punishment whereby a reinforcing stimulus is removed from the environment following a response (Weiner, 1962). Weiner established points on a counter as conditioned reinforcers. When he then subtracted one point after each response, making the response cost one point, responding was immediately and often almost completely suppressed. The effect was greater than typically obtained with time-out, and did not require as much attention to discriminative stimuli since the removal of the point is a distinct cue in itself. Response cost, then, apparently functions as an aversive event similar to shock, but probably usually requires a conditioned reinforcer (since removing primary reinforcers seems implausible). Response cost procedures are readily used in token economies, just as they are in real monetary economies. In one study using Veterans' Administration (VA) hospital patients, response cost was applied directly to money rather than to tokens, since the hospital staff could control patient access to their VA allotments, upon which patients depended for cigarettes, papers, and beverages. Harmatz and Lapuc (1968) placed obese male patients on an 1800-calorie diet and weighed each man weekly. Those who failed to lose weight over the week forfeited a proportion of their allotments. The experimental group did not differ immediately in post-treatment in weight loss from men in group therapy, or in diet-only control groups. However, the experimental subjects continued to lose weight during a one-month follow-up period whereas the controls regained the weight they lost. Similar clinical case reports aimed at reducing smoking by requiring that the patient tear up a one dollar bill prior to each cigarette taken, indicate practical use and some success with response cost manipulations.

An ingenious use of response cost has been described by Nathan and his colleagues (Nathan, Andberg, and Patch, undated) in treatment of stuttering. A young woman patient was allowed to communicate to her therapist only through a two-way audio-video system, termed TRACCOM by Nathan, for Televised Reciprocal Analysis of Conjugate Communication. The patient had to press a switch at a given rate to maintain optimal visual clarity and volume of the picture; light signals indicated "free" periods when pressing was not required, and when there would be a period of no image or sound, regardless of switchpressing. The S^{Δ} signal and loss of TRACCOM communication was then made contingent upon stuttering during the patient's talking with her therapist. A progressive ratio schedule was used, with fewer stutters per response cost as the rate of stuttering decreased. The S^{D} signal and a "free" period of communication followed stutter-free utterances. The patient dropped to one-fourth of base line rate of stuttering and more than doubled her stutter-free speech; gains were maintained at a six-month follow-up both within and outside the therapeutic setting.

The term *response cost* has also been used in another context of behavioral control. In training a response in the laboratory animal, the amount of effort or number of responses for one unit of reinforcement is gradually increased. A pigeon, for example, may begin under a fixed ratio schedule, which offers one grain of food for three keypecks. The ratio gradually increases to five pecks, then to 10, 25, 50, or even 100. At some point, either when the step increase is too large or the effort is too great, the animal's performance weakens and eventually he may stop working altogether (Ferster and Skinner, 1957). In technical language, the decrease in performance under those conditions is called *strain*

(Ferster and Perrott, 1968). In addition to its importance as a disturbing feature in a behavior modification program with low payoff ratios, this phenomenon also has its practical utility for reduction of a response. A literal example of increase in response cost to reduce an undesirable response is the raising of parking meter fees per time unit to control downtown congestion, or the addition of prerequisites for admission to a popular course. With compulsive patients, the authors have used this technique by gradually adding small required steps prior to execution of a compulsive act until the cost of executing the ritual, for example, skin picking or excessive eating, reached the point of strain and the behavior decreased. The use of increased response cost to *maintain* a behavior, however, is common in all training programs due to its economy and effectiveness. Thus, praising a child is gradually less frequent as he improves in his behavior, token cultures reduce the value of each token as the patient improves, and lesser bonus incentives are offered when a worker has reached a maximum rate of work. The aversive potential of increased response cost thus is dependent on the past history of reinforcement for the behavior and the capacity of the organism with regard to the cost. It lies somewhat beyond the point at which maximum behavior can be maintained for the lowest payoff.

PROBLEMS IN USE OF AVERSIVE CONTROL

The long neglect of punishment, clinically and experimentally, was in large part due to a number of undesirable or harmful effects that were supposed to accompany aversive control, limiting its utility. More recent laboratory and clinical investigations have laid many of these fears to rest, or at least diminished them greatly.

One remaining problematic issue is the degree to which punishment-produced response suppression will generalize. When punishment is associated with one set of stimuli but not with another, in a fairly consistent fashion, suppression may be generalized initially but the responses soon recover in the presence of the set of "safe" stimuli (see, for example, Azrin, 1956). Indeed, a contrast effect may boost responding in the safe context above what it had been before treatment (Brethower and Reynolds, 1962). Birnbrauer (1968) provides a clinical illustration of the effects of punishment being so highly discriminated as to thwart therapeutic goals. An adolescent retardate had to be kept in restraints constantly because of his biting and other destructive acts. In laboratory sessions intense shock was contingent upon destructive acts, and the specific target behaviors were quickly eliminated. However, verbal warnings, paired with shock in an effort to make them conditioned aversive stimuli, were effective only when spoken by the person who had actually administered shock. Concurrent attempts to reduce another destructive act (napkin-tearing during meals) by reinforcing competing responses and time-out contingent upon the target behavior had no effect. Only when shock was administered for this specific response was it also suppressed. Ward attendants then began administering shock for destructive acts and positive reinforcement for prosocial acts, and for five months the boy's destructive behaviors were infrequent while sociability increased. However, verbal threats never became effective as punishment, and suppression remained specific to response and situation. Moreover, the behavioral offenses thereafter returned to their prepunishment levels.

Birnbrauer concluded that application of punishment requires safeguards "against the formation of discriminations—between responses, between a response at one time from the same response at other times, between situations, and between people" (p. 209). The effects of shock punishment had initially been rapid and powerful, leading Birnbrauer to advocate complete and prolonged suppression of a response as early as possible in order to take full advantage of the effects of shock at the outset, especially since later reinstitution of shock could not produce suppression as it had earlier. Two other variables were proposed for special attention: the timing of punishment, and the availability of an alternative response. The patient reacted to verbal warnings only when they were given while the response was in progress, supporting the conclusion of others (see, for example, Aronfreed and Reber, 1965) that punishment timed to coincide with response onset is the most effective procedure with normal children. Shock also appeared to be an effective suppressor when an alternative specific response was available, suggesting that provision of alternatives must be programmed into any punishment therapy.

Among others, Risley (1968b), Bucher and Lovaas (1968), and Wolf, Mees and Risley (1964) assert the importance of guarding against antitherapeutic discriminations. Application of the aversive event in a range of naturalistic settings, by a variety of persons, for a variety of examples of the target response class, and rapid and complete suppression of the naturally occurring behaviors are suggested as safeguards.

In addition to the problems of generalizing the effects of punishment, other characteristic problems must be noted. Deliberate use of aversive control in behavior modification runs the common risks of the patient modeling the therapist's behavior. If the administration of punishment is viewed as the behavior of the therapist model, imitation learning of aggressive behavior would be expected, both in self-control and in the patient's handling of his interpersonal relationships. The delivery of aversive stimulation has also been postulated as one of the antecedents of aggression (Buss, 1961; Ulrich and Azrin, 1962). Although several clinical reports have indicated awareness of the possible aggression toward the therapist in aversive conditioning, these behaviors are not widely reported with adult patients. At the extreme, the use of aversive agents in therapy might even be expected to result in additional neurotic symptoms, if one accepts the conflict-anxiety-avoidance model about the formation of neurotic symptoms. In actual practice, safeguards that include the careful planning of their use and constant monitoring of behavior changes suffice to minimize the side effects of aversive control techniques.

Many investigators who have used aversive control have reported deliberate efforts to assess other areas of behavior as well as the target response. For example, Risley (1968b) monitored a number of other behaviors while punishing climbing by shock, and autistic rocking by shouting and shaking, in a six-year-old girl. Punishment was applied in the laboratory and at home, both by the investigator and by the mother. In both cases, the target behaviors were rapidly eliminated. Initially, the laboratory and the experimenter were discriminative jointly but not separately for response suppression, until this stimulus control was deliberately counteracted.

Among the side effects noted were increases in similar behaviors (for example, climbing on a chair) when the target acts were suppressed (for example, climbing a book case). However, when this response was also punished, no other substitute appeared. No general avoidance of the situations or of punishing agents was found. Instead, avoidance responses were highly specific. For the most part they were intentionally reinforced, for example, sitting in a chair. No other behaviors were suppressed, nor did any aggressive behaviors occur. When a previously acquired aggressive behavior (attacking brother) was punished, no pain-elicited or substitute aggression was found. Despite the stimulus control exerted by the investigator over response rate, the girl increased her eye contact with him after punishment began, thereby enhancing other training activities, and otherwise behaved no differently with him. Risley concludes:

"The most significant side effect was the fact that eliminating climbing and autistic rocking with punishment facilitated the acquisition of new desirable behaviors. . . . Some deviant behaviors, maintained by unknown variables, interfered with the establishment of new behaviors. This interference was not primarily due to a physical incompatibility between the behaviors. This interference, which might be termed "functional incompatibility," suggests that the elimination of such deviant behaviors may be a necessary prerequisite to the establishment of new behaviors" (pp. 25–26).

Bucher and Lovaas (1968) report similar results for their clinical use of punishment. After self-destructive behaviors were suppressed by shock and generalization was promoted by use of several punishing agents in several environments, their autistic boy exhibited less avoiding of adults and less crying. Freed from previously necessary physical restraints, he also rapidly developed many desirable behaviors. Comparable "positive side effects" were noted in other children.

In summary, despite the theoretical and animal experimentation bases for fearing harmful side effects of punishment, the evidence from clinical studies is preponderantly on the other side. Positive rather than negative side effects seem to be the typical result of punishment of specific disruptive behaviors. It remains to be seen to what extent desirable and undesirable side effects depend on such variables as the ratio of positive reinforcement to punishment, the nature of the response and its role in the patient's total behavioral ecology, and the frequency and nature of the aversive stimulation. While clinicians will undoubtedly continue to approach the use of punishment with humane circumspection, the therapeutic utility of punishment can no longer be neglected nor can the parameters governing its effects in patient populations remain unexplored.

SUMMARY

Until recently, the role of aversive stimulation in behavior control has been relatively neglected in research and clinical application because of misgivings about possible undesirable side effects. Now, however, many of the variables that influence the outcomes of aversive control can be defined and some guidelines for its effective application can be specified. The procedures entailed in the several major paradigms of aversive stimulation can be specified as well, but in actual practice laboratory and clinical applications of aversive stimulation usually involve elements of several paradigms that cannot be separated empirically or theoretically. For example, punishment procedures often entail classical conditioning to the aversive stimuli as well, and theoretical explanations of punishment often appeal to the avoidance paradigm as the basic underlying mechanism. The clinician, by his awareness of the overlapping of models in actual practice, can both check out his basic procedure against guidelines for its maximal effectiveness and also use the other operations that are inherent in his tactics to enhance therapeutic effectiveness. For instance, in applying punishment, he may use what is known about punishment to insure that he is maximizing its effect and also make deliberate use of the classical conditioning component by adding an aversion relief element to his procedure.

The chief models of aversive control are: (1) contingent removal of positive reinforcement (time-out, response cost); (2) contingent application of aversive stimuli (punishment); (3) contingent removal of aversive stimuli (escape and avoidance); and (4) classical aversive conditioning of neutral or positive stimuli by pairing them with aversive events. Other manipulations considered in this chapter include extinction as an aversive event and the effects of noncontingent aversive stimulation.

Because of their importance as modification tools, as topics for theoretical inquiry, and as presumed factors in the origin of problematic behaviors, particular attention has been given to escape and avoidance training, and punishment. Escape and avoidance behaviors are contingently reinforced by removal (escape) or omission (avoidance) of aversive stimuli. Escape and avoidance training build new behaviors, affecting old behaviors only by competing with them. Punishment deals specifically with suppression of an old behavior and does not in itself determine what new behaviors occur to replace the punished response. Animal work suggests that effective escape-avoidance training is dependent on such factors as ease of discrimination of the aversive situation, prior history with the particular aversive stimuli and with escape and avoidance procedures in general, stimulus intensity, the extent to which the desired behaviors are "reflexive" reactions to fear, and the presence of undesired alternative responses that successfully escape or avoid the aversive event.

Punishment, the contingent application of aversive stimuli, can rapidly and efficiently suppress an undesired response. Among the parameters that influence the effectiveness and durability of punishment are the stimulus intensity and contingency schedule, the immediacy and frequency of punishment, the possibility of undesired escape responses, the absence of positive reinforcement as a predictable sequel to punishment, and simultaneous development of alternative desirable behaviors which produce positive reinforcement. As in the case of escape and avoidance, punishment can produce paradoxical results unless these and related factors are taken into account. Available evidence does not support earlier suspicions that punishment and other operations with aversive stimuli need have harmful side effects, when the procedures are properly constructed and applied to suit the individual circumstances.

Part IV

Verbal Mediation and Self-Regulation

CHAPTER 8

Verbal Behavior and the Interview

In previous chapters we have studied the principles and methods by which behavior modification can be applied to clinical problems through systematic control of the patient's environmental stimulation or the social consequences of his behavior. Under those conditions, the crucial elements of the behavioral equation are directly accessible to observation and manipulation by the therapist. In the treatment procedure that is modeled after the classical conditioning paradigm, the S components in the equation consist of external environmental stimuli; their rearrangement is the gist of therapy. When the response is a clearly defined symptomatic (deviant) verbal or motor act, isolated by the therapist for its importance in the patient's interaction with his social and physical environment, the environmental consequences of the target behavior, either manipulatable rewards or aversive stimuli, are varied for therapeutic purposes. The therapeutic methods parallel operant conditioning procedures in the laboratory. But in many cases, verbal and thought behaviors, interposed between stimulus identification and action, represent the problematic behavioral process. The attack on these disturbances is difficult to accomplish by direct conditioning procedures.

In dealing with human behavior, the engineering of fully controlled environments for individuals encounters many obstacles. Not only are there strong social injunctions against rigorous control of individual behavior but there are also characteristic limitations to any such attempts due to man's unique capacity to create his own subjective environment. The result of this special property of human behavior is man's greater independence from his physical environment than is true of any other species and his capacity for regulating his behavior on the basis of these private processes.

A study of Findley, Migler, and Brady (1963) yields an interesting illustration of the role of these private events even when nearly total control of the external environment could be obtained for experimental purposes. A volunteer subject was housed in a totally controlled environment, simulating the isolation one might encounter in a one-man space chamber. For 152 days the volunteer lived under conditions in which all of his daily activities were strictly programmed. For example, use of toilet facilities, presentation of foods, access to a bed for sleeping, and availability of recorded music, art supplies, and reading material were controlled by the experimenter. The subject's motor behavior could be measured with regard to frequency and duration, and accessibility of items could be controlled by making materials available only after the subject had gone through a specified series of activities.

Although the subject's performance indicated that it is possible for a human being to maintain himself and his physical health in a tightly programmed environment, the experiment showed the development of increasing behavioral stress after approximately ninety days. The subject tended to sleep for briefer periods and more frequently, he spent increasing time in toilet activities, and there was a decline in the time spent in intellectual and creative activities. In the later stages of the experiment the record of the subject's comments, made over an intercom, showed an increase in frequency of negative statements. This rigorously controlled experiment leads to essentially the same conclusions as the reports by men whose dependency on programmed and usually severely reduced environmental stimulation was created by such cultural conditions as incarceration or accidental isolation. The isolation experiment suggests that good nutrition, adequate environmental stimulation, opportunity for physical activity and availability of physical comforts are not sufficient to maintain efficient psychological functioning. Whether the lack of contact with other human beings, the space confinement, or the imposition of a rigorously programmed and automated provision of "the worldly goods" represents the major variable in disruption of normal behavior patterns is uncertain, but the outcome of the isolation experiment certainly suggests that total environmental control is not easily accepted, even when physical needs are fully met.

In sensory deprivation experiments all external stimulation is severely reduced during periods varying from several hours up to several days. Subjects in these studies report efforts toward self-stimulation by reciting nonsensical lyrics, engaging in mental "games" and otherwise providing themselves with a verbal stimulus-environment that maintains some activity. The interposition of a verbal-subjective stage between behavioral input and output is all too evident in many studies on complex psychological functions. The subject's interpretations of the physical input, his past experiences, his attitudes toward the experiment, and his expectations about the experimenter's demands turn up as important independent variables over which the experimenter has little control. Although unwanted in the studies that emphasize the input-output relationships in behavior (because of the methodological problems they present and their great individual variations), these private experiences constitute the core of what is often regarded as the source of man's most magnificent experiences. A behavioral viewpoint cannot disregard the importance of these subjective experiences and their influence in modifying the role of the physical environment.

The distinction between the achievement of behavioral change by an externally controlled program and by self-initiated changes parallels a major distinction made by many writers in contrasting behavior therapy methods and traditional psychodynamic approaches. The primary distinction lies in the conceptualization of the integrative mechanisms by which a person utilizes his past and present experiences in the determination of his action. Psychological theories range along a continuum from one extreme at which all human behavior is viewed as learned by simple association of stimulus and response links, much in the tradition of Locke's tabula rasa hypothesis, to the other extreme at which phenomenological theory and existentialism endow the human organism with inherent powers of self-determination and control almost independent of environmental influences. The locus of the position taken along this dimension determines a crucial frame of reference for a psychological worker. It has far-reaching implications for his theoretical assumptions as well as his interest and approach to experimental and clinical problems.

For expository purposes we have separated several facets of these issues that are of importance in clinical research and practice. In this chapter we summarize some research on verbal behavior that has implications for clinical practice. The use of verbal methods of behavior control underlies most traditional dynamic psychotherapies and all procedures that use interview methods. In the following chapter we deal with examples of somewhat more restricted areas of research and clinical application, associated with the problem of an individual's interaction with himself. The understanding of man's capacity to regulate his own behavior, to initiate, reward, and criticize his own actions, and to bring about therapeutic changes through self-control and self-programming is an intriguing and challenging problem for which only a thin theoretical basis has been constructed to date. Yet these capacities are constantly used in clinical treatment and sometimes it is their deficiencies that are the target of therapy.

THE INTERNAL ENVIRONMENT

In any living organism, biological processes create a continuous bombardment of stimulation within the skin of the organism at all levels of integration from the simple cell to complex organ systems. Commonly, the healthy person will not focus on these internal cues unless they change in quality and intensity. Among clinical patients, subjective complaints frequently do include descriptions of such somatic events. Since localization of such stimuli is often very difficult to pinpoint, vague complaints about pain, discomfort, or unusual sensations make up the majority of such complaints in neurotic patients. Our discussion of the internal environment, however, will not deal with these physiological and biological processes, which may be components of neurotic symptoms, but with psychological behaviors. Many of these are private behaviors, composed of verbal and motor responses, are equally difficult to assess. Our emphasis on processes by which the person can create an internal psychological environment without any external support for long periods of time does not underestimate the importance of biological processes correlated with such experiences. Prolonged sensory deprivation, for example, has been shown to result in changed sensory and physiological function as well as psychological disorganization. However, it is an arbitrary restriction upon the subject matter of this book to deal with learning processes at the level of psychological behavior only.

The most significant area of research required for an understanding of interpersonal clinical interactions lies in the realm of thinking, problem-solving, imagining, dreaming, fantasizing, speaking, and similar activities. It is inconceivable to construct a psychology of human behavior without accounting for these processes. Yet, most of the time devoted to analysis of these complex behaviors has been spent on argumentation, speculation, and theorizing. In fact, a half century of psychological research has contributed very little toward establishing a workable model of thought processes. Recent work in the area of thinking has provided several models that treat these behaviors as computer analogies (see, for example, Miller, Galanter, and Pribram, 1960; Reitman, 1965; and others). These authors focus attention on the characteristics of the thinking *process* rather than its contents. They consider language and thinking as relatively independent psychological activities, in the sense that the former serves to fill in the raw material with which the latter operates. Rules for thinking processes may thus turn out to be generally applicable to different verbal behaviors and may yield some understanding of the inferred processes by which perceptual and sensory cues are transformed and organized in the service of problem solving, planning, and verbal output.

These approaches are relatively new, however. In 1960 Hebb, in his presidential address to the American Psychological Association entitled *The American Revolution* (1960), sounded a strong plea for psychologists to progress to the second phase of the American revolution, the application to the study of thought of the same serious systematic experimental analysis that had been successful in studying learning phenomena. The analysis of thought should have a direct bearing on a better understanding of individual experiences and processes generally characterized under the term "the self." It should also yield evidence about psychological events that undoubtedly influence human affairs but that are not directly observable. Hebb's challenge includes one further point that sets him apart from the many other writers who have also proposed that the study of the subjective domain represents the core problem of psychology. Despite the methodological problems in the exploration of covert behaviors, Hebb insists on maintenance of the same experimental rigor and the same criteria for replicability, verifiability, and public accessibility of both the methods and results in the study of these complex processes.

In our description of the behavioral equation we have pointed out that the locus of the various elements in the equation is not confined to the external environment. Both stimulus and response components can occur in that part of the total psychological space that is considered *private* because it is not shared with anyone else. The special properties of such private behaviors carry both advantages and disadvantages in social functions. For example, an individual can respond to such cues as a toothache, sexual arousal, or the memory of a funny incident. The information about such events as potential determinants of the person's behavior is usually not available to an observer. Consequently, a man is often able to relate his own actions to antecedent conditions more accurately than an observer. On the other hand, the development of verbal labels for events in the internal environment occurs mainly in childhood when an adult helps the child to discriminate among such stimuli on the basis of the child's observation of well-known correlated external events. For example, the child learns to describe his emotions on the basis of correspondences between stimulus events and his own total response. He learns to localize sources of pain and to describe his moods, his likes, his hates, and his personality characteristics on the basis of information provided initially by others.

As a result of the intermittent nature of opportunities for corrective social action during a person's development of his reactions about himself and of his observation of his internal events, the repertoire about such events is usually unreliable, and varies from one person to another. Despite all these problems there is no reason to assume, however, that private behaviors are essentially different from publicly observable behaviors, or that their relationships to each other and to external events follow special laws. On these grounds, Skinner (1953, 1963) has proposed that private events, including language behaviors, be treated within the framework of the same experimental analysis developed for animal behaviors and for overt human responses.

Mediational Models

Many authors have proposed models to account for private behaviors as intervening events. Osgood's *mediation hypothesis* (1953) presents this theoretical approach in a form most closely associated with a behavioral approach. The hypothesis is derived from Hull's learning theory and assumes a representational mediation process in higher mental activities which can be expanded to cover various phenomena of language behavior. Osgood bases this hypothesis on a distinction between stimulating events associated with the actual object or external event, and others that are associated with, but not totally dependent upon, the presence of the external event and can occur by themselves. The former represent the "object-tied" portion of the stimulus and the latter represent the "detachable" stimulus elements. Both classes of stimuli elicit some proportion of object-tied and detachable response patterns. The latter reactions constitute the representational processes and may occur when some symbol associated with the original stimulus object is presented. The mediational hypothesis thus attempts to explain the effect of such symbolic controlling stimuli as words, or partial recurrence of a stimulus event, or internal cues associated with stimulus objects, in eliciting responses that are similar to those originally conditioned to an object. The mediational process is also invoked to account for the development of meaning. For example, the sight of an insect elicits some fear response. The word "spider" is simultaneously heard or said. The "detachable" portions of the response to the live insect become conditioned to the word. This mediating reaction (r_m) produces a distinct stimulational pattern (s_m) that can elicit a series of behaviors. The substitution of the word for the original object and its capacity to evoke similar behavior defines the meaning of the word. A study by Staats, Staats, and Crawford (1962) illustrates supporting research. Subjects were instructed to learn a list of words and a shock or harsh sound always followed presentation of the word "large." The procedure conditioned a GSR response to the word "large" alone. Subjects also changed their original rating of the meaning of "large" toward greater unpleasantness, and the intensity of the unpleasantness rating was significantly related to the intensity of the conditioned GSR response.

The essential feature of mediation theory lies in its attempt to deal with internal events by assuming that some partial representation of the total reaction occurs either verbally, autonomically, or kinesthetically and that these partial representations possess essentially the same characteristics as the usual events (described as stimuli) and responses in overt behavior. Since the mediational processes may occur in the absence of external stimulation and without any observable response events associated with them, they provide a schematic description of the various linkages and arrangements that occur among verbal and kinesthetic cues and responses during the function of so-called higher mental processes. A number of studies on verbal behavior have shown the utility of the mediational hypothesis. But its reliance on associationistic S–R theory for the analysis of events into discrete stimulus and response elements and their bonding relationship has caused some to criticize it as too narrow and limited for the explanation of all language acquisition and thought processes (which include large and complex verbal patterns in the natural environment).

A slightly different form of the mediational model is presented by Dollard and Miller (1950). These authors conceptualize verbal responses as cue-producing responses. They assume that thinking can be described as a series of verbal responses, essentially similar to talking aloud. Verbal responses can facilitate discriminations by providing clear labels for event classes, and they can mediate the transfer of already learned responses when a new label is attached to an event. For instance, therapists often use labeling to promote a patient's discrimination of originally disturbing events from presently safe ones. Differential labeling of childhood and adult contexts of similar situations, for example, sexual or competitive, can facilitate the execution of well-practiced behaviors, once they are cued off by the new label. A further illustration is given by relabeling of an anxiety attack as a transitory and nonfatal somatic reaction. Upon onset of the attack, the patient's labeling of the event as a nuisance rather than as a threat to his life can help him to initiate appropriate behaviors reducing the duration of the attack. Verbal behavior also mediates rewards and enables a person to combine responses into new and adaptive original sequences. The mediational approach of Dollard and Miller essentially analyzes complex covert responses into chains of behaviors and then applies the learning theory model to describe the operation of these elements in unison.

Other writers in the behavioristic camp have similarly attempted to bridge the gap between observable and inferred internal processes by mediational constructs that assign the same properties to internal or "minimally observable" events as are assigned to external stimulus and response events. The crucial distinction between these theories and others lies in the assumption that no supplementary models of man's machinery for processing of information, integrating it, and acting upon it are introduced into their system. This approach has faith in the feasibility of eventually attacking the internal processes as behavioral events that can be observed (at least under special laboratory conditions) and related to other variables.

Psycholinguistic Models

Recently, a number of other conceptual approaches have been proposed by theorists who believe that the behavioral processes associated with language and thinking can best be understood by testing of complex models that are derived from an analysis of human language development. These latter systems place emphasis on man's apparent capacity to organize information not by simple additive and associative categories but in such a way that rules for behavior are extracted from specific instances and applied to novel situations. Recent research by a number of linguists has addressed itself to such difficult problems as the explanation of several well-substantiated facts about language acquisition that defy a simple associationistic interpretation. Language develops in a remarkably short time, it manifests a richness, flexibility, and creative character that would hardly be expected if speech were based only on reproduction of previously heard or associated strings of words. Cross-cultural studies on verbal and nonverbal communications further raise the puzzling problem of accounting for similarities in signals, interactional patterns, methods of proceeding from evidence to inference, and similar activities for which no easy environmentalistic interpretation is available. The capacity of a young child to order and to reproduce sentences that are grammatically correct in his language and to reject incorrect ones also remains a puzzling problem for behavioristic psychologists. Such language production cannot be explained by simple word learning, imitation, or generalization when new forms are generated by the child or new word arrangements are correctly judged.

In general, recent linguistic theories have given more weight than do behavioral theories to some inherent competence of the human organism to organize his perceptual and linguistic experiences in some predetermined way. Central attention is given to the rules of some structural biological mechanism equivalent to innate preprogrammed machinery that acts upon a perceptual and verbal input and orders it. A most influential proponent of this new linguistic approach is Chomsky (1965). He makes a distinction between *competence* and *performance* in verbal behavior. The former describes a person's knowledge of his language and the latter refers to his actual use of such knowledge in concrete situations. The basic regularities of a language can be analyzed by a system of rules. This system is called a *generative grammar*. It is not a model used deliberately by a speaker—it is the scientist's conceptualization to describe the person's intrinsic competence as a speaker or listener. Chomsky distinguishes between the surface structure of a sentence and its underlying base structure. Sentences of the form "John washed the car" and "The car was washed by John" share the same meaning, thus they are related to the same base structure. But it is by rules of transformation that both derive different surface structures, either as active or passive forms. One interesting feature of this approach is the suggestion that every human being possesses some innate linguistic competence. The extent of this capacity should be demonstrable by the discovery of universals (similarities in the rules of all human languages), which guide the development of language for children in different language environments. The conflict between S–R theories and those that take the view that humans are endowed with a biologically based capacity for complex language processing represents the modern sequel to the historical debate between nativistic and environmentalistic views concerning the relative contributions of experience and innate competence in the higher mental processes. Research in neurophysiology has added the exciting possibility that recently conceptualized biochemical and bioelectrical changes in the nervous system, correlated with the organization and storage of information, may also contribute to our understanding of changes involved in thinking on a much more molecular level than is attacked by behavioral scientists. This brief review of theoretical approaches to language reflects the dearth of facts and plethora of speculation in this area. As a consequence, a large portion of the clinician's behavior and of the behavior that he observes in his patients remains open to speculative instead of scientific analysis.

Verbal Therapy: The Interview

The nature of verbal processes and their relationship to observable social and motor acts is especially relevant to the interview, the major instrument in clinical assessment and treatment. The verbal interchange between a patient and a therapist constitutes the oldest and most widely used vehicle for psychotherapy. By persuasive, manipulative, or explanatory actions the therapist hopes to affect the patient's thoughts and speech. In turn the patient's new outlook is expected to ameliorate his defective behaviors. In preceding chapters and the following ones we discuss recent techniques for behavior modification that rest on the assumption that therapeutic intervention can be applied directly to the symptomatic behavior. The use of the interview differs by its indirect approach. For most complaints it is not the personal interaction in the therapist's office but some other behavior that is the target of therapy. Even during direct manipulation of environmental contingencies, or desensitization, or classical conditioning, the powerful influence of verbal control over behavior is evident, as we have seen in our discussion about the importance of instructions and attitudes in these methods. In the diagnostic stage of the clinical interaction, the interview is used widely as a convenient way of obtaining information and making observations about the patient's interaction patterns, regardless of the subsequently chosen treatment method. Finally, verbal behavior itself may be the target of the therapeutic enterprise when a patient's delusional speech, his attitudinal responses to his fellowmen, and similar verbal behaviors represent the core problem. Although it has been demonstrated convincingly that neither a patient's insight or verbalization, nor a full verbal description of his difficulties or the nature of the treatment are necessary for improvement, the patient's verbal interaction with the therapist and with members of his daily environment cannot be disregarded as sources of information and influences on treatment progress.

In Figure 8-1 the relationship between techniques using the interview as a therapeutic device and other behavior modification techniques is described. The figure illustrates the choices open to the therapist for changing behavior. It will be noted that only those methods that attack physiological responses or motor operants do not utilize language as a medium for behavior change. In most clinical cases, simultaneous intervention at several of the treatment loci described in Figure 8-1 are utilized. However, various treatment schema can be characterized by their emphasis on intervention at different points. For example, traditional psychoanalysis is primarily concerned with the relationship between R-0 and R-3, and only incidentally with the behaviors R-1 and R-5; the medium of therapy is mainly verbal. Insight therapy attempts to relate R-0 to R-1 and hence

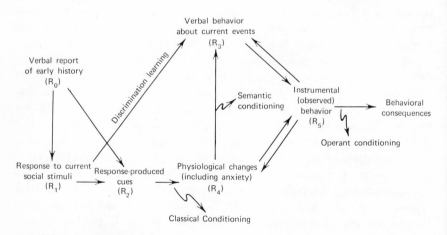

Figure 8-1   Locus of treatment (from Kanfer and Phillips, Archives of General Psychiatry, 1966, **15**, p. 116).

to R-3; realignment of verbal labels with different classes of events defines the verbal nature of this procedure. Wolpe's reciprocal inhibition technique concentrates mainly on R-1 and R-4. But even in this approach we have noted the use of the verbal medium when hierarchy items are imagined. Although interview therapy may utilize other techniques as well, its main focus is on changes in the type of behavior characterized in the figure as R-3, or on verbal instances of R-5.

Of all the clinical techniques, the interview is not only the most widely used but also the least understood. In the remainder of this chapter we will attempt to summarize some research relevant to the psychological variables known to affect the therapist-patient interaction and its product, the verbal behavior of the patient. We will examine only several representative questions about this interaction and the research related to these questions, since the interview has been given only a secondary role in the development of behavior therapy methods. A voluminous literature in clinical psychology and psychiatry has as its main goal the study of the numerous ways in which verbal therapy can be conducted. The work on verbal therapy techniques and on their effectiveness will not be discussed here. Instead we will consider several problems that are common to all interview methods. Our first question concerns the methodological problem in the treatment of the verbal report. We then examine the available literature on the relationship between verbal behavior and motor acts. The last section of this chapter is devoted to a review of some contributions from investigations on verbal conditioning and on interpersonal factors to the understanding of the diverse variables affecting interview behavior.

The nature of the verbal report. In experimental psychology the meaning of a person's self-report as an indicant of his actual experience has been of special interest for methodological reasons. Although sensory input can induce some behavior changes in the organism, the response to sensory stimulation and the subject's report about it must be carefully distinguished. For example, a subject's report in a perception experiment about the relative magnitude of two objects to be discriminated is a function not only of the actual physical size of the objects but also of many other social and learning influences. Natsoulas (1967) has suggested that verbal *reports* be defined as distinct from the more general term *response*. When a response can be presumed or shown to have a direct relationship to some specified external event it can be characterized as a *report*. As the uncertainty about the event to which the report refers increases, the report character of the response is reduced. When a large number of possible events influence the response, the verbal report can no longer be relied upon as a source of information concerning the event. If the subject is to be treated as a reporter who simply provides the therapist or the experimenter with information about an event, care must be taken to ascertain the existence of such an event by some independent means. Although it is still possible to study the nature of the person's verbal utterances as responses, they cannot be accepted as reports unless some independent verification is obtained. For example, a patient's description about the aggressive behavior of another person toward him may be correlated with specifiable aggressive acts on the part of the person. On the other hand, it may have been influenced by the patient's history in relation to that person, by his inferences about the person's actions from other sources of information, or by many other features that distort the report validity.

Some authors have made the distinction between reports about *phenomenal* versus *cognitive* experiences. In the first case it is generally assumed that the report is determined mainly by the effects of a stimulus object; whereas in the second case it is determined by other verbally mediated inferences about these effects. The skilled clinician will attempt to differentiate between these two sets of determinants of the patient's conversation, since he can use information both about the patient's actual experiences and about the manner in which his past history and the interview setting affect the form and manner of the report. But different consequences may result from each type of information. Therefore, the clinician evaluates the patient's behavior or obtains information before deciding whether to accept the patient's story as factual. Unfortunately, little scientific basis is available for these judgments, and in practice report validity is more quickly assumed than questioned. It is in these decisions that the clinician's experiences and skills play a major role.

Hefferline (1962) follows a behavioristic approach in defining a reporting response as one that has been attached to a prior response through continuous selective reinforcement by the social community for accurate correlations of the response and the report. Hefferline suggests a paradigm in which a chain of two correlated responses to a stimulus eventuates, expressed as: $S \rightarrow R_1 \cdot R_2$. The term R_1 represents an inaccessible event and R_2 is a report or verbal response. This view sketches the origin of self-descriptive verbal responses as a process beginning in early childhood with the parental offering of labels for the child's apparent private experiences. For example, the child's behavior and the known antecedents lead the parent to infer that little Johnny is suffering from a stomachache due to overeating, or a headache due to fatigue. The parent helps the child to localize and describe pain stimuli for the purpose of facilitating remedial action. Emotional responses are similarly linked to verbal responses to describe happy, sad, or angry states and questions serve to stimulate reports of past experiences (memories) that the parent has shared with the child. This constant social monitoring of verbal reports establishes a verbal repertoire with which the child learns to communicate internal events and past experiences to others. The unreliability of such reports, however, has already been noted in the studies by Schachter and others (Chapter 4) in the labeling of emotions. Monitoring by the community of the correspondence between external events and observable responses continues throughout a person's life but the continuing correspondence between internal events, covert responses and verbal reports is increasingly difficult to ascertain with progressive language development and independence of the child.

Only a few isolated studies are available in which efforts were made to compare the characteristics of a particular event and the verbal reports about it. Haggard, Brekstad, and Skard (1960) conducted interviews with mothers who had participated in a longitudinal study in a children's clinic. When the children were between seven and eight years old the mothers were given an interview that was built around historical information available from the records of interviews at the child's birth, and at ages one and six. It was found that the mothers' statements during the last interview were not particularly accurate as reports of prior events. The length of time interval by itself was not related to the reliability of the report. Whereas specific and discrete events, such as the weight of the child at birth, were reported with some reliability, the mothers' attitude and child-rearing practices were not recalled accurately. Rosenthal (1963) studied the accuracy of reports by adults who had participated in a longitudinal study during their last two years of high school. Although Rosenthal's data revealed significant correlations between many retrospective reports and adolescent events, the findings also demonstrated inaccuracy in memories, especially among women and specifically in the area of parental relationships. In addition to distortions that could be attributed to memory, the mode of response per se may affect the report content. Leibowitz (1968) compared three techniques for measuring aggression: (1) by means of a self-report inventory, (2) a behavioral technique in which a subject executes aggressive behavior by administering electric shock to another person, and (3) a role playing procedure for acting out aggression. The correlations among these measures suggest that verbal and physical aggression do not correlate highly, but that subjects are fairly consistent in repeated trials of the same measure.

The experimental tests of the congruence between verbal statements on questionnaires and personality inventories and direct behavior measurement constitute a large portion of the literature dealing with the validation of various personality tests. Although behavioral tests for such personality characteristics as leadership, test anxiety, or homosexuality can be designed, the degree of correlation between verbal report and the directly measured behavior varies widely among individuals and varies as a result of the particular conditions under which the experiment is conducted.

Azrin, Holz, and Goldiamond (1961) administered a questionnaire that had been used to question combat flyers about their fears in combat. College students were given the questionnaire under two conditions. One group was told to assume that they had never experienced any of the listed symptoms, whereas another group was told to assume they had experienced all of the symptoms. All subjects were instructed to answer in terms of what is expected, regardless of what behavior is presumed actually to have occurred. In addition, they were told that all symptoms were experienced equally often. The students' lists of symptoms were ranked by their order of frequency, and this rank order was then correlated with reports by other experimenters who had previously administered the same questionnaire to combat flyers within two months following their combat experiences. It was found that the rank order of the responses was highly similar between the students and the flyers. Students who were told to imagine that they had not experienced the symptoms and those who were told that they had did not differ from each other. The authors concluded that the same type of response bias operating in their students may have operated in the combat flyers and that any report concerning the actual symptoms in combat flyers would have to be validated by direct and objective measurement of the symptoms. Studies such as this clearly point to the limited credibility of verbal reports and their inadequacy as substitutes for observation of the reported behavior. However, as Leibowitz's study indicates and as we have noted in studies examining the effects of desensitization (Chapter 4), this lack of interchangeability cannot always be interpreted as a weakness in verbal report measures. The lack of high correlation between verbal and nonverbal measures does not imply a subordination of one response system to another. Instead, it demonstrates the need for selecting response measures that are relevant to the question to be answered. For example, a patient's verbal denial of his fears may coexist with physiological indicants of emotionality. Despite this lack of correlation, the verbal behavior can be examined for its determinants and its effects on the social environment and on the patient himself. For some situations it may be as important to know what the patient says as to know how he "feels" or responds physiologically.

A very subtle biasing effect which distorts verbal reports is produced by the tendency of persons to conform to the demands that they perceive as imposed by the situation. This tendency has been demonstrated as a contaminating factor in several important psychological areas. In the area of psychological assessment it has been repeatedly found that answers to personality test items are affected by the subject's tendency to respond

by saying what he perceives to be the proper answer. Subjects unintentionally slant their answers in the direction of socially desirable response
patterns. In fact, current test construction procedures give careful attention
to the social desirability factor in order to eliminate this source of contamination in individual assessment. In experimental work with human
subjects, especially when complex verbal or social behaviors are involved,
the subject's perceptions of the purpose of the experiment and his interpretation of what the experimenter might wish him to do has been shown
to affect the outcome of experimental findings (Orne, 1962). A third
and equally important source of bias in verbal reports has been carefully
studied by Rosenthal (1966). In a series of studies, Rosenthal and his
co-workers have shown that experimenters in psychological research tend
to influence their subjects' behavior in very subtle ways toward support
of the experimental hypotheses. These experimenter-expectancy effects
have been demonstrated both in human subjects and in animals. In many
of these studies the precise means by which such expectancies are communicated by the experimenter to the subject are not clear. The ubiquity
of these findings, however, suggests the overriding importance of situational variables other than the planned experimental procedures on the
output obtained from a subject.

It is not surprising that the clinical interview should be affected by
these same biases. Although no studies have been encountered in which
clinical interviews were examined with the same rigorous methods as those
used to demonstrate the effects of laboratory experimenters on their subjects, numerous clinical reports have indicated the influence of the
clinical setting, the professional and individual characteristics of the interviewer, and the implicit purpose of the interview on the verbal productions
of the patient. One recent study by Braginsky and Braginsky (1967)
illustrates the type of effects that can be expected to follow subtle variations in structuring clinical interviews. The subjects were hospitalized
schizophrenics. Patients in one group were told that the purpose of the
interview was to see whether they might be ready for discharge, while
another group was told that the interview was for the purpose of deciding admission to an open or closed ward. A third group was told that
the interview was aimed at evaluation of their feelings and their progress
in the hospital. The results supported the expectations that schizophrenic
patients presented themselves as "healthy" and eligible for open ward
living when their ward status was questioned, but appeared as more "sick"
and ineligible for discharge when their residency status was questioned.
The data clearly confirmed the hypothesis that patients responded in a
manner that maximized their chances of accomplishing the implicit purpose
of the interview. Since the interviewers were unaware of the conditions

to which the patients were assigned, the different impressions on which their judgments were based reflect primarily the changes in interview behavior produced by the different experimental instructions to the patients. Thus we note that interview material obtained in clinical interactions is subject not only to distortions inherent in the dubitable validity of verbal reports about events and internal states, but also due to the strong and subtle influence of situational variables that determine what the patient says and how he expresses it. The results of many other studies (summarized in Goldstein, Heller, and Sechrest, 1966) also indicate that a variety of factors associated with the personality of the therapist, the patient, and the relationship between the two serves to modify both the patient's verbal output and his response to psychotherapeutic intervention.

The Relationship Between Words and Action. Although the traditional interview methods assume the modifiability of behavior by means of changes in thoughts and speech, it is by no means clear that verbal responses can always serve as controlling stimuli for other acts. In social relationships some congruence between verbal statements and motor acts is essential for fulfillment of everyday interpersonal agreements. For example, the entire fabric of social cooperation rests on the general confidence that a man's verbal promise can be counted upon to eventuate in execution of the appropriate behaviors. The promise to keep an appointment at a specified place, to deliver merchandise or to carry out an assignment represents the verbal controlling stimuli that presumably initiate a series of complex motor acts, culminating in the fulfillment of such a promise. Social mores and legislation enforce these contractual agreements by providing positive reinforcements for the congruence between words and actions and aversive consequences for failure to follow the verbal statements with appropriate actions. Perhaps because of the ubiquity of this correspondence little research effort has been devoted to exploration of the specific processes by which words and actions are related. In fact, the absence of such correlations in sufficiently infrequent in social intercourse that it is often taken as evidence of a behavior disorder or pathological condition. Its seriousness is emphasized by the stringent measures taken, including the deprivation of civil rights, for those patients who are judged "mentally incompetent" and not expected to show the common correspondence between words and action.

The relationship between verbal and motor behaviors has been examined in only a few studies by observation of the actual effects of modifying verbal responses on the occurrence of related motor behaviors. Lovaas (1961) reported that conditioning of aggressive verbal responses increased subsequent nonverbal aggressive behavior in children. In a second study, the same author (Lovaas, 1964) reported that reinforcement of the naming of selected foods (carrots, apples, celery, and raisins) during a conditioning session with nursery school children resulted in an increase of actual consumption of these foods. However, these results were not obtained for all subjects and decreased intakes were observed on successive dates of conditioning. Brodsky (1967) investigated the relationship between verbal and nonverbal behavior change in a behavior modification study with two retarded females. One girl was reinforced for statements concerning social behavior in a series of interviews. Although the frequency of verbal statements rose during the interview session, the author did not find a corresponding increase in the girl's social behaviors in the natural living environment. The second subject was reinforced for initiating social interactions in a structured laboratory situation. Increased social behavior in the laboratory generalized to the natural setting and to the verbal statements about social interactions during the interview.

The focus of some behavior therapists on changes in general behavior instead of general attitudes is based on the clinically observed effects of behavior changes on subsequent attitudes and self-evaluations. For example, Cautela (1965) has suggested that changes in verbalizations during psychotherapy, commonly called "insight," frequently *follow* rather than precede behavioral changes. Clinicians have reported similar incidents of insight following new behaviors. These observations suggest that the traditional psychotherapy sequence of progression from attitude to behavior may be reversed with good effects.

Even in verbal tasks, such as the performance of mathematical problems, verbalization prior to making a response can lead to improved accuracy. Lovitt and Curtiss (1968) report such improvement in performance with an 11-year-old boy whose work in mathematics had been erratic. When the boy was no longer required to verbalize aloud, his improvement was maintained. In subsequent experiments with different problems, his accuracy was again low. This single case finding alone cannot support the popular notion that verbalization of a problem aids in its solution, nor can it explain the mechanisms by which improvement occurs. Additional feedback from oral recitation, increased attention, improved discrimination by labeling could all be contributing factors. However, the study suggests the kind of approach that can aid in isolating the parameters affecting the verbal control of other behavior.

The facilitation of discrimination learning and concept formation by use of verbal labels has been studied extensively. However, the generalization of training from verbal to content-related nonverbal behaviors has not been subjected to systematic investigation. The method is illustrated in one laboratory situation by Phelan, Hekmat, and Tang (1967), who trained subjects to associate nonsense syllables with wooden blocks. Some syllables were then paired with unpleasant words. When subsequently asked to select the blocks that they liked most, subjects tended to avoid the blocks that had been associated with the negative label. The authors suggest that conditioning of affective word labels tends to influence the subject's nonverbal behavior in choosing the previously labeled objects. Studies in this area are few, however, and many questions remain. For example, the parameters affecting the degree of verbal control are not well known. The conditions required for self-regulation by verbal control are similarly uncharted; and the range of stimulus functions across verbal and nonverbal modalities has remained relatively unexplored. The role of verbal responses in controlling other motor behaviors in the same organism seems of central importance in the study of human behavior since frequent instances are encountered in clinical psychology in which a person appears to "know" or verbally describe a behavioral episode or to indicate what behaviors are expected of him, but he is unable to execute them. In such instances the verbal and motor repertoires appear to be uncorrelated.

Several recent studies suggest that the development of verbal control over motor behavior in the young child can be accelerated by training. Luria (1961) reports a series of observations in Russian laboratories that focus on the development of the regulatory role of language in children and on its disruption following cerebral pathology. These experiments trace the self-regulatory function of verbal responses in the young child from his early dependence on environmental cues or feedback from his own motor responses, through stages of partial control in which initiation of inhibitory responses is gradually shifted from control by sensory cues to control by verbal responses, to the final stage of inner speech. The experiments by Luria, and the replications of these studies in the United States, deal with the specific relationship of verbal behavior to the control of the person's own motor acts. It is apparent that such self-regulatory control is necessary if a person is to execute behaviors indicated in his verbal utterance to others. In other words, a child must be able to control his own motor behavior by some verbal response if he is to fulfill his promise to mother that he would take only two cookies, or that he would turn off his light at 9:00 P.M.

Luria's experiments demonstrated that three to four year olds typically cannot respond to verbal instructions requiring control over their motor behavior in absence of external stimuli. One of Luria's experiments has been replicated by Bem (1967). She found that three year olds were unable to press a lever corresponding to the number of lights previously exposed on a display. To distinguish between a maturational and learning hypothesis for explanation of this deficiency, Bem established a training procedure in which the children were first trained to respond correctly in the presence of external feedback. This was accomplished by training the child to count the lights and to repeat the count as the lights were gradually dimmed. Control of the counting responses thus shifted from the disappearing external stimuli to self-generated verbal stimuli. Motor training was then given in which the children pressed the lever to turn off one light at a time. Counting and pressing were then combined and the light intensities were gradually reduced until no discriminable light cue accompanied the motor behavior. The subject's successful matching of the light count by lever presses thus was shifted to self-generated stimuli. The success of this training indicated that verbal self-control can be established experimentally in three year olds, enhancing the child's independence of external cues. These studies suggest that development of the controlling function of verbal stimuli over a person's own behavior can be accelerated by early training in childhood, and that perhaps similar methods could be utilized to increase self-control through verbal self-instructions in adults.

The authors of this book have applied this experimental approach to several brain injured patients in the clinic. These men were taught to give themselves verbal instructions aloud before undertaking simple motor tasks. At first a therapist carried out parallel instructions and activity to serve as a model. As the patient acquired skill in self-instruction, such help was gradually faded. The procedure aided the patients in executing simple tasks that they could not do prior to training. Thus Luria's method may have use in retraining adults as well as in training children.

In an analysis of the functions of verbal behavior in psychotherapy, Greenspoon and Brownstein (1968) suggest that many patient problems may be associated with the lack of training in the execution of motoric behaviors under control of the verbal behavior of others. Similarly, failure to establish early stimulus control over one's own motoric acts through verbal statements may result in behavior deviations in adulthood. Persons for whom the verbal controlling stimuli of others have not acquired control over their own responses, are likely to respond poorly to verbal psychotherapy methods, because the therapist's verbalizations would have little effect on their behavior. Similarly, patients who have failed to bring their motor behavior under control of their own verbal behavior, are also likely to show only limited benefits from interview methods, since these techniques usually require that the patient exert verbal control over his actions after his verbal behavior is modified and after he leaves the therapist's presence.

Verbal Conditioning. In traditional psychotherapy it has generally been assumed that the patient's verbal productions and his interpersonal behaviors reflect long-established and well-ingrained behavior patterns that are relatively invariant under minor changes in the environmental setting. Consequently, the sensitive clinician was expected to make general inferences about his patient's "basic personality structure" from a series of brief observations. This assumption has been held especially with regard to the interview and projective personality tests. In therapy interviews the clinician has been viewed as a catalyst who facilitates expressions of thoughts and feelings reflective of habitual personality patterns of the patient. Although many personality theorists, especially the psychoanalysts, called attention to the importance of the interactional process in therapy, the main practical focus in interview therapy has remained on the analysis of the patients' story content. Dream analysis, the use of responses to pictures on the Thematic Apperception Test, and the detailed analysis of therapy protocols illustrate this attempt to make inferences about personality processes and structures from verbal content. In the early 1950's investigators began to examine the extent to which a clinician can influence the patient's verbal productions through very simple and inconspicuous behaviors. The impetus for research in the area of verbal conditioning came from attempts to demonstrate that several variations of Skinner's operant conditioning model can be fruitfully applied to verbal behavior.

Among the experiments that received the widest attention was a study by Greenspoon (1951). In this investigation, Greenspoon examined the effects of introducing a brief verbal response by the experimenter on the frequency of occurrence of a verbal response class in the continuous verbal output of subjects who were instructed to say aloud all the words that occurred to them. Subjects were asked to say only individual words and not to use sentences, numbers, or phrases. Either verbal stimuli, "mmm-hmm" or "huh-uh", a red light flash, or a tone stimulus were used contingently whenever the subject emitted a plural noun word. The effect of the four different contingent stimuli on the frequency of plural noun responding was clear-cut. The introduction of the verbal stimulus "mmm-hmm" by the experimenter, the visual stimulus, or the auditory stimulus resulted in a significant increase in the number of plural nouns when compared to a control group. The verbal stimulus "huh-uh" tended to depress the frequency of plural nouns. The clinical implications of Greenspoon's study were almost immediately taken up by Dollard and Miller (1950). While Greenspoon emphasized the paradigm as an analogue to animal operant conditioning, Dollard and Miller stressed the automatic unconscious aspects of the effects of reinforcement and the potential applications of this line of research to clinical psychology. The experimental method presented an interesting analogue to clinical interviews in that the free associations of psychoanalytic patients are also interrupted only by minimal verbal cues from the therapist. The potential role of therapist behaviors as reinforcers was thus brought to the attention of clinicians.

A second basic paradigm was developed from Taffel's (1955) sentence construction procedure. Taffel introduced greater stimulus control than Greenspoon by use of discrete trials, and modified the analogue from that of a free operant to that of a discrimination task. On each trial in Taffel's procedure subjects were shown cards on which were printed several pronouns and a verb. They were requested to make up sentences with the words on the card. Choice of a first person pronoun was reinforced with the verbal stimulus "Good." The contingent verbal stimulus clearly resulted in increased emission of the reinforced response class.

The similarity between these two experimental paradigms and the clinical interview were quickly seen by clinical psychologists and the number of studies in verbal conditioning increased rapidly. Although some of these studies were concerned with investigation of the effects of specific parameters on the rate of acquisition of verbal responses (for example, characteristics of the experimenter, of the reinforcing stimuli, of the nature of the interaction between experimenter and subject, of the personality characteristics of the subject, and so on), other studies used this experimental vehicle for direct tests of hypotheses derived from clinical practice and theory (for example, the effect of interpretations on verbal productivity, or the role of awareness in acquisition). The results of verbal conditioning studies clearly make it necessary to reexamine the assumption that a patient's interview behavior is mainly determined by his thought content, personality, or past experience. It is also necessary to pay careful attention to the interviewer's behavior and the clinical setting as determinants of the obtained interview material. The conditionability of verbal responses in laboratory situations similar to the clinical interview also suggests that the process of behavior modification by interview may be partially described by the verbal operant conditioning paradigm.

The generalization of findings from verbal conditioning studies to interview conduct are facilitated by many similarities in the two situations. The subject's dependence on rules established by the experimenter, the lack of specific instructions concerning the task, and the verbal nature of the interaction with its implicit consequence of heavy use of generalized verbal reinforcers provide an excellent parallel between the interview and the verbal conditioning situation. Many of the variables believed to affect an interviewee's behavior have been examined carefully in studies using modified verbal conditioning procedures and these studies are discussed in recent summaries by Kanfer (1968) and Krasner (1958, 1962a, 1967). In this section we briefly review only several studies with direct clinical implications and some of the unresolved problems that have been formulated as a result of the many experiments in the area.

The unreliability of early memories has been discussed in connection with the problem of validating self-descriptions. The verbal conditioning procedure underlies an experiment by Quay (1959) that demonstrated that the recall of emotional and personal materials may be manipulated by use of minimal social reinforcement for appropriate response classes. Quay asked a number of college students to report memories of their early childhood. After establishing a base rate of occurrence of memories concerned with families and memories concerned with people outside the family, the interviewer differentially reinforced the reports of the family or nonfamily classes of memories in different groups by following these verbalizations with a low "uh-huh" sound intended as a minimal verbal reinforcer. The results demonstrated that the systematic utilization of the generalized reinforcer increased the proportion of memories in the particular category for which the reinforcing stimulus was given. The strong effect of interviewer behavior on the content of subject productions has also been demonstrated by Rogers for positive and negative self-references during interviews (1960), by Salzinger and Pisoni (1958) for the rate of self-referred affect statements in schizophrenic patients, by Kanfer and McBrearty (1962) for the time spent on predetermined topics in interviews with college students, by Waskow (1962) for the rate of interview statements referring to feelings and attitudes or to intellectual content, and by many others for interview content that had previously been held to reflect mainly past experiences or intrapsychic processes.

In fact, the breadth of the literature suggests that there may be few areas of verbal content that cannot be manipulated in the interview situation by the simple expedient of subtle reinforcing cues from the interviewer. Such reinforcing stimuli as head nods, smiles, verbal gruntlike signs of affirmation and similar minimal behaviors have shown considerable effectiveness when systematically applied. Even when the therapist is not deliberately attempting to modify the patient's verbal output by contingent reinforcement, his general attitude toward the patient's productions and his style of interviewing can achieve the same results as the systematic reinforcement approach. Truax (1966) explored the possibility that reinforcement effects may occur even when the therapist derives his theoretical background from a school of psychotherapy that believes that the clinician is essentially nondirective and permits the patient complete choice about the content of conversation. Truax analyzed excerpts from tape recordings of a therapy case handled by Carl Rogers. He hypothesized that empathy, warmth, and directiveness serve as reinforcing stimuli for particular classes of therapeutic content and that these contingent reinforcing stimuli were applied differentially to various types of patient behavior in nondirective therapy interviews. Truax found that significant differential reinforcing effects were embedded in the transactions of client-centered psychotherapy. The therapist's empathetic comments and those that could be characterized as conveying the therapist's warmth were shown to be positive reinforcing stimuli for the behavior that they selectively followed. Truax's data were consistent with predictions of patient change made on the basis of a reinforcement viewpoint. The finding of results compatible with a behavioristic model of the psychotherapeutic process, even when the verbal strategy of such a process is couched in a nonlearning theoretical framework, strongly points to the important contributions of verbal conditioning effects during therapy interviews. A number of studies (see, for example, Adams and Frye, 1964; Noblin, Timmons, and Reynard, 1963; and Timmons, Noblin, Adams, and Butler, 1965) have also shown that interviewer comments such as interpretations, confrontations, or reflections, representing the classical means for implementing the production of insight in the patient, can themselves be used as contingent reinforcing stimuli. Their systematic application can produce predictable changes in the patient's productions.

The verbal conditioning effect may be one factor underlying the reports of several studies that the patient's verbal behavior and his value system tend to move toward similarity with the therapist's in successful therapeutic interactions. Whether intentional or not, consistent communication of cues for particular behaviors that the therapist may wish to see in his patient could result in changes in moral values by the patient which have been repeatedly reported in the research literature and in clinical observation (Palmore, Lennard, and Hendin, 1959; Rosenthal, 1955; Welkowitz, Cohen, and Ortmeyer, 1967). The modification of verbal content, of duration of verbal utterances, and speaker order has also been demonstrated in groups of three or more people. The underlying purpose of these studies has been to explore the role of the therapist in guiding group psychotherapy by subtle reinforcement of group members or particular content.

Most of the earlier studies in verbal conditioning purported to provide laboratory demonstrations that could be used as evidence that the psychotherapeutic process contains significant elements of operant conditioning methods. In direct application to clinical procedures, two separate types of studies can be distinguished. The first group of studies comprises efforts to modify the verbal behavior of a patient, because such disordered verbal behavior may represent a target symptom whose removal may have far-reaching beneficial effects. This direct attack of symptomatic verbal behavior by use of reinforcement contingencies is illustrated in a study by Sherman (1965). Three long-term mute psychotic patients were exposed to reinforcement procedures for reinstatement of some verbal behavior. The techniques included the numerous operant conditioning methods with which we are familiar from the animal laboratory. Shaping, fading procedures, and rewarded imitation represented some of the procedures. All three patients had had histories of mutism for at least twenty years. In all three persons some verbal behavior was reinstated, ranging from a verbal repertoire of approximately thirty words to full use of simple sentences in common conversation. Rickard, Dignam, and Horner (1960) modified the emission of delusional speech in a chronically hospitalized patient by attending to him only when rational speech was emitted. Ayllon and Haughton (1964) used contingent reinforcement by nursing personnel to modify delusional and symptom-centered talk in psychotic patients. A number of similar studies and case reports are available and some have been summarized in Chapter 6 on operant conditioning. In these studies the modality of the critical response was of relatively little importance. The same procedures were executed with verbal behavior as would be applied to motor behavior of various types.

The second group of studies concerns itself with the modification of verbal behavior, not for its own sake but because it is assumed that such changes in the verbal repertoire would in turn have effect upon the patient's other behaviors. These studies concern either demonstrations or practical applications of operant conditioning procedures in the modification of attitudes, self-descriptive statements, quantity of verbal output, proportion of feeling and emotion statements. Whether such procedures are used in the laboratory or in the clinic, the main test of their effectiveness lies in the degree to which such changes can be shown to generalize to extra-test situations. For example, Nuthmann (1957) found that verbally reinforced subjects increased in frequency of self-accepting statements when presented items from a personality test. Taken at face value, such subjects presented a better picture of themselves and their personality test protocol could be judged to be healthier. The actual therapeutic effect of such a procedure, however, can only be judged if it were known whether other interactional and thought behaviors of the patient were also changed by it.

The evidence concerning generalization of successful changes in responding is not very conclusive. In a diagnostic interview setting, Aiken and Parker (1965) administered positive reinforcement for positive self-evaluations and negative reinforcement for negative self-evaluations. After completion of the interview, a test form was administered consisting of positively and negatively phrased self-descriptions in random order. They found some generalization from the conditioning interview effects to the postinterview measures. On the other hand, Rogers (1960) was able to successfully condition self-references in quasi-therapy interviews but failed to find any changes in scores on tests of anxiety, or in emotional adjustment, or self-references outside the sessions. Dicken and Fordham (1967) reinforced positive self-references and statements of positive affect in experimental interviews with college students. These subjects showed significantly greater changes from pre- to postexperimental scores on the California Psychological Inventory than subjects who were treated in the interview according to the rules for "client-centered" therapy and control subjects who had no interviews. The subjects also participated in group discussions. The experimental group tended to talk more following the interview than the other groups. In group therapy patients, the effects of verbal conditioning on ratings of adequacy of interpersonal relationships following conditioning were reported to be beneficial (Ullmann, Krasner, and Collins, 1961; Ullmann, Krasner, and Ekman, 1961). The changes in test responses taken to reflect attitudes appear to persist over a relatively long period. Bugelski and Hersen (1966) conditioned college students' answers to ambiguous statements about old age by administration of verbal reinforcement. Three weeks after the conditioning sessions a sample of subjects was retested to determine the residual effects of the training session. A significant conditioning effect was found on the retest.

Awareness in Verbal Conditioning. Although modification of verbal response frequencies by contingent verbal reinforcement has been clearly demonstrated, investigators have questioned that the mechanism operating in these studies is essentially similar to the process of simple operant conditioning. The main attack on the conditioning position has come from cognitive theorists. It is the position of the cognitivists that the demonstration of verbal conditioning can best be interpreted *not* as conditioning that is automatic and unrelated to the subject's conscious and aware dispositions to change his behavior, but as a result of changes in cognitive processes such as hypotheses that direct the subject's responding. What is learned in verbal conditioning is held to be the correct response-reinforcement contingency and no learning is expected unless a correct or partially correct hypothesis is present. Thus, the verbal conditioning effect is said to depend on the subject's awareness, his motivation for obtaining the various reinforcing stimuli, the adequacy with which he can form a hypothesis about the critical response class, and other variables that affect these processes (Spielberger and DeNike, 1966). The behavioristic position (see, for example, Kanfer, 1968; Krasner, 1967) stresses the empirical relationships between the conditions for response acquisition and the resultant performance pattern. Although numerous studies have demonstrated that those subjects who can describe various elements of the task (on a postexperimental questionnaire) show better learning of the task, it is not clear whether improvement in performance follows or precedes awareness. Some studies have suggested that learning may be a process of several concurrent changes at different levels. Increased verbalizing and hypothesizing about the task could thus proceed at the same time as the acquisition of the critical verbal responses. The interdependence of these two levels of learning would vary on different tasks and in different situations. For instance, instructions presenting the task as a problem to be solved, ease of description of the critical class, and narrowness of the reinforced class are among the variables expected to enhance the interrelationship between learning and awareness measures. The empirical results have not clearly supported the hypothesis that awareness is a prerequisite for learning. Many experimenters have reported the occurrence of learning in only those subjects who could verbalize the correct response-reinforcement contingency on postexperimental questionnaires. Other researchers have found learning in unaware subjects, and some investigators have reported learning in both groups of subjects, with some greater amounts of learning in aware subjects. The conflicting findings have given rise to considerable debate about methodological issues concerning questionnaire tests for awareness and about the role of awareness as either a mediating or a correlated process.

It should be remembered that in the verbal conditioning model a critical response class is generally chosen that has many easily available members in the subject's repertoire. In this sense, no new responses are learned; only existent responses are either brought under control of a discriminative stimulus or increased in overall rate of emission. This feature of operant conditioning increases the importance of the manner in which the task is presented to a person. The more easily the response class can be discriminated and the response-reinforcement contingency can be observed, the more quickly learning should occur. The importance of *ambiguity* as a variable in verbal conditioning was tested by Kanfer and Marston (1961). College students were exposed to series of word pairs consisting of one neutral and one hostile word. Three degrees of ambiguity were obtained by changing the following factors: (1) information about the task; (2) the nature of the reinforcing stimulus; and (3) ease of discriminability of the stimuli. The different degrees of ambiguity were obtained by changing instructions, using either the verbal reinforcing stimulus "good" or a light flash, and increasing the discrepancy between the two members of the stimulus pair by varying the degree of hostile connotation of one member. The results supported the proposition that learning in verbal conditioning experiments is attenuated by the unstructured nature of the procedure. All groups receiving more information via instructions showed significantly greater learning, steeper and more negatively accelerated learning curves, greater transfer of learning, and higher awareness ratings. The effects of the two reinforcing stimuli interacted both with the task information variable and the stimulus discriminability variable. Under conditions of higher ambiguity (minimal task information) the social reinforcer was more effective than the signal light. The more widely discrepant stimulus pairs were more effective with the light as reinforcing stimulus but less effective with the social reinforcer. The correlation between awareness ratings on a postexperimental questionnaire and learning scores varied from 0.34 to 0.63 in the groups, supporting the hypothesis that learning and awareness can be treated as separate dependent variables with shifting coavariation in different treatment groups.

Several studies have shown the importance of the social characteristics of both subject and experimenter and their interactional relationship in verbal conditioning. For example, the nature of prior interaction between subject and experimenter on a different task, the subject's perception of the experimenter as a person who is of compatible or incompatible personality to himself, the avowed purpose of the experimental procedure, and many similar interactional variables tend to modify the conditioning effect.

Verbal conditioning has also been shown to vary as a function of the typical variables employed in other verbal learning studies. The size of the response class, the nature of the reinforcing stimulus, the schedule of reinforcement, and similar variables have been reported to affect verbal conditioning. Despite the wealth of research findings, the data of the verbal conditioning literature have not yet been integrated into the traditional interview framework. The lack of utilization of these research findings in the revision of therapy techniques makes it doubtful that they will find extensive application in interview therapy until a general theory of behavior provides firmer guidelines for the overall strategies in psychotherapy. Nevertheless the impact of research on verbal conditioning, on the reinforcing effects of various therapy operations, and the other work on the process of interview interactions has been to increase the awareness of clinicians of the importance of their behavior in guiding the content of interview materials.

Other Mutual Influences in Interviews. In addition to the type of findings illustrated in the verbal conditioning area, extensive studies are available on the subtle interactional effects between therapist and patient on verbal content and structural features of speech, such as the duration of utterances, the frequency of interruptions, silence, speech disturbances, and similar variables.

In experimental interviews in which the interviewer attempted to limit the duration of his own verbal utterances to five seconds, the interviewee's average duration of speech utterances was found to remain reasonably constant across two different interviewers on the same day and on retests ranging from one week to eight months (Saslow and Matarazzo, 1959). The same group of investigators also reported differences in average speech duration and related structural speech variables in normal and psychotic subjects (Matarazzo and Saslow, 1961). Deliberate increase in the duration of the interviewer's comments from five seconds to 10 and 15 seconds produced corresponding increases in the average duration of the interviewee's speech. The extensive research of several groups of investigators on the noncontent aspects of interviews is barely illustrated by the findings mentioned above. Use of standardized interview methods, measurement of lengths, pauses, speaker shifts, silences, speech errors, latencies, and other microscopic analyses of interview behavior have enabled researchers to accumulate increasing knowledge about subtle mutual cues that direct and maintain conversation in two person groups. The advent of computers and application of sophisticated mathematical models for interactional behavior (Jaffe, 1964; and Jaffe, Feldstein, and Cassotta, 1967) have advanced theory construction and data analysis in the efforts toward understanding mutual speaker-listener influences and the formal aspects of verbal interactions.

The two person therapeutic communication system is heavily influenced by the role that each participant assumes for himself on the basis of his expectations about the nature of the relationship. To examine the effects of such role playing on the flow of communication, Kanfer (1965b) asked female nurses to discuss their personal experiences in dyads, allowing only one girl at a time to use a one-way intercom. When the subjects acted as peers, they spent approximately the same time speaking and listening, as shown in Figure 8-2, for Sessions 1 and 2. For Sessions 3 and 4 the experimental subjects were instructed to assume complementary patient and therapist roles. In these sessions, a significant shift is noted in the distribution of time for talking. As Figure 8-2 shows, the girls who assumed the patient role (Group CP) now talked more than two thirds of the time, while girls in the therapist role (Group CT) restricted themselves to speaking less than 30 percent of the time. It is noteworthy that this relationship, once established for Sessions 3 and 4, continued to affect Session 5, for which the subjects were instructed to carry out "unrestrained conversation" in free interaction, with the intercom removed. By contrast, the subjects in the control group maintained a stable distribution of time over all five sessions. The remarkable uniformity of the time distributions among all pairs suggests that the perception of the proper communication roles for peers and for doctor-patient pairs in therapy is widespread and stable. Extrapolation from these data to a wide range of behaviorally disturbed patients cannot be made easily

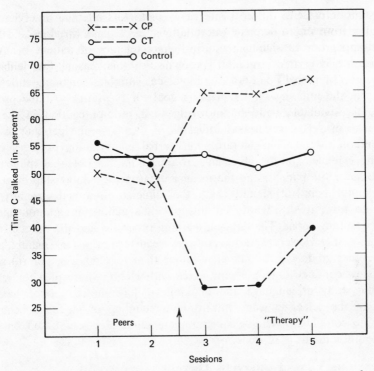

Figure 8-2 Description of time (in percent) C talked in all sessions as a function of role instructions (from Kanfer, 1965b, p. 329).

because the subjects in this study were healthy young women. However, the importance of each participant's perceived role in the interaction is clearly demonstrated by its strong effect on the pattern of conversational exchange.

In addition to the large body of research on structural variables in interviews, physiological behavior patterns have been studied in relation to interviewer operations. For instance, a host of studies on "interpersonal physiology" has examined the effects of the interviewer's anxiety, hostility, specificity of inquiry, and other independent variables on moment-to-moment physiological changes in the interviewee. The concomitance of physiological changes in both interviewer and interviewee has also been demonstrated and proposed as an index of rapport in therapy (Coleman, Greenblatt, and Solomon, 1956). Numerous studies have demonstrated the effects of drugs on interview behavior; others have shown the impact of sensory deprivation and neurological disabilities on verbal behavior. The many studies on structural and physiological dimensions of verbal interactions present an impressive array of factors affecting interview behavior. However, to date the interrelationship of these variables and their relative potency in shaping enduring characteristics of patient behaviors during the interview is not well known. For this reason, the deliberate utilization of verbal operations or biological variables for therapeutic purposes in the interview still remains a goal for the future. At the present time, the available body of knowledge can prompt caution in the acceptance of verbal reports as indicants of events in the patient's life or his internal states. The literature on verbal conditioning provides compelling evidence for the clinician's awareness of his potential influencing power over the patient, and the meager data on the relationship of verbal and motor behavior should cause the clinician to attend carefully not only to his patient's words but his patient's actions in and outside of the consulting room. The data on learning processes and the mutual influences of interviewers and interviewees seem to be useful mainly as a conceptual guide for the clinician rather than to offer a set of rules for interview conduct. One can only agree with Hebb, whose plea for a systematic study of language and thinking we have noted above, that the bulk of the scientific work toward understanding of language behavior and the complex psychological and therapeutic processes based on language still remains to be done.

A Learning View of Interview Therapy

A review of the variables affecting the patient's verbal output during diagnostic or therapeutic interviews makes it clear that a behavioral point of view differs considerably from traditional psychodynamic therapies in the conceptualization of the mechanisms and purposes of the interviews. For example, Wolberg (1954) describes the rationale of interviewing as follows:

"One of the aims of psychotherapy is to restore to the patient a control over his emotions. Before this can be done, he must be able to make the proper symbolic connections with his emotions. Therapeutic interviewing helps to accomplish this, and enables him to scrutinize, identify and elaborate on his feelings and their sources" (p. 158).

It is the bringing into awareness of "the forces within himself which produce his symptoms and interfere with a successful life adaptation" (p. 155) that Wolberg sees as the major therapeutic mechanism in interviews. Unlike the interview in the traditional vein, verbal behavior therapy is characterized by Storrow (1967) as stressing reportable or observable behavior, instead of hypothetical states or dynamics, and the present instead of the past. In contrast to the traditional approach, presented by

Wolberg, the interview is not employed primarily to permit the patient to develop his own insights and understanding of his unconscious motivation, of his feelings, and of the events in his past history that have resulted in his maladaptive behavior. However, the importance of the therapeutic relationship in interview therapy is not denied. The relationship between therapist and patient can serve to promote behavioral change through the therapist's efforts to establish himself as a potential source of reinforcement during each interview. Therapeutic tactics in later interviews consist in selectively reinforcing verbal behaviors that promise to serve as controlling stimuli for more effective action on the part of the patient. Storrow (1967) describes what is meant by establishing the therapist as a source of reinforcement in the following way:

"A potent source of reinforcement is to be recognized by the fact that it has a marked impact on behavior. I know that my reinforcing value has risen to a useful level when I note a certain change in the patient's behavior, when he begins to express positive feelings for me and to look forward to the sessions. When he begins to show respect for me as a competent professional person. When he begins to value my opinions. When he tries to act upon my suggestions. When he begins to value and to seek my approval and to be at least mildly upset at signs of my disapproval" (pp. 144–145).

Storrow's description does not imply that relationship therapy is carried out only by tactics which make the patient dependent upon the therapist's approval or disapproval. Although such utilization of the therapist's role as an instrument in interviews may be helpful for particular purposes and for short periods of time, the major goal is to teach the patient how to analyze his own environment and his behavioral potentials, and to provide himself with opportunities for more effective actions.

Since the interview has such a long history in traditional diagnostic and therapeutic efforts, innumerable books and articles are available that describe different interview methods and strategies designed to maintain the patient's verbal output, to help him to describe his environment and his past behavior more effectively, and to consider alternatives in behavior. In fact, long-range interview strategies over the course of therapy make up the different "schools" of psychotherapy; they form the basis for the operations derived from different underlying assumptions about the therapeutic process, for example about the role of transference, dream analysis, or interpretation. The behavior modification techniques described in the preceding chapters have been devised as alternatives for cases in which interview therapy is neither feasible nor efficient. Current research makes it clear that behavior modification can be produced by direct control of the environment, as well as by interview methods. An integration of both approaches in the total clinical enterprise represents the optimal use of available methods, since the interview is uniquely suited for information gathering and for some individual patients (Kanfer, 1966a). The question is not whether to *substitute* conditioning methods for all interviewing methods, but how to use the interview, or conditioning, or both most effectively for a particular patient. For proper use of interviews it must be recognized that psychological and physiological determinants affect the therapist's observations, and interpretations of interview behavior must take into account the impact of these variables.

The emphasis on conditioning techniques in behavior modification approaches has a second implication. It is that the major consequence of the increasing use of conditioning methods is not merely a minor revision in interview methods but a drastic change in the relative importance of interviews as therapeutic instruments. Improvement in conditioning techniques may eventually relegate interview therapy to the status of an *adjunct* for behavior modification techniques. As psychologists make increasing use of the same direct methods of modifying behavior in psychotherapy as used in the laboratory, they should become more effective in treating patients whose symptoms had previously been resistant to attack by interview therapy. When the focal symptoms consist of public behaviors, understanding the patient's thinking becomes less important and treatment requires fewer interviews and a less intimate personal relationship if direct modification techniques can be applied.

Interviewing techniques, however, retain their great value for treatment of individuals who require counseling, attitude changes, or information, but who are capable of executing effective social behaviors without further retraining. The replication of a close personal relationship in interview therapies also makes it an ideal vehicle for modifying directly those problems that consist of a patient's difficulties in relating to another person and in using appropriate interactional behaviors. Cases in which the target behaviors are verbal behaviors for efficient assessment of life situations, evaluation of feelings, or decision-making are also well suited for treatment by interviews. In these cases the problematic behavior can be examined during the interview and changed by the same principles of behavior modification as are used for motoric, social, or interactional responses.

Several features of the nature of learning in interview therapy have been examined in a paper by Kanfer (1961). Three major assumptions can be made with reasonable support from research findings:

1. Major behavioral modifications in verbal therapy are generated by systematic application of external controls. Conclusions about the influence

of the therapist on the patient's behavior come from the previously mentioned studies of dyadic influences, verbal conditioning, and the psychology of persuasion. This view differs from the assumptions that change is due to spontaneous growth for which the therapist serves only as a catalyst; or that *internal* processes are simply directed or set free by the therapist. Behavior change in interviews is rooted in the patient-therapist interaction and guided by therapist behaviors.

2. Learning in interviews can be conveniently separated into two stages—learning to perceive the environment differently (discrimination learning) and learning new behaviors in social interactions (operant conditioning). Either of these stages, or both, may serve the treatment goal. When a person learns to change his perceptions of the environment or of himself, with prompting and reinforcement from the therapist, he may have already in his repertoire responses that are adequate, once they are connected to appropriate (realistic) discriminations. When the patient is unable to discriminate among the various stimulating conditions leading to a given problematic response, the therapist often intervenes by supplementing from his own experiences those probable contingencies between stimulus dimensions and responses that are appropriate for the situation. Interview techniques for this purpose are described by many traditional therapists in detail, and in learning terms by Dollard and Miller (1950). Thus the problematic response can be modified by alteration of the prior verbal contingencies on which it may depend.

The second stage, learning of new instrumental responses, can be achieved in interviews if these responses are interpersonal and verbal ones, of the kind that can naturally occur in the therapeutic relationship. If they are responses that cannot be practiced and reinforced, the interview can serve for planning and instigation of these behaviors under favorable circumstances outside the clinician's office. Chapter 9 describes many of these methods for training a person to modify his own behavior in the therapist's absence.

3. The dependent variables in interview therapy are not only the primary content of a patient's communications, as in traditional therapy. They include all other behavioral changes during the interview. Although their relation to the interview process is not always clear, behaviors outside of therapy are also recorded as an index of progress, though not unequivocally as a measure of therapy effectiveness. The role of interviews as an information-giving device resembles the well-supported effectiveness of verbal instructions in laboratory learning tasks. In both cases it is easier to demonstrate effects than to elucidate the processes by which they occur.

When the dependent variable is an autonomic response, for instance an anxiety response, the common techniques of extinction, counter-conditioning, or narrowing stimulus control can sometimes be used directly, as illustrated by those mixed-model techniques in Chapter 4 that employ interviews. For example, in desensitization, relaxation training and establishment of anxiety hierarchies are usually conducted in interviews. It will be recalled that these operations are also influenced by many of the same variables that affect other therapy interactions.

We have reviewed briefly some of the issues arising from the assumptions of traditional psychotherapists that the patient's verbal interview behavior can be taken as the sole focus of concern for the entire therapeutic enterprise, and that his verbal and emotional behaviors can be viewed as manifestations of more basic internal personality processes. The presented research on factors affecting verbal behavior should serve a clear cautionary function to guard against treating interview data and interview content as reliable or primary information about the events or internal states that the patient describes, unless the conditions under which the report is given are taken into account and the report-reliability is independently established. On the other hand, once such cautions are taken, the observations of a patient in the interview can be very useful, and interview techniques can provide an excellent method for implementation or supplementation of the behavior modification techniques in a comprehensive treatment program.

SUMMARY

Interview therapy typically aims to change social behaviors indirectly by modifying the patient's attitudes, his perception of the environment, and his self-perceptions. It has also been used to change the patient's interpersonal and verbal behavior, as manifested in the therapy session, and to instigate the patient toward changing his environment and his own behavior. But the main rationale for its employment has been that verbal behavior is a symbolic surrogate for other behaviors. Once verbal behaviors have been modified, it is expected that all other responses under their control, including emotional and social acts, would change accordingly.

Since interview therapy uses language as the major mode for interaction, the conceptualization of verbal behavior becomes a crucial factor in the use of interview strategies. Currently, no complete account of the determinants of language is available. The mediation hypothesis has been proposed in various forms to explain the process by which some representation of external stimuli, or of past events, serves to actuate verbal behaviors and controlling stimuli for other actions. These mediational models conceptualize verbal behaviors as learned responses that serve to relate and differentiate experiences and to organize a person's information processing and perception, bridging the gap between environmental inputs and behavioral outputs. The psycholinguistic model, on the other hand, endows the human organism with competence to organize his perceptual and linguistic experiences in some predetermined way and gives less weight to the role of learning in the development of language and language-derived processes, such as thinking and perception.

When a person describes his experiences or his internal states in an interview, care must be taken to recognize this behavior as a response that is under control of both the person's history and the interview situation, instead of as a true record of past or of internal events. The history of the development of self-descriptive behaviors and their vagueness in most adults reflects the relatively poor control of this behavior by environmental contingencies and social agents. Consequently, the congruence between verbal reports and observational data of the same event is often far from perfect.

In interview situations, abundant evidence indicates that even minimal subtle cues by a listener will affect the content and structural characteristics of a person's verbal output. Such verbal conditioning is assumed to go on in all interviews and can be used deliberately by the therapist to modify some characteristic of the patient's utterances. Research findings have not clearly established, however, how much and under what conditions verbal behavior changes achieved during interview therapy generalize to the patient's behavior out of therapy. The degree of success in verbal conditioning methods has demonstrated clearly the strong influence of the therapist's subtle responses. However, the effect is not an inevitable result of the presence of a listener. It varies with the type of reinforcing stimulus used, the relationship between the subject and the behavior modifier, the characteristics of the critical response class, and other variables. In addition, changes in verbal behavior are also affected by the person's awareness of the response-reinforcement contingency, and his attitude toward change.

The mutual influences in interviews have been examined not only in verbal exchanges but also by physiological measures in both participants. At present, the interview continues to be used for collection of data about the patient's history, for observation of his behavior under varying interviewing conditions, and for behavior modification. As the variety of noninterview techniques in therapy increases, interview techniques are gradually receding from their central and multipurpose role in treatment. In most behavior therapies interview methods are selected for specific purposes, rather than as a vehicle for all psychological treatment, and with some patients interview methods are not used at all.

CHAPTER 9

Self-Regulation and its Clinical Application

The earlier chapters in this book have described the supporting research and methodology for clinical procedures that bring about behavior changes by environmental control of the stimulus, or of reinforcement for the patient's behavior, or both. These therapeutic techniques require the presence of the therapist during the critical periods of behavior change. Little responsibility for changing is left in the hands of the patient. The last chapter differs from the earlier ones in that it describes techniques of behavioral change that are carried out mainly by verbal methods. These techniques comprise all interview methods and presume that extensive changes in the patient's behavior occur as a secondary result of attitudinal and verbal-ideational changes. Although some direct modification of verbal behavior may be attempted by contingent reinforcement in the same manner as we have encountered in verbal conditioning studies, the patient is an active participant in the interview therapy process and considerable reliance is placed on his ability to utilize interview information and insights for his guidance in daily life outside the therapy sessions.

In the present chapter we discuss some experiments on the process of self-regulation and some in which the patient takes the major responsibility for regulating his own environment and actions, according to a therapeutic plan worked out jointly with the therapist. The interpersonal relationship required to foster such a program is not unique to psychotherapy. It essentially consists of a training or tutoring relationship in which one person is helped by a more experienced person to learn new skills. In the case of therapy these skills concern the person's ability to regulate his own behavior more effectively. Recent techniques based on behavioral principles include highly specific training for the execution of particular behavioral acts and guidance in the acquisition of special social skills that can enlarge the patient's repertoire in the control and regulation of his own behavior. We have described these techniques elsewhere under the name of *instigation therapy* (Kanfer and Phillips, 1966). The major distinguishing features of this technique are the use of the teacher-learner relationship for joint planning and for instigating action by encouraging and supporting the patient. The actual process of gradual behavior change is expected to occur during the self-monitored execution of new responses in the absence of any observer, therapist, or counselor. The beneficial effects of the patient's active role are not limited to maintaining treatment progress. Experiments as well as clinical experience have suggested that the patient's perception of himself as the major agent in bringing about improvement increases his predisposition toward further change and toward expanding his horizons for continuing personal development. In the environmentally oriented behavior therapies, these attitudes of participation and self-regulation are especially important in maximizing cooperation among patients who are opposed to external manipulations. The patient's active role is also indispensable for execution of programs in his natural environment, particularly applicable when the symptoms do not warrant institutionalization or interference by the therapist in the patient's private life.

THE SELF CONSTRUCT

Many schools of psychotherapy demand that the patient reorganize his own life pattern and his attitudes toward himself and others. However, the therapeutic interaction is often viewed as a catalyst that brings about changes in the self. These changes in turn result in the adoption of personally satisfying and psychologically more effective behaviors. Realistic self-reactions and awareness of the important relationships in one's life appear as crucial forces that promote reorganization toward more effective adjustment. In these theories the self, or an equivalent psychological force, such as the ego, is viewed as an active inner structure that can be put into the service of rehabilitation, once the therapist has resolved the conflicts or removed the obstacles that had previously blocked the effective functions of this inner force. For example, in Carl Rogers' theory of client-centered therapy, the revision of the patient's self-structure is the major goal. It is accomplished by creation of a permissive accepting environment in which revision and expansion of the self-structure can take place (Rogers, 1951). Sullivan (1954b) regards the self-system as an organization of experiences that serves to protect the individual from experiencing anxieties and results in constraining his range of experiences by avoiding threatening situations. In therapy the basis for these avoidance-reactions (security operations) is examined and the self-system is modified.

On the other hand, modern learning approaches do not view the self as a unitary personality structure. Cameron (1947) describes this view in summarizing his discussion of the development of self-reactions:

"Because people become so easily superstitious over the word *self*, let us repeat here in closing that self-reactions, whether verbal or non-verbal, overt or covert, are no more and no less than acquired patterns of behavior. They are reactions of a biosocial man, woman or child to his own appearance, behavior and status as a social object, originally learned and practiced overtly in the company of others, and secondarily carried over into silent speech and socially organized thinking. Self-reactions always remain human behavior, never becoming transmuted into static substance, never reified or transformed by diagrams into a compartmentized *psyche*. There is no single, united self at the core of our being. We are, as we have seen and shall see again more clearly, many persons in a house divided. The basis of much frustration and many conflicts is in this universal circumstance, that no man ever fuses all his self-reactions together into a single, unambiguous, coherent whole" (p. 102).

A somewhat similar view is expressed by Rotter, who also emphasizes the dependence of the self-concept on particular behaviors and situations. Rotter (1954) states:

"Social learning theory does not utilize a construct of the self or the self concept. It does make use of some of the implications of these constructs. . . . If we mean by this self a person as abstracted from the total situation, then clearly such an abstraction is important and necessary. If it is possible to substitute the word *person* for *self* then there can be no objection to the term. It is acceptable and obviously of great significance that the person as a whole may react to one of his parts. He may have an attitude about himself as a unit, or about himself as he may function in a given situation, or about some part of himself, or about how other people perceive him. The basic formulation of social learning theory states that one of the major predictors of behavior is the subject's expectancy regarding the outcome of his behavior in a given situation. One might refer to such expectancies as self concepts or say that a person's conception of himself in a given situation is a determiner or major determiner of his behavior. In this sense, every time we mention the word *expectancy,* since expectancy always deals with a person's expectancy of the outcome of his own behavior, one might put in parentheses *self concept*" (pp. 239–240).

Skinner similarly rejects the traditional cultural assumption of the self as the unitary directing system responsible for integrating psychological function. ". . . a self is simply a device for representing *a functionally unified system of responses.* In dealing with the data, we have to explain the functional unity of such systems and the various relationships which exist among them" (1953, p. 285). The unifying feature of a functional system may consist of a set of common reinforcements that leads the person to establish a distinct class of related instrumental behaviors. Or, consistent behavior patterns may be organized around particular situations, such as the behavior toward one's mother, one's playmates or toward one's self. Thus, many separate "self-systems" may appear in a person, with varying degrees of congruence among them.

The behavioristic conception of the evolution of coherent systems of attitudes and self-reactions supposes that these responses are learned, similar to the way in which responses to external objects and events are learned. Language serves to combine and interrelate response classes and events and contributes to the coherence of such attitudes by bridging temporal and spatial gaps between situations. Thus, a child develops knowledge about himself on the basis of descriptions by many people about himself, his body, his social behavior, his speech, from his infancy on and under innumerable conditions. He labels his own behavior and its effect upon others. He learns what he can do and what he cannot do, how others respond to him, and what consequences various actions have for him and for others. Even when this knowledge is not correct, it may serve as a cue for his behavior, all the same. Since the cues constitute a connected set of criteria for action, these self-prescribed standards can have far-reaching motivational effects. The most striking feature about self-knowledge, however, is that it is often absent in areas that are most crucial to social functioning. The social environment provides direct and immediate feedback about the individual's effects on it only rarely. Although a person's behavior has continuing consequences, these are often not immediately recognized by him and environmental feedback is frequently delayed, too vague, or withheld. What a man's best friend will not or cannot tell him is often the discrepancy between judged and actual effectiveness of his social response pattern. In turn, foggy self-knowledge reduces the capacity for planning and for executing behavior at its most efficient level. In any therapy program that is partly based on the patient's veridical appraisal of his own actions and their social consequences, the therapist's task must include some assessment and observation of the congruence between the patient's acts, their consequences and their antecedent conditions, and his ability to observe and report them adequately.

Once it is denied that the *self* is a process entity or a mental structure, it is necessary to outline some of the particular areas in which psychologists have been able to accumulate research data on the functionally related response systems that we call *self.* One large area of research concerns the various conditions determining the standards of performance that a person accepts as desirable or sufficient. Research in this area was begun by Kurt Lewin and his students and is known as *level of aspiration* research. In early work in this area, Hoppe (1930) gave his subjects different tasks and invited them to discuss their efforts. He noted that their goals were initially modest and that their level of aspiration for succeeding tasks was lowered after failures and raised after successes. The changes in level of aspiration were interpreted as reflections of the subject's set toward the tasks and his characteristic level of self-evaluation. A large number of later studies, using quantitative procedures to measure the subject's estimates of his future performance, found these scores to vary under different motivational conditions and as a function of prior experiences in the laboratory or in the person's life history. It was also noted that predictions differed when subjects were asked to state their expected score, the best or worst score they hoped (or feared), or the score that would satisfy them. Numerous variables, such as the subject's rate of improvement, the importance of the goal to be achieved, and the proximity of the task's end were found to affect the self-evaluative measures. The research findings indicate the importance of the many considerations by the subject, some realistic, some imagined, that affect his assessment of his capacities. Since these assessments also influence a person's future behavior, knowledge of their determinants is of great importance to the clinician who wishes to predict behavior.

The regulation of one's own behavior is not only a function of the appraisal of one's performance but also of the relative relationship of this performance to a social frame of reference. Festinger (1954) has posited the existence of a drive in the human organism to evaluate his opinions and his abilities. The implication of the existence of this drive is that we would expect persons to engage in behaviors that enable them to make accurate evaluations on the basis of objective nonsocial criteria. In the absence of clear criteria, comparisons with the opinions and abilities of other persons serve as the source of information. These hypotheses led Festinger to a series of predictions. For example, subjective evaluations should be unstable when neither physical nor social comparisons are possible. Festinger draws on the level of aspiration literature to show supporting evidence for this prediction. Further, in the case of availability of both objective and social bases for self-evaluation, the former should be preferred. Although Festinger establishes additional hypotheses, it suffices here to note that his theory of social comparison processes also roots self-reactions in the person's past experiences and calls attention to the continuing dependence of these reactions on feedback from the social environment. The content of self-reactions thus is constantly subject to modification and, according to Festinger's motivational hypothesis, the person is actively seeking verification of this content. These psychological processes should aid in the therapeutic process when a clinician can offer controlled information about the patient's opinions and abilities, for the purpose of producing behavior changes.

In addition to serving as a sounding board for his patient and to providing direction for self-evaluating and standard-setting behaviors, the clinician also encourages self-adjusting behaviors in the execution of therapy prescriptions. These behaviors are often based on comparisons with the therapist's statements, or on goals discussed in interview sessions. In verbal therapy with adults, the clinician often assists only in the development of a program for behavior change. Responsibility for execution of the program is relegated to the patient. The psychological processes underlying these self-directing therapeutic actions have not been investigated directly in the laboratory and are only poorly understood. For example, the likelihood that a patient will carry out an agreement to execute the therapist's assignments or to change his environment in a specified way may relate to his evaluation of his own capacity to do so, his motivation for change, his standards for what constitutes "improvement" and other factors. None of these variables has been extensively studied. To aid the patient in establishing standards and to provide incentives, the therapist can use the interview for establishing a set of appropriate responses. These can serve as therapy surrogates to the patient who can recall and rehearse statements that the therapist has made to him. Although such statements would clearly appear to have discriminative stimulus functions, the mechanisms by which they are recalled and by which they affect behavioral control in the absence of the therapist are complicated and not easily derived from available laboratory data.

SELF-CONTROL

One major requirement in the execution of instigation therapy is the capacity of the patient to put behavior under his own control. The theoretical dilemma, shared by all psychological approaches, lies in explaining behavioral relationships in which the same person is both object and subject, both the doer and the target of the action. The practical management of self-control has been easier to achieve than the conceptual formulation. As long as 4000 years ago, Homer reported some good advice for exercise of self-control through the admonitions of Circe to the sea faring Odysseus. To prevent the disastrous exposure to the bewitching songs of the Sirens, Odysseus was warned to plug his oarsmen's ears with soft beeswax. For his own control, he let himself be tied to the mast after cautioning the crew not to release him, "shout as may, begging to be untied." Odysseus' successful strategy for eliminating stimuli that present the temptation to engage in an undesirable or destructive behavior, or preventing the response by physical restraint well in advance of exposure to the critical situation, is used in current treatment of alcoholics, sexual offenders, and with similar problems of self-control. It is also among the list of potential controlling devices listed by contemporary psychologists (Skinner, 1953). Yet, the mechanisms that permit a person to control his own behavior in the face of competing environmental controls still require explanation. Behavioristic writers have attempted to circumvent this dilemma, by treating it as a special case of the situation in which one person acts upon another. For example, Skinner writes "when a man controls himself, chooses a course of action, thinks out the solution to a problem, or strives toward an increase in self-knowledge, he is *behaving*. He controls himself precisely as he would control the behavior of anyone else—through the manipulation of variables of which behavior is a function" (1953, p. 228).

Skinner believes that in describing self-control the question of who controls whom can be answered by examination of the relationship among various organized systems of responses within a person and by study of the extent to which these systems stand in controlling relationships to each other. This approach collapses the environment-person distinction, implicit in our behavioral equation. S, R, K, and C components all lie in the same person, O. In clinical application, this view suggests that the probability that a person will learn to control some deviant behavior, such as overeating, depends on the response-reinforcement contingencies for eating and noneating, the environmental opportunities for food-getting, all other features associated with the maintenance of the eating response, and the availability of controlling responses in the person's general repertoire. If the instrumental behaviors for self-control are available and can be increased by changing stimulus conditions and by contingent reinforcement, the patient should show a reduction in his tendency to overeat because the probability of exercising the self-controlling response would now be strengthened to the point that it exceeds the strength of the eating response. The additional complexity due to the variables affecting the patient-therapist relationship and the probability that the patient will act on the therapist's suggestions presents a practical but not theoretical problem in such an approach. The person's past experience in controlling his own environment and in securing reinforcements for such control would also play a large role in his therapeutic success with self-directing methods. The major practical problem lies in the initial predominance of available reinforcement for the undesirable response, since resistance to the temptation to execute it has much lower and less immediate favorable consequences than engaging in a self-controlling alternative.

The process of self-control always involves the change of the probability of executing a response that has both rewarding and aversive consequences, and the selective initiation of a controlling response by a person even though the tempting response is available and more immediately rewarding. After repeated trials, the tempting response occurs again if the controlling response is blocked or the conditions change. If the tempting response no longer occurs, because its associated rewarding consequences have been reduced or the controlling response is now a well-established alternate response to the stimulating conditions, we no longer speak of a self-control situation. The process has been described by Skinner as one in which "an organism may make the punished response less probable by altering the variables of which it is a function. Any behavior which succeeds in doing this will automatically be reinforced. We call such behaviors self-control" (1953, p. 230). Skinner lists several methods for the exercise of self-control, all of which involve the manipulation of *controlling responses*. These are a set of responses that are characterized by a special relationship to the *controlled* response so that their execution makes the tempting behavior either impossible or less probable. Common examples of controlling responses are the application of a time-lock on a refrigerator to avoid between-meal snacks, or on a cigarette case to avoid excessive smoking, or the intentional failure to put money in one's pockets in order to avoid going on a shopping spree, or to a tavern. Numerous other examples in everyday life illustrate the techniques by which prior manipulation of the subject's social, physical, or physiological environment accomplishes a reduction of the probability of the controlled response. Although genuine examples of self-control (since the person initiates the changes), these methods aid the person by shifting behavioral control to an environment so changed that the undesirable behavior is not as easily stimulated or maintained. The outstanding feature of these methods is the interruption of a behavioral sequence at an *early* stage, when the transitional probabilities from one link to the next are still low and alternate responses are more easily strengthened. For example, it is easier to avoid the entire sequence of drinking behaviors, in the absence of alcohol, prior to entry into a bar than after a drink is served.

A favorite social method of controlling temptation is based on the effects of punishment. The emotional concomitants of strong aversive stimulation are rearoused when a child finds himself in a situation in which he had previously been punished. Both the external cues and those arising from his own behavior generate aversive stimuli generally characterized as anxiety. If the emotional responses occur in the context of a transgression or of responses leading to commission of a previously punished act, they are called *guilt*. Any action that lowers the probability of executing the guilt-arousing behavior sequence thus serves as an escape response, and is reinforced by removing the child from the guilt-situation. From the observer's point of view, the net effect is the child's failure to execute what appears as an attractive action. Strictly speaking, however, such training methods do not lead to "self"-control in the sense of our definition, since it is the aversive component of the controlled response which is directly altered to reduce its probability of occurrence. Only if the child initiates an independent and originally unrewarding response, or if he sets the occasion for the occurrence of the aversive stimulus, for example, by spanking his "bad, cookie-stealing" hand, or if he generates recall of aversive consequences, such as thinking of the terrible consequences, can one speak of self-control. Thus it is important to distinguish between the results of direct modification of the controlled response by aversive consequences, including withdrawal of positive reinforcement, and the case of self-control with interposition of a controlling response, *without* direct reduction of the attractiveness of the controlled response.

In addition to the controlling techniques mentioned so far, application of self-reinforcement and self-punishment in self-control can be used. The conceptualization of the role of these processes in self-control is even more problematic. In fact, as we have noted, two simple explanations could be advanced that dispense with a self-regulatory concept altogether and still seem to account for some instances of "self-control": (1) these are special cases in which a chain of responses is interrupted because an alternative (for example, a controlling response) is ultimately followed by greater positive reinforcement than the original sequence; or (2) the anticipatory anxiety responses associated with the aversive conditions (such as guilt) following execution of the original behavior chain, set the stage for an escape response (that is, any behavior changing the sequence). However, neither explanation makes clear how the individual can *actively* alter the course of his behavior, nor how such self-initiated behavior stands in relation to other variables. The problems of self-control and self-reinforcement are defined by the absence of any *current* external reinforcement contingencies, and by the person's *selective* manipulation of his environment in counteracting the natural effects of external control.

Skinner's discussion of self-control deals primarily with the process by which a controlled response is reduced in frequency or is inhibited. A broader definition of self-control includes cases in which a response is maintained despite its noxious effects. Thus, at least two separate cases of self-control can be distinguished: (1) the case in which a highly valued event or reinforcing stimulus is available ad lib and the subject *fails* to execute the behavior; and (2) the case in which a behavior is *executed* despite its known aversive consequences. The first case is illustrated by situations commonly described under resistance to temptation; the second case includes situations in which pain, unpleasant stimulation, or similar events are tolerated even when an escape response is available. In human situations commonly considered to lie in the domain of self-control, the response to be controlled always has conflicting consequences. It is only when the controlled behavior has immediate positive reinforcing value and long-range aversive consequences (for example, in drinking or smoking), or when it has immediate aversive consequences but long-range positive effects (such as heroic acts, tolerance of pain), that any question at all arises whether the person is executing self-control.

Both cases—strengthening of the resistance to temptation or increasing tolerance of noxious stimulation—usually involve the provision of supplemental controlling variables to counteract the effect of the precurrent reinforcers. Generalized social reinforcement and self-descriptive statements with social reinforcing properties can be made contingent on the execution of self-control. Thereby some behaviors may be strengthened that, at first look, appear to be detrimental to the organism. The segment of behavior observed in these situations may seem to present an exception to the basic motivational assumption that organisms avoid pain and approach positive reinforcers. Neither in self-imposed failure to respond to positive reinforcers nor in tolerance of noxious stimuli can one expect the behavior to occur in the absence of strong additional variables; nor would such self-control be expected to endure very long when parameter values change so that the tempting behavior becomes more attractive or the controlling response weakens. For instance, a controlling response such as counting or doing exercises is likely to be of value only for a transitory temptation. If the situation is unchanged, a breakdown in self-control can be expected eventually, as fatigue or satiation weakens the controlling response. The stability of self-controlling behaviors therefore relates directly to situational variables and momentary fluctuations in the state of the organism and the environment. Such vernacular expressions as "every man has his price," or "everybody has a breaking point" seem to refer to this relative instability of self-control.

Ferster (1965) distinguishes three forms of self-control. The most widely encountered form is applied to performances that alter the relation between the individual's behavior and his environment so that ultimately aversive consequences to the person are reduced. The control of eating behavior in an obese person is an example of this first form. A second form of self-control involves the performance of behaviors that increase a person's long-range effectiveness, even when the consequences are long delayed or even immediately aversive. This type of self-control is exemplified by a person engaging in such educational activities as piano practice. A third form of self-control involves the alteration of the physical environment rather than of the person's own behavior. Hiding a whiskey bottle in a highly inaccessible place is an example of this form of self-control. In all three forms the person engages in behavior that has beneficial long-range consequences. Ferster's analysis suggests the importance of examining these consequences also in terms of optimizing the individual's relationship to the social and physical environment for the eventual obtainment of reinforcers available in a given cultural and physical setting. In other words, one underlying feature of all self-controlling behaviors seems to lie in their utility for a better adjustment to the cultural and social demands of the individual's environment. The vacillations encountered when a person initiates a program that may eventually require changes in the distribution of available reinforcers and in postponement of some, can often be observed in the behavior of making voluntary contact with a therapist. The arrangement of a definite appointment or a commitment to a husband or wife to seek therapy are some ways by which a patient makes therapeutic contact more probable. At the same time, active efforts may be made to obtain reassurance from friends who had seen psychotherapists, from reading in popular magazines, and other similar activities to reduce the aversiveness of therapy.

In several examples we have suggested that the beginning of a self-control program involves the temporary abandonment of immediate or near reinforcers for the sake of later and more important ones. The study of variables affecting the delay of reinforcement-consumption (gratification) is thus relevant to the planned engineering of a self-control program. The factors that enable a person to delay gratification should also facilitate execution of self-control. In a series of experiments with children many of these determinants were explored by Mischel and Gilligan, 1964; Mischel and Metzner, 1962; and Mischel and Staub, 1965. Self-control was defined by the investigators as the ability to postpone gratification by choosing a delayed but larger reward over an immediate but smaller one. Variables such as a person's generalized expectancies of the reinforcement consequences following either choice, the subject's reinforcement history, situational manipulations, the reward value of the chosen item, and the duration of the temporal delay were among the factors that determined the experimental outcomes. These findings point to the value of widely practiced methods of altering the probability of immediate reward consummation by training, by promises of future rewards, or by modifying the desirability of the reward. This paradigm is useful in illustrating the *relative* nature of self-control; it suggests variables that a patient can use to alter management of his personal problems, under guidance of a therapist.

In the studies by Mischel and his co-workers the future delivery of rewards was controlled by the experimenter even though the child's choices were generally honored. The laboratory procedure resembled practical situations in which individuals postpone reward consumption for the sake of natural long-range consequences that are not completely under their control. A classic example is that of the disciplined money saver who foregoes immediate pleasures for the sake of later ones. However, the risk of such choices is obvious. The possibility of currency devaluation, depression, or robbery, or similar external interventions tends to weaken such "self-controlling" behaviors, as long as the ultimate consequences remain uncertain. Individuals who have had many experiences in which delayed rewards were forefeited or who have little trust in the credibility of their environment would thus be reluctant to work for delayed rewards or exert self-control for their sake.

Early manifestations of self-control are encouraged during childhood training by many parents, especially in American middle-class families. Developmental psychologists have often called attention to the frequent and continuing parental reinforcement of children's self-regulatory behavior during the child's early socialization training, especially in the case of nonexecution of responses. For example, in early toilet training or in training a child not to handle a fragile object, the consequences of inhibiting such behaviors often consist of the adult's administration of large measures of verbal approval, material rewards, and other reinforcements associated by words and actions to the child's controlling behavior.

As we noted in our discussion of the use of guilt to control socially undesirable but personally attractive behavior, common social practices lean heavily on aversive methods for development of resistance to temptation. The major goal of early socialization training, in fact, has been regarded by many to be the development of a conscience, or the internalization of social norms. Society highly prizes the inhibitions of many behaviors, such as aggressive or sexual transgressions, because these are difficult to enforce by continuing external controls. An extensive survey of research and theory related to mechanisms of socialization by Aronfreed (1968) reflects the centrality of this topic for understanding the transition of the infant to a social being. In turn, the survey indicates how various learning mechanisms, including vicarious learning, aversive and positive control of behavior, respondent conditioning, and self-reinforcement are brought into play in the child's socialization.

In turning next to consideration of the tolerance of noxious stimulation, we find that the critical requirement for a definition of self-control is the availability of responses that could avoid or escape the aversive stimulation. Since the cues for these antagonistic responses can be self-administered and their execution can be covert, an observer is often moved to conclude that the person's actions represent disciplined voluntary acts that defy natural behavioral principles. In fact, this conclusion is often based on an incomplete analysis of the controlling variables. In a demonstration of the effects of simple controlling responses on the tolerance of painful ice-water immersion of the hand, Kanfer and Goldfoot (1966) provided verbal responses or distractions by environmental objects to different groups of female students. Tolerance time was significantly affected by the availability of these controlling responses. The greatest tolerance was observed in subjects for whom external stimulation was provided. However, availability of verbal responses also altered tolerance. The study illustrates, in principle, the modifiability of self-controlling behavior by the mechanism suggested in the behavioral analysis of this process.

The sufferance of noxious stimulation, (especially the apparent "voluntary" procurement of pain stimuli) has often been characterized as an example of abnormal behavior, because of its apparent contradiction of common motivational principles. There are many examples in the literature of situations in which both animals and men seem to seek out noxious stimulation. The relevance of these studies for an understanding of self-control lies in the demonstration that time-limited observations of behaviors cannot serve as the sole basis for a behavioral analysis. Sandler (1964) has reviewed a series of experiments in which characteristic responses to pain in animals were modified by experimental operations. Both Sandler (1964) and Brown (1965) conclude from their analyses of masochism that the disregard of other relevant variables, for example, change in the biological state of the organism, or the presence of some other contingencies in the organism's history, often leads to deceptively narrow definitions. In such situations momentary observations reflect only a fragment of the behavioral episode in which conflicting avoidant and approach responses have intricately related histories, determining their respective dominance at any point in time. Appeal to such concepts as masochism to name these behaviors serves to obscure rather than to explain the processes under observation. When the observer cannot describe a particular compelling set of concurrent controlling stimuli in the environment whose operation would account for the behavioral outcome, he is often tempted to conclude that his observations are inconsistent with a motivational principle. Observation of human behavior are the more baffling because the determinants of the observed behavior may be related to highly idiosyncratic antecedent factors of which the observer has little knowledge. But the multiple and complex series of determining events in a person's life history can be studied in laboratory demonstrations in which unusual outcomes of natural situations are replicated by selecting particular antecedents or combinations of training variables. The studies cited so far demonstrate that the ultimate origin of self-regulatory behaviors may lie in the social and biological environment of the person, but that the aggregate of an individual's experiences does shape a person who can, to some extent, influence his own behavior by deliberate alteration of influences to which he exposes himself.

MOTIVATIONAL ASPECTS OF SELF-REGULATION (SELF-REINFORCEMENT)

When behavior must be maintained without external reinforcement, the individual may supply some parallel motivating operations in the form of self-reinforcement. Such reliance on self-generated stimulation enables humans to persist in, or change, their actions with relatively lesser dependence on their environment than infrahuman organisms. The establishment of specific contingencies for the administration of self-reward or self-punishment by early training can alter a person's response to environmental stimuli by introducing self-presented cues originating in his past social history. As we have noted earlier, Skinner and Ferster have described techniques for self-control that consist of altering the consequences of a person's own behavior in order to maximize the reinforcement potential of the environment. Self-reinforcement of operant behaviors represents a special type of self-initiated behaviors that can have far-reaching consequences in maintaining or modifying almost any behavior in a man's repertoire.

The act of self-reinforcement is not one that can be related easily to the variables controlling it. Skinner has defined one property of positive self-reinforcement by stating that "it presupposes that the individual has it in his power to obtain reinforcement but does not do so until a particular response has been emitted" (1953, pp. 237–238). While this supposition emphasizes the contingency of self-reinforcement on particular discriminative stimuli, it does not provide a full definition of the class of behaviors encompassed under self-reward and self-punishment. Self-reward is often contingent not only on external events but on the incidence of a wide range of previously established patterns. For example, self-reward may be predicated on achievement of a given performance level or on the feeling of fatigue after an exercise. Self-castigation may follow a disturbing thought or a disapproved social act. To clarify these processes, data are needed to account for the incidence of self-reinforcement and for the conditions under which a person refrains from continuous administration of available positive reinforcers. In the case of noxious stimuli not only the conditions under which a man withholds or stops their administration must be known, but also the variables that account for those cases in which more painful externally delivered aversive stimuli can be avoided by self-administered mild negative reinforcement. It is on this basis that a patient's painful self-recriminations or atonement can often be understood as escape from stronger stimuli, be they anxiety or anticipated external aversive consequences.

To provide firmer grounds for the simile between reinforcing properties of social or physical stimuli and self-administered stimuli, it is also necessary to demonstrate that the operations designated as self-reinforcement share some of the motivational, discriminative, and maintaining properties claimed for other reinforcing stimuli. The empirical support from studies on self-reinforcement provides increasing evidence for the operation of a self-regulatory mechanism that has the special function of controlling the person's behavior, independent of momentary environmental circumstances, thereby fostering the autonomy of human organisms.

The bulk of studies on the self-reinforcement process in the laboratory have followed three major paradigms: (1) the directed learning paradigm for the study of various variables affecting the rate of self-reinforcing responses; (2) the vicarious learning paradigm for the examination of the different modelling effects on self-evaluation and self-reinforcement; and (3) the temptation model for the study of variables affecting the self-administration of rewards contrary to social sanction.

1. *The directed learning paradigm.* In this procedure, reported by Kanfer and his co-workers (Kanfer and Marston, 1963a,b; Marston and Kanfer, 1963b; Kanfer, 1966b; Kanfer and Duerfeldt, 1967a; Kanfer, Duerfeldt, and Le Page, 1969) the reinforcing stimulus is freely available to the subject and is self-administered. The subject is instructed to reward or criticize himself after he has made a response. Usually he is exposed first to a learning task in which external reinforcement is provided until a low level of learning is achieved. Thus the subject is not able to reach a high degree of subjective certainty of the correctness of his response. The subject is then asked to take over the experimenter's function of administering a reinforcing stimulus. He is instructed to do so whenever he believes that he has responded correctly. This paradigm has been used to investigate the motivational properties of self-reinforcement, the variables affecting the frequency of self-rewards, and the relationship between self-reinforcement and other dependent variables commonly investigated in learning tasks. In a series of studies it was found that the rate of self-administered reward on a task for which the subject has only low skills tends to match or exceed slightly the rate of prior external reinforcement on the same task. When incorrect responses are followed by negative reinforcement from an experimenter in training, subjects tend to administer self-criticism subsequently on the same task at a rate related to prior external reinforcement but somewhat lower in magnitude.

When a person performs a task with very few errors, there are few occasions on which he stops and evaluates his performance. It is even more unlikely that he would reward or criticize his achievements following such self-assessment, unless his performance on the task were unusually good or bad. Under laboratory conditions, the requirements for overt self-appraisal and contingent self-reinforcement on each trial results in increased accuracy and higher frequency of self-rewards as a function of higher competence on the experimental task. In the studies using this procedure it was also found that the rate of self-rewards remains quite stable over many trials, even after external feedback is discontinued. Self-criticism, on the other hand, tended to show a somewhat lower rate after training, increasing as trials progress and subsequently decreasing to a stable level.

When a person is trained on an ambiguous task and is given external reinforcement, such as poker chips, for his self-rewards, the rate of self-rewards tends to generalize to similar learning tasks. These findings suggest that self-reinforcing operations can be modified by external reinforcement. In turn, the clinical implications of these findings suggest the possibility of deliberately manipulating a person's frequency of self-reinforcements during his daily life in order to bolster his self-confidence and self-evaluation. The frequency of self-rewards was also affected by experimental instructions. When subjects were told to adopt stringent criteria for administration of self-reinforcement, they tended to reward themselves less frequently than subjects who were instructed to be liberal, even when they were equally accurate. It was also shown that a subject's judgment of the performance of another person on the same task is affected by his own prior rate of self-rewards.

Although self-reward and self-criticism have often been related in the past to generalized attitudes about one's own performance and might therefore be expected to show a reciprocal relationship, several studies have shown that self-criticism and self-rewarding behaviors are not highly correlated. For example, if a person is trained to increase his tendency to reward himself on a given task, his tendency to criticize himself for incorrect performance on the same task does not change concurrently. Similarly, a person's broad evaluation of his own performance level and the particular behavior of rewarding himself on single trials do not show high consistency. Consequently, it is possible to train a person to reward himself only infrequently but to evaluate his overall performance, relative to a reference group, either as very good or very poor, depending on independent training for such statements (Kanfer and Duerfeldt, 1967a).

A review of experimental findings in this area (Kanfer, 1967b) suggests that self-reinforcing operations can be modified by a number of experimental variables and that the study of the self-reinforcing process may make some contribution to understanding the means by which people maintain their behavior without recourse to support from the external environment. However, full exploration of the self-reinforcement concept requires demonstration that the defining operations affect subsequent behavior, that is, have reinforcing properties. Several studies (Kanfer, 1967b) have been reported that demonstrate that the incidence of self-rewarding and self-critical responses affects accuracy of performance on subsequent trials, or maintains the same response over many trials. If such self-reinforcing mechanisms can be shown to control subsequent behaviors they would find increased applications in clinical procedures. Interviews could then be used to teach the patient to establish criteria for appropriate behaviors and to reinforce his own actions in accordance with the newly learned self-generated responses. Motivational resources can thereby be placed directly in the patient's hands, facilitating a behavioral change process even when the therapist is not present to guide and to motivate the patient by external reinforcement.

2. *The vicarious learning paradigm.* Although rate of self-rewards can be directly affected by contingent response consequences, its incidence can also be varied through previous observations of self-rewarding behavior in models. Bandura and his co-workers have studied transmission of self-rewarding patterns in children in different experimental procedures. Several studies in this series have been mentioned in Chapter 5 in our discussion of vicarious learning. One paradigm involves the exposure of a child to a model who plays a skill game, such as a miniature bowling game. Upon attainment of a prearranged score, the model takes self-rewards in the form of candy or tokens from a freely available supply. The score contingency and criteria for self-reinforcement are made explicit by the model's verbal comments about the contingencies, his self-evaluative statements, and his accompanying self-praise or self-criticism. Following the observation, the child is asked to play the same game, and he can obtain scores similar to those

of the model. The dependent variable is generally the number of self-rewards, or of trials on which the child takes rewards. This design permits control of the child's performance level on this apparent game of skill by systematic manipulation of the scores. It is especially suited for study of model characteristics and observer-model relationships as parameters in the transmission of self-reinforcing behaviors.

In a series of studies by Bandura and his colleagues the characteristics of the model, the standards set for self-rewards, the discrepancy between model and subject standards, and the relationship of the model to the subject were found to be the most potent variables in changing self-rewarding patterns. For example, Bandura and Kupers (1964) found that children who observed adult models tended to match closely the self-reward patterns exhibited by their models, with regard to the criterion for which they rewarded themselves with candy. In addition, self-approving and self-critical verbalizations given by the model were imitated by the children. Peer models were not as effective as adult models in setting standards for nonreinforcement of low level performance. Further, a higher percentage of the children who had observed peer models exceeded the magnitude of candy rewards taken by the model on each occasion than those who had seen the adult models.

But the adoption of high criteria for self-reward is not a direct function of observation of a model alone. Bandura and Whalen (1966) presented the bowling game after the children had undergone success or failure experiences on games appearing to measure physical strength, problem-solving ability and psycho-motor dexterity. Groups of children saw the bowling game played by models who set high, moderately high, or low criteria for self-rewards. Different effects of treatment were found for varying performance levels. The prior experience of success or failure influenced self-reward rates only at a low level of performance. In this group, children who had failed on the prior task rewarded themselves less often after observation of inferior models while children in the success condition took more self-rewards than those who observed equally competent superior models. These results point to the complex interaction between modeling cues, prior history, and performance as joint determinants of self-reward administration.

3. *The temptation paradigm.* Many different studies have been reported on children's cheating, but only a few show relevance of the data to the area of self-reinforcement. The common element among these studies lies in the provision of ad lib rewards administered at the subject's discretion, a set of explicit rules describing the proper standards for self-reward, and apparent lack of control by the experimenter to enforce or even to observe the subject's adherence to the stated con-

tingencies. The experimenter's knowledge of the subject's actual performance, by observation or by constraints built into the task, permits tabulation of the administration of undeserved or inappropriate self-rewards. When desirable rewards are made available, the procedure is one that invites behavior commonly known as cheating or dishonesty.

Mischel and Gilligan (1964) have used a procedure in which children play a shooting gallery game. The object of the game is to obtain a high score, ostensibly by skillful marksmanship. However, a moving target and a rigged score indicator permit manipulation of scores which are unrelated to the subject's skill. The child is asked to keep his score and prizes are promised for achieving a given level of performance. When the experimenter leaves the room the child can cheat on his score-keeping and obtain undeserved prizes. The inflated point scores represent the inappropriate self-reward. Kanfer (1966b) and Kanfer and Duerfeldt (1968) used a class procedure in which children were asked to think of a number on each trial, prior to the experimenter's drawing a slip from a lottery box. The children were instructed to reward themselves with a point recorded in their scoring booklet, whenever the number drawn by the experimenter coincided with their anticipated guess. The frequency of undeserved self-rewards was found to relate to the child's age, his academic standing in his class, the magnitude of the reward, the availability of an adult model who also took undeserved rewards and similar variables.

Knowledge of the relationships governing the genesis and operations of these classes of "self-responses" is an essential requirement for clinical practice. Recent developments in behavior therapy have increasingly tended to include self-reactions in the treatment of behavior problems and have utilized self-regulatory mechanisms to effect behavior change. Techniques in which the patient assumes some part of the therapist's role and attempts to modify his own behavior are not an innovation of behavior therapy. The importance of self-regulation in achieving happiness has been stressed by ancient philosophers and moralists and is encountered in many religions. Behavior therapists differ not in application of these general techniques, but in their efforts to incorporate them into a theoretically consistent model of behavior modification and to provide the patient with supplementary behaviors that make self-regulation easier. These newly learned controlling responses are generally derived from an experimental analysis of the clinical problem. The obvious advantage in transferring control to the patient lies in the fact that it can not only shorten the therapeutic process but can also maintain and extend the changes initiated in therapy.

CLINICAL USE OF SELF-CONTROL PROCEDURES

The skillful engineering of the environment for facilitation of self-control by the patient is illustrated in an early description by Fox (1962) of the treatment of ineffective study habits in college students. The author set as his task the establishment of three elements: (1) the initiation of study under stimulus control; (2) the use of the study period as an effective discriminative stimulus for behaviors called "good study habits;" and (3) the accomplishment of such a program without continuing professional help. College students met individually with the experimenter to analyze their schedules, and described their current study habits. Then, each student received a series of written instructions that specified particular sequences of behavior. For example, a student was requested to go to the library at a certain time, to leave all his books on the first floor, except those relevant to his physics studies, to go to a specified room and to engage in studying physics. He was asked to leave the library immediately if he experienced discomfort or began to daydream. He was told that, once he had decided to leave, he should read one page of the physics text carefully or solve the easiest problem assigned to him and leave immediately even when his interest had been renewed. Each day thereafter the student was told to increase the amount of work he performed after deciding to leave the study room. After a week additional course studies were added. Different rooms and different hours were set aside for each subject.

These procedures tend to minimize the aversive consequences of studying and to provide conditions for positive reinforcement by completing at least a small assignment in each session. Successive approximations and fixed-ratio schedules of reinforcement also are inherent in this program. The students are trained in recitation during which the material of the book is outlined, recited, or reviewed. New techniques useful in recitation, such as the asking of questions or survey of material, are taught to the student. Fox reported good success with this technique, which he attributed to the utilization of stimulus control methods. The essential feature of this approach lies in training the patient to arrange his environment in a way that would minimize his difficulties in performing the required task.

Goldiamond (1965) presents three studies that illustrate the procedure of instructing a person to set up behaviors that change the environment, thereby bringing his own behavior under different control. In the process of setting up a program for himself, the patient can be taught the methods of behavioral analysis so that he can apply them to himself when appropriate. Examples of this approach are given in the treatment of obesity by Ferster, Nurnberger, and Levitt (1962). The therapeutic procedure involved four steps: (1) determining what variables influence eating; (2) determining how these variables can be manipulated; (3) identifying the unwanted effects of overeating; and (4) arranging a method of developing required self-control. Obese women learned to control their own eating behavior at home by applying operant learning methods acquired in the clinic. Daily accounts were obtained of the conditions associated with food intake and of the behavior chains culminating in eating. Since actual weight gain is too distant from the act of eating to have any immediate aversive effects, verbal practice was conducted to increase the patient's active verbal repertoire concerning the ultimate aversive consequences of obesity. Thus, the verbal stimuli were easily available as immediate negative reinforcers. To achieve narrower stimulus control, the therapist prescribed that eating could occur only in a designated place, at specified times, and all food-related activities had to be controlled closely.

The emphasis of deliberate stimulus control arrangements is illustrated by arrangement of specific eating routines. Reduction in the disposition to eat can also be accomplished by introduction of other activities incompatible with eating. For instance, telephoning a friend (a practice commonly used by Alcoholics Anonymous) might interfere with the tendency to indulge in customary between-meal snacks at a time when the tendency to eat is high. The patient might arrange to postpone reading his evening newspaper until some time later when a peak tendency to eat occurs. Another example in the use of prepotent repertoires to lessen an undesirable behavior consists of the undertaking of a strongly reinforced activity that requires some time and attention. For example, going for a walk or a car ride, beginning a conversation, or similar activities would be prepotent over eating because of the temporary aversive consequences resulting from their interruption. In some cases the prepotent repertoires physically remove the individual from the place where eating usually occurs. Ferster et al. applied these techniques in a short-term small group therapy program in which the basic principles of stimulus control, utilization of prepotent repertoires, amplification of aversive consequences, and other self-regulatory techniques were taught to the patients.

In individual interview therapy, Stuart (1967) carried out treatment for overeating by training the patient to manage his own behavior through rearrangement of behavioral sequences. Stuart gives a detailed outline of the content of the series of interviews. The initial interview includes recording of the time, nature, quantity, and circumstance of all food and drink intake. Recording of weight four times daily is requested, both as a reminder of the therapeutic program and as a means of ascertaining fluctuations in gross bodily weight. The patient is also asked to list behaviors that may be used as positive reinforcers and his greatest weight-related fears. Following the recording procedures the first step in the therapy program requires the patient to interrupt his meals for a predetermined period of time. At first two to three minutes are suggested and the time is gradually increased to five minutes. The patient is instructed to put down utensils and merely to sit in place at the table for the specified time. This maneuver is intended to strengthen self-control and to demonstrate that eating is a response that can be broken down into components and successively mastered.

In later interviews the patient is instructed to remove food from all places in the house other than the kitchen and to keep in the house only foods that require preparation. He is instructed to make eating "a pure experience," that is, to pair eating with no other activity such as reading, listening to the radio, watching television, or talking on the telephone. These steps use the method of narrowing stimulus control for the eating response and dissociation of eating from other interrelated behaviors that could serve as cues for eating. The patient's weight chart is reviewed in successive interviews as a reminder of progress. In subsequent sessions the patient is required to eat more slowly, thus increasing direct control of the eating response; alternate responses for eating are suggested. These procedures are similar to Ferster's for establishment of substitute distracting behaviors. In later sessions covert sensitization (Cautela, 1966) is also used. In this procedure the patient is trained to relax and to imagine that he is about to indulge in eating. He must follow this image by visualizing the occurrence of a highly aversive event. Essentially, this procedure is similar to stimulus control methods for behavior modification, discussed in an earlier chapter. The image of the forbidden object (CS) is paired with the aversive UCS, thus forestalling the occurrence of the undesired behavior. Stuart reports follow-up data for eight patients under this program after one year. In all eight patients considerable weight loss, ranging from 26 to 47 pounds, was reported over a 12-month period.

Covert Sensitization

The method of covert sensitization utilized by Stuart was originally proposed by Cautela (1966, 1967). In this procedure the patient is taught to relax in the same manner as in the desensitization procedure. He is then asked to visualize very clearly the pleasurable object, that is, food, liquor, homosexual person. He is then instructed to visualize that he is about to commit the undesirable act and to imagine the onset of this sequence. When he reaches the near final point of approaching the undesirable response he is told to imagine that he begins feeling sick to his stomach. A number of suggestions for aversive and imaginative stimuli are offered. A feeling of relief is offered as positive reinforcement for imagined successful avoidance or escape from the problematic sequence. For example, the patient is told to imagine that he rushes outside into the fresh air after refusing a drink or engagement in a homosexual act, and that the feeling of nausea goes away and he now feels fine. After several practice trials in the therapist's office the patient is instructed to continue self-administered treatment between visits. As therapy progresses the self-control technique is increasingly monitored by the patient. Cautela suggests that this approach can be used with obesity, homosexuality, and similar problems. The essential feature of covert sensitization lies in the fact that the patient is taught techniques similar to those used in the aversion therapies. However, the actual behavioral events are replaced by verbal responses, and the patient takes responsibility for practice and execution of the treatment without direct assistance from the therapist.

Barlow, Leitenberg, and Agras (1969) tested the assumption that the pairing of the verbal description of a noxious scene with the undesirable behavior is crucial to the effectiveness of covert sensitization in two cases of sexual perversion. The authors established the appropriate hierarchies of sexually arousing scenes for each patient, a pedophiliac and a homosexual. The patients were asked to keep a record of their daily sexual arousals. The hierarchy items were typed on individual index cards and before each treatment session the patients were requested to sort them into four groups by strength of arousal. Finally, a GSR recording of reactions to six selected scenes from the hierarchy was taken during each preparatory session and before every second treatment session. These measures constituted the dependent variables for evaluation of treatment effects. Following training in deep muscle relaxation eight scenes from the hierarchy were presented in each session. Four scenes were coupled with imagery of nausea, while the remaining scenes suggested the beginning of nausea and relief on leaving the arousing scene. After acquisition (pairings of noxious and arousing scenes), an extinction procedure was introduced. The sessions consisted of presentation of the arousing scene for ten seconds; a 30-second-blank was then used to take the place of the previous nausea-invoking scene. At the end of the interval the therapist said: "Stop imagining that." After eight extinction sessions, the acquisition procedure was reintroduced.

The results are shown in Figure 9-1 for the pedophilic patient. Both the record of sexual urges and the score on the sorting of hierarchy item cards show a clear decrease as acquisition progressed. Omission of the noxious scene during extinction reveals the increase in sexual urges several days after the change in procedure. The reduction of these urges can

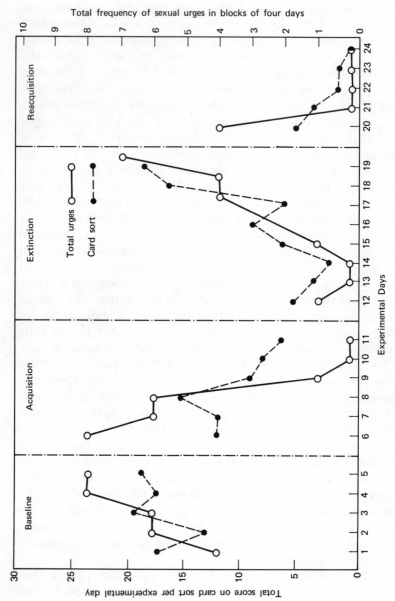

Figure 9-1 Total score on card sort per experimental day and total frequency of pedophilic sexual urges in blocks of four days surrounding each experimental day. Lower scores indicate less sexual arousal (from Barlow, Leitenberg, and Agras 1969, p. 599).

be seen to follow reintroduction of the acquisition procedure. The same changes were observed in the second subject. The GSR data showed recovery during extinction only in the pedophilic patient. The study points to the pairing of the noxious and arousing stimuli as the conditioning mechanism that may underlie the therapeutic effects of covert sensitization.

Contingency Management

Homme (1965, 1966) has suggested a technique of behavioral engineering in which the patient exercises self-control through rearranging behaviors by means of covert verbal responses that serve as controlling cues for desirable behaviors. Homme uses the term *coverant* (covert and operant) to describe responses that are verbal operants usually inaccessible to the observer. They include such behaviors as thinking, imagining, reflecting, relaxing, and fantasizing. Homme assumes that the frequency of behaviors of this sort can be controlled according to the same principles that control overt behaviors.

Homme's main thesis is that the symptomatic behavior can be reduced by specific antecedent verbal behaviors that are incompatible with the target response. In the self-management of contingencies, the patient is first helped to relax as completely as possible. This physical attitude is used to provide a discrimination between feedback from tense and nontense musculature and the patient is taught to associate this physical state with the self-command "relax." The relaxation coverant is especially useful because it permits attachment of high probability behaviors contingent on its execution. Another type of coverant, the self-mastery coverant, which is equivalent to a statement such as "I am in charge of my own behavior," can be used because of its incompatibility with statements of inadequacy and inferiority. When the coverant is interjected prior to a highly probable response, its rate of occurrence is strengthened, according to the principles proposed by Premack (1965). Contingency management can be applied either by a therapist or by the person himself and relies on the assumption that a response is strengthened when followed by a highly probable behavior.

Contingency self-management is illustrated by requiring the patient to make positive coverant statements in specific situations prior to a highly probable behavior. For example, the patient is asked to repeat to himself "I am master of my own fate" or "I am a likable person" or similar "procoverants" prior to making a telephone call, starting a car, taking money from one's purse or wallet, and so on. Increased operant rates of these responses should lower the frequency of the antagonistic symptomatic response. Homme (1966) compares this approach with that advocated in behavior control by positive thinking and moralistic self-persuasion. Coverant control therapy aims to accomplish the same purpose, to induce a person to change the frequencies of his procoverants and thereby to control his moods and self-attitudes. Homme's method simply suggests a way in which the frequency of positive statements can be more easily manipulated, since their insertion prior to an existing response of high probability should increase their frequency in line with associationistic principles.

Self-control Techniques in the Modification of Smoking Behavior

Current statistics on cigarette consumption attest to the disappointing results of various public campaigns to curb smoking. Since this habit is maintained in part by social stimuli, it is practiced in innumerable situations and often associated with pleasant experiences. Research reports suggest that systematic attempts to aid a person in the self-control of smoking behavior have not yielded much success. These failures may be due to the fact that social control of smoking has not been undertaken by obvious means such as discontinuing the manufacture of cigarettes, the advertising of the product, or a public positive reinforcement for cessation of smoking or for nonsmoking. Thus the person who attempts to stop smoking continues to be exposed to situations in which the behavior is under temptation (by the presence of S^Ds for smoking) or even reinforced. Because our social community appears reluctant to infringe upon a person's individual right to make independent personal choices in this area, none of the methods of environmental control have been widely applied to smoking. Consequently ,the application of self-controlling procedures has been most widespread in the management of such behaviors as smoking, overeating, and drinking in which environmental support or inherent gratification create conflicting consequences, and external controls are not practical.

Many of the clinical procedures used in control of smoking are similar to those described for obesity. For example, Homme (1965) suggests the following steps for the coverant control of smoking. The person is instructed to make a list of verbal events that he finds aversive in relation to smoking. He then selects one activity that occurs with high frequency during a day. This activity represents a reinforcing consequence (C^+) for the preceding antismoking coverant at any time that the person thinks about or begins to reach for a cigarette. Antismoking coverants are rehearsed and include items such as recital of the damaging physical consequences of smoking (for instance, "I will feel better" or "my physical condition will improve"). A well-established response is then carried out following the antismoking coverant. Preferably the controlling response is one that takes the person out of the situation, for example, getting out of an office chair or turning on the radio change the stimulus situation. The effectiveness of these procedures has not yet been evaluated by research data. In essence, this procedure aims to generate a high rate of responses antagonistic to the target behavior and its antecedents.

Tooley and Pratt (1967) combined three methods of behavior modification strategies in their successful treatment of smoking with a husband and wife. The procedure combined coverant control, covert sensitization, and contractual management. The last technique involves the negotiation of behavioral contracts wherein the smokers agreed to meet certain non-smoking obligations in exchange for approval from the therapist and for other social rewards. Contractual management had previously been described by the same authors (Pratt and Tooley, 1964a,b) as a technique in which an agreement is established between the patient and the therapist with clearly stated obligations on the part of both parties. The patient is reinforced for successful accomplishment of the established goals according to the conditions of the contract. In their discussion of the smoking case history, the authors illustrate many of the current therapeutic techniques for self-management, including the requirement that the patient keep records of his own behavior, the establishment of aversive consequences for breaking a contract, and the rehearsal of controlling responses designed to strengthen the behavior incompatible with a symptomatic response.

Since smoking involves behavior that can potentially be executed anywhere in the patient's environment, even aversive procedures established in the laboratory or clinic must be supplemented by self-controlling behaviors. Keutzer, Lichtenstein, and Mees (1968) have reviewed a series of studies in which aversion therapy procedures were practiced. These techniques employ the methods of stimulus control that we have discussed in Chapters 3, 4, and 7.

One modification of aversive techniques is reported by Mees (1966a) in which the subjects were required to hold their breath while imagining the inhalation of a cigarette. Breath-holding was also practiced outside the laboratory and was reported to be very effective. It falls within the scope of self-controlling devices, since the subject must initiate a controlling response (holding his breath) in the presence of stimulation that had previously served as an S^D for the symptomatic response of smoking.

A method of self-control commonly employed in clinical practice is the successive narrowing of the conditions under which a symptomatic behavior is permitted to occur. The underlying learning concept is that of decreasing the range of discriminative stimuli that control the inappropriate behavior. An illustration of this approach has been reported by Nolan (1968). The subject of the study was the author's wife. Nolan selected a particular chair placed in such a way that she could not conveniently watch television, carry on a conversation, or engage in other activities. When she wished to smoke she sat in the smoking chair. A daily record of cigarette consumption and time spent in the smoking chair revealed a gradual decline of cigarettes consumed over a period of one month. This method permits the gradual reduction of auxillary reinforcing stimuli (such as reading, drinking coffee or alcohol) usually associated with the smoking habit. In this therapeutic technique self-control is facilitated because there is no demand for sudden and complete elimination of the response. Instead, environmental changes are arranged that inherently reduce the potentials for the occurrence of maintaining stimuli associated with the habit by disruption of the behavioral pattern and their association with the response.

A similar technique of stimulus control has been used successfully by the authors of this book for the control of nail-biting and hair-pulling in adolescents. In its practical application patients are required to restrict the symptomatic response gradually, both in time and location. For example, the patient is asked to smoke or bite his nails only in a specific room or at a specific time. The restriction is increased slowly and demands for antagonistic substitutive responses are slowly increased until the symptom occurs at tolerable frequency or extinguishes altogether. The additional responses are introduced to prevent the execution of the symptomatic response. By establishing competing responses that initially are not overly restrictive or novel, the patient is aided in not giving up self-control as impossible before he even makes his first attempts. At the same time, the requirement of interpolating some new behaviors serves to interrupt an old response chain, increase the cost of the final response, provide opportunities for self-observation, and delay the symptomatic response. The engineering of new behavior sequences aids the person to manipulate controlling stimuli earlier in the total sequence when it is less difficult for him to interrupt the chain than at the point when the final symptomatic response is made. The demands that the patient sit in a particular chair, go to a designated room, make an entry in his observation book, or put on a particular piece of jewelry all meet the requirement of interrupting the firmly established chain of behaviors.

Ober (1968) compared self-control techniques with aversion treatment and an insight technique based on Berne's *Games People Play* (1964). The author obtained smoking rates on the basis of the patient's self-reports and the reports of informants, and found that these two sources of information correlated very highly. The experimental groups showed a smoking reduction of approximately 50 percent with no significant difference between the operant and aversive procedures. Both methods were more effective than the transactional analysis treatment. Rutner (1967) compared subjects assigned to a covert sensitization group, a "breath-holding" group (using Mees' method previously reported), a contractual management group (Tooley and Pratt, 1967), and a self-monitoring group (Kanfer, 1967b). All subjects were seen for one treatment session. They were instructed in the procedure and given sufficient practice to carry out treatment by themselves. At the end of 21 days, data were collected on their smoking behavior during the interim. All five groups significantly reduced smoking behavior after treatment. The contract management group was more successful than the others. Rutner also administered the Rotter IE scale, which differentiates people who see either themselves or the external world as the major agents responsible for controlling their behavior. There was no correlation between the scores on this scale and success in behavior modification. Keutzer (1967) compared Homme's covert control procedure, Mees' breath-holding technique, and a negative practice group for their effectiveness in reducing smoking behavior. In addition, several control groups were used. Subjects were asked to practice the various techniques between experimental sessions. Although there was a significantly greater decrease in smoking in the treated groups than in the controls, there was no significant difference among the various types of treatments. The reports of successful control of smoking behavior have not been general, however. Inadequate follow-up of therapy adherence and post-therapy measurements and poor design of clinical studies have raised questions about adequacy of the reported research and the general effectiveness of the techniques (Bernstein, 1969).

Other Self-Administered Behavior Control Techniques

In principle, the arrangement of any response-reinforcement contingency could be applied by a subject to his own behavior, if the person is capable of observing the occurrence of the response and executing the contingent reinforcement only when called for by the treatment program. Numerous reports by clinicians indicate that the application of electric shock, following an aversion therapy paradigm, has been put under the subject's own control with beneficial effects. For example, McGuire and Vallance (1964) describe the use of a simple apparatus for administering mild shock contingent upon particular symptomatic behaviors. In this procedure a fetishist may be asked to administer shock after the onset of fetishistic fantasies. Obsessive ruminations, excessive alcohol intake, and other behavior disorders have been treated by introducing the patient first to the aversion therapy procedure and then requesting that he administer the treatment to himself at home with a portable electric shock generator. McGuire and Vallance report treatment of a series of cases by this technique with good success and relatively few treatment dropouts.

An illustration of the direct application of self-reinforcement and self-monitoring concepts in clinical procedures is offered in a well-controlled study by Rehm and Marston (1968). The procedure essentially used manipulation of overt self-reinforcement to effect a positive change in self attitudes and social behaviors, with associated anxiety reduction and increased approach to feared situations. Male college students who reported dating problems were first screened to eliminate those with serious emotional problems. Subjects in the self-reinforcement (SR) group were asked to construct a desensitization type hierarchy from 30 standard items describing heterosexual situations, ranging from contacts such as taking a seat next to a girl in class to kissing a girl. Each student arranged these items according to the degree of discomfort he would experience in the situation. An information sheet was also given to each subject, briefly describing the theoretical basis of the treatment. Finally, a battery of tests was given to permit evaluation of therapeutic effects. It consisted of several questionnaires and taped social situations to which subjects were asked to respond, as if they were actual encounters with a girl. The gist of the procedure was the subject's assignment to attempt to get into the situations described in his hierarchy by steps, and to evaluate and reward his performance with self-approval for each successful attempt. A detailed record was kept by the subject and his self-reward was further reinforced by the therapist in five weekly sessions. Control groups involved traditional nondirective sessions or supportive sessions in which subjects were encouraged to conceptualize their problem and to work on it. In addition to a posttreatment session, a follow-up was conducted seven to nine months after the end of the study. The SR group showed the greatest improvement on measures of self-reported anxiety and overt behavior in specific situations, of verbal behavior in simulated social interactions, and on tests of general anxiety and self-description. The study demonstrates the utility of a systematic learning approach to a therapy-procedure that assumes that changes in social behavior can be mediated by changes in the self-reactions on which they depend. This assumption is also the one made in traditional insight therapy. But the learning approach, by contrast, uses methods of training based on reinforcement theory, with recording and identification of specific responses as targets and utilization of self-reward as ingredients of the procedure.

Rutner and Bugle (1969) report utilization of self-monitoring procedures in which the individual is required to keep a record of the frequency of the symptomatic behavior. This record-keeping is intended to interrupt the behavior and to permit the individual to label and recognize the onset of the behavior, thus helping him to bring it under his own control. A schizophrenic patient, who had been hospitalized for 13 years, was particularly distressed that her behavior was controlled by "voices." The patient was instructed to record the frequency of her hallucinatory behavior for a three-day period and the resulting frequency charts were posted on the ward. Reported hallucinations decreased from a base line of 91 to zero on the first experimental day, increased to 60 on the following day and then declined to zero. No remissions were reported for a subsequent three-month period. The authors suggest that the public placement of the chart on the ward changed the patient's hallucinations from their status as private events with no feedback from the social community, to public events subject to social disapproval and negative reinforcement. The same patient also showed changes in many social behaviors on the ward. This dramatic reduction of a psychotic symptom by relatively simple techniques is consistent with the assumption that the maintenance of psychotic behavior is closely related to its inaccessibility to public evaluation and reinforcement. Rutner and Bugle's study on one patient is consistent with other clinical experiences. Nevertheless, an understanding of the underlying process and evaluation of the general effectiveness of this technique must await more extensive reports.

The gradual transfer of behavior therapy techniques from therapist to patient usually includes the initial training and execution of the treatment program. Subsequently the clinician asks the patient to take over the clinician's role. Mees (1966b) reports one such transfer with successful results in a patient who learned to control sadistic fantasies during masturbation by means of self-administered aversive stimuli. Although no published reports are available of similar clinician-to-patient transfers for operant conditioning with positive reinforcement, the previously reviewed literature on self-reinforcement suggests that positive reinforcement may also be self-administered contingent upon particular criteria. Attempts to use verbal self-reinforcing stimuli and material reinforcers, such as buying a hat or going to a movie contingent upon accomplishment of a prescribed behavioral sequence, have been used widely in treatment and are consistent with the daily experiences of most people. However, the majority of reported research in the area of self-control techniques is at the demonstration and case report stage and closely controlled studies of the effectiveness of specific variables are still lacking.

Contract Management

Many earlier writers have emphasized that a psychotherapeutic interaction requires the implicit or explicit agreement between patient and therapist about the conditions for treatment. Sulzer (1962) and Pratt and Tooley (1964b) have described more explicitly the utility of a therapeutic contract in behavior modification techniques. In these procedures there is deliberate negotiation of contracts that demand specific behaviors of the patient and for whose successful achievement the therapist provides a predetermined reinforcement. The contracts constitute an agreement between the two parties that makes the behavior of each party contingent upon the behavior of the other and reciprocal exchanges of behavior are then defined in the contract. Although no research is available at present concerning the processes underlying the contract, previously reviewed studies have already indicated the pragmatic utility of this procedure. The establishment of a contract may provide specific targets that the patient can aim for, and it clearly specifies the means and consequences of fulfilling the contract. It is probable that the general tendency of most members in our society to fulfill obligations that they have accepted in formal agreements with others enhances the motivational resources for the behavioral changes specified in the contract. Although contract management has certain similarities to the type of agreement an individual may make with himself in New Year's resolutions or with "good intentions," it has the added power of providing an opportunity to discuss methods for achieving desired results and establishing reinforcing consequences with another individual. In this sense, self-control is enhanced by the method of relinquishing partial control over one's behavior to another individual who acts so as to aid the person to establish controlling responses and who takes responsibility for administering contingent reinforcers.

Self-Confrontation

Numerous therapeutic techniques share the principle of providing objective feedback to the patients to give them an opportunity to "see themselves as others see them." The advent of closed-circuit television has resulted in a renewal of interest in this technique. Conceptually, these approaches provide the patient with objective information about his behavior that can then become the cue for self-regulatory action. Gallup (1968) in a review of the literature, notes the responsiveness of animals and men to their mirror-images and suggests that these self-confronting devices have therapeutic utility in modifying the patient's distorted inferences about himself, based on the appraisals of others. In clinical studies, Moore, Chernell, and West (1965) and Stoller (1968) report the beneficial effects of exposure of patients to a replay of videotape recordings in individual therapy interviews and therapy groups, respectively. Cornelison and Arsenian (1960) exposed psychotic patients to photographs of themselves and noted favorable changes as a result of this self-confrontation.

Self-Control by Imagined Aversive Consequences

Davison (1969a) reports a self-control technique used with an eleven-year-old boy with serious difficulties at home. After ascertaining the conditions under which the child was unruly and other situations in which he was well behaved, Davison asked the boy to "imagine as hard as he could" the factors that had controlled obedient behavior in the past. These discriminative stimuli turned out to be the father's angry mood, or the stern control by counselors in a summer camp where the boy had been well behaved. With brief practice in the consultation room, the boy was able to generate both the inhibiting imaginative stimuli as well as the anxiety associated with these stimuli. Training in what Davison calls "imaginal aversive contingency" technique resulted in rapid improvement in the child-father relationship. Several other techniques were used with this child in subsequent sessions. Davison also points out the importance of the relationship of the boy to the therapist and its usefulness for providing effective reinforcement and some stimulus control in producing the boy's behavior change. The technique is similar to Homme's control of coverants in that self-generation of controlling responses is sought, with the consequence of reducing the probability of the undesirable behavior. It is also a technique that has been reported by Ferster for strengthening the effects of ultimate aversive consequences of a habit on the particular occurrence of a single instance.

Behavioral Analysis Training

A related group of techniques for training in self-control has been suggested by Goldiamond (1965). Assuming that part of the difficulty in self-control lies in the patient's inability to analyze the external and internal stimulus conditions, the environmental contingencies, and the schedule under which he operates, the patient's response pattern remains helplessly bound to controlling variables beyond the patient's reach. By training a person to carry out a behavioral analysis, that is, to recognize the functional relationships between his actions and antecedent and subsequent environmental events, he can then gain greater control over external and internal determinants of his actions. Once he is "master of his fate" to a greater degree, more effective behavior can be expected. This method is similar to the one used by Ferster to control obesity, as described earlier in this chapter. The essential feature of this method lies in helping the patient to attend to his own behavior more objectively, to appraise his environment, to note the consequences of his behavior in a more detached fashion, and, finally, to treat his own "case" by manipulating controlling variables as the clinician might for another person. In the clinical application of this procedure the patient is guided through a formal didactic course in behavioral analysis, with counseling by the therapist about potential operations that could produce the desired behavior change according to behavioral principles. Use of this technique is limited to persons with sufficient educational background, strong motivation, and interest to undertake a program that at first seems to have only distant relevancy to his current behavioral problems. It is an approach that is well suited, however, for intelligent adult patients whose behavioral problems stem from their lack of techniques for changing their environment and their own behavior.

SOME THEORETICAL CONSIDERATIONS ABOUT SELF-REGULATION IN THERAPY

A major criticism of early operant learning approaches to psychiatric problems has been that the techniques used only external controls in treatment. It has been argued by traditional therapists that only reorganization of the personality, increased self-awareness, and broader understanding of the determinants of one's own behavior can bring about lasting personality changes. Symptom removal and learning of more effective behaviors have been viewed solely as incidental by-products of changes in more fundamental psychological processes. These criticisms appear most cogent for early attempts at behavior modification, which concentrated on reduction of motoric symptoms that can be more easily controlled by direct environmental manipulations. Indeed, treatment of clearly definable response classes has been most successful with institutionalized psychotics and with children, over whose environment considerable control can be exercised. In adult neurotics, the greater independence of the problematic behaviors from the controlling social environment has posed problems in definition of the target behavior, in arranging more favorable response-reinforcement contingencies, and in providing effective reinforcers. These problems are especially pronounced in patients whose symptomatic behaviors consist mainly of covert, unshared, often inaccessible, private responses. Furthermore, these behaviors constitute what have been called "mental events" and, on methodological and philosophical grounds, they were excluded from the early behavioristic systems. Contemporary approaches are attempting to provide coverage for the full range of problematic behaviors covering all human functions, including "self-responses." These internal events make up a domain of important behaviors governing the individual's actions in relation to himself and others, even though they are only distantly initiated or maintained by the social and physical environment. Current efforts to expand behavioristic systems to these private behavior patterns are faced with several problems, which we will summarize here. All of them arise out of the limited knowledge of (1) the particular psychological processes governing a person's reaction to himself and to the variables that represent sources of external control over his behavior; (2) the means by which these reactions are integrated

into the person's total action systems; and (3) the events that can serve
to reinforce and maintain these covert patterns.

The Person as Object and Subject

We have briefly noted the problem of dual roles of a behaving person
in connection with our discussion of verbal interactions. In the laboratory,
self-administration of procedures is not new. In fact, nineteenth century
researchers frequently performed experiments in learning and psycho-
physics on themselves. For example, psychologists collated series of
paired-associate nonsense syllables and then examined their recall for lists
of various lengths, as a function of different presentation variables. Similarly, in psychophysical experiments, investigators arranged random series
of stimulus presentations and then noted their own responses on each
trial. Although there undoubtedly was some biasing effect due to the investigators' previous knowledge, the obtained data essentially reflected the
same learning pattern as obtained when naive subjects were used. Contemporary investigators have reported similar success in obtaining the
usual acquisition curves for classical conditioning even when the procedure
is self-administered. Nevertheless, there is as yet not sufficient work to
judge the extent to which administration of a learning series by another
person would differ from self-administered learning.

In clinical practice, use of self-administered techniques encounters an
additional problem. Patients frequently seek advice from friends and often
reject it as too difficult to follow. As a result they may obtain considerable
social reinforcement for expressing inability to control their own behavior.
In fact, in human interactions it is not uncommon to observe that a man's
statement of incapacity to control himself has beneficial consequences
by its controlling effect on others who respond to him sympathetically
and reduce aversive stimulation to the patient. Reinforcement for expressions of inability or inadequacy is illustrated in child-rearing when teachers
or parents lower their standards for the child's achievement, extend a
helping hand, or even reward the child for "trying" when he persists
in protesting that he is unable to accomplish a task, or that he cannot
control some parts of his own response system.

Self-Monitoring

In the study of self-regulatory processes it must be demonstrated what
conditions initiate the effort of a person to modify his own behavior,
what methods and mechanisms are used for the modification, and under
what conditions these modifying efforts cease. Some basis for speculation
about self-monitoring processes can be taken from the experimental litera-

ture on human vigilance and human attention. Studies in these areas have demonstrated that attending behaviors are affected by the variation in some property of the presented stimulus materials as well as the contingent reinforcement for attending and the natural consequences associated with attending or failure to attend to particular signal inputs. In continuous adult behavior there are points at which self-monitoring processes begin and the cues for the onset of such processes need to be examined. On a speculative basis, Kanfer (1967b) has proposed that self-regulatory processes are triggered when self-monitoring reveals a departure from a range of consensually acceptable behaviors in a situation that may have ultimate aversive consequences. To understand the nature of self-monitoring, one can take an example from childhood learning. A mother or teacher functions as a monitor for a young child by interfering only when a behavioral sequence signals a tendency to deviate from the range of behaviors that the adult considers appropriate for the situation. Training in self-monitoring is facilitated when the trainer labels the cues for detecting deviations and assists the child in rectifying his behaviors by direct guidance or by permitting the child to observe corrections in the trainer's own monitoring. A useful model may be one that is similar to the feedback circuitry involved in quality control analysis. At first the feedback loop affects only the mother of a child who is the "inspector" and initiates corrective behaviors in the child. Eventually, direct feedback to the child is established by training and the necessity for the mother's labeling and corrective response no longer exists. This hypothesis proposes that self-regulation is *not* a continuous process but is invoked only as a self-correcting procedure when discrepancies, cues of impending danger, or conflicting motivational states activate the monitoring system.

A number of studies seem to indicate that fully adequate self-observation is rarely encountered in people, and that the opportunity to observe one's own behavior objectively results in changes of relatively large magnitude, in contrast to the minimal effects due to information about oneself that is verbal, abstract, and based on the observations of others. For example, Holzman, Rousey, and Snyder (1966) studied the effects of being confronted by one's own voice. Physiological responses showed greater activation by one's own voice than by that of another, whether or not the subjects consciously recognized their own voices. When playback was delayed for three months after taping, the significant activation by one's own voice persisted for those who recognized their own voices and continued as a tendency for those who did not recognize their own voices. The authors conclude that hearing one's own voice is indeed a different experience from hearing the voices of others. Confronting a person with a videotape or picture of himself has repeatedly been shown to produce marked changes in behavior (Cornelison and Arsenian, 1960; Miller, 1962; Walz and Johnston, 1963). Boyd and Sisney (1967) presented playbacks of videotapes of a standardized interview to neuropsychiatric patients. The self-image confrontation produced changes in the patient's responses on the Leary Interpersonal Check List, suggesting that interpersonal concepts of the self, the ideal self, and the public self became less pathological and less discrepant with one another than for control subjects who were not exposed to a playback of their own interviews. These differences were apparent two weeks after the original self-confrontation.

We have proposed (Kanfer, 1967b) that learning to monitor one's own behavior and to observe one's actions with some objectivity is an essential prerequisite for initiation of useful self-regulatory behaviors. It therefore is expected that adequate self-control would be encountered to a greater extent in individuals who have had better training in self-observation and self-monitoring and can activate self-regulatory processes when called for. Deviations from the culturally determined and commonly accepted behavioral band which trigger self-regulatory processes may be in terms of physical response characteristics, functional consequences, the rate of the behavior, or appropriateness for the given stimulus conditions. A clear example of the use of self-monitoring as a preliminary step in behavior modification is found in the frequent requests by behavior therapists that the patient begin treatment by recording the frequency of occurrence of his symptoms, their consequences, and the stimulus conditions under which they occur. For example, Lindsley, at the Kansas University Medical Center, has used portable counters that are similar to the commercial type used for keeping golf scores and are strapped on the wrist. By means of this counter the patient can tally the exact rate of a specified response class over a period of time. In the analysis of his problem the patient is taught to recognize the relationships of many symptomatic responses to particular circumstances or reinforcing contingencies. Construction of graphs showing response distributions and plots of behavior changes represents further training devices to aid the patient in developing methods for accurate self-monitoring. The patient's monitoring of his behavior can also help him toward better discriminations among his behaviors and can reveal the various social contexts with which particular responses are associated.

In daily life a number of cues for the onset of self-monitoring behaviors seem to be available. Among these are (1) intervention by others, for instance, the threat of punishment, or the focus on one's own behavior by an external event. A mother's critical comment or a boss' low performance rating for a specific job are examples in this class; (2) the presence of extreme activation levels may serve as cues for self-monitoring. For instance, physiological feedback of hyperactivity, excitement, emotional states, boredom, and depressed behavior may serve as cue functions for self-monitoring; (3) the failure to achieve predicted consequences or desired effects may occasion self-monitoring, such as when operation of an unfamiliar car does not lead to starting the engine, telling a joke in a social situation does not lead to laughter, or a verbal response fails to exert control over physical or social stimulus objects; and (4) the availability of several different roles or response sets with approximately equal strengths. This cue of self-monitoring is inherent in most choice or conflict situations. Once elicited, the nature of the self-monitoring behavior, in turn, is a function of the person's previous training. For example, the conditions that we have hypothesized for the onset of self-monitoring may lead one person to seek additional information by observing the reactions of others to himself or by obtaining objective information about his performance; but another person may turn to introspective ruminations instead. The persistent patterns of action in self-monitoring represent an important personality dimension since their relative contributions toward effective self-regulation or self-correction differ widely.

The acquisition of self-descriptive behaviors has been analyzed in detail by Skinner (1953, 1957) and have recently been elaborated by Bem (1967). In this framework, self-descriptive statements are viewed as dependent on multiple controlling stimuli. They are determined in part by internal stimuli, but they may also be controlled by discriminative stimuli provided by the subject's social community. Self-descriptions represent the product of a person's information about himself from many sources. One significant yardstick for evaluating such information is derived from the social norms to which the person is exposed. In fact, social comparison processes have been suggested by several authors as the major sources of self-evaluative statements. For instance, a player's evaluation of his tennis game and his consequent plan for practice would depend upon the number and kind of self-observations and upon the normative group with which he compares his performance. A champion player will hardly be satisfied with top spot among a class of high school varsity players. A study by Kanfer and Duerfeldt (1967a) explored the effects of an experimenter's evaluation on a subject's later self-evaluation on an ambiguous task. The experimenter's judgment was ostensibly based on the performance of a peer reference group. The result showed significant effects of these judgments on the subject's evaluation of his own behavior, although the frequency of his self-reinforcements did not change. The importance of available social performance standards in the development of children's self-reward patterns has been demonstrated in several studies by Bandura and his colleagues described earlier.

Self-Persuasion

Once a person has made a self-descriptive statement and compared his behavior with a reference group he may be faced with the next step in the process, that is, modifying his own behavior. Festinger (1957) has been dealing with problems arising from the contradictions created when a person receives information that is inconsistent with his prior behavior. Festinger holds that the coexistence of two cognitions that are inconsistent with each other creates an aversive motivational state that will result in alteration of one of the two dissonant cognitions. Since the past behavior cannot be changed, the person will tend to reduce the discrepancy by any maneuver that realigns the two events. A somewhat different approach to the same problem has been advanced by Bem (1967), who suggests that an individual bases his subsequent beliefs and attitudes on the evaluation of his own previous behaviors, judging them as another observer would. If a person can be induced to engage in some behavior that is not fully consistent with his previously held attitudes, he may then exhibit attitudes or judgments that can be viewed as interpersonal judgments in which the observer and the observed happen to be the same individual.

The experimental basis is illustrated in two studies on self-persuasion by Bem. In the first study (Bem, 1965), subjects were trained to tell the truth in the presence of one colored light and to lie in the presence of another. They were then required to state attitudes with which they disagreed, while one of the two colored lights was illuminated during each statement. It was found that the attitude statements uttered in the presence of the "truth light" were later endorsed significantly more often than those made in the presence of the "lie light." The lights determined the degree to which subjects believed what they had heard themselves say. Bem also reported that the subjects were not aware of the influence exerted by their previous statements or by the color of the lights. In another study, the same technique was employed to demonstrate that an individual can be induced to believe his "false confessions," if there are external cues present that characteristically set the occasion for telling the truth (Bem, 1966). Similarly, "true confessions" associated with cues for lying led to self-disbelief, that is, distortions in the recall of the actual experiences. These studies suggest that attitude statements can be regarded as a person's inferences from observations of his own overt behavior and the accompanying stimulus variables (when internal stimuli are not sufficiently strong to overshadow these effects). Bem argues that a person's own statements are therefore functionally similar to those that any outside observer would make about his behavior, because both originate in the observation of a person's response and its controlling factors.

When a person believes that a noticeable behavior change can be attributed to his own actions rather than to an external agent, he shows a greater persistence in this behavior. Davison and Valins (1969) tested this hypothesis in an experiment that represented an analogue to psychiatric treatment with tranquilizing drugs. All subjects were given a drug (actually a placebo), ostensibly to test its effect on skin sensitivity to electric shock stimuli. Pain threshold and shock tolerance were tested prior to and following ingestion of the pill. On the second test the shock intensities were surreptitiously reduced by half. All subjects believed that the drug had changed their performance. Half of the subjects were than told that they had actually received a placebo, whereas the other half continued to believe that they received a true drug. On a subsequent test it was found that subjects who attributed their lower sensitivity to drug action perceived the shocks as more painful and tolerated significantly fewer than subjects who were informed of the placebo effect (those who attributed their behavior change on the prior test to their own actions). A replication of the study with minor procedural refinements yielded the same results. In another experiment (Bandler, Madaras, and Bem, 1968), subjects were asked to rate their discomfort after receiving electric shocks in either an escape or a no-escape condition. The authors argued that a person may use his own overt behavior in response to an aversive stimulus as a basis for inferring its painfulness. Therefore, even though the physical shock intensity is constant in all conditions, subjects should perceive the shock as more painful when they terminated (escaped) it. The results verified this prediction. Appropriate control conditions ruled out alternate explanations of the findings; records of the galvanic skin responses suggested that differences in actual physiological arousal did not serve as a basis for the subjects' discomfort ratings. These experiments support the general assumption that observations of one's own past behavior can have a striking effect on a person's later attitudes and behavior. This effect may be further enhanced when the actions can be attributed to the person's own initiative.

In clinical application, several schools of therapy utilize techniques that are consistent with this conceptual framework. For example, George Kelly (1955) advocates a role playing technique in which the patient is asked to engage in behaviors, uncharacteristic of himself, but consistent with the behavior of the person he would like to be. Repeated execution of this type of behavior is expected to lead the person not only to act differently but also to think of himself as a different person. Similarly, the emphasis of behavior therapy on the execution of behaviors instead of on insight is supported by the assumption that changes in behavior will lead a person to change his attitude about himself, yielding new insights after new behaviors have appeared. A considerable body of research from Rogers' nondirective approach has dealt with changes during psychotherapy affecting the discrepancy between a person's self-image and ideal image. It is presumed that therapeutic benefits can be measured by a decrease in discrepancy between these two different sets of attitudes. From the behavioral viewpoint, it is expected that increased correspondence between real and ideal self-attitudes would be accompanied or perhaps preceded by increased change toward the behavior attributed to the ideal self-image.

In addition to description of the mechanisms by which changes in self-perception can occur, one must also ask what are the motivational bases for initiating efforts toward attitude change. A number of personality theories have incorporated a motivational construct that assumes an innate human drive toward consistency, self-fulfillment, self-improvement, or self-actualization, ascribing to man constant effort to achieve higher and improved levels of functioning. Although behavioristic approaches do not accept the innate qualities of such a motivational system, its existence might be demonstrated on the basis of common early experiences for many children in the Western cultures in which the positive qualities of continued striving for self-consistency and self-improvement are emphasized and the instrumental behaviors are reinforced. Despite the importance of this question in understanding human functioning, there is little experimental work that yields empirical support to a description of the features that initiate and maintain self-corrective behavior processes.

Servomechanisms and Self-Regulation

As we have indicated in our discussion of the behavioral equation in Chapter 2, internal or organismic variables constantly modify the response to the environment. A person's own behavior can serve as input and can be further modified by past experiences, present motivational conditions, or other individual factors. Numerous psychological theories in the areas of learning, perception, and motivation accommodate the concept of a feedback loop, that is, the continued adjustment of a person's behavior as a function of his own response. The area of research on response feedback offers some thoughts for further consolidation of the theoretical basis for self-corrective behaviors. The idea that response probability is affected by the person's previous state of arousal, by his success expectations, or by self-imposed performance criteria has appeared from time to time in various contexts. All of these proposed mechanisms share the concept of some adjustive device triggered by the feedback effects of a response that continues to affect further responses until the imposed standard or response level is met.

The recent literature on verbal learning yields several illustrations of the phenomena of human self-adjustment with which we are concerned. For instance, the facilitative effect of knowledge of results upon learning and performance has been widely described. In a review of the literature on the motivational effects of knowledge of results, Locke, Cartledge, and Koeppel (1968) suggested that these effects are modified by the learner's standards of evaluation, the goals that he sets himself for performing the task. Thus the simple concept of knowledge of results as a reinforcing event is expanded by these writers to include some type of prior goal or reference level against which performance is compared. Brown and McNeill (1966) describe tip-of-the tongue behavior in which a subject runs through several responses similar to the correct one before making his final choice. Adams describes this behavior:

"As the subject runs through a series of similar responses, he has the clear feeling that he knows the correct response, has it on the tip of his tongue, and can give it in just a moment. Moreover, the subject not only knows he is in error and must reject wrong responses, but also knows the relative magnitude of the errors. For example, a subject might be asked to give the capitol of the State of Illinois. He might say, "The capitol of Illinois is Bloomington. No, that's wrong! Plainfield! No, that isn't it either! Summerfield! That's close! Springfield! That's it!" The subject certainly seems to know that his first response is a relatively large error and should be summarily rejected, that the second response has smaller error and is in the general region of the correct response, that the third response is very close to being correct, and so on" (Adams, 1967, pp. 284–285).

Hart (1965) presented subjects with verbal paired associates and then gave them a recall test. After recall, he asked them to judge whether they had a *feeling of knowing* the missed items. In a subsequent recognition test, in which correct answers had to be selected among four alternatives, he found that the subjects' "feeling of knowing" had good accuracy in predicting success on the recognition task.

These experiments suggest that the effects of a person's own behavior can be viewed as a link by which his actions are immediately converted into stimuli for following responses, or for matching against a performance standard. These feedback effects can be differentiated from the environmental consequences of a response. Considerable experimental work has been devoted to isolating these effects in animal studies, since early S–R theory placed heavy reliance on the role of proprioceptive feedback as response-produced cues, triggering off the next response element in the chain of motor behaviors, such as maze-running. In contrast, S–S theory emphasizes cognitive learning of stimuli and requires no peripheral response trigger to account for learning. The results of these studies were not unequivocal. Although proprioceptive feedback was shown to be useful in learning, it did not turn out to be indispensable (Solomon and Turner, 1962).

A critical expansion of response feedback theory was proposed by Miller, Galanter, and Pribram (1960), Adams (1967, 1968) and others who incorporate an error-correcting phase in the feedback loop, patterned after the servo theory of engineering, which describes the self-correction of devices such as a thermostat, or an automatic aircraft pilot. In these models an input (for example, a signal from the organism's muscle system) is compared to a reference mechanism. Any deviation from the standard (an error) is corrected until the error is reduced to zero. Studies in motivation and learning have demonstrated the overt outcome of these presumed corrective maneuvers and have even shown that the corrective actions of a learner follow his own response and *precede* external reinforcement. The main theoretical problem lies in accounting for the process of storing past experiences and for the mechanisms by which the living organism compares present and past performance, or matches standards and continues or ceases corrective behavior as a result of this comparison. In the hypothetical model of a comparison mechanism, which somehow matches the evaluation (or feedback) of the present response and the established criterion, the state of no-discriminable-difference between evaluation of one's performance and the standard could serve as a signal for cessation of further correction responses and administration of self-reinforcement. In fact, reaching the criterion may be the reinforcing event itself. This reinforcement (similar to the mechanism proposed by Adams (1968), Eimas and Zeaman (1963), and others) would have informational properties in stopping the error-correcting sequence, and motivational properties if one accepts the assumption that man is inherently motivated by goal achievement. Although the empirical support for this theoretical formulation is mainly based on analogues, the treatment of verbal learning and perceptual data by a theory incorporating response feedback and a mechanism for criteria-matching may be of heuristic value in organizing our thinking about self-regulation. A tentative view of self-regulation along the proposed lines has the advantage of clarifying the conceptual relationship between self-monitoring (as the deliberate attending to response feedback), performance criteria (as social or personal standards), and self-reinforcement (as a result of certain outcomes of discrimination between performance and standard). The overwhelming advantage, however, lies in the possibility of bringing this area of human functioning into direct contact with other learning research, thus providing a broader empirical basis for refinement of this very coarse model.

The clinical procedures issuing from the self-regulation model are consistent with the techniques illustrated in preceding pages. When patients are requested to keep a record of their own behavior, the explicit description of discrete responses should enhance the ease of discriminability between these behaviors and a standard proposed by the therapist or the patient, in comparison to vague self-reports or casual and anecdotal reconstruction. Furthermore, the selection of a target behavior is usually accompanied, explicitly or implicitly, by a simultaneous statement of more appropriate responses to be substituted, thus providing some fundamental dimension along which the magnitude of "error" can be measured in assessing the degree to which one's behavior deviates from the ideal or proposed standard. Finally, these specifications should permit the therapist to assist the patient in selecting appropriate "error-correcting" behaviors, thus hastening the acquisition of new responses to be substituted for the undesirable ones.

From these considerations one would also predict that favorable behavior changes are obtained only when the self-monitored response contains some aversive elements. For example, self-reporting of successful social behaviors, or failure of the patient to agree with the therapist that the proposed criterial response is indeed a more desirable one, should result in little change. In effect, clinical observations and incidental comments from experimental subjects in behavior modification studies suggest that the effects of self-monitoring show great individual differences. Some of these differences may be attributable to the combination of a target response and the person's view of the desirability of the response. The importance of selecting a particular response for self-observation is illustrated in a study by McFall (1970). Students were asked to record their frequency of smoking during class periods. One group was instructed to record the actual frequency of cigarette smoking while a second group was told to tally the occasions on which they considered smoking but, for whatever reason, did not do so. The instructor did not discourage smoking. McFall found that self-monitoring significantly changed smoking frequency over a previous base rate period, during which unobtrusive measures were taken by an observer. However, during the self-monitoring period, subjects who recorded smoking increased their rate, but those who recorded thinking of smoking but did not smoke decreased their smoking rate. Clearly, in this study self-monitoring had the opposite effects for the two response classes.

Most application of self-directed behavior therapies is undertaken with patients who are voluntary candidates for psychotherapy. Under these conditions, the desirability of behavior change and acceptability of a proposed response is rarely a serious question. The features of the hypothetical mechanism of self-regulation proposed above are illustrated also in a paper by Kolb, Winter, and Berlew (1968). In two studies on self-directed change, graduate students, who were members of a laboratory training group, set goals for changing their personal behavior relevant to their group interactions. The authors hypothesized that people are more likely to make permanent changes if they feel themselves responsible for the change. They also assumed that their subjects were motivated toward achieving the stated goals. Each subject was asked to select a particular goal toward which he would work. The subject observed his own behaviors relevant to the target response and prepared daily graphs on their frequency of occurrence. In this procedure the authors emphasized the importance of setting a specific goal. They further predicted that the observed change in behavior would be related to the degree of the subject's commitment. The procedures involved two sources of feedback, from self-observations and from observations and opinions expressed by members of the group during the meetings. During a ten-week series of meetings 54 subjects underwent this procedure. Half the group was encouraged to discuss their project in the sessions and the group members reacted to the subject's project (feedback condition). The remaining subjects did not discuss their project in the group (no-feedback condition). By this design the amount of feedback was experimentally varied for the groups. The authors found significantly more change for those subjects whose projects were discussed in the groups. In addition, there was a low significant correlation with a measure of degree of commitment, evaluated from a questionnaire filled out by the subject. In a second study all subjects underwent the same procedure except that, in addition to self-perceived records of change in the target behavior, the group leaders also rated the amount of observed change. In general, group leaders tended to rate the change somewhat lower than subjects rated their own change. However, it was found that the amount of discussion was significantly related to self-perceived change and to the change reported by the group leader. Thus the study illustrates the effectiveness of establishing a specific target, monitoring the initial behavior and the successive behavioral changes. The relevance of the amount of feedback from self observations and from group ratings for facilitating change tends to support the general notion of the importance of feedback in self-initiated behavior modification. Similarly, the relevance of initial commitment or willingness to adhere to a specific criterion of performance reflects the influence of the initial goal level of the person on the amount of behavior change to be expected. It remains for further experiments in this area to determine to what extent therapeutic manipulations of the comparison standards and amount of feedback can affect a course of treatment.

ARRANGEMENTS FOR SELF-CONTROL

As we have previously indicated, the decision to change one's own behavior requires deliberate disruption of previously well-coordinated, smoothly functioning procedures. Our theoretical analysis suggests that the disruption of undesirable response sequences can be best carried out if a person can (1) intervene early in the response sequence; (2) utilize environmental controls so that the burden of nonexecution of a symptomatic response does not come at a point where its potential payoff and its response strength due to past experience are too great; (3) execute alternate behaviors that have a reasonably high potential for reinforcement; (4) practice controlling responses and expect that they will be reinforced by his social environment; (5) specify the desired terminal behavior; and (6) obtain clear feedback during his attempts to change. The techniques of contract management, coverant therapy, deliberate self-observation, labeling of discriminative stimuli for symptomatic behaviors, and other arrangements of positive consequences for self-control all serve to facilitate the substitution of new behaviors by self-controlling procedures. It is noteworthy that exhortation, moral persuasion, and appeal to the patient's will power differ from the described treatment methods in that they do not train the patient in the analysis of behavior and particular techniques that would enable him to achieve the results suggested by good advice.

Our review of current work on self-reinforcement indicates that the pattern of self-administered rewards and criticisms can be influenced by social manipulations once a self-monitoring process has been initiated. Relatively little work is available from clinical practice to support the laboratory findings and the theoretical contentions of the importance of this mechanism in self-regulation.

Although this chapter has dealt with behavioral approaches to the most challenging area of human functioning, that of man's capacity to guide his own destiny, we have seen that both laboratory work and clinical practice have more speculations to offer than solid experimental or clinical evidence. Nevertheless, a natural extension of behavior therapy to these areas remains a proving ground for the adequacy of the behavioristic approach in covering human behavior in its entity. Therefore, it is in this area more than others that continued research is needed to assure a firmer footing of clinical applications of learning psychology.

SUMMARY

Training methods for helping a person control his own behavior have been applied only recently in behavior therapy. Nevertheless, they represent a series of techniques that can be used to extend behavior therapy to new problems, especially with patients whose behavior is sufficiently intact to permit their cooperation and whose environment is not easily controlled.

In conceptualizing the process of self-regulation, the assumption is made that self-attitudes, self-evaluations, and self-reinforcement originate in the selective reinforcement of the child's self-related behaviors by his social environment. Eventually, a pattern of such reactions is established for different behavior segments by imitation and by contingency learning. For convenience, these functionally related response patterns have been characterized as the self-system.

The process of self-control has been described as one in which a person alters the probability of occurrence of a behavior by changing the variables that have controlled its occurrence in the past. The most common self-controlling methods are those in which the person initiates a shift in stimulus control from one feature of the environment to another, originates a competing response, or provides reinforcement for any controlling response. Self-control includes two types of situations: (1) a highly valued event or reinforcing stimulus is available and a person fails to execute behaviors that would bring the event or object within reach; and (2) a person continues to tolerate aversive stimulation and fails to make available avoidance or escape responses. The target behavior for self-control always has conflicting consequences (positive and negative), with nearly equal potential for maintaining an approach or avoidance response.

We have noted that training to tolerate delay of reinforcement represents one facet of a self-control program. Numerous other self-control programs are available and include increase in reinforcement for controlling responses, deliberate alteration of environmental controlling stimuli early in the behavior sequence (when the probability of making the target response is still fairly low), utilization of self-reinforcement for nonexecution of the target response, execution of a incompatible behaviors, removal of the physical stimuli serving as S^D for the undesired response, and similar strategies.

Since self-control eventually occurs in the absence of external support, self-reinforcement is an important feature in this procedure. The determinants of self-reinforcement, its motivational properties, and the conditions for learning its schedule of dispensation have been examined in a series of studies on self-reinforcement. Three major laboratory paradigms have been used for the investigation of this process: (1) The directed learning model for the study of variables affecting the rate of self-reinforcing responses; (2) the vicarious learning paradigm for examination of modeling effects; and (3) the temptation model for the study of variables affecting self-administration of rewards, contrary to social sanction. The accumulated studies have demonstrated the modifiability of self-rewards and self-punishments by a host of variables. They have also suggested that these self-administered operations can maintain behavior, that is, have some motivational properties.

In the clinic, self-control procedures can be taught directly by instructing the patient in general learning principles and by helping the patient to arrange programs that reduce the undesirable behaviors gradually. Control of smoking behavior, excessive eating, inability to study, and similar problems have been treated in this way. In *covert sensitization,* the patient is trained to present himself with imaginal aversive stimuli just as he approaches temptation to execute the undesired behavior. In *contingency management,* the person is taught to make covert verbal responses that are incompatible with the undesirable target behavior. Contingency self-management can also be executed by a patient when he makes positive covert statements just prior to highly probable behaviors, thus increasing the strength of these positive behaviors in his repertoire. Changes in stimulus control have been used therapeutically, by gradually narrowing the conditions under which a symptomatic behavior is permitted to occur. The use of self-administered shock and self-reinforcement for accomplishing each step in a hierarchy (arranged in order of difficulty for execution) has also been reported.

Clinical and research evidence suggest that even attending to one's behavior in a systematic way, as frequently demanded by a behavior therapist for record keeping, may have beneficial therapeutic effects. Other authors have reported the advantages of an explicit agreement between patient and therapist about the conditions for treatment, a method termed *contract management.* In this approach the behavior of each party is contingent upon the behavior of the other and the reciprocal exchange of behaviors is defined in the contract. The advent of recent audio and video devices has fostered the therapeutic utilization of objective feedback to the patient about his own behavior in *self-confrontation* techniques.

The introduction of self-regulatory techniques into the storehouse of behavior therapies is of special importance, since the earliest and most successful methods of behavior therapy have relied almost exclusively on control of the patient's treatment environment. This extension demonstrates the attempts to extend behavior therapy to a wide range of problems. Theoretical issues concerning the conceptualization of behaviors in which the person may be both object and subject of the behavior have not yet been resolved. However, these techniques have brought sharply into focus the problems and potentials of a behavioristic theory for dealing with those inaccessible, private experiences which early behaviorism had attempted to rule out of psychology.

Part V

Issues Arising in Clinical Application of Behavior Modification

The Larger Context of Behavior Therapy: Social, Organismic, and Assessment Issues

The two introductory chapters of this text deal with a general frame of reference and paradigm within which the philosophy, goals, and operations of the behavior therapies can be described. The bulk of Chapters 3 to 9 present the research and theoretical bases of a number of specific techniques for modifying behavior. From time to time we have described ways in which behavior therapy techniques fit into the total clinical enterprise, and we have noted some of their assets and deficiencies in meeting the needs of the practicing clinician. Trends in our society that have influenced the growth and development of the behavior therapies have been alluded to at times, and the fact that parameters outside of the behavioral learning paradigm affect behavior and its change has been acknowledged, if only briefly. However, there has been little opportunity to move outside of the area of learning to other fields of research or clinical practice relevant to the methods presented here. These omissions are in keeping with the purpose of this text. Nonetheless, now that the therapies and their learning foundations have been surveyed, it seems desirable to round out the picture of clinical practice by illustrating the potential contribution of other frames of reference to the behavior therapist's work. In addition, a number of issues of general relevance to all therapies, and to behavioral approaches in particular, have been touched upon in connection with some particular model but were not considered earlier as topics in themselves, for example, ethical issues of behavior control, or applied and theoretical issues in the field of assessment.

It is the purpose of these final two chapters to generally sample the total context of behavior modification. We cannot attempt either broad coverage of all the many pertinent topics nor even in-depth discussion of a number of topics. Instead, several areas have been singled out for brief discussion as illustrations of the larger social and psychological context in which the behavior therapist operates. Our selections are based on current psychological literature with particular relevance to the behavior therapies. The sections in this chapter and the next are largely unrelated to one another, except as they exemplify topics indirectly mentioned in other chapters.

The first section of this chapter deals with a few variables selected from the extensive literature on behavior influence and behavior change. Conceptualizations of the traditional psychotherapy process have increasingly drawn upon the experimental literature of attitude change, interpersonal attraction, social influence, role theory, expectancy, and similar areas. From this literature specific variables have emerged that are being evaluated for their effects within psychotherapy, and hypotheses have been formulated to explain and improve therapeutic effectiveness. In a recent *Annual Review* survey of psychotherapy research, Cartwright (1968) emphasized this trend:

"One major impression, which is inescapable to the person who surveys the current literature, is that psychotherapy as a field of inquiry no longer forms a distinctive problem area for which special theories and techniques need to be devised. More and more it is apparent that the present perspective is that psychotherapy represents one kind of dyadic relationship to which the findings from the study of other social relationships are relevant . . . . This perspective of psychotherapy as an example of one kind of social relationship which has similarity to others and of the problems brought to this relationship as learning problems has resulted in removing a good deal of the mystique from the field and in introducing more direct research attacks through the use of analogue methods. There is now a flavor to the literature that a new era has dawned almost equivalent in its effect on the craftsman therapist to that which followed the rationalizing of production methods by the industrial revolution" (Cartwright, 1968, p. 387).

For several decades, psychologists concerned with strengthening the empirical basis of psychotherapy have pleaded the importance of attempts to extrapolate findings from the social and experimental psychological laboratories to the clinical enterprise. Investigations of personality and psychopathology, which drew upon laboratory variables and operations, made even more clear the relevance of the larger body of psychological knowledge to behavior change in clinical settings. However, it is only recently that clinicians have been affected by publications dealing with behavior influence from the perspective of the social, physiological, and personality laboratories. One reason for delay in the penetration of meth-

ods and knowledge from general psychological research into the psychotherapeutic hour has been the conviction of some therapists that extrapolation from artificial experiments to "real-life" therapy is antithetical to
the humanist spirit of therapy, and unscientific in its reliance on the untested overextension of limited findings. Krasner (1962b) has replied to
this sort of criticism with a point of view that underlies the new era
emphasized by Cartwright:

"Conditioning studies have been termed 'laboratory' studies or experimental analogues of psychotherapy. I feel that these terms may be mis-
nomers. Most of us are so involved in the psychotherapy process both
in research and in clinical practice, that there had developed an aura
of sacredness about the process . . . . Many investigators imply that the
process of psychotherapy, as now practiced, is the royal and only road
to changing peoples' behavior. The yardstick for the acceptability of research then becomes 'how close is this to the real psychotherapy process?'
I feel strongly that we are losing sight of the purpose of psychotherapy,
which is to change peoples' behavior. The purpose of psychotherapy is
not 'to do' psychotherapy, as such . . . . It is good for the therapist
to enjoy psychotherapy and to feel that he is doing something important,
but this is not the purpose of psychotherapy. The apologetic tone in papers
which experimentally investigate behavior is uncalled for. These so-called
laboratory studies have important implications for the psychotherapy process and derive some of their hypotheses from psychotherapy. However,
I am less and less inclined to call them "experimental analogues" of psychotherapy. Rather, I see them as part of a broader psychology of behavior
control which is oriented toward devising techniques for the deliberate
control, manipulation, and change of behavior. . . . our basic aim is
not to create an analogue of psychotherapy, but to devise techniques
of behavior control" (Krasner, 1962b, p. 103).

Among the variables that have attracted particular attention as possible
bases for experimentally derived therapeutic operations are the factors
associated with the interpersonal-influence nature of the clinical setting.
Such variables are not technique-specific. Presumably, they are part of
any approach to behavior change, including the behavior therapies, in
which any personal contact with a clinician is required. Some critics have
characterized behavior therapies as mechanistic and dehumanizing, meaning in part that attention to and utilization of interpersonal influence variables are neglected. The heavy reliance of behavior therapies on social
reinforcement, modeling, and vicarious reinforcement demonstrates that
this is by no means the case.

In addition, however, behavioral clinicians can also make use of research on interpersonal parameters that are less directly derived from social learning models. For example, the social reinforcement construct becomes more clinically useful when related to research on parameters governing social influence. Those personal and behavioral attributes that characterize a person as a potent influencer in social psychology research presumably are closely related to his potency as a social reinforcer. In our opinion, behavior therapy can be more effective if its practitioners draw on as broad an experimental base as possible and accommodate new knowledge as it emerges from the psychological laboratory. This will require the behavior therapist to view his own specialty as only one area of application of knowledge from the broader field of behavior influence and interpersonal communication. In keeping with this opinion, we discuss in this chapter a few illustrative variables and studies selected for their demonstrated relevance to behavior control. Our sampling from these other fields is suggestive, not inclusive. The variables are discussed neither as techniques nor as mechanisms, but as correlates of behavior influence.

A second broad area of investigation germaine to learning-based modification techniques is the research that relates personality and organismic characteristics to learning. Again, the relevant literature that could be reviewed here is prohibitively large. It reveals that the relationships between learning and personality variables are tenuous and too easily affected by an individual's unique historical and environmental background to warrant detailed coverage in a survey of general therapeutic procedures. Nonetheless, the evidence suggests that prediction of the effects of a particular technique, such as desensitization, may be improved by giving consideration to some durable personality characteristics of the patient, such as his extraversion-introversion scores. In the second section of this chapter we describe a small sample of this literature to illustrate the potential importance of personality and organismic parameters in the application of behavior therapies. The variables discussed are viewed as correlates of learning effects. Although they often evolved from particular personality theories, the emphasis here is on their implications as moderating factors for behavioral approaches, instead of on the intervening processes or traits that they are sometimes theorized to represent. Thus they serve to supplement our understanding of the person in relation to his environment and his problem; they do not alter the basic frame of reference proposed in Chapters 1 and 2.

Finally, a third section of this chapter discusses behavioral diagnosis. Diagnosis is the crossroad at which critical decisions must be made in order to meet the goals of the total clinical enterprise. At this juncture the available techniques we have explored, the personal and organismic characteristics of therapist and patient, and the environmental resources available to the patient and the therapist are blended for integration into a series of flexible treatment strategies. The product of this encounter within the interpersonal clinical setting is the choice of a therapeutic program. Diagnosis or behavior assessment is, then, the common meeting ground in the applied setting of all that has been discussed up to this point. As yet the decision-making processes of the behavioral clinician are poorly understood. There is little scientific basis for the selection of the best course of treatment for particular patient-target-environment combinations. The clinician tries to match and sort variables on the basis of a functional analysis to achieve the optimal solution of the problems presented by an individual patient, with only the crudest rules to guide him. Many of the factors that influence the chosen treatment approach are not specific to behavior therapies, although they are described in behavioral terms. Similarly, as we noted in Chapter 2, the clinician's assessment still largely depends upon traditional clinical interviewing and observational skills. Despite this overlapping with more traditional approaches, the behavior modifier does have a somewhat unique view of assessment procedures and goals that differentiates him from other clinicians. Thus, behavioral assessment seems a particularly appropriate topic with which to end this chapter, since its content of necessity connects the theory and techniques of learning-based behavior therapies with issues and variables of clinical practice as a whole.

One perspective from which to view the three topics discussed in this chapter is in terms of the range of variables that are potentially important in determining therapeutic outcome. Paul (1969a) has proposed four large classes or domains of variables that must be described, measured, and/or controlled in outcome studies of any therapy. Each domain, in turn, includes a number of subclasses of variables that must be taken into account. Figure 10-1 summarizes Paul's outline. The figure suggests that effectiveness of any therapy is likely to be influenced by client characteristics, including the particular complaints that are targets of change in a given case, relatively enduring traits, and the total context in which the client lives. Each subcategory in turn may have many specific variables relevant to outcome. Each of the other three domains—the therapist or other modification agent, events correlated with the passage of time, and the dependent behavioral variables used to assess outcome—similarly encompasses numerous discrete variables likely to influence therapeutic effectiveness. The ultimate goal of the clinician is to write a therapeutic prescription that takes into account the relevance of each of these variables. For more detailed assessment of the role and contribution of one component in a therapeutic paradigm, control of all of the others is necessary. Presumably the ideal evaluation research design would be factorial in nature,

I. *Clients* (for example, subjects, patients, students, and so on)
    A. *Target Behaviors*
        (for instance, symptoms or complaints that involve motoric, autonomic, physiological, ideational, or verbal responses)
    B. *Relatively Stable Personal-Social Characteristics*
        (such as sex, age, education, experiences, socioeconomic level, anxiety level, extroversion)
    C. *Life Environment*
        (for example, family, work, recreational resources, hygiene conditions, drugs, and so forth)
II. Behavior Modifiers (for instance, therapist, automated device, counselor, technician)
    A. *Behavior Modification Technique*
        (such as discrete actions, treatment, strategy, variables manipulated)
    B. *Relatively Stable Personal-Social Characteristics*
        (for example, empathy, experience, prestige, theoretical orientation, warmth, likeability, liking for client)
    C. *Treatment Environment*
        (such as, clinic, ward, home, school, laboratory)
III. *Time* (for example, assessment made at initial contact, pretreatment, during treatment, posttreatment)
IV. *Outcome Criteria* (for instance, dependent variables based on target behaviors, measured by a variety of instruments with controls for instrumental errors)

Figure 10-1 Domains of Variables Relevant to Evaluation of Therapeutic Outcome (Adapted from Paul, 1969a).

systematically manipulating all four domains and many subvariables in each domain. For example, therapist empathy may cause different effects with different types of patients undergoing different forms of treatment. Its effect might be trivial in the desensitization treatment of monophobic patients, but it could be a significant factor in teaching chronically anxious patients new social skills through role playing.

All of the behavior therapies that we have reviewed can usefully be viewed within the context of the variables listed in Figure 10-1. Domains III and IV were briefly mentioned in Chapter 1 and in discussions of evaluation studies of particular techniques. Domain II has been the major substance of preceding chapters, which concentrated on (A) modification techniques, and at times took account of (C) treatment environment. From Domain I, suitable target behaviors (A) have been considered in association with each modification technique, with some attention to the influence of life environment (C) on choice and effectiveness of modification technique. Discussion of the stable personal-social characteristics (B) of patient and of therapist, in Domains I and II, has been reserved for this chapter. The diagnostic process, which simultaneously assesses all domains in order to achieve a treatment strategy, also remains to be considered as a separate topic.

The interacting subdomains of client and therapist characteristics form the treatment relationship. The variables relevant to these two subdomains often are less well defined and understood than are those of other subdomains. In many cases little is known about the mechanisms responsible for their effects. Nonetheless, client and therapist characteristics apparently can profoundly effect treatment outcome, in ways that can be considered separate from the intentional learning that is planned within the treatment setting.

SPECIFIC VARIABLES IN PATIENT-THERAPIST INTERACTIONS

Variables from research fields as diverse as interpersonal attraction and role theory can often be accommodated within the framework of the behavioral equation in order to expand the behavioral approach to a broader range of patient problems and therapist decisions. The cognitive models underlying these research fields are more complex, more molar, more concerned with hypothetical mediating mechanisms and general transituational traits than is the behavioral model we have been using. However, the empirical relationships and sometimes even a set of procedures from one model can be translated into the terms of the other and used to enrich it. It is at the level of the theory, not the level of experimentation, that the difference exists. The behavioral model does not deal separately with the verbal-logical operations of cognitive or dynamic models. It makes no attempt to use structure or process analogues to simplify comprehension or create an abstracted sketch of the locus of behavior. However, at the behavioral level of observation, data, prediction, and empirical test, the two approaches can often complement each other with mutual benefit.

Not only is it obvious that most treatments take place in an interpersonal setting consisting of at least one patient and one therapist in interaction with each other, but there is also general consensus, supported by research data, that this interpersonal relationship has significant effects on the process and outcome of therapy regardless of the techniques or theory of behavior change used. Clinicians with very different orientations agree that the quality of the therapeutic relationship is important in all approaches to behavior modification. Behavioral clinicians may speak of the therapist as a "social reinforcement machine" and acknowledge that the therapy process is affected by the same variables as are other interpersonal situations (Krasner, 1962a). Lazarus has acknowledged: "Both Wolpe and I have explicitly stated that relationship variables are often extremely important in behavior therapy. Factors such as warmth, empathy, and authenticity are considered necessary but often insufficient" (Klein, Dittmann, Parloff, and Gill, 1969, p. 262). Rogerian client-centered therapists have always emphasized interactional behaviors and relational variables such as empathy or warmth as the prime movers in behavior change (see, for example, Rogers, Gendlin, Kiesler and Truax, 1967). Similarly, psychoanalytically oriented investigators, using general concepts (such as transference and countertransference) and more specific variables (such as empathy, liking, and experience) have explored the therapist's personal as well as technical interactional contribution to therapeutic process and outcome (Strupp, 1960). A number of studies (see, for example, Adams and Frye, 1964; Truax, 1966) have indicated that the actual *operations* of Rogerians and analysts alike can be described and ordered in terms of their reinforcing effects on the patient's verbal productions.

The general assumption that relationship factors may be central to, or even the sole determinant of, behavior change has gained support from observations that very different psychotherapeutic approaches have about the same degree of success, and that experienced psychotherapists, whatever their theoretical predilections, are very similar to one another in how they relate to patients. As a sophisticated example of the first sort of finding, Cartwright (1966) used matched pairs of patients and therapists, the latter highly experienced in either client-centered or psychoanalytic therapy, to ascertain whether there would be greater similarity in therapeutic processes across different types of patients in the same type of treatment, or across similar types of patients in different types of treatment. Criterion measures were designed to reflect both client-centered, psychoanalytic, and relatively nontheoretical (neutral) indicators of patient changes during a series of therapy sessions. Therapist behaviors, coded in categories appropriate to each school, were found to differ greatly between the two schools of therapists. Within each therapist group, on the other hand, therapist behaviors were homogeneous. Despite the different behaviors of their theoretically divergent therapists, the matched patients moved very similarly through therapy and reached similar levels of goal relevant behavior. Cartwright notes:

"Matched therapists from the different orientations produced similar levels of therapeutic progress in their matched patients although the immediate precipitant of a peak patient response would be categorized as a typical client-centered response, i.e., clarification, from the client-centered therapist, but a typically psychoanalytic response, i.e., interpretation, from the psychoanalytic therapist" (Cartwright, 1968, pp. 398–399).

These findings underscore the fact that specific technical differences in two theoretically distinct verbal types of therapy are relatively much less important than the interactional relationship of therapist and patient.

Similarly, a number of studies have indicated more directly that "experienced" or "successful" therapists are very similar along relationship variables, whatever their differences in theory or technique. Measures and constructs that are used to represent relationship variables vary widely, with little consensus about which aspects of the therapeutic interaction are crucial in producing change. Despite the range of variables examined, however, the results generally agree in indicating the importance of the relationship. An example is a study by Parloff (1961) that assessed therapist-patient relationship in a group therapy setting by means of Q-sort ratings by observers. The Q-sort items (Fiedler, 1950) described the therapist's ability to understand and communicate with the patient, the emotional distance between them, and the "status" dimension reflected in the therapist's behaviors. Patients and clinicians rated patient change in symptomatic comfort, effectiveness, and objectivity at the beginning and end of treatment. The closer the patient-therapist relationship approached an "ideal standard," the more the patient was rated by himself and others as showing therapeutic benefits in symptom loss, increased dominance, and increased objectivity. Thus quality of relationship was significantly related to patient improvement.

To the extent that the behavior therapist relies on traditional clinical *modes* of interacting with patients (as opposed to automated electromechanical modes such as Lang's DAD—see Chapter 4), the therapist may enhance or detract from the effectiveness of his behavioral techniques through the impact of his own personal and interactional characteristics. Thus the greater reliance on the *clinician* as an instrument in verbal therapy magnifies the effects of his individuality (not only his unreliability) in comparison to machine devices. Consider, as an extreme example, a case known to the authors, in which a blind male behavior therapist treated an adolescent girl whose major behavioral pattern with men was seductiveness. Her usual flirtatious and seductive efforts to gain support for her asocial and antisocial behaviors failed since the therapist received none of the visual sexual stimuli on which she usually relied for control. Nor could the therapist's lack of reinforcement for her behaviors be conveniently denigrated by the girl since it was clearly his vision and not his manliness that was responsible for her failure to control his behavior. When her habitual, sexually inviting behaviors were extinguished in therapy, the girl began to interact with the therapist in a more constructive fashion and settled down to work on reorganizing her own self-concept and defining the consequences of alternative behavior patterns. Other, less conspicuous therapist characteristics can be expected to affect the therapist's enactment of a prescribed approach in similar ways.

In selecting the personal and interactional characteristics that may be used for deliberate enhancement of therapeutic efforts, the behavior modifier is confronted with two interrelated problems. First, the specific variables for whose effectiveness there is empirical support are numerous and overlapping. They have been defined in many ways and are difficult to operationalize and measure. For example, therapist *empathy* has received a great deal of theoretical and experimental attention but its relationship to other constructs, such as warmth, is uncertain; it is defined differently from study to study; and it is usually measured by judges' ratings of the "accuracy" of responses to feelings instead of in more behavioral terms. This lack of specific definition can lead to such anomolies as an interview protocol being rated as showing accurate therapist responses to a patient's expressed and "deeper, more hidden feelings" when the therapist utters nothing other than one "Mhm" during each pause in the patient's speech (Traux and Carkhuff, 1967, p. 49). At the other end of the spectrum, some interactional variables have been operationalized and assessed at a detailed behavioral level. For example, *attending* behaviors by a therapist have been defined as eye contact, relaxed posture, and verbal following. The learnability and positive effects of attending behaviors have been experimentally studied (Ivey, Normington, Miller, Morrill, and Hasse, 1968).

The second obstacle to judicious use of interactional and personal-social characteristics in promoting behavior change is the lack of knowledge about any superordinate factor to which the individually studied variables may relate. That is, not only are the interrelationships among specific variables obscure, but also it seems likely that many separate variables reflect the action of a superordinate class or factor with which each is correlated, in turn. Until the mechanisms responsible for the effects of warmth, empathy, status, and so on, are better understood and any interactions of the mechanisms are described, the behavior therapist runs the risk of concentrating upon use of an interactional variable whose effects are relatively trivial and indirect.

Two broad factors are particularly attractive candidates as classes under which many more specific interactional variables might be subsumed: positive social reinforcement and expectancy congruence. Many of the characteristics attributed to especially successful therapists, such as empathy, warmth, and genuineness (Traux and Carkhuff, 1967), or specificity and topical focus in his communications (see, for example, Pope and Siegman, 1968), or liking for the patient (Strupp, 1960) appear to fit well into a social reinforcement framework. Therapist variables such as sex, age, status, emotional climate, and value system have been experimentally manipulated within the verbal conditioning paradigm and have been found to have effects parallel to those expected from clinical theories and psychotherapy research (Kanfer, 1968; Krasner, 1962a). Similarly, variables such as "ambiguity" have been studied in laboratory verbal conditioning experiments, social affiliation and influence experiments, and analogue and actual therapy, with parallel findings at all levels. Although precise definitions have varied, experimenter-therapist ambiguity has usually entailed the absence of clear evaluative responses (being noncommittal or implying unspoken reservations) and of directive statements that would structure the situation and the behaviors expected in it for the subject-client (see, for example, Heller, 1968). It has also been suggested that the lack of a clear-cut end point for the therapy process heightens its ambiguity for the patient and makes him more open to therapist influence (Frank, 1961b). The usual failure to tell the patient the specific rules and desired outcome responses in most traditional and verbal therapy creates the ambiguous conditions that can maximize therapist influence (Kanfer, 1968). Thus, the patient feels he must keep working toward "cure," but since the criteria for this goal are not specified, he is unable to assess his progress and looks to the therapist for any cues that might help him to know where he is going and what he should do to get there. Krasner, in summarizing work on ambiguity and instructional set carried out within many varied frames of reference, concludes: "These findings are consistent in interpreting ambiguity as enhancing the reinforcing value of the therapist" (1962a, p. 76).

The second major class under which specific relationship variables may be subsumed is variously termed "cognitions," "expectancies," or "role-taking." Frank (1962), for example, believes that a therapist's social role and "personal magnetism" are therapeutic because they enhance the patient's expectation of help. A warm, emphatic relationship is important, he feels, mainly in promoting the patient's trust and his perception of the therapist as potentially helpful. This effect is especially desirable with some patients (for instance, schizophrenics) whose general mistrust of others precludes these elements from developing from role definition and personal characteristics alone. Thus Frank considers warmth, empathy, genuineness, and other relationship variables that have been demonstrated to influence therapy process and outcome as subsidiary to the cognitive expectancies of patient and therapist, and particularly to the mutuality of their expectancies. In support of his view Frank cites studies, such as one by Freedman, Engelhardt, Hankoff, Glick, Kaye, Buchwald, and Stark (1958), that showed that the effect of therapist "warmth" is a function of the schizophrenic patient's view of his illness and his expectancies regarding appropriate care. Patients who tended to deny their psychological problems dropped out of treatment more often if their psychiatrist was rated high on a relationship index than if he was rated low. The reverse was true of patients who accepted the existence of their problems.

Prognostic expectancies, that is, expectancies regarding the degree of anticipated patient improvement, have been shown to be predictive of actual improvement. Goldstein (1962), after reviewing the available research literature, concluded that these prognostic expectancies are differentiated from actual prognosis and that patient expectancies relate to improvement in a curvilinear fashion. Patients who hold moderate prognostic expectations show the most therapeutic change. Similarly, the therapist's prognostic expectancies apparently influence outcome of the treatment, regardless of the type of treatment used.

We now turn briefly to several concrete illustrative areas of research on therapist-patient interactions. Frequently we mention potential connections with social reinforcement and with expectancies, but in each case the relevance of these or alternative superordinate variables can often only be speculated upon. Hopefully, as studies use more complex designs and multiple variables, these relationships will be given empirical clarification.

Therapist Characteristics

A variety of relatively stable personal-social therapist characteristics has been studied in recent years when the therapist's individual contribution to treatment began to attract increasing attention. Warmth, empathy, value systems, class origin, theoretical orientation, and authoritarianism are examples of the variables studied (see, for example, Levinson, 1962).

As an illustration of this line of inquiry, the programmatic investigations by Betz and Whitehorn (Betz, 1967; Carson, 1967) of differential therapist success with schizophrenic and neurotic patients offer an unusually clear example. Their work is of particular interest since the stable therapist variables they have studied have, in turn, been related to interview behaviors and to therapist and patient expectancies.

The research began with the finding that some psychiatric residents consistently achieved relatively high improvement rates with hospitalized schizophrenics while others showed poor rates, although both did equally well with other types of patients. Betz and Whitehorn first identified differences in clinical "styles" and then in values or interests on the Strong Vocational Interest Inventory that discriminated between the two groups of residents (Whitehorn and Betz, 1954, 1960). On the Strong Inventory therapists categorized as "A's" (those usually successful with schizophrenic patients) indicate distaste for activities of a manual, technical, or mechanical nature but resemble lawyers in preferring problem-solving activities. Therapist categorized as *"B's"* (those residents who do poorly with schizophrenics in comparison with *A* therapists) endorse the opposite Strong items. In clinical style, as judged from case research, the *A* therapists were found to prefer personality-oriented instead of psychopathology-oriented therapeutic goals, to actively set limits on undesired patient behaviors, and to express more freely their own attitudes about problems being discussed. *B* therapists were more permissive, didactic, interpretive, and concerned with symptomatic change.

Other correlates of therapist *A-B* status (as the scores on the special *A-B* Strong scale are termed) include field-dependence-independence (with *B's* more field independent; Pollack and Kiev, 1963), and self-descriptions of reactions to stress (Sandler, 1965). Interestingly, in the Sandler study male college students classified as *A* or *B* types described their own stress adjustments in terms *opposite* to those descriptive of patients most responsive to *A* or *B* therapists. The *A* men more often described themselves as trusting, intropunitive, and collaborative, quite contrary to the personality of schizophrenic patients with whom *A* therapists best succeed.

The suggestion in Sandler's study that complementarity of therapist and patient characteristics may in part mediate the differential effectiveness of *A* and *B* therapists has been partially supported by a study of *A* and *B* type *patients* (Berzins, Friedman, and Seidman, 1969). Male college clinic patients were classified by the usual *A-B* Strong scale and rated for their presenting symptoms and complaints and role expectancies. The *A* patients, like *A* therapists, were more intropunitive, but also indicated that they expected to unburden themselves actively and productively in therapy. The *B* patients expected to seek rational guidance and correction from an analytical teacher-like therapist. The *A* and *B* patients thus seemed to expect a form of treatment very similar to the style offered by *B* and *A* therapists, respectively, suggesting to the investigators that patients do best with therapists opposite in personal style to themselves. Betz (1962) similarly states the basic difference in *A* and *B* therapists in terms of expectancy. She recalls Frank's view, described earlier, that the ability to arouse expectancies for positive interaction is especially important with schizophrenics, the patient group with whom *A* therapists excell.

"Physicians whose attitudes tend to expect and respect spontaneity tend to evoke self-respectful social participation more effectively than those whose attitudes tend to restrict spontaneity by preference for more conventionalized expectations. This appears to be the basic difference between A and B therapists" (Betz, 1962, p. 52).

Although behavioral differences in modeling and in directly reinforcing particular spontaneous self-expression have not been directly examined, Betz's statement suggests these as possible mechanisms for producing the differential therapeutic effectiveness of A and B therapists.

One of the major goals that Betz and Whitehorn had set for their research program was to determine whether the crucial determinants of treatment success lay in the therapists. Their strategy, in first finding outcome differences, then personal therapist differences, and finally looking for mechanisms transmitting personal characteristics into outcome differences is, as we have seen, somewhat indirect in identifying what are crucial behaviors for the therapist. Since an A type therapist differs from a B in many respects at once, and since the primary classification into A and B may be only a weak and indirect reflection of any crucial behavioral differences, more direct and experimental approaches to the same issues seem necessary.

Numerous studies have attempted more direct assessment of the impact of particular therapist characteristics and behaviors, by either correlational or experimental approaches. The focus may be on therapy-specific variables, for instance, the speech-retarding effects of interpretive statements in analogue interviews (Kanfer, Phillips, Matarazzo, and Saslow, 1960), or on the degree of interviewer participation sought by the interviewee as a function of the topic being discussed and the type of interviewer comments (reflection, agreement, disagreement, and so on) (Kanfer and Marston, 1964). Other studies have focused on the general affect-arousing qualities of particular therapist behaviors, for example, the correlation of patient GSR to therapist "gentleness" and "attentiveness," as assessed in small units of interaction within each session (Dittes, 1957). The effects of the therapist's personal attitudes toward the patient, such as the poorer prognosis of a patient who is disliked by his therapist (Strupp, 1960), or the retention of patients in treatment by therapists who evidence more than ordinary interest in the patient's problems (McNair, Lorr, and Callahan, 1963) have been investigated. Still others have focused on more enduring characteristics of the therapist, such as his typical temporal speech patterns (Goldman-Eisler, 1952; Matarazzo, Wiens, Matarazzo, and Saslow, 1968).

Until this diversity of findings, variables, and functional relationships can be ordered by some superordinate variables, it will be difficult to interpret and integrate the available empirical results. The therapy-oriented studies referred to above are now paralleled only in part by learning laboratory studies of the characteristics of effective models and social reinforcers and by experiments on effective attitude change agents in social psychological research. When these laboratory investigations afford some theoretical rapprochement with each other, their integrated conclusions should also clarify the meaning of related clinical studies. For example, interpersonal attraction theory already has been translated into stimulus-response language. A series of studies has shown that when another person is associated with direct or vicarious reinforcement of the subject, the subject develops a "liking" for the other person (James and Lott, 1964; Lott, Lott and Matthews, 1969). Liked persons have been found to function as more effective models and reinforcers (see, for example, Lott and Lott, 1969; Sapolsky, 1960), to be more persuasive and less likely to elicit dissonance reduction in getting subjects to perform distasteful acts such as eating grasshoppers (Zimbardo, Weisenberg, Firestone, and Levy, 1965), and so on. As the nature of the events that lead two persons to develop "liking" for one another are further explicated, and the interactions of the therapist's responses and reinforcement value with various subject response classes are elaborated, a pattern may emerge that will partially unify seemingly diverse therapist characteristics such as gentleness, warmth, verbal rate, *A-B* type, or expectancy.

Another interesting example of a more direct approach to therapist influence involves assessing the relative degree to which therapists and patients are interdependent or mutually influential. In a study by Houts, MacIntosh, and Moos (1969) seven patients were rotated for therapy sessions among four different therapists. A number of patient and therapist behaviors were noted by observers. After each session both the patient and the therapist indicated how he expected patients and therapists *should* behave with respect to the same behaviors the observers had coded. The results indicated that therapists were more influenced behaviorally by patients than were patients influenced by therapists. That is, therapist behaviors were less stable (or more flexible) across patients than were patient behaviors across therapists. However, on the expectancy questionnaires, both therapist and patient differences exerted a strong influence on each other. The investigators concluded that:

". . . differences between therapists convey more weight in the [expectation] questionnaires than they do in the behavior ratings for both therapist and patient. This indicates discrepancy between what therapists think should happen and that, in part, these discrepancies are due to the fact that differences between therapists are more important in the thinking of therapists than they are in the behavior of either therapists or patients" (Houts et al., 1969, p. 44).

These findings, like those of Cartwright (1966), suggest that global effects of different therapist characteristics are not likely to be useful or instructive until they can be given demonstrable behavioral referents.

Relationship Variables

"Relationship" is a term that refers to a large number of variables that cluster into behaviors or effects called "liking," "attraction," and so forth. We include only a few sample variables in this section, selecting on the basis of their apparent influence on patient and therapist behavior and on therapeutic outcome.

Interpersonal influence within therapy is an interactive process. Each participant is influenced by the cues and reinforcers the other emits, by the behavior presented to him for reaction. The *inter*active nature of therapeutic transactions has already been mentioned, as for example in the study by Houts et al. (1969). At every response level, similar findings exist. There is ample evidence of mutual influence, even at the level of physiological responses, as described in Chapter 8 and elsewhere. Coleman, Greenblatt, and Solomon (1956), for instance, found parallel heart rate changes, indicating momentary shifts in affect in patient and therapist over a series of 44 therapy sessions. At a verbal behavioral level, the percentages of interview time utilized in speaking by therapist and patient are highly correlated (Matazarro, Wiens, Matarazzo, and Saslow, 1968). Correlational analyses of patient and therapist behaviors over five-minute interview segments have shown concurrence of disrupted communications for both participants (Tourney, Lowinger, Schorer, Bloom, Auld, and Grisell, 1966). And at a very different level, patient and therapist have been shown to influence each other's perceptions and evaluations of the key issues in therapy as measured over the course of treatment (Pande and Gart, 1968).

Integration and clinical application of the wealth of studies in this area are difficult because of the range of variables and mechanisms proposed for predicting and controlling the interactional influences. Presumably, for example, the reciprocal social reinforcement value of each participant for the other is important in determining their interactions. Unlike the laboratory experimenter, the therapist is not tightly programmed in his behavior and is influenced in what he does immediately, as well as over time, by the patient's behavior toward him. The therapist is, of course, affected by new information from his patient in his momentary decisions about goals and techniques. But beyond this deliberate, task-oriented receptivity to influence by the patient's verbal reports and other behavior, the therapist's interpersonal behavior can also be directly shaped by patient reinforcements in ways not dictated by tactical therapeutic decisions (Kanfer, 1961).

A particularly interesting area in which the effects of patient-therapist interaction have been examined is that of mutual expectations. We referred earlier to Frank's (1962) proposition that "the ability of patient and therapist to meet each other's expectations is an important component of healing" (p. 6). In describing their reactions to a period of intense observation of the clinical work of Wolpe and Lazarus, Klein, Dittmann, Parloff, and Gill (1969) comment:

"Perhaps the most striking impression we came away with was of how much use behavior therapists make of suggestion and of how much the patient's expectations and attitudes are manipulated. Behavior therapists are not at all silent on this point in their descriptions of technique, but the literature did not prepare us for the unabashed suggestions that therapists directed toward their patients. The major arena for suggestion is in the orientation period of treatment. Here the therapist tells the patient at length about the power of the treatment method, pointing out that it has been successful with comparable patients and all but promising similar results for him, too. The patient is provided with a detailed learning-theory formulation of the etiology of his problems and is given a straightforward rationale for the way in which the specific treatment procedures will 'remove' his symptoms. The patient's motives and values may also be considered so as to 'correct misconceptions' which block desirable courses of action or restrict the effect of treatment. Indeed it seemed to us that treatment plans and goals were laid out in such a detail that the patient was taught precisely how things would proceed and what responses and changes were expected of him all along the way" (p. 262).

The effects of patient and therapist expectancies on therapy process and outcome have been studied separately and as they interact with each other. Findings have been interpreted in relation to laboratory studies of interpersonal perception and interpersonal attraction (Goldstein, 1962). The effects of therapist expectancies on patient behavior have been postulated to depend upon cognitive similarity and interpersonal attraction, which in turn influence communication effectiveness by the process of operant conditioning. The degree to which a patient is attracted to his therapist, and the later change in his attraction, is significantly related to the therapist's prognostic expectancy at the beginning of treatment (Heller and Goldstein, 1961). In reviewing this and related studies, Goldstein (1962) concluded that cognitive similarity between two persons covaries with their interpersonal attraction and their communication effectiveness (Newcomb, 1956; Triandis, 1960) and that, in turn, transmission to the patient of the therapist's prognostic expectancies is facilitated by the patient's attraction to the therapist, who thereby becomes a potent reinforcer. Since Rosenthal and Fode (1963) found that experimenters' biasing of subjects was correlated with their liking or disliking of the subjects, Goldstein suggests that therapist attraction to the patient also contributes to communication of therapist prognostic expectancies. In turn, patient prognostic expectancies have been found to have a curvilinear relation to outcome (Brady, Zeller, and Reznikoff, 1959; Goldstein and Shipman, 1961), as mentioned earlier in this chapter—patients who expect moderate improvement have a more favorable result from therapy than do patients who expect either very little or very much improvement. Patient prognostic expectancies are in turn a function of the amount of distress felt by the patient (Lipkin, 1954) and locus and type of referral (Heine and Trosman, 1960), among other variables.

When role expectations are examined, the interactional influence of such beliefs becomes even more evident. Patient pretherapy expectations about how their therapist would behave were classified by Apfelbaum (1958) as *nurturant* (expecting a protective, uncritical therapist), *critic* (expecting a therapist who would push responsibility, be analytical and critical), or *model* (expecting the therapist to neither judge nor protect, but to listen and himself be well-adjusted). Apfelbaum found that duration of treatment, dropout rate, severity of pathology, and improvement were all related to the role expectations initially held by the patient. Lennard and Bernstein (1960) went further in demonstrating that strain in the relationship between patient and therapist is a function of degree of dissimilarity of their mutual role expectations. Goldstein (1962) has summarized a number of other studies supporting this general conclusion. For example, congruence of therapist and patient expectations regarding the benefits the patient would derive from therapy is predictive of whether a patient will remain in treatment (Gliedman, Stone, Frank, Nash, and Imber, 1957). Although neither presenting complaint nor expected efficacy of treatment predicted early termination, patient expectations about the nature and form of treatment did predict termination, presumably as a function of mutuality with the therapist's notions on the same issue (Heine and Trosman, 1960).

Many operant behavior therapists have a tendency to exclude "cognitions," "expectancies," and similar constructs from their model. Despite this tendency, a learning-oriented approach to behavior modification is by no means incompatible with attention to the behavioral events to which these constructs often refer if they are clearly defined, operational, and repeatable (as was discussed in Chapter 8). Learning-oriented researchers can both test the limits of coverage of their constructs and seek to make more explicit and concrete the *behavioral* precursors, constituents, and consequences of phenomena such as "mutuality of role expectations" whose importance in affecting dyadic interactions has been demonstrated in clinical studies and in the laboratory. The variables of concern can usually be translated into the terms of the behavioral equation, and then subjected to further tests of their effective parameters and mechanisms. "Expectancies" can, for example, be defined as "a shorthand expression for the degree to which one has learned environmental contingencies" (Ullmann and Krasner. 1969, p. 72). The effects of one's expectancies on one's own and other persons' behavior can similarly be put in behavioral terms:

". . . the behavior of labeling the situation, i.e., the 'prophecy' or expectancy, is likely to alter the cues to which a person attends and responds. Because the person's behavior provides stimuli for other people, his prophecy is an aspect of the situation and alters it. Behavior leads to consequences, and as the person changes his behavior, new consequences occur, so that gradually environmental events are shaped in the direction of expectancies" (Ullmann and Krasner, 1969, p. 73).

On the other hand, a patient's expectancies about the behaviors or role of his therapist can be viewed as reinforcers for which entering therapy is seen as an S^D by the patient, on the basis of past learning. When the expected reinforcement is not forthcoming, therapy-attending behavior is extinguished unless new reinforcing stimuli, not only of equal potency but also sufficient to overcome the effects of extinction, have been made available in the meantime. Similarly, the acquisition of new attitudes and "meaning," which is postulated to occur as a consequence of the therapy interaction, has been investigated as a classical conditioning process. The controlling effects of attitudes and meaning on other behavior have been tested as reflecting secondary positive and aversive reinforcement properties (Staats, 1968), suggesting that these reinforcing properties are the basis for the utility of expectancy confirmation, interpretations, and other "cognitive" phenomena in psychotherapy.

Placebo Effects and Experimenter Bias

Recent investigations of placebo effects and experimenter bias offer additional illustrations of the mutual enrichment that occurs when lines of investigation from different frames of reference are integrated in relation to phenomena that seem empirically similar. In this case, the concerns of clinician and experimenter, behavior modifier and cognitive theorist overlap in their interest in the prediction and control of influence effects. Research on expectancies as predictors of placebo and bias effects may enrich the armamentarium of the behavior therapist. In complementary fashion, investigations of the contributions of reinforcement operations and modeling mechanisms to production of the effects can add to the cognitive theorist's hypotheses about the translation of expectancies into overt behavior.

Shapiro (1960) has defined the placebo reaction as the "psychological, physiological, or psychophysiological effect of any medication or procedure given with therapeutic intent, which is independent of or minimally related to the pharmacological effect of the medication or to the specific effects of the procedure, and which operates through a psychological mechanism" (p. 110). He points out that although the practice of medicine has relied mainly on placebo effects for most of its history, there has been little effort to investigate placebos until recently. Contemporary research has examined placebo reactions as a function of the administrator, receiver, nature of the distress, form of placebo, and the situation in which it is administered (Haas, Fink, and Hartfelder, 1963; Honigfeld, 1964a).

Placebo effects have been drawing increasing attention as central phenomena to be explored and explained in the clinical realm, just as experimenter effects have come to be recognized as important in relation to laboratory activity. These related phenomena are capturing interest not only because of their relevance in forming research control groups and taking base line comparison measures, but because they also involve effects that are often desirable and that could be deliberately utilized in therapy when the responsible mechanisms are better understood. In clinical outcome studies placebo effects must be controlled for, but they may also be sought after to enhance therapeutic effect. The mechanisms are presumably akin to those involved in other influence operations. Placebo reactions thus offer both a common meeting ground for behavioral and cognitively oriented therapists and investigators, and an outcome to be capitalized upon by therapists of all orientations. Placebo reactions, like the therapist and patient characteristics discussed earlier, form part of the ubiquitous context of behavior influence affecting outcome, within which the specific techniques of the behavior therapies are carried out.

Frank (1961a), in line with his emphasis on expectancies as the curative agent in psychotherapy and other healing processes, proposes that

". . . the effectiveness of the placebo lies in its ability to mobilize the patient's expectancy of help. . . . the ability to respond favorably to a placebo is not so much a sign of excessive gullibility, as one of easy acceptance of others in their socially defined roles. . . . if part of the success of all forms of psychotherapy may be attributed to the therapist's ability to mobilize the patient's expectation of help, then some of the effects of psychotherapy should be similar to those produced by a placebo" (pp. 70–71).

It is not known to what extent "acceptance of others in their socially defined roles" or an expectancy for help from others is cross-situational, that is, a generalized trait. The search for a "placebo reactor" personality, that is, an enduring trait or tendency to respond favorably to placebos (and suggestion) across clinical complaints and placebo administrators has been a particularly active area of research. Results thus far are controversial. The dispute on this topic reflects in part the differences between those who construe personality in terms of stable traits and states and those who emphasize situational determinants of behavior. Ullmann and Krasner (1969) state "under the appropriate set of contingencies (i.e., what is reinforcing to them) most people will enact the role of placebo reactor. The problem can be put in terms of finding the environmental stimuli that make the placebo response likely, rather than of finding who is or is not a placebo reactor" (p. 79).

On the other hand, when groups of patients differing in placebo response have been compared, it has been usual to find other significant differences between groups as well, although the particular correlates vary widely from study to study. For instance, when surgical patients suffering severe and lasting pain from wounds were given saline injections, some 30 to 40 percent reported relief from their pain (Lasagna, Mosteller, Felsinger, and Beecher, 1954). Those who reported pain relief were found to be more dependent, reactive emotionally, and conventional, while nonreactor patients tended to be mistrustful and isolated. In other studies, a negative reaction on the part of schizophrenic patients to placebo medication given at a post-hospital follow-up clinic has been reported to be a very good predictor of ultimate readmission to hospital (Hankoff, Freedman, and Engelhardt, 1958).

Frank (1961a) has proposed that the direct effect of placebo is to reduce anxiety and related emotions that exaggerate painful sensations. Whatever the mode of action, there is ample evidence that placebo reactions occur in a large number of persons (32 percent, according to a review by Beecher, 1955) for a wide variety of complaints, and that they are in large part a function of the placebo administrator's and recipient's expectations.

Honigfeld (1964a) concluded from his extensive literature review that the placebo-reactor is a fictitious character. Since investigators rarely test for placebo reactions in the same population across placebos, complaints, administrators, and situations, there is as yet little ground for supporting the notion of placebo reaction as a general personality trait. It may be that when constant conditions of stress, authoritative setting, positive expectancy on the part of the placebo administrator, and marked discomfort are used, reliable individual differences in placebo reactivity can be established. This would permit direct comparisons of the parameters affecting placebo reactions, suggestibility, response to other's and one's own expectancies—all phenomena that seem to be related to each other and to effectiveness of psychotherapy and related psychological therapies. Goldstein (1962), after reviewing the literature on placebo reactions and effects of expectancies, concludes:

". . . several clear similarities emerge between positive placebo reactors on the one hand, and therapy patients with favorable prognostic expectancies and those receptive to their therapist's expectancies, on the other. For both placebo and psychotherapy patients of these types, anxiety level, degree of subjective distress, attraction to the therapist, field dependence, and suggestibility appear to be important influences determining reaction to treatment. The possibility, therefore, that in both instances we are examining individuals who are similar in several major respects, adds further to the meaningfulness we have suggested is associated with viewing the psychotherapeutic process in the light of placebo constructs" (Goldstein, 1962, p. 110).

An interesting research link between work on compatibility of patient and therapist expectations and placebo reactions exists in a pair of studies by Freedman and his coworkers. Freedman, Engelhardt, Hankoff, Glick, Kaye, Buchwald, and Stark (1958) determined that there is a significant relationship between duration of therapeutic contact and the congruence of initial patient and therapist expectancies regarding the goals and nature of their imminent interactions. Hankoff et al. (1958) used many of Freedman's schizophrenic subjects in the study mentioned earlier that found that initial negative placebo reactions predicted rehospitalization. The patients who had negative placebo reactions were found to have been among those with incompatible expectancies in the Freedman et al. study. Hankoff et al. concluded that the sequence of incompatible expectancies, absence of placebo effect, dropout from other drug and clinic treatment, and readmission to the hospital suggest a factor common to any treatment success, namely expectancies. The authors summarize that "the placebo response may therefore serve as an indicator of the nature and quality of the therapeutic relationship, specifically with respect to mutual expectations, and hence function as a useful predictor of treatment success" (p. 550).

As we indicated earlier, the placebo reaction may be regarded as a nonspecific influence on behavior that is present in all therapeutic endeavors, just as experimenter bias may exert a nonspecific influence on laboratory behaviors (Rosenthal, 1966). Critical effects on experimental outcomes from the experimenter's expectations, hypotheses, or wishes have been demonstrated in a number of studies by Rosenthal and his co-workers. Their work implies that these biasing effects are relatively easily demonstrated, pervasive, and robust. Other investigators have experienced difficulty in producing the biasing effect, have found alternative mechanisms (such as misrecording) to explain those instances of the bias effect that did occur, and have criticized the statistical analyses used in many of the positive studies (Barber, Calverley, Forgione, McPeake, Chaves, and Bowen, 1969; Barber and Silver, 1968). While the extent and seriousness of the effect thus remain uncertain, it is of interest to note that many of the same parameters appear to influence the experimenter bias effect as have been implicated in placebo reactions, in therapist influence, and in the influence of the therapist-patient relationship (see, for example, Kintz, Delprato, Mettee, Persons, and Schappe, 1965). These consistencies suggest strongly that the effectiveness of any behavior modification technique can be evaluated only with proper controls for placebo or experimenter effects, that specific versus nonspecific contributions to outcome need to be partialed out, and that behavioral approaches to parametric and analytical studies of the effects of expectancies can be very fruitful. Particularly, the communalities suggest that the behavior therapist would sacrifice an important source of influence for therapeutic benefit were he to ignore, rather than control and use, these nonspecific (expectancy) variables.

LEARNING AS A FUNCTION OF ORGANISMIC VARIABLES

Thus far we have been discussing factors within the therapeutic setting that influence learning in a nonspecific way and that therefore may affect the result of any therapy. There is another large domain of variables that also influence learning and therapeutic outcome but that operate outside as well as within the therapy setting. This domain, which may be roughly termed organismic, includes a host of physiological, genetic, constitutional, and other biological variables.

The behavioral equation, $S-O-R-K-C$, serves to remind us of the fundamental governing role of biology in all human behavior. The O factors that concern us here, however, are not molecular physiological, biochemical, or electrical functions and structures. Instead, organismic features that are associated with lasting behavior patterns are the focus here. As in the case of expectancies and other cognitive variables, biological influences on learning and hence on therapy are somewhat tangential to our presentation of behavior therapy techniques. Our purpose is not, then, to provide any comprehensive view of the types and mechanisms of biological-personality influences on behavior change; it is to acknowledge their importance and the need to take them into account in devising therapeutic approaches and in predicting treatment outcomes for both individuals and particular classes of people.

Just a few examples may serve to emphasize the complex interactions involved, and their profound behavioral effects, when we consider individual differences in basic biological characteristics. Figure 10-2 from Pribram (1962) depicts changes in the dominance hierarchy of a colony of rhesus monkeys subsequent to surgical production of lesions in the amygdaloid region of the temporal lobes of the brain of several of the monkeys, one at a time. Not only general social dominance but also specific correlated approach-avoidance, aggressive behaviors, and activity level of all of the colony members were affected by the biological alteration of one member. Pribram (1962) found that the effects of the amygdolectomy were a function of the lesion itself and of the immediate preoperative dominance pattern. Biological and complex social variables thus interact to produce behavior changes in all members of a group of monkeys.

Genetic endowment, early experiences, and constitutional changes in later life can produce physiological differences that fundamentally limit or alter learned behavior patterns. Exposure early in life to an environment rich in stimuli and response possibilities, as opposed to an impoverished environment, leads to differences in brain chemistry and thickness of the cortex in rats (Bennett, Diamond, Krech, and Rosenzweig, 1964). Gross pre- and postnatal physiological impairments, including those on a genetic basis, are presumed to account for the distribution of very severe mental retardation, which is far in excess of what would be predicted on the basis of the normal curve (Dingman and Tarjan, 1960). Brain damage, ranging in etiology from prenatal anomolies and birth trauma to infections, systemic diseases, and toxicity, has complex effects on behavior depending on its location, severity, and on individual characteristics such as age of trauma and level of previous functioning. Even when brain damage is the original source of behavioral excesses and deficits, for instance, hyperactivity or inability to engage in simple self-care, behavior modification procedures can often lead to significant improvement. Rohan and Provost (1966), for example, describe an operant training procedure that restored self-feeding behaviors in a blind and severely brain-damaged man who had not responded to other teaching approaches. Patterson (1965a) has reported an operant program in the schoolroom that reduced hyperactivity and increased attention and academic productivity in a brain-damaged nine-year-old boy.

The range of possible examples is almost limitless; any biological characteristic that affects the person's ability to perceive and discriminate relevant stimuli, to respond symbolically or motorically, to react to common reinforcing stimuli, or to tolerate particular reinforcement schedules will affect the size and quality of the behavior repertoire he can acquire and maintain. These characteristics may be as general as genetically influenced activity level, or as specific as a hearing loss for sounds in a given frequency range. Although the behavioral significance of biological characteristics is obvious, they are often of little practical importance in planning a therapeutic program. Most patients with psychological problems are, as far as is known, within the normal range of biological variation. Furthermore, unless a given biological characteristic can be identified and the behaviors related to it manipulated in some way, biological deviations are more likely to set limits on therapeutic goals or to require a prosthetic environment (see Chapter 6) than they are to suggest specific therapeutic operations. Clearly, most behavior therapy techniques assume certain biological capacities in their recipients. Although a shock avoidance procedure can be used successfully with a very young infant, treatment using tokens as generalized reinforcers, for example, requires such complex functions as delay of primary reinforcement, use of symbols, and memory of past contingencies. These are beyond the capacities of an infant, although not beyond the severely retarded or schizophrenic. Desensitization, role-playing, and other techniques demanding greater participation by the patient obviously require more complex biological capacities as well, for instance, the ability to "visualize," to respond autonomically to self-presented symbolic stimuli, to observe and describe one's own and other's behaviors. Self-regulatory behaviors instigated by less direct forms of behavior therapy demand even greater intellectual development and whatever biological and social substrata are needed for this level of discrimination, cooperation, and determination to change.

One of the achievements of behavior therapy has been to extend the repertoire of biologically defective persons. Behavior therapy techniques have successfully developed self-help and academic skills in the severely retarded, social and work behaviors in psychotics, and self-control and attending responses in brain-damaged children. As the earlier discussion of behavioral prosthetics pointed out (Chapter 6), a basic premise of behavior therapy is that environmental-behavioral engineering can overcome, circumvent, or ameliorate many biologically determined deficiencies. Nonetheless, hereditary and constitutional variables do set final limits on behavior change and maintenance. In addition, they influence the choice of techniques and target responses in treatment.

The biological parameters we take up here are of a different sort, however, than those that represent physical deficiencies. Instead we very briefly consider a few general biological characteristics that interact with other terms of the behavioral equation to influence learning. For a more comprehensive view of this topic, the reader can consult any of a number of

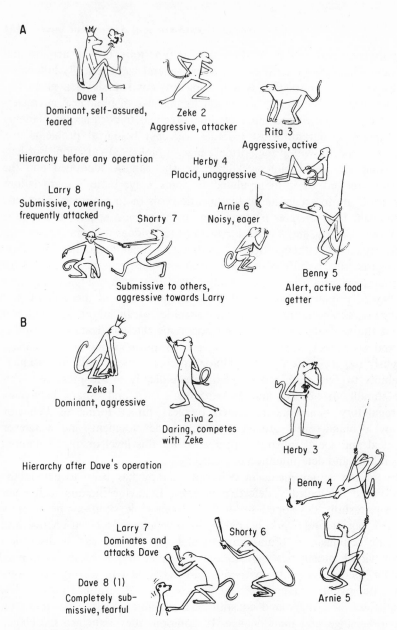

A

Dave 1
Dominant, self-assured,
feared

Zeke 2
Aggressive, attacker

Rita 3
Aggressive, active

Hierarchy before any operation

Herby 4
Placid, unaggressive

Larry 8
Submissive, cowering,
frequently attacked

Arnie 6
Noisy, eager

Shorty 7

Submissive to others,
aggressive towards Larry

Benny 5
Alert, active food
getter

B

Zeke 1
Dominant, aggressive

Riva 2
Daring, competes
with Zeke

Herby 3

Hierarchy after Dave's operation

Benny 4

Larry 7
Dominates and
attacks Dave

Shorty 6

Dave 8 (1)
Completely sub-
missive, fearful

Arnie 5

Figure 10-2. **A,** dominance hierarchy of a colony of eight preadolescent male rhesus monkeys before any surgical intervention. **B,** same as **A** after bilateral amygdalectomy had been performed on Dave. Note his drop to the bottom of the hierarchy. **C,** same as **A** and **B,** except that both Dave and Zeke have received bilateral amygdalectomies. **D,** final social hierarchy after Dave, Zeke and Riva have all had bilateral amygdalectomies. Minimal differences in extent of locus of the resections do not correlate with differences in the behavioral results. Herby's

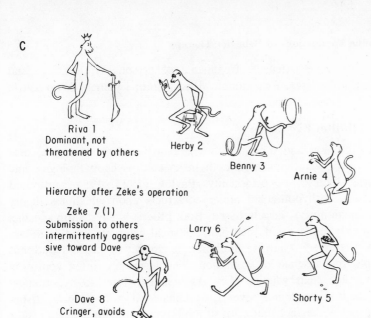

C

Riva 1
Dominant, not
threatened by others

Herby 2

Benny 3

Arnie 4

Hierarchy after Zeke's operation

Zeke 7 (1)
Submission to others
intermittently aggres-
sive toward Dave

Larry 6

Dave 8
Cringer, avoids
interaction

Shorty 5

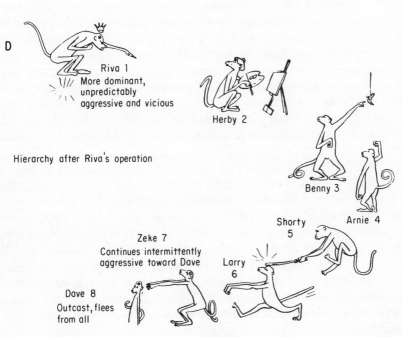

D

Riva 1
More dominant,
unpredictably
aggressive and vicious

Herby 2

Hierarchy after Riva's operation

Benny 3

Shorty
5

Arnie 4

Zeke 7
Continues intermittently
aggressive toward Dave

Larry
6

Dave 8
Outcast, flees
from all

nonaggressive "personality" in the second position of the hierarchy accounts for the disparate effects of similar lesions. (From Pribram, 1962, appearing in Thompson, 1967, pp. 560–561).

texts that give more extensive treatments of personality, learning, and biological variables (see, for example, Buss, 1966; Eysenck, 1960 1961; Kruse, 1957; Maher, 1966).

Central Inhibition-Excitation

Cortical excitation and inhibition are among the prime biological processes that have been implicated both in specific psychopathologies and in some trait theories of personality. Pavlov (1927, 1957) proposed these processes as hypothetical molar constructs upon which his theory of cortical functioning is largely based. Both processes have more specific, if as yet poorly understood, neurophysiological referents, and both are positive in character. That is, inhibition is an active process and not at all simply the absence of excitation. The terms are often confusing unless it is made clear whether they are meant to refer to hypothetical constructs, neurophysiological events, or behavioral consequences. Especially confusing is the fact that cortical inhibition in Pavlov's sense results in the *opposite* of inhibition in overt behavior, that is, cortical inhibition produces behavioral arousal (see Franks, 1961, for a more extended discussion).

Pavlov proposed many hypotheses regarding the cortical concomitants of psychopathology. However, his ideas were often contradictory and he did not offer experimental work to support them. Pavlov suggested that neurasthenic patients have an excess of central excitatory activity and hysterics have an excess of central inhibition. This would imply that neurasthenics would condition rapidly and extinguish slowly, whereas hysterics would condition with difficulty and would extinguish rapidly. A very large amount of literature has accumulated on conditionability, arousal and vigilance levels, extinction, development of reactive inhibition, and related learning phenomena in various diagnostic groups in an effort to test the relevance of cortical inhibition and excitation to specific psychopathologies. For example, it has been suggested, especially by Russian workers, that some categories of schizophrenics are defective in cortical inhibition, while others have massive amounts of inhibition (Lang and Buss, 1965). Among the studies supporting this view, Stanishevskaya (1955), using blood pressure as a measure of the orienting reflex, found that normals initially give a generalized response to presentation of a new stimulus but rapidly narrow down to a localized response, presumably as a consequence of inhibition. He found that simple schizophrenics show only the general arousal stage, and that catatonics show neither, that is, no orienting response at all.

A number of other Russian investigators have found an absence or depression of the orienting response in chronic, and specially in catatonic schizophrenics. Inhibition is presumed to underlie extinction and discrimination learning: non-reinforced responses are assumed to be centrally inhibited or suppressed. It follows that schizophrenics who are deficient in inhibition (for example, those showing only the generalized orienting response) would extinguish poorly, overgeneralize, and fail to acquire discriminations. Massive inhibition, as in catatonics, would leave the patient essentially "decorticate." Research results mostly support the inferences that can be made from the Russian hypotheses regarding the role of inhibition in schizophrenia (see Lynn, 1963, for a summary). Since a number of other hypotheses fit the data equally well, however, and inhibition as used here has the status of a loosely defined hypothetical construct, it has been difficult to confirm more stringently the relevance of the theory to the etiology of schizophrenia.

Despite the rather direct connections hypothesized between excitation-inhibition and various learning parameters, the literature on these brain activities offers the behavior therapist no specific suggestions for improvement of his assessment and treatment operations. In this regard, excitation-inhibition is similar to a number of other biological variables or constructs which thus far are of far greater theoretical than practical importance. Presumably, as our understanding of these biological processes increases, extrapolation from the psychobiological laboratory to the clinic will become more feasible, just as variables such as "interpersonal attraction" or "expectancy" are being extrapolated from the social and cognitive psychology literature and applied to clinical problems. Some day it may be possible, for example, to classify a schizophrenic according to his cortical excitation-inhibition patterns, to predict the particular techniques most likely to alter his behavior, and to state the limits imposed on any therapeutic efforts by his central nervous system characteristics. At present, theories and research data about excitation-inhibition do not offer this direct clinical relevance except insofar as they form the basis of current work on extraversion-introversion.

Russell (1958) has made a similar point in connection with biochemical correlates of behavior:

"Some forms of behavior are linked more directly to their biochemical correlates than others. Where the linkage is direct, changes in biochemical events are reflected in specific changes in behavior. But where the linkage is diffuse, changes in biochemical events may affect a variety of behavior patterns. In this latter instance a particular biochemical state may facilitate change of behavior, but the actual change may not occur without learning or the application of some other psychological procedure for altering behavior. . . . Despite the considerable number of examples of both specific and diffuse relations between biochemical events and behavior, it is quite correct to say that our general knowledge of the biochemical correlates of behavior is still very primitive. We have little knowledge of the processes by which biochemical events are, to use a recent phrase (Grenell, 1957), 'transduced into general behavior patterns.' Present theoretical models purporting to describe these processes are couched in terms of diffuse physiological mechanisms, metabolic events in specific regions of the brain, synaptic transmission, and molecular shifts and interactions in nerve cell membranes. A decision as to which, if any, of these models is adequate awaits much more information than we now possess. This information can only be obtained by research which includes among its approaches systematic observations of the effects of 'biochemical lesions' on behavior" (p. 211).

Introversion—Extraversion

Another extension of Pavlov's theories of cortical inhibition and excitation is found in Eysenck's work on the personality dimension of introversion-extraversion (Eysenck, 1957; Eysenck and Rachman, 1965). Eysenck has postulated that "high degrees of extraversion are found in people in whom inhibitory processes occur quickly, strongly, and persistently, and in whom excitatory processes occur slowly, weakly, and non-persistently; high degrees of introversion are found in people of whom the reverse is true" (Eysenck and Rachman, 1965, p. 35). Figure 10-3 outlines Eysenck's notions of how biological differences in cortical processes interact with environmental influences to produce differences in the personality dimension of extraversion-introversion. The level of extraversion-introversion is manifested, in turn, by a number of differences in conditionability, traits, and habits. In the diagram, excitation-inhibition balance is used as a theoretical construct (L_1) to explain individual differences in conditionability and related phenomena observed in the laboratory (L_2). These differences are presumed to interact with multiple environmental influences to produce various observable traits (such as activity level and sociability) that form two trait clusters, extraversion and introversion (L_3). Attitudes are similarly the product of environmental influences interacting with the individual's basic extraversion-introversion makeup.

Eysenck's theories of personality and psychopathology rest on another bipolar dimension, as well—that of *neuroticism*. By this term he denotes persons whose emotions are labile, intense, and easily aroused. This emotional lability and the general behavior of persons high in neuroticism are presumed to be caused by an innate predisposition to rapid, strong, and lasting autonomic nervous system responses. In Eysenck's scheme, various disorders can be located on a two-dimensional grid representing

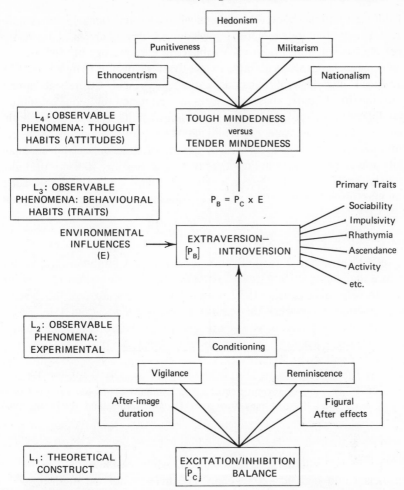

Figure 10-3   Eysenck's theory of extraversion-introversion. Diagrammatic picture of the interaction between genetic and environmental influences giving rise to phenotypic behavior patterns (from Eysenck and Rachman, 1965, p. 41).

various degrees of neuroticism and extraversion-introversion. Diagnostic groups, such as hysterics and psychopaths, have been assessed by paper-and-pencil tests for their location on these two trait dimensions. Most often their scores place them at the locus on the grid that would be predicted by Eysenck's theory. Figure 10-4 presents the grid locations of various diagnostic groups based on their standard scores on such measures as the Maudsley Personality Inventory.

As Figure 10-4 indicates, anxious and obsessional (dysthymic) patients

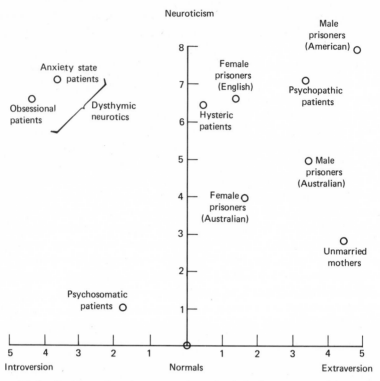

Figure 10-4   Position of various neurotic and criminal groups on the two factors of neutroticism and introversion-extraversion (from Eysenck and Rachman, 1965, p. 21).

are high in neuroticism and introversion, while psychopaths are low in neuroticism and high in extraversion. Dysthymic patients, predisposed to neuroticism by a labile, overactive autonomic nervous system, also are predisposed biologically (by high cortical excitation) to form conditioned responses rapidly, strongly, and durably. Therefore they readily develop the conditioned dysthymic symptoms of phobias, obsessions, and so on, and do not extinguish these symptoms quickly. Psychopaths, on the other hand, are hypothesized by Eysenck to represent a failure of conditioning. This failure is due to the biological predisposition of extraverts (high in cortical inhibition) to form conditioned responses only weakly and with difficulty, and to be slow in autonomic reactions. Thus psychopaths tend not to form conditioned anxiety responses that normally inhibit asocial acts.

A large body of experimental and clinical investigation supports Eysenck's theories. As in the case of other cortical process theories, alternative explanations are, of course, possible. For those who emphasize the role of social reinforcement in symptom formation and who focus on situation-specific behaviors instead of hypothesizing general personality states or traits, Eysenck's approach has less appeal than an operant conditioning one, particularly as long as the relevant biological factors remain hypothetical constructs.

Since there is sufficient predictive validity attached to measures of extraversion-introversion with respect to learning and conditioning, behavior therapists often take this dimension into account in formulating research designs and treatment plans. For example, Eysenck's theory would predict that aversive conditioning therapy would be relatively slow and ineffective with psychopaths and other extraverts, although it is often just these persons who exhibit target behaviors (alcoholism, unacceptable sexual responses) that appear most suited for treatment by aversive conditioning. Other observations relevant to treatment planning include the greater tolerance for pain (including shock and other aversive CS) reported for extraverts (Lynn and Eysenck, 1961), and the ability of strong stimuli to overcome the inhibition of extraverts so that they then condition as readily as do introverts (Eysenck, 1965a). Stimulating drugs can be employed to overcome the central inhibition of extraverts when a conditioning therapy is to be used (Eysenck, 1963). On the other hand, the autonomic lability and readiness to respond with anxiety of the highly neurotic patient can also pose difficulties for conditioning therapies. Eysenck's theory predicts (with clinical and laboratory support) that highly anxious persons do not condition as readily as do those with lower levels of anxiety. Most reports, for example, indicate greater success for systematic desensitization with moderately anxious patients (see, for example, Marks and Gelder, 1966; Gelder, Marks, Wolff, and Clarke, 1967).

Lader and Wing (1966) have proposed innate differences in central habituation, resembling Eysenck's neuroticism and introversion dimensions, to explain morbid anxiety and the effects of desensitization. Like Eysenck, Lader and Wing predict that habituation and desensitization occur most rapidly when a patient is at as low a level of activity or arousal as possible, and cite experimental evidence for this prediction. Should the Lader-Wing hypothesis gain further support, a change in desensitization procedure would be necessitated, as Rachman has pointed out: "The emphasis would have to move from the present concern with superimposing an antagonistic response whenever anxiety is elicited, to a procedure which can effect a reliable and enduring decrease in arousal level such that desensitization to the hierarchy items can proceed with ease and speed" (Rachman, 1968, p. 58). Depressed persons, who are low in neuroticism but introverted according to Eysenck's schema, apparently may respond poorly to desensitization and other conditioning therapies because of their low reactivity, despite the predicted ease of conditioning of introverts (Meyer and Crisp, 1966).

The preceding discussion implies that the literature now available on neuroticism and extraversion-introversion offers more possibilities for direct extrapolation of experimental data to clinical application than is the case for cortical inhibition-excitation. Extraversion-introversion appear as constructs, in some guise, in many, if not most, personality theories (for instance, field dependence-independence, inner-outer directedness). However, their actual practical importance for treatment remains to be established. For example, it is not known whether the usual shock levels used in aversive conditioning are sufficient to override the tolerance for pain asserted to exist in psychopaths. If not, can sufficient levels be established, perhaps on the basis of extroversion scores? Can cutoff points on scales of neuroticism and introversion be established, beyond which desensitization will probably fail? Do these cutoff points depend on the nature, extensiveness, and intensity of a patient's particular phobic symptoms? Until clinical investigations help to answer these questions, the behavior therapist can take account of these variables in his practice only in a general way.

Arousal

Arousal or activation as an overall biological state, measured by such indices as EEG desynchronization, GSR, heart rate, or muscle tension, is highly related to theories of central excitation and inhibition. However, the work on arousal has tended to focus on the nonspecific effects of stimulation on directly measurable autonomic nervous system responses instead of on the hypothesized central governing processes. The intercorrelations between different measures of arousal are far from perfect. Individuals show a characteristically different pattern of autonomic responses to a variety of stimuli or stresses. Therefore, "arousal" must be considered a general state of the organism, not necessarily reflected in overt behavior nor in any one given physiological measure (see, for example, Lacey, Bateman, and VanLehn, 1953). Much of the discussion in Chapter 4 of the problems in measurement of anxiety is relevant here; but, in addition, there is only low agreement about the defining properties of arousal—its response characteristics and the stimuli that elicit it.

Differences in absolute arousal level, in general patterns of change with stimulation, and in specific responses to stimulation have all been investigated as variables that may underlie either particular disorders or general classes of psychopathology. For instance, neurotic patients have been found to show continuing increases on measures such as blood pressure rise in response to stressful stimuli, long after normals have leveled off or begun to return to base line (Malmo and Shagass, 1952). Acute schizophrenics appear to be more aroused than normals by stressful stimuli, and chronic schizophrenics seem to be less reactive than normals (Malmo, Shagass, and David, 1951). Venables (1964) has theorized that schizophrenics are chronically in a high state of arousal and therefore unable to show any increase under added stimulation. Venables' hypothesis is supported by a number of studies showing improved functioning of schizophrenics when they have been given depressant drugs. Another line of support comes from studies such as Venables and Wing (1962) that showed that GSR level (as an arousal measure) and extent of social withdrawal are positively correlated in chronic schizophrenics. As Maher (1966) has suggested, Venables' findings indicate that schizophrenic withdrawal may represent an effort to cut down external stimulation in order to keep an already high arousal level within bearable limits. As can be seen, at the level of data and behavior, theories of central inhibition-excitation and of arousal are not very different, except for the greater reliance on hypothetical constructs of the former.

Venables' notions of high arousal in behaviorally unresponsive schizophrenics are similar to those of Schachter regarding psychopaths (Schachter and Latané, 1964). Schachter has proposed that emotion is a function of the interaction of a state of physiological arousal and cognitions appropriate to the arousal (Schachter. 1964a). Neurotics who suffer from chronic anxiety have been found to be emotionally volatile and overreactive in their autonomic responses. Schachter reasons that "the cognitive system and personality structure of this sort of individual is such that he constantly interprets his world in threatening or emotional terms—an interpretation that triggers autonomic activity" (Schachter and Latané, 1964, p. 269). Unlike Eysenck, Schachter hypothesizes that the high level and ease of arousal in neurotics is cognitively, not genetically or constitutionally determined. However, other investigators have found that subjects who report high awareness of autonomic changes under stress actually show larger physiological responses and also overestimate the magnitude of the changes at these times. That is, both their actual arousal level and their labeling of their feelings are in the more intense direction (Mandler, Mandler, and Uviller, 1958). Psychopaths, on the other hand, are found in Schachter's work to be less anxious and emotionally reactive than normals but, surprisingly, to be *more* autonomically responsive to a variety of mild and severe stresses than are normals. Since Schachter had found that autonomic arousal alone is not sufficient for the report of an emotional state, but must be coupled with cognitive and situational factors that determine that the arousal will be labeled as an emotion, the issue with psychopaths appears to be one of the labeling: How does the psychopath label his sensations of bodily arousal? Schachter argues:

"Sociopaths appear to be more responsive to virtually every titillating event . . . . Such generalized, relatively indiscriminate reactivity is, we would suggest, almost the equivalent of no reactivity at all . . . . Only intense states of autonomic reactions, presumably stronger than, and differentiable from his normal reactions, acquire emotional attributes for the sociopath subject. . . . sociopaths are individuals characterized by marked autonomic reactivity, who over the course of their development have learned *not* (or have not learned) to apply emotional labels to their states of arousal" (Schachter and Latané, 1964, pp. 266–267).

Differences in arousal thresholds, if not innate, may be acquired early in life as a result of training in labeling stimuli and bodily sensations under arousal. Whether learned or innate, differences in arousal thresholds and intensities have important general implications for learning-based therapies. In the case of psychopaths, whether their lack of relative arousal is due to a ceiling effect or a very high threshold, the consequence of relative unreactivity is that they condition only with difficulty in a pain-avoidance procedure. They learn as well as do normals under positive reinforcement however, and markedly improve in avoidance learning when given an autonomic activating drug like adrenalin (see, for example, Lykken, 1957; Schachter and Latané, 1964). Thus the work of both Eysenck and Schachter indicates that aversive conditioning is difficult with psychopaths and that arousing drugs facilitate treatment. Both also agree in regarding neurotics as emotionally hyperresponsive and as easily conditioned toward persistent arousal and emotion. With respect to treatment, however, Schachter's view would emphasize changes in the patient's cognitive labeling of his environment and his own sensations, while Eysenck's stress on innate cortical differences in neurotics would support the use of drugs to reduce arousal thresholds.

Similarly, Venables' (1964) hypotheses about schizophrenics implicate arousal effects on learning ability and imply the need for medication to correct arousal level. The acute schizophrenic is, in Venables' view, unable to restrict the range of his attention, engage in necessary selective ignoring, or distinguish figure and ground relationships among stimuli because of a chronically low level of arousal. Drugs or stimulation that produce arousal should enable these patients to narrow their attention and thereby learn discriminations and new behaviors, otherwise beyond their capacity. If Venables is correct, intense stimulation or adrenalin-like drugs are likely to be necessary adjuncts to conditioning therapies with acute schizophrenics. On the other hand, according to Venables, chronic schizophrenics have unusually high arousal levels and suffer from a narrowing of attention. Many stimuli necessary for learning and performance maintenance are not perceived at all. For behavior therapy to succeed with such patients, reduction of arousal by drugs or other means would be necessary.

Some General Comments

In this section we have been able to discuss only briefly three areas from the immense literature relevant to biological foundations of learning and behavior control. A lengthy list of unmentioned topics remains. The three topics we have discussed may nevertheless exemplify some of the potentials and some of the difficulties and present disappointments in trying to integrate biological and behavioral approaches to psychopathology and in applying this integration to clinical problems.

Cohen (1969) has surveyed a large number of current developments in neurobiology for their potential contributions to behavior therapy. The survey was motivated by his

". . . concern about the increasing gap between neurobiological studies of brain mechanisms and efforts to establish a more scientific basis for the diagnosis and treatment of disturbances in cognition, behavior, and interpersonal relations. There is the need for psychopathological studies to move closer to the stream of biological research concerned with nervous-system functioning. It is this research which should constantly replenish or support the diagnostic and therapeutic practices as well as the research efforts of the clinician" (Cohen, 1969, p. 589).

Psychological research and its constructs and measures have had very little impact on nosology and diagnosis, prognostic schemes, therapeutic techniques, or outcome evaluation. The nature of the material covered in Cohen's review helps to clarify why this impact has been so slight. What is lacking for the behavior therapist is any feeling for even a few central constructs or principles that might be directly applied to clinical problems. Instead, the literature provides either detailed studies, demanding technical knowledge and judgments in a discipline other than psychology, or abstract summaries of data and theories, lacking concrete substance and guidance.

Serious obstacles to clinical utilization of neurobiological advances occur at a number of different levels in the clinician's functioning. A first obstacle is one of conceptual level and unit of analysis. Lord Brain (1965), the great English neurophysiologist, himself has questioned the idea "that current physical concepts of causation, which are valid at the molecular level, necessarily completely explain the interrelated activities of the millions of nerve cells which must be involved in all our higher mental activities . . . . the naive physical determinism, which appealed particularly to some 19th century writers, may not be applicable to present-day interpretation of the brain-mind relationship" (p. 196).

Quite aside from any special logical and semantic difficulties in dealing with mind-brain interactions, many psychobiological and learning constructs are too nebulous or not yet well enough established to permit any precise and concrete application to clinical practice. For instance, a general factor of conditionability, which plays an important role in many hypotheses about the nature or etiology of specific disorders, has yet to be firmly established as a real parameter. Cortical inhibition and excitation as used by Pavlov have little to do with processes directly measured in electrophysiology since they are abstractions about rather global or summated cortical functions. A clear description of autonomic reactivity is complicated by the low correlations between verbal report, behavior, and physiological measures as indices of arousal. For this reason, some investigators have urged that relationships between behavior and biological manipulations be studied directly without interposing another set of theoretical constructs, such as extraversion-introversion, between the observed behaviors and biological measures.

Another obstacle is the lack of competence in psychobiology of theoretically oriented clinicians to use its techniques and constructs on a level other than "cookbook." Even the use of autonomic measures, such as GSR, to monitor changes in desensitization can pose serious technical and conceptual difficulties for the behavior therapist. Lacey (1959) has pointed out that clinicians too often incorrectly use one measure of "arousal" as if all autonomic measures were highly intercorrelated, or as if one measure is a suitable indicant across individuals. Furthermore, they often fail to use the mathematical procedures necessary to achieve stable measures of lability. Lacey also criticizes the use of traditional concepts, such as homeostasis or arousal, in psychophysiological studies of clinical problems since these concepts do not encompass a sufficient quantity of data. Instead, Lacey holds, new concepts are needed to explain how autonomic activity controls and modulates behavior, and autonomic activity itself should be viewed from a transactional point of view instead of being used merely as an indicant. Sophistication of this level is simply not found among most clinicians.

A different level of obstacle to application of psychobiological methods and data in therapy planning has to do with the specificity of many biology-behavior relationships and their small order of magnitude. Franks (1961), for example, has pointed critically to the "diminutive magnitude" of the obtained correlations between conditioning variables and personality-constitutional variables such as extraversion-introversion. These correlations are likely to have little practical utility, whatever their theoretical interest. Similarly, biological effects on behavior can rarely be characterized in a general fashion without taking into account the specific conditions surrounding and eliciting the behavior. Cook and Kelleher (1963) cite the effects of meprobamate on "aggressiveness" as an illustration of this point. The drug reduces attack behavior elicited in pairs of animals by electric shock or isolation, but increases attacks by cats on mice when the attacks have been suppressed by electric shock. The drug, as Brady (1967) has pointed out, apparently suppresses or releases attack behavior depending on the situation because in both cases it decreases the effects of a shock, but the different behavioral functions of shock in the two situations lead to different outcomes.

Finally, many difficulties in experimental control arise when decline in learning rate or performance decrement are the dependent variables used to test hypotheses about biological determinants of behavior in abnormal groups. The presence of correlated variables, effects of hospitalization, and unreliable diagnoses pose their own set of problems. In addition, however, the difficulty in separating peripheral from central nervous system effects, and learned from innate effects on attention and arousal, conditionability, and so on make it difficult to choose among theories and to apply isolated or controversial findings in the clinic.

The behavior therapist seems to be left in the position of having to maintain his attention to biological variables and his interest in research and theoretical developments in these areas with little direct and immediate reinforcement for doing so. At present, he is usually restricted in direct use of psychobiological variables to rather simple manipulations on an empirical basis, such as giving arousing drugs to psychopaths prior to conditioning. Ultimately, the clinician may have available predictive assessment devices that, unlike general trait measures, are able to isolate specific biological variables that have significant and quantitative relationships to learning and perceptual tasks involved in treatment procedures.

BEHAVIORAL ASSESSMENT

The preceding two sections illustrated the importance of general, nonspecific influences on the processes of behavior change. Social-interpersonal characteristics of therapist and patient indirectly affect the outcome of the therapist's efforts at influence. The patient's biological characteristics will govern how and to what extent he accomplishes the learning that comprises the therapeutic goal. With increased knowledge about these parameters and their effects on behavior, additional arenas for intervention or control should improve the efficacy of behavior therapy. The goal for behavior therapies, and the reason for expanding their roots in basic psychological research is to have available a consistent behavioristic view, a complete set of psychological principles that can be applied to an individual patient from initial presentation of complaint to discharge from treatment. In order to apply a behavioral model comprehensively to the entire treatment process, however, the behavior therapist needs systematic methods by which to collect information to appraise the patient's difficulties and to reach decisions concerning the most appropriate treatment program.

To operate within a behavioristic framework in the clinic it is necessary to: (1) locate the problem to be exposed to therapeutic attention and (2) translate the initial complaint about the patient into a language and set of questions that can be fruitfully pursued by available behavioral technology. The total situation, as well as, for example, the specific behaviors of the aggressive child, the anxious and unhappy adult, the promiscuous adolescent, or the unreliable psychotic patient, must be assessed before an effective treatment strategy can be initiated. In the early stages of behavior therapy, this process of *assessment* or *diagnosis* has been given inadequate attention. Behavioral clinicians have usually relied on traditional methods, diagnostic classifications, and the backlog of their personal clinical experiences. In an evaluation of behavior therapy, Klein, Dittmann, Parloff, and Gill (1969) point to this elusive skill: "Although the behavior therapist would not wish to ascribe his results to any 'dynamic' theories he may have learned in the past, it is clear that many clinical decisions in the treatment are based on an understanding of some functional organization of behavior . . ." (p. 265). As has been stated previously, the behavior therapist has remained as much artist as scientist, relying on his sensitivity, his past experience, and his general knowledge of psychology and human behavior in making decisions about priorities for target responses, selection of treatment, and critical points at which treatment changes are required.

Eventually behavioral technology must expand to include not only the treatment tools but also the interactions between therapist and patient from the first contact to final discharge. A full account of the clinical enterprise, therefore, would include a formulation of the uses of information obtained from referring sources, initial interviews, or other observations, a formulation of the bases for the clinician's hypotheses that in turn lead to choices of target behaviors, and of the features during therapy that lead the clinician to change his therapeutic tactics or to terminate treatment. Knowledge of the rationale for clinical decisions and the relevancy of various behavioral and social-environmental dimensions for treatment success should make it easier to develop assessment techniques that would have validity in predicting which treatment methods would produce optimal benefit for an individual patient.

In this section, to a greater extent than in previous chapters, we attempt to deal with trends, tentative directions, and future potentials instead of laboratory and clinical research. This section deals with that part of behavior therapy to which least systematic attention has been given at this time. Nevertheless, recent writers have begun to suggest new models and techniques suitable for behavioral diagnosis. There are heuristic beginnings that are consistent with the behavioristic framework but that are only vaguely described and not yet tested by research. First, however, we will present a brief description of one behavioral model of abnormal behavior to set the stage for reviewing the general functions of assessment and some of the drawbacks of traditional practices and concepts. Recent efforts at behavioral analysis and the remaining problems in this area are then discussed.

Behavioral Models of Pathology

To the extent that the goals of therapy are vague, nonspecific, and subjective, assessment and diagnostic nosologies are likely to continue to rely on nonspecific dynamic personality formulations and unreliable labels. To the extent that behavior therapists develop more discrete and specific criteria for success and specifiable therapeutic operations, their need for particularistic assessment information increases. Their ability to promote these developments depends in part on having available a compatible conception of disordered behavior. Chapters 1 and 2 outlined some of the characteristics of a behavioral conception of pathology upon which it may be possible to build assessment techniques and classification schemes suited to the needs of behavior therapy. A relatively consistent view of the nature of behavior disorders has been encountered in the succeeding chapters and studies cited. It seems appropriate to review the main features of such a model here, however, since they have special implications for assessment and also are likely to be more meaningful now that the various therapeutic techniques have been described.

The "medical model" has become by now a familiar target of criticism, although the term varies in connotation as it is used by various critics (see, for example, Sarbin, 1967, Szasz, 1960, Ullmann and Krasner, 1969). "Medical model" usually implies: (1) reliance on the logic and goals of the traditional medical diagnostic process; (2) adherence to the view that pathological internal processes lead to behavioral "symptoms" and that such "symptoms" are not in themselves legitimate targets of treatment.

Instead treatment should be directed toward underlying causes; and (3) persons showing behavior problems should be treated as "ill," consonant with the social role model assigned to patients with medical complaints.

Two closely related models of disordered behavior may be contrasted with the medical model. One usually is called upon in connection with stimulus control therapies, and the other is especially suited to consequence control therapies. The differences in patient populations, therapeutic technologies, and models of psychopathology typically involved in these two types of therapies have interacted to increase their theoretical differences and the relative separation of the two therapeutic approaches. Therapists of both classical and operant conditioning persuasion usually agree in regarding maladaptive behavior as being *learned*. However, therapists relying on classical conditioning techniques of treatment concentrate on neurotic behaviors, viewed as classically conditioned respondents (anxiety) and as behaviors reinforced by a reduction of the anxiety drive. A second group of behavior disorders represent a "failure of conditioning processes to occur which would produce socially desirable habits" (Eysenck and Rachman, 1965, p. 7) or "where there may have taken place a type of positive, appetitive conditioning which is contrary to the rules and laws of the country in question" (p. 8). Sociopathic and homosexual behaviors are examples of the second group. Psychotic behaviors represent the outcome of an entirely different etiology. They have an endogenous nature, although open to modification by learning. Eysenck reserves the term "behavior therapy" for Pavlovian type procedures. He refers to "cures" achieved with neurotics by these therapies and describes operant conditioning of psychotic symptoms as "rehabilitation," underscoring the different assumed etiologies of the two types of behavior disorders.

In contrast to this position is that of behavior modifiers who rely primarily upon operant conditioning for etiological assumptions and therapeutic methods. Ferster (1965), for example, outlines a functional analysis of deviant behavior that ascribes neurotic and psychotic behaviors alike to untoward reinforcement processes, past and present. Basic physiological defects, postulated by Eysenck as the etiology of psychosis, are accepted by Ferster as a possible but unproven cause of failure to develop normal performances because of disruption of reinforcement operations.

Ferster and many other behavior therapists view all symptomatic behavior in terms of its discrepancy from the desired consequences of a given social-cultural environment as viewed and practiced by the community.

". . . the milieu specifies the behaviors potentially available to an individual in contact with it. An individual's environment might be thought of as an infinite variety of response keys, all of which are set to produce a reinforcer or avoid an aversive stimulus if—and only if—the individual's repertoire contains the required behavioral items . . . . The use of the milieu as a standard of reference provides a classification system that is cross-culturally general, because it does not refer to specific items of behavior or a specific environmental practice. Two entirely different repertories from two entirely different cultures might, for example, have in common that all the performances in the repertoires are maintained by positive reinforcement, and that the individual repertoires are the maximum that could be maintained by such environments. Conversely, various items of behavior may be absent because of the absence of a history of experiences that were necessary in order to approximate a complex form by slow stages; or because the particular schedule of reinforcement currently maintaining the performance reduced the disposition to engage in the performance. Such an evaluation of the discrepancy between the actual repertoire of an individual and the potential behavior supported by the individual's milieu does not depend upon the particular performance that is evaluated. Two very different performances might be absent from a repertoire for the same reason, or a single performance might be absent from the repertoire of two individuals for different reasons.

"The basic processes by which behavior is strengthened, weakened, maintained, extinguished, put under stimulus control, and so forth, can provide a framework for specifying the relation between the individual's existing repertoire and the milieu potentially available to him" (Ferster, 1965, pp. 12–13).

The operant model views problematic behavior, then, as the outcome of the same functional processes that affect all behavior, with the reinforcement history (and physiological, anatomical, and other constitutional influences on that history) as the primary etiological agent. The focus is on symptoms, not on internal mediating processes. Since a given behavior may result from a multitude of possible interactions in an individual reinforcement history, direct evidence that symptoms have actually been so formed is difficult to achieve. Even the evidence from animal work that problematic behaviors *can* be so produced is not satisfactory; in part this follows from the social effectiveness instead of the autonomic-disease definition of "symptoms." Animal work has demonstrated that an infinite variety of behaviors can be established, for example, by differential positive reinforcement and chaining schedules. Whether a given "problem" behavior has been produced in this manner is a different matter. Further, whether a given response, known to have been so produced, is viewed as a neurotic or psychotic symptom depends on the range of tolerance for behavior deviations in the patient's cultural milieu. Thus the definition of a behavior as a symptom is often a sociological question, not a question that can be answered by the psychology of learning.

Because of the basic difference in number and complexity of potential etiological variables in the respondent and operant models of pathology, the operant-oriented model can never have as clear cut a *post hoc* explanation of symptom production. Longitudinal studies may at least establish that various reinforcement patterns can and do produce problematic behaviors in the natural environment, just as controlled therapeutic trials can demonstrate relevance of certain variables to current maintenance of symptoms—as, for example, when temper tantrums are extinguished following removal of adult attention as their usual consequence.

There are numerous hypotheses regarding possible environmental contingencies that may engender particular abnormal behaviors. Salzinger (1968), for instance, has extrapolated from laboratory research operations to propose the symptoms that these operations seem likely to produce. He has made inferences from observations of abnormal behaviors to the learning operations that might have caused these behaviors. Similar formulations have frequently appeared throughout the preceding chapters. In discussing the implications of research on intermittent reinforcement for abnormal behavior, Salzinger states:

"The intermittent reinforcement literature tells us that the inconsistent reinforcing behavior by the mother and/or father most likely serves all the better, for its inconsistency, to produce stable abnormal behavior in the child. The fact that the mother tries very hard not to give into the child having a temper tantrum, but gives in some of the time, is of course the very paradigm which maintains the behavior she is trying to eliminate. The precise results of schedule research are probably less important than the finding that many different kinds of reinforcement are effective in the maintenance of behavior. . . . the fact that conditioning is more rapid than extinction is what makes the intermittent schedule a good candidate for the production of abnormal behavior. It is also worthwhile to mention here that the specification of a schedule must include specification of the behavior the animal brings to the experiment . . . . Although it has become the fashion among some behavior therapists to ignore the patient's reinforcement history (with the exception of the most closely related last event), findings in the behavior theory literature appear to show that behavior on the current schedule of reinforcement depends not only on the reinforcement contingency it specifies, but also on the organism's reinforcement history, and in addition, on the way in which the current schedule was introduced" (p. 6).

Just as assessment aspects of a behavioral approach to clinical problems must rest on a behavioral conception of the nature and origins of pathology, so too, traditional psychiatric diagnosis has taken as its conceptual justification a particular view of the nature of illness and its cure, based on an early general medical model. We can now contrast this model and its associated diagnostic processes with the behavioral framework for viewing pathology.

Traditional Models and Functions of Diagnosis

The medical model can be illustrated best in the case of infectious diseases. For instance, in the case of malaria, medical science has provided a clear description of the ecological and biological mechanisms involved in contraction of the disease, its effects on the human body, and its manifestations or "signs and symptoms." Its prognosis in response to various therapeutic agents, and its natural course when no treatment is offered, can be described on the basis of empirical evidence. *Etiology, diagnosis,* and *prognosis* are clearly interconnected and tied either to available knowledge or, in other instances, to a theory about the disease process. Such a model presumes that knowledge of the main causative factors and of their manifestation in signs and symptoms offer a firm basis for the doctor's decisions concerning treatment and for his predictions of the future course of the disease. When specific pathological processes are known to respond to particular treatment agents, diagnosis becomes the central task of the doctor. Once an illness is properly diagnosed, appropriate remedial measures are quickly applied. Even in current medical practice, however, this simple model does not take into account the complexity of factors involved and a much more elaborate model must be used. Tuberculosis and other diseases result from multiple influences in which an interplay of the characteristics of the host, the pathological agent, and the environment combine to modify the particular quality and course of the disease.

In traditional psychiatric approaches to diagnosis, attempts were made to imitate the simple medical model by discovery of signs or symptoms indicative of a particular personality structure that would permit assignment of a patient to a given class of people. The personality theory is then used to make inferences about etiology, prognosis, and treatment outcome on the basis of sparse knowledge and rich theory.

In clinical psychology, as in psychiatry and medicine, conceptualizations and methods of diagnosis are in a state of ferment. In medicine, the ferment reflects the feeling "that we are standing on the threshold of a new era of medicine—a revolutionary period when there will be profound changes in the way we think about disease and medical diagnosis"

(Engle, 1964, p. 17). Sophisticated analyses of the logical processes and statistical models underlying diagnosis, designs for computer programs for conducting diagnosis, new and refined laboratory assessment procedures, and increased understanding of the basic biological processes underlying pathology are among the developments contributing to this revolutionary expectation in medicine (see, for example, Jacquez, 1964). While diagnostic theorists in medicine are wrestling with whether the diagnostic process can best be described by mathematical models of conditional probability, psychiatry still struggles with the selection of the most useful classification categories in the absence of any coherent set of unifying concepts. Gerard and Mattsson (1964) discuss the problem in describing their efforts to improve the classification of schizophrenia.

"It is too universally believed by scientists and laymen that scientific progress depends essentially on improved quantitation. This is not the case. Progress begins with improved 'entitation', a word one of us has coined for finding the right entities to quantitate; and this is the problem that all here are facing. The problem has been presented to you of finding how to split an amorphous and confused universe into some kind of entities, either individuals or groups, with which one can effectively operate. It has also been pointed out that it is more difficult to make a diagnosis of a disease than a classification of an organism or of a species . . . .

"In the area of mental disturbance the problem has, of course, been confounded by the fact that the diagnosis has originally been reached by clinicians in terms of, mainly, subjective evaluation of behavioral phenomena. Over the centuries, many objective criteria—biochemical, physiological, anthropometric, all sorts—have been put forth as able to separate schizophrenics from non-schizophrenics. Unfortunately, none of them has turned out as even reasonably consistently and sharply discriminating one group of individuals, diagnosed clinically as schizophrenic, from another group, diagnosed clinically as anything else" (pp. 81–82).

Reflecting a lack of a unifying conception on which to base classificatory categories, the language used in psychiatric diagnosis has usually shown an undifferentiated mixture of various personality theories, syndromes of presumed symptomatic communality, and proposed disease entities sharing an assumed etiology and prognosis. The Diagnostic and Statistical Manual of the American Psychiatric Association (1952), for example, based its categories on a combination of dimensions. A typology was established on the basis of presumed primary defense mechanisms, inferred abstract internal processes (for instance, "anxiety . . . unconsciously and automatically controlled by the utilization of various psychological defense mechanisms"), and various etiological factors (for example, alcoholic psychosis, senile dementia, or psychosis with undiagnosed physical condition) presume structural or functional biological changes as primary causes of the behavior disturbance. The mixture of dimensions also include symptom clusters, such as phobic neurosis, marital maladjustment, or withdrawal reaction of adolescents. Duration and severity provide a further modifying part of the diagnosis, as when psychotic reactions are characterized as acute or chronic. Tolerance on the part of the community defines some disorders in terms of the extent to which an individual deviates from the range of acceptable behavior, for instance, inadequate personality, homosexuality, or pathological stealing. Dissatisfaction with this classificatory approach resulted in the revision of the psychiatric nomenclature in 1968 (APA Manual, 1968), but minor changes in the classification schema did not essentially alter its conceptual approach.

During the last few decades, in his role as a diagnostician, the clinical psychologist devised and utilized a series of assessment techniques, including projective tests and questionnaires, which aimed at providing diagnostic labels. As a result of accumulating evidence that these tests lacked clinical utility, predictive validity, or even reliability, there has been a gradual shift away from attempts to evaluate personality traits. Instead, there is a movement toward increased use of behavioral observations, assessment of situation-specific variables, and inclusion of the patient's social environment in assessment. At the same time, diagnosis has become more problem-centered than person-centered. Efforts to characterize the person in terms of a particular type of mental illness have been replaced with attempts to discover the "problems in living" (Szasz, 1960), following a social-psychological instead of medical-psychiatric model.

Functions of Psychological Assessment. The combination of diverse purposes and different organizational schema in the diagnostic model has also affected the state of the field of psychological assessment. Mischel (1968a), in his book *Personality and Assessment,* has described the situation from a behavioral point of view:

"Personality theory, experimental research, and assessment have quite different histories and their mutual implications have not been explored thoroughly. Courses on personality theory usually review the concepts advocated by different authors and offer omnibus surveys of psychological conceptions of man. Personality assessment, on the other hand, typically is relegated into the 'how to do it' practical domain, and is inserted as an applied, independent course on assorted measurement techniques. Especially distressing, most approaches to personality still remain largely separated from developments in behavior theory and experimental research, in spite of many protests and some major efforts to the contrary . . . .

"Progress in the area of personality psychology and assessment has been hindered by the failure to apply relevant principles about the conditions that produce, maintain, and modify social behavior. The principles that emerge from basic research too often have not been seen as directly relevant to the understanding of the determinants of test responses in the clinic or the assessment project. It is as if we live in two independent worlds: the abstractions and the artificial situations of the laboratory and the realities of life . . . .

"Traditional separations between theory, basic research, and assessment practices come from historical accidents and professional biases rather than from logical necessity or convenience, and they take their toll in the training of personality and clinical psychologists. The resulting schisms within the field are reflected in the reactions of students who begin their practicum training and soon wonder, quite rightly, what their theoretical seminars in basic psychology have to do with their new daily activities. These frequent dissonances are being recognized increasingly" (pp. 1–2).

When the focus of assessment is on practical clinical utility, the most reasonable goal at present would appear to be that it yield an analysis of the patient's behavior that is related to the conceptual and empirical framework of treatment. In a recent panel discussion, this point of view was expressed by several psychiatrists. In private practice the lack of pressure to categorize patients for administrative purposes has resulted in even greater rejection of traditional diagnosis in institutions. Lack of knowledge about the relationship between diagnosis and response to treatment robs diagnosis of practical value in individual cases.

Behavioral assessment is aimed neither at personality description nor patient assignment to particular personality types. Behavioral diagnosis or analysis can be used for several purposes: (1) identification of therapeutic target responses and their maintaining stimuli; (2) assessment of functional relationships among response classes and among discriminative and reinforcing stimuli; (3) determination of available social resources, personal assets, and skills for use in a therapeutic program, as well as of limitations and obstacles in the person and in the environment; and (4) availability of specific therapeutic strategies or behavioral techniques most consonant with the personal and environmental factors in the patient's life situation.

Behavioral diagnosis attempts to provide information that permits the clinician to define targets for change, to identify conditions maintaining the undesirable behavior, and to select the most practical means for producing the desired changes. For research, statistical, or administrative purposes it may be necessary to seek some key dimension in the patient's total situation that would permit his placement in a more encompassing class of problems. For example, for these purposes large behavioral patterns or socially significant events, such as psychosis or suicide, may be singled out as a distinguishing feature of a patient. When this is done, however, the label has little utility for treatment.

Other Inadequacies of Traditional Systems. In emulating the ideal of the simple medical model, psychiatric and psychological diagnosticians have prematurely accepted deviant behaviors as manifestations of an illness and set their goals higher than permitted by current knowledge in the field. Various concerns with the character of current psychiatric classification have not remedied this basic problem, and the tenuous linkage between assignment to diagnostic categories and therapeutic strategies has made proper evaluation of treatment effectiveness an almost impossible task.

"Numerous criticisms have dealt with the internal consistency, the explicitness, the precision, and the reliability of psychiatric classifications. It seems to us that the more important fault lies in our lack of sufficient knowledge to categorize behavior along those pertinent dimensions which permit prediction of responses to social expectations, social stresses, life crises, or psychiatric treatment. This limitation obviates anything but a crude and tentative approximation to a taxonomy of effective and ineffective behavior. A reasonable expectation of a practical diagnostic schema is that the taxonomic system be closely related to the conceptual and empirical framework of treatment" (Kanfer and Saslow, 1969, p. 419).

At the descriptive level, traditional nosological categories (such as hysteria and paranoid schizophrenia) have been found to be unreliable in application (Kanfer and Saslow, 1969; Schmidt and Fonda, 1956) and inconsistent in the symptom and behavior patterns subsumed in each classification (Katz, Cole, and Lowery, 1964; Lorr, Klett, and McNair, 1963; Zigler and Phillips, 1961). Factor analyses have generally produced contradictory and heterogeneous subclusters of behaviors for patients in the same traditional diagnostic category. Efforts to derive more reliable categories empirically by identifying homogeneous clusters of behaviors have been generally disappointing. Rater stereotypes, rather than patient homogeneity, have been a frequent result. Wittenborn (1962), for example, obtained low inter-rater reliability for many of his symptom-behavior scales, and the factors that emerged corresponded closely to traditional diagnostic categories. In addition to the limitations of factor analysis as a means of identifying new dimensions, this approach does not deal directly with the problem of identifying target behaviors or selecting a therapeutic strategy.

Actuarial approaches to assessment, intended to overcome unreliability and low validity of clinical judgments by using objective, quantitative techniques, have encountered similar problems (Mischel, 1968a). Tests or ratings used for actuarial predictions suffer from a number of defects. Meaningful criteria for the behavior pattern that the tests are intended to predict are difficult to achieve, and the predictive validities are often not very impressive even though they are generally superior to clinical judgments. The act of assigning a diagnostic label may at times serve as a self-fullfilling prophecy, altering the behavior of the treatment staff in order to direct the patient toward the predicted behaviors (see, for example, Ullmann, 1967b). More importantly, diagnostic and predictive statements available from current methods generally have relatively little utility for making practical clinical decisions. Treatment decisions have been found to be relatively unaffected by diagnostic evaluations performed ostensibly to guide clinical decision making (Dailey, 1953). Meehl (1960) reported that only 17 percent of a sample of therapists found prior testing of any value in their treatment. McPartland and Richart (1966) have illustrated how an approach that focuses on disordered subjective states and clinical "symptoms" may lack utility. Such an approach often errs in treating by-products of larger behavior patterns. Diagnosis by symptoms alone tends to focus on behaviors that may be irrelevant to the total life pattern of the patient. The economically disadvantaged patients treated in a public clinic, who were studied by McPartland and Richart, improved in clinical symptoms but not in their problems of daily living. A patient may have lost his acute symptoms of depression but did not gain marital harmony or employment as a result of therapy. McPartland and Richart concluded that symptom improvement is not usually followed by a less problematic way of life and that plights of living usually precede disordered thoughts and feelings, instead of being their results. The investigators noted that clinical decisions were rarely influenced by the complex problems of living presented by their clients.

At the theoretical level, the hypothetical nature of dynamic personality theories has encouraged the use of unverifiable processes or structures as diagnostic constructs. Dynamic theorists have advocated the importance of interactional and configural relationships of internal *states* (conflicts, defenses) and trait theorists have concerned themselves with discrete, quantifiable variables that are presumed to be cross-situational. Both have in common, however, the use of "responses as signs (indirect or direct) of pervasive underlying mental structures; both assume that these underlying inferred dispositions (whether called traits, states, processes, dynamics, motives, or labeled in other ways) exert generalized and enduring causal effects on behavior; and both have been devoted to a search for signs that serve as reliable indicators of these hypothesized underlying dispositions" (Mischel, 1968a, p. 8). Hypothesized constructs are unsatisfactory as foundations for diagnostic assessment to the extent that they are not verifiable, or are not parsimonious for behavior description and prediction, or are only weakly and indirectly related to overt behavior patterns.

Conceptually, trait and state models presume a high degree of consistency of predispositions within the person as the basis for prediction of behavior across situations. Although this assumption has much appeal, it has not gained the necessary empirical support. The trait-state approach to description and prediction for this reason has come under increasing criticism: "the real trouble is that it has not worked well enough, and despite the huge volume of literature it has stimulated, it seems to lead to a dead end" (Vernon, 1964, p. 239). This point of view is by no means generally accepted among either practitioners or theorists (see, for example, Block, 1968). However, the research that demonstrates the dependency of behavior on specific situational stimuli is highly consonant with the practical needs of the therapist for specific guidelines when he is designing a treatment program. The evidence is also consonant with the behavioral model's assumption of the crucial role of specific environmental control of behavior.

Assessment for Behavior Modification

The model of assessment suited to the behavior therapies differs from the traditional one in several important respects. It does not attempt to describe the total personality but instead narrows its focus to those variables particularly relevant for treatment. Present nosological systems and standard diagnostic tests are rarely relevant to the task of devising a behavior therapy strategy. In selecting his treatment technique, the clinician needs information about the target behaviors, the reinforcement parameters maintaining them, opportunities in the patient's environment for maintaining other more desirable responses, therapist characteristics, the patient's ability to observe and reinforce himself, the requirements of the learning paradigm to be applied, and so forth. Exhibit 10-1, an interview and history-taking guide developed by Kanfer and Saslow (1969), indicates the wide range of specific data that is likely to be involved in a clinical functional analysis. It includes historical, social, cognitive, and biological factors as well as directly observable behavior. Such information is specific, often objective, and oriented toward direct use in therapeutic intervention. Contrary to the assertion that behavior therapy

Exhibit 10-1   Components of a Behavioral Diagnosis (Adapted from Kanfer and Saslow, 1969)

1. *Analysis of a Problem Situation.* The patient's major complaints are categorized into classes of behavioral excesses and deficits. For each excess or deficit the dimensions of frequency, intensity, duration, appropriateness of form, and stimulus conditions are described. In content, the response classes represent the major targets of the therapeutic intervention. As an additional indispensable feature, the behavioral assets of the patient are listed for utilization in a therapy program.

2. *Clarification of the Problem Situation.* Here we consider the people and circumstances that tend to maintain the problem behaviors, and the consequences of these behaviors to the patient and to others in his environment. Attention is given also to the consequences of changes in these behaviors that may result from psychiatric intervention.

3. *Motivational Analysis.* Since reinforcing stimuli are idiosyncratic and depend for their effect on a number of unique parameters for each person, a hierarchy of particular persons, events, and objects that serve as reinforcers is established for each patient. Included in this hierarchy are those reinforcing events that facilitate approach behaviors as well as those that, because of their aversiveness, prompt avoidance responses. The purpose of obtaining this information is to lay plans for utilization of various reinforcers in prescription of a specific behavior therapy program for the patient, and to permit utilization of appropriate reinforcing behaviors by the therapist and significant others in the patient's social environment.

4. *Developmental Analysis.* Questions are asked about the patient's biological equipment, his sociocultural experiences, and his characteristic behavior development. They are phrased in such a way as (a) to evoke descriptions of his habitual behavior at various chronological stages of his life, (b) to relate specific new stimulus conditions to noticeable changes from his habitual behavior, and (c) to relate such altered behavior and other residuals of biological and sociocultural events to the present problems.

5. *Analysis of Self-Control.* This section examines both the methods and the degree of self-control exercised by the patient in his daily life. Persons, events, or institutions that have successfully reinforced self-controlled behaviors are considered. The deficits or excesses of self-control are evaluated in relation to their importance as therapeutic targets and to their utilization in a therapeutic program.

6. *Analysis of Social Relationships.* Examination of the patient's social network is carried out to evaluate the significance of people in the patient's environment who have some influence over the problematic behaviors, or who in turn are influenced by the patient for his own satisfactions. These interpersonal relationships are reviewed in order to plan the potential participation of significant others in a treatment program, based on the principles of behavior modification. The review also helps the therapist to consider the range of actual social relationships in which the patient needs to function.

7. *Analysis of the Social-Cultural-Physical Environment.* In this section the preceding analysis of the patient's behavior as an individual is extended by consideration of the norms in his natural environment. Agreements and discrepancies between the patient's idiosyncratic life patterns and the norms in his environment are defined so that the importance of these factors can be decided in formulating treatments goals that allow as explicitly for the patient's needs as for the pressures of his social environment.

is ahistorical and superficial, Exhibit 10-1 illustrates the rich mass of information that the clinician will often need for a behavior analysis sufficient for selection of a treatment strategy.

Another characteristic of behavioral approaches to assessment is that their data are often direct samples of behavior in specific situations, instead of indirect and generalized indicants of behavioral predispositions. Assessment and prediction continue throughout treatment, and the type of intervention used at any moment is constantly reconsidered and revised if the data from the therapeutic operations warrant a change in the program. Moreover, continuing adjustment of the parameter values of treatment variables occurs on the basis of the patient's reaction. Amount and timing of reinforcement, size of behavior units recorded, frequency of treatment sessions, or steps in a desensitization hierarchy are all subject to constant reevaluation and adjustment.

Functional analysis of behavior is part and parcel of treatment: "the behavior assessor introduces into the test situation, either directly or symbolically, the conditions of interest, and instead of seeking to tap signs of durable internal state, he systematically varies these stimulus conditions and observes their effects on behavior . . . . His interest is in how learning conditions change an individual's performance, and not in estimates of the subject's performance level in comparison to other persons" (Mischel, 1968b, p. 2).

The operant behavior therapies have generally employed single case, experimental behavior-sample methods of assessment. The stimulus-substitution and mixed model therapies, since they include mediating constructs, such as anxiety, have more often included trait assessment by standardized tests and questionnaires. However, these tests are used not for traditional psychodynamic inference but for actuarial description and prediction. Simple and straightforward measures of reported past behavior, population base rates, patient self-ratings, and observed behaviors have greater utility for prediction of future behaviors, including treatment outcome, than do complex clinical evaluations that rely on inferred states and traits. The bahaviorally oriented clinician, when he does use trait measures to guide decisions, therefore tends to do so on an actuarial, quantitative basis. The consideration of individual extraversion or anxiety scores in deciding whether to apply desensitization or aversive conditioning illustrates such usage.

To the extent that therapy operations and outcome criteria for the behavior therapies can be defined in observable and objective ways, an actuarial, decision-making model of assessment should be more useful and feasible than it is in the case of traditional psychotherapies. Although operant conditioning therapies have made little use of actuarial prediction thus far, there is no conceptual obstacle to doing so. Cronbach and Gleser (1965) have proposed a decision making model of assessment that takes into account the values and outcomes of alternative decisions, as well as the cost of making the assessment and predictions. Such as utilitarian model would seem to fit well the pragmatic orientation of the behavior therapies.

Certainly there are a number of factors that the clinician must somehow weight differentially in deciding which behaviors he will attempt to modify. The modifiability of a particular behavior in therapy partly will depend on what is currently maintaining the behavior. The choice of target responses is affected by the extent to which the modification would entail beneficial or detrimental consequences not only for the patient but also for other persons close to him. Some target behaviors offer the possibility of indirect beneficial changes in other responses that are functionally related to the symptomatic behavior; for example, elimination of bed-wetting can result in improved mother-child relationships when the latter may also be a possible target for its own sake. The practical resources (social, temporal, physical, and economic), which can be brought to bear on various potential target behaviors, are likely to differ; availability of a cooperative spouse, employer, teacher, or of funds for intensive treatment can alter the therapeutic goal. The setting in which the therapist and patient interact will make some treatment techniques and hence some targets, more practical than others. Table 10-1 lists a few alternative techniques that could be applied to target responses defined in terms of the behavioral equation. A decision making model based on objective assessment and actuarial data could aid the clinician in selecting among available techniques. A prior question, however, entails the decision of whether to define the behavioral problem in terms of, for instance, a response deficiency or weak stimulus control. Alternative psychological formulations may suggest the same treatment; but often the practical significance of the choice can be made clearer by consideration of the requirements and consequences that can be foreseen for each of several alternate strategies dictated by different emphasis in the formulation. As yet, the behavior therapist has little in the way of scientifically based procedures for deciding which element within a complex behavioral chain to attack.

Methods of Response Assessment. The clinician has several requirements with respect to assessment of response repertoires. As was noted in Chapters 2 and 6, the clinician needs to identify the defining dimensions for significant response classes, the range of class members to be included, and functional relationships of these behaviors to stimuli and other responses and consequences in the daily environment. The clinician also needs diagnostic tools to identify key target responses in individual pa-

Table 10-1   Illustrative Manipulations of Behavior Relevant to
Different Therapeutic Targets

Element of Behavioral Equation	Status of Element	Potential Therapeutic Operations	Example
R	Absent	Shaping by successive approximation (response differentiation).	Training autistic children in speech.
		Modeling and imitation, with vicarious and direct reinforcement.	Training social skills with modeling and role playing.
R	Deficient	With eliciting conditions maximized, reinforce 100 percent and then gradually shift to an intermittent schedule; remove any punishment of target response.	Reward, not punish, self-assertion in therapy group.
		Suppress a competing, more probable response by extinction, removal of eliciting stimuli, satiation, or aversive conditioning.	Aversive conditioning of homosexual fantasy to increase heterosexual fantasy and activity.
		Make the response the only source for crucial reinforcement.	Teacher attention available only when child is playing with peers.
		Use a more potent reinforcer.	Use of tokens, money, or other generalized reinforcer. Escape of shock for spitting out alcohol.
		Reinforce any responses that are links in a behavior chain that terminates in the desired response.	Reinforce getting out of bed on time, which is necessary for punctual job arrival.
		Enhance stimulus generalization by reinforcing response in association with many different situations that can serve as S^Ds.	Role play self-assertion with many different persons.
R	Excessive	Extinction.	"Time-out" and no attention given contingent upon temper tantrums.

Table 10-1   (Continued)

Element of Behavioral Equation	Status of Element	Potential Therapeutic Operations	Example
R	Excessive	Reinforce a less probable competing response. Suppress by punishment. Remove an early link in the behavioral chain terminating in the response.	Reinforce constructive play to reduce autisms. Shock self-mutilative acts of autistic children. Patient doesn't buy fattening groceries.
		Enhance stimulus and schedule control and then extinguish.	Obese women trained to eat *full* meals but only in certain settings at specified times before calories per meal are decreased.
S	Control Ineffectual Response Inappropriate	Stimulus discrimination training, supplying clear S^Δs, and S^Ds, beginning with 100 percent schedule.	Training social skills appropriate for use with different classes of persons, for example, males versus females, peers versus supervisors.
S	Control Overly Rigid	Fade out one S^D while adding new ones.	In speech training, substituting objects and pictures for trainer's spoken cues.
S	Control Too Weak	Reinforce only in connection with selected S^Ds and suppress responses to other stimuli, for example by punishment, extinction.	Play roughly with child in family room, impose "time out" when he begins rough play in the living room.
		Train attention to internal events as S^Δs and S^Ds.	Wandering attention when studying is cue to stop, rather than practice not-studying in the study situation.
		Enhance potency of relevant S^Ds by using more powerful reinforcer.	Use attractive and full regular meals to attain stimulus control over eating (e.g., eliminating random snacks) before reducing food intake.

Table 10-1   (Continued)

Element of Behavioral Equation	Status of Element	Potential Therapeutic Operations	Example
C	Deficient in Range or Type	Secondary reinforcement, pair ineffective with effective stimuli.	Therapist says "good" and smiles and hugs autistic child when delivering food reinforcers.
		Deprivation of competing reinforcers.	Isolate to enhance value of social reinforcement by other persons.
		Switch from aversive to positive reinforcement control.	Parents change from nagging and complaining to praise and affection as controlling reinforcers.
C	Excessive Potency	Aversive conditioning.	Pair homosexual fantasy or alcohol intake with electric shock.
		Extinguish value as a secondary reinforcer, changing an S^D into an S^Δ.	Remove all social reinforcement associated with being in a tavern.
K	Schedule Weak or Strained	Provide more frequent reinforcement.	For a depressed salesman, enrich his territory with good prospects.
		Provide clearer S^Δ to prevent ineffectual responding.	Clarify through discussions the cues a wife provides that she is not receptive to the husband's attentions at that time.
		Provide a variable intermittent schedule if responses occur only in a burst right before a predictable reinforcement.	Use frequent surprise quizzes to avoid preexam cramming.
K	Schedule Required To Be Too Fat.	Place on 100 percent reinforcement and then gradually thin to a variable intermittent schedule to promote resistance to extinction.	Patient learning new social skills gives up if met with rebuffs and so needs guaranteed success early in acquisition.
O		The state of the organism, and operations affecting it, influence many S, R, C and K events, setting limits on or enhancing effects of manipulations of them.	Drugs, painful stimulation, deprivation, prostheses represent some of the ways to manipulate the state of the organism.

tients. Current developments in assessment theory and advances in behavior observation methods are likely to be more helpful with the first need than with the second. There is little basis in current behavior theory or in a behavioral framework of personality development to point to historical or behavioral segments that are especially sensitive indicators of maladjustment or disturbance. Without such a guide for pinpointing primary response dimensions or behavior content, quick recognition of critical mechanisms or response patterns representing prime therapy targets is difficult. Thus, the behavior therapist often relies on both traditional personality theories to direct his probing and on adaptation of traditional measuring techniques for evaluation. For example, self-rating and questionnaires have been developed to identify significant fears (Geer 1965; Wolpe and Lang, 1964). Table 10-2 presents Geer's research version of the Fear Survey Schedule, along with some normative data, as an illustration of this approach. The behavioral correlates of scores on tests such as the MMPI, Maudsley Personality Inventory, and the Rorschach are being explored (Brady, Pappas, Tausig, and Thornton, 1962; Greenspoon and Gersten, 1967; Morgenstern, Pearce, and Rees, 1965).

Direct observation on a time and situation sampling basis is also coming into greater use for response assessment. Observations in homes, wards, or natural settings often are used simultaneously for assessment, hypothesis testing, and treatment (see, for example, Martin, Weinstein, and Lewinsohn, 1968). Representative observational data appeared in several figures in Chapter 6, where some of the work on reliability, validity, sampling needs, and observation effects was referred to as well (Cronbach, Gleser, Nanda and Rajaratnam, 1967; Patterson and Harris, 1968). To deal with the issues of situational specificity in responses, some investigtors are using a P-technique analysis of observed frequencies of behaviors across environmental contexts. This sort of analysis permits scaling of individuals on trait and situational (discriminative stimuli) continua (Patterson and Bechtel, 1970).

Technological advances are providing assistance with assessment by observational techniques. A number of these were mentioned in earlier chapters. Strain gauges for measuring sexual responses (Bancroft, Jones, and Pullan, 1966; Freund, 1963) and conjugate audiovisual communication devices for measuring communication patterns (Nathan, Bull, and Rossi, 1968) are examples. Elwood (1969) has described the development of an automated system that provides a standardized environment and is capable of administering commonly used psychological tests. The system has been employed to administer all items of the WAIS, to record all responses, and to score several of the subtests without use of a professional examiner. Devices that make the task of behavior observation simpler,

Table 10-2 Items of the Fear Survey Schedule-II with Some
Illustrative Normative Data (from Geer, 1965)[a]

Item	Mean Score		Item-Total Score Correlations	
	Men	Women	Men	Women
1. Sharp objects	1.60	1.87	0.477	0.434
2. Being a passenger in a car	0.60	0.93	0.411	0.527
3. Dead bodies	1.70	1.98	0.592	0.400
4. Suffocating	2.05	2.04	0.510	0.476
5. Failing a test	3.30	3.32	0.411	0.380
6. Looking foolish	2.79	2.94	0.467	0.575
7. Being a passenger in an airplane	1.26	1.79	0.513	0.448
8. Worms	0.27	1.32	0.355	0.402
9. Arguing with parents	1.27	1.37	0.493	0.287
10. Rats and mice	1.03	2.33	0.568	0.316
11. Life after death	0.86	1.22	0.445	0.426
12. Hypodermic needles	1.50	1.89	0.607	0.312
13. Being criticized	1.98	2.30	0.612	0.573
14. Meeting someone for the first time	1.30	1.52	0.496	0.493
15. Roller coasters	1.32	1.99	0.332	0.222
16. Being alone	0.70	1.23	0.548	0.489
17. Making mistakes	2.22	2.52	0.492	0.578
18. Being misunderstood	1.74	1.94	0.468	0.471
19. Death	1.96	2.39	0.538	0.659
20. Being in a fight	1.83	1.78	0.585	0.481
21. Crowded places	0.72	0.77	0.424	0.431
22. Blood	0.77	0.84	0.550	0.306
23. Heights	1.76	1.73	0.461	0.368
24. Being a leader	1.02	1.45	0.497	0.557
25. Swimming alone	0.96	1.43	0.474	0.395
26. Illness	1.25	1.86	0.568	0.426
27. Being with drunks	1.16	2.63	0.518	0.463
28. Illness or injury to loved ones	3.11	4.08	0.534	0.627
29. Being self-conscious	2.18	2.41	0.648	0.537
30. Driving a car	0.48	1.06	0.558	0.492
31. Meeting authority	1.27	1.66	0.546	0.514
32. Mental illness	1.29	1.97	0.516	0.519
33. Closed places	0.78	1.16	0.434	0.477
34. Boating	0.53	1.88	0.555	0.532
35. Spiders	1.20	2.19	0.466	0.472
36. Thunderstorms	0.45	1.03	0.482	0.428
37. Not being a success	2.79	2.28	0.442	0.597
38. God	1.35	1.50	0.382	0.313
39. Snakes	1.97	3.05	0.482	0.482
40. Cemeteries	0.71	1.24	0.549	0.546
41. Speaking before a group	2.59	2.87	0.487	0.484

[a] Subjects scale the amount of fear they feel toward the object or situation on a
7 point scale; 1 = none, 7 = terror.

more reliable, and more sensitive to response changes range from interval timers attached to clipboards, to multichannel event recorders, to miniature radio transmitters worn by the subject (Purcell and Brady, 1966).

As yet, only a beginning has been made in using traditional operant methodology and equipment as analogue behavior samples to identify excessive and deficient behaviors. Much of this work has used traditional psychiatric diagnoses and other questionable criteria to evaluate the assessment power of rate or other operant response characteristics, reducing the value of the results. (See Weiss, 1969, and Lindsley, 1962 for reviews of operant conditioning techniques in assessment). Among the interesting developments in this area is Weiss' (1969) work on the extent and skill with which people emit responses that function as social reinforcers for others. The subject uses a simple motor response (for instance, a lever press) to indicate attending to a speaker. The rate and locus of his motor responses are compared with group norms. Effectiveness in reinforcing speakers has been found to be related to sociometric status, therapeutic skill, scores on self-report measures such as the Edwards Personal Preference Schedule, and other interpersonal behaviors.

Assessment of Motivational and Maintaining Variables

A second assessment task of the clinician is to define the conditions maintaining problem behavior and the reinforcing consequences available for therapeutic manipulation that are most potent in affecting the patient's behavior. When a patient's access to important reinforcers can be controlled, generalized reinforcers (for example, tokens)—for which a variety of backup reinforcers are available—may work very well without further knowledge of the patient's reinforcement hierarchies. Similarly, for nursery school children, contingent administration of teacher attention may be sufficient for retraining. But when we move to outpatient adults living in a complex social system, motivational analysis is much more difficult to achieve. What are the most potent reinforcers that the therapist, spouse, or the patient himself can manipulate to achieve behavior change? What operations in such a complex system are currently maintaining the symptomatic behaviors? Objective personality tests may prove to have some value in addressing these questions. Need-oriented instruments, such as the Edwards Personal Preference Schedule, may be adaptable in yielding broad reinforcer hierarchies. Cautela and Kastenbaum (1967) devised a self-report Reinforcement Survey Schedule to evaluate on a five-point scale the "pleasurable feelings" subjects associate with a large number of objects and events. In general, however, little more than hunches based on observed coincidences of target responses and consequences is available for identification of factors maintaining problem behaviors.

When the clinician needs to know whether deficits or deviations in the patient's motivational system underlie problem behaviors, several experimental analogues may suggest fruitful directions to pursue. For example, Patterson (1967) used rate of lever pressing for producing pictures of aggressive interactions as a measure of the aversive characteristics of this class of stimuli in individual children. Response rates were validated against frequency of victimization to aggression from peers during a five-week observation period in the classroom. Patterson was able to establish satisfactory concurrent validity for this laboratory measure. In another study. Patterson (1965b) used an operant task with children in which social reinforcement was administered by peers or parents. Differential responsiveness to different purveyors of social reinforcement was found to correlate with the child's sex and with teachers' descriptions of the child's personality and problem behaviors. These studies differ from other diagnostic techniques in two ways. First, they utilize a simple and quantifiable response in a standardized laboratory procedure. Traditional diagnostic methods often yield volumes of complex verbal output that are difficult to categorize. Secondly, the new techniques limit prediction to a highly specific response class instead of striving for global assessment of the individual's entire response repertoire.

General Comments

The exploratory developments described above suggest that construction of behavioral assessment procedures is a feasible but difficult task. It is possible to visualize future diagnostic procedures in which several standardized tasks yield measures with predictive validity for a wide range of related behaviors, and in which each patient undergoes additional observations or tests specific to his case. It remains to be seen whether a short set of analogue situations or standardized observations can yield differential predictions of patient responsiveness to different treatment procedures. Observations that could clearly establish particular response deficits or excesses in standardized situations would reduce the therapist's dilemma in selecting target behaviors. They would also provide him with a series of goals that can be measured at the end of each treatment stage for evaluation of treatment success.

Another area for future development entails identifying the crucial commonalities among patients with similar problems, either in their past learning histories or in their characteristic ways of responding to significant social stimulation. Clinicians' choices of targets are now based in part on the relative discomfort or social disharmony that a particular symptom creates for an individual. Frequently this approach results in emphasis on the by-products or long-range coincidental consequences of the patient's actions, which can obscure the target behaviors that should be attacked in therapy. For example, complaints by a mother that a child is unmanageable or truant, actions by a marital partner toward divorce, homosexual or delinquent behaviors leading to police action, or a man's failure to support his family are outcomes of behavior patterns. The most effective focus in treatment may not be on these events but on the responses of the patient and his social environment leading to these final consequences.

Traditional classification of symptoms has been based on the content of the patient's experiences, for instance, his dependent or hostile relationship to members of his family, his psychosexual experiences, or his confident or deprecatory self-attitudes. Another set of dimensions for organization of pathological behaviors can be built on the basis of the common modifiability of responses by a particular treatment due to the similarity of the learning parameters accompanying their acquisition. This approach would be relatively content-free. It would stress reinforcement schedules, range of discriminative stimuli, concurrent control by positive and aversive consequences, or similar learning constants in the acquisition of basic social behaviors. An interesting illustration of this approach is offered in investigations (see, for example, Ferster, 1958b; Weiner, 1965) of particular acquisition histories that result in "maladaptive behavior." "Maladaptive" is defined by the organism's failure to obtain available reinforcers, or by his continued responding when the consequences are injurious to himself.

Behavioral assessment in the future is likely to depend upon elaboration and extension of laboratory analogue or response sampling techniques similar to those discussed. Their development and usefulness will depend upon better understanding of the ecological structure of behavior. For instance, the implication that "what is wrong" with the mama's boy who isolates himself from peers is that only mother is a potent social reinforcer for him. Patterson (1967) suggests that treatment might be directed at expanding the range of important social reinforcers instead of directly reinforcing peer play with primary reinforcers. Both approaches, if successful, would probably eventually increase the social reinforcement value of peers for the previously isolated child. Which strategy to employ would then be a matter of efficiency, but the interplay between response change and reinforcer change would remain as a basic relationship needing definition.

SUMMARY

This chapter has dealt with several disparate topics: interpersonal influence and cognitive expectancies, biological influences on behavior, and the logic and functions of assessment. The uniting factor is their role as context for the more specific operations of behavior therapy and, indeed, of any approach to behavior change.

Variables that have been investigated in the social psychology laboratory and the clinic and that fall within the field of interpersonal influence were discussed with particular attention to their relevance for clinical practice. They were selected for their current prominence but are meant to represent the much larger domain of personal-social variables that may indirectly help or hinder the specific effects of a particular behavior therapy technique. Although some authors would assert that prognostic and role expectancies, interpersonal attraction, or empathic warmth and genuineness from the influencer are the major effective variables in all efforts at behavior change, we believe that they have nonspecific effects that may enhance or detract from the outcome of primary therapeutic operations. The behavior therapist therefore needs to take into account the research findings concerning these and many similar variables in order to maximize his effectiveness with patients. Until recently, there was little rapprochement between applied clinical work, whether assessment or therapy, and the relatively rapid developments in personality, social, developmental, and other fields of scientific psychology. Just as learning research has led, after a period of lag, to application in the behavior therapies, so too other investigative fields are beginning at a slower rate to have a direct impact on clinical practice. The several social and cognitive variables were briefly touched upon in order to exemplify these advances and the ability of the behavioral model to incorporate them at the level of empirical data.

A similar but more difficult problem exists in the case of our second topic—biological or organismic variables. It is obvious that biological functions set limits on which behaviors can be acquired by and maintained in a given individual. Despite the very impressive recent additions to scientific understanding by psychobiology, including genetics, pharmacology, neurophysiology, and so on, it is as yet very difficult for the clinician to grasp the essentials of these discoveries and to extrapolate from them to his work with patients. Our very brief discussion of a small sample of variables currently thought to be especially important for learning and performance illustrates some of the obstacles for the behavior therapist in trying to incorporate biological factors in his treatment planning at other than a very general level. Among these, besides the clinician's relative ignorance of theory, data, and procedures in this area, are the low order of correlation between these variables, such as extraversion, and any particular response or reinforcement parameter; the nature of many of the variables as hypothetical intervening variables, for example, cortical inhibition; the nonspecific effects of many of the variables, for instance, arousal; and the instability and idiosyncrasy of other variables, such as autonomic responses. Despite these difficulties, biological variables are beginning to establish themselves as predictors of behavior and as factors to be taken into account when planning therapy programs, for example, by inclusion of drugs in work with patients who are handicapped biologically in acquiring new behaviors. The particular variables we selected for illustrative purposes are all related in some way to the excitation and inhibition constructs and have been hypothesized to relate to learning processes in important ways. They form a continuum from relatively high to low levels of abstraction and illustrate the problems of applying empirical data to support constructs at different levels of abstraction.

The third area covered behavioral assessment and diagnosis. Here the centextual influence is a more indirect one. It relates to the conceptual and procedural tools available to the behavior therapist for collecting and processing information relevant to *all* of the domains affecting outcome, in order to reach the best practical decisions regarding treatment strategy. Assessment is a continuing and integral part of behavior therapy. Quantitative evaluation of change in target behaviors and restructuring of therapeutic tactics on the basis of continuing monitoring of progress are ideals to which behavior therapy is committed. Assessment and diagnosis have the very practical goal of guiding the decision-making of the clinician toward maximum utility. The behavioral model of abnormal psychology has no place at all for traditional diagnostic labels in the formulation of treatment strategies. Nor are traditional trait tests of much value to the behavior therapist except in the case of a few variables that may prove to be predictive of outcome for stimulus substitution therapies. By and large, the behavioral clinician must rely on self-reports, reports by others, and direct observations to make his functional analysis. Research and innovation seem likely to provide improved observational techniques, sophisticated instrumentation for assessment, and analogue behavior samples using operant methodology that can be used to evaluate a patient's response repertoire, range and type of effective reinforcement contingencies, and other learning parameters. It seems likely for some time to come that the behavior therapist will operate on the basis of his "clinical lore" in evaluating the role of other factors influencing treatment choice, such as resources in the patient's physical-social environment, cultural norms and expections of those with whom the patient lives, and in deciding where, in the complex chains of interrelated behavioral patterns of daily life, the therapist should attempt to intervene.

CHAPTER 11

Some Issues in Ethics, Training and Theoretical Foundations of Behavior Modification

In addition to specific problems in individual application of research findings to behavior therapy, there are more general issues that affect the entire field of psychology. Other problems raise the question of the role of behavior therapy in our changing culture. In the preceding chapters we have touched upon specific aspects of these rather general controversies in professional clinical practice and the psychological models from which professional practice derives. To none of these issues can extended consideration be given in a text that concentrates on relating behavior therapy techniques to basic research. Yet, it seems suitable that in the final chapter we should attempt to pull together some of the conceptual, social, and practical dilemmas that form another aspect of the significant context for behavior modification techniques and that thus far have been only alluded to. The issues selected are those that confront the profession in general, not just the individual practitioner whose concrete therapeutic conduct is subject to a number of other choices and questions not considered here. Similarly, in discussing some theoretical problems, we will refer not to individual assertions or findings regarding parameters of learning, but to more general trends in the foundations of behavior theory.

These general issues seem appropriate as the closing content of this book, partly because of their implications for the present evaluation and future utility of behavior therapy. Equally important, these issues remind us that behavior therapy can be evaluated only by considering its place in the broader context of current professional and scientific developments. Our view is that behavior therapy cannot be isolated from the mainstream of clinical practice and, in fact, for a proper understanding of behavior therapy it must be integrated into the mainstream of psychology, biology, technology, and social-cultural change. The behavioral orientation reflects and acts upon the current *zeitgeist,* which in turn reflects rapid and often unpredictable change at every level of our culture. The future viability of any therapeutic approach seemingly will depend upon its capacity to accommodate itself to new knowledge, to society's changing criteria for effective behaviors, and to changing modes of professional practice stemming from new social demands on the behavioral sciences. Similarly, the present status of any therapy is largely a function of its relationship to the current nature of these other fields and social pressures. To assess the present and future status of behavior therapy and how viable it is likely to be, we must consider its larger context.

In this chapter, we consider four interrelated aspects of this broader context, each seemingly important as a determinant of the future form and significance of clinical psychology. First to be briefly reviewed are social-cultural changes as they influence the opportunities afforded and the demands placed upon clinical practices. Second, we take up some of the ethical dilemmas that are inherent in clinical practice and research. Initially, ethics are considered from the broader viewpoint of social change and professional responsibility in general, and then specifically as they relate to clinical psychology and behavior therapy. Since social-cultural developments form the backdrop for all other influences, each section of this chapter follows this general organization. The third section discusses models and goals of education in clinical psychology. Likely effects of developments in behavior therapy on training programs are examined. The last section reviews some of the problems in current S–R theories and in their application to clinical problems. A discussion is included of the conceptual and practical changes that will probably be needed if the behavioral model is to continue to become increasingly influential.

SOCIAL-CULTURAL CHANGE AND CLINICAL PRACTICE

The four topics of this chapter are highly interrelated and interdependent. The rapid and complex changes currently taking place in clinical practice and in the conceptualizations and activities in the mental health field in general exemplify this interdependence. Traditional models and assumptions used for describing disordered behavior, the method used to attempt to ameliorate or "cure" psychopathology, the personnel involved, and the mode of delivery of mental health services—indeed, the whole image society has of the disturbed individual—are being reexamined, discarded, and replaced. Cowen and Zax (1967) have summarized some of the major reasons for general discontent with previous approaches to mental health problems.

1. Inability of available resources to meet the demands, much less the needs, for services. Chronic shortages of facilities, personnel, and

money has meant inadequate service, long waiting lists, and delay in innovation.

2. Inability of traditional therapeutic approaches to significantly help large classes of disorder. Senile, schizophrenic, retarded, and other chronic patients have often been given only minimal custodial care, not treatment or rehabilitation.

3. Inability of individual psychotherapy—the most prized approach—to show significant effectiveness, much less to live up to the large claims made for it. Available outcome data do not yield support for the utility of individual psychotherapy in numerous types of behavior disorders.

4. Inability of the usual modes of delivery of service to avoid profound inequities, particularly with respect to differences in race, age, education, and social class. The type, amount, and quality of care have repeatedly been shown to depend upon these clinically extraneous variables.

5. Inability of traditional modes of treatment and their delivery systems to adapt to the social needs and life styles of the largest group of potential recipients, most of whom do not receive the help they need. A gulf often exists between the lofty goals of personality reconstruction in many therapies and the realistic life requirements of a socially, vocationally, or sexually disabled or ineffectual patient. This gulf is most apparent in the case of the uneducated, poor, and aged.

These and other sources of dissatisfaction are compelling mental health workers to revise goals and models and to innovate new techniques and organization. Behavioral disorders are being defined as *community* problems instead of individual problems, as exemplified in President Kennedy's 1963 Message to Congress in which he advocated federal help for state planning of local comprehensive services. Support for treatment is being shifted to local community centers, ranging from storefronts and home visits to halfway houses and day hospitals (for example, Community Mental Health Centers Act, 1963). Emphasis is increasingly being placed primarily on prevention, and secondarily on rehabilitation, instead of on "cure" (see, for example, Fairweather, 1964; Caplan, 1964; Sanford, 1965). Such basic alterations are already creating new issues and dislocating old patterns in training, definition of the clinician's role, and ethical constraints on the clinician's responsibilities and rights.

Instigators of Change

The mental health worker, like any other professional, bears a responsibility toward society to be guided in his services by the values, needs, and demands of the public. His therapeutic tools and the behavioral problems he faces are constantly changing through the development of new knowledge and technology. His strategy is influenced, in addition, by changes in the frames of reference dominant in the basic psychological science upon which he draws and in the agencies in which he works. Rapid alterations in these areas have instigated much of the ferment and change in clinical practices.

The most powerful influences on psychological treatment projects in the community, state, and nation are perhaps the most difficult to encompass and assess for future implications. Their existence is a truism, although their importance is so great as to be difficult to comprehend. We refer here to the enormous and increasingly rapid changes in the social-cultural-physical environment as a consequence of technological development, population growth, socio-political reorganization, and diffusion of knowledge. Change in psychology and in mental health operations is embedded in and parallel to these much larger social changes, which are profoundly altering the whole pattern of daily living for the ordinary person. Technological advances in the physical and social sciences and their impact on the existing cultural order create new needs, new values, and new problems that are only temporarily met by new cultural-political structures; they soon become obsolete or create problems of their own. New influences on behavior patterns and urgent requirements for radical changes in previously stable social institutions constantly emerge. From TV to the birth control pill, from affluence to automated factories, from environmental destruction to grassroots political activism, the inventions and events of the past several decades, which at their initiation often seemed remote from the average citizen, have led to behavioral changes so profound that they are often termed revolutions—for examples, the sexual revolution, the civil rights revolution, the revolution in education. Other labels equally emphasize the rapidity and drama of behavioral and attitudinal change—the drug crisis, the urban crisis, the generation gap, the affluent society, the population explosion.

Carl Rogers (1968), in looking ahead to the year 2000, has written:

". . . I should like to point to the greatest problem which man faces in the years to come. It is not the hydrogen bomb, fearful as that may be. It is not the population explosion, though the consequences of that are awful to contemplate . . . . It is the question of how much change the human being can accept, absorb, and assimilate, and the rate at which he can take it. Can he keep up with the ever-increasing rate of technological change, or is there some point at which the human organism goes to pieces? Can he leave the static ways and static guidelines which have dominated all of his history and adopt the process ways, the continual changingness which must be his if he is to survive?" (p. 266).

For the clinician, the greatest problem is his relative inability to keep up with the changing psychological demands and the material and social resources in the "real world." Inventions of new "hardware" both disrupt the work and living patterns of many people and initiate new methods for changing instrumental behavior before these inventions can be evaluated in miniature or analogue studies. Changes in education, employment patterns, urbanization, intergroup relations, financial equalities and expectations lead to new concepts and attitudes. In turn, these new viewpoints affect the problems and expectations brought to the clinician as well as the manner in which he construes his own goals, role, and proper locus of intervention.

Technological progress, when broadly defined as "the organization of knowledge for practical purposes" (Mesthene, 1968, p. 44), can serve as a keystone in discussing most of the profound alterations in influences on man's pattern of life. This is so because technology, so defined, impinges on or directly leads to most instances of change. Schon (1968) has summed up the nature of current social change in advanced societies: "The nature of the transformations we are now groping for is as yet unclear, but seems to be expressing itself in a series of elemental shifts: from product to process, from component to system and to network, from static organizations (and technologies) to flexible ones, from stable institutions to temporary systems, to ways of knowing capable of handling greater informational complexity, from stable, substantive values to values for the process of change" (p. 16). The "elemental" nature of these shifts "makes the interrelated tasks of profiting from (technology's) opportunities and containing its dangers a major intellectual and political challenge of our time" (Mesthene, 1968, p. 48).

Analysis of the broad and long-lasting changes outlined by Schon entails a triple challenge to clinical psychology: (1) to help alleviate the "social and psychological displacement" imposed by rapid social-cultural change; (2) to develop a more viable and effective technology of its own; and (3) to capitalize on its own progress while containing the dangers inherent in the creation of more effective means of behavior control. In more concrete form, technological and social change has raised new issues of conflicting values and potentialities of control, for instance, in the use of electronic bugging or television propaganda. New ecological conceptions of the environment and man's interventions in the environment have become necessary (for example, urban redevelopment, new conceptions of conservation, pollution control). Technological and social change also has fostered new aspirations and new fears for society and the individual (for instance, economic and social equality, threats to civil liberties). The same issues and effects are evident within clinical psychology and are briefly discussed within the more general social-technological context in following sections.

At quite a different level, a number of recent trends in psychological theory and research programs provide a particularly relevant background against which to view behavior therapy. Current research in personality, motivation, and other areas of psychology has been characterized as a "disconcerting sprawl" abandoning the "simple and sovereign ideas" of the past (Sanford, 1968). That is, present research tends to focus on diverse, discrete empirical domains with little concern for large-scale theories.

Emphasis on "action now" has led to an empirical and molecular stance in research, as is the case in practice, and has often led to a divergence from previously accepted methodologies and conceptual systems, for example, the increasing use of single case methods, or partial abandonment of trait psychology. Later in this chapter we will take up a few of the issues in learning research that impinge particularly on behavior therapy. At this point, the matter to be stressed is that just as behavior therapy has been enhanced by its compatibility with the stance of present-day psychology, so its future will depend in equal measure on its adaptability to new resolutions of conceptual and methodological issues within psychology and to the trends that will replace current viewpoints.

VALUES, LOYALTIES, AND CONTROL: SOME ETHICAL ISSUES

In the past, the phrase "ethical issues" has connoted to the average professional psychologist mainly prohibitions against sexual exploitation of clients, overstepping legitimate competency, or breach of confidentiality. The phrase may also have aroused some chauvinistic pride in the American Psychological Association's pioneering comprehensive and detailed Ethical Standards (APA 1953, 1963), which long was unique as an officially adopted ethical code of a scientific organization.

More recently, concern with ethics has become more prominent, more general, and more controversial, not just within applied psychology but also within governmental policy-making bodies, scientific research, and professional practice in all fields. Changes in the content of these issues over time has made them more salient and more acute, in part as a result of the social and technological changes referred to earlier.

Conflict of Science and Social Morality

Increasing power and control stemming from new knowledge, new roles, and new technology have created situations in all disciplines in which values, society's demands, and the professional's and scientist's own loyalties come into new or exacerbated conflict. Novel opportunities and demands on science and the professions create difficult ethical problems. Brayfield (1968) has noted that "ethical issues in the development and application of psychological knowledge are becoming more complex, more extensive, more open to public scrutiny and more demanding of our professional interest and attention than at almost any other time in the history of our discipline" (unnumbered page). The same condition holds in most, if not all, other fields touched by the knowledge and technology explosion. From among the many critical areas of concern, we single out for special attention the issues of control, privacy, and research with human subjects. In each instance, the researcher and the applied psychologist are faced with conflicts between opposing values and priorities. The psychologist as researcher may have priorities for his work and its conduct that conflict with the values of society at large, or with the primary self-interest of his human subject. The subject's priorities are different from the primary needs of science. The importance of accumulating knowledge is of a different magnitude for a scientific discipline than for society in general. The clinician-researcher is simultaneously a member of many social units with potentially incompatible loyalties. As a citizen, a scientist, a clinician, an employee, and a trusted confidant he has responsibilities to various segments of society, to his discipline, to an individual patient or research subject, to his employer, and to other people and principles whose demands on his loyalties may conflict.

At a concrete level, evidence of growing concern with ethical problems is exemplified in recent laws and administrative rulings by the Federal government to tighten controls over drug research and to enforce guidelines governing the use of human subjects in federally supported research (see, for example, Curran, 1969). Other examples of increasing public interest in professional decisions with ethical overtones include the many discussions about equitable allocation of scarce clinical resources, such as kidney dialysis or transplantable organs (see, for instance, deWardener, 1966), or about the criteria of death in cases of organ removal for transplantation (Ad Hoc Committee, 1968). Congressional hearings on psychological tests, invasion of privacy, and behavioral research that intersects with foreign policy (APA, 1965a, 1966a,b) have demonstrated acute public sensitivity to ethical issues within psychology and related disciplines.

In the case of any of these examples, the conflicting values to be sorted and weighed against each other and the decisions to be made are subtle and complex. Kidney dialysis, for instance, is very expensive in terms of personnel, time, and equipment. It is available only in major medical centers where its costs are largely subsidized. Facilities are not sufficient for treating all patients who could benefit, even if ability to pay were not a factor. Patients who would otherwise die in a rather short time can lead relatively normal productive lives so long as they are regularly treated by dialysis. The administrators and physicians controlling access to dialysis must decide what criteria should be applied to select recipients of this treatment from among the much larger group of applicants. With few precedents to guide them, they must decide how to weigh variables such as age, vocational productivity, family responsibilities, medical prognosis with and without therapy, and psychological adjustment. The life-and-death quality of the decision and its value-laden quality have led the public and professionals alike to ask: Who should be empowered to make such decisions? Should they be made by medical personnel because of the technical aspects, or by representatives of the taxpayers who help to pay for the facilities, or by civic and religious leaders of the community because their value judgments represent society? Often hospitals assign the decision making to boards containing representatives of all of these interests. Such boards establish their own criteria to select patients for treatment from a group of candidates who have successfully passed prior medical screening.

In application of scientific findings to public affairs and in the far-reaching decisions of which scientific enterprises should receive financial support, a central issue is how to ascertain the ultimate benefits to society of any decision. Policy decisions can be evaluated in terms of their behavioral consequences. Just as is done in making a functional analysis of an individual's behavior or of a social system, all elements of the behavioral equation can be considered in terms of their effects, cost, or accessibility to change. The resulting policy decision parallels the treatment strategy prepared in the clinical case. Despite the practical limitations on finding an answer to the question "What price science?" it would be easier to achieve if prior analysis fully describes the relevant antecedents and outcomes of policy decisions in behavioral terms.

As the example of kidney dialysis illustrates, foremost among the values likely to be in conflict for professional decision makers are those related to the concept of control. Who should be empowered to influence whom, under what conditions, and toward what ends? In clinical work the question becomes: How does one achieve the ideal balance in helping a patient to change without exerting "undue" influence?

Issues of Control

"Control" in its various guises has become a paramount concern for humanists, scientists, and government policy-makers. Two major contradictory aspects are stressed by social critics. On the one hand, fears of impersonal central control and of replacement of humanistic moral values by materialistic, pragmatic ones permeate most discussions of behavior modification, systems design, and social ecological intervention. On the other hand, the plea is made for an increase in organized social-environmental control at a national level in order to limit the dangers and maximize the benefits of society's new capabilities. The *Bulletin of the Atomic Scientists* in recent years has moved the hands of its symbolic clock closer to the midnight of "doomsday" because of current destruction of the biophysical environment. To quote one author in that journal:

"Man has proceeded some distance in the direction of influencing and ordering his natural surroundings . . . . Now a point has been reached where further control of nature for human improvement is threatened by a failure to carry forward the organization of man's social structure to correspond to the heightened levels of technological interdependence. How and whether this restructuring will be accomplished presents western society with its paramount challenge in the decades ahead" (Schiller, 1968, p. 14).

Schiller goes on to assert that there is a Western myth that identifies freedom with limitless individual choice. He believes that this myth will lead ultimately to a far greater loss of freedom unless comprehensive centralized actions are taken to anticipate and avoid disruption of the entire social fabric as the consequence of technologically related change:

"Ironically, the concern with safeguarding individual freedom against an alleged onrushing regimentation may have overlooked what is a very real and present danger to liberty . . . . For, in fact, the image of an intemperate state imposing its arbitrary will in America, at least, caricatures existing reality, where truly national functions go untended, or at best, are administered feebly, all in the name of preserving liberty. Indeed, the time is overdue to clarify the relation of the individual to his community in an age of massive technical innovation" (Schiller, 1968, p. 17).

All component parts of an ecological system are, by definition, interrelated and interdependent. It follows that planning and management are distorted when elements are focused upon singly, since alterations of any one element result in changes in the entire system. Unexpected and unwanted distortions in an ecology become apparent at only a very slow rate, however, making their correction tardy and difficult. The effects of an intervention may become visible only in a crisis at some distant time. Because of the number and complexity of relationships involved, at present we lack the ability to make the predictions that would permit the engineering of an improved balance in an ecological system, whether biological or social.

The myth of unrestricted individual choice as the guarantee of freedom for all breaks down as the human ecology increases in size and complexity. The farmer, who in the past was the bastion of individualism in his self-sufficiency and freedom of choice, now depends not only on price supports and productivity quotas but must also be restricted in his use of the products of scientific discoveries, such as DDT, in order to prevent biological damage to all animal life and ultimate loss of his own productivity from chemically-resistant insects. The government's headaches in managing farm subsidies and food prices illustrate very well the general difficulties in comprehending and controlling ecological systems. In general, policy planning and decisions for change have to take into account many interrelated variables. Schiller asserts that we must curb those random individual choices that have far-reaching social consequences because these choices can produce restraints on others which ultimately far exceed the restraints of coercive social regulations. Society's failure to regulate behaviors that affect others can destroy the hope for individual fulfillment implicit in current material and technological progress. According to many ecologists (see, for example, Hardin, 1968; Odum, 1969), in order to meet the crisis in our biological-physical environment a whole new order of thinking, a different order of "mutually agreed upon coercion" is required. Thus, the concept of "freedom" appropriate to our pioneer era, when the population was small and the unexploited resources seemingly limitless, is not tenable when use of individual freedoms can combine to threaten the welfare or very survival of the social group, as in water pollution or land utilization.

When the social-cultural environment is the target for change, obstacles to prediction and control seem even greater than in the individual case. Among the measures that have been proposed to improve the management of the human ecology are scientific systems of decision making, national data banks, and regular assessment of the social performance and status of the country (Bauer, 1966; Gross, 1966; Price, 1969).

Advocates and critics alike point to practical and attitudinal obstacles to the use of such technical solutions to problems in managing the human ecology. All social institutions resist change and react adversely to the threat implied by the power of knowledge. When social organizations are altered to make use of new opportunities, equally important previous goals may no longer be adequately served. Even when new goals and methods can be agreed on, there are no moral, legal, or political leadership groups who are clearly authorized to decree large-scale constraints on individual and community behavior. The problems are compounded by lack of public understanding of and involvement in the issues. This has led to a laissez-faire attitude toward scientific and technological innovation. The political solution of control by a totalitarian government is equally inadequate, not only because of its political and social effects, but also because contemporary totalitarian systems have shown no greater effectiveness in ecological control than democratic forms of government. As a final problem, which all of us have confronted all too often at various levels, it is apparently very difficult to establish appropriate checks on the use of power without risking strangulation of decision-making in bureaucratic red tape and power struggles.

Opposition to greater science-based social control is particularly generated by the dread that an impersonal "machine" civilization is rapidly oppressing the individual and dehumanizing society. It is feared that injustices are occurring increasingly because actuarial predictions are being placed above human values. For example, when a policeman stops a "suspicious" looking pedestrian, the officer is reacting on an actuarial basis to the person's clothes, movements, indications of socio-economic status, and so forth. Minority group members and youths, whose appearances are deviant from the larger society, complain of unjustified harassment and police bias when they are stopped and searched on the basis of what may or may not be a correct prediction. The actuarial method is not to be blamed in such cases. Instead, the fault lies in the decision about how and when actuarial methods are appropriate. Few persons complain when the largest police force is assigned to duty—on the basis of actuarial methods—for periods when the risk of crime is greatest. The same confusion between ascribing the danger to the tools instead of to their inappropriate application also applies to methods and devices for psychological prediction and control. Availability of hypnosis, conditioning, or persuasion methods does not constitute the danger. Rather, their indiscriminate use is the hazard.

Scientists have been blamed for providing new sources of control of individuals and labeled as "sorcerers who are totally blind to the human adventure . . . a dictatorship of test tubes rather than hobnailed boots" (Ellul, 1964, p. 434–435). A French sociologist, generally favorable to modern scientific management practices, has warned: "Beware of the temptation—difficult to resist—of the arrogance of rationality. . . . it is a kind of folly to assume that a rational view of the world based on the inevitability of scientific progress can cope with a fragmented, culturally diverse society full of complex emotional problems . . . . It means to be blind to cultural and institutional diversity, to see everybody as an abstract entity" (Crozier, 1969). Dogmatic or totalitarian control can result from blind faith in a "technological fix" for all human woes, or from misusing scientific knowledge as if it provides a logical rationale to replace humane values or moral judgments in making policy decisions.

The conflicting values and dilemmas of the science professions are also apparent in the mental health professions. Questions regarding ethical judgments and conflicting goals loom importantly in all current treatment approaches. In many of his moment-to-moment treatment decisions, each therapist is guided in part by his belief in himself as an agent of society, of some minority power group within society, or of the individual client. Each therapist asks himself questions such as: To what extent do techniques of behavior control violate the individual's freedoms? Does *failing* to apply a potential technology for behavior change represent ultimate loss of freedom for the individual and society and an unjustified waste, or a necessary caution against manipulation? Actuarial predictions and laboratory-devised methods of therapy may be seen as threatening the place of humanistic values and the respect for individual dignity and choice. Social prescription of behavior may ignore experiential and emotional needs, which are perhaps more basic to human fulfillment.

These and countless other related questions have been raised in connection with all treatment approaches to behavior disorders. The potential for "control of the mind," for an outsider's determination of one's value choices was recognized as inherent in psychopharmacological and neurophysiological advances early in their development. Also realized was the conflict involved in the unique scientific role of the psychologist as both researcher-developer and practitioner-applier. This pair of concurrent roles means that value problems could not be evaded by leaving the application of one's findings and the moral dilemmas that accompany practice to other social groups. Symposia were organized to promote an exchange of ideas about these issues among a wide range of concerned groups: psychologists, pharmacologists, physiologists, philosophers, theologians, historians, artists (Farber and Wilson, 1961, 1963). Some have suggested that "society must so organize itself that a proportion of the very ablest and most imaginative of scientists are continually concerned with trying to foresee the long-term effects" of new knowledge and practices, the monitoring of which otherwise would depend "on the alertness of individuals to foresee danger and to form pressure groups that try to correct mistakes . . . ." (Solandt, 1969, p. 445).

Similarly, whenever a social institution such as a mental hospital is reorganized, the delicate balance between beneficial guidance and total control must be carefully managed. For example, Saslow (1964) compared the features of a therapeutic community ward and Chinese thought reform as described by Lifton (1961). Saslow noted qualitative similarities with only quantitative differences in the control of communication flow, manipulation of drive state, demand for "virtue" or purity as defined by the controllers, cult of personal confession, prohibition against questioning basic assumptions, and use of language that terminates thought. Saslow concluded that although thought reform emphasizes coercion and exhortation whereas milieu wards emphasize therapy and self-realization, both depend on the same procedures, the same assumption of social control "for your own good" by persons protected from counter-controls by doctrinaire superiority and by legal and social prerogatives. He noted that re-entry into America's pluralistic society may help psychiatric patients to combat the absolutist tendencies of hospital wards. Nevertheless, a hospital staff must remain constantly vigilant to the ethical dilemma of differentiating treatment from coercion and in executing the former without the latter. The same precautions apply with even greater force to the more totally "engineered" environments described in the chapter on operant-based approaches. Whatever the setting, the danger is that a therapist may assume the right to decide how the patient and environment *should* act, using his own criteria of desired social effectiveness instead of the criteria offered by the recipient of the therapeutic influence or society.

When the problems of social control came under scrutiny for new therapies (such as milieu therapy or operant conditioning), the same yardstick was applied to traditional psychotherapies as well. They too were found not to be free of influence and control dilemmas although this issue had not been seriously raised in the past. Studies on the effects of expectancies, of value and attitude congruences, and indeed, the very dependence of therapeutic benefit on the therapist's social reinforcements and on the shaping up of mutual role expectancies on the part of patient and therapist (Frank, 1961b; Goldstein, 1962) have amply demonstrated that all psychotherapists exercise influence and control over their clients (see Chapter 10). These findings have been among the points made in their own defense by therapists using new approaches in which controlling operations are more explicit and obvious. Among all the techniques touched by the controversy over control, however, the conditioning therapies have been singled out for the greatest criticism. May, for example, has depicted the behavior therapist as a sort of robot, valuing behavior control for its own sake:

"Now obviously this kind of conditioning approach to psychotherapy means that the patient is conditioned to the goals of the therapist, as the therapist controls the patient, but the therapist also takes no real responsibility for this, because the therapist, himself, is a programmed IBM machine, and one does not need to go into detail to indicate that the full meaning of human freedom—freedom and responsibility in any meaningful sense—is thereby undermined, but to the extent that if this would be our approach to therapy, freedom would be destroyed" (May, 1962, as cited in Krasner, 1965b, p. 16).

Critics in the popular press, discussing operant approaches to child rearing, have put it even more strongly: "Behaviorism is a psychology of despair and self-contempt. If man is simply a complex machine, then ethics and decency are nonsense and our philosophers, both ancient and modern, were fools" (LeShan and LeShan, 1968, p. 100).

Control in Therapy

Kanfer (1965a), in reviewing ethical issues in behavior manipulation, identified several features around which controversy and concern usually center: (1) the degree and extent to which behavior control is possible and present in therapeutic transactions. All concerns rest on the assumption that control is *possible*. (2) the *methods* which are used to achieve control, (3) the *behavioral domain* which is to be controlled, and (4) the *discrepancy* between personal values and cultural meta-values. Each of these features is discussed in some detail in the following sections.

Existence of Therapist Control. The growing potential for scientific control of human behavior has really not been a disputed topic between humanistic or traditional therapists and behaviorists. Carl Rogers, in his classic debate with Skinner on issues of control, readily acknowledged their agreement on that score.

"I am sure we agree that men—as individuals and as societies—have always endeavored to understand, predict, influence, and control human behavior—their own behavior and that of others.

"I believe we agree that the behavioral sciences are making and will continue to make increasingly rapid progress in the understanding of behavior, and that as a consequence the capacity to predict and to control behavior is developing with equal rapidity" (Rogers and Skinner, 1956, p. 307).

Less clear is the extent to which dynamic therapists admit that all therapy involves a process of control, whether or not it is premeditated and programmed. Certainly, many existential therapists would deny their directive influence. Gendlin (1967), for example, asserts that this approach:

". . . does not base the psychotherapy process on values, but rather bases values on the nature of the psychotherapy process. . . . we do not (and cannot) with value-conclusions choose the outcomes we call therapeutic. Rather, the order is reversed: What outcomes are "therapeutic" we learn empirically from the process. . . . In short, it is not my values that determine what therapy process we get. Rather, the nature of a therapy process (if it is to occur at all) determines certain basic aspects of what it is to be a therapist" (pp. 191–192).

Despite such extreme views, many therapists acknowledge that much of the success of psychotherapy rests on control and influence, at least within the limits set by patient cooperation and mutuality of patient and therapist goals and expectations. If controlling processes have been of less concern until recently, it is because they have been relatively inefficient and covert. Once presence of control is granted, the issue changes, as Ulrich (1967) has pointed out:

"It is concluded that controlled human behavior is an existing fact which cannot be altered and individuals concerned with personal freedom should at least consider that perhaps the only meaningful form of behavioral freedom must be based on a knowledge of the factors which, indeed, control us" (p. 229).

If it is granted that the therapist exerts significant influence on his patient, then the differences of opinion and the ethical-moral controversy center on who controls whom, by what methods, in respect to which behaviors, and according to whose set of values.

Methods of Control. A key controversial factor is the use of therapy that emphasize "techniques" for behavior change that are subtle but powerful, that rely on positive reinforcement, or that restrict alternative responses—including pathological ones. Descriptions of "techniques" and the laboratory research from which they derive apparently imply to many readers that a cold automaton has replaced a living and caring therapist. Actually, our knowledge of the importance of warmth, spontaneity, and genuineness in promoting social reinforcement value and therapeutic effects leads us to quite the opposite argument—that is, a behavioral therapist will usually need to embody the same personal characteristics prized in other therapists. Nevertheless, this image of the callous behaviorist has been difficult to dispel.

Similarly, when methods of influence are subtle and planned in advance, they appear more objectionable. Paradoxically, the more acceptable approaches advocated in their place may be just as subtly coercive but only less openly labeled as such and less carefully planned to maximize effectiveness. For example, Rogers (Rogers and Skinner, 1956) asserts it is akin to brainwashing if therapeutic molding by external control is subtle. He then goes on to advocate as the alternative to loss of freedom and choice in a fast-approaching *Walden Two* or *1984,* a selection of fluid processes (rather than static behaviors) such as self-actualization, creative adaptation to a changing environment, or the process of becoming as proper goals for whose achievement control is exerted. Despite the fact that they are selected, prescribed, and facilitated by the therapist and not by the client, Rogers contends that these process goals guarantee an open society in which individual choice is preserved. However, as soon as such abstract process goals are operationalized in more concrete, discrete terms, there is little to separate them from the goals that behavior therapists are also likely to pursue. Apparently, to Rogers the subtle but self-proclaimed, self-conscious influence operations of modeling, social reinforcement, and other behavior therapy techniques are more objectionable than are equally subtle but more covert operations that reliably produce therapist-prescribed behavior change, but with less active, less programmed therapist intervention. Although Rogers has faith in the natural evolution of mental health in the individual, in actual therapy it remains the prerogative of the therapist to characterize as beneficial that which he, the therapist, judges to be self-actualization and therefore meritorious. By this value judgment, the Rogerian therapist guides the patient's direction as much as do other therapists.

Another characteristic of controlling methods that seems to provoke criticism is the use of positive reinforcement instead of punishment. The open *act* of rewarding is generally viewed with favor and the *act* of punishment with disfavor. In contrast, effective *control* of individuals as a result of positive reinforcement is viewed as less detectable by the controlled person, less likely to elicit counter-control efforts, and more effective in influencing "private" events (see Chapter 8). Hence it is seen as more dangerous, potentially threatening, and of lesser moral virtue than control based on aversive stimuli (Kanfer, 1965a). Many teachers and parents object to the use of positive reinforcements to control behavior, characterizing them as "bribes" and temporary expedients. Positive reinforcement is a prominent device in maintaining culturally prescribed behaviors. Yet aversive stimulation is more frequently focused on as a vehicle for control in social institutions, education, religion, and traditional psychology. Psychology has emphasized the role of anxiety as a central motivating force in social adjustment. Many philosophers, theologians, and personality theorists have viewed man as engaged in a struggle against his "bad" natural tendencies and hence as relying on aversive control by himself and others to suppress his evil dispositions. Perhaps it is the novelty of emphasis on positive reinforcement which arouses antagonism.

The Behavioral Domain Selected For Control. The third feature identified by Kanfer (1965a) as affecting perceptions of control is the domain of manipulated behavior. Control in the acquisition of driving skills is generally valued as desirable whereas control of interpersonal skills and behaviors may be seen as more questionable, and control of sexual or assertive skills (except perhaps to remove them) is often attacked. Some critics see behavioral approaches as useless in affecting man's most important and unique functions: "The machine approach works well on simple levels. It can teach a child French grammar or simple forms of obedience. It cannot do anything about creativity, flexibility, empathy, love and courage" (LeShan and LeShan, 1968, p. 100). Most behavior therapists, as well as many of their sophisticated critics, would disagree with this statement. Indeed, it is potential control of exactly such complex functions as creativity, self-control, empathy, or value formation, that is either most feared or most sought after.

The content of private values or processes seems to many people to be most intimate, personal, and in greatest need of safeguards against external influence. Therapeutic influence is seen as especially ominous when applied to apparently well-functioning persons—not to very defective organisms—precisely because it is then likely to deal with private events. Behavioral methods of control are acceptable in our society in situations where a high degree of conformity is expected (for example, in reestablishing minimal social behaviors in disturbed psychotics or in removing phobic behaviors), but they are often not acceptable for influence of those characteristics that determine a person's choices. The issue here is closely related to conflicts in meta-values discussed in the next section. Indeed, most methods of persuasion, whether thought reform or psychotherapy, require the target individual to expose his private experiences, fears, beliefs, and personal attitudes for examination and modification, even though these behaviors are rarely shared with anyone. This is cause for concern both because of the very nature of the material and because such self-accusation and self-revelation enhance external control.

"Privacy, the inaccessibility of much personal behavior in a democratic society, probably represents the bulwark of democracy because it allows for variability, and for divergence of attitudes and beliefs. What is jealously guarded as a right to privacy in everyday life is, in fact, surrendered in the psychotherapeutic hour . . . . The potentials for controlling important behavioral sequences, usually not subject to control by direct social reinforcement, increase very much the extent of the therapist's influence" (Kanfer, 1965a, p. 191).

Personal Values and Meta-Values. The fourth characteristic affecting the way behavioral control is perceived in psychotherapy has to do with the relationship between personal values and those values generally accepted by most members of a given culture (meta-values). Personal values encompass a variety of alternative behaviors and goals that are equally acceptable to the individual in achieving satisfactions. As an agent of society, the therapist acts to enlarge the alternatives available to a patient within the limits imposed by cultural meta-values. Since the latter are often vague or conflicting, especially for private behaviors, the therapist may come to act as interpreter and arbiter of cultural values. Diversity of subcultures, personal values, and therapists' interpretations has probably helped to avoid totalitarianism in psychotherapists heretofore, along with the inefficiency of therapeutic methods for exerting influence. The more potent therapeutic control becomes and the more consistent are the values pursued by therapists as interpreter-agents of society, the more totalitarian therapeutic procedures could become.

There are many ways in which people may decide to live that reflect personal values—homosexual versus heterosexual, married or divorced, using many drugs or none, concentrating on recreation or on work. The culture actually permits behaviors toward both extremes of many bipolar choices in daily life patterns, although open advocacy of only one polar choice is sanctioned publicly. For example, although verbal sanctions remain in our culture against divorce, there are It's Great To Be Single Clubs and very high rates of divorce. With regard to alcohol, cigarette, and drug use there are even more conflicting cultural signals for guidance of individual behaviors. Meta-values are increasingly offering more choices to the individual, and are becoming increasingly permissive in some respects. If a therapist represents only one pole of a pair of values, clients lose freedom to exercise available options by exposure to therapeutic influence.

Behavior therapists tend to be as concerned about the ethics of control as are their critics. They can point to certain positive aspects of their approach to therapeutic behavior manipulation: It is explicit in that its goals and operations are openly stated and subject to rejection by client or society; it is doing in a planned and efficient way what other procedures strive for but approach with less efficiency or clarity; and the therapeutic goals are defined by society, its agents, or the patient and not by the theory underlying the modification process itself. For instance, when an enuretic child is treated by the bell-and-pad method, his parents as society's agents have sanctioned explicit control of the target behavior that brought them to the therapist. If such a child were given a course of psychoanalytic play sessions, the therapist would introduce a new set of values from his own theoretical orientation, since this type of session seeks far more extensive changes than removal of the presenting complaint.

At the same time, concern about "who controls the controllers" and what social agency should be empowered to establish legitimate goals for manipulation remains an unsolved fundamental issue for discussion among behavior therapists. Emphasis in professional training on the value implications of therapeutic influence, the role of the therapist in enacting society's goals, and the personal and social consequences of therapeutic decisions has been frequently urged (see, for example, Krasner, 1965a). Roe (1959) has suggested that awareness is a major potential defense against manipulation and, hence, that psychological activism in changing society should be matched by openness in doing so. Others have urged increased research on ethical values and value choices as they enter into behavior control (Krasner, 1964). Basically, however, the dilemma remains, and public education for awareness, debate, and ultimate regulation of behavior control appears to be the major process for resolving the behavior therapist's choices and conflicts.

London (1964) has made some particularly cogent observations relating to public perceptions of and reactions to the issues of behavior control. He asserts that man apparently inherently must see himself as controlling his own behavior, must experience himself as having freedom of will. But, London further asserts, man cannot function effectively without external control: "this sense of freedom of will is as surely a part of man's nature as is the fact that he does not have it" (p. 170). He concludes:

"Psychotherapists have an important job to do, and it looks as if they will learn to do it well. As their ability to control and manipulate behavior improves, the moral character of their enterprise will become more visible, and more embarrassing. But at the same time, their knowledge of man should also improve, and their moral stand thus becomes more defensible. When that happens, their title to guild status will be free and clear, and their ability to serve men, individually and in society, precious" (London, 1964, p. 173).

Socio-Political Matrix of Privacy

Respect for an individual's or a group's right to protection from intrusive surveillance is a highly prized social value in western society. On the other hand, society needs information about individuals and groups in order to serve other values, including those concerned with survival of the society and its members. This is the case with diseases that doctors are required to report to public health officials. To illustrate the conflict between these two sets of values, let us consider that the knowledge and tools of behavioral science are increasingly being used as instruments of government in trying to solve the complex social-behavior problems of our society (see, for example, NRC Advisory Committee, 1968). This in turn has led to proposals for new means of collecting, integrating, and evaluating social-behavioral data. A National Data Bank has been proposed in which all relevant social science information and records would be collated in a centralized computer facility. A National Data Bank could draw upon commercial, educational, and governmental sources to produce huge quantities of information about the characteristics and behavior of any individual or group. The cost of retrieving and assembling the data from the many available but scattered records has previously protected the public from the loss of privacy that access to these data would create. Advances in computer technology have reduced both the cost and time required for storage and retrieval of large masses of data. Population-wide social-behavioral data banks would be invaluable for basic research, evaluation and systems research, and enlightened policy planning and decision making. Even if their users had the purest of disinterested motives, the mere existence of such a storehouse could be a basic violation of the right to privacy. The additional danger is that the data are equally open to those with baser motives. A national data center thus epitomizes the growing conflict between two values: society's need to know, to plan, and to decide on the basis of knowledge, and the individual's right to determine the extent and conditions under which personal information is shared with others.

A panel of the Office of Science and Technology, appointed to examine issues of privacy in behavioral research, described research as "the root of the conflict between the individual's right to privacy and society's right to discover" (Executive Office of the President, 1967, p. 4). The dangers to privacy of a federal central data bank have been investigated in House and Senate hearings and discussed widely by behavioral scientists and others (Harrison, 1967; Ruebhausen and Brim, 1965; Westin, 1967).

Privacy is at issue in the ethics of behavior change not only because private events may be targets of change, but because effective influence on any behavior (public or private) is likely to require extensive behavioral-social assessment and hence violation of privacy. For the patient's therapeutic benefit extensive data may be needed prior to effective planning and conduct of a behavior modification procedure. Conflict of this need with the client's right to privacy is a dilemma confronting everyone involved in behavior influence. The conflicting loyalties and responsibilities of the professional are amply illustrated in the extensive discussions and Congressional hearings about use of psychological tests for personnel decisions in government (see, for example, APA, 1965a). Related objections have been raised about the investigative practices of agencies such as Welfare.

Mostly, the assessment activities of individual psychologists and smaller agencies are only beginning to come under scrutiny for possible violations of the patient's right to privacy. Even with respect to the data collection process which is part of behavior change procedures used by individual practitioners and is much less extensive than, for example, a National Data Bank, practical guidelines for safeguarding the individual's privacy and yet accomplishing the therapeutic goal have not been developed. For example, "confidentiality" between clinician and client used to be categorically asserted. However, the changing nature of clinical practice and mental health intervention has made the matter more complex and conflictual. Peterson (1968a), for instance, has pointed out that increasing socialization of psychosocial welfare functions obligates the professional as an agent of change less to the individual client than to organized society. The welfare caseworker, regardless of her empathy for the recipient's plight and needs, represents the public interest in proper financial management of the agency's funds. She usually maintains control over the client's allotted budget by telling the client what to buy and how to buy it, how to dress her children and what to feed them, and influences numerous other behaviors. With the client's loss of economic and administrative controls go other subtler controls, including loss of the client's former right to determine the limits of inquiries to be conducted about him. The welfare worker can assume the right to interview neighbors or to inspect the kitchen and under the bed, without fear of meeting protest. Since clinical intervention is moving from the therapist's office into the natural environment, observation and data collection are also moving increasingly into previously private realms of the client's life. And as Peterson (1968a) notes, when intervention involves an organization or a group, such as a family, the identity of the persons whose rights to privacy and whose informed consent are involved can become quite obscure. Suppose a parent consults a behavior therapist who decides that a functional analysis of the child's behavior in the home is necessary for diagnostic assessment and treatment planning. Whose consent and what protection are required in behalf of the other family members whose intimate home behaviors will be observed and recorded? When intervention is located in larger organizations, the situation is even more complex with respect to who is the client, who must be informed of the nature and purposes of data collection, and whose consent is required for collection and distribution of what information.

As an example of what has become technically possible in the field of behavioral monitoring, Purcell and Brady (1966) (see Chapter 10 also) have described the use of miniature radio transmitters to record all of the verbal behavior, over a period of days, of a group of institutionalized children and of everyone with whom they interacted. Their evidence suggests rapid adaptation to the monitoring by all parties, so that even the inherent protection of privacy by guardedness and awareness

of being observed did not last long—at least for these volunteer, cooperative subjects. Instrumentation of this sort seemingly offers a partial solution
to remedy the distortion of natural social interactions that has been reported when, for example, families have been directly observed in the
home (Patterson and Harris, 1968). Instrumented behavioral monitoring
is therefore likely to be used much more frequently for both clinical and
research efforts in natural settings. Naturalistic observations and with them,
the occurrence of privacy invasion seem destined to increase because of
the desirability of direct observation as a basis for behavioral diagnosis,
and because of increased technical ease in making the observations in
the patient's natural environment.

Issues In Human Research

The investigator who works with human subjects is often faced with
a complex dilemma. Society values the protection of individual rights
and welfare, but it also values the advancement of knowledge. The scientist
himself holds multiple allegiances and interests, with respect to his scientific discipline and his own career, as well as to his research subjects and
the general pursuit of knowledge. When a researcher is determining what
procedures are permissible with human subjects in attempting to answer
a particular research question, he must try to balance these conflicting
values in order to arrive at an ethical, equitable solution. Potential risks
to individual subjects must be weighed against potential value of the research findings for society. Because the scientist's capabilities and methods
are becoming ever more sophisticated and his goals of understanding are
becoming more ambitious, the potential seriousness of his manipulations
of subjects has increased correspondingly.

As noted, research on organ transplantation and genetic intervention
has dramatized ethical concerns about human experimentation. It has produced intensive reassessment of the issues and guidelines confronting the
investigator. Even in the popular press, publications as diverse as the
Wall Street Journal (1964, 1966) and the *Saturday Review* (1966) have
devoted extensive coverage to controversies in research ethics. Among
scholars, interest has been even more keen. *Daedalus,* the journal of the
American Academy of Arts and Sciences, for example, recently devoted
an entire issue to the ethical aspects of experimentation with human subjects. Although medical experimentation was used as a paradigm for the
issues in general, the editor readily acknowledged the relevance of the
discussion to other fields of experimentation.

"There is reason to believe that ethical issues will increasingly preoccupy
social scientists, and not only because of a growing resistance to their

research proposals. The school and the ghetto are two of the more obvious sites for experimentation with human subjects, and their inhabitants may need to be "protected" in very much the same way that hospital patients and experimental subjects in medical research now are. Alternatives will have to be weighed so that the needs of society are taken into account while the rights of the individual are not neglected. The medical paradigm—with its emphasis on consent, professional competence, review mechanisms, adequacy of research design, legal liability, protection of privacy, governmental regulation, and the like—may prove to have more than a little relevance to the kinds of psychological and educational experimentation that will be countenanced in the future" (Graubard, 1969, pp. vi–vii).

If it is presumed that the more tangible precautions from the above list have been or readily will be established by administrative and legal codes, the issue of informed consent remains a particularly complex and difficult problem. The requirement of consent by an informed subject prior to an experiment is a protection of the individual's rights and welfare and helps to balance the pressures on a researcher caused by his personal values or his or society's obligations to pursue new knowledge. The Nuremberg Code, written as a reaction to atrocities committed by Nazi researchers, required that a subject be able to make an understanding and enlightened decision to participate in a study on the basis of full knowledge of its nature and purpose, its methods and duration, and all of its hazards, inconveniences, and possible effects on himself. The Code attempts to forestall any future recurrence of the senseless tortures and inhumanities perpetrated under the guise of scientific experimentation in Nazi concentration camps. But full, free, and informed consent involves complex elements and subjective evaluations (Beecher, 1966; Boston University, 1963; Pappworth, 1967). Among the difficult problems that arise are questions of how severe a risk a normal volunteer should be allowed to assume, and whether consent can ever be truly free of influence when the researcher is also a clinician ministering to a patient in physical or psychological discomfort. It is difficult to decide who, if anyone, should be allowed to give consent for those unable to act for themselves (for example, retardates, psychotics, minors), or how full an account of methods and possible risks must be given for a subject to be "fully informed." The nature of experimentation rests on the uncertainty of outcome. Thus no researcher can ever honestly assure his subjects that the listed hazards exhaust the possible range of consequences of his experimental procedures. Since the scientific complexities of an investigation are often meaningful only to a specialist, it seems doubtful that the ordinary lay person can act freely on his own judgment and comprehension. What about the imponderables that influence motivation to give consent—the prestige and persuasiveness of the investigator, trust and gratitude toward experts, implied sanctions or benefits as in the case of students or prisoners, or "neurotic" needs of various sorts? The concrete operations necessary in any given case to assure that consent is "free" and "informed" are extremely difficult to prescribe.

These general issues form the core of controversy in all fields engaging in human research. In the area of behavior modification and psychological research the possible effects of informed consent on the results of research further complicate the dilemma. For example, "awareness" of the experimental purpose may be the independent variable to be manipulated by the investigator. Even when it is not, deception about both the purpose of the study and dimensions of measurement is frequently required and practiced in psychological studies. Kelman (1967) has discussed many of the ethical and methodological problems that arise when deception is used in psychological research. For example, he points out that the usual safeguard of debriefing a subject afterwards about the true nature of an experiment may impose the added burden on a subject of knowing how easily he has been gulled. No amount of *post hoc* understanding can fully erase the effects of having engaged in some demeaning behaviors during a psychological experiment (Walster, Berscheid, Abrahams, and Aronson, 1967). On the other hand, foreknowledge by all subjects would make much psychological research impossible.

Kelman has also pointed out the methodological implications of deception in psychological experiments. Large populations of potential subjects (such as college students) come to hold unknown and uncontrolled suspicions and expectations toward any psychological study in which they participate. Subjects may be trying to "psych out" the experimenter who is perceived to be trying to "psych out" the subjects. In this case, it may be the experimenter who is most deceived about the meaning of his results. Only rarely does the researcher make sufficient inquiries to safeguard himself against overlooking subject expectations and deceptions (see, for example, Stricker, 1967; Stricker, Messick, and Jackson, 1967).

Outcome studies of behavioral therapies contain similar issues with regard to deception of subjects and informed consent, despite the generally overt and open nature of behavior therapy procedures. Outcome studies may require participation of uninformed placebo treatment subjects as controls. Base-rate observations in the natural environment may subject families or individuals to unexpected self-revelations to which they would not have consented in advance. Manipulations of reinforcement systems are carried out in many studies under necessarily misleading instructions.

Investigations of naturally occurring contingencies and their effects, for example, on a hospital ward, often involve deception of the subjects. Were the true nature of the observations and purpose known, consent might often have been withheld. For example, a nursing staff might be expected to refuse permission for a study of the antitherapeutic effects of the reinforcement contingencies they apply to patients, such as attention contingent on bizarre behavior, and positive reinforcement of passivity.

The use of control groups in studying treatment effectiveness raises not only the issue of deception but also the question of withholding treatment or giving a placebo or presumably less effective treatment to persons seeking help because of disability or discomfort. Of course, the best rebuttal to objections against use of controls in clinical studies is that until such research is done, there is no evidence that the experimental procedure or treatment that is withheld has any beneficial effects at all. In fact, it may turn out to be detrimental to the therapeutic goal. But more often, partial evidence already attests to possible effectiveness; in any case, placebo or no-treatment or "wait" groups are denied those procedures commonly applied to similar complaints, whatever their merits. "Standard clinical practice" is the norm against which malpractice complaints are assessed. Hence, withholding or delaying treatments which are "standard practice" in given clinical circumstances is often unacceptable to society although there is little evidence that the standard treatment has any efficacy. The use of analogue studies can get around this problem in the early stages of research. Still, as previously noted, clinical studies using actual target populations are ultimately required to verify analogue results and to answer questions about prognosis, applicability to a range of complaints and patient characteristics, and situational limitations. If earlier studies have demonstrated any benefits of the method at all, the ethical problem of control groups then appears in the clinical verification stage of research.

The opposite problem in clinical practice has to do with the ethics of continued reliance on traditional practices whose utility has yet to be demonstrated despite years of investigation. Does "informed consent" require that patients receiving shock or insight psychotherapy first be told the discouraging figures on the effectiveness of such treatments? If psychotherapy does not alter the rate or extent of recovery from neurosis, as many investigations suggest (see, for example, Eysenck, 1965a), then is it improper to accept a client's trust, time, and money for psychotherapy, or to train students in inefficient procedures? Although very few clinician's may be willing to take such an extreme position, increasing skepticism about the efficacy of traditional psychotherapies and consequent reluctance to rely upon them has resulted in greater openness to experimentation with alternative methods and some feeling of urgency in designing more powerful and conclusive research. Increasingly, statements are made like that of Wolfensberger (1967):

"An invalidated medical treatment, like bloodletting as practiced in the 18th century, can be worse than no treatment at all. Is it really so inconceivable that some widely current but insufficiently validated human-management practices (psychotherapy, for example) may constitute the bloodletting of the 20th century?" (p. 49).

Golann (1969), in reviewing emerging ethical concerns of psychologists, has raised the same issue in a somewhat different way:

"For the most part (emerging ethical issues) concern the relationship of psychologists to their clients, colleagues, or subjects. Some of the problems are particularly pertinent to professional practice, others to basic or applied research. Perhaps a larger problem of ethics is that the distinction between these approaches has become so clearly drawn. How much of professional practice is based upon research findings? How much influence has validity or outcome data had upon technology? How many new programs or techniques are designed in such a way that they are simultaneously practice and research . . . or at least designed so as to obtain some estimate of efficacy?" (pp. 457–458).

The behavior modifier who seeks to do as Golann advocates, combining technique development with evaluation research, faces the difficulties inherent in combining two roles that involve subtle distinctions in purpose, concern, and attitude, as discussed in Chapter 1. Ladimer (1967) has pointed out a number of these distinctions: in clinical practice the client seeks out the practitioner whereas the researcher seeks out specific clients for study; diagnosis and therapy are provided by the clinician as long as they are needed for treating his client, whereas the researcher has a limited contact defined by his investigative needs rather than the client's; patients usually pay for clinical services, whereas a researcher may compensate a subject for his trouble; and clinical work depends upon standard accepted modes of practice, whereas research typically involves untested procedures. Ladimer further points out that the role and obligations of the patient and of the research subject also differ.

The behavior modifier can turn to both methodological aids and codes of conduct for help in combining the roles of clinician and scientist. Campbell (1969), for instance, has described political and administrative constraints on evaluative studies of social-behavioral demonstration programs and suggests particular designs and procedures to reduce the consequent ethical and methodological problems. Many of his suggestions are readily adapted to research with individual clinical subjects as well. For example, when a treatment cannot be withheld from some subject-patients, special research designs may still permit adequate control comparisons. Several sets of preliminary guidelines for human research have been proposed as bases for more formal and extensive codes. Wolfensberger (1967), for example, discusses permissible and advisable activities by the researcher, given various combinations of risks incurred, rights yielded by the subject, and demands of research designs (rigor, potential gain of knowledge, predictability of procedural effects). Various combinations of rights, risks, and research types suggest different forms of subject instruction, consent release, review of proposal by peers, and so on.

Ultimately, however, the clinical investigator is compelled to rely upon his own judgment and upon consultation with colleagues when confronting ethical issues in his own work. He may then be reminded of the statement of a French biologist some years ago to the effect that science has taught us how to be gods before we have learned how to be men.

The clinical psychologist, as therapist and researcher, is continually faced with responsibility for safeguarding the rights and welfare of patients and subjects. Clinical methods of behavior control as well as innovative experimentation require serious consideration of possible detrimental consequences including infringement of rights of privacy.

TRAINING AND MODELS OF CLINICAL PRACTICE

Another important set of influences affecting the direction of clinical psychology and clinical practice consists of innovations and controversies in professional-scientific education. The knowledge explosion, while providing access to previously undreamed of wealth of fact and instrumentation, has confronted all scientific and professional educators with the need to revise old teaching principles. It is no longer possible to impart to a student *all* the knowledge in even a specialized area. In most fields, the latest discoveries are often superseded by the time they appear in textbooks. The outpouring of books and journals also leads to training students in retrieval of knowledge rather than its commitment to memory. Readiness to absorb new information, to evaluate its sources, and to grasp basic concepts are likely to be more useful for the modern professional than the total recall of his lecture notes or textbooks.

Rapid introduction of new knowledge and techniques is also a problem for the practicing professional. In medicine, for example, the same scientific advances that provide the means to arrest a myriad of pathological processes that had formerly been inevitably fatal also confront the physician with "dangerous complexities": "The conscientious physician is staggered by the rapidity with which changes are taking place so that it becomes more and more difficult for him to introduce them into his practice"

(Rutstein, 1967, p. 30). In practice, availability of new cures has also produced occasional laxity in early diagnosis or treatment. Rutstein defines as the paradox of modern medicine the discrepancy between rapid mushrooming of medical science and a growing lag in its application for improved medical care of the general population. This paradox has its analogue in all fields of knowledge.

Another cause of ferment in professional education is increasing public pressure for revised goals and teaching practices. A rapidly expanding proportion of the population is now entering higher education, including graduate education, with a proportionate increase in public expenditures to support education. The public insists that education be "relevant" for the student and for society, that the quality, availability, and individualization of education be increased for all segments of the population, and that educators be better trained and more effective in their jobs.

The same forces affecting general education and training seem to be operative in clinical psychology as well. Sharp criticism of graduate programs comes from students, faculty, and practicing clinicians alike. Trends toward increasing specialization, in response to growing complexity in psychology, are in conflict with public needs for generalist skills. Commitment to research in order to develop depth in substantive knowledge clashes with mushrooming opportunities for clinical services. External demands for more mental health manpower foster growth in the number and size of training programs and in the financial investment they represent. New roles and functions created to meet public demands for novel services are resulting in reexamination of the content, goals, and assumptions of clinical training programs.

Clinical psychology may even be experiencing the general social influences on education more acutely than some other professions and sciences because it is a relatively new field, developing with great self-consciousness and making repeated efforts at self-examination and explicit self-direction. In this section we will be concerned with the relevance for training programs, and for behavior therapies in particular, of alternative answers proposed to several basic issues. The first issue is the ambiguity of proper roles of the clinician and the substantive content required to fulfill these roles. The second major question concerns itself with the level of training required to carry out various clinical activities. The first deals with alternative models of the professional clinician, the second with training of subprofessional therapeutic agents.

Models of Clinical Roles and Training

When the growth of clinical psychology as a discipline became almost explosive immediately following World War II, its leaders initiated a remarkable effort at introspective self-direction that has continued to the present. The results were a series of conferences in which various models for clinical practice and hence for graduate training were formulated and recommendations to university departments were made. Building on the 1947 report of the Committee on Training in Clinical Psychology (Shakow report, APA, 1947), the Boulder Conference (Raimy, 1950) in 1949 outlined desirable curricula and evaluation procedures for producing scientist-professionals with generalist skills. Implementation of the recommendations of the Boulder Conference has made it the model that is most typical of present graduate psychology department.

A major conclusion of the Boulder Conference was that research should be given importance equal to that of practice in the functioning and, hence, in the graduate training of all clinical psychologists. Consistent with this decision, the title of "psychologist" was to be reserved for persons who had completed a research degree, the Ph.D. A second principal decision was to institute a core curriculum covering theory construction, conceptual tools, and scientific method in order to insure that each student was solidly grounded in the knowledge and methods of basic psychology. Clinical training was to give equal emphasis to theory and practice with closely supervised practicum experience coordinated with course work. Field training was to progress from laboratory to clerkship to internship as the student's competence developed. Diagnostic testing and psychotherapy were the critical skills to be acquired. The overall goal of training was to produce a scientifically oriented professional, broadly educated in substantive psychology, who also possessed journeyman clinical skills.

Later conferences on clinical training at Stanford in 1955, Miami in 1958, and Chicago in 1965 generally confirmed the Boulder perspective, with only minor differences in conclusions and recommendations (Lloyd and Newbrough, 1966). However, in considering many of the same issues, the later conferences produced different priorities and points of view. Changes have occurred in the past twenty years in the operations that are nominally intended to train the Boulder-model product of graduate education. Among these are increased flexibility in the choice of first-year core courses, decreased emphasis on skillful performance with a few specific diagnostic instruments, greater attention to training in therapy, and growing use of university affiliated facilities for practicum and internship training (Alexander and Basowitz, 1966). A number of factors have prevented the "ideal" Boulder program from becoming a reality. Some recommendations were never actually enacted Graduate student self-selection usually favored service interests, and probably some of the original goals lacked practicality. The result has been that few graduates have actually embodied both parts of the hyphenated Boulder model, and proportionately few have been scientifically productive. Many critics add that even in patient contact or in evaluation of the instruments and methods that they select, recent graduates have not evidenced in their roles as clinicians any of the skepticism and empirical problem-solving approach acquired in their scientific training.

Changing Goals of Training Programs

Despite the seeming generality of support by succeeding conferences for the Boulder model, today there is far less uniformity of opinion and far less confidence in the feasibility or desirability of a generally applicable training model. Separate professional schools for producing clinical practitioners have been suggested (APA, 1965b). The most salient changes in these schools would be decreased training in research and experimental psychology, the absence of a dissertation requirement, and increased practicum training. Behavior therapy, with its emphasis on derivation of applied techniques from the content and methods of experimental, social, personality, and learning psychology and on empirical evaluation of its operations and effectiveness, cannot accommodate these proposals.

A number of issues, long present as undercurrents in discussions of training, are now more sharply debated, acted upon, and taken up as missions by formally organized interest groups. Table 11-1, taken from Frederick (1969b), outlines some of these issues, or as he terms them, dichotomies, as they apply to psychotherapy training. Frederick's issues cover the questions of what the clinician should do (role models), what content background he needs in order to carry out these activities, and who should be trained for clinical work. By and large, in Table 11-1 the left-hand column describing issue content reflects a Boulder model. The right-hand column represents diverse current trends, including those within behavior therapy and those within the new professional schools. The issues are not new. They have been the foci at each of the training conferences. But whereas Boulder seemingly came to a consensus on these issues, Miami evidenced more uncertainty about "right" choices between the dichotomized poles and admitted more flexibility in approaches, and Chicago saw the enactment of extremes in concrete programs (see, for example, Peterson, 1968b).

Shifting Content of Clinical Practice

Hersch (1968) has characterized all mental health fields as currently suffering a "discontent explosion." Evidence of discontent is found in disillusionment with past clinical approaches existing side by side with the assertion that training in traditional clinical theories and techniques needs to be strengthened. The fluidity of the boundaries defining appro-

Table 11-1   Dichotomies in Psychotherapy Training
(adapted from Frederick, 1969b, pp. 394–395)

Issue	Content		
General vs. Specific	Broad. Encompasses wide curriculum. Little or no specific expertise, e.g., psychological testing. Community psychology and mental health concepts advocated.	vs.	Focus on high degree of skill in specialized areas. Skill in psychological testing emphasized. Established curriculum in both institutional and field placements.
University vs. Field Settings	Primary responsibility for training and clinical information should be located in university.	vs.	University actually should be an "Ivory Tower" devoted to theoretical research issues. All practicum training should be in Field Settings.
Formal vs. Informal	Professional faculty only. Formal accredited courses should be required.	vs.	Anyone knowledgeable and interested ought to give training.
Medical model vs. Psychological	Patients viewed as sick; diagnosis and treatment provided accordingly.	vs.	Persons seen as learning aberrant psychological and emotional responses to life. Not sick. Concepts of "care and treatment" not necessary or appropriate.
Scientist vs. Practitioner	Experimental. Emphasis upon research, language proficiency, scientific curricula.	vs.	Entirely clinical. Little or no research, no language proficiency, professional degree. Perhaps no doctoral thesis.
Doctoral vs. Subdoctoral	Doctoral training is a *sine qua non* for professional competence.	vs.	Subdoctoral persons, if carefully selected, can function well, often with little professional supervision.
Private Practitioner vs. Public Servant	Free enterprise espoused; fees are necessary part of treatment to motivate patient.	vs.	Service and welfare to society are chief goals for the future. Fees are not necessary for patient motivation.

priate clinical practice has led to uncertainty about the goals and content of training programs. In analyzing the sources of the "discontent explosion," Hersch (1968) emphasizes several failures.

1. Inability of clinical psychology and psychiatry to ameliorate refractory social-behavioral problems, such as delinquency, multiproblem families, and mental retardation. These problems are associated in part with socioeconomic status and hence interwoven with the problems of civil rights and the war on poverty, as part of the current change in the social organization of this country.
2. Inability to utilize the traditional individual clinical model—or its derivative for small groups—for more than a small fraction of the persons needing service within the limits of trained manpower available or ever likely to be available.
3. Lack of evidence that long-term individual psychotherapy, the bulwark of clinical practice (and training), has any beneficial effect. To this could be added the accumulation of evidence that traditional diagnostic techniques and diagnostic systems have little functional utility in guiding decisions (see Chapter 10). Uncritical acceptance of traditional assumptions about diagnosis and psychotherapy has led to sharp disillusionment even though training in these practices continues to be central to most programs. This anomaly is demonstrated in the case of projective techniques, for example. A recent survey showed that 86 percent of faculty members questioned characterized projective tests as unsupported by research and unimportant. Yet the same respondents felt that projective techniques should continue to be required course work in graduate education (Thelen, Varble, and Johnson, 1968).
4. Inability to achieve any progress in preventing behavioral disability through application of prevalent practices and conceptions, despite the conviction that prevention instead of treatment must be the ultimate goal.

Discontent with the past have produced novel roles, target populations, and arenas for professional activity for many young clinicians of today. These changes have been much slower in affecting the content and methods of training programs. This lag may be due to views of new practices as being chaotic and as seeking innovation without drawing on available knowledge and without evaluating one approach in depth before becoming expansionistic (Bloom, 1969). At the same time, future roles and practices for the clinician seem to be unpredictable and obscured by demands for involvement in general social betterment. Entry into the field of promoting social change can lead to exceeding the usual political role of a professional and the substantive competence of a psychologist. Bloom describes most psychologists in selected innovative clinical settings as using least those skills they were most specifically trained to carry out (diagnosis and research). His subjects were engaged mainly in functions for which they had received no training (for example, community analysis and intervention, administration, demographic assessment, consultation). Their activities were largely undifferentiated from agency colleagues in other disciplines, both professional and nonprofessional. Critics have voiced concern that ill-considered and hasty breaks with the traditional past of clinical psychology, based on frustration with its deficiencies, may result in a discarding of positive past developments as well. The result would be the creation of new programs, equally unsatisfactory and hence likely to provide grounds for yet another explosion of discontent (Bloom, 1969; Hersch, 1968).

Training for the Future

If current models of clinical psychology and goals of training reflect controversy, questions of how to train for the future are even more difficult to answer. The kinds of continuing changes to which we have repeatedly referred—in society, in mental health generally, and clinical psychology specifically—make it difficult to predict the nature of the target populations and their presenting difficulties, the goals of intervention and appropriate training for practitioners for meeting these goals, and the theoretical substrata of future therapeutic efforts. Certain general trends do seem likely to continue, however, for the next several decades. For one, advances in biology and social science are already affecting psychological theory and practice. They are likely to do so far more profoundly in the future, both in terms of the tasks presented to the practitioner, and in the conception of man and the tools that become available to influence his behavior. The increasing life span already made possible by biological advances has, for instance, confronted psychological research and practice with new problems of understanding and alleviating the loss of social role, the psychological stresses, and mental and physical impairments accompanying old age. The field of mental retardation offers a prime example of increasing challenges because children who previously would have died now survive with severe impairment, at the same time as biochemical and genetic discoveries permit prevention or control of the effects of other processes usually leading to retardation. In the future, possibilities of genetic control, chemical manipulation of fine nuances of affective-cognitive experience, discovery of neuro-physiological processes isomorphic with cognitive processes and subjective experiences, and a host of other developments will present psychology with unsuspected insights into the nature of man, and unsuspected new human problems with which to cope (Murphy, 1969).

Similarly, development of new fields, such as social ecology and social systems analysis, points to the increasing relevance, indeed, dependence of psychological theory and practice on other social sciences. At present this trend is shown, for instance, by the attention given to therapeutic methods that achieve individual change by intervention in some supraindividual social unit—whether a marital pair, family, ward, institution, or community—and by rapidly expanding utilization of many different group approaches for therapeutic change or personal enrichment. Hopefully, advances in sociological and social psychological concepts and methods will keep pace with the trend toward social and institutional definitions of and interventions in problematic behavior. The applied social psychologist, broadly trained in administration, community organization, institution of change, and allied areas, may well replace to a great extent the individually oriented clinical psychologist of today. To what extent the present substantive content of clinical psychology will contribute to community and social group interventions is uncertain. There are examples of very fruitful combinations of the two approaches. Paul (1969b), for example, concluded that a combination of milieu and learning treatments of chronic hospital patients offers the greatest promise of reducing the size of this "hard-core" group. If the biological and social sciences continue to present new types of tasks to the clinician, as well as new tools for achieving solutions, the dilemma of whether to train specialists or generalists will be exacerbated. Paul's suggestion implies that the student would need to be trained in learning theory and behavior therapy, as well as in social system theory and analysis, administration, and so forth.

Another trend that is certain to continue in its influence on clinical psychology is the increasing rapidity with which changed perceptions of self, human nature, and society are brought about by large scale forces, such as urbanization, education, technology, population growth, and exploration of the physical and biological world. Albee (1967) has noted the effects on symptomatology and therapy of social-cultural changes in the recent past:

"An examination of the history of psychoanalysis shows that a dramatic change in the kinds of cases seeking professional help emphasizes the cultural rather than biological origins of emotional disorder . . . . Psychoanalytic theory was in large part derived from clinical experience with persons living in Victorian Vienna. Turn-of-the-century Vienna was an inner-directed culture . . . .

"In an inner-directed, urbanizing society the prevailing requirement for individually mobile, upwardly striving people is an individual conscience for each individual. Strict repression of sexuality in the middle class is necessary until education is completed, or the achievement of a sufficient measure of financial success permits the financial burden of marriage and family. Children are taught to repress and control strong but unacceptable urges. Such delay of gratification must be individually controlled, whereas in earlier, tradition-directed societies the stable small community itself provided external control for a population which lived and died within the hills of home.

"This inner-directed pattern was particularly characteristic of the middle-class *nouveau riche,* from which hysterial group were drawn the conflicted neurotics who represented psychoanalysis's first subjects" (Albee, 1967, p. 71).

What kind of people will the psychologist face in three or four decades? Imagine people far more crowded together in homogeneous urban environments, working far less and served at home and in clinic or hospital by automated devices, increasingly secularized and educated, facing new conceptions of the universe as science expands and deepens its discoveries, with the means for far more deliberately controlling their own behavior, and with freedom to explore new behaviors and experiences formerly banned.

It is almost impossible to anticipate the skills and knowledge needed by the clinician, to guess what services he will be called upon to provide in the year 2000. Yet graduate training will have to evolve, and not so slowly at that, in new directions and with sufficient flexibility to provide clinicians who can adapt to and exploit these changes without having had explicit training for them. This outlook implies that we cannot train students in particular content areas for tackling specific problems or social conditions of the future. We can only train educated generalists who will be able to apply new knowledge and skills to new problems, and to use new research methods to evaluate and improve their efforts.

Technicians and Nonprofessionals as Therapeutic Agents

As Guerney (1969) has pointed out, inadequate professional manpower to provide mental health services has been a fact for decades; hence, it alone cannot explain the present growth of programs to develop nonprofessional therapeutic agents. Recent social action movements and concern with poverty and racial discrimination have undoubtedly added significantly to recognition of unmet needs and created a feeling of urgency about inventing ways to meet them. Guerney points to a new optimistic belief that something can be done about manpower shortages and about behavioral problems as the key element in producing ferment in mental health practices and personnel utilization. As he puts it:

"There is a feeling that innovations may be at hand which may be able to meet the need. For one thing, the mental health field, at this point in its development, already has a record of some success in attempting to increase its therapeutic effectiveness and to make more efficient use of its personnel . . . .

"There are other developments which also seem to have paved the way for a higher level of public participation in the psychotherapeutic and rehabilitative processes. These have to do with . . . the question of whether, even in individual psychotherapy, it was necessary to have an intellectual-emotional understanding of the genesis of one's problems in order to overcome them. The view that this was necessary came from the psychoanalytic tradition. As long as this assumption prevailed, truly significant expansion of psychotherapeutic effectiveness via the inclusion of large segments of the population in the rehabilitative effort remained blocked . . . . More recently, and most significantly, the views of Rogers and of Skinner (foremost among several learning theorists) helped the therapist to break out of his self-imposed handicap of demanding near-omnipotence of himself. They did so by offering alternative approaches, which were mainly *ahistorical*.

"Neither of their approaches requires a therapist to play Virgil for the patient. The techniques which adherents of their views employ, while they call for personal qualities certainly not found in everyone, do not by any means call for the very special attributes and training of therapists following a psychoanalytic model. Both of these more recent approaches do require a reasonably adequate intellect, patience, interpersonal sensitivity, self-control, and a strong motivation to help others. These qualities alone are not sufficient for a person to become a professional person or a scientist. But given an individual with these qualities, or even the potential for developing these qualities, it is possible for a follower of Rogers or of Skinner to consider training him, in a reasonable period of time, to begin helping others with their problems of psychosocial adjustment" (Guerney, 1969, pp. 1–3).

The extent and speed with which the use of nonprofessional agents is progressing is exemplified by Bloom's (1969) description of a set of innovative community-oriented mental health services. There was no task carried out by professionals that was not also accomplished, and with apparently equal success, by untrained nonprofessionals. Although extensive research evidence is lacking, a number of studies support Bloom's observations of the effectiveness of nonprofessional therapeutic agents. There is the demonstration by Rioch, Elkes, Flint, Usdansky, Newman, and Silber (1963) that mature and carefully selected housewives can, by intensive training, be turned into effective individual psychotherapists. Poser (1966) has shown that undergraduate students with no training or experience achieved results as good or better than did professional therapists in group therapy with hospitalized chronic schizophrenics. Stollak (1967) found significant changes in both children's and therapists' behaviors when volunteer college students were trained over ten weeks to conduct play therapy. These and other innovators in the use of nonprofessional therapists concur with Rioch (1966):

"More important even than saving of traditional professional time, these new workers have a double advantage. They bring fresh points of view, flexible attitudes, and sometimes new methods into the field. They also solve their problems in helping to solve the problems of others. They become constructive, better integrated citizens themselves, which is the most important thing of all, for in doing so they add to the community's pool of good will, rather than to its pool of discontent and suspicion" (p. 291).

Rioch's comments probably apply even more to some of the innovative community-service roles being developed with indigenous workers than they do to nonprofessionals in traditional psychotherapeutic roles. According to Riessman (1967), some 150,000 nonprofessional positions have been established in the United States by new social action legislation. Although many of these positions do not involve literally the roles of therapeutic agents, the majority do entail some social-personal interventions relevant to community mental health in the broadest sense. The delivery of advice, support, or training has its beneficial effects on the agent as well as the recipient. Riessman, like Rioch, emphasizes what he terms "the helper principle"—the therapeutic benefits accruing to the giver as well as to the receiver of help (Riessman, 1965). The problems in making this principle work are mostly those of proper selection and training of helpers, and providing them with supervision and opportunities for advancement.

When the many aides and other nonprofessional care-giving workers in mental hospitals are added to those in community settings, the total of nonprofessionals serving clients with behavioral problems is estimated to be over half a million. Although even in his traditional role the hospital aide has enormous impact on the patient, Ellsworth (1968) and others have demonstrated that when the aide's role is deliberately altered and enhanced, he is more effective in rehabilitating precisely those chronic patients whom the trained professional has been unable to help. Ellsworth's experimental program resulted in marked patient improvement, which remained significantly greater in comparison to control groups at a six-year follow-up.

The changes in professional models, training goals, and personnel utilization that we have sketched affect and are affected in turn, by the growth of the behavior therapies. In closing this section, it is appropriate to review some of these interactive effects.

Training Implications of the Behavior Therapy Model

The behavior therapies, initiated during a period of ferment in graduate education in psychology, from the first have included concern with the training of practitioners (see, for example, Krasner, 1965b; Ullmann, 1967b). The behavioristic frame of reference, as it is translated into a philosophy of training, also has implications for the issues within mental health training in general (see Figure 11-1). The practice of behavior therapy as it has been described in this text involves a unique combination of clinical finesse and broad acquaintance with the theories and techniques of experimental psychology. Behavior therapy technology can be carried out by technicians, but formulation of a strategy of treatment requires clinical and psychological expertise. New solutions to clinical problems demand both depth and breadth in psychological science. Thus training for behavior therapy represents a third choice in place of Frederick's dichotomy of general versus specific training. Behavior therapy requires little training in traditional skills, such as diagnostic testing, but it does require clinical competence in working with patients combined with an extensive background in the basic science of psychology.

The behavior therapy model of the clinical psychologist differs from the Boulder model primarily in its advocacy of intimate integration of clinical and research wisdom into one role and one set of activities. The Boulder model called for competence in both but treated them as two separate, though concurrent, functions.

Similar to the Boulder model, the behavior therapy model frequently implies trying to have the best of both worlds, not only with regard to generalist versus specialist training, but with regard to the other dichotomies presented in Figure 11-1 as well. The behavior therapist clearly requires thorough academic grounding in substantive areas, gained in the University curriculum. But only by combining this knowledge with simultaneous field experience in extrapolating techniques and principles to individual clinical problems can he test their relevance and develop conceptualizations and skills relevant to their application. On two of the dimensions in Figure 11-1, the behavior therapist represents a strong stand. A research background is essential not only for appropriate application of laboratory-based techniques but also to fit the empirical stance of the approach. Continuous monitoring of treatment effects by means of quantitative data is so much a part of the process of treating individual cases that an experimentalist point of view seems inherent in the role of behavior therapist. The behavior therapist requires training in the active and responsible role of a practitioner, as well. In these respects, the model of the clinician toward which training is directed is traditionalist, but, in the case of behavior therapy, is strengthened by the additional requirements for general psychological knowledge and experimental sophistication.

Its model of the practitioner defines much of the content demanded for training behavior therapists. Aspects of the behavioral model itself have further implications for the content of training. A behavioral model that views all behavior, including the targets of treatment, as the product of the same fundamental learning and biological processes focuses attention in training not on psychopathology, then, or on diagnostic tests, but on functional analysis of complex patterns of responses. A trainee in behavior therapy therefore must have a nonjudgmental view of his clients:

"The first thing a behavior therapy trainee then must learn is a new view of people. This means that the target behavior is a normal, appropriate, reasonable outcome of past and continuing experience. This is a very therapeutic thing in and of itself. It leads the behavior therapist to address his client as a normal individual and one to be respected for the strengths he manifests in the majority of his activities. Such strengths are not defenses or reaction formations. The person's difficulties are not the outgrowth of his totally distorted psyche and are not the result of a compromise between intrapsychic conflicts. The person is a unique person and not a label or a diagnostic categorization . . . . If people still want abstractions and formulations of abnormality, all human behavior, especially normal acts, become adequate models. For example, I think that anyone who can explain how a college girl comes to emit such biologically implausible behavior as maintaining her virginity, or who can explain how a decent college boy comes to drop jellied gas on civilians has a perfect model for such utterly sick behaviors as sitting on a chair staring at a wall, failure of a New Yorker to assert himself, or that ultimate of vile behavior, drinking too much at an APA convention. Looking at behavior, truly there is nothing as far out as a square and nothing as bizarre as a rule abiding mid twentieth century American" (Ullmann, 1967b, pp. 3–4).

As Ullmann (1967b) also points out, the trainee in behavior therapy is taught to focus on *what* rather than *why:* what responses under what circumstances occur with what undesired effects, replaceable with what other behaviors, and so forth. Learning to formulate useful *what* questions is a crucial task for the trainee.

The nature of behavioral techniques and formulations has implications for the types of satisfaction that a trainee learns to derive from his work. For any therapist, personal rewards may include the one-to-one close relationship with the patient, the power to control and influence another person's life, the understanding of the patient's personality, or the patient's improvement. For the behavior therapist, a major reinforcer maintaining his professional efforts must be the observation of changes in the patient's behavior and not the satisfaction derived from formulating an elegant theoretical *post hoc* explanation of the patient's development.

With regard to what types of personnel are to be trained as therapeutic agents, the behavior therapies complement current efforts to make more effective use of nonprofessionals. As was described in Chapter 6, not only hospital aides and other technicians, but teachers, parents, spouses, peers, and even a patient's young children have been trained to affect changes in a patient's behavior. Often this is accomplished without direct intervention but only by consultation with the behavior therapist. This is possible because the goals, specific techniques, and vocabulary of behavior therapy are fairly explicitly stated and readily taught. The use of surrogate therapists for intervention in the patient's natural environment is implicit in the orientation of behavior therapy. Therapeutic agents who are a natural part of the patient's environment can enhance immediate effects, assure the maintenance of change, and provide generalization of newly acquired behaviors. Since the therapeutic agent is often part and parcel of the problem behavior or problematic system of behavioral interaction, as when family members reinforce each other's undesirable behavior, intervention by the people who are actually on the spot involves Riessman's "helper" principle in a very direct way. By its very nature, behavior therapy should continue to expand in the use of nonprofessional intervention agents, complementing and enlarging the movement in this direction in mental health activities.

Finally, several attributes of behavior therapy fit well the more general social-cultural changes which are influencing clinical practices. For example, technological innovations can be easily incorporated into many aspects of behavior-oriented treatment. We have seen a number of instances in earlier chapters, such as automated devices for desensitization (Lang, 1968), mechanical dispensing of reinforcers in the classroom (Patterson, 1965a), and automatic recording of response frequency for desired and undesired behaviors (Lovaas, Freitag, Gold, and Kassorla, 1965). Emphasis on pragmatic results instead of on hypothetical mediating constructs fits naturally with the goal-oriented, intervention-minded programs of social welfare, which currently are tackling problems of delinquency, school dropouts, and underemployment. Similarly, the large scale social engineering potentials of behavior therapy complement the direction of mental health programs toward community definitions of and interventions in problematic behaviors. There is currently renewed general interest in outcome research and in investigations of the mechanisms producing therapeutic success. Behavior therapy not only shares in this empirically-minded approach, but its advocates have been among the initiators in reinstituting evaluation research (see, for example, Eysenck, 1965a; Paul, 1966).

GENERAL ISSUES IN LEARNING PARADIGMS

We have touched upon a number of limitations in the various learning paradigms that are the foundations of the behavior therapies. It seems useful, in a closing section, to provide a brief integration of some of the gaps in knowledge, definitional problems, and theoretical difficulties that challenge behavior theory in a more general way. A review of several limitations of behavior theory as a model for clinical practice will lead us to related recent criticisms of S–R psychology. Several specific areas of practical or conceptual difficulty will also be briefly described.

Criticisms of Behavior Therapy As Applied Learning Principles

A frequent objection to descriptions of the nature of behavior therapy has been that behavior therapies do not, in fact, embody application of scientific principles but simply assume the scientific mantle by incorrect use of laboratory terminology to describe what are in fact pragmatic *ad hoc* procedures (Breger and McGaugh, 1965; Simkins, 1966). This criticism has been stated a number of ways:

". . . there are discernible in the behavior modification literature certain tendencies to go further than is warranted either by data or by logic" (Davison, 1967, p. 1).

". . . once we have established our functional relationships, then the . . . applicationist will be in a position to know beforehand what he must do to accelerate or decelerate a given behavior. Until such functions are established, psychotherapy, behavior therapy, psychoanalysis, or any other attempts to modify behavior will depend upon the individual 'ingenuity' or idiosyncracies of the therapist, and not on the application of scientific principles. Viewed in this perspective, the modification of behavior still retains its status as an art" (Simkins, 1967, p. 13).

This argument, as in Simkins' case, may be based on the belief that learning laboratory research has not yet established generalizable and reliable functional relationships at a level warranting the label "theory" or "principle." Others, like Davison, accept the availability of useful generalizations about acquisition and maintenance of behavior but caution behavior therapists to be circumspect in their language, claims, and logical inferences. Behavior therapy cannot be treated as an accomplished technology. Instead, it is a growing and changing, temporarily expedient use of laboratory derived methods, bolstered by other resources from the therapist's experience. Published reports and case conferences offer many examples of claims of therapeutic success as a function of a specific operation in the absence of good evidence of a clear cause-and-effect relationship. Loose and ambiguous use of terms such as reinforcement, often in a circular fashion or in conjunction with variables from quite inappropriately used paradigms of behavior change, are frequent. Inferences about the etiology of behavior from knowledge of the variables affecting the present response represent still another logical error often encountered.

However, these flaws lie mostly in the practical operations or speech and thinking habits of some behavior therapist-researchers, not in the model itself. In all therapeutic endeavors, a clinician's aspirations and his hypotheses about present operations outstrip what is available as established knowledge ready to be applied. The danger to clinical practice lies in not recognizing the tentativeness of clinical formulations, in failing to provide controls for testing the original hypotheses, and in attributing success to various mechanisms in the absence of a design for measuring their effects. The fact that application exceeds well-established experimental bases is not in itself objectionable when its pragmatic exploratory nature is explicit.

Problems in Extrapolation from Animal Research

Questions about the adequacy of learning models as paradigms for treatment often relate less to the substantive assertions of the models than to their structural applicability to complex naturalistic human behavior. For example, can a behavioristic model adequately explain the development of language and thinking, or the correlations of behavior disturbances in schizophrenics? In its simplest form, this objection is based on the fact that most of the learning principles upon which behavior therapy models draw are the products of animal laboratory research. The white rat and the highly constrained laboratory environment are of questionable value as analogues for clinical treatment settings, much less for the patient in his complex natural environment. Most basic animal experiments have relied upon food, water, and shock as controlling incentives. They have measured simple discrete motor responses, such as lever presses or leg flexion, while organismic factors and past history have been carefully controlled. Social processes of a nature and complexity that would provide better justification for analogic extrapolation to human problems have rarely been studied at the animal level. A number of interesting beginnings have been made in this direction, however. Several of these studies were mentioned in earlier chapters, for example, Azrin's (1964) work on aggression, Solomon's on avoidance learning (Solomon and Wynne, 1953; Solomon and Brush, 1956), and studies of imitation and coaction in animals (Simmel, Hoppe, and Milton, 1968). Although intriguing in their approach, these studies have yet to demonstrate their relevance to human communities. Transmission of behavior and culture from one generation to the next is the hallmark of man, the characteristic that distinguishes him from infrahumans. Direct study of crucial problems through experiments with animals is impossible when this unique characteristic is involved. Despite all efforts at constructing realistic analogues, some human problems cannot be studied in the white rat. Laboratory animals are not good subjects for study of the "generation gap," or the clash of new with traditional cultural mores, or acquisition of moral behavior, or attitude change, and so forth. The existence of man's verbal and symbolic functions raises even greater obstacles to extrapolating from animal research to human behavior than does his social-cultural nature. Implications of verbal processes for the behavior therapies were discussed in Chapter 8.

Given all of the limitations of animal, and even of human laboratory research as a replication of naturalistic complex human behavior, the adequacy of such studies as direct empirical foundations for any therapy may be questioned. Nevertheless, it may be argued that simple principles and procedures have been demonstrated to be sufficient to predict, control, and explain large and significant proportions of human behavior and that, as long as research continues to provide useful generalizations in this sense, its asserted "oversimplicity" is a trivial issue. General principles in any model are those that can be demonstrated at any level and that yield guidelines for action in different species or levels of complexity. Principles dealing with processes such as osmosis in biology or reinforcement in learning psychology, have relevance to rats and men alike. Rat sociology is nonexistent, however. Thus animal experimentation as the major basis for general behavior theory must be a temporary expedient. The amount and subtlety of human research in behavior acquisition and modification is rapidly increasing, promising a much more sophisticated and inclusive behavioristic basis for therapy models in the future. In the preceding chapters many human studies were cited that are compatible with a behavioristic viewpoint and that have immediate implications for behavior therapy. These range from studies of relationships between verbal, behavioral, and physiological indices of anxiety (Lang, 1968), to work on verbal labels, physiology, and context as variables controlling emotional states (Schachter, 1964a), to studies of self-regulation (Kanfer, 1967b), to research on social learning and complex social interactions as these affect behavior acquisition and change (see, for example, Bandura and Walters, 1963; Patterson, 1969). Ultimately, human research should permit (1) a more direct test of the behavioral model as it has developed in the animal laboratory; (2) greater understanding and control over verbal and social variables within the behavioristic model; and (3) an expansion of the model to include parameters unique to humans.

Generality of Behavior Change

Whether obtained behavior changes prove to be durable and widespread in a patient's daily life is a crucial issue for all therapies. Behavior theory may be criticized as unable to provide any clear set of parameters that a therapist may assess or manipulate in order to predict or insure that therapeutic benefits are lasting and occur in all of the relevant natural environments of the patient's life. No single paradigm within behavior theory is adequate for this purpose. The behavior therapy model therefore has recourse to a number of separate, less encompassing principles from which to derive techniques enhancing durability and generality.

Generalization is often called upon as the most widely applicable set of principles, but traditional laboratory handling of stimulus and response generalization cannot be transferred directly to the therapy situation. Most research on generalization in the laboratory has involved simple, measureable continua of physical stimuli, motor responses, and powerful incentives (for example, frequency of a tone, running speed, hunger and thirst) that are not characteristic of the complex stimulus contexts of daily life or the clinical setting. Both the relevance of functional relationships discovered in the laboratory and their use in constructing therapeutic strategies are at present unsupported by more naturalistic research on generalization. Even in the animal laboratory, dimensions along which generalization can be measured are found only for the simplest and most concrete stimuli. In humans, mediation along unknown and unsuspected similarity dimensions, differing from individual to individual, hamper or facilitate transfer of therapeutic effects to everyday life. As one illustration, it is not uncommon for a patient to tell his therapist that some particular experience reminded him of a recent therapy session and that he drew upon recall of the session to act in new ways. Or because he sees it as "less artificial", a real-life stimulus may elicit a phobic response that had been successfully desensitized in therapy.

In view of the conceptual and practical problems in measuring similarity of stimuli within complex naturalistic settings, generalization is likely to remain an inadequate model for predicting therapeutic effects. Critics who charge that behavior therapists use the term *generalization* in "nonscientific" ways are therefore quite correct, if they mean that the laboratory operations defining generalization experiments are not characteristic of therapy research or practice. The therapist can only be crudely guided by extrapolation from laboratory findings. Nevertheless, he can attempt to take into account apparent functional similarities and differences between clinical and life situations, or between the contexts in which a patient shows deviant or adequate behaviors.

Some writers characterize behavior therapy, and indeed, all therapies, as discrimination training. In their view, a response is abnormal when it is under inadequate or inappropriate stimulus control. Therapy would then consist of building or reversing discriminations (Greenspoon, 1961). To deal with deficient stimulus discrimination as a target behavior, the therapist may extend stimulus control by artificial means (see Chapter 8). Some contrived stimulus may be provided for the patient to serve as a cue for desirable behaviors. An obese person may be given a distinctively colored table cloth and trained to eat only in its presence, for example. Stimulus generalization may, on the other hand, be enhanced by therapeutic instructions or practice, as when a patient role plays self-assertion with a number of different types of persons in order to increase the range of social stimuli eliciting this behavior.

Response generalization is the goal when one or several responses are treated with the expectation that a large class of related behaviors will change in similar ways. A shy young man may be trained in the social skills of asking for a date in the college coffee house, with the expectation that he will also improve in his skill at phoning for a date, chatting before class, and so forth.

Skepticism has often been voiced about whether programming of behaviors, no matter how complex and subtle, can ever be resilient enough to equip a patient to cope with the onslaught of environmental changes. The sources, nature, and frequency of reinforcement contingencies and of discriminative cues change. In the changing human social environment new behaviors may be called for and old ones become inappropriate. Treatment always necessitates the establishment of some artificial relationships, even if only at its start. If therapy is not conducted in the natural environment, but on a token ward of a hospital, for instance, the therapist must anticipate the behaviors and controlling stimuli that will be required for maintenance of a desirable repertoire when the patient leaves the ward. The hospital environment has to simulate circumstances and to provide these conditions. The problem is lesser but not absent when treatment occurs in the natural environment. A therapeutic intervention carried out in the home may provide parents with very adequate means of altering a child's problematic behavior. But the typical behaviors occurring in the home, and the stimuli controlling them, change as the child matures and as other family events, such as birth of a sibling, create a different set of environmental factors. To what extent can a therapeutic regimen be expected to equip any patient for future changes in his life-environment?

Several points seem pertinent here. Therapeutic efforts vary by design in the extent to which they are intended to enable patients to cope with environmental variations. At one extreme, token cultures for severely impaired institutionalized patients may anticipate making a patient's life more satisfying, independent, and dignified, and less burdensome to others while he remains permanently in the same institutional environment. Or a program such as Fairweather's (1967) may aim at moving patients out of an institution and into a new environment—one that is kept relatively constant and stable, with the level of demand on the patient controlled as much as possible. Toward the other end of the continuum, parents may be taught general principles of behavior control that can be applied to different targets as their child matures; or a patient may learn new modes of self-regulation that he applies in a variety of new contexts. The behavioral model has potentials for flexibility as well as for building up specific and highly discriminated responses. A patient's tolerance for low reinforcement schedules for a particular response can be increased so that he can cope with the limited natural payoffs of his world; or a patient can be taught to apply a behavioral principle to a large variety of problematic situations—for example, to use relaxation or desensitization techniques to cope with any anxiety-arousing situation. When a therapeutic strategy provides general rules for many different problems the clinician does not attempt to build in specific behaviors that might prove inappropriate in the future. However, in the final analysis, the behavior therapist does not expect to make a patient resistant to all stresses or to equip him competently to handle all new circumstances. Instead, the therapist deals with current complaints, achieving as lasting and general a solution to them as is possible.

Several tactics have been described in the preceding chapters with which behavior therapists try to accomplish therapeutic benefits. In order to attain viability of a newly established behavior pattern in the face of complex changes one may need to increase the probability of (1) a class of behaviors, shaped in one setting, occurring in another setting; (2) an entire class of related responses increasing in frequency when only several members of that class are strengthened in therapy; or (3) extinction or punishment of a behavior in one setting resulting in decreased performance of the behavior in many other settings.

One approach, relevant to stimulus generalization, has been to conduct treatment precedures in as many different contexts as possible. For example, aversive conditioning may be carried out with different stimuli, in varied settings, by several therapists. The extreme of this approach is illustrated by the use of relevant social agents in the changing natural environment, such as when parents are taught to shape new behaviors in their child in the home. Since they can intervene on many occasions, using alternative cues and reinforcers, and acting on many members of a single response class, transfer of effects is built into the therapy operations. Discovery of what Baer and Wolf (1967) term "entry behaviors" direct transfer of treatment effects, however. A small response class is (see Chapter 6) implies that less effort need be expended toward gaining identified that, when altered, results in reinforcement by the natural environment of many other desired behaviors as well.

By such devices, the behavior therapist copes pragmatically with several issues to which research may provide more reliable answers in the long run. One of these is the above-mentioned inability to specify with confidence, much less measure, naturalistic dimensions of stimuli or responses along which generalization might be predicted and enhanced. Still to be understood, and hence better utilized, are those surprising circumstances in which the effects of aversive conditioning or punishment are far more generally effective than a therapist has any right to hope. Rachman and Teasdale (1969), among others, have pointed out that what is surprising about the aversion paradigm is not that it is not more effective, but that it works at all in affecting many responses with a long history of reinforcement in a variety of environments seemingly quite unlike the treatment setting. Presumably some symbolic responses or other mediating mechanisms are responsible. How to describe and make more effective use of these is a key issue for behavior therapy. Mediation of behavior change by self-regulatory responses, discussed in an earlier chapter, has as one of its greatest assets the potential for providing generality of effect, which otherwise is difficult to engineer in the treatment program.

Deficiencies in Behavior Theories

The goal of any science is the construction of a model that best fits the natural phenomena. Psychological models, including those of learning, are as yet far from ingenious enough to fit the complexity of natural behaviors outside of the highly controlled laboratory experiment. The behavior therapist cannot draw on a comprehensive theory of human learning for his work. At best he has available a methodology rooted in scientific tenets and a rather small set of substantive principles, which he applies by extrapolation or analogy. In this sense, behavior therapy is a pragmatic application of laboratory technology and empirical generalizations. It does not constitute, as it is sometimes described, the scientific application of laws of learning. The preceding chapters enumerate many instances in which a conceptually "pure" model becomes impure when applied to learning processes other than those encountered in the defining experiments, for example, in applying the classical conditioning model to aversive therapies. Basic operations and variables of a model, such as "reinforcement" as an operation, or "reinforcer" as a stimulus event, are difficult to define in the real world. Available principles and their underlying empirical data have not yet been fitted into a framework for predicting in advance what particular methods will be effective for various problematic behaviors and particular people.

Critiques of behavior therapy often focus on its S–R theory roots (see, for example, Breger and McGaugh, 1965), but the deficiencies that we are addressing here characterize learning theories in general. Thus Breger and McGaugh espouse, in place of the behavioral model as a foundation for therapy, an information-processing model of learning based on that of Miller, Galanter, and Pribram (1960). However, although this cognitive view has the advantage of focusing on uniquely human and subjective processes, and is asserted by Breger and McGaugh to be the contemporary replacement for "outmoded" behavorial learning principles, it is not sufficiently developed to provide a schema for organizing clinical data, and is far less able to provide concrete techniques or tactics. In fact, in contrast to the data and generalizations reviewed in this text, a therapist would have not even these few solid anchor points if he were to embark on therapy with the Breger and McGaugh model. Breger and McGaugh put the potential contribution of the cognitive model in these terms:

"The view of learning we have outlined does not supply a set of ready-made answers to clinical problems that can be applied from the laboratory, but it indicates what sort of questions will have to be answered to achieve a meaningful learning conceptualization of neurosis and symptoms. Questions such as 'What are the conditions under which strategies are acquired or developed?' stress the fact that these conditions may be quite different from the final observed behavior. That is to say, a particular symptom is not necessarily acquired because of some learning experience in which its stimulus components were associated with pain or fear-producing stimuli. Rather, a symptom may function as an equipotential response, mediated by a central strategy acquired under different circumstances" (Breger and McGaugh, 1965, p. 356).

This statement seemingly implies that behavior therapists hold beliefs that in fact they do not hold, for example, that observed problematic behaviors are equivalent to or isomorphic with the earlier conditions under which they were developed, or that all symptoms are determined by associations of responses with pain or anxiety. More importantly Breger and McGaugh's statements clarify that the main contender against behavioral learning models is not at all ready—conceptually or pragmatically—to contribute directly to any therapeutic formulations or technologies. As one rejoinder put it, in discussing Breger and McGaugh's reformulation of therapy in terms of a cognitive model of learning:

"Their reformulation provided only a different manner of speaking—one characterized more by its resemblance to the language of common sense than by its promise of greater precision. They provided no evidence that their "reformulation" . . . is superior to the models they criticize. Instead, they apparently argued . . . that a cognitive theory (or one employing central, mediating constructs) must necessarily be superior to a conceptual system that remains more closely linked to the language of observation" (Wiest, 1967, p. 215).

The exchange of criticism and rejoinder (see, for example, Rachman and Eysenck, 1966) between advocates of behavioral and other models of learning has clarified the claims and current positions of both groups, as well as some of the deficiencies of any current learning theory to handle the subtle complexities of clinical cases. Kendler (1968) has argued:

"Perhaps, if one really desires to be pessimistic, consensus will never be achieved in psychology because of the intrinsically different kinds of phenomena that interest those who identify themselves as psychologists. Although we aspire some day to integrate the facts of behavior, phenomenal experience, and physiology, no a priori reason exists to insure our success. For the present our attention should be focused on the lack of any clearcut frame of reference to judge the issues which confront us" (pp. 391–392).

The gist of these arguments is, then, that no adequate model of learning is available, even within the more limited goals that a given model sets for itself; that at present neither argument nor evidence permit choice between competing models; that the debates between paradigm adherents tend to be fruitless of solutions. However, as the accumulation of research in this book demonstrates, the behavior-oriented model has provided both hypotheses and data to permit continuing tests of its theoretical framework. Frontier areas of research suggest that expansion, instead of abandonment, of the model may remedy its shortcomings.

Some critics, as the earlier quotation from Simkins (1967) illustrated, assert that there is "no such thing as modern learning theory" and that generalizations at a level warranting the title of "laws" or "principles" are not yet available for prediction and manipulation of human behavior.

Yet as the preceding chapters have demonstrated, a large number of empirically supported generalizations can be marshaled, whether under the label of "laws" or "principles" or not, that have utility in behavioral prediction and control. Their weakness lies in a relative lack of complexity, that is, in an inability to define analytically and make predictions for situations in which multiple influences are operating simultaneously on a complex set of behaviors.

Further Criticisms of S–R Theory

According to Kendler (1965, 1968), both the difficulties faced by S–R models and criticisms of them can contribute more to conceptual and investigative progress if they are clearly addressed to particular components. Kendler believes that there is no general *S–R theory*. Instead, he proposes four independent components of the S–R model: (1) a technical language system; (2) a methodological orientation that is physicalistic, operational, and experimental but by no means any longer bound to logical positivism or pure operationism; (3) a pretheoretical model; and (4) a group of competing theories.

S–R As A Language. Criticism of S–R language as a system for describing behavioral events is frequently and easily made. In Chapter 2 and again in later chapters, we noted some of the problems in specifying and delimiting referents of terms such as "stimulus," "response," or "reinforcement." Some criticisms are more suited to an earlier era of reflexology than to current behavioral usage, and theoretically and empirically meaningful investigations and applications have readily been conducted with the present language system. Since, as Kendler (1968) notes, stimulus-response language in itself neither excludes other concepts for describing behavior nor imposes empirical relationships, it should be able to adapt flexibly to new information and thereby maintain its pragmatic utility. The preceding chapters have underscored the need for clarification of the structure of naturally occurring behaviors in the natural environment. The explanatory scope and clinical utility of the behavioral model will be greatly enhanced when we can group behaviors and stimuli into classes on the basis of their actual *functional* equivalence. As therapeutic interventions expand into the natural environment and deal with spontaneously occurring social interactions, the need will increase for more information about natural, functional units of behavior.

S–R as Methodology. Criticisms of the methodological orientation of S–R paradigms have been partially discussed in the sections in this chapter on issues of control and extrapolation to humans from animal laboratory research, and in earlier presentations (see Chapters 1 and 6) of attacks by humanistic psychologists on the operational, physicalistic stance of behavior therapy. As Wiest (1967) has indicated, criticisms of behavioristic methodology often seem to be directed at structures (for instance, hypothetico-deductive system, reductionism) no longer generally adhered to by behavioral investigators (see, for example, Koch, 1964). From the viewpoint of the behavior therapist, the development of more sophisticated methods for the following purposes would be most helpful: (1) to integrate idiographic and nomothetic approaches; (2) to isolate behavioral effects in the natural environment; (3) to construct analogues or miniature models of therapeutic interventions, including social engineering; and (4) to deal with subjective processes, such as self-regulation or vicarious reinforcement. These represent procedural developments instead of a change in methodological orientation.

S–R as a Pretheoretical Model. It is as a pretheoretical model that behavior therapy has been drawn almost exclusively from S–R associationism. Principles or empirical generalizations forming the substantive results of research within the model comprise the content and technology of behavior therapy. Models for describing the nature of problematic behaviors, their acquisition, maintenance, and change, are based on the behavioral S–R system. The S-O-R-K-C behavioral formula we have used as our model includes explicit recognition of organismic variables that, however, have received less attention and are in need of greater integration with the other components. The principal limitation of the behavioral model has been in handling subjective events, just as S–R language and methodology have tended to lead to an underemphasis of investigation in this area. By the clinical demands placed on them, behavior therapies have highlighted the lack of behavioral research in the areas of complex intraindividual functioning. Many of the psychological processes previously covered under the term "cognition" now seem more amenable to analysis by behavioristic methods. Among these are the areas of self-regulation, self-reinforcement, vicarious learning, the relationship between motor control and verbal control, and the role of respondents in determining operant behaviors.

Currently, the most serious challenge to the behavioral model comes not so much from its clash with the information-processing models of learning, as from the need to account for a number of observations about verbal behavior and thinking, especially the linguist's descriptions of acquisition of grammar (see, for example, Jenkins, 1968). Bem and Bem (1968), in reviewing Lenneberg's (1967) volume on language, summarize the difficulty facing empirically oriented behaviorists in this way:

"Except in their guarded moments, the linguists do not equate their formal model with a psychological theory per se, but they do maintain that any psychological model of linguistic *performance* must necessarily incorporate their formal model of linguistic *competence,* or something very much like it. Their Nativist position will hold the fort until some learning theory can either define the syntactical relations with anything simpler than a full transformational grammar and/or show "how it got there." That day may come, but it seems unlikely that the successful theory will look much like a simple extension of any current Empiricistic notions of "what is learned" and how. When linguists assert that current behavioral theories are inadequate *in principle,* it is tempting to allude to previous formal proofs that bumble-bees could not possibly fly. The sober fact is, however, that no bumble-bee could fly if it adhered to aero-dynamic principles of flight that apply to other insects but that fail him because of his species-specific construction.

"That, in short, is the secret weapon of the linguists. And that is why Empiricists are becoming Nativists in these latter days" (Bem and Bem, 1968, p. 500).

It remains to be seen whether research and theory based on Skinner's (1957) interpretation or some alternative behavioral model can ultimately account for the facts of verbal behavior (but not for the linguist's constructs *about* verbal behavior, which a competing model need not deal with, as Wiest (1967), among others, has discussed). Meanwhile, behavioral investigations and interpretations of "cognitive" processes are progressing sufficiently to offer a model for training people to be efficient and effective thinkers. Skinner's (1968) recent book on *The Technology of Teaching* describes a number of component behaviors of thinking and a systemic approach to "teaching thinking." Neimark (1970) proposes a computer analogy that describes acquisition by children (in development sequences paralleling Piaget's stages) of "programs" for sustained attention and other components of adult problem-solving. She concludes that discouraging results thus far in training thinking may be due to inadequate analysis of the component skills or incorrect sequencing of training. Neimark's model represents the sort of rapprochement of cognitive and behavioral theories that may in the long run offer the greatest dividends for behavioral theory as well as for clinical application.

S–R as a Group of Competing Theories. Although critics often attack S–R theories as if they represented a unified stand, there are actually a number of competing theories that may differ drastically in their basic 'assumptions and variables. The behavior therapist, faced with the need to draw eclectically from whichever model best fits his pragmatic task, should be familiar with many theories in order to achieve a personal integration of available principles and establish a frame of reference for his theoretical thinking. Obstacles to such an integration are likely to lessen as continued research and conceptual advances permit the discarding of inadequate theoretical formulations (as has been the case with some concepts in Hullian theory), or integration of competing models (as, for example, in two-factor learning theory), or a more concrete integration of variables that can be shown to interact and interlock (as in the case of classical and operant conditioning of autonomic responses).

We have given only a few of the many possible criticisms not only of applications of the behavioral model but of the model per se. Given the choice of following traditional clinical theories that have little contact with the general body of psychological research, or a highly respectable theory with limited data, such as information-processing theories, the behavioral model seems to provide a better heuristic framework for clinical application and for research than any other model.

SUMMARY

This chapter, like the preceding one, has dealt with several very diverse topics, which have in common, however, a significant role as part of the professional and scientific context of behavior therapy. To introduce these topics we first sketched out how the current dramatic changes in our social and physical environment are affecting contemporary clinical practice and are pointing to certain requirements for any therapy to remain viable in the future. Included in these requirements are adaptability to changing social goals and mores, a pragmatic approach, ability to adapt to and use technology and nonprofessional manpower, and receptiveness to new theory and knowledge. In our view, behavior therapy is better suited than any other to these requirements, although it is far from a completed model.

The social change influences directing and impelling behavior therapy and mental health practices in general have equal impact on moral-ethical issues and training practices in the professions and in clinical psychology. Within behavior therapy in particular, increasing effectiveness brings increasing behavior control, with all of the dangers and benefits to the recipient and to society that control implies. Issues of invasion of privacy also impinge with particular importance on behavior therapy since its practice often requires direct observation of events usually held to be private. Similarly, current concerns about adequate safeguards when human subjects are used in research and concerns about the practice of deceiving subjects are especially relevant to research in behavior therapy since it involves direct manipulation of human behavior, often of necessity without the subject's full knowledge of what is being observed, manipulated, or expected of him. In clinical practice, on the other hand, behavior therapy has certain attributes that alleviate some of these ethical dilemmas. It is the usual case that target behaviors are openly specified and mutually decided upon, that controlling operations and behavioral observations are similarly open and defined in their purpose and nature. Indeed, the patient may often be instructed in behavioral principles and techniques and asked to share in monitoring by observing and recording his own responses.

Ferment in education in general is paralleled by controversy and change in present training practices and goals in clinical psychology. Disillusion with traditional clinical techniques and availability of new ones combine with the demands of society for more service in the interests of new goals and new client populations to produce great variability in training programs and a gradual departure from clinical psychology's traditional Boulder model of the scientist-professional. Training for the practice of behavior therapy fits the Boulder model well, since a broad background in basic psychology and research, as well as traditional clinical skills are required for the design and evaluation of new therapeutic programs. On the other hand, the technical nature of behavior therapy operations often allows nonprofessional workers to carry out many of the actual operations of treatment, both alleviating manpower problems and increasing the therapeutic effectiveness of the behaviors of caretaking personnel, such as hospital aides.

The third topic discussed briefly in this chapter involved inadequacies in the behavioral model *for* therapy and how it is actually applied *in* therapy. Criticisms of this model have come from two sides, humanistic and scientific. Despite the stereotype of behavior therapy as mechanistic and depersonalized, the flexible quality of its techniques permits it to serve the most humanistic goals. In application, the operations of therapy may be only analogues of the laboratory research from which they are derived, and the research bases are limited in so far as they rest on animal research. On the other hand, critics of the behavioral model and of the therapy based on the model as being unscientific and outmoded have no alternative model to offer that is as well founded. As our knowledge of S–R psychology and of cognitive and social processes increases, the behavioral model will certainly change. Behavior therapy is a temporarily expedient method for achieving desired changes in behavior. It requires constant revision and improvement. But for the present it can offer valuable techniques for humane goals in an open system that contains greater flexibility, verifiability, and coverage than any of the traditional schools of psychotherapy.

References

Ad hoc Committee of Harvard Medical School to Examine the Definition of Brain Death. A definition of irreversible coma. *J. Amer. Med. Assoc.,* 1968, **205,** 337–340.

Adams, H. E., & Frye, R. L. Psychotherapeutic techniques as conditioned reinforcers in a structured interview. *Psychol., Rep.,* 1964, **14,** 163–166.

Adams, J. A. *Human memory.* New York: McGraw-Hill, 1967.

Adams, J. A. Response feedback and learning. *Psychol., Bull.,* 1968, **70,** 486–504.

Aiken, E. G., & Parker, W. H. Conditioning and generalization of positive self-evaluations in a partially structured diagnostic interview. *Psychol. Rep.,* 1965, **17,** 459–464.

Albee, G. W. Needed: A conceptual breakthrough. In M. Klutch (Ed.), *Mental health manpower,* Vol. II. Sacramento: California Dept. of Mental Hygiene, June 1967.

Alexander, I. E., & Basowitz, H. Current clinical training practices: An overview. In E. L. Hoch, A. O. Ross, & C. L. Winder (Eds.), *Professional preparation of clinical psychologists.* Washington: American Psychological Association 1966.

Alfert, E. Comparison of responses to a vicarious and a direct threat. *J. Exp. Res. Pers.,* 1966, **1,** 179–186.

Allen, K. E. & Harris, F. R. Elimination of a child's excessive scratching by training the mother in reinforcement procedures. *Beh. Res. & Ther.,* 1966, **4,** 79–84.

Allen, K. E., Hart, B. M., Buell, J. S., Harris, F. R. & Wolf, M. M. Effects of social reinforcement on isolate behavior of a nursery school child. *Child Dev.,* 1964, **35,** 511–518.

American Psychiatric Association. *Diagnostic and statistical manual of mental disorders.* Washington: American Psychiatric Association, 1952.

American Psychiatric Association. *Diagnostic and statistical manual of mental disorders* (2nd ed.) (DSM-II). Washington: American Psychiatric Association, 1968.

575

American Psychological Association. Committee on Training in Clinical Psychology. Recommended graduate training program in clinical psychology. *Amer. Psychol.*, 1947, 2, 539–558.

American Psychological Association. *Ethical standards of psychologists.* Washington, D.C.: American Psychological Association, 1953.

American Psychological Association. Committee on Ethical Standards for Psychology. Ethical standards of psychologists. *Amer. Psychol.*, 1963. **18**, 56–60.

American Psychological Association. Special issue: Testing and public policy. *Amer. Psychol.*, 1965a, **20**, Whole No. 11.

American Psychological Association. Committee on the Scientific and Professional Aims of Psychology. Preliminary Report (Clark Report). *Amer. Psychol.*, 1965b, **20**, 95–100.

American Psychological Association. Testimony before House Special Subcommittee on invasion of privacy of the Committee on Government Operations. *Amer. Psychol.*, 1966a, **21**, 404–422.

American Psychological Association. Testimony before House Subcommittee on international organizations and movements of the Committee on Foreign Affairs. *Amer. Psychol.*, 1966b, **21**, 455–470.

Anant, S. S. Comment on "A follow-up of alcoholics treated by behavior therapy." *Beh. Res. & Ther.*, 1968, **6**, 133.

Annau, Z., & Kamin, L. J. The conditioned emotional response as a function of intensity of the US. *J. Comp. Physiol. Psychol.* 1961, **54**, 428–432.

Apfelbaum, B. *Dimensions of transference in psychotherapy.* Berkeley: University of California Press, 1958.

Aronfreed, J. *Conduct and conscience: The socialization of internalized control over behavior.* New York: Academic Press, 1968.

Aronfreed, J., & Reber, A. Internalized behavioral suppression and the timing of social punishment. *J. Pers. Soc. Psychol.*, 1965, **1**, 3–16.

Ashem, B., & Donner, L. Covert sensitization with alcoholics: A controlled replication. *Beh. Res. & Ther.*, 1968, **6**, 7–12.

Atthowe, J. M. Jr., & Krasner, L. The systematic application of contingent reinforcement procedures (token economy) in a large social setting: A psychiatric ward. Paper presented at American Psychological Association, Chicago, Sept. 1965.

Atthowe, J. M. Jr., & Krasner, L. A preliminary report on the application of contingent reinforcement procedures (token economy) on a "chronic" psychiatric ward. *J. Abnorm. Psychol.*, 1968, **73**, 37–43.

Ax, A. F. The physiological differentiation between fear and anger. *Psychosomatic Medicine,* 1953, **15**, 433–442.

Ayllon, T. Intensive treatment of psychotic behavior by stimulus satiation and food reinforcement. *Beh. Res. & Ther.*, 1963, **1**, 53–61.

Ayllon, T., & Azrin, N. H. Reinforcement and instructions with mental patients. *J. Exp. Anal. Beh.*, 1964, **7**, 327–331.

Ayllon, T., & Azrin, N. H. The measurement and reinforcement of behavior of psychotics. *J. Exp. Anal. Beh.*, 1965, **8**, 357–383.

Ayllon, T., & Azrin, N. H. *The token economy: A motivational system for therapy and rehabilitation.* New York: Appleton-Century-Crofts, 1968.

Ayllon, T., & Haughton, E. Control of the behavior of schizophrenic patients by food. *J. Exp. Anal. Beh.*, 1962, **5**, 343–352.

Ayllon, T., & Haughton, E. Modification of symptomatic verbal behavior of mental patients. *Beh. Res. & Ther.*, 1964, **2**, 87–97.

Ayllon, T., & Michael, J. The psychiatric nurse as a behavioral engineer. *J. Exp. Anal. Beh.*, 1959, **2**, 323–334.

Azrin, N. H. Some effects of two intermittent schedules of immediate and non-immediate punishment. *J. Psychol.* 1956, **42**, 3–21.

Azrin, N. H. Aggressive responses of paired animals. Paper presented at Symposium on Medical Aspects of Stress. Washington, D.C.: Walter Reed Institute of Research, April 1964.

Azrin, N. H., & Holz, W. C. Punishment. In W. K. Honig (Ed.), *Operant behavior: Areas of research and application.* New York: Appleton-Century-Crofts, 1966.

Azrin, N. H., Holz, W. C., & Goldiamond, I. Response bias in questionnaire reports. *J. Consult. Psychol.*, 1961, **25**, 324–326.

Azrin, N. H., Hutchinson, R. R., & Hake, D. F. Extinction-induced aggression. *J. Exp. Anal. Beh.*, 1966, **9**, 191–204.

Bachrach, A. J., Erwin, W. J., & Mohr, J. P. The control of eating behavior in an anorexic by operant conditioning techniques. In L. P. Ullmann & L. Krasner (Eds.), *Case studies in behavior modification.* New York: Holt, Rinehart & Winston, 1965.

Baer, D. M. Some remedial uses of the reinforcement contingency. In J. M. Shlien (Ed.), *Research in psychotherapy:* Vol. III. Washington, D.C.: American Psychological Association, 1968.

Baer, D. M., & Sherman, J. A. Reinforcement control of generalized imitation in young children. *J. Exp. Child Psychol.*, 1964, **1**, 37–49.

Baer, D. M., & Wolf, M. M. The entry into natural communities of reinforcement. Paper presented at American Psychological Association, Washington, D.C., September 1967.

Baer, D. M., & Wolf, M. M. The reinforcement contingency in preschool and remedial education. In R. D. Hess & R. M. Bear (Eds.), *Early education: Current theory, research, and action.* Chicago: Aldine, 1968.

Baker, B. L. Symptom treatment and symptom substitution in enuresis. *J. Abnorm. Psychol.*, 1969, **74**, 42–49.

Baldwin, J. M. *Mental development in the child and in the race.* New York: Macmillan, 1895.

Bancroft, J. H. J. Aversion therapy. Unpublished DPM dissertation, University of London, 1966.

Bancroft, J. H. J., Jones, H. G., & Pullan, B. R. A simple transducer for measuring penile erection, with comments on its use in the treatment of sexual disorders. *Beh. Res. & Ther.,* 1966, 4, 239–241.

Bancroft, J. H. J., & Marks, I. M. Electrical aversion therapy of sexual deviations. *Proc. Roy. Soc. Med.,* 1968, **61,** 796–799.

Bandler, R. J. Jr., Madaras, G. R., & Bem, D. J. Self-observation as a source of pain perception. *J. Pers. Soc. Psychol.,* 1968, **9,** 205–209.

Bandura, A. Social learning through imitation. In M. R. Jones (Ed.), *Nebraska symposium on motivation, 1962.* Lincoln: University of Nebraska Press, 1962.

Bandura, A. Influence of models' reinforcement contingencies on the acquisition of imitative responses. *J. Pers. Soc. Psychol.,* 1965a, **1,** 589–595.

Bandura, A. Vicarious processes: A case of no-trial learning. In L. Berkowitz (Ed.), *Advances in experimental social psychology.* Vol. II. New York: Academic Press, 1965b.

Bandura, A. Modeling approaches to the modification of phobic disorders. In Ruth Porter (Ed.), *CIBA Foundation Symposium on the role of learning in psychotherapy.* London: Churchill, Ltd., 1968.

Bandura, A., Blanchard, E. B., & Ritter, B. J. The relative efficacy of desensitization and modeling therapeutic approaches for inducing behavioral, affective, and attitudinal changes. Unpublished manuscript, Stanford University, 1968.

Bandura, A., Grusec, J. E., & Menlove, F. L. Observational learning as a function of symbolization and incentive set. *Child Dev.,* 1966, **37,** 499–506.

Bandura, A., Grusec, J. E., & Menlove, F. L. Vicarious extinction of avoidance behavior. *J. Pers. Soc. Psychol.,* 1967, **5,** 16–23.

Bandura, A., & Huston, A. C. Identification as a process of incidental learning. *J. Abnorm. Soc. Psychol.,* 1961, **63,** 311–318.

Bandura, A., & Kupers, C. J. Transmission of patterns of self-reinforcement through modeling. *J. Abnorm. Soc. Psychol.,* 1964, **69,** 1–9.

Bandura, A., & McDonald, F. J. The influence of social reinforcement and the behavior of models in shaping children's moral judgements. *J. Abnorm. Soc. Psychol.,* 1963, **67,** 274–281.

Bandura, A., & Menlove, F. L. Factors determining vicarious extinction of avoidance behavior through symbolic modeling. *J. Pers. Soc. Psychol.,* 1968, **8,** 99–108.

Bandura, A., & Rosenthal, T. L. Vicarious classical conditioning as a function of arousal level. *J. Pers. Soc. Psychol.,* 1966, **3,** 54–62.

Bandura, A., Ross, D., & Ross, S. A. A comparative test of the status envy, social power, and secondary reinforcement theories of identificatory learning. *J. Abnorm. Soc. Psychol.,* 1963a, **67,** 527–534.

Bandura, A., Ross, D., & Ross, S. A. Imitation of film-mediated aggressive models. *J. Abnorm. Soc. Psychol.,* 1963b, **66,** 3–11.

Bandura, A., Ross, D., & Ross, S. A. Vicarious reinforcement and imitative learning. *J. Abnorm. Soc. Psychol.*, 1963c, **67**, 601–607.

Bandura, A., & Walters, R. H. *Social learning and personality development.* New York: Holt, Rinehart and Winston, 1963.

Bandura. A., & Whalen, C. K. The influence of antecedent reinforcement and divergent modeling cures on patterns of self-reward. *J. Pers. Soc. Psychol.*, 1966, **3**, 373–382.

Barber, T. X., Calverley, D. S., Forgione, A., McPeake, J. D., Chaves, J. S., & Bowen, B. Five attempts to replicate the experimenter bias effect. *J. Consult. Clin. Psychol.*, 1969, **33**, 1–6.

Barber, T. X., & Silver, M. J. Fact, fiction, and the experimenter bias effect. *Psychol. Bull. Monogr. Suppl.*, 1968, **70**, #6 part 2, 1–62.

Barlow, D. H., Leitenberg, H., & Agras, W. S. Experimental control of sexual deviation through manipulation of the noxious scene in covert sensitization. *J. Abnorm. Psychol.*, 1969, **74**, 596–601.

Barnard, G. W., Flesher, C. K., & Steinbook, R. M. The treatment of urinary retention by aversive stimulus cessation and assertive training. *Beh. Res. Ther.*, 1966, **4**, 232–236.

Baron, A., Kaufman, A., & Rakauskas, I. Ineffectiveness of "time out" punishment in suppressing human operant behavior. *Psychon. Sci.*, 1967, **8**, 329–330.

Baron, R. M. Social reinforcement effects as a function of social reinforcement history. *Psychol. Rev.*, 1966, **73**, 527–539.

Bauer, R. A. *Social indicators,* Cambridge: M.I.T. Press, 1966.

Baum, M. Rapid extinction of an avoidance response following a period of response prevention in the avoidance apparatus. *Psychol. Rep.*, 1966, **18**, 59–64.

Beam, J. C. Serial learning and conditioning under real life stress. *J. Abnorm. Soc. Psychol.*, 1955, **51**, 543–551.

Becker, W. C., Madsen, C. H. Jr., Arnold, C. R., & Thomas, D. R. The contingent use of teacher attention and praise in reducing classroom behavior problems. Mimeograph, 1967.

Beecher, H. K. The powerful placebo. *J. Amer. Med. Assoc.*, 1955, **159**, 1602–1606.

Beecher, H. K. Consent in clinical experimentation: Myth and reality. *J. Amer. Med. Assoc.*, 1966, **195**, 34–35.

Beecroft, R. S. *Classical conditioning.* Goleta, Calif.: Psychonomic Press, 1966.

Bell, R. Q. A reinterpretation of the direction of effects in studies of socialization. *Psychol. Rev.*, 1968, **75**, 81–95.

Bem, D. J. An experimental analysis of self-persuasion. *J. Exp. Soc. Psychol.*, 1965, **1**, 199–218.

Bem, D. J. Inducing belief in false confessions. *J. Pers. Soc. Psychol.*, 1966. **3**, 707–710.

Bem, D. J. Self-perception: An alternative interpretation of cognitive dissonance phenomena. *Psychol. Rev.,* 1967, **74,** 183–200.

Bem, D. J., & Bem, S. L. Nativism revisited: A review of Eric H. Lennenberg's *Biological Foundations of Language. J. Exp. Anal. Beh.,* 1968, **11,** 497–501.

Bem, S. L. Verbal self-control: The establishment of effective self-instruction. *J. Exp. Psychol.,* 1967, **74,** 485–491.

Bennett, E. L., Diamond, M. C., Krech, D., & Rosenzweig, M. R. Chemical and anatomical plasticity of the brain. *Science,* 1964, **146,** 610–619.

Berger, S. M. Incidental learning through vicarious reinforcement. *Psych. Rep.,* 1961, **9,** 477–491.

Berger, S. M. Conditioning through vicarious instigation. *Psychol. Rev.,* 1962, **69,** 450–466.

Berger, S. M. Observer practice and learning during exposure to a model. *J. Pers. Soc. Psychol.,* 1966, **3,** 696–701.

Berger, S. M. Vicarious aspects of matched-dependent behavior. In E. C. Simmel, R. A. Hoppe, & G. A. Milton (Eds.), *Social facilitation and imitative behavior.* Boston: Allyn and Bacon, Inc., 1968.

Bergin, A. E. A technique for improving desensitization via warmth, empathy and emotional re-experiencing of hierarchy events. In R. D. Rubin, C. M. Franks & A. A. Lazarus (Eds.), *Proceedings of the Association for Advancement of the Behavioral Therapies.* New York: Academic Press, 1969.

Berkowitz, L. *Aggression: A social psychological analysis.* New York: McGraw-Hill, 1962.

Berkowitz, L. Aggressive cues in aggressive behavior and hostility catharsis. *Psychol. Rev.,* 1964, **71,** 104–122.

Berkowitz, L., & LePage, A. Weapons as aggression-eliciting stimuli. *J. Pers. Soc. Psychol.,* 1967, **7,** 202–207.

Berlyne, D. E. Arousal and reinforcement. In D. Levine (Ed.), *Nebraska symposium on motivation, 1967.* Lincoln, Nebraska: University of Nebraska Press, 1967.

Berne, E. *Games people play: The psychology of human relationships.* New York: Grove Press, 1964.

Bernstein, D. A. Modification of smoking behavior: An evaluative review. *Psychol. Bull.,* 1969, **71,** 418–440.

Berzins, J. I., Friedman, W. H., & Seidman, E. Relationship of the A-B variable to patient symptomatology and psychotherapy expectancies. *J. Abnorm. Psychol.,* 1969, **74,** 119–125.

Betz, B. J. Experiences in research in psychotherapy with schizophrenic patients. In H. H. Strupp and L. Luborsky (Eds.), *Research in psychotherapy.* Vol. 2. Washington, D.C.: American Psychological Association, 1962.

Betz, B. J. Studies of the therapist's role in the treatment of the schizophrenic patient. *Am. J. Psychiat.,* 1967, **123,** 963–971.

Bijou, S. W., & Orlando, R. Rapid development of multiple-schedule performances with retarded children. *J. Exp. Anal. Beh.,* 1961, **4,** 7–16.

Birk, L., Crider, A., Shapiro, D., & Tursky, B. Operant electrodermal conditioning under partial curarization. *J. Comp. Physiol. Psychol.,* 1966, **62,** 165–166.

Birnbrauer, J. S. Generalization of punishment effects—A case study. *J. Appl. Behav. Anal.,* 1968, **1,** 201–211.

Birnbrauer, J. S., Bijou, S. W., Wolf, M. M., & Kidder, J. D. Programmed instruction in the classroom. In L. P. Ullmann & L. Krasner (Eds.), *Case studies in behavior modification.* New York: Holt, Rinehart, and Winston, 1965.

Black, A. H. Heart rate changes during avoidance learning in dogs. *Canadian J. Psychol.,* 1959, **13,** 229–242.

Black, A. H., & Morse, P. Avoidance learning in dogs without a warning signal. *J. Exp. Anal. Beh.,* 1961, **4,** 17–23.

Blake, B. G. The application of behavior therapy to the treatment of alcoholism. *Beh. Res. & Ther.,* 1965, **3,** 75–85.

Blake, B. G. A follow-up of alcoholics treated by behavior therapy. *Beh. Res. & Ther.,* 1967, **5,** 89–94.

Blake, P., and Moss, T. The development of socialization skills in an electively mute child. *Beh. Res. & Ther.,* 1967, **5,** 349–356.

Block, J. Some reasons for the apparent inconsistency of personality. *Psychol. Bull.,* 1968, **70,** 210–212.

Bloom, B. L. Training the psychologist for a role in community change: A report of the first institute on innovations in psychological training. Mimeograph, 1969.

Blough, D. S. The study of animal sensory processes by operant methods. In W. K. Honig (Ed.), *Operant behavior: Areas of research and application.* New York: Appleton-Century-Crofts, 1966.

Boe, E. E., & Church, R. M. *Punishment: Issues and experiments.* New York: Appleton-Century-Crofts, 1968.

Bolles, R. C. What reinforces avoidance behavior? Mimeograph, University of Washington, 1968.

Boren, J. J., & Sidman, M. Maintenance of avoidance behavior with intermittent shock. *Canadian J. Psychol.,* 1957, **11,** 185–192.

Boston University. Law-Medicine Research Institute. *Clinical investigation in medicine: Legal, ethical and moral aspects. An anthology and bibliography.* Boston: Boston University, 1963.

Boyd, H. S., & Sisney, V. V. Immediate self-image confrontation and changes in self-concept. *J. Consult. Psychol.,* 1967, **31,** 291–294.

Brady, J. D., Zeller, W. W., & Reznikoff, M. Attitudinal factors influencing outcome of treatment of hospitalized psychiatric patients. *J. Clin. Exp. Psychopathol.,* 1959, **20,** 326–334.

Brady, J. P. Brevital-relaxation treatment of frigidity. *Beh. Res. & Ther.,* 1966, **4**, 71–77.

Brady, J. P. Drugs in behavior therapy. Paper presented at the Sixth Annual Meeting of the American College of Neuropsychopharmacology, San Juan. Puerto Rico, December 1967.

Brady, J. P., Pappas, N., Tausig, T. N., & Thornton, D. R. MMPI correlates of operant behavior. *J. Clin. Psychol.,* 1962, **18**, 67–70.

Brady, J. V. Ulcers in executive monkeys. *Sci. Amer.,* 1958, **199**, 95–103.

Brady, J. V., Porter, R. W., Conrad, D. G., & Mason, J. W. Avoidance behavior and the development of gastroduodenal ulcers. *J. Exp. Anal. Beh.,* 1958, **1**, 69–72.

Braginsky, B. M., & Braginsky, D. D. Schizophrenic patients in the psychiatric interview: An experimental study of their effectiveness at manipulation. *J. Consult. Psychol.,* 1967, **31**, 543–547.

Brain, W. R. Science and antiscience. *Science,* 1965, **148**, 192–198.

Brayfield, A. H. Ethical problems of the application of psychology. Address at the XVI International Congress of Applied Psychology, Amsterdam, the Netherlands, August 1968.

Breger, L., & McGaugh, J. L. Critique and reformulation of "learning theory" approaches to psychotherapy and neurosis. *Psychol. Bull.,* 1965, **63**, 338–358.

Brethower, D. M., & Reynolds, G. S. A facilitative effect of punishment on unpunished behavior. *J. Exp. Anal. Beh.,* 1962, **5**, 191–199.

Brodsky, G. D. The relation between verbal and non-verbal behavior change. *Beh. Res. & Ther.,* 1967, **5**, 183–191.

Brogden, W. J., Lipman, E. A., & Culler, E. The role of incentive in conditioning and extinction. *Amer. J. Psychol.,* 1938, **51**, 109–117.

Broughton, R. J. Sleep disorders: Disorders of arousal? *Science,* 1968, **159**, 1070–1078.

Brown, E. C., & L'Abate, L. An appraisal of teaching machines and programmed instruction with special reference to the modification of deviant behavior. In C. M. Franks (Ed.), *Behavior therapy: Appraisal and status.* New York: McGraw-Hill, 1969.

Brown, J. S. A behavioral analysis of masochism. *J. Exp. Res. in Pers.,* 1965, **1**, 65–70.

Brown, R., & McNeill, D. The "tip of the tongue" phenomenon. *J. Verb. Learn. Verb. Beh.,* 1966, **5**, 325–337.

Browning, R. M. Operantly strengthening UCR (awakening) as a prerequisite to treatment of persistent enuresis. *Beh. Res. & Ther.,* 1967a, **5**, 371–372.

Browning, R. M. A same-subject design for simultaneous comparison of three reinforcement contingencies. *Beh. Res. & Ther.,* 1967b, **5**, 237–243.

Bryan, J. H., & Test, M. A. Models and helping: Naturalistic studies in aiding behavior. *J. Pers. Soc. Psychol.,* 1967, **6**, 400–407.

Bucher, B., & Lovaas, O. I. Use of aversive stimulation in behavior modification. In M. R. Jones (Ed.), *Miami Symposium on the prediction of behavior, 1967: Aversive stimulation.* Coral Gables, Florida: University of Miami Press, 1968.

Buchwald, A. M., & Young, R. D. Some comments on the foundations of behavior therapy. In C. M. Franks (Ed.), *Behavior therapy: Appraisal and status.* New York: McGraw-Hill, 1969.

Buehler, R. E., Patterson, G. R., & Furniss, J. M. The reinforcement of behavior in institutional setting. *Beh. Res. & Ther.,* 1966, **4,** 157–167.

Bugelski, B. R., & Hersen, M. Conditioning acceptance or rejection of information. *J. Exp. Psychol.,* 1966, **71,** 619–623.

Buss, A. *The psychology of aggression.* New York: Wiley, 1961.

Buss, A. *Psychopathology.* New York: Wiley, 1966.

Cameron, N. *The psychology of behavior disorders: A bisocial interpretation.* New York: Houghton-Mifflin, 1947.

Campbell, B. A., & Church, R. M. (Eds.), *Punishment and aversive behavior.* New York: Appleton-Century-Crofts, 1969.

Campbell, D., Sanderson, R. E., and Laverty, S. G. Characteristics of a conditioned response in human subjects during extinction trials following a single traumatic conditioning trial. *J. Abnorm. Soc. Psychol.,* 1964, **68,** 627–639.

Campbell, D. T. Reforms as experiments. *Amer. Psychol.,* 1969, **24,** 409–429.

Caplan, G. *Principles of preventive psychiatry.* New York: Basic Books, 1964.

Carlin, A. S., & Armstrong, H. E., Jr. Aversive conditioning. Learning or dissonance reduction.? *J. Consult. Clin. Psychol.,* 1968, **32,** 674–678.

Carlsmith, J. M. The effect of punishment on avoidance responses: The use of different stimuli for training and punishment. Paper presented at Eastern Psychological Association, Philadelphia, 1961.

Carson, R. C. A and B therapist "types": A possible critical variable in psychotherapy. *J. Nerv. Ment. Dis.,* 1967, **144,** 47–54.

Cartwright, R. D. A comparison of the response to psychoanalytic and client-centered psychotherapy. In L. A. Gottschalk, A. H. Auerbach (Eds.), *Methods of research in psychotherapy.* New York: Appleton-Century-Crofts, 1966.

Cartwright, R. D. Psychotherapeutic processes. *Annual Review of psychology,* 1968, **19,** 387–416.

Cautela, J. R. Desensitization and insight. *Beh. Res. & Ther.,* 1965, **3,** 59–64.

Cautela, J. R. Treatment of compulsive behavior by covert sensitization. *Psychol. Rec.,* 1966, **16,** 33–41.

Cautela, J. R. Covert sensitization. *Psych. Rec.,* 1967, **20,** 459–468.

Cautela, J. R., & Kastenbaum, R. A reinforcement survey schedule for use in therapy, training, and research. *Psych. Rep.,* 1967, **20,** 1115–1130.

Chomsky, N. *Aspects of a theory of language.* Cambridge, Massachusetts: M.I.T. Press, 1965.

Christian, J. J., Lloyd, J. A., & Davis, D. E. The role of endocrines in the self-regulation of mammalian populations. *Recent Progress in Hormone Research,* 1965, **21,** 271–278.

Church, R. M. Emotional reactions of rats to the pain of others. *J. Comp. Physiol. Psychol.,* 1959, **52,** 132–134.

Church, R. M. The varied effects of punishment on behavior. *Psychol. Rev.,* 1963, **70,** 369–402.

Church, R. M. Response suppression. In B. A. Campbell, & R. M. Church (Eds.), *Punishment and aversive behavior.* New York: Appleton-Century-Crofts, 1969.

Cofer, C. N., & Appley, M. H. *Motivation: Theory and research.* New York: Wiley, 1964.

Cohen, H. L. Behavioral architecture. *Architect. Assoc. J.,* 1964, 7–13.

Cohen, H. L., Filipczak, J., & Bis, J. S. *Case I: An initial study of contingencies applicable to special education.* Silver Spring, Maryland: Institute for Behavioral Research, 1967.

Cohen, S. I. Neurobiological considerations for behavior therapy. In C. M. Franks (Ed.), *Behavior therapy: Appraisal and status. Assessment and appraisal.* New York: McGraw-Hill, 1969.

Colby, K. M. Psychotherapeutic process. *Annual Review of Psychology,* 1964, **15,** 347–370.

Coleman, R., Greenblatt, M., & Solomon, H. C. Physiological evidence of rapport during psychotherapeutic interviews. *Dis. Nerv. System,* 1956, **17,** 71–77.

Community Mental Health Centers Act, Public Law 88–164, Title II. 88th Congress, First Session, 1963. A bill to provide for assistance in the construction and initial operation of community mental health centers and for other purposes.

Cook, L., & Kelleher, R. T. Effects of drugs on behavior. *Annual Review of Pharmacology,* 1963, **3,** 205–222.

Cook, S. W. The psychologist of the future: Scientist, professional, or both. In J. R. Braun (Ed.), *Clinical psychology in transition,* rev. ed. Cleveland: The World Publishing Company, 1966.

Cooke, G. The efficacy of two desensitization procedures: An analogue study. *Beh. Res. & Ther.,* 1966, **4,** 17–24.

Cooke, G. Evaluation of the efficacy of the components of reciprocal inhibition psychotherapy. *J. Abnorm. Psychol.,* 1968, **73,** 464–467.

Cooper, A. J. A case of fetishism and impotence treated by behavior therapy. *Brit. J. Psychiat.,* 1963, **109,** 649–652.

Cooper, J. E., Gelder, M. G., & Marks, I. M. Results of behavior therapy in seventy-seven psychiatric patients. *Brit. Med. J.,* 1965, **1,** 1222–1225.

Cornelison, F. S., & Arsenian, J. A study of the responses of psychotic patients to photographic self-image experiences. *Psychiat. Quart.*, 1960, **34**, 1–8.

Cowen, E. L., & Zax, M. The mental health fields today: Issues and problems. In E. L. Cowen, E. A. Gardner, & M. Zax (Eds.), *Emergent approaches to mental health problems*. New York: Appleton-Century-Crofts, 1967.

Craig, K. D. Vicarious reinforcement and noninstrumental punishment in observational learning. *J. Pers. Soc. Psychol.*, 1967, **7**, 172–176.

Craig, K. D. Physiological arousal as a function of imagined, vicarious, and direct stress experiences. *J. Abnorm. Psychol.*, 1968, **73**, 513–520.

Craig, K. D., & Weinstein, M. S. Conditioning vicarious affective arousal. *Psychol. Rep.*, 1965, **17**, 955–963.

Craig, K. D., & Wood, K. Physiological differentiation of direct and vicarious affective arousal. *Canadian J. Beh. Sci.*, 1969, **1**, 98–105.

Creelman, M. B. *The experimental investigation of meaning: A review of the literature*. New York: Springer, 1966.

Cronbach, L. J., & Gleser, G. C. *Psychological tests and personnel decisions* (2nd ed.). Urbana: University of Illinois Press, 1965.

Cronbach, L. J. , Gleser, G. C., Nanda, H., & Rajaratnam, N. The dependability of behavioral measurements: Multifacet studies of generalizability. Technical Report OE6-10-268, Sept. 1967, U.S. Office of Education.

Crozier, M. Quoted by Raymond, H. *New York Times*, 1969.

Curran, W. J. Governmental regulation of the use of human subjects in medical research: The approach of two federal agencies. *Daedalus*, 1969, **98**, 542–594.

Dailey, C. A. The practical utility of the clinical report. *J. Consult. Psychol.*, 1953, **17**, 297–302.

D'Amato, M. R., Etkin, M., & Fazzaro, J. Cue-producing behavior in the Capuchin monkey during reversal, extinction, acquisition and overtraining. *J. Exp. Anal. Beh.*, 1968, **11**, 425–433.

D'Amato, M. R., & Gumenik, W. E. Some effects of immediate versus randomly-delayed shock on an instrumental response and cognitive processes. *J. Abnorm. Soc. Psychol.*, 1960, **60**, 64–67.

Darby, C. L., & Riopelle, A. J. Observational learning in the Rhesus monkey. *J. Comp. Physiol. Psychol.*, 1959, **52**, 94–98.

Davison, G. C. Anxiety under total curarization: Implications for the role of muscular relaxation under desensitization of neurotic fears. *J. Nerv. Ment. Dis.*, 1966, **143**, 443–448.

Davison, G. C. Some problems of logic and conceptualization in behavior therapy research and theory. Paper presented at the First Annual Meeting of the Association for the Advancement of the Behavioral Therapies. American Psychological Association, Washington, D.C., 1967.

Davison, G. C. Elimination of a sadistic fantasy by a client-controlled counter-conditioning technique: A case study. *J. Abnorm. Soc. Psychol.,* 1968a, **73**, 84–90.

Davison, G. C. Self-control through "imaginal aversive contingency" and "one-downsmanship." In J. D. Krumboltz & C. E. Thoresen (Eds.), *Behavioral counseling: Cases and techniques.* New York: Holt, Rinehart & Winston, 1969a.

Davison, G. C. Systematic desensitization as a counterconditioning process. *J. Abnorm. Psychol.,* 1968b, **73**, 91–99.

Davison, G. C. Appraisal of behavior modification techniques with adults in institutional settings. In C. M. Franks (Ed.), *Behavior therapy: Appraisal and status.* New York: McGraw-Hill, 1969b.

Davison, G. C., & Valins, S. Maintenance of self-attributed and drug-attributed behavior change. *J. Pers. Soc. Psychol.,* 1969, **11,** 25–33.

Davitz, J. R., & Mason, D. J. Socially facilitated reduction of a fear response in rats. *J. Comp. Physiol. Psychol.,* 1955, **48,** 149–151.

deWardener, H. E. Some ethical and economic problems associated with intermittent hemodealysis. In CIBA, *Ethics in medical progress: CIBA foundation symposium.* Boston: CIBA, 1966.

Dicken, C., & Fordham, M. Effects of reinforcement of self-references in quasi-therapeutic interviews. *J. Counsel. Psychol.,* 1967, **14,** 145–152.

DiLollo, V., & Berger, S. M. Effects of apparent pain in others on observer's reaction time. *J. Pers. Soc. Psychol.,* 1965, **2,** 573–575.

Dingman, H. F., & Tarjan, G. Mental retardation and the normal distribution curve. *Amer. J. Ment. Deficiency,* 1960, **64,** 991–994.

Dinsmoor, J. A. A quantitative comparison of the discriminative and secondary reinforcing functions of a stimulus. *J. Exp. Psychol.,* 1950, **40,** 457–472.

Dinsmoor, J. A. Escape from shock as a conditioning technique. In M. R. Jones (Ed.), *Miami symposium on the prediction of behavior 1967: Aversive stimulation.* Coral Gables, Florida: University of Miami Press, 1968.

Ditrichs, R., Simon, S., & Greene, B. Effect of vicarious scheduling on the verbal conditioning of hostility in children. *J. Pers. Soc. Psychol.,* 1967, **6,** 71–78.

Dittes, J. E. Galvanic skin responses as a measure of patient's reaction to therapist's permissiveness. *J. Abnorm. Soc. Psychol.,* 1957, **55,** 295–303.

Dollard, J., & Miller, N. E. *Personality and psychotherapy: An analysis in terms of learning, thinking and culture.* New York: McGraw-Hill, 1950.

Dorcus, R. M., & Shaffer, G. W. *Textbook of abnormal psychology.* Baltimore: The Williams and Wilkins Company, 1945.

Duffy, E. *Activation and behavior.* New York: Wiley, 1962.

Duke, M. P., Frankel, A. S., Sipes, M., & Stewart, R. W. The effects of different kinds of models on interview behavior and feelings about an interview situation. Unpublished manuscript, Indiana University, 1965.

Eimas, P. D., & Zeaman, D. Response speed changes in an Estes' paired-associate "miniature" experiment. *J. Verb. Learn. Verb. Beh.,* 1963, **1**, 384–388.

Eisenberger, R., Karpman, M., & Trattner, J. What is the necessary and sufficient condition for reinforcement in the contingency situation? *J. Exp. Psychol.,* 1967, **74**, 342–350.

Ellsworth, R. B. *Nonprofessionals in psychiatric rehabilitation.* New York: Appleton-Century-Crofts, 1968.

Ellul, J. *The technological society.* New York: Knopf, 1964.

Elwood, D. L. Automation of psychological testing. *Amer. Psychol.,* 1969, **24**, 287–289.

Engle, R. L. Medical diagnosis. In J. A. Jacquez (Ed.), *The diagnostic process.* Ann Arbor, Michigan: University of Michigan Press, 1964.

Estes, W. K. An experimental study of punishment. *Psychol. Monogr.,* 1944, **57**, #263.

Estes, W. K. The problem of inference from curves based on group data. *Psychol. Bull.,* 1956, **53**, 134–140.

Estes, W. K., & Skinner, B. F. Some quantitative properties of anxiety. *J. Exp. Psychol.,* 1941, **29**, 390–400.

Evans, D. R. Masturbatory fantasy and sexual deviation. *Behav. Res. & Ther.,* 1968, **6**, 17–19.

Executive Office of the President, Office of Science and Technology. *Privacy and behavioral research.* Washington, D.C., February 1967. Summarized in *Amer. Psychol.,* 1967, **22**, 345–349.

Eysenck, H. J. *The dynamics of anxiety and hysteria.* London: Routledge, and Kegan Paul, 1957.

Eysenck, H. J. (Ed.). *Experiments in personality.* New York: Praeger, 1960.

Eysenck, H. J. (Ed.). *Handbook of abnormal psychology.* New York: Basic Books, 1961.

Eysenck, H. J. (Ed.). *Experiments with drugs.* Oxford: Pergamon Press, 1963.

Eysenck, H. J. The effects of psychotherapy. *Internatl J. Psychiat.,* 1965a, **1**, 99–142.

Eysenck, H. J. (Ed.). *Experiments in behavior therapy.* London: Pergamon Press, 1965b.

Eysenck, H. J. Extraversion and the acquisition of eyeblink and GSR conditioned responses. *Psychol. Bull.,* 1965c, **63**, 258–270.

Eysenck, H. J. *The biological basis of personality.* Springfield, Illinois: Thomas, 1967.

Eysenck, H. J., & Rachman, S. *The causes and cures of neuroses.* London: Routledge, and Kegan Paul, 1965.

Fairweather, G. W. (Ed.). *Social psychology in treating mental illness: An experimental approach.* New York: Wiley, 1964.

Fairweather, G. W. *Methods for experimental social innovation.* New York: Wiley, 1967.

Farber, S. M., & Wilson, R. H. L. (Eds.). *Man and civilization: Control of the mind.* Vol. 1, 1961. *Conflict and creativity.* Vol. 2, 1963. New York: McGraw-Hill.

Farrar, C. H., Powell, B. J., & Martin, L. K. Punishment of alcohol consumption by apneic paralysis. *Beh. Res. & Ther.,* 1968, **6**, 13–16.

Feldman, M. P. Aversion therapy for sexual deviations: A critical review. *Psychol. Bull.,* 1966, **65**, 65–79.

Feldman, M. P., & MacCulloch, M. J. The application of anticipatory avoidance learning to the treatment of homosexuality. I. Theory, technique and preliminary results. *Beh. Res. & Ther.,* 1965, **2**, 165–183.

Ferster, C. B. Withdrawal of positive reinforcement as punishment. *Science,* 1957, **126**, 509.

Ferster, C. B. Control of behavior in chimpanzees and pigeons by time out from positive reinforcement. *Psychol. Monogr.,* 1958a, **72**, No. 8, Whole No. 461.

Ferster, C. B. Reinforcement and punishment in the control of human behavior by social agencies. *Psychiat. Res. Rep.,* 1958b, **10**, 101–118.

Ferster, C. B. Essentials of a science of behavior. In J. I. Nurnberger, C. B. Ferster, & J. P. Brady (Eds.), *An introduction to the science of human behavior.* New York: Appleton-Century-Crofts, 1963.

Ferster, C. B. Classification of behavioral pathology. In L. Krasner & L. P. Ullmann (Eds.), *Research in behavior modification: New developments and implications.* New York: Holt, Rinehart & Winston, 1965.

Ferster, C. B., & Appel, J. B. Punishment of S^Δ responding in matching to sample by time out from positive reinforcement. *J. Exp. Anal. Beh.,* 1961, **4**, 45–56.

Ferster, C. B., Nurnberger, J. I., & Levitt, E. B. The control of eating. *J. Mathetics,* 1962, **1**, 87–109.

Ferster, C. B., & Perrott, M. C. *Behavior principles.* New York: Appleton-Century-Crofts, 1968.

Ferster, C. B., & Skinner, B. F. *Schedules of reinforcement.* New York: Appleton-Century-Crofts, 1957.

Festinger, L. A theory of social comparison processes. *Human Relations,* 1954, **7**, 117–140.

Festinger, L. *A theory of cognitive dissonance.* Stanford: Stanford University Press, 1957.

Fiedler, F. E. The concept of an ideal therapeutic relationship. *J. Consult. Psychol.,* 1950, **14**, 39–45.

Findley, J. D. An experimental outline for building and exploring multi-operant behavior repertoires *J. Exp. Anal. Beh.,* 1962, **5**, 113–166.

Findley, J. D., Migler, B. M., & Brady, J. V. A long-term study of human performance in a continuously programmed experimental environment. Technical Report, Space Research Laboratory, University of Maryland. Submitted to the National Aeronautics and Space Administration, 1963.

Flanders, J. P. A review of research on imitative behavior. *Psychol. Bull.*, 1968, **69,** 316–337.

Folkins, C. H., Lawson, K. D., Opton, E. M. Jr., & Lazarus, R. S. Desensitization and the experimental reduction of threat. *J. Abnorm. Psychol.*, 1968, **73,** 100–113.

Fox, L. Effecting the use of efficient study habits. *J. Mathetics,* 1962, **1,** 75–86.

Frank, J. D. *Persuasion and healing.* Baltimore: Johns Hopkins Press, 1961a.

Frank, J. D. The role of influence in psychotherapy. In M. I. Stein (Ed.), *Contemporary psychotherapies.* New York: Free Press of Glencoe, 1961b.

Frank, J. D. The role of cognitions in illness and healing. In H. H. Strupp & L. Luborsky (Eds.), *Research in psychotherapy.* Vol. II. Washington, D.C.: American Psychological Association. 1962.

Franks, C. M. Conditioning and abnormal behavior. In H. J. Eysenck, (Ed.), *Handbook of abnormal psychology.* New York: Basic Books, 1961.

Franks, C. M. Behavior therapy, the principles of conditioning and the treatment of the alcoholic. *Quart. J. Stud. Alcohol,* 1963, **24,** 511–529.

Franks, C. M. Conditioning and conditioned aversion therapies in the treatment of the alcoholic. *Internatl. J. Addictions,* 1966, **1,** 61–98.

Frederick, C. J. (Ed.). *The future of psychotherapy.* Boston: Little, Brown & Co., 1969a.

Frederick, C. J. Future training in psychotherapy. In C. J. Frederick (Ed.), *The future of psychotherapy.* Boston: Little, Brown & Co., 1969b.

Freedman, N., Engelhardt, D. M., Hankoff, L. D., Glick, B. S., Kaye, H., Buchwald, J. & Stark, P. *Arch. Neurol. Psychiat.,* 1958, **30,** 657–666.

Freund, K. A laboratory method for diagnosing predominance of homo- or hetero-erotic interest in the male. *Beh. Res. & Ther.,* 1963, **1,** 85–93.

Friedman, D. E. A new technique for systematic desensitization of phobic symptoms. *Beh. Res. & Ther.,* 1966, **4,** 139–140.

Friedman, D. E., & Silverstone, J. T. Treatment of phobic patients by systematic desensitization. *Lancet,* 1967, March 4, 470–472.

Fuller, P. R. Operant conditioning of a vegetative human organism. *Amer. J. Psychol.,* 1949, **62,** 587–590.

Fuller, R. B. *Education automation.* Carbondale, Illinois: Southern Illinois University Press, 1962.

Gallup, G. G. Jr. Mirror-image stimulation. *Psychol. Bull.* 1968, **70,** 782–793.

Gambrill, E. Effectiveness of the counterconditioning procedure in eliminating avoidance behavior. *Beh. Res. & Ther.,* 1967, **5,** 263–274.

Geer, J. H. The development of a scale to measure fear. *Beh. Res. & Ther.*, 1965, **3**, 45–53.

Gelder, M. G., & Marks, I. M. Severe agoraphobia: A controlled prospective trial of behavior therapy. *Brit. J. Psychiat.*, 1966, **112**, 309–319.

Gelder, M. G., Marks, I. M., Wolff, H. H., & Clarke, M. Desensitization and psychotherapy in the treatment of phobic states: A controlled inquiry. *Brit. J. Psychiat.*, 1967, **113**, 53–73.

Gelfand, D. M., Gelfand, S., & Dobson, W. R. Unprogrammed reinforcement of patients' behavior in a mental hospital. *Beh. Res. & Ther.*, 1967, **5**, 201–207.

Gellhorn, E. Motion and emotion: The role of proprioception in the physiology and pathology of the emotions. *Psychol. Rev.*, 1964, **71**, 457–472.

Gendlin, E. T. Client-centered developments and work with schizophrenics. *J. Counsel. Psychol.*, 1962, **9**, 205–212.

Gendlin, E. T. Values and the process of experiencing. In A. H. Mahrer (Ed.), *The goals of psychotherapy*. New York: Appleton-Century-Crofts, 1967.

Gerard, R. W., & Mattsson, N. The identification of schizophrenia. In J. A. Jacquez (Ed.), *The diagnostic process*. Ann Arbor, Michigan: University of Michigan Press, 1964.

Gewirtz, J. L., & Stingle, K. G. Learning of generalized imitation as the basis for identification. *Psychol. Rev.*, 1968, **5**, 374–397.

Gilmore, J. B. Toward an understanding of imitation. In E. C. Simmel, R. A. Hoppe, & G. A. Milton (Eds.). *Social facilitation and imitative behavior*. Boston: Allyn & Bacon, 1968.

Gliedman, L. H., Stone, A. R., Frank, J. D., Nash, E. H. Jr., & Imber, S. D. Incentives for treatment related to remaining or improving in psychotherapy. *Amer. J. Psychother.*, 1957, **11**, 589–598.

Goffman, E. *Asylums*. New York: Aldine, Chicago, 1962.

Golann, S. E. Emerging areas of ethical concern. *Amer. Psychol.*, 1969, **24**, 454–459.

Gold, S., & Neufeld, I. A. A learning theory approach to the treatment of homosexuality. *Beh. Res. & Ther.*, 1965, **2**, 201–204.

Goldberg, J., & D'Zurilla, T. J. Demonstration of slide projection as an alternative to imaginal stimulus presentation in systematic desensitization therapy. *Psychol. Rep.*, 1968, **23**, 527–533.

Goldiamond, I. Self-control procedures in personal behavior problems. *Psychol. Rep.*, 1965, **17**, 851–868.

Goldman-Eisler, F. Individual differences between interviewers and their effect on interviewees' conversational behavior. *J. Ment. Sci.*, 1952, **98**, 660–671.

Goldstein, A. P. *Therapist-patient expectancies in psychotherapy*. New York: Pergamon, 1962.

Goldstein, A. P., Heller, K., & Sechrest, L. B. *Psychotherapy and the psychology of behavior change*. New York: Wiley, 1966.

Goldstein, A. P., & Shipman, W. G. Patient's expectancies, symptom reduction, and aspects of the initial psychotherapeutic interview. *J. Clin. Psychol.,* 1961, **17,** 129–133.

Goodwin, D. L. Training teachers in reinforcement techniques to increase pupil task-oriented behavior: An experimental evaluation. Stanford University, Mimeograph, 1966.

Gormezano, I., & Moore, J. W. Effects of instructional set and UCS intensity on latency, percentage, and form of the eyelid response. *J. Exp. Psychol.,* 1962, **63,** 487–494.

Grastyán, E., Karmos, G., Vereczkey, L., & Kellényi, L. The hippocampal electrical correlates of the momeostatic regulation of motivation. *Electroenceph. Clin. Neurophysiol.,* 1966, **21,** 34–53.

Graubard, S. R. Preface. Ethical aspects of experimentation with human subjects. *Daedalus,* 1969, **98,** No. 2.

Greenspoon, J. The effect of verbal and non-verbal stimuli on the frequency of numbers of two verbal response classes. Unpublished doctoral dissertation, Indiana University, 1951.

Greenspoon, J. Behavioristic approaches to psychotherapy. In F. J. Shaw (Ed.), *Behavioristic approaches to counseling and psychotherapy.* University of Alabama Press, 1961.

Greenspoon, J., & Brownstein, A. J. Psychotherapy from the standpoint of a behaviorist. *Psychol. Rec.,* 1968, **17,** 401–416.

Greenspoon, J., & Gersten, C. D. A new look at psychological testing: Psychological testing from the point of view of a behaviorist. *Amer. Psychol.,* 1967, **22,** 848–853.

Greenwald, A. G., & Albert, S. M. Observational learning: A technique for elucidating S-R mediation processes. *J. Exp. Psychol.,* 1968, **76,** 267–272.

Grings, W. W., & Carlin, S. Instrumental modification of autonomic behavior. *Psychol. Rec.,* 1966, **16,** 153–159.

Grings, W. W., Lockhart, R. A., & Dameron, L. E. Conditioning autonomic responses of mentally subnormal individuals. *Psychol. Monogr.,* 1962, **76,** Whole No. 558.

Gross, B. M. The state of the nation: Social systems accounting. In R. A. Bauer (Ed.), *Social indicators.* Cambridge, Massachusetts: M.I.T. Press, 1966.

Grossberg, J. M., & Wilson, H. K. Physiological changes accompanying imagined fear situations. Paper presented at the Western Psychological Association meetings, San Francisco, May 1967.

Guerney, B. G. (Ed.). *Psychotherapeutic agents: New roles for nonprofessionals, parents and teachers.* New York: Holt, Rinehart & Winston, 1966.

Gwinn, G. T. The effects of punishment on acts motivated by fear. *J. Exp. Psychol.,* 1949, **39,** 260–269.

Haas, H., Fink, H., & Hartfelder, G. The placebo problem. *Psychopharm. Service Center Bull.,* 1963, **2,** 1–65.

Haggard, E. A., Brekstad, A., & Skard, A. G. On the reliability of the anamnestic interview. *J. Abnorm. Soc. Psychol.,* 1960, **61,** 311–318.

Hake, D. F., & Laws, D. R. Social facilitation of responses during a stimulus paired with electric shock. *J. Exp. Anal. Beh.,* 1967, **10,** 387–392.

Hall, R. V., Lund, D., & Jackson, D. Effects of teacher attention on study behavior. *J. Appl. Beh. Anal.,* 1968, **1,** 1–12.

Hankoff, L. D., Freedman, N., & Engelhardt, D. M. The prognostic value of placebo response. *Amer. J. Psychiat.,* 1958, **115,** 549–550.

Hardin, G. The tragedy of the commons. Science, 1968, **162,** 1243–1248.

Harrison, A. The problem of privacy in the computer age: An annotated bibliography. Memorandum RM-5495-PR/RC. Santa Monica: Rand Corporation, December 1967.

Harlow, H. F., & Zimmerman, R. R. Affectional responses in the infant monkey. *Science,* 1959, **130,** 421–432.

Harmatz, M. G., & Lapuc, P. Behavior modification of overeating in a psychiatric population. *J. Consult. Clin. Psychol.,* 1968, **32,** 583–587.

Hart, J. D. Fear reduction as a function of the assumption and success of the therapeutic role. Unpublished Master's Thesis, University of Wisconsin, 1966.

Hart, J. T. Memory and the feeling-of-knowing experience. *J. Educ. Psychol.,* 1965, **56,** 208–216.

Hartup, W. W. Peers as agents of social reinforcement. *The young child: Reviews of research.* Washington, D.C., National Association for the Education of Young Children, 1967.

Hartup, W. W., Glazer, J. A., & Charlesworth, R. Peer reinforcement and sociometric status. *Child Dev.,* 1967, **38,** 1017–1024.

Hawkins, R. P., Peterson, R. F., Schweid, E., & Bijou, S. W. Behaivor therapy in the home: Amelioration of problem parent-child relation with the parent in a therapeutic role. *J. Exp. Child Psychol.,* 1966, **4,** 99–107.

Hearst, E. Stress-induced breakdown of an appetitive discrimination. *J. Exp. Anal. Beh.,* 1965, **8,** 135–146.

Hebb, D. O. The American revolution. *Amer. Psychol.,* 1960, **15,** 735–745.

Hefferline, R. F. Learning theory and clinical psychology—an eventual symbiosis? In A. J. Bachrach (Ed.), *Experimental foundations of clinical psychology.* New York: Basic Books, 1962.

Heine, R. W., & Trosman, H. Initial expectations of the doctor-patient interaction as a factor in continuance in psychotherapy. *Psychiat.,* 1960, **23,** 275–278.

Heller, K. Ambiguity in the interview interaction. In J. M. Shlien (Ed.), *Research in psychotherapy,* Vol. III. Washington, D.C.: American Psychological Association, 1968.

Heller, K., & Goldstein, A. P. Client dependency and therapist expectancy as relationship maintaining variables in psychotherapy. *J. Consult. Psychol.*, 1961, **25**, 371–375.

Heller, K., & Marlatt, G. A. Verbal conditioning, behavior therapy, and behavior change: Some problems in extrapolation. In C. M. Franks (Ed.), *Behavior therapy: Appraisal and status.* New York: McGraw-Hill, 1969.

Helmer, J. E., & Furedy, J. J. Operant conditioning of GSR amplitude. *J. Exp. Psychol.*, 1968, **78**, 463–467.

Herrnstein, R. J. Superstition: A corollary of the principles of operant conditioning. In W. K. Honig (Ed.), *Operant behavior: Areas of research and application.* New York: Appleton-Century-Crofts, 1966.

Hersch, C. The discontent explosion in mental health. *Amer. Psychol.*, 1968, **23**, 497–506.

Herz, M. J. Drugs and the conditioned avoidance response. In C. C. Pfeiffer, & J. R. Smythies (Eds.), *International review of neurobiology*, Vol. II. New York: Academic Press, 1960.

Hetherington, E. M., & Frankie, G. Effects of parental dominance, warmth, and conflict on imitation in children. *J. Pers. Soc. Psychol.*, 1967, **6**, 119–125.

Hicks, D. J. Imitation and retention of film-mediated aggressive peer and adult models. *J. Pers. Soc. Psychol.*, 1965, **2**, 97–100.

Hill, F. A. Effects of instructions and subject's need for approval on the conditioned galvanic skin response. *J. Exp. Psychol.*, 1967, **73**, 461–467.

Hill, W. F. Learning theory and the acquisition of values. *Psychol. Rev.*, 1960, **67**, 317–331.

Hill, W. F. Sources of evaluative reinforcement. *Psychol. Bull.*, 1968, **69**, 132–146.

Hillix, W. A., & Marx, M. H. Response strengthening by information and effect in human learning. *J. Exp. Psychol.*, 1960, **60**, 97–102.

Hingtgen, J. N., Sanders, B. J., & DeMyer, M. K. Shaping cooperative responses in early childhood schizophrenics. In L. P. Ullmann & L. Krasner (Eds.), *Case studies in behavior modification.* New York: Holt, Rinehart & Winston, 1965.

Hinsey, C., Patterson, G. R., & Sonoda, B. Validation of a procedure for conditioning aggression in children. Paper presented at meeting of Western Psychological Association, 1961.

Hoffman, H. S. The analysis of discriminated avoidance. In W. K. Honig (Ed.), *Operant behavior: Areas of research and application.* New York: Appleton-Century-Crofts, 1966.

Hogan, R. A. Implosive therapy in the short-term treatment of psychotics. *Psychother.: Theory, Res. Pract.*, 1966, **3**, 25–32.

Hogan, R. A., & Kirchner, J. H. Preliminary report of the extinction of learned fears via short-term implosive therapy. *J. Abnorm. Psychol.*, 1967, **72,** 106–109.

Holz, W. C., & Azrin, N. H. Interactions between the discriminative and aversive properties of punishment. *J. Exp. Anal. Beh.*, 1962, **5,** 229–234.

Holz, W. C., & Azrin, N. H. Conditioning human verbal behavior. In W. K. Honig (Ed.), *Operant behavior: Areas of research and application.* New York: Appleton-Century-Crofts, 1966.

Holz, W. C., Azrin, N. H., & Ayllon, T. A comparison of several procedures for eliminating behavior. *J. Exp. Anal. Beh.*, 1963, **6,** 399–406.

Holzman, P. S., Rousey, C., & Snyder, C. On listening to one's own voice: Effects on psycho-physiological responses and free associations. *J. Pers. Soc. Psychol.*, 1966, **4,** 432–441.

Homme, L. E. Perspectives in psychology—XXIV Control of coverants: The operants of the mind. *Psychol. Rec.*, 1965, **15,** 501–511.

Homme, L. E. Contiguity theory and contingency management. *Psychol. Rec.*, 1966, **16,** 233–241.

Homme, L. E., deBaca, P. C., Devine, J. V., Steinhorst, R., & Rickert, E. J. Use of the Premack principle in controlling the behavior of nursery school children. *J. Exp. Anal. Beh.*, 1963, **6,** 544.

Honig, W. K. (Ed.). *Operant behavior: Areas of research and application.* New York: Appleton-Century-Crofts, 1966.

Honigfeld, G. Non-specific factors in treatment. I: Review of placebo reactions and placebo reactors. *Dis. Ner. Syst.*, 1964a, **25,** 145–156.

Honigfeld, G. Non-specific factors in treatment. II: Review of social-psychological factors. *Dis. Nev. Syst.*, 1964b, **25,** 225–239.

Hoppe, F. Erfolg und misserfolg. *Psychol. Forsch.*, 1930, **14,** 1–62.

Hoppe, R. A. Interrelationships: Conceptual and behavioral. In E. C. Simmel, R. A. Hoppe, & G. A. Milton (Eds.), *Social facilitation and imitative behavior.* Boston: Allyn & Bacon, 1968.

Houts, P. S., MacIntosh, S., & Moos, R. H. Patient-therapist interdependence: Cognitive and behavioral. *J. Consult. Clin. Psychol.*, 1969, **33,** 30–45.

Humphery, J. Behavior therapy with children: An experimental evaluation. Unpublished doctoral dissertation, University of London, 1966.

Hunt, H. F., & Brady, J. V. Some effects of punishment and intercurrent "anxiety" on a simple operant. *J. Compt. Physiol. Psychol.*, 1955, **48,** 305–310.

Hunt, H. F., & Dyrud, J. E. Commentary: Perspective in behavior therapy. In J. M. Shlien (Ed.), *Research in psychotherapy:* Vol. III. Washington, D.C.: American Psychological Association, 1968.

Hurwitz, H. M. B. Periodicity of response in operant extinction. *Quart. J. Exp. Psychol.*, 1957, **9,** 177–184.

Ingram, E. M. Discriminative and reinforcing functions in the experimental development of social behavior in a preschool child. Unpublished Master's Thesis, University of Kansas, 1967.

Isaacs, W., Thomas, J., & Goldiamond, I. Application of operant conditioning to reinstate verbal behavior in psychotics. *J. Speech Hearing Disord.,* 1960, **25,** 8–12.

Ivey, A. E., Normington, C. J., Miller, C. D., Morrill, W. H., & Hasse, R. F. Microcounseling and attending behavior. *J. Counsel. Psychol., Monogr., Suppl.,* 1968, **15,** No. 5, Part 2.

Jacobson, E. *Progressive relaxation.* Chicago: University of Chicago Press, 1938.

Jacquez, J. A. *The diagnostic process.* Ann Arbor, Michigan: University of Michigan Press, 1964.

Jaffe, J. Verbal behavior analysis in psychiatric interviews with the aid of digital computers. In D. Mck. Rioch & E. O. Weinstein (Eds.), *Disorders of communication,* Vol. 42. Baltimore: Williams & Wilkins, 1964.

Jaffe, J., Feldstein, S., & Cassota, L. A stochastic model of speaker switching in natural dialogue. In K. Salzinger & S. Salzinger (Eds.), *Research in verbal behavior and some neurophysiological implications.* New York: Academic Press, 1967.

James, G., & Lott, A. J. Reward frequency and the formation of positive attitudes toward group members. *J. Soc. Psychol.,* 1964, **62,** 111–115.

Janis, I. L., & Mann, L. Effectiveness of emotional role-playing in modifying smoking habits and attitudes. *J. Exp. Res. Pers.,* 1965, **1,** 84–90.

Jenkins, J. J. The challenge to psychological theorists. In T. R. Dixon & D. L. Horton (Eds.), *Verbal behavior and general behavior theory.* Englewood Cliffs, New Jersey: Prentice-Hall, 1968.

Johnson, S. M., & Sechrest, L. Comparison of desensitization and progressive relaxation in treating test anxiety. *J. Consult. Clin. Psychol.,* 1968, **32,** 280–286.

Jones, H. G. Personal communication, 1967.

Jones, M. C. A laboratory study of fear: The case of Peter. *Pedagog. Sem.,* 1924, **31,** 308–315.

Kahn, M., & Baker, B. Desensitization with minimal therapist contact. *J. Abnorm. Psychol.,* 1968, **73,** 198–200.

Kamin, L. J. "Attention-like" processes in classical conditioning. In M. R. Jones (Ed.), *Miami symposium on the prediction of behavior, 1967: Aversive stimulation.* Coral Gables, Florida: University of Miami Press, 1968.

Kanfer, F. H. The effect of a warning signal preceding a noxious stimulus on verbal rate and heart rate. *J. Exp. Psychol.,* 1958, **55,** 73–80.

Kanfer, F. H. Incentive value of generalized reinforcers. *Psychol. Rep,* 1960, **7,** 531–538.

Kanfer, F. H. Comments on learning in psychotherapy. *Psychol. Rep., Monogr. Suppl.,* 1961, **9,** 681–699.

Kanfer, F. H. Experimental analogues of psychotherapy. Paper presented at meeting of American Psychological Association, St. Louis, Missouri, 1962.

Kanfer, F. H. Issues and ethics in behavior manipulation. *Psychol. Rep.* 1965a, **16**, 187–196.

Kanfer, F. H. Structure of psychotherapy: Role-playing as a variable in dyadic communication. *J. Consult. Psychol.*, 1965b, **29**, 325–332.

Kanfer, F. H. Implications of conditioning techniques for interview therapy. *J. Counsel. Psychol.*, 1966a, **13**, 171–177.

Kanfer, F. H. Influence of age and incentive conditions on children's self-rewards. *Psychol. Rep.*, 1966a, **19**, 263–274.

Kanfer, F. H. Directions in behavior modification research. Paper presented at the Second Annual Institute on Man's Adjustment in a Complex Environment: The Behavior Therapies. Veterans Administration Hospital, Brecksville, Ohio, May 1967a.

Kanfer, F. H. Self-regulation: Research, issues, and speculations. Paper presented at the Ninth Annual Institute for Research in Clinical Psychology, "Behavior Modification in Clinical Psychology," at the University of Kansas, April, 1967b.

Kanfer, F. H. Verbal conditioning: A review of its current status. In T. R. Dixon & D. L. Horton (Eds.), *Verbal behavior and general behavior theory*. Englewood Cliffs, New Jersey: Prentice-Hall, 1968.

Kanfer, F. H., & Duerfeldt, P. H. Effects of pretraining of self-evaluation and self-reinforcement. *J. Pers. Soc. Psychol.*, 1967a, **7**, 164–168.

Kanfer, F. H., & Duerfeldt, P. H. Learner competence, model competence and number of observation trials in vicarious learning. *J. Educ. Psychol.*, 1967b, **58**, 153–157.

Kanfer, F. H., & Duerfeldt, P. H. Age, class-standing and commitment as determinants of cheating in children. *Child. Dev.*, 1968, **39**, 545–557.

Kanfer, F. H., Duerfeldt, P. H., & LePage, A. L. Stability of patterns of self-reinforcement. *Psychol. Rep.*, 1969, **24**, 663–670.

Kanfer, F. H., & Goldfoot, D. A. Self-control and tolerance of noxious stimulation. *Psychol. Rep.*, 1966, **18**, 79–85.

Kanfer, F. H., & McBrearty, J. F. Minimal social reinforcement and interview content. *J. Clin. Psychol.*, 1962, **18**, 210–215.

Kanfer, F. H., & Marston, A. R. Verbal conditioning, ambiguity, and psychotherapy. *Psychol. Rep.*, 1961, **9**, 461–475.

Kanfer, F. H., & Marston, A. R. Conditioning of self-reinforcing responses: An analogue to self-confidence training. *Psychol. Rep.* 1963a, **13**, 63–70.

Kanfer, F. H., & Marston, A. R. Determinants of self-reinforcement in human learning. *J. Exp. Psychol.*, 1963b, **66**, 245–254.

Kanfer, F. H., & Marston, A. R. Human reinforcement: Vicarious and direct. *J. Exp. Psychol.*, 1963c, **65**, 292–296.

Kanfer, F. H., & Marston, A. R. Characteristics of interactional behavior in a psychotherapy analogue. *J. Consult. Psychol.,* 1964, **28,** 456–467.

Kanfer, F. H., & Matarazzo, J. D. Secondary and generalized reinforcement in human learning. *J. Exp. Psychol.,* 1959, **58,** 400–404.

Kanfer, F. H., & Phillips, J. S. Behavior therapy: A panacea for all ills or a passing fancy? *Arch. Gen. Psychiat.,* 1966, **15,** 114–128.

Kanfer, F. H., & Phillips, J. S. A survey of current behavior therapies and a proposal for classification. In C. M. Franks (Ed.), *Behavior therapy: Appraisal and status.* New York: McGraw-Hill, 1969.

Kanfer, F. H., Phillips, J. S., Matarazzo, J. D., & Saslow, G. Experimental modification of interviewer content in standardized interviews. *J. Consult. Psychol.,* 1960, **24,** 528–536.

Kanfer, F. H., & Saslow, G. Behavioral diagnosis. In C. M. Franks (Ed.), *Behavior therapy: Appraisal and status.* New York: McGraw-Hill, 1969.

Kantorovich, N. V. An attempt at associative-reflex therapy in alcoholism. *Nov. Reflexol. Fiziol. Nerv. Sist.,* 1929, **3,** 436–447.

Karsh, E. B. Changes in intensity of punishment: Effect on running behavior of rats. *Science,* 1963, **140,** 1084–1085.

Katkin, E. S., & Murray, E. N. Instrumental conditioning of autonomically mediated behavior: Theoretical and methodological issues. *Psychol. Bull.,* 1968, **70,** 52–68.

Katz, M. M., Cole, J. O., & Lowery, H. A. Nonspecificity of diagnosis of paranoid schizophrenia. *Arch. Gen. Psychiat.,* 1964, **11,** 197–202.

Katzev, R. Extinguishing avoidance responses as a function of the delayed warning signal termination. *J. Exp. Psychol.,* 1967, **75,** 339–344.

Kelleher, R. T. Schedules of conditioned reinforcement during experimental extinction. *J. Exp. Anal. Beh.,* 1961, **4,** 1–5.

Kelleher, R. T., & Gollub, L. R. A review of positive conditioned reinforcement. *J. Exp. Anal. Beh.,* 1962, **5,** 543–597.

Keller, F. S. "Good-bye, teacher . . ." *J. Appl. Beh. Anal.,* 1968, **1,** 79–89.

Kelly, G. A. *The psychology of personal constructs.* New York: Norton, 1955.

Kelman, H. C. Manipulation of human behavior: An ethical dilemma for the social scientist. *J. Soc. Issues,* 1965, **21,** 31–46.

Kelman, H. C. Human use of human subjects: The problem of deception in social psychological experiments. *Psychol. Bull.,* 1967, **67,** 1–11.

Kendler, H. H. Motivation and behavior. In D. Levine (Ed.), *Nebraska symposium on motivation, 1965.* Lincoln, Nebraska: University of Nebraska Press, 1965.

Kendler, H. H. Some specific reactions to general S-R theory. In T. R. Dixon & D. L. Horton (Eds.), *Verbal behavior and general behavior theory.* Englewood Cliffs, New Jersey: Prentice-Hall, 1968.

Kennedy, J. F. Message from the President of the United States relative to mental illness and mental retardation, Feb. 5, 1963. 88th Congress, 1st Session, Document No. 58. U.S. Gov Printing Office: 1956 0-767-476.

Kennedy, W. A., & Foreyt, J. P. Control of eating behavior in an obese patient by avoidance conditioning. *Psychol. Rep.,* 1968, **22,** 571–576.

Kessen, W., & Mandler, G. Anxiety, pain, and the inhibition of distress. *Psychol. Review,* 1961, **68,** 396–404.

Keutzer, C. S. Behavior modification of smoking: A review, analysis, and experimental application with focus on subject variables as predictors of treatment outcome. Unpublished doctoral dissertation, University of Oregon, 1967.

Keutzer, C. S., Lichtenstein, E., & Mees, H. L. Modification of smoking behavior: A review. *Psychol. Bull.,* 1968, **70,** 520–533.

Kimble, G. A. *Hilgard and Marquis' Conditioning and Learning.* (2nd Ed.) New York: Appleton-Century-Crofts, 1961.

Kimble, G. A., & Kendall, J. W., Jr. A comparison of two methods of producing experimental extinction. *J. Exp. Psychol.,* 1953, **45,** 87–90.

Kimmel, H. D., & Hill, F. A. Operant conditioning of the GSR. *Psychol. Rep.,* 1960, **7,** 555–562.

King, G. F., Armitage, S. G., & Tilton, J. R. A therapeutic approach to schizophrenics of extreme pathology: An operant-interpersonal method. *J. Abnorm. Soc. Psychol.,* 1960, **61,** 276–286.

Kinsman, R. A., & Bixenstine, V. E. Secondary reinforcement and shock termination. *J. Exp. Psychol.,* 1968, **76,** 62–68.

Kintz, B. L., Delprato, D. J., Mettee, D. R., Persons, C. E., & Schappe, R. H. The experimenter effect. *Psychol. Bull.,* 1965, **63,** 223–232.

Klee, J. B. The relation of frustration and motivation to the production of abnormal fixations in the rat. *Psychol. Monogr.,* 1944, **56,** 4, Whole No. 257.

Klein, M. H., Dittmann, A. T., Parloff, M. B., & Gill, M. M. Behavior therapy: Observations and reflections. *J. Consult. Clin. Psychol.,* 1969, **33,** 259–266.

Kobasigawa, A. Observation of failure in another person as a determinant of amplitude and speed of a simple motor response. *J. Pers. Soc. Psychol.,* 1965, **1,** 626–630.

Koch, S. Psychology and emerging conceptions of knowledge as unitary. In T. W. Wann (Ed.), *Behaviorism and phenomenology.* Chicago: University of Chicago Press, 1964.

Kolb, D. A., Winter, S. K., & Berlew, D. E. Self Directed Change: Two Studies. *J. Appl. Beth. Sci.,* 1968, **4,** 453–471.

Krasner, L. Studies of the conditioning of verbal behavior. *Psychol. Bull.,* 1958, **15,** 148–171.

Krasner, L. The therapist as a social reinforcement machine. In H. H. Strupp and L. Luborsky (Eds.), *Research in psychotherapy.* Vol. II. Washington, D.C.: American Psychological Association, 1962a.

Krasner, L. The therapist's contribution. In H. H. Strupp and L. Luborsky (Eds.), *Research in psychotherapy.* Vol. II. Washington, D.C.: American Psychological Association, 1962b.

Krasner, L. Behavior control and social responsibility. *Amer. Psychol.,* 1964, **17,** 199–204.

Krasner, L. The behavioral scientist and social responsibility: No place to hide. *J. Soc. Issues,* 1965a, **21,** 9–30.

Krasner, L. Societal and professional implications of the "behavior therapies." *ETS Res. Memo.,* Princeton, N.J.: Educational Testing Service, June 1965b.

Krasner, L. Verbal operant conditioning and awareness. In K. Salzinger & S. Salzinger (Eds.), *Research in verbal behavior and some neurophysiological implications.* New York: Academic Press, 1967.

Kreitzer, S. F. College students in a behavior therapy program with hospitalized emotionally disturbed children. Paper presented at California State Psychological Association, January, 1966.

Krumboltz, J. D., Varenhorst, B. B., & Thoresen, C. E. Non-verbal factors in the effectiveness of models in counseling. *J. Counsel. Psychol.,* 1967, **14,** 412–418.

Kruse, H. D. (Ed.) *Integrating the approaches to mental disease.* New York: Hoeber, 1957.

Kuhn, T. S. *The structure of scientific revolutions.* Chicago: University of Chicago Press, 1962.

Lacey, J. I. Psychophysiological approaches to the evaluation of psychotherapeutic process and outcome. In E. A. Rubinstein and M. B. Parloff (Eds.), *Research in psychotherapy.* Vol. I. Washington, D.C.: American Psychological Association, 1959.

Lacey, J. I., Bateman, D. E., & VanLehn, R. Autonomic response specificity: An experimental study. *Psychosom. Med.,* 1953, **15,** 18–21.

Lacey, J. I., Kagan, J., Lacey, B. C., & Moss, H. A. The visceral level: Situational determinants and behavioral correlates of autonomic response patterns. In P. H. Knapp (Ed.), *Expression of the emotions in man.* New York: Internal. Universities Press, 1963.

Lacey, J. I., & Lacey, B. C. The relationship of resting autonomic activity to motor impulsivity. In H. C. Solomon, S. Cobb, & W. Penfield (Eds.), *The brain and human behavior,* Baltimore: Williams and Wilkins, 1958.

Lader, M. H., & Wing, L. Physiological measures, sedative drugs, and morbid anxiety. *Maudsley Monogr.,* No. 14, 1966.

Ladimer, I. Rights, responsibilities, and protection of patients in human studies. *J. Clin. Pharmacol. and New Drugs,* 1967, 7, 125–130.

Lang, P. J. Fear reduction and fear behavior: Problems in treating a construct. In J. M. Shlien (Ed.), *Research in psychotherapy, Vol. III.* Washington, D.C.: American Psychological Association, 1968.

Lang, P. J. The mechanics of desensitization and the laboratory study of human fear. In C. M. Franks (Ed.), *Behavior therapy: Appraisal and status.* New York: McGraw-Hill, 1969.

Lang, P. J., & Buss, A. H. Psychological deficit in schizophrenia. II. Interference and activation. *J. Abnormal Psychol.,* 1965, **70,** 77–106.

Lang, P. J., & Lazovik, A. D. Experimental desensitization of a phobia. *J. Abnorm. Soc. Psychol.,* 1963, **66,** 519–525.

Lang, P. J., Lazovik, A. D., & Reynolds, D. J. Desensitization, suggestibility, and pseudotherapy. *J. Abnorm. Psychol.,* 1965, **70,** 395–402.

Lang, P. J., & Melamed, B. G. Avoidance conditioning therapy of an infant with chronic ruminative vomiting. *J. Abnorm. Psychol.,* 1969, **74,** 1–8.

Lasagna, L., Mosteller, F., Felsinger, J. M., & Beecher, H. K. A. A study of the placebo response. *Amer. J. Med.,* 1954, **16,** 770–779.

Latané, B., & Schachter, S. Adrenalin and avoidance learning. *J. Comp. Physiol. Psychol.,* 1962, **55,** 369–372.

Lawson, P. R. *Frustration. The development of a scientific concept.* New York: Macmillan, 1965.

Lazarus, A. A. Crucial procedural factors in desensitization therapy. *Beh. Res. & Ther.,* 1964, **2,** 65–70.

Lazarus, A. A. Behavior therapy, incomplete treatment, and symptom substitution. *J. Nerv. Ment. Dis.,* 1965a, **140,** 80–86.

Lazarus, A. A. Towards the understanding and effective treatment of alcoholism. *South African Med. J.,* 1965b, **39,** 736–741.

Lazarus, A. A. Behavior rehearsal vs. non-directive therapy vs. advice in affecting behavior change. *Beh. Res. & Ther.,* 1966, **4,** 209–212.

Lazarus, A. A. A plea for technical and theoretical breadth. *AABT Newsletter,* June 1968, **3,** 2.

Lazarus, R. S. *Psychological stress and the coping process.* New York: McGraw-Hill, 1966.

Lazarus, R. S. Emotions and adaptation: Conceptual and empirical relations. In D. Levine (Ed.), *Nebraska symposium on motivation, 1968.* Lincoln: University of Nebraska Press. 1968.

Lazarus, R. S., Speisman, J. C., Nordkoff, A. M., & Davidson, L. A. A laboratory study of psychological stress produced by a motion picture film. *Psychol. Monogr.,* 1962, **76,** 34, Whole Number 553.

Lazowick, L. On the nature of identification. *J. Abnorm. Soc. Psychol.,* 1955, **51,** 175–183.

Leibowitz, G. Comparison of self-report and behavioral techniques of assessing aggression. *J. Consult. Clin. Psychol.*, 1968, **32**, 21–25.

Leitenberg, H. Is time-out from positive reinforcement an aversive event? A review of the experimental evidence. *Psychol. Bull.*, 1965, **64**, 428–441.

Leitenberg, H. Punishment training with and without an escape contingency. *J. Exp. Psychol.*, 1967, **74**, 393–399.

Leitenberg, H., Agras, W. S., Barlow, D. H., & Oliveau, D. C. The contribution of selective positive reinforcement and therapeutic instructions to systematic desensitization therapy. *J. Abnorm. Psychol.* 1969, **74**, 113–118.

Leitenberg, H., Agras, W. S., Thompson, L. E., & Wright, D. E. Feedback in behavior modification: An experimental analysis in two phobic cases. *J. Appl. Beh. Anal.*, 1968, **1**, 131–137.

Lemere, F., & Voegtlin, W. L. An evaluation of the aversion treatment of alcoholism. *Quart. J. Stud. Alcohol*, 1950, **11**, 199–204.

Lennard, H. L., & Bernstein, A. *The anatomy of psychotherapy.* New York: Columbia University Press, 1960.

Lennenberg, E. H. *Biological foundations of language.* New York: Wiley, 1967.

Leonard, G. B. *Education and ecstasy.* New York: Delacorte Press, 1968.

LeShan, E., & LeShan, L. A home is not a lab. *New York Times Magazine,* April 7, 1968, 97–107.

Levis, D. J., & Carrera, R. Effects of ten hours of implosive therapy in the treatment of outpatients: A preliminary report. *J. Abnorm. Psychol.*, 1967, **72**, 504–508.

Levinson, D. J. The psychotherapist's contribution to the patient's treatment career. In H. H. Strupp and L. Luborsky (Eds.), *Research in psychotherapy.* Vol. II. Washington, D.C.: American Psychological Association, 1962.

Lewis, M., Wall, A. M., & Aronfreed, J. Developmental change in the relative value of social and non-social reinforcement. *J. Exp. Psych.*, 1963, **66**, 133–137.

Liberman, R. A view of behavior modification projects in California. *Beh. Res. & Ther.*, 1968, **6**, 331–341.

Lichtenstein, E., Keutzer, C. S., & Himes, K. H. "Emotional" role-playing and changes in smoking attitudes and behavior. *Psychol. Rep.*, 1969, **25**, 379–287.

Lichtenstein, P. E. Studies of anxiety: I. The production of a feeding inhibition in dogs. *J. Comp. Physiol. Psychol.*, 1950, **43**, 16–29.

Liebert, R. M., & Allen, M. K. The effects of rule structure and reward magnitude on the acquisition and adoption of self-reward criteria. *Psychol. Rep.*, 1967, **21**, 445–452.

Lifton, R. J. *Thought reform and the psychology of totalism: A study of brainwashing in China.* New York: W. W. Norton, 1961.

Lindley, R. H., & Moyer, K. E. Effects of instructions on the extinction of a conditioned finger-withdrawal response. *J. Exp. Psychol.*, 1961, **61**, 82–88.

Lindsley, O. R. Operant conditioning methods applied to research in chronic schizophrenia. *Psychiat. Res. Rep.*, 1956, **5**, 118–139.

Lindsley, O. R. Operant conditioning methods in diagnosis. In J. H. Nodine and J. H. Moyer (Eds.), *Psychosomatic medicine: The first Hahnemann Symposium*. Philadelphia: Lea & Febiger, 1962.

Lindsley, O. R. Experimental analysis of social reinforcement: Terms and methods. *Amer. J. Orthopsychiat.*, 1963a, **33**, 624–633.

Lindsley, O. R. Free operant conditioning and psychotherapy. In J. Masserman (Ed.), *Current psychiatric therapies*. New York: Grune and Stratton, 1963b.

Lindsley, O. R. Direct measurement and prosthesis of retarded behavior. *J. Educ.*, 1964a, **147**, 62–81.

Lindsley, O. R. Geriatric behavioral prosthetics. In R. Kastenbaum (Ed.), *New thoughts on old age*. New York: Springer, 1964b.

Lindsley, O. R. Training teachers and parents in behavior modification. Paper presented at Behavioral Technology Conference, University of Oregon, July 1968.

Lipkin, S. Clients' feelings and attitudes in relation to the outcome of client-centered therapy. *Psychol. Monogr.*, 1954, **68**, Whole No. 372.

Liversedge, L. A., & Sylvester, J. D. Conditioning techniques in the treatment of writer's cramp. *Lancet*, June 1955, 1147–1149.

Lloyd, D. N., & Newbrough, J. R. Previous conferences on graduate education in psychology: A summary and review. In E. L. Hoch, A. O. Ross, & C. L. Winder (Eds.), *Professional preparation of clinical psychologists*. Washington, D.C.: American Psychological Association, 1966.

Lockard, J. S. Choice of a warning signal or no warning signal in an unavoidable shock situation. *J. Comp. Physiol. Psychol.*, 1963, **56**, 526–530.

Locke, E. A., Cartledge, N., & Koeppel, J. Motivational effects of knowledge of results: A goal-setting phenomenon? *Psychol. Bull.*, 1968, **70**, 474–485.

Lomont, J. F. Reciprocal inhibition or extinction? *Beh. Res. & Ther.*, 1965, **3**, 209–219.

Lomont, J. F., & Edwards, J. E. The role of relaxation in systematic desensitization. *Beh. Res. & Ther.*, 1967, **5**, 11–25.

London, P. *The modes and morals of psychotherapy*. New York: Holt, Rinehart & Winston, 1964.

Lorr, M., Klett, C. J., & McNair, D. M. *Syndromes of psychosis*. New York: Macmillan, 1963.

Lott, A. J., & Lott, B. E. Liked and disliked persons as reinforcing stimuli. *J. Pers. Soc. Psychol.*, 1969, **11**, 129–137.

Lott, A. J., Lott, B. E., & Matthews, G. M. Interpersonal attraction among children as a function of vicarious reward. *J. Educ. Psychol.*, 1969, **60**, 274–283.

Lovaas, O. I. Interaction between verbal and nonverbal behavior. *Child Dev.* 1961, **32**, 329–336.

Lovaas, O. I. Control of food intake in children by reinforcement of relevant verbal behavior. *J. Abnorm. Soc. Psychol.*, 1964, **68**, 672–678.

Lovaas, O. I. A behavior therapy approach to the treatment of childhood schizophrenia. In J. Hill (Ed.), *Minnesota Symposium on Child Psychology*, Minneapolis: University of Minnesota Press, 1967.

Lovaas, O. I., Baer, D. M., & Bijou, S. W. Experimental procedure for analyzing the interaction of social stimuli and children's behavior. Paper read at SRCD Convention, Berkeley, Calif., 1963.

Lovaas, O. I., Freitag, G., Gold, V. J., & Kassorla, I. C. Recording apparatus and procedure for observation of behaviors of children in free play settings. *J. Exper. Child Psychol.*, 1965, **2**, 108–120.

Lovaas, O. I., Freitas, L., Nelson, K., & Whalen, C. The establishment of imitation and its use for the development of complex behavior in schizophrenic children. *Beh. Res. & Ther.*, 1967, **5**, 171–181.

Lovaas, O. I., Schaeffer, B., & Simmons, J. Q. Building social behavior in autistic children by use of electric shock. *J. Exp. Res. Pers.*, 1965, **1**, 99–109.

Lovitt, T. C., & Curtiss, K. A. Effects of manipulating an antecedent event on mathematics response rate. *J. Appl. Beh. Anal.*, 1968, **1**, 329–333.

Lovibond, S. H. *Conditioning and enuresis.* New York: Pergamon Press, 1964.

Luborsky, L., & Strupp, H. H. Research problems in psychotherapy: A three-year follow-up. In H. H. Strupp & L. Luborsky (Eds.), *Research in psychotherapy*, Vol. II. Washington, D.C.: American Psychological Association, 1962.

Lumsdaine, A. A., & Glaser, R. (Eds.) *Teaching machines and programmed learning: A source book.* Washington, D.C., National Education Association, 1960.

Lundin, R. W. *Personality: A behavioral analysis.* London: The Macmillan Company, 1969.

Luria, A. R. *The role of speech in the regulation of normal and abnormal behavior.* New York: Liveright, 1961.

Lykken, D. T. A study of anxiety in the sociopathic personality. *J. Abnorm. Soc. Psychol.*, 1957, **55**, 6–10.

Lynn, R. Russian theory and research on schizophrenia. *Psychol. Bull.*, 1963, **60**, 486–498.

Lynn, R., & Eysenck, H. J. Tolerance of pain, extraversion and neuroticism. *Percept. Mot. Skills*, 1961, **12**, 161–162.

MacCulloch, M. J., Feldman, M. P., Orford, J. F., & MacCulloch, M. L.

Anticipatory avoidance learning in the treatment of alcoholism: A record of therapeutic failure. *Beh. Res. & Ther.*, 1966, **4**, 187–196.

MacCulloch, M. J., Feldman, M. P., & Pinschof, J. M. The application of anticipatory avoidance learning to the treatment of homosexuality. II. Response latencies and pulse rate changes. *Beh. Res. & Ther.*, 1965, **3**, 21–44.

McFall, R. M. The effects of self-monitoring on normal smoking behavior. *J. Consult. Clin. Psychol.*, 1970 (in press).

McDavid, J. W. Imitative behavior in preschool children. *Psychol. Monogr.*, 1959, **73**, Whole No. 486.

McDavid, J. W. Effects of ambiguity of environmental cues upon learning to imitate. *J. Abnorm. Soc. Psychol.*, 1962, **65**, 381–386.

McDavid, J. W. Effects of ambiguity of imitative cues upon learning by observation. *J. Soc. Psychol.*, 1964, **62**, 165–174.

McGuire, R. J., Carlisle, J. M., & Young, B. G. Sexual deviations as conditioned behavior: A hypothesis. *Beh. Res. & Ther.*, 1965, **2**, 185–190.

McGuire, R. J., & Vallance, M. Aversion therapy by electric shock: A simple technique. *Brit. Med. J.*, 1964, **1**, 151–153.

McNair, D. M., Lorr, M., & Callahan, D. M. Patient and therapist influences on quitting psychotherapy. *J. Consult. Psychol.*, 1963, **27**, 10–17.

McPartland, T. S., & Richart, R. H. Social and clinical outcomes of psychiatric treatment. *Arch. Gen. Psychiat.*, 1966, **14**, 179–184.

Madill, M. F., Campbell, D., Laverty, S. G., Sanderson, R. E., & Vanderwater, S. L. Aversion treatment of alcoholics by succinylcholine-induced apneic paralysis. *Quart. J. Study Alcohol*, 1966, **27**, 483–509.

Madsen, C. H. Jr., Becker, W. C., & Thomas, D. R. Rules, praise and ignoring: Elements of elementary classroom control. *J. App. Beh. Anal.*, 1968, **1**, 139–150.

Maher, B. A. *Principles of psychopathology: An experimental approach.* New York: McGraw-Hill, 1966.

Malmo, R. B. Anxiety and behavioral arousal. *Psychol. Rev.*, 1957, **64**, 276–287.

Malmo, R. B., Boag, T. J., & Smith, A. A. Physiological study of personal interaction. *Psychosom. Med.*, 1957, **19**, 105–119.

Malmo, R. B., & Shagass, C. Studies of blood pressure in psychiatric patients under stress. *Psychosom. Med.*, 1952, **14**, 82–93.

Malmo, R. B., Shagass, C., & David, F. H. Electromyographic studies of muscular tension in psychiatric patients under stress. *J. Clin. Exp. Psychopath.*, 1951, **12**, 45–66.

Maltzman, I. Awareness: Cognitive psychology vs. behaviorism. *J. Exp. Res. Pers.*, 1966, **1**, 161–165.

Mandler, G. The interruption of behavior. In D. Levine (Ed.), *Nebraska symposium on motivation, 1964.* Lincoln, Nebraska: University of Nebraska Press, 1964.

Mandler, G., Mandler, J. M., & Uviller, E. T. Autonomic feedback: The perception of autonomic activity. *J. Abnorm. Soc. Psychol.,* 1958, **56,** 367–373.

Mann, L. The effects of emotional role-playing on smoking attitudes and behavior. *J. Exp. Soc. Psychol.,* 1967, **3,** 334–348.

Mann, L., & Janis, I. L. A follow-up study on the long-term effects of emotional role-playing. *J. Pers. Soc. Psychol.,* 1968, **8,** 339–342.

Marks, I. M., & Gelder, M. G. A controlled retrospective study of behavior therapy in phobic patients. *Brit. J. Psychiat.,* 1965, **111,** 561–573.

Marks, I. M., & Gelder, M. G. Common ground between behavior therapy and psychodynamic methods. *Brit. J. Med. Psychol.,* 1966, **39,** 11–23.

Marks, I. M., & Gelder, M. G. Transvestism and fetishism: Clinical and psychological changes during faradic aversion. *Brit. J. Psychiat.,* 1967, **113,** 711–729.

Marlatt, G. A. Exposure to a model and task ambiguity as determinants of verbal behavior in an interview. Paper presented at meeting of Western Psychological Association, San Diego, 1968.

Marlatt, G. A., Jacbson, E. A., Johnson, D. L., & Morrice, D. J. Effect of exposure to a model receiving varied informational feedback upon subsequent behavior in an interview. Paper presented at meeting of Midwestern Psychological Association, Chicago, 1966.

Marston, A. R. Variables in extinction following acquisition with vicarious reinforcement. *J. Exp. Psychol.,* 1964, **68,** 312–315.

Marston, A. R. Imitation, self-reinforcement, and reinforcement of another person. *J. Pers. Soc. Psychol.,* 1965, **2,** 255–261.

Marston, A. R. Determinants of the effects of vicarious reinforcement. *J. Exp. Psychol.,* 1966, **71,** 550–558.

Marston, A. R., & Kanfer, F. H. Group size and number of vicarious reinforcements in verbal learning. *J. Exp. Psychol.,* 1963a, **65,** 593–596.

Marston, A. R., & Kanfer, F. H. Human reinforcement: Experimenter and subject controlled. *J. Exp. Psychol.,* 1963b, **66,** 91–94.

Martin, B. The assessment of anxiety by physiological-behavioral measures. *Psychol. Bull.,* 1961, **58,** 234–255.

Martin, M. L., Weinstein, M., & Lewinsohn, P. M. The use of home observations as an integral part of the treatment of depression: The case of Mrs. B. Unpublished manuscript, University of Oregon, 1968.

Masserman, J. H. *Behavior and neurosis.* Chicago: University of Chicago Press, 1943.

Masserman, J. M., & Pechtel, C. Neurosis in monkeys: A preliminary report of experimental observations. *Ann. N.Y. Acad. Sci.,* 1953, **56,** 253–265.

Matarazzo, J. D., & Saslow, G. Differences in interview interaction behavior among normal and deviant groups. In I. A. Berg and B. M. Bass (Eds.), *Conformity and deviation.* New York: Harper, 1961.

Matarazzo, J. D., Wiens, A. N., Matarazzo, R. G., & Saslow, G. Speech and silence behavior in clinical psychotherapy and its laboratory correlates. In J. M. Shlien (Ed.), *Research in psychotherapy,* Vol. III. Washington, D.C.: American Psychological Association, 1968.

May, R. Discussion on existentialism and current trends in psychology. Conference at Sonoma State College, Sonoma, California, 1962. Quoted in L. Krasner, Societal and professional implications of the behavior therapies. *ETS Res. Memo.,* RM-65-9, June 1965.

Mayer, J., & Thomas, D. W. Regulation of food intake and obesity. *Science,* 1967, **156,** 328–337.

Meehl, P. E. The cognitive activity of the clinician. *Amer. Psychol.,* 1960, **15,** 19–27.

Meehl, P. E. Psychopathology and purpose. In P. H. Hoch & J. Zubin (Eds.), *The future of psychiatry.* New York: Grune and Stratton, 1962.

Mees, H. L. Placebo effects in aversive control: A preliminary report. Paper presented at the joint meeting of the Oregon-Washington State Psychological Associations, Ocean Shores, Washington, May 1966a.

Mees, H. L. Sadistic fantasies modified by aversive conditioning and substitution: A case study. *Beh. Res. & Ther.,* 1966b, **4,** 317–320.

Mertens, G. C., & Fuller, G. B. *The therapist's manual.* Mimeograph, Willmar State Hospital, Minnesota, 1964.

Mesthene, E. G. The role of technology in society: Some general implications of the program's research. In *Fourth annual report, Program in technology and society.* Cambridge: Harvard University Press, 1968.

Meyer, V. Modification of expectations in cases with obsessional rituals. *Beh. Res. & Ther.,* 1966, **4,** 273–280.

Meyer, V., & Crisp, A. H. Aversion therapy in two cases of obesity. *Beh. Res. & Ther.,* 1964, **2,** 143–148.

Meyer, V., & Crisp, A. H. Some problems in behavior therapy. *Brit. J. Psychiat.,* 1966, **112,** 367–381.

Meyer, V., & Gelder, M. G. Behavior therapy and phobic disorders. *Brit. J. Psychiat.,* 1963, **109,** 19–28.

Migler, B., & Wolpe, J. Automated self-desensitization: A case report. *Beh. Res. & Ther.,* 1967, **5,** 133–135.

Millenson, J. R. *Principles of behavioral analysis.* New York: Macmillan, 1967.

Miller, E., Dvorak, B., & Turner, D. A method of creating aversion to alcohol by reflex conditioning in a group setting. In C. M. Franks (Ed.), *Conditioning techniques in clinical practice and research.* New York: Springer, 1964.

Miller, G. A., Galanter, E. H., & Pribram, K. H. *Plans and the structure of behavior.* New York: Holt, Rinehart & Winston, 1960.

Miller, J. O. Diffusion of the intervention effects in disadvantaged families. Undated mimeo. George Peabody College, Nashville, Tennessee.

Miller, M. F. Responses of psychiatric patients to their photographed images. *Dis. Nerv. Syst.,* 1962, **23,** 296–298.

Miller, N. E. Learnable drives and rewards. In S. S. Stevens (Ed.), *Handbook of experimental psychology.* New York: Wiley, 1951.

Miller, N. E. Learning resistance to pain and fear: Effects of overlearning, exposure, and rewarded exposure in context. *J. Exp. Psychol.,* 1960, **60,** 137–145.

Miller, N. E., & Dollard, J. *Social learning and imitation.* New Haven: Yale University Press, 1941.

Miller, R. E., Banks, J. H. Jr., & Ogawa, N. Communication of affect in "cooperative conditioning" of Rhesus monkeys. *J. Abnorm Soc. Psychol.,* 1962, **64,** 343–348.

Mischel, W. *Personality and assessment.* New York: Wiley, 1968a.

Mischel, W. Implications of behavior theory for personality assessment. Paper presented at meeting of Western Psychological Association, San Diego, March 1968b.

Mischel, W., & Gilligan, C. Delay of gratification, motivation for the prohibited gratification, and responses to temptation. *J. Abnorm. Soc. Psychol.,* 1964, **69,** 411–417.

Mischel, W., & Liebert, R. M. Effects of discrepancies between observed and imposed reward criteria on their acquisition and transmission. *J. Pers. Soc. Psychol.,* 1966, **3,** 45–53.

Mischel, W., & Liebert, R. M. The role of power in the adoption of self-reward patterns. *Child Dev.,* 1967, **38,** 673–683.

Mischel, W., & Metzner, R. Preference for delayed reward as a function of age, intelligence, and length of delay interval. *J. Abnorm. Soc. Psychol.,* 1962, **64,** 425–431.

Mischel, W., & Staub, E. The effects of expectancy on working and waiting for larger rewards. *J. Pers. Soc. Psychol.,* 1965, **2,** 625–633.

Montagu, A. Chromosomes and crime. *Psychology Today,* 1968, **2,** 42–49.

Moore, F. J., Chernell, E., & West, M. J. Television as a therapeutic tool. *Arch. Gen. Psychiat.,* 1965, **12,** 217–220.

Moore, O. K. Autotelic responsive environments and exceptional children. In O. J. Harvey (Ed.), *Experience, structure and adaptability.* New York: Springer, 1966.

Morgenstern, F. S., Pearce, J. F., & Rees, W. L. Predicting the outcome of behaviour therapy by psychological tests. *Beh. Res. & Ther.,* 1965, **2,** 191–200.

Morrill, C. S. Teaching machines: A review. *Psychol. Bull.,* 1961, **58,** 363–375.

Morse, W. H. Intermittent reinforcement. In W. K. Honig (Ed.), *Operant behavior: Areas of research and application.* New York: Appleton-Century-Crofts, 1966.

Mowrer, O. H. Apparatus for the study and treatment of enuresis. *Amer. J. Psychol.,* 1938, **51,** 163–166.

Mowrer, O. H. A stimulus-response analysis of anxiety and its role as a reinforcing agent. *Psychol. Rev.,* 1939, **46,** 553–565.

Mowrer, O. H. Preparatory set (expectancy): Some methods of measurement. *Psychol. Monog.,* 1940, **52,** No. 2, Whole No. 43.

Mowrer, O. H. On the dual nature of learning—a reinterpretation of "conditioning" and "problem-solving." *Harvard Educ. Rev.,* 1947, **17,** 102–148.

Mowrer, O. H. *Learning theory and personality dynamics.* New York: Ronald Press, 1950.

Mowrer, O. H. *Learning theory and behavior.* New York: Wiley, 1960a.

Mowrer, O. H. *Learning theory and the symbolic processes.* New York: Wiley, 1960b.

Mowrer, O. H., & Jones, H. M. Extinction and behavior variability as functions of effortfulness of task. *J. Exp. Psychol.,* 1943, **33,** 369–386.

Murphy, G. Psychology in the year 2000. *Amer. Psychol.,* 1969, **24,** 523–530.

Murphy, J. V., Miller, R. E., & Mirsky, I. A. Interanimal conditioning in the monkey. *J. Comp. Physiol. Psychol.,* 1955, **48,** 211–214.

Murray, H. A. *Explorations in personality.* New York: Oxford University Press, 1938.

National Research Council Advisory Committee on Government Programs in the Behavioral Sciences, National Research Council, National Academy of Sciences. The behavioral sciences and the federal government: Summary and recommendations. *Amer. Psychol.,* 1968, **23,** 803–809.

Narrol, H. G. A learning therapy for alcoholics: Upon what behavior should retraining focus? Paper presented at meeting of American Psychological Association, Los Angeles, September, 1964.

Nathan, P. E., Andberg, M., & Patch, V. D. Behavior therapy and psychotherapy: A combined procedure for the successful treatment of severe stuttering. Undated mimeograph, Harvard Medical School.

Nathan, P. E., Bull, T. A., & Rossi, A. M. Operant range and variability during psychotherapy: Description of possible communication signatures. *J. Nerv. Ment. Dis.,* 1968, **146,** 41–49.

Nathan, P. E., Schneller, P., & Lindsley, O. R. Direct measurement of communication during psychiatric admission interviews. *Beh. Res. & Ther.,* 1964, **2,** 49–57.

Natsoulas, T. What are perceptual reports about? *Psychol. Bull.,* 1967, **67,** 249–272.

Neimark, E. D. Model for a thinking machine: Mark .04. *Merrill-Palmer Quart.,* 1970, in press.

Newcomb, T. M. The prediction of interpersonal attraction. *Amer. Psychol.,* 1956, **11,** 575–586.

Nisbett, R. E., & Schachter, S. The cognitive manipulation of pain. *J. Exp. Soc. Psychol.,* 1966, **2,** 227–236.

Noblin, C. D., Timmons, E. O., & Reynard, M. C. Psychoanalytic interpretations as verbal reinforcers: Importance of interpretation content. *J. Clin. Psychol.,* 1963, **19,** 479–481.

Nolan, J. D. Self-control procedures in the modification of smoking behavior. *J. Consult. Clin. Psychol.,* 1968, **32,** 92–93.

Nuthmann, A. M. Conditioning of a response class on a personality test. *J. Abnorm. Soc. Psychol.,* 1957, **54,** 19–23.

Ober, D. C. Modification of smoking behavior. *J. Consult. Clin. Psychol.,* 1968, **32,** 543–549.

Odum, E. P. The strategy of ecosystem development. *Science,* 1969, **164,** 262–270.

Olds, J., & Olds, M. Drives, rewards and the brain. In F. Barron, W. C. Dement, W. Edwards, H. Lindman, L. D. Phillips, J. Olds, & M. Olds. (Eds.), *New directions in psychology II.* New York: Holt, Rinehart & Winston, 1965.

Orne, M. T. On the social psychology of the psychological experiment: With particular reference to demand characteristics and their implications. *Amer. Psychol.,* 1962, **17,** 776–783.

Osgood, C. E. *Method and theory in experimental psychology.* New York: Oxford University Press, 1953.

Palmore, E., Lennard, H. L., & Hendin, H. Similarities of therapist and patient verbal behavior in psychotherapy. *Sociometry,* 1959, **22,** 12–22.

Pande, S. K., & Gart, J. J. A method to quantify reciprocal influence between therapist and patient in psychotherapy. In J. M. Shlien (Ed.), *Research in psychotherapy,* Vol. III. Washington, D.C.: American Psychological Association, 1968.

Panman, R. A., Arenson, S. J., & Rosenbaum, M. E. The value of demonstration in human maze learning. *Iowa Acad. Sci.,* 1962, **69,** 490–495.

Pappworth, M. H. *Human guinea pigs: Experimentation on man.* London: Routledge, and Kegan Paul, 1967.

Parloff, M. B. Therapist-patient relationship and outcome of psychotherapy. *J. Consult. Psychol.,* 1961, **25,** 29–38.

Parsons State Hospital. Detailed Progress Report. A demonstration program for intensive training of institutionalized mentally retarded girls. January 1967.

Patterson, G. R. An application of conditioning techniques to the control of a hyperactive child. In L. P. Ullmann & L. Krasner (Eds.), *Case studies in behavior modification.* New York: Holt, Rinehart & Winston, 1965a.

Patterson, G. R. Responsiveness to social stimuli. In L. Krasner & L. P. Ullmann (Eds.), *Research in behavior modification.* New York: Holt, Rinehart & Winston, 1965b.

Patterson, G. R. A learning theory approach to the treatment of the school phobic child. In L. P. Ullmann & L. Krasner (Eds.), *Case studies in behavior modification.* New York: Holt, Rinehart & Winston, 1965c.

Patterson, G. R. Prediction of victimization from an instrumental conditioning procedure. *J. Consult. Psychol.,* 1967, **31,** 147–152.

Patterson, G. R. Social learning: An additional base for developing behavior modification technologies. In C. Franks (Ed.), *Behavior therapy: Appraisal and status.* New York: McGraw-Hill, 1969.

Patterson, G. R., & Bechtel, G. G. Formulating the situational environment in relation to states and traits. In R. B. Cattell (Ed.), *Handbook of modern personality study.* Chicago: Aldine, 1970, in press.

Patterson, G. R., & Fagot, B. I. Selective responsiveness to social reinforcers and deviant behavior in children. *Psychol. Rec.,* 1967, **17,** 369–378.

Patterson, G. R., & Gullion, M. E. *Living with children. New methods for parents and teachers.* Champaign, Illinois: Research Press, 1968.

Patterson, G. R., & Harris, A. Some methodological considerations for observation procedures. Paper presented at meeting of American Psychological Association, San Francisco, California, September 1968.

Patterson, G. R., Littman, R. A., & Bricker, W. Assertive behavior in children: A step towards a theory of aggression. *Soc. Res. Child Dev. Monogr.,* 1967, **32,** 1–43.

Patterson, G. R., Littman, I., & Brown, T. R. Negative set and social learning. *J. Pers. Soc. Psychol.,* 1968, **8,** 109–116.

Patterson, G. R., Hawkins, N., McNeal, S., Phelps, R. Reprogramming the social environment. *J. Child Psychol. Psychiat.,* 1967, **8,** 181–195.

Patterson, G. R., Ray, R., & Shaw, D. Direct intervention in families of deviant children. Paper presented at meeting of Oregon Psychological Association-Washington State Psychological Association, May 1968.

Patterson, G. R., & Reid, J. Reciprocity and coercion: Two facets of social systems. Paper presented at Ninth Institute for Research in Clinical Psychology, University of Kansas, Lawrence, Kansas, April 1967.

Patterson, G. R., & White, G. D. It's a small world: The application of "Time-out from reinforcement." *Oregon Psychological Association Newsletter,* 1969, **15,** No. 2 Suppl.

Paul, G. L. *Insight versus desensitization in psychotherapy: An experiment in anxiety reduction.* Stanford: Stanford University Press, 1966.

Paul, G. L. Behavior modification research: Design and tactics. In C. Franks (Ed.), *Behavior therapy: Appraisal and status.* New York: McGraw-Hill, 1969a.

Paul, G. L. Chronic mental patient: Current status—future directions. *Psychol. Bull.,* 1969b, **71,** 81–94.

Paul, G. L., & Shannon, D. T. Treatment of anxiety through systematic desensitization in therapy groups. *J. Abnorm. Psychol.,* 1966, **71,** 124–135.

Pavlov, I. P. *Conditioned reflexes.* London: Oxford University Press, 1927.

Pavlov, I. P. *Lectures on conditioned reflexes.* Vol. 2: *Conditioned reflexes and psychiatry.* New York: International Publishers, 1941.

Pavlov, I. P. *Experimental psychology and other essays.* New York: Philosophical Library, 1957.

Petoney, P. Value change in psychotherapy. *Human Relations,* 1966, **19,** 39–45.

Perkins, C. C. Jr. An analysis of the concept of reinforcement. *Psychol. Rev.,* 1968, **75,** 155–172.

Perloff, B., & Lovaas, O. I. Effect of non-contingent aversive stimulation on learned behaviors in an autistic child. Unpublished manuscript, University of California at Los Angeles, 1967.

Peters, H. N. An experimental evaluation of learning as therapy in schizophrenia (Abstract). *Amer. Psychol.,* 1952, **7,** 354.

Peters, H. N. Learning as a treatment method in chronic schizophrenia. *Amer. J. Occupat. Ther.,* 1955, **9,** 185–189.

Peterson, D. R. *The clinical study of social behavior.* New York: Appleton-Century-Crofts, 1968a.

Peterson, D. R. The doctor of psychology program at the University of Illinois. *Amer. Psychol.,* 1968b, **23,** 511–516.

Phelan, J. G., Hekmat, H., & Tang, T. Transfer of verbal conditioning to nonverbal behavior. *Psychol. Rep.,* 1967, **20,** 979–986.

Pierrel, R., & Sherman, J. G. Train your pet the Barnabus way. *Brown Alumni Monthly,* 1963, February, 8–14.

Polin, A. T. The effect of flooding and physical suppression as extinction techniques on an anxiety-motivated avoidance locomotor response. *J. Psychol.,* 1959, **47,** 235–245.

Pollack, I. W., & Kiev, A. Spatial orientation and psychotherapy: An experimental study of perception. *J. of Nerv. Ment. Dis.,* 1963, **137,** 93–97.

Pope, B., & Siegman, A. W. Interviewer warmth in relation to interviewee verbal behavior. *J. Consult. Psychol Clin. Psychol.,* 1968, **32,** 588–595.

Poser, E. V. The effect of therapists' training on group therapeutic outcome. *J. Consult. Psychol.,* 1966, **30,** 283–289.

Pratt, S., & Tooley, J. Contract psychology: Some methodological considerations and the research contract. Mimeo, Wichita State University, 1964a.

Pratt, S., & Tooley, J. Contract psychology and the actualizing transactional field. Special Edition #1 (Theoretical Aspects in Research), *Internat. J. Soc. Psychiat.,* 1964b, 51–69.

Premack, D. Toward empirical behavioral laws: I. Positive reinforcement. *Psychol. Rev.,* 1959, **66,** 219–233.

Premack, D. Reinforcement theory. In D. Levine (Ed.), *Nebraska symposium on motivation, 1965.* Lincoln, Nebraska: University of Nebraska Press, 1965.

Pribram, K. H. Interrelations of psychology and the neurological disciplines. In S. Koch (Ed.), *Psychology: A study of a science, Vol. 4.* New York: McGraw-Hill, 1962.

Price, D. K. Purists and politicians. *Science,* 1969, **163,** 25–31.

Purcell, K., & Brady, K. Adaptation to the invasion of privacy: Monitoring behavior with a miniature radio transmitter. *Merrill-Palmer Quart.,* 1966, **12,** 242–254.

Quay, H. The effect of verbal reinforcement on the recall of early memories. *J. Abnorm. Soc. Psychol.,* 1959, **59,** 254–257.

Rachman, S. Aversion therapy: Chemical or electrical? *Beh. Res. & Ther.,* 1965a, **2,** 289–300.

Rachman, S. Studies in desensitization: I. The separate effects of relaxation and desensitization. *Beh. Res. & Ther.,* 1965b, **3,** 245–252.

Rachman, S. Sexual fetishism: An experimental analogue. *Psychol. Rec.,* 1966a, **16,** 293–296.

Rachman, S. Studies in desensitization: II. Flooding. *Beh. Res. & Ther.,* 1966b, **4,** 1–6.

Rachman, S. *Phobias: Their nature and control.* Springfield, Illinois: Charles Thomas, 1968.

Rachman, S., & Eysenck, H. J. Reply to a "critique and reformulation of behavior therapy." *Psychol. Bull.,* 1966, **65,** 165–169.

Rachman, S., & Hodgson, R. J. Experimentally-induced "sexual fetishism": Replication and development. *Psychol. Rec.,* 1968, **18,** 25–27.

Rachman, S., & Teasdale, J. D. Aversion therapy: An appraisal. In C. M. Franks (Ed.), *Behavior therapy: Appraisal and status.* New York: McGraw-Hill, 1969.

Raimy, V. C. (Ed.), *Training in clinical psychology* (Boulder Conference). New York: Prentice-Hall, 1950.

Ramsey, R. W., Barends, J., Breuker, J., & Kruseman, A. Massed versus spaced desensitization of fear. *Beh. Res. & Ther.,* 1966, **4,** 205–207.

Rapaport, D. A critique of Dollard and Miller's "Personality and psychotherapy." *Amer. J. Orthopsychiat.,* 1953, **23,** 204–208.

Raymond, M. J. Case of fetishism treated by aversion therapy. *Brit. Med. J.,* 1956, **2,** 854–857.

Raymond, M. J. The treatment of addiction by aversion conditioning with apomorphine. *Beh. Res. & Ther.,* 1964, **1,** 287–291.

Razran, G. The observable unconscious and the inferable conscious in current

Soviet psychophysiology: Interoceptive conditioning, semantic conditioning and the orienting reflex. *Psychol. Rev.,* 1961, **68,** 81–147.

Rehm, L. P., & Marston, A. R. Reduction of social anxiety through modification of self-reinforcement: An instigation therapy technique. *J. Consult. Psychol.,* 1968, **32,** 565–574.

Reitman, W. R. *Cognition and thought: An information-processing approach.* New York: Wiley, 1965.

Rescorla, R. A., & Solomon, R. L. Two-process learning theory: Relationships between Pavlovian conditioning and instrumental learning. *Psychol. Rev.,* 1967, **74,** 151–182.

Reynolds, G. S. *A primer of operant conditioning.* Glenview, Illinois: Scott, Foresman, 1968.

Rickard, H. C., Dignam, P. J., & Horner, R. F. Verbal manipulation in a psychotherapeutic relationship. *J. Clin. Psychol.,* 1960, **16,** 364–367.

Rickard, H. C., & Dinoff, M. Behavior modification in a therapeutic summer camp. In H. C. Rickard (Ed.), *Behavioral intervention in human problems.* New York: Pergamon, 1970, in press.

Riessman, F. The "helper" therapy principle. *Social Work,* 1965, **10,** 27–31.

Riessman, F. Strategies and suggestions for training nonprofessionals. *Comm. ment. Health J.,* 1967, **3,** 103–110.

Rioch, M. J. Changing concepts in the training of therapists. *J. Consult. Psychol.,* 1966, **30,** 290–292.

Rioch, M. J., Elkes, C., Flint, A. A., Usdansky, B. S., Newman, R. G., & Silber, E. National Institute of Mental Health pilot study in training mental health counselors. *Amer. J. Orthopsychiat.,* 1963, **33,** 678–689.

Risley, T. R. Learning and lollipops. *Psychology Today,* 1968a, **1,** 28–31, 62–65.

Risley, T. R. The effects and side effects of punishing the autistic behaviors of a deviant child. *J. Appl. Beh. Anal.,* 1968b, **1,** 21–34.

Risley, T. R., & Wolf, M. Establishing functional speech in echolalic children *Beh. Res. & Ther.,* 1967, **5,** 73–88.

Ritter, B. The group treatment of children's snake phobias using vicarious and contact desensitization procedures. *Beh. Res. & Ther.,* 1968, **6,** 1–6.

Roe, A. Man's forgotten weapon. *Amer. Psychol.,* 1959, **14,** 261–266.

Rogers, C. R. *Client-centered therapy.* New York: Houghton-Mifflin Co., 1951.

Rogers, C. R. Interpersonal relationships: U.S.A. 2000. *J. Appl. Beh. Sci.,* 1968, **4,** 265–280.

Rogers, C. R. (Ed.) and Gendlin, E. T., Kiesler, D. J., & Traux, C. B. *The therapeutic relationship and its impact: A study of psychotherapy with schizophrenics.* Madison, Wisconsin: University of Wisconsin Press, 1966.

Rogers, C. R., & Skinner, B. F. Some issues concerning the control of human behavior: A symposium. *Science,* 1956, **124,** 1057–1066.

Rogers, J. M. Operant conditioning in a quasi-therapy setting. *J. Abnorm. Soc. Psychol.*, 1960, **60**, 247–252.

Rohan, W. P., & Provost, R. J. Reestablishment of eating habits in a blind and brain damaged patient: A case report. *J. Psychiat. Nurs.*, 1966, **4**, 458–466.

Rosenbaum, M. E., Chalmers, D. K., & Horne, W. C. Effects of success and failure and the competence of the model on the acquisition and reversal of matching behavior. *J. Psychol.*, 1962, **54**, 251–258.

Rosenbaum, M. E., Horne, W. C., & Chalmers, D. K. Level of self-esteem and the learning of imitation and non-imitation. *J. Pers.*, 1962, **30**, 147–156.

Rosenbaum, M. E., & Tucker, I. F. The competence of the model and the learning of imitation and non-imitation. *J. Exp. Psychol.*, 1962, **63**, 183–190.

Rosenthal, D. Changes in some moral values following psychotherapy. *J. Consult. Psychol.*, 1955, **19**, 431–436.

Rosenthal, I. Reliability of retrospective reports of adolescence. *J. Consult. Psychol.*, 1963, **27**, 189–198.

Rosenthal, R. On the social psychology of the psychological experiment: The experimenter's hypothesis as unintended determinant of experimental results. *Amer. Scientist*, 1963, **51**, 268–283.

Rosenthal, R. *Experimenter effects in behavioral research.* New York: Appleton-Century-Crofts, 1966.

Rosenthal, R., & Fode, K. L. Psychology of the scientist. V: Three experiments in experimenter bias. *Psychol. Rep.*, 1963, **12**, 491–511.

Rosenthal, R., Kohn, P., Greenfield, P. M., Carota, N. Data desirability, experimenter expectancy, and the results of psychological research. *J. Pers. Soc. Psychol.*, 1966, **3**, 20–27.

Rothaus, P., Johnson, D. L., & Lyle, F. A. Group participation training for psychiatric patients. *J. Counsel. Psychol.*, 1964, **11**, 230–238.

Rotter, J. B. *Social learning and clinical psychology.* Englewood Cliffs, New Jersey: Prentice-Hall, 1954.

Rubinstein, E. A., & Parloff, M. B. (Eds.), *Research in psychotherapy.* Vol. I. Washington, D.C.: American Psychological Association, 1959.

Ruebhausen, O. M., & Brim, O. G. Jr. Privacy and behavioral research. *Columbia Law Review*, 1965, **65**, 1184–1211. Reprinted in *Amer. Psychol.*, 1966, **21**, 423–437.

Russell, R. W. Effects of "biochemical lesions" on behavior. *Acta Psychologica*, 1958, **14**, 281–294.

Rutner, I. T. The modification of smoking behavior through techniques of self-control. Unpublished Master's Thesis, Wichita State University, 1967.

Rutner, I. T., & Bugle, C. An experimental procedure for the modification of psychotic behavior. *J. Consult. Clin. Psychol.*, 1969, **33**, 651–653.

Rutstein, D. D. *The coming revolution in medicine.* Cambridge, Massachusetts: M.I.T. Press, 1967.

Salzinger, K. Behavior theory models of abnormal behavior. Paper presented at the Biometrics Research Workshop on Objective Indicators of Psychopathology, Tuxedo, New York, February 1968.

Salzinger, K., & Pisoni, S. Reinforcement of affect responses of schizophrenics during the clinical interview. *J. Abnorm. Soc. Psychol.,* 1958, **57,** 84–90.

Sampson, E. E., & Insko, C. A. Cognitive consistency and performance in the autokinetic situation. *J. Abnorm. Soc. Psychol.,* 1964, **68,** 184–192.

Sandler, D. Investigation of a scale of therapeutic effectiveness: Trust and suspicion in an experimentally induced situation. Doctoral dissertation, Duke University, Ann Arbor, Michigan: University Microfilms, 1965. No. 66-1382.

Sandler, J. Masochism: An empirical analysis. *Psychol. Bull,* 1964, **62,** 197–204.

Sanford, N. The prevention of mental illness. In B. Wolman (Ed.), *Handbook of clinical psychology.* New York: McGraw-Hill, 1965.

Sanford, N. Personality: I. The field. *International encyclopedia of the social sciences.* 2nd ed. New York: Macmillan, 1968.

Sapolsky, A. Effect of interpersonal relationships upon verbal conditioning. *J. Abnorm. Soc. Psychol.,* 1960, **60,** 241–246.

Sarbin, T. R. On the futility of the proposition that some people be labeled "mentally ill." *J. Consult. Psychol.,* 1967, **31,** 447–453.

Saslow, G. The use of a psychiatric unit in a general hospital. In A. F. Wessen (Ed.), *The psychiatric hospital as a social system.* Springfield, Illinois: C. C. Thomas, 1964.

Saslow, G., & Matarazzo, J. D. A technique for studying changes in interview behavior. In E. A. Rubenstein and M. B. Parloff (Eds.), *Research in psychotherapy.* Vol. I. Washington, D.C.: American Psychological Association, 1959.

Saturday Review, February 5, 1966.

Schachter, S. The interaction of cognitive and physiological determinants of emotional state. In L. Berkowitz (Ed.), *Advances in experimental social psychology.* Vol. I. New York: Academic Press, 1964a.

Schachter, S. The interaction of cognitive and physiological determinants of emotional state. In P. H. Leiderman and D. Shapiro (Eds.), *Psychobiological approaches to social behavior.* Stanford: Stanford University Press, 1964b.

Schachter, S. Obesity and eating. *Science,* 1968, **161,** 751–756.

Schachter, S., & Latané, B. Crime, cognition, and the autonomic nervous system. In D. Levine (Ed.), *Nebraska symposium on motivation, 1964,* Lincoln: University of Nebraska Press, 1964.

Schachter, S., & Singer, J. E. Cognitive, social & physiological determinants of emotional state. *Psychol. Rev.,* 1962, **69,** 379–399.

Schaefer, E. S., & Furfey, P. H. Intellectual stimulation of culturally-deprived infants during the period of early verbal development. Mimeograph, June 1967.

Schaefer, H. H., & Martin, P. L. *Behavioral therapy.* New York: McGraw-Hill, 1969.

Schiller, H. I. Social control and individual freedom. *Bull. Atomic Scientists,* May 1968, 16–21.

Schmidt, H. O., & Fonda, C. P. The reliability of psychiatric diagnosis: A new look. *J. Abnorm. Soc. Psychol.,* 1956, **52,** 262–267.

Schoenfeld, W. N. An experimental approach to anxiety, escape and avoidance. behavior. In P. J. Hoch and J. Zubin (Eds.), *Anxiety.* New York: Grune & Stratton, 1950.

Schoenfeld, W. N., Bersh, P. J., & Notterman, J. M. Interaction of instrumental and autonomic responses in avoidance conditioning. *Science,* 1954, **120,** 788.

Schon, D. A. Quoted in *Fourth Annual Report, Program on Technology and Society.* Cambridge: Harvard University, 1968.

Schutz, W. C. *Joy: Expanding human awareness.* New York: Grove Press, 1967.

Schwartz, A. N., & Hawkins, H. L. Patient models and affect statements in *group therapy. Proceed. 73rd Annual Conven. Amer. Psychol. Assoc.,* In *Amer. Psychol.,* 1965, **20,** 548.

Schwitzgebel, R. L. A survey of electromechanical devices for behavior modification. *Psychol. Bull.,* 1968, **70,** 444–459.

Segal, E. F. The urban learning village: A community training program for problem slum families, based on behavior modification methods. Paper presented at Western Psychological Association, San Diego, May 1968.

Seligman, M. E. P., & Maier, S. F. Failure to escape traumatic shock. *J. Exp. Psychol.,* 1967, **74,** 1–9.

Seligman, M. E. P., Maier, S. F., & Geer, J. H. Alleviation of learned helplessness in the dog. *J. Abnorm. Psychol.,* 1968, **73,** 256–262.

Selye, H. *The physiology and pathology of exposure to stress.* Montreal: Acta, Inc., 1950.

Shaffer, L. F. The problem of psychotherapy. *Amer. Psychol.,* 1947, **2,** 459–467.

Shapiro, A. K. A contribution to a history of the placebo effect. *Beh. Sci.,* 1960, **5,** 109–135.

Shapiro, D., Crider, A. B., & Tursky, B. Differentiation of an autonomic response through operant reinforcement. *Psychon. Sci.,* 1964, **1,** 147–148.

Shapiro, D., Tursky, B., Gershon, E., & Stern, M. Effects of feedback and reinforcement on the control of human systolic blood pressure. *Science,* 1969, **163,** 588–590.

Shapiro, M. M. Salivary conditioning in dogs during fixed-interval reinforcement contingent upon lever pressing. *J. Exp. Anal. Beh.,* 1961, **4,** 361–364.

Shaw, F. J. A stimulus-response analysis of repression and insight in psychotherapy. *Psychol. Rev.,* 1946, **53,** 36–42.

Sherman, A. R. Therapy of maladaptive fear-motivated behavior in the rat by the systematic gradual withdrawal of a fear-reducing drug. *Beh. Res. & Ther.,* 1967, **5,** 121–129.

Sherman, J. A. Use of reinforcement and imitation to reinstate verbal behavior in mute psychotic. *J. Abnorm. Psychol.,* 1965, **70,** 155–164.

Shoben, E. J. Psychotherapy as a problem in learning theory. *Psychol Bull.,* 1949, **46,** 366–392.

Sidman, M. Normal sources of pathological behavior. *Science,* 1960a, **132,** 61–68.

Sidman, M. *Tactics of scientific research.* New York: Basic Books, 1960b.

Sidman, M. *The Lavers Hall project.* Mimeograph, June 1965.

Sidman, M. Avoidance behavior. In W. K. Honig (Ed.), *Operant behavior: Areas of research and application.* New York: Appleton-Century-Crofts, 1966.

Sidman, M., Herrnstein, R. J., & Conrad, D. G. Maintenance of avoidance behavior by unavoidable shock. *J. Comp. Physiol. Psychol.,* 1957, **50,** 553–557.

Sidman, M., & Stoddard, L. T. The effectiveness of fading in programming a simultaneous form discrimination for retarded children. *J. Exp. Anal. Beh.,* 1967, **10,** 3–15.

Silverman, R. E. Eliminating a conditioned GSR by the reduction of experimental anxiety. *J. Exp. Psychol.,* 1960, **59,** 122–125.

Simkins, L. Behavior modification: Research or engineering. Paper presented at Southwestern Psychological Association, Arlington, Texas, 1966.

Simkins, L. Problems of response definition in clinical psychology. Paper presented at Western Psychological Association, San Francisco, 1967.

Simmel, E. C., Hoppe, R. A., & Milton, G. A. *Social facilitation and imitative behavior.* Boston: Allyn & Bacon, 1968.

Skinner, B. F. *The behavior of organisms: An experimental analysis.* New York: Appleton-Century, 1938.

Skinner, B. F. *Walden two.* New York: Macmillan, 1948.

Skinner, B. F. *Science and human behavior.* New York: Macmillan, 1953.

Skinner, B. F. *Verbal behavior.* New York: Appleton-Century-Crofts, 1957.

Skinner, B. F. Two "synthetic social relations." *J. Exp. Anal. Beh.,* 1962, **5,** 531–533.

Skinner, B. F. Behaviorism at fifty. *Science,* 1963, **140,** 951–958.

Skinner, B. F. Discussion of behaviorism at fifty. In T. W. Wann (Ed.), *Behaviorism and phenomenology.* Chicago: University of Chicago Press, 1964.

Skinner, B. F. *The technology of teaching.* New York: Appleton-Century-Crofts, 1968.

Sloane, R. B., Davison, P. O., Staples, F., & Payne, R. W. Experimental reward and punishment in neurosis. *Compre. Psychiat.,* 1965, **6,** 388–395.

Smith, F. J., & Marston, A. R. Effects of inter- and intraresponse class differences upon learning via vicarious reinforcement. *J. Verb. Learn. Verb. Beh.,* 1965, **4,** 360–364.

Snyder, R. L. Some correlates of interaction rate in natural populations of woodchucks. *Ecology,* 1962, **44,** 637–643.

Solandt, O. M. The control of technology. *Science,* 1969, **165,** 445.

Sollod, D., & Sturmfels, G. *Reciprocal inhibition and the conditioned emotional response.* Unpublished manuscript, Washington University, 1965.

Solomon, R. L. Punishment. *Amer. Psychol.,* 1964, **19,** 239–253.

Solomon, R. L., & Brush, E. S. Experimentally derived conceptions of anxiety and aversion. In M. R. Jones (Ed.), *Nebraska symposium on motivation, 1956.* Lincoln, Nebraska: University of Nebraska Press, 1956.

Solomon, R. L., Kamin, L. J., & Wynne, L. C. Traumatic avoidance learning: The outcomes of several extinction procedures with dogs. *J. Abnorm. Soc. Psychol.,* 1953, **48,** 291–302.

Solomon, R. L., & Turner, L. H. Discriminative classical conditioning in dogs paralyzed by curare can later control discriminative avoidance responses in the normal state. *Psychol. Rev.,* 1962, **69,** 202–219.

Solomon, R. L., & Wynne, L. C. Traumatic avoidance learning: Acquisition in normal dogs. *Psychol. Monogr.,* 1953, **67,** No. 4, Whole No. 354.

Solyom, L., & Miller, S. B. Reciprocal inhibition by aversion relief in the treatment of phobias. *Beh. Res. & Ther.,* 1967, **5,** 313–324.

Sommer, R. Hawthorne dogma. *Psychol. Bull.,* 1968, **70,** 592–595.

Sommer, R. *Personal space: The behavioral basis of design.* Englewood Cliffs, New Jersey: Prentice-Hall, 1969.

Spielberger, C. D., & DeNike, L. D. Descriptive behaviorism vs. cognitive theory in verbal operant conditioning. *Psychol. Rev.,* 1966, **73,** 306–326.

Staats, A. W. *Learning, language and cognition.* New York: Holt, Rinehart & Winston, 1968.

Staats, A. W., Minke, K. A., Goodwin, W., Landeen, J. Cognitive behavior modification: "Motivated learning" reading treatment with sub-professional therapy-technicians. *Beh. Res. & Ther.,* 1967, **5,** 283–299.

Staats, A. W., Staats, C. K., & Crawford, H. L. First-order conditioning of word meaning and the parallel conditioning of a GSR. *J. Gen. Psychol.*, 1962, **67**, 159–167.

Stahelski, A. J., & Lovaas, O. I. Two studies to increase spontaneity in autistic children. Paper presented at meeting of Western Psychological Association, San Francisco, 1967.

Stampfl, T. G., & Levis, D. J. Essentials of implosive therapy: A learning-theory-based psychodynamic behavioral therapy. *J. Abnorm. Psychol.*, 1967, **72**, 496–503.

Stanishevskaya, N. N. A plethismographic investigation of catatonic schizophrenics. In *Proc. all-union theoretical-practical conf.* Moscow: Madgiz, 1955.

Sternbach, R. A. The effects of instructional sets on autonomic responsivity. *Psychophysiol.*, 1964, **1**, 67–72.

Sternbach, R. A. *Principles of psychophysiology.* New York: Academic Press, 1966.

Stevenson, H. W. Social reinforcement of children's behavior. In L. P. Lipsitt & C. C. Spiker (Eds.), *Advances in child development and behavior*, Vol. 2. New York: Academic Press, 1965.

Stimbert, V. E., Schaeffer, R. W., & Grimsley, D. L. Acquisition of an imitative response in rats. *Psychon. Sci.*, 1966, **5**, 339–340.

Stollak, G. E. The experimental effects of training college students as play therapists. Paper presented at meeting of Midwestern Psychological Association, Chicago, 1967.

Stoller, F. H. Focused feedback with video tape: Extending the group's function. In G. M. Gazda (Ed.). *Basic innovations to group psychotherapy and counseling.* Springfield, Illinois: C. C. Thomas, 1968.

Storrow, H. A. *Introduction to scientific psychiatry: A behavioristic approach to diagnosis and treatment.* New York: Appleton-Century-Crofts, 1967.

Straughan, J. H. Treatment of child and mother in the playroom. *Beh. Res. & Ther.*, 1964, **2**, 37–41.

Stricker, L. J. The true deceiver. *Psychol. Bull.*, 1967, **68**, 13–20.

Stricker, L. J., Messick, S., & Jackson, D. N. Suspicion of deception: Implications for conformity research. *J. Pers. Soc. Psychol.*, 1967, **5**, 379–389.

Strupp, H. H. *Psychotherapists in action.* New York: Grune & Stratton, 1960.

Stuart, R. B. Behavioral control of overeating. *Beh. Res. & Ther.*, 1967, **5**, 357–365.

Sturm, I. E. The behavioristic aspect of psychodrama. *Group Psychother.*, 1965, **18**, 50–64.

Sullivan, H. S. Basic concepts in the psychiatric interview. In H. S. Perry & M. L. Gawel (Eds.), *The psychiatric interview.* New York: Norton, 1954a.

Sullivan, H. S. *The psychiatric interview.* New York: W. W. Norton, 1954b.

Sulzer, E. S. Reinforcement and therapeutic contract. *J. Consult. Psychol.,* 1962, **9,** 271–276.

Szasz, T. S. The myth of mental illness. *Amer. Psychol.,* 1960, **15,** 113–118.

Taffel, C. Anxiety and the conditioning of verbal behavior. *J. Abnorm. Soc. Psychol.,* 1955, **51,** 496–501.

Terrell, G. Jr., Durkin, K., & Wiesley, M. Social class and the nature of the incentive in discrimination learning. *J. Abnorm. Soc. Psychol.* 1959, **59,** 270–272.

Thelen, M. H., Varble, D. L., & Johnson, J. Attitudes of academic clinical psychologists toward projective tests. *Amer. Psychol.,* 1968, **23,** 517–521.

Thiessen, D. D., & Rodgers, D. A. Population density and endocrine function. *Psychol. Bull.,* 1961, **58,** 441–451.

Thomas, D. R., Becker, W. C., & Armstrong, M. Production and elimination of disruptive classroom behavior by systematically varying teachers' behavior. *J. Appl. Beh. Anal.,* 1968, **1,** 35–46.

Thorndike, E. L. *Educational psychology, Vol. II: The psychology of learning.* New York: Teachers College, Columbia University, 1913.

Thorndike, E. L. Reward and punishment in animal learning. *Comp. Psych. Monogr.,* 1932, **8,** Whole No. 39.

Thorne, F. C. Rules of evidence in the evaluation of the effects of psychotherapy. *J. Clin. Psychol.,* 1952, **8,** 38–41.

Thorpe, J. G., Schmidt, E., Brown, P. T., & Castell, D. Aversion-relief therapy: a new method for general application. *Beh. Res. & Ther.,* 1964, **2,** 71–82.

Thorpe, J. G., Schmidt, E., & Castell, D. A comparison of positive and negative (aversive) conditioning in the treatment of homosexuality. *Beh. Res. & Ther.,* 1963, **1,** 357–362.

Tilton, J. R. The use of instrumental motor and verbal learning techniques in the treatment of chronic schizophrenics. Unpublished doctoral dissertation, Michigan State University, 1956.

Timmons, E. O., Noblin, C. D., Adams, H. E., & Butler, J. R. Operant conditioning with schizophrenics comparing verbal reinforcers vs. psychoanalytic interpretations: Differential extinction effects. *J. Pers. Soc. Psychol.,* 1965, **1,** 373–377.

Tolman, C. W. The role of the companion in social facilitation of animal behavior. In E. C. Simmel, R. A. Hoppe, & G. A. Milton (Eds.), *Social facilitation and imitative behavior.* Boston: Allyn & Bacon, 1968.

Tooley, J. T., & Pratt, S. An experimental procedure for the extinction of smoking behavior. *Psychol. Rec.,* 1967, **17,** 209–218.

Tourney, G., Bloom, V., Lowinger, P. L., Schorer, C. Auld, F., & Grisell, J. A study of psychotherapeutic process variables in psychoneurotic and schizophrenic patients. *Amer. J. Psychother.,* 1966, **20,** 122–124.

Triandis, H. C. Cognitive similarity and communication in a dyad. *Human Relations*, 1960, **13**, 175–183.

Truax, C. B. Reinforcement and non-reinforcement in Rogerian psychotherapy. *J. Abnorm. Psychol.*, 1966, **71**, 1–9.

Truax, C. B., & Carkhuff, R. R. *Toward effective counseling and psychotherapy: Training and practice.* Chicago: Aldine, 1967.

Traux, C. B., Wargo, D. G., Carkhuff, R. R., Kodman, F. Jr., & Moles, E. A. Changes in self-concept during group psychotherapy as a function of alternate sessions and vicarious therapy pre-training in institutionalized mental patients and juvenile delinquents. *J. Consult. Psychol.*, 1966, **30**, 309–314.

Turner, L. H., & Solomon, R. L. Human traumatic avoidance learning: Theory and experiments on the operant-respondent distinction and failures to learn. *Psychol. Monogr.*, 1962, **76**, No. 40, Whole No. 559.

Turner, R. K., & Young, G. C. CNS stimulant drugs and conditioning treatment of noctural enuresis: A long term follow-up study. *Beh. Res. & Ther.*, 1966, **4**, 225–228.

Tyler, V. O. Jr., & Brown, G. D. Token reinforcement of academic performance with institutionalized delinquent boys. *J. Educ. Psychol.*, 1968, **59**, 164–168.

Ullmann, L. P. Abnormal psychology without anxiety. Paper presented at meeting of Western Psychological Association, San Francisco, 1967a.

Ullmann, L. P. The major concepts taught to behavior therapy trainees. Paper presented at meeting of American Psychological Association, Washington, D.C., September, 1967b.

Ullmann, L. P. Behavior therapy as social movement. In C. M. Franks (Ed.), *Behavior therapy: Appraisal and status.* New York: McGraw-Hill, 1969.

Ullmann, L. P., & Krasner, L. (Eds.), *Case studies in behavior modification.* New York: Holt, Rinehart & Winston, 1965.

Ullmann, L. P., & Krasner, L. *A psychological approach to abnormal behavior.* Englewood Cliffs, New Jersey: Prentice-Hall, 1969.

Ullmann, L. P., Krasner, L., & Collins, B. J. Modification of behavior through verbal conditioning: effects in group therapy. *J. Abnorm. Soc. Psychol.*, 1961, **62**, 128–132.

Ullmann, L. P., Krasner, L., & Ekman, P. Verbal conditioning of emotional words: Effects on behavior in group therapy. Research Reports of the Veterans Administration, Palo Alto, California, No. 15, 1961.

Ulrich, R. Behavior control and public concern. *Psychol. Rec.*, 1967, **17**, 229–234.

Ulrich, R. E., & Azrin, N. H. Reflexive fighting in response to aversive stimulation. *J. Exp. Anal. of Beh.*, 1962, **5**, 511–520.

Valins, S., & Ray, A. Effects of cognitive desensitization on avoidance behavior. *J. Pers. Soc. Psychol.,* 1967, **7**, 345–350.

Venables, P. H. Input dysfunction in schizophrenia. In B. A. Maher (Ed.), *Progress in experimental personality research,* Vol. I. New York: Academic Press, 1964.

Venables, P. H., & Wing, J. K. Level of arousal and the subclassification of schizophrenia. *Arch. Gen. Psychiat.,* 1962, **7**, 114–119.

Verhave, T. The functional properties of a time out from an avoidance schedule. *J. Exp. Anal. Beh.,* 1962, **5**, 391–422.

Vernon, P. E. *Personality assessment: A critical review.* New York: Wiley, 1964.

Wahler, R. G., Winkel, G. H., Peterson, R. F., & Morrison, D. C. Mothers as behavior therapists for their own children. *Beh. Res. & Ther.,* 1965, **3**, 113–124.

Walder, L. O., Breiter, D. E., Cohen, S. I., Daston, P. G., Forbe, J. A., & McIntire, R. W., Teaching parents to modify the behavior of their autistic children. Paper presented at meeting of American Psychological Association, New York, 1966.

Wall Street Journal. August 31, 1964, and January 21, 1966.

Walster, E., Bercheid, E., Abrahams, D., & Aronson, V. Effectiveness of debriefing following deception experiments. *J. Pers. Soc. Psychol.,* 1967, **6**, 371–380.

Walters, G. C., & Rogers, J. V. Aversive stimulation of the rat: Long term effects on subsequent behavior. *Science,* 1963, **142**, 70–71.

Walters, R. H., & Brown, M. A test of the high magnitude theory of aggression. *J. Exp. Child Psychol.,* 1964, **1**, 376–387.

Walz, G. R., & Johnston, J. A. Counselors look at themselves on video tape. *J. Counsel. Psychol.,* 1963, **10**, 232–236.

Waskow, I. E. Reinforcement in a therapy-like situation through selective responding to feelings or content. *J. Consult. Psychol.,* 1962, **26** 11–19.

Watson, J. B. *Psychology from the standpoint of a behaviorist.* Philadelphia: Lippincott, 1924.

Watson, J. B. *Psychological care of infant and child.* New York: Norton, 1928.

Watson, J. B., & Rayner, R. Conditioned emotional reactions. *J. Exp. Psychol.,* 1920, **3**, 1–14.

Watson, L. S. Jr. Application of operant conditioning techniques to institutionalized severely and profoundly retarded children. Paper presented at meeting of American Psychological Association, Chicago, 1965.

Webb, W. B. (Ed.), *The profession of psychology.* New York: Holt, Rinehart & Winston, 1962.

Weiner, H. Some effects of response cost upon human operant behavior. *J. Exp. Anal. Beh.,* 1962, **5**, 201–208.

Weiner, H. An operant conditioning analysis of past experience and maladaptive human behavior. Technical Report No. 26, Washington, D.C.: St. Elizabeth's Hospital, 1965.

Weiss, R. L. Operant conditioning techniques in psychological assessment. In P. W. McReynolds (Ed.), *Advances in psychological assessment.* Vol. 1. Palo Alto: Science & Behavior Books, 1969.

Weitzman, B. Behavior therapy and psychotherapy. *Psychol. Rev.,* 1967, **74,** 300–317.

Welkowitz, J., Cohen, J., & Ortmeyer, D. Value system similarity: Investigation of patient-therapist dyads. *J. Consult. Psychol.,* 1967, **31,** 48–55.

Westin, A. F. *Privacy and freedom.* New York: Atheneum, 1967.

White, J. D., & Taylor, D. Noxious conditioning as a treatment for rumination. *Ment. Retard.,* 1967, **5,** 30–33.

Whitehorn, J. C., & Betz, B. J. A study of psychotherapeutic relationships between physicians and schizophrenic patients. *Amer. J. Psychiat.,* 1954, **111,** 321–331.

Whitehorn, J. C., & Betz, B. J. Further studies of the doctor as a crucial variable in the outcome of treatment with schizophrenic patients. *Amer. J. Psychiat.,* 1960, **117,** 215–223.

Wickens, D. D. A study of voluntary and involuntary finger conditioning. *J. Exp. Psychol.,* 1939, **25,** 127–140.

Wiest, W. M. Some recent criticisms of behaviorism and learning theory with special reference to Breger and McGaugh and to Chomsky. *Psychol. Bull.,* 1967, **67,** 214–225.

Wilson, A., & Smith, F. J. Counterconditioning therapy using free association: A pilot study. *J. Abnorm. Psychol.,* 1968, **73,** 474–478.

Wilson, G. D. An electrodermal technique for the study of phobias. *New Zealand Med. J.,* 1966, **65,** 696–698.

Wilson, G. D. Efficacy of "flooding" procedures in desensitization of fear: A theoretical note. *Beh. Res. & Ther.,* 1967, **5,** 138.

Wilson, G. T., Hannon, A. E., & Evans, W. I. M. Behavior therapy and the therapist-patient relationship. *J. Consult. Clin. Psychol.,* 1968, **32,** 103–109.

Wittenborn, J. R. The dimensions of psychosis. *J. Nerv. Ment. Dis.,* 1962, **134,** 117–128.

Wittenborn, J. R., Adler, E., Lukacs, A., Sharrock, J., & Simmons, J. J. III. A contingent reinforcer. *Psychol. Rev.,* 1963, **70,** 418–431.

Wolberg, L. R. *The technique of psychotherapy.* New York: Grune & Stratton, 1954.

Wolf, M. M., Giles, D. K., & Hall, R. V. Experiments with token reinforcement in a remedial classroom. *Beh. Res. & Ther.,* 1968, **6,** 51–64.

Wolf, M. M., Risley, T., & Mees, H. L. Application of operant conditioning procedures to the behavior problems of an autistic child. *Beh. Res. & Ther.,* 1964, **1,** 305–312.

Wolfensberger, W. Ethical issues in research with human subjects. *Science,* 1967, **155,** 47–51.

Wolpe, J. *Psychotherapy by reciprocal inhibition.* Stanford: Stanford University Press, 1958.

Wolpe, J. Some methods of behavior therapy. In Camarillo State Hospital Mimeograph Report: *Behavior therapy and theory in 1966.* Camarillo State Hospital, Camarillo, California, 1966.

Wolpe, J., & Lang, P. J. A fear survey schedule for use in behavior therapy. *Beh. Res. & Ther.,* 1964, **2,** 27–30.

Wolpe, J., & Lazarus, A. A. *Behavior therapy techniques: A guide to the treatment of neuroses.* New York: Pergamon Press, 1966.

Wolpin, M., & Raines, J. Visual imagery, expected roles and extinction as possible factors in reducing fear and avoidance behavior. *Beh. Res. & Ther.,* 1966, **4,** 25–37.

Woodworth, R. S., & Schlosberg, H. *Experimental psychology.* New York: Holt, Rinehart & Winston, 1954.

Woody, R. H. *Behavioral problem children in the schools.* New York: Appleton-Century-Crofts, 1969.

Zajonc, R. B. Social facilitation. *Science,* 1965, **149,** 269–274.

Zajonc, R. B. Social facilitation in cockroaches. In E. C. Simmel, R. A. Hoppe, & G. A. Milton (Eds.), *Social facilitation and imitative behavior.* Boston: Allyn & Bacon, 1968.

Zeiler, M. D. Fixed and variable schedules of response independent reinforcement. *J. Exp. Anal. Beh.,* 1968, **4,** 405–414.

Zeiner, A., & Grings, W. W. Backward conditioning: A replication with emphasis on conceptualizations by the subject. *J. Exp. Psychol.,* 1968, **76,** 232–235.

Zeisset, R. M. Desensitization and relaxation in the modification of psychiatric patients' interview behavior. *J. Abnorm. Psychol.,* 1968, **73,** 18–24.

Zigler, E., & Phillips, L. Psychiatric diagnosis: A critique. *J. Abnorm. Soc. Psychol.,* 1961, **63,** 607–618.

Zimbardo, P. G., Weisenberg, M., Firestone, I., & Levy, B. Communicator effectiveness in producing public conformity and private attitude change. *J. Pers.,* 1965, **33,** 233–256.

Zimmerman, D. W. Sustained performance in rats based on secondary reinforcement. *J. Comp. Physiol. Psychol.,* 1959, **52,** 353–358.

Zimmerman, J., & Ferster, C. B. Chained VI performance of pigeons maintained with an added stimulus. *J. Exp. Anal. Beh.,* 1964, **7,** 83–89.

Zytowski, D. G. The study of therapy outcomes via experimental analogues: A review. *J. Counsel. Psychol.,* 1966, **13,** 235–240.

Author Index

625

MacCulloch, M. J., 115, 117, 122
MacIntosh, S., 471
Madaras, G. R., 446
Madill, M. F., 121
Madsen, C. H. Jr., 280, 303
Maher, B. A., 484, 491
Maier, S. F., 336, 337
Malmo, R. B., 138, 211, 212, 491
Maltzman, I., 26
Mandler, G., 142, 337, 491
Mandler, J. M., 491
Mann, L., 234
Marks, I. M., 30, 105, 117, 118, 156, 157, 489
Marlatt, G. A., 45, 229
Marston, A. R., 204, 207, 208, 396, 421, 436, 470
Martin, B., 147
Martin, M. L., 514
Martin, P. L., 307
Marx, M. H., 230
Mason, D. J., 206
Mason, J. W., 349
Masserman, J. H., 295, 356
Matarazzo, J. D., 258, 398, 470, 472
Matarazzo, R. G., 470, 472
Matthews, G. M., 471
Mattsson, N., 502
Mayer, J., 64
Meehl, P. E., 272, 506
Mees, H. L., 118, 300, 365, 433, 435, 437
Melamed, B. G., 331
Menlove, F. L., 190, 204, 225, 226
Mertens, G. C., 284
Messick, S., 544
Mesthene, E. G., 525
Mettee, D. R., 479
Metzner, R., 417
Meyer, V., 123, 152, 228, 340, 490
Michael, J., 38, 281, 283, 298, 299, 305
Migler, B., 157
Migler, B. M., 371
Millenson, J. R., 249
Miller, C. D., 263, 466
Miller, E. C., 120
Miller, G. A., 374, 449, 568
Miller, M. F., 443
Miller, N. E., 79, 81, 139, 187, 196, 218, 229, 336, 357, 377, 390, 403
Miller, R. E., 212
Miller, S. B., 161, 345

Milton, G. A., 563
Minke, K. A., 269, 270
Mirsky, I. A., 212
Mischel, W., 19, 204, 216, 417, 418, 425, 503, 506, 507, 509
Mohr, J. P., 331
Moles, E. A., 228
Montagu, A., 65
Moore, F. J., 438
Moore, J. W., 144
Moore, O. K., 58, 316
Moos, R. H., 471
Mordkoff, A. M., 213
Morgenstern, F. S., 115, 514
Morrice, D. J., 229
Morrill, C. S., 310
Morrill, W. H., 263, 466
Morrison, D. C., 292, 300
Morse, P., 354
Morse, W. H., 267
Moss, H. A., 215
Moss, T., 283
Mosteller, F., 477
Mowrer, O. H., 78, 124, 139, 219, 286, 328, 337, 344, 348
Moyer, K. E., 100, 144
Murphy, G., 553
Murphy, J. V., 212
Murray, E. N., 100
Murray, H. A., 59

Nanda, H., 514
Narrol, H. G., 309, 310
Nash, E. H. Jr., 474
Nathan, P. E., 256, 298, 363, 514
Natsoulas, T., 381
Neimark, E. D., 572
Nelson, K., 197
Neufeld, I. A., 127
Newbrough, J. R., 549
Newcomb, T. M., 473
Newman, R. G., 556
Nisbett, R. E., 145
Noblin, C. D., 393
Nolan, J. D., 433
Normington, C. J., 263, 466
Notterman, J. M., 102
Nurnberger, J. I., 288, 427
Nuthmann, A. M., 394

Ober, D. C., 434

Subject Index